FRENCH ALPS

Fr. Isler/MICHELIN

Executive Editorial Director   David Brabis
Chief Editor   Cynthia Clayton Ochterbeck

THE GREEN GUIDE FRENCH ALPS

Editor   Gwen Cannon
Principal Writer   Margaret LeMay
Production Coordinator   Allison M. Simpson
Cartography   Alain Baldet, Michele Cana, Peter Wrenn
Photo Editor   Lydia Strong, Stephanie Quillon
Layout & Design   Nicole Jordan, Tim Schulz, Frank Ladd
Cover Design   Ute Weber

Contact Us: The Green Guide
       Michelin Maps and Guides
       One Parkway South
       Greenville, SC 29615
       USA
       ☎ 1-800-423-0485
       www.michelintravel.com
       michelin.guides@us.michelin.com

       Michelin Maps and Guides
       Hannay House
       38 Clarendon Road
       Watford, Herts WD17 1JA
       UK
       ☎ (01923) 205 240
       travelpubsales@uk.michelin.com

Special Sales: For information regarding bulk sales,
       customized editions and premium sales,
       please contact our Customer Service
       Departments:
       USA   1-800-423-0485
       UK   (01923) 205 240
       Canada 1-800-361-8236

Note to the reader
While every effort is made to ensure that all information printed in this guide is correct and up-to-date, Michelin Maps and Guides (Michelin Tyre PLC, Michelin North America, Inc.) accepts no liability for any direct, indirect or consequential losses howsoever caused so far as such can be excluded by law.

One Team …
A Commitment to Quality

There's just one reason our team is dedicated to producing quality travel publications—you, our reader. We want you to get the maximum benefit from your trip—and from your money. In today's multiple-choice world of travel, the options are many, perhaps overwhelming.

In our guidebooks, we try to minimize the guesswork involved with travel. We scout out the attractions, prioritize them with star ratings, and describe what you'll discover when you visit them.

To help you orient yourself, we provide colorful and detailed, but easy-to-follow maps. Floor plans of some of the cathedrals and museums help you plan your tour.

Throughout the guides, we offer practical information, touring tips and suggestions for finding the best views, good places for a break and the most interesting shops.

Lodging and dining are always a big part of travel, so we compile a selection of hotels and restaurants that we think convey the feel of the destination, and organize them by geographic area and price. We also highlight shopping, recreational and entertainment venues, especially the popular spots.

If you're short on time, driving tours are included so you can hit the highlights and quickly absorb the best of the region.

For those who love to experience a destination on foot, we add walking tours, often with a map. And we list other companies who offer boat, bus or guided walking tours of the area, some with culinary, historical or other themes.

In short, we test and retest, check and recheck to make sure that our guidebooks are truly just that: a personalized guide to help you make the most of your visit. After all, we want you to enjoy traveling as much as we do.

The Michelin Green Guide Team

PLANNING YOUR TRIP

INTRODUCTION TO FRENCH ALPS

SYMBOLS

- 🔖 **Tips to help improve your experience**
- 🔖 **Details to consider**
- 🔖 **Entry Fees**
- 🔖 **Walking tours**
- 🔖 **Closed to the public**
- 🕐 **Hours of operation**
- 🕐 **Periods of closure**

CONTENTS

DISCOVERING FRENCH ALPS

HOW TO USE THIS GUIDE

Orientation

To help you grasp the "lay of the land" quickly and easily, so you'll feel confident and comfortable finding your way around the region, we offer the following tools in this guide:

- Detailed table of contents for an overview of what you'll find in the guide, and how it is organized.
- Map of the Alps at the front of the guide, with the principal sights highlighted for easy reference.
- Detailed maps for major cities and villages, including driving tour maps and larger-scale maps for walking tours.
- Map of ten Regional Driving Tours, each one numbered and color coded.
- Map showing the local specialities and activities for each area and town.

Practicalities

At the front of the guide, you'll see a section called "Planning Your Trip" that contains information about planning your trip, the best time to go, different ways of getting to the region and getting around, basic facts and tips for making the most of your visit. You'll find driving and themed tours, and suggestions for outdoor fun. There's also a calendar of popular annual events. Information on shopping, sightseeing, kids' activities and sports and recreational opportunities is also included.

LODGINGS

We've made a selection of hotels and arranged them within the cities, categorized by price category to fit all budgets (see the Legend on the cover flap for an explanation of the price categories). For the most part, we selected accommodations based on their unique regional quality, their local charm, as it were. So, unless the individual hotel or bed & breakfast embodies local ambience, it's rare that we include chain properties, which typically have their own imprint. If you want a more comprehensive selection of accommodations in the alps, see the red-cover Michelin Guide France.

RESTAURANTS

We thought you'd like to know the popular eating spots in the region. So we selected restaurants that capture the Alpine experience—those that have a unique regional flavor and local atmosphere. We're not rating the quality of the food per se. As we did with the hotels, we selected restaurants for many towns and villages, categorized by price to appeal to all wallets. If you want a more comprehensive selection of dining recommendations in the region, see the red-cover Michelin Guide France.

Attractions

Principal Sights are arranged alphabetically. Within each Principal Sight, attractions for each town, village, or geographical area (such as the Vercors) are divided into local Sights or Walking Tours, nearby Excursions to sights outside the town, or detailed Driving Tours—suggested itineraries for seeing several attractions around a major town. Contact information, admission charges and hours of operation are given for the majority of attractions. Unless otherwise noted, admission prices shown are for a single adult only. Discounts for seniors, students, teachers, etc. may be available; be sure to ask. If no admission charge is shown, entrance to the attraction is free.

If you're pressed for time, we recommend you visit the three- and two-star sights first: the stars are your guide.

STAR RATINGS

Michelin has used stars as a rating tool for more than 100 years:

★★★	Highly recommended
★★	Recommended
★	Interesting

SYMBOLS IN THE TEXT

Besides the stars, other symbols in the text indicate tourist information ⓘ; wheelchair access ♿; on-site eating facilities ✕; camping facilities △; on-site parking 🅿; sights of interest to children Kids; and beaches ⌒.

See the box appearing on the Contents page for other symbols used in the text.

See the Maps explanation below for symbols appearing on the maps.

Throughout the guide you will find peach-coloured text boxes or sidebars containing anecdotal or background information. Green-coloured boxes contain information to help you save time or money.

Maps

All maps in this guide are oriented north, unless otherwise indicated by a directional arrow. See the map Legend at the back of the guide for an explanation of other map symbols. A complete list of the maps found in the guide appears at the back of this book.

Addresses, phone numbers, opening hours and prices published in this guide are accurate at press time. We welcome corrections and suggestions that may assist us in preparing the next edition. Please send your comments to:

Michelin Maps and Guides
Hannay House
39 Clarendon Road
Watford, Herts WD17 1JA
UK
travelpubsales@uk.michelin.com
www.michelin.co.uk

Michelin Maps and Guides
Editorial Department
P.O. Box 19001
Greenville, SC   29602-9001
USA
michelin.guides@us.michelin.com
www.michelintravel.com

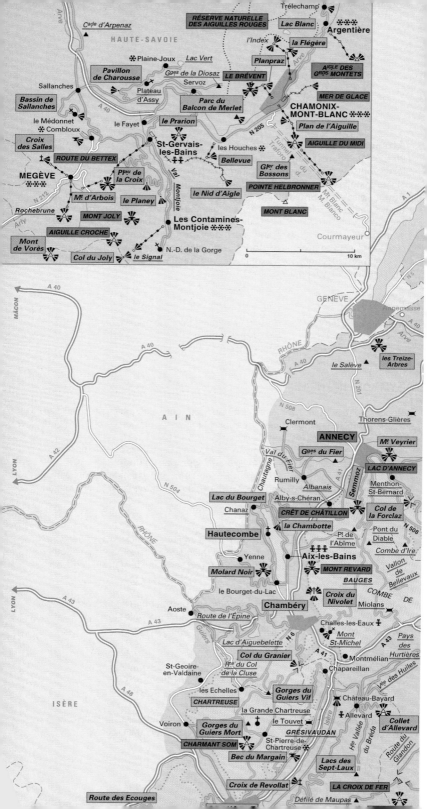

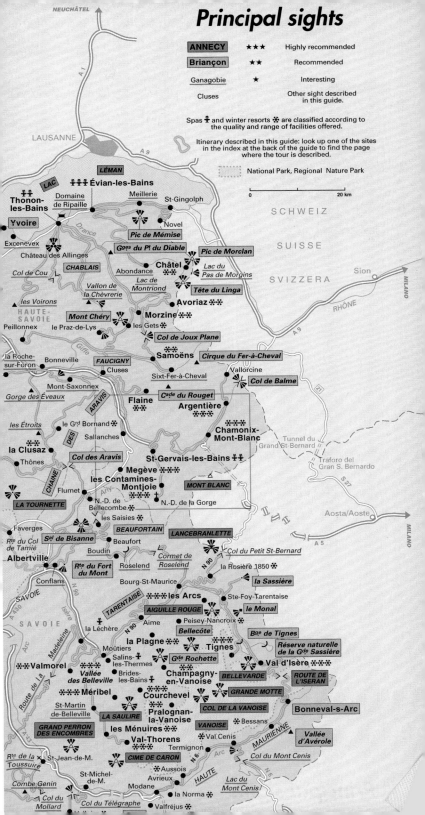

Principal sights

ANNECY	★★★	Highly recommended
Briançon	★★	Recommended
Ganagobie	★	Interesting
Cluses		Other sight described in this guide.

Spas ‡ and winter resorts ✳ are classified according to the quality and range of facilities offered.

Itinerary described in this guide: look up one of the sites in the index at the back of the guide to find the page where the tour is described.

National Park, Regional Nature Park

0   20 km

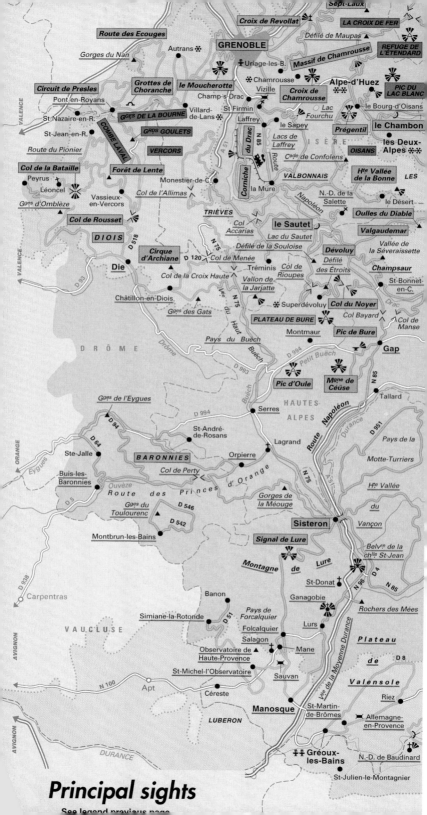

Principal sights

See legend previous page

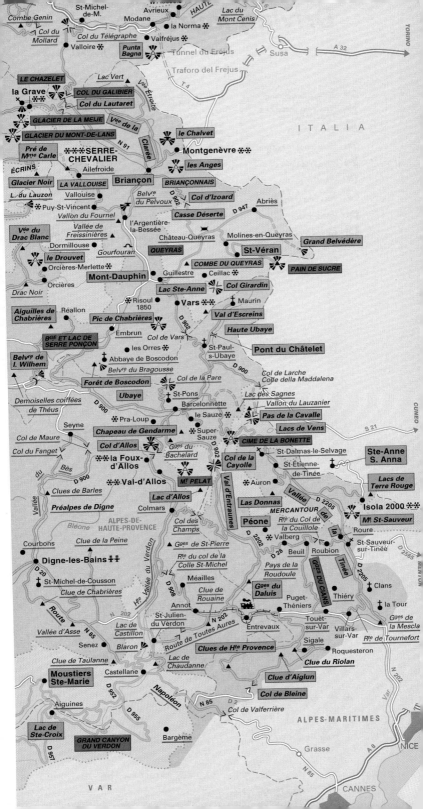

Driving tours

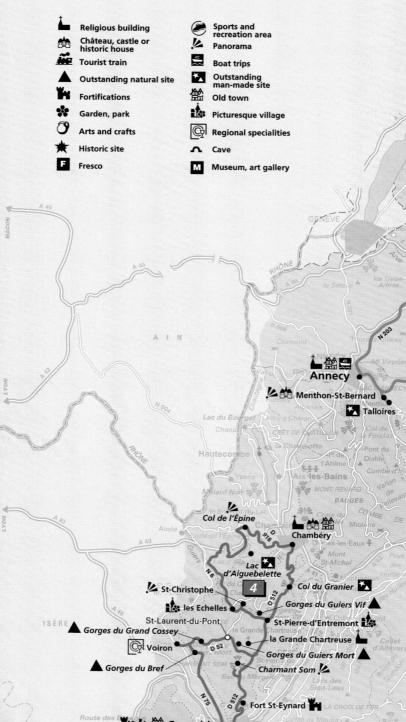

Religious building

Château, castle or historic house

Tourist train

Outstanding natural site

Fortifications

Garden, park

Arts and crafts

Historic site

F **Fresco**

Sports and recreation area

Panorama

Boat trips

Outstanding man-made site

Old town

Picturesque village

Regional specialities

Cave

M **Museum, art gallery**

Annecy

Menthon-St-Bernard

Talloires

Aix-les-Bains

Col de l'Épine

Chambéry

Lac d'Aiguebelette

4

St-Christophe

Col du Granier

les Echelles

Gorges du Guiers Vif

St-Laurent-du-Pont

St-Pierre-d'Entremont

Gorges du Grand Cossey

la Grande Chartreuse

Voiron

Gorges du Guiers Mort

Gorges du Bref

Charmant Som

Fort St-Eynard

Grenoble

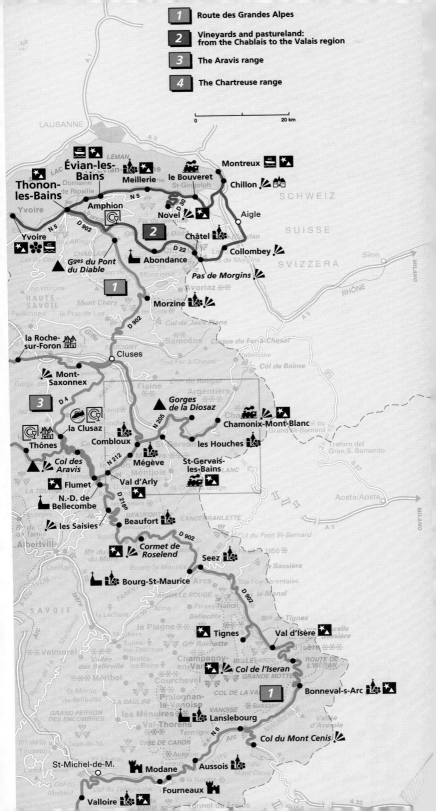

1 Route des Grandes Alpes

2 Vineyards and pastureland: from the Chablais to the Valais region

3 The Aravis range

4 The Chartreuse range

0   20 km

LAUSANNE

LÉMAN

Évian-les-Bains

Meillerie

le Bouveret

St-Gingolph

Montreux

Chillon

Thonon-les-Bains

Domaine de Ripaille

Amphion

Yvoire

Novel

Aigle

SCHWEIZ

SUISSE

SVIZZERA

Sion

MILANO

RHÔNE

Châtel

Abondance

Collombey

Ggesdu Pont du Diable

Pas de Morgins

Avoriaz

HAUTE-SAVOIE

Mont Chéry

le Praz-de-Lys

Morzine

Col de Joux Plane

Samoëns

Cirque du Fer-à-Cheval

Sixt-Fer-à-Cheval

Col de Balme

la Roche-sur-Foron

Cluses

Mont-Saxonnex

Flaine

Argentière

3

la Clusaz

Gorges de la Diosaz

Chamonix-Mont-Blanc

Traforo del Gran S. Bernardo

Thônes

Combloux

les Houches

Col des Aravis

Mégève

St-Gervais-les-Bains

Flumet

Val d'Arly

Montjoie

N.-D. de Bellecombe

BEAUFORT

les Saisies

Beaufort

LANCEBRANLETTE

Col du Petit St-Bernard

Aosta/Aoste

MILANO

Cormet de Roselend

Seez

Bse de Tignes

Bourg-St-Maurice

SAVOIE

la Plagne

Tignes

Val d'Isère

Col de l'Iseran

GRANDE MOTTE

ROUTE DE L'ISERAN

Bonneval-s-Arc

1

Pralognan-la-Vanoise

Lanslebourg

Col du Mont Cenis

Vallée d'Avérole

St-Michel-de-M.

Modane

Aussois

Fourneaux

Valloire

Tunnel du Fréjus

Driving tours

See legend previous page

1	Route des Grandes Alpes
5	Vercors, the green fortress
6	Drac and Romanche, corniches and gorges
7	Durance and Ubaye
8	Route Napoléon
9	Haute Provence between Verdon and Durance
10	Vineyards and trees of the Diois region

The perched village of Roubion

WHEN AND WHERE TO GO

Driving Tours

🕹 *See the Driving Tours map on pp14-17.*

THEMED ITINERARIES

Ville et Pays d'art et d'histoire
– Tours led by guides approved by the Ministry of Culture and Communication are offered in important cities and sites throughout the region. Contact the local tourist offices or go to www. vpah.culture.fr.

Themed circuits – La Fondation pour l'action culturelle internationale en montagne (FACIM) has developed four thematic circuits for the French Alps: **Les Chemins du baroque**, which follows expressions of this style (rarely found elsewhere in France) around more than 60 sites and 500km/312.5mi of roads in the Savoie; **Les Pierre Fortes**, which takes you around castles and fortresses, often on vertiginous mountain faces, along the French-Italian frontier; **Terre des Alpes**, which explores Alpine farms and pastures and rural traditions; and **Archipels d'altitude,** which looks at ski resorts and their often innovative designs. FACIM – 81 place St-Léger 73000 Chambéry -☎04 79 60 59 00 - www.savoie-patrimoine.com

In Vauban's footsteps – The comprehensive defence system designed by Vauban during Louis XIV's reign is unique in the history of military architecture. Some of these former strategic sites can now be visited: citadels in Mont-Dauphin and Briançon, the castle in Château-Queyras, the citadel in Seyne-les-Alpes and the two forts in Colmars-les-Alpes are the finest examples of Vauban's work. Later military fortifications by Vauban's successors are also open to the public: 18C works are centred round Briançon whereas 19C defences are situated further afield. A fort by Maginot, known as Janus, can be visited by appointment. For detailed information, contact the Office du Tourisme in Briançon: Maison des Templiers, Cité Vauban, Place du Temple 05105 Briancon Cedex - ☎04 92 21 08 50 - www. ot-briancon.fr

The upper Ubaye Valley also boasts several defence works, among them Fort de Tournoux, Fort de Roche-Lacroix and the St-Ours Fortifications. Visits are organised by appointment with the Association des Fortifications de l'Ubaye : 4 av. des Trois-Frères-Arnaud - 04400 Barcelonette - ☎04 92 81 52 92 - www. ubaye.com/fortifications

In Jean Giono's footsteps – The Jean Giono centre at Manosque organizes walks all year long, led by qualified guides, around natural sites that inspired the famed novelist. The entire itinerary is handicapped-accessible, thanks to cooperation with Handi Cap Évasion. Centre Jean Giono, 3 bd Élémir-Bourges, Manosque - ☎ 04 92 70 52 54, www.centrejeangiono.com.

Routes des cadrans solaires – There are detailed itineraries with a sundial theme in four areas of the Hautes-Alpes region. The departmental tourist office has brochures listing the most important sundials: Maison des Alpes de Haute Provence, Immeuble François-Mitterand, BP 170 04005 Digne-les-Bains Cedex - ☎04 92 21 08 50, www.alpes-haute-provence.com

The **Briançonnais** offers a variety of mostly 18C or contemporary sundials; there are 20 of them in Briançon alone as well as very original ones in the villages of Prelles, Puy-St-Vincent, Les Alberts, Val-des-Prés, Plampinet, La Salle-les-Alpes and Névache.
The **Vallouise** Valley has a choice of sundials mainly by Zarbula.
In the **Queyras**, sundials are often decorated with exotic birds; they were designed by Zarbula or other artists influenced by him.

How to Tell the Time by Looking at a Sundial

A vertical sundial consists of a panel, usually facing south, and of a metal rod, or gnomon, representing the Earth's axis. Its length must not extend the shadow beyond the panel at the time of the summer solstice and be sufficient for the shadow to be visible at the time of the winter solstice. Reading the time on a sundial is relatively easy but the conversion into accepted, "normal" time is rather involved and requires three factors to be taken into account: the longitude which, in the south of France results in a 20 to 30min difference from Paris; real time (solar time) and average time (24-hour day) corresponding to the variation in the Earth's rotating speed (in summer, it can vary from + 3min to – 6min); and finally, the difference between summer and winter time.

There are also interesting sundials in the **pays du Boëch** to the west and in the **Ubaye** Valley to the south; contact the Maison de la Vallée de l'Ubaye, 4 avenue des 3 frères Arnaud, 04400 Barcelonnette - ☎04 92 81 03 68, www.barcelonnette.com

Route des fruits et des vins – This itinerary stretching from the shores of the Serre-Ponçon Lake to Sisteron has opportunities for tastings (dégustations) in various wine and fruit cooperatives, according to the season. The Comité départemental du Tourisme in Gap will provide a list of orchards and wine cellars in Chorges, Espinasses, Tallard, Théus, Laragne and many other villages: 2A, cours Frédéric-Mistral, 05000 Gap - ☎ 04 92 52 56 56, www.tourisme.fr/gap.

Route de l'Olivier – A number of routes in the Bouches-du-Rhône and Drôme départements are devoted to the symbol of Provence and Provençal cuisine, the olive. An itinerary around les Barronies and the Plateau de Valensole takes in mills where oil is produced and sold as well as restaurants which make a point of using local produce. Further information is available from the Association Française Interprofessionelle de l'Olive (Afidol), 22 rue Henri-Pontier, 13626 Aix-en-Provence Cedex 01- ☎ 04 42 23 01 92, www.afidol.info

ON THE WATER

Several large lakes situated in shallow valleys, such as the Lac du Bourget, Lac d'Annecy, Lac Léman (Lake Geneva) and Lac d'Aiguebelette offer a wide range of outdoor activities

R. Mattes/ MICHELIN

Clarée Valley

(sailing, water-skiing, diving, wind-surfing etc). The mildness of the climate is underlined by the presence of vineyards and olive groves.

Lake Geneva cruises – There are 30 landings around the French and Swiss shores of the lake, with many boat trips and cruises (restaurants on board) available. All year long, a daily, 35-minute route links **Évian** and **Lausanne** in Switzerland and a daily service (20min) links **Yvoire** and **Nyon**. By taking a boat, you can pass time in Vevey, Lausanne and Geneva while avoiding road traffic. In summer, there are also round trips at night. Information from the Compagnie générale de navigation sur le lac Léman in Lausanne - ☎ (00 41) 848 811 848, and the tourist office in Yvoire ☎ 04 50 72 80 21- www.yvoiretourisme.com.

Several clubs offer **yachting facilities and sailing courses:** Société nautique du Léman français, port de Rives, 74200 Thonon-les-Bains, ☎ 04 50 71 07 29 and Cercle de la voile d'Évian, port des Mouettes - BP 103 - 74500 Évian-les-Bains - ☎ 04 50 75 06 46. There is a colourful gathering of yachts on the lake in mid-June, called the Bol d'or de Genève.

Lac du Bourget – The largest natural lake in France also offers a variety of water-based activities. Cruises starting from the Grand Port in Aix-les-Bains, Portout-Chanaz, de Lavours, de Belley or Le Bourget-du-Lac include a choice of trips from a 1hr tour of the lake to a day trip to the Savière Canal and the River Rhône. You can enjoy lunch or dinner aboard new yacht, the *Alain Prud'homme*, which sails from Aix-les-Bains. Contact the tourist office in Aix-les-Bains or the Compagnie des bateaux du lac du Bourget, Grand Port, 73100 Aix-les-Bains - ☎ 04 79 88 92 09 or 04 79 63 45 00 - www. gwel.com The lake is exposed to high winds and sailing conditions are similar to those encountered at sea, so ideal for windsurfing. There are also several sailing clubs in Aix-les-Bains and Le Bourget-du-Lac.

Lac d'Annecy – The superb scenery is the major attraction of the lake. There is a tour of the lake starting from the Thiou pier in Annecy and cruises are organised by the Compagnie des bateaux d'Annecy, 2 place aux Bois, 74000 Annecy, ☎ 04 50 51 08 40 – www.annecy-croisieres.com. The best period to sail on the lake is from March to early November. **Sailing courses** are organised by various clubs including Base nautique des Marquisats in Annecy - ☎ 04 50 33 65 20 and Cercle de la voile in Sévrier, ☎ 04 50 52 40 04- www.cvsevrier.com

Lac du Monteynard – In high season, the cruises on this charming lake on the edge of the Parc régional du Vercors also take in the breathtaking gorges of the Drac and the Ebron, which can be seen only from the water. Ask about sailing times at Bateau-Croisières La Mira, 38650 Treffort - ☎ 04 76 34 14 56.

Lac d'Esparron-du-Verdon – Cruises on the *Perle du Verdon* tour the lake in season, and the local yachting club offers sailing courses and rentals. For information contact the tourist office at Hameau du Port, 04800 Esparron-du-Verdon - ☎ 04 92 77 15 97.

TOURIST TRAINS

Chemin de fer de la Mure – The 30km/19mi itinerary of this former mining railway between St-Georges-de-Commiers and La Mure includes an impressive number of engineering works and offers exceptional views of the Gorges du Drac. Today, it is powered by electric engines dating from the 1930s (&see Lacs de LAFFREY).

Chemin de fer de Montenvers – This line, opened in 1908, transports you from the valley of Chamonix to the Mer de Glace glacier high on Mont Blanc (1 913m/6 276ft), through exhilarating scenery. From the terminus, you can follow a footpath or take a gondola up to sites on the glacier.

Chemin de fer de la Provence – The famous **Train des Pignes** – so-called because the old steam locomotives used to burn pine cones – links Nice and Digne-les-Bains, covering a distance of 150km/93mi via Puget-Théniers, Entrevaux, Annot and St-André-les-Alpes, along a route which once continued to Toulon on the coast. The line, built between 1890 and 1911, includes some 60 metal bridges, viaducts, tunnels and other daring works of engineering. A three-hour journey through five mountain valleys opens up a world of magnificent landscapes, dotted with hilltop villages. **For hikers and ramblers,** designated stopping points, in addition to the stations, allow walkers to strike off into open countryside and rejoin the train further along the line. On Sundays from June to mid-October, a **steam train** runs on the section between Puget-Théniers and Annot. The line allows access all year round to the Lac de Castillon, the Gorges du Verdon and skiing resorts of the Alpes-Maritimes region. In winter the **Train des Neiges** runs daily to the resorts in the Val d'Allos. Information about the Chemin de Fer de Provence from the Gare du Sud, 4 bis rue Alfred-Binet, BP 1387, 06007 Nice, Cedex 1, ☎ 04 97 03 80 80, www. trainprovence. com; or contact the Gare des CP, avenue P.-Semard 04000 Digne-les-Bains - ☎ 04 92 31 01 58.

INDUSTRIAL SITES

These sites, some still operational, some now preserved as cultural monuments, offer an insight into traditional and contemporary industries.

Caves de la Chartreuse – The famous liqueur distillery; 10 boulevard Kofler, BP 102 – 38500 Voiron - ☎ 04 76 05 81 77 (*see Massif de la CHARTREUSE*).

Coopérative laitière de haute Tarantaise – Co-operative dairy; ZA des Colombières – 73700 Bourg-St-Maurice - ☎04 79 07 08 28 -

National park and protected peripheral area

Regional Nature Park

▲ Nature reserve

www.fromagebeaufort.com (👜see BOURG- ST-MAURICE)

Coopérative laitière du Beaufortain – Co-operative dairy; 73270 Beaufort - ☎ 04 79 38 33 62 - www.cooperative-de-Beaufort (👜 see BEAUFORT).

Eaux minérales d'Évian – Mineral water bottling plant (👜 See ÉVIAN-LES-BAINS).

Centre scientifique et technique de Grenoble – Tours and temporary exhibits in a science and technology centre; La Casemate, 1 place Laurent, Grenoble - ☎ 04 76 44 88 80- www.ccsti-grenoble.org

Musée Opinel – Museum devoted to the famous Savoyard knife (👜 See ST-JEAN-DE-MAURIENNE).

Hydrelec – Energy museum; 38114 Allemont - ☎ 04 76 80 78 00 - www.musee-hydrelec.fr (👜see Route de la CROIX DE FER).

La Mine-Image – Coal mine; 38770 La Motte-d'Aveillans - ☎04 76 30 68 74 - www.mine-image.com (👜see Lacs de LAFFREY).

Centrale hydroéléctrique de La Bâthie (beneath the Roselend Dam) – Hydroelectricity generator; 73540 La Bâthie -☎ 04 79 31 06 60.

FOR NATURE-LOVERS

A number of organisations offer natural history excursions in the Alps; a list of locations is available from UNCPIE (Centre permanent d'initiatives pour l'environnement), 26, rue Beaubourg, 75003 Paris - ☎ 01 44 61 75 35 - www. uncpie.org.

On **Mont Blanc**, 50 footpaths have been developed along Alpine themes such as pastures, marshes, lakes, animal life, agriculture, daily life, industry, etc. Explanatory panels follow the trails, which are generally very easy and short, so ideal for families. Contact Espace Mont-Blanc – 175 rue Paul-Corbin, 74190 Chedde - ☎04 50 93 66 73 – www.espace-mont-blanc.com

Nature Parks and Reserves

The protected areas, parks and reserves of the French Alps offer wonderful opportunities for ramblers, cyclists and other nature-lovers. The parks have visitor centres, called "Maisons" at several sites; these are noted in the Sights section. You will find organized nature walks, exhibits and other activites for adults and children.

Parc naturel régional des Bauges – Maison du Parc, 73630 Le Châtelard -☎04 79 54 86 40 - www. pnr-massif-bauges.fr

Parc naturel régional de la Chartreuse – Maison du Parc, 38380 St-Pierre-de-Chartreuse -☎04 76 88 75 20 - www.parc-chartreuse. net, www.chartreuse-tourism.com

Parc national des Écrins – Domaine de Charance, 05000 Gap - ☎ 04 92 40 20 10 - www. les-ecrins-parc-national.fr (7 Maisons du parc 👜 see BRIANÇON, l'EMBRUNAIS, VALOUISE, VALGAUDEMAR, CHAMPSAUR, OISANS, VALBONAIS)

The **Parc national du Mercantour** – 23 rue d'italie - BP 1316, 06006 Nice Cedex - ☎04 93 16 78 78 - www.parc-mercantour.fr (Maison du parc at 👜 BARCELONNETTE)

Parc national de la Vanoise – 135 rue du Dr-Julliand -BP 705, 73007 Chambéry Cedex -☎04 79 62 30 54 - www.vanoise.com Maison du parc at 👜TERMIGNON, contact tourist office ☎04 79 20 51 67

Parc naturel régional du Vercors – Maison du Parc, 255 ch. des Fusiliés, 38250 Lans-en-Vercors -☎04 76 94 38 26 www.pne-vercors.fr

Parc naturel régional du Verdon – BP 14, 04360 Moustiers-Sainte-

Marie -☎04 92 74 68 00 (*See Gorges du VERDON*)

Réserve géologique de Haute-Provence- ☎ 04 92 36 70 70 - www.resgeol04.org (*see DIGNES*)

La Maison des Gorges de Verdon – Le Château, 04120 La-Palud-sur-Verdon - ☎ 04 92 77 32 02, www.lapaludsurverdon.com (*see VERDON*) In the summer, outings are organized to observe **Verdon's famous vulture colony.** Contact the tourist office in Castellane- ☎ 04 92 83 67 14 - www.castellane.org

Parc naturel régional du Queyras – La Ville, 05350 Arvieux -☎04 92 46 88 20 - www.pnr-queyras.com

When to Go

CLIMATE

Sports and leisure in the French Alps changes with the seasons. The region's resorts are at their liveliest in winter, when snowy villages and landscapes, and the frequently brilliant blue skies of the south, offer the best-known images of alpine holidays. Weather in the spring and fall, while lovely and mild, is more unpredictable, with sometimes violent storms and, in south, the notorious springtime *mistral*. In the summer, the south generally remains drier than the lush north, but is also considerably hotter, except in the higher hills. Climbers and walkers flock to the whole area in search of striking panoramas and clean mountain air and the water sports centres around Geneva, Le Bourget and Annecy come into their own. Be aware, however, that heat haze may obscure some of the best views in the height of summer. For any outdoor activity on sea or land, it is useful to have reliable weather forecasts. For **Metéo France** (national weather bureau)reports in French, dial 3250, then select from the recorded choices. For **départemental reports**, dial 08 92 68 02 followed by the two-digit number of the *département* (0.34 €/min):

Alpes de Haute Provence ☎ 04
Alpes Maritimes ☎ 06
Drôme ☎ 26
Haute-de-Savoie ☎ 74
Hautes-Alpes ☎ 05
Isère ☎ 38
Savoie ☎ 73
Var ☎ 83
Vaucluse ☎ 06

For weather on the Web, consult **www.meteo.fr**
See also the chapter on Safety in the Mountains.

WHAT TO PACK

As little as possible! Cleaning and laundry services are available everywhere. Most personal items can be replaced at reasonable cost. Try to pack everything into one suitcase and a tote bag. Porter help may be in short supply, and new purchases will add to the original weight. Take an extra totebag for carrying new purchases or for shopping at open-air markets, for carrying a picnic, etc. Be sure luggage is clearly labelled and old travel tags removed. Do not pack medication in checked luggage, but keep it with you; be sure the prescription is with the medication.

Carry-on luggage is now severely restricted on airplanes; make sure you have enough room in your checked luggage for eventual purchases. To avoid last-minute drama, find out from your airline exactly what is permitted in both your carry-on and checked luggage, and any other security restrictions, which are different on continental Europe from those in Britain or the US.

KNOW BEFORE YOU GO

Useful Web Sites

www.ambafrance-us.org
The French Embassy in the USA website provides a wealth of information and links to other French sites (regions, cities, ministries).

www.franceguide.com
The French Government Tourist Office / Maison de la France site has practical information and links to more specific guidance. The site includes a list of facilities accessible to handicapped people.

www.francekeys.com
This site has practical information covering all the regions, with links to tourist offices and related sites.

www.day-tripper.net
This site offers a information and links to many commercial sites for services such as hotels, car hire, ferry tickets, and whatever France has to sell.

www.fr-holidaystore.co.uk
This website offers links to companies offering ferrry tickets, car rentals, hotels and tours.

www.visiteurope.com
The European Travel Commission provides useful information on travelling in 30 European countries, and includes links to commercial services, rail schedules, weather reports, etc.

www.holidayfrance.org.uk
The Association of British Travel Organisers to France has created this tidy site which covers just about everything.

www. france.com
This is a well-organized site for finding apartments, hotels, rail tickets, car rental, tours, cell phone rental, shuttles etc. There are also background articles and links to relevent sites.

www.justfrance.com
This site offers detailed information on French culture, history, business, education, media etc., useful travel information, as well as links to commercial sites. Notably, there is information about handicapped access.

Tourist Offices

FRENCH TOURIST OFFICES

For information, brochures, maps and assistance in planning a trip to France you should apply to the French Tourist Office in your own country:

Australia – New Zealand
Sydney – Level 22, 25 Bligh Street, NSW 2000 Sydney - ☎ (02) 9231 5244 - http://au.franceguide.com

Canada
Montreal – 1981 Avenue McGill College, Suite 490, Montreal PQ H3A 2W9 - ☎ (514) 288-2026 - http://ca-uk.franceguide.com
Eire
Dublin – No office - ☎ 15 60 235 235 (Irish information line), http://ie.franceguide.com

South Africa
P.O. Box 41022, 2024 Craighall - ☎ 00 27 11 880 80 62 - http://za.franceguide.com

United Kingdom
178 Piccadilly, London WIJ 9AL - ☎ 09068 244 123 - http://uk.franceguide.com

United States
http:// us.franceguide.com
East Coast – New York – 444 Madison Avenue, 16th Floor, NY 10022-6903 - ☎ (514) 288-1904 (Montreal office)
Mid West – Chicago – Consulate General of France, 205 North Michigan Avenue, Suite 3770, Chicago, IL

60601-2819 - ☏ (514) 288-1904 (Montreal office)

West Coast – Los Angeles – 9454 Wilshire Boulevard, Suite 715, Los Angeles, CA 90212-2967 - ☏ (514) 288-1904 (Montréal office)

TOURIST OFFICES IN FRANCE

Visitors will find more precise information through the network of tourist offices in France. The addresses and telephone numbers of local tourist offices, called *syndicats d'initiative* in smaller towns, are listed after the symbol 🛈 in the introductions to individual sights. Addresses for regional tourist offices (covering several *départements*) and *départements* covered in this guide are listed below:

Comité Régional du Tourisme (CRT):

Rhône-Alpes – 104 route de Paris, 69260 Charbonnières-les-Bains - ☏ 04 72 59 21 59 - www.rhone-alpes-tourisme.co.uk

Provence-Alpes-Côte d'Azur – Les Docks, Atrium 10.5, 10 place de la Joliette, BP 46214, 13567 Marseille Cedex 02 - ☏ 04 91 56 47 00 - www.decouverte-paca.fr/us

Riviera-Côte-d'Azur – 55 promenade des Anglais, BP 1602 06011 Nice Cedex 1 - ☏ 08 92 70 74 07 - www.guideriviera.com

Comité Départemental du Tourisme (CDT)

Alpes-de-Haute-Provence – Immeuble François-Mitterand, BP 170, 04005 Digne-les-Bains Cedex - ☏ 04 92 31 57 29 - www.uk.alpes-haute-provence.com

Drôme – 8, rue Baudin BP 531, 26005 Valence - ☏ 04 75 82 19 26 - www.drometourisme.com/anglais

Hautes-Alpes – 8 bis rue Capitaine-de-Bresson BP 46, 05002 Gap Cedex - ☏ 04 92 53 62 00 - www.hautes-alpes.co.uk

Haute-Savoie – 1, rue Jean-Jaures, 74000 Annecy - ☏ 04 50 45 00 33 - www.tourism.savoiehautesavoie.com

Isère – 14 rue de la République, BP 227, F-38019 Grenoble Cedex - ☏ 04 76 54 34 36 - www.isere-tourisme.com

Savoie – Agence touristique départemental de la Savoie, 24 bd de la Colonne, 73000 Chambéry - ☏ 04 79 33 42 47 - www.savoiehautesavoie.com

Var – 1, bd du Mar.-Foch, BP 99, 83003 Draguignan Cedex - ☏ 04 94 50 55 50 - www.tourismevar.com

International Visitors

EMBASSIES AND CONSULATES

Australia
Embassy – 4 rue Jean-Rey, 75724 Cedex 15 Paris - ☏ 01 40 59 33 00 - www.france.embassy.gov.au

Canada
Embassy – 35 avenue Montaigne, 75008 Paris - ☏ 01 44 43 29 00 - www.amb-canada.fr

Eire
Embassy – 4 rue Rude, 75016 Paris - ☏ 01 44 17 67 00 - www.foreignaffairs.gov.ie/irishembassy/france.htm

New Zealand
Embassy – 7 ter rue Léonard-de-Vinci, 75016 Paris - ☏ 01 45 01 43 43 - www.nzembassy.com

South Africa
Embassy – 59 quai d'Orsay, 75007 Paris - ☏ 01 53 59 23 23 - www.afriquesud.net

UK
Embassy – 35 rue du Faubourg St-Honoré, 75383 Paris Cedex 08 - ☏ 01 44 51 31 00 - www.britishembassy.gov.uk

Consulate – 18 bis rue d'Anjou, 75008 Paris- ☎ 01 44 51 31 00

Consulate – Bordeaux – 353 bd du Président-Wilson, 33073 Bordeaux Cedex - ☎05 57 22 21 10

Consulate – Marseille – 24 av du Prado, 13006 Marseille - ☎ 04 91 15 72 10

USA
Embassy – 2 avenue Gabriel, 75382 Paris Cedex 08- ☎ 01 43 12 22 22 - www.amb-usa.fr.

Consulate – 2 rue St-Florentin, 75001 Paris Cedex 08 - ☎ 01 43 12 22 22

Consulate – Marseille – Place Varian Fry 13006 Marseille Cedex 06 - ☎ 04 91 54 92 00 - www.amb-usa.fr/marseille

DOCUMENTS

Passport – Nationals of countries within the European Union entering France need only a national identity card (or in the case of the British, a passport). Nationals of other countries must have a valid national passport.

Visa – No **entry visa** is required for Canadian, US or Australian citizens travelling as tourists and staying less than 90 days, except for students planning to study in France. If in doubt, apply to your local French Consulate. US citizens should obtain the booklet *Safe Trip Abroad* (US$2.75): Government Printing Office - ☎ (202) 512-1800 – or order at http://bookstore. gpo.gov or consult on-line and download at www.pueblo.gsa.gov (click on travel publications). General passport information is available by phone toll-free from the Federal Information Center (item 5 on the automated menu), ☎ 800-688-9889. US passport application forms can be downloaded from http://travel.state.gov

CUSTOMS

In Britain, go to the Customs Office (UK) website at http://customs.hmrc. gov.uk for information on allowances, travel safety tips, and to consult and download documents and guides. For questions contact the National Advice Service at 0845 010 9000. The **US Customs Service** offers a publication *Know Before You Go* for US citizens, to consult and download at www. customs.ustreas.gov (click on travel). **Canadians** can consult or download "I Declare" at www.canadaonline. about.com; for **Australians**, "Know Before You Go" is at www.customs. gov.au; for **New Zealanders,** "Advice for Travellers" is at www.customs. govt.nz

Americans can bring home, tax-free, US$800 worth of goods; **Canadians** CND$750; **Australians** AUS$900 and **New Zealanders** NZ$700. Persons living in a Member State of the European Union are not restricted in regard to goods for private use, but the recommended allowances for alcohol and tobacco are shown in the table.

Spirits (whisky, gin, vodka etc)	10l
Fortified wines (vermouth, port etc)	20l
Wine (not more than 60l sparkling)	90l
Beer	110l
Cigarettes	3 200
Tobacco products (other than cigarettes)	3 kg
Cigars	200
Smoking tobacco	1kg

HEALTH

First aid, medical advice and chemists' night service rota are available from chemists/drugstores *(pharmacie)* identified by the green cross sign. You should take out comprehensive insurance coverage as the recipient of medical treatment in French hospitals or clinics must pay. Nationals of non-EU countries should check with their insurance companies about policy limitations. All prescription drugs should be clearly labelled; it is essential that you carry the prescription.

British and Irish citizens (and all EU citizens) should apply for a European Health Insurance Card (EHIC), which has replaced the E111 and entitles the holder to urgent treatment for accident or unexpected illness in EU countries. **British citizens** apply online to www.dh.gov.uk/travellers, or telephone to 0845 606 2030, or pick up an application at the Post Office. **Irish citizens** may contact info@health.gov.ie or www. ehic.ie. **Americans and Canadians** can contact the International Association for Medical Assistance to Travelers: ☎ for the US (716) 754-4883 or for Canada (416) 652-0137 or (519) 836-0102, www.iamat.org.

The American Hospital of Paris is open 24hr for medical and dental emergencies as well as consultations, with English-speaking staff, at 63 boulevard Victor-Hugo, 92200 Neuilly sur Seine - ☎ 01 46 41 25 25 - www.american-hospital.org. Accredited by major insurance companies.

The Hertford British Hospital is just outside Paris at 3 rue Barbès, 923000 Levallois-Perret - ☎ 01 46 39 22 22 - www.british-hospital.org.

Accessibility

The sights described in this guide which are easily accessible to people of reduced mobility are indicated in the *Admission times and charges* by the symbol &.
Since 2001, the designation **Tourisme et Handicap** has applied to a thousand sites accessible to the handicapped: go to **www.franceguide.com**.
The principal French source for information on facilities is the **Association des Paralysés de France**, Direction de la Communication, 17 bd Auguste-Blanqui, 75013 Paris - www.apf.asso.fr E-mail: faire-face@apf.asso.fr The APF publishes a *Guide vacances* (4.70€) where you will find addresses for APF offices in each *département*, also listed on the website.
For English-speakers, go to **The Access Project**, 39 Bradley Gardens, West Ealing, London WI3 8HE, www.accessproject.phsp.org.
The **Michelin Guide France** and the **Michelin Camping Caravaning France** indicate hotels and campsites with facilities suitable for physically handicapped people.
The **French railways** (SNCF) (www.voyages-sncf.com), **Air France** (www.airfrance.fr) and major ski resorts, through **Handi-Ski** (found on the site for French ski schools: www.esf.net), offer facilities for the handicapped.

GETTING THERE

By Air

The various national and other independent airlines operate services to Paris (Roissy-Charles-de-Gaulle and Orly airports). Major companies offering regularly scheduled flights from the UK and the US to one of the key gateway airports (Geneva, Lyon-Satolas and Chambéry) include Air France, American Airlines, Delta and British Airways. Discount flights within Europe offer wide choice but conditions change often, so check the websites. Top discounters include **Ryanair**, www.ryanair.com; and **Easyjet** at www.easyjet.com; **Flybe** at www.flybe.com; **Jet2.com**, a subsidiary of Dart Group PLC, at www.jet2.com. Within France, air travel generally compares unfavorably with rail, both for price and time, and when you consider transport to and from airports.

Air travel for the handicapped

Air France offers "Saphir" services for the handicapped - ☎08 20 01 24 24 - www.airfrance.fr A guidebook on services in French airports, *L'Aeroguide France*, is available from Aeroguide Éditions, 47 av. Léon-Gambetta, 92120 Montrouge - ☎01 46 55 93 43 - 59€, plus postage.

By Sea

There are numerous **cross-Channel passenger and car** ferry services from the United Kingdom and Ireland, as well as the 35-minute rail trip through the Channel Tunnel between Folkestone and Calais: **Eurotunnel,** ☎ 08705 35 35 35 (in the UK) or 08 10 63 03 04 (in France) - www.eurotunnel.com. To choose the most suitable route between your port of arrival and your destination use the Michelin Tourist and Motoring Atlas France, Michelin map 911 (which gives travel times and mileages) or Michelin maps from the 1:200 000 series (with the yellow cover). For details apply to travel agencies or to:

P & O Ferries

Channel House, Channel View Road, Dover CT1& 9TJ - ☎ 08705 980 333 (in the UK) or 08 35 12 01 56 (in France)- www.poferries.com Service between Dover and Calais.

Norfolk Line

Norfolk House, Eastern Docks, Dover, CT16 1JA Kent - ☎ 870 870 10 20 (in the UK) 03 28 28 95 50 (in France)- www.norfolkline-ferries.com Service between Dover and Dunkerque.

Brittany Ferries

Millbay Docks; Plymouth, Devon. PL1 3EW, - ☎ 0873 665 333 (in the UK), 02 98 29 28 00 (in France) - www.brittany-ferries.com Service between Portsmouth, Poole and Plymouth and ports in France and Spain.

Irish Ferries

PO Box 19, Alexandra Road, Dublin 1 - ☎ 8705 17 17 17 (in the UK) 00 353 818 300 400 (Northern Ireland) 0818 300 400 (Republic of Ireland) - www.irishferries.com Service between Dublin and Rosslane and Roscoff and Cherbourg.

Seafrance Ferrries Ltd.

Whitfield Court, Honeywood Close, Whitfield, Kent CT16 3PX - ☎ 0870 443 1653, www.seafrance.com Service between Dover and Calais.

www.ferries.co.uk

On-line ferry booking through 11 companies as well as accomodation, travel insurance, coverage for vehicle breakdowns - ☎0871 222 3312 (in the UK) +44 (0) 871 222 3312 (outside the UK)

By Rail

The Eurostar Group, composed of British, French and Belgian railways, operates a 3hr passenger service between **London** (Waterloo International Station) and **Paris** (Gare du Nord), with up to 16 trains daily. Passengers can connect to the high-speed TGV train at either Lille or Paris. In 2007, with completion of a high-speed line to London St. Pancras station, time from London to Paris will be reduced to 2hrs 15 minutes. The TGV, speeding at up to 297 kph (186 mph), travels from Paris to Albertville in approximately 3hrs 40min (3hrs 40min in winter), to Annecy in 3h 45min, to Chambéry in 3hrs, to Grenoble in 3hrs, to Thonon-les-Bains in 4h 30min, to Moutiers in 4hrs. From Lille, add one hour. From Lille and Paris, there are direct TGV connections to Bourg-St-Maurice and St-Jean-de-Maurienne. For French railways (SNCF) reservations and information: direct line - ☎3635 (0.34€/min) or 0 892 35 35 35 (only from abroad) or 3615 SNCF (0.21€/min) - www.voyages-sncf.com Regional trains, called TER, and SNCF buses link the whole region in an efficient network. However, you will often have to transfer between lines if you want to go from the Tarentaise to the Maurienne regions, or to Faucigny. Direct line same as for the SNCF or 3615 TER (0.21€/min) - www.ter-sncf.com/paca During the winter, special ski trains leave from Waterloo on Friday evening and Saturday morning, connecting through Paris Gare du Nord to the stations of Bourg St-Maurice, Aime la Plagne, Moûtiers, Albertville and Chambéry: Snow Train Call Centre - ☎0871 244 646. In summer, direct Eurostar service connects Waterloo to Avignon on Saturdays: ☎0875 186 186 - www.eurostar.com.

Eurailpass, Flexipass, Eurailpass Youth, EurailDrive Pass and **Saverpass** are travel passes which may be purchased by residents of countries outside the European Union. In the Western Hemisphere, go to www.raileurope.com. In the **US**, contact your travel agent or **Rail Europe** ☎ 1-877-257-2887. In **Canada**, contact 1-800-361-RAIL. **Australians** go to www.railplus.com.au, ☎1300 555 003, and for **New Zealanders**, go to www.railplus.com.nz, ☎ 649 377 5415. **European residents** can buy an individual country pass if not a resident of the country where you plan to use it. In the UK, contact Rail Europe Ltd. at Rail Europe House, 34 Tower View, Kings Hill, West Malling, Kent ME19 4ED. ☎ 08705 848 848, www.raileurope.co.uk. At the SNCF (French railways) site, www.sncf.fr, you can book ahead, pay with a credit card, and receive your ticket in the mail at home.

There are numerous **discounts** available, from 25-50% below the regular rate. These include discounts for using senior cards and youth cards, group rates and seasonal promotions. You can procure special passes and ID cards in all SNCF stations and boutiques; bring an ID photo. The SNCF also operates a **travel service** for accomodation, car rentals and holiday packages. Remember to validate (composter) French railway tickets using the orange automatic date-stamping machines at the platform entrance. Failure to do so may result in a fine. SNCF also operates a **telephone information, reservation and prepayment service in English** from 7am to 10pm (French time). In France call ☎ 08 36 35 35 39 (when calling from outside France, drop the initial 0 and add 33).

Rail travel for the handicapped

A free brochure describing services for the handicapped is available at French railway (SNCF) stations and boutiques or at www.voyages-sncf.com: Mémento du voyageur handicappé. Or telephone SNCF Accessibilité Service - ☎08 00 15 47 53.

By Coach/Bus

The Alps can also be reached by coach via Paris. **Eurolines,** Europe's largest regular coach network, operates ski season services to Chamonix, Grenoble, Annecy, Chambéry and Lyon.

London: National Express Ltd, Ensign Court, 4 Vicarage Road, Edgbaston, Birmingham B15 3ES - ☎ 08705 808080, Disabled Persons Hotline: 0121 423 8479 - www.nationalexpress.com/euroline.

Paris: Gare Routière internationale de Paris Gallieni, Boite 313, 28 av du Général-de-Gaulle, 93541 Bagnolet- ☎ 01 49 72 51 52 - www.eurolines.fr.

GETTING AROUND

Driving in France

The area covered in this guide is easily reached by main motorways and national routes. Refer to the listing of Michelin maps and plans at the back of the guide. The latest Michelin route-planning service is available on Internet, **www.ViaMichelin.co.uk.** Travellers can work out a precise route using such options as shortest route, scenic route, route avoiding toll roads or the Michelin-recommended route. The site also provides tourist information (hotels, restaurants and attractions).

The roads are very busy during the holiday period, particularly at weekends in July and August, and to avoid traffic congestion it is advisable to follow the recommended secondary routes (signposted as *Bison Futé – itinéraires bis).*

DOCUMENTS

Travellers from other European Union countries and North America can drive in France with a valid national or home-state **driving licence.** An **international driving licence** is advisable, however. **In the US,** contact the National Automobile Club, 1151 East Hillsdale Blvd., Foster City, CA 94404 - ☎ 650-294-7000, 1-800-622-2136, www.nationalautoclub.com; or contact your local branch of the American Automobile Association, ☎1-866-968-7222, www.aaa.com. The IDP costs US$10. **In Canada**, contact www.caa.ca for provincial clubs; the permit costs CDN$15. The **Australian Automobile Association** at www.aaa.asn.au and the **New Zealand Automobile Association** at www.aa.co.nz - ☎0800 500 444 also provide the IDP. Most car rental agencies will ask for it, even if not required, and it is useful identification even for those not planning to drive. For the vehicle, it is necessary to have the registration papers (logbook) and a nationality plate of the approved size.

Certain motoring organisations (AAA, CAA, AA, RAC) offer accident **insurance** and breakdown service schemes for members. Check with your current insurance company in regard to cover while abroad. If you plan to hire a car using your credit card, check with the company, which may provide liability insurance automatically.

HIGHWAY CODE

The minimum driving age is 18. Traffic drives on the right. All passengers, front and back, must wear **seat belts.** Children under age 10 must ride in the back seat, unless in a specially approved seat facing backwards. Headlights must be switched on in poor visibility and at night.

In the case of a **breakdown,** a red warning triangle or hazard warning lights are obligatory. In the absence of stop signs at intersections, cars must **yield to the right.** Vehicles must stop when the lights turn red at road junctions and may filter to the right only when indicated by an amber arrow. The regulations on **drinking and driving** (limited to .05% or 0.50g/l, two or three glasses of wine) and **speeding** are strictly enforced – usually by an on-the-spot fine and/or confiscation of the vehicle. Remember that on **steep, single lane roads in the Alps**, as elsewhere in France, the driver heading downhill is expected to pull over or reverse to allow oncoming vehicles to pass. For an official text of the Highway Code, go to www.legifrance.gouv.fr

Parking Regulations – In town there are zones where parking is either restricted or subject to a fee; tickets should be obtained from the ticket machines *(horodateurs* – small change necessary) and displayed inside the windscreen on the driver's side; failure to display may result in a fine, or towing and impoundment. Other parking areas may require you to take a ticket when passing through a barrier. To exit, you must pay the parking fee (usually there is a machine located by the exit – *sortie)* and insert the paid-up card in another machine which will lift the exit gate. Where a blue parking zone is marked by a blue line on the road and a 🅿 sign, a cardboard disc *(disque de stationnement)* gives 1hr 30min parking, or 2hr 30 min over lunchtime. Discs are available in supermarkets or petrol stations and occasionally given away free.

Tolls – In France, most motorway sections are subject to a toll *(péage)*. You can pay in cash or with a credit card (Visa, Mastercard).

Petrol (US: gas) – French service stations dispense: *sans plomb* 98 (super unleaded 98), *sans plomb* 95 (super unleaded 95), *diesel/gazole* (diesel) and *GPL* (LPG). Gas in France is much more expensive than in the US. It is usually cheaper off the motorway; check the large hypermarkets on the outskirts of town.

CAR RENTAL

There are car rental agencies at airports, railway stations and in all large towns throughout France. Most European cars have manual transmission; automatic cars are available only if an advance reservation is made. Drivers must be over 21; between ages 21-25, drivers are required to pay an extra daily fee; some companies allow drivers under 23 only if the reservation has been made through a travel agent. It is relatively expensive to hire a car in France; North Americans in particular should take advantage of fly-drive offers, or seek advice from a travel agent, specifying requirements.

Rental agencies have offices all over France; to find the one near where you want to rent, consult the websites.

- **Avis:** Online booking at www. Avis.fr
- **AutoEurope:** ☎1-888-223-5555 (US and Canada), www.autoeurope.com
- **Budget France:** ☎08 25 00 35 64 - www.budget.fr
- **Hertz France:** www.hertz.fr
- **Europcar:** www.europcar.fr
- **SIXT-Eurorent:** ☎08 20 00 74 98 - www.e-sixt.com
- **National-CITER:** www.citer.fr
- **Baron's Limousine:** (chauffeur-driven) ☎01 45 30 21 21- www. barons-limousines.com

- **Worldwide Motorhome Rentals** www.mhrww.com or call (US toll-free) ☎ 1-888- 519-8969; outside the US ☎ 1-530-389-8316

- **Overseas Motorhome Tours Inc.** in the US ☎ 800-322-2127; outside the US ☎ 1-310-543-2590 , www.omtinc.com

By Rail

♿ *See Getting There*

By Coach/Bus

♿ *See Getting There*

WHERE TO STAY AND EAT

Where to Stay

FINDING A HOTEL

Turn to the Address Books in the *Discovering the Sights* section for descriptions and prices of typical places to stay and eat with local flair. Use the **map of Places to stay** below to identify recommended places for overnight stops. For an even greater selection, use the red-cover **Michelin Guide France,** with its famously reliable star-rating system and hundreds of establishments all over France. For further assistance, **La Fédération Loisirs Accueil**, 280 bd St-Germain, 75007 Paris - ☎01 44 11 10 44 - www. loisirsaccueilfrance.com offers booking services. The website gives the addresses and telephone numbers of Fédération offices in 62 *départements*; or you can ask for a list by e-mail: info@loisirsaccueilfrance. **La Fédération nationale Clévacances** offers a huge list of rental properties and rooms in 79 départements. You can also request a list for specific *départements* at 54 bd de l'Embouchure, BP 52116, 31022 Toulouse Cedex 2 - ☎05 61 13 55 66 - www.clevacance.com

A guide to good-value, family-run hotels, **Logis et Auberges de France,** is available from the French Tourist Office - www.tourisme.fr. The website gives an extensive list of accomodations for each *département*, as well as links for making reservations, and a list of tourist offices all over France; you can order the brochure by e-mail on the site.

Relais et châteaux , www.relais-chateaux.com, provides information on luxury hotels with character. The guide can be ordered or downloaded online: 15 rue Galvani, 75017 Paris, ☎ 08 25 32 32 32. From the US: 1-800-735-2478 . From Canada: 1-866-390-0090. From the UK: 00 800 2000 00 02.

Economy Chain Hotels – If you need a place to stop en route, these can be useful, as they are inexpensive (35-45€ for a double room) and generally located near the main road. While breakfast is available, there may not be a restaurant; rooms are small and simple, with a television and bathroom.

Rather than sort through hotels yourself, you can go to websites that cover several chains, from modest to luxurious. These sites allow you to select your hotel based on geographical location, price and level of comfort, and to book online.

- **www.viamichelin.com** covers hotels in France, including famous selections from the Michelin Guide as well as lower-priced chains.
- **www.activehotels.com** covers a wide range of hotels, and offers customer reviews.
- **www.day-tripper.net** covers reasonably priced hotels, by location, throughout France.

Here are some modestly-priced chains:
- **Akena** - ☎ 01 69 84 85 17 - www.hotels-akena.com
- **B&B** - ☎ 02 98 33 75 00 (in France); 33 02 98 33 75 00 (when calling from outside France) - www.hotel-bb.com
- **Mister Bed** - ☎ 01 46 14 38 00 You book through a bigger website such as en.venere.com
- **Best Hôtel** - ☎ 03 28 27 46 69 - www.besthotel.fr

The hotels listed below are slightly more expensive (from 45€), and offer a few more amenities and services.
- **Campanile, Kyriad, Bleu Marine, Première Classe, Louvre -** ☎ 01 64 62 46 46 - www.envergure.fr

A Typical French Menu

La Carte	The Menu
ENTRÉES	STARTERS
Crudités	Raw vegetable salad
Terrine de lapin	Rabbit terrine (pâté)
Frisée aux lardons	Curly lettuce with bacon bits
Escargots	Snails
Salade au crottin de Chavignol	Goat cheese on a bed of lettuce
PLATS (VIANDES)	MAIN COURSES (MEAT)
Bavette à l'échalote	Sirloin with shallots
Faux filet au poivre	Sirloin with pepper sauce
Pavé de rumsteck	Thick rump steak
Côtes d'agneau	Lamb chops
Filet mignon de porc	Pork fillet
Blanquette de veau	Veal in cream sauce
Nos viandes sont garnies	Our meat dishes are served with vegetables
PLATS (POISSONS, VOLAILLE)	MAIN COURSES (FISH, FOWL)
Filets de sole	Sole fillets
Dorade aux herbes	Sea bream with herbs
Saumon grillé	Grilled salmon
Truite meunière	Trout fried in butter
Magret de canard	Duck breast
Poulet rôti	Roast chicken
FROMAGE	CHEESE
DESSERTS	DESSERTS
Tarte aux pommes	Apple pie
Crème caramel	Cooled baked custard with caramel sauce
Sorbet: trois parfums	Sherbet/sorbet: choose 3 flavours
BOISSONS	BEVERAGES
Bière	Beer
Eau minérale (gazeuse)	(Sparkling) mineral water
Une carafe d'eau	A carafe of tap water (no charge)
Vin rouge, vin blanc, rosé	Red wine, white wine, rosé
Jus de fruit	Fruit juice
MENU ENFANT	CHILDREN'S MENU
Jambon	Ham
Steak haché	Minced beef
Frites	French fried potatoes

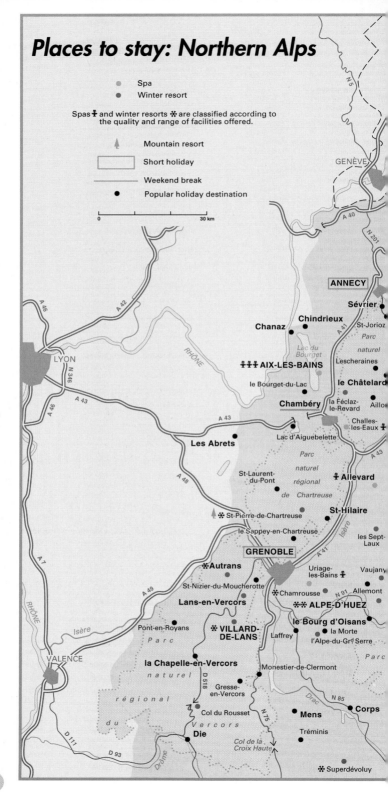

Places to stay: Northern Alps

- ● Spa
- ● Winter resort

Spas ‡ and winter resorts ✳ are classified according to the quality and range of facilities offered.

- ▲ Mountain resort
- ▢ Short holiday
- — Weekend break
- ● Popular holiday destination

0 ———————— 30 km

GENÈVE

ANNECY

Sévrier
St-Jorioz
Chanaz Chindrieux
Parc
naturel
Lescheraines
‡‡‡ AIX-LES-BAINS
le Bourget-du-Lac
le Châtelard
la Féclaz-
le-Revard Aillon
LYON
Chambéry
Challes-
les-Eaux ‡
Lac d'Aiguebelette
Les Abrets
Parc
St-Laurent-
du-Pont
naturel
régional
‡ **Allevard**
de Chartreuse
▲✳ St-Pierre-de-Chartreuse
St-Hilaire
le Sappey-en-Chartreuse
les Sept-
Laux
GRENOBLE
✳**Autrans**
Uriage-
les-Bains ‡ Vaujany
St-Nizier-du-Moucherotte
✳Chamrousse Allemont
Lans-en-Vercors
✳✳ ALPE-D'HUEZ
Pont-en-Royans
✳ **VILLARD-**
DE-LANS
le Bourg d'Oisans
Laffrey la Morte
l'Alpe-du-Grᵈ Serre
la Chapelle-en-Vercors
Parc
VALENCE
Monestier-de-Clermont
naturel
Gresse-
en-Vercors
régional
du
Col du Rousset
Mens
Die
Tréminis
Vercors
Col de la
Croix Haute
Corps
✳ Superdévoluy

34

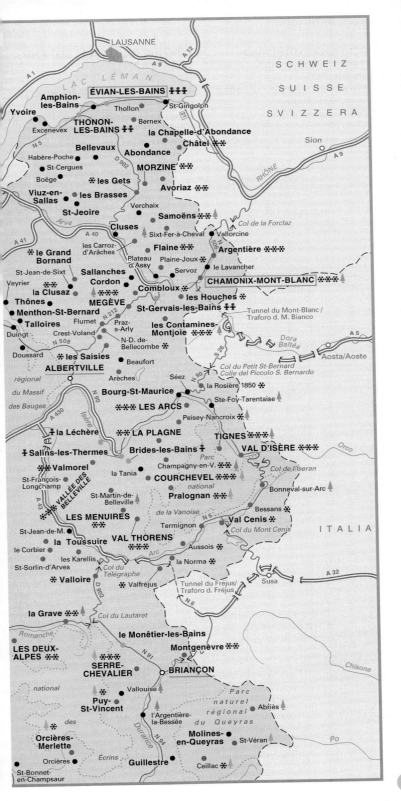

Other online chain reservations:

- 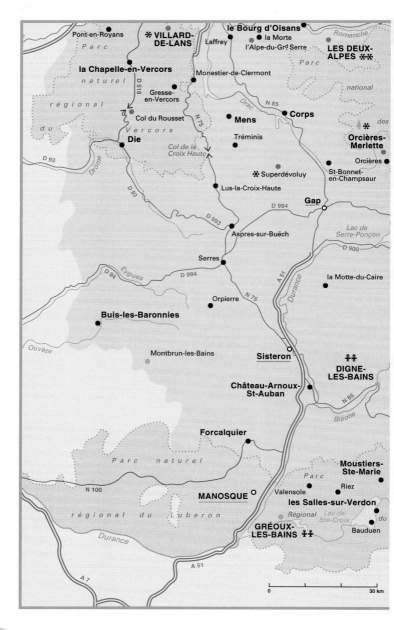 www.ichotelsgroup.com (Holiday Inn)
- www.choicehotels.com (Comfort)
- www.bestwestern.fr (Best Western)
- www.etaphotel.com (Étap Hotels)
- www.ibishotel.com (Ibis Hotels)

RENTING A COTTAGE, BED AND BREAKFAST

The **Maison des Gîtes de France** lists self-catering cottages or apartments, or bed and breakfast accommodation *(chambres d'hôtes)* at a reasonable price: 59 rue St-Lazare, 75439 Paris

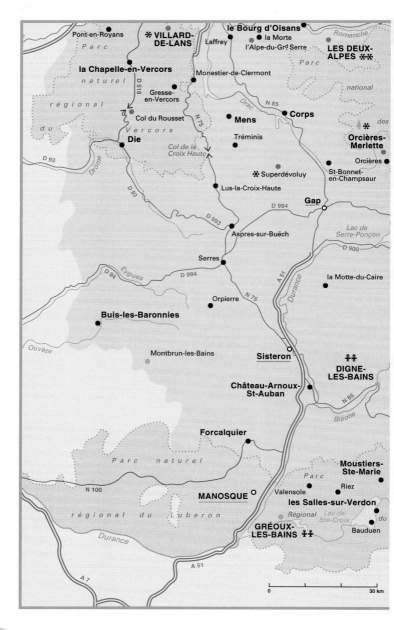

Cedex 09 - ☎ 01 49 70 75 75 - www. gites-de-france.com

La Fédération des Stations Vertes lists some 588 country and mountain sites ideal for families: BP 71698, 21016 Dijon Cedex - ☎03 80 54 10 50 - www. stationsvertes.com

The Association of British Travel Organizers to France, **www.holi-dayfrance.org.uk** lists companies offering self-catering apartments or houses. There is also **Bed and Breakfast France**, PO Box 47085, London SW18 9AB, ☎ 0871 781 0834-www. bedbreak.com, and **Mountain Base**

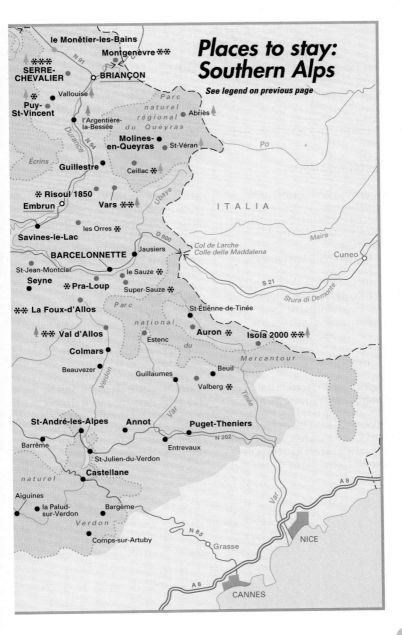

Places to stay: Southern Alps

See legend on previous page

specialising in self-catering apartments and chalets in the Chamonix Valley, ☎ 33 (0)4 50 90 67 45 www.mountain-base.com.

The **Fédération des Logis de France** offers hotel-restaurant packages geared to hiking, fishing, biking, skiing, wine-tasting and enjoying nature: ☎01 45 84 83 84 - www.logis-de-france.fr

The adventurous can consult **www.gites-refuges.com** where you can order a guidebook, *Gîtes d'étapes et refuges*, listing some 4 000 shelters for hikers, mountaineers, rock climbers, skiers, canoe/kayakers etc: 74 rue A. Perdreaux , 78140 Vélizy ☎01 34 65 11 89.

HOSTELS, CAMPING

To obtain an International Youth Hostel Federation ("Hosteling International") card (there is no age requirement), contact the IYHF in your own country:
- ◆ **US** - ☎ (202) 783-6161, www.hiusa.org;
- ◆ **UK** ☎ 1707 324 170, www.iyhf.org;
- ◆ **Canada** - ☎ (613) 273- 7884 - www.hihostels.ca;
- ◆ **Australia** - ☎ 61-2-9565-1669 - www.yhg.com.au.

You can book through: www.hihostels.com

In France, the **Fédération Unie des Auberges de Jeunesse (FUAJ)** is associated with Hosteling International: 27 rue Pajol, 75018 Paris - ☎ 01 44 89 87 27 - www.fuaj.org The **Ligue Française pour les Auberges de la Jeunesse** (LFAJ) can be contacted at

67, rue Vergniaud, Bât. K, 73013 Paris - ☎ 01 44 16 78 78 - www.auberges-de-jeunesse.com

The **Michelin Camping Caravaning France** guide lists a selection of campsites. The Alps are popular with campers in the summer months, particularly the areas around the Lac d'Aiguebelette and the Lac d'Annecy, so it is wise to reserve in advance.

Where to Eat

Turn to the Address Books in the *Discovering the Sights* section for descriptions and prices of selected places to eat. Use the red-cover **Michelin Guide France,** with its famously reliable star-rating system for an even greater choice. If you would like to dine at a highly rated restaurant from The Michelin Guide, book ahead! In the countryside, lunch is served between noon and 2pm and dinner between 7.30-10pm. However, a hungry traveller can usually get a sandwich in a café, and ordinary hot dishes may be available in a *brasserie*.

Restaurants usually charge for meals in two ways: a fixed-price *menu,* with 2 or 3 courses and sometimes a small pitcher of wine, or the more expensive *à la carte,* with each course ordered separately.

Cafés have different prices, depending on location. The price is cheaper if you stand at the counter *(au comptoir)* than if you sit down in the main room *(dans la salle)* and often it is even more expensive outdoors *(sur la terrace).*

WHAT TO DO AND SEE

Outdoor Fun

SAFETY IN THE MOUNTAINS

Mountain areas are potentially dangerous, even for the most experienced enthusiasts. Avalanches, falling rocks, bad weather, fog, treacherous terrain and snowfields, icy water, loss of one's bearings and wrong assessment of distances are the dangers threatening mountaineers, skiers and hikers.

Driving in Mountain Areas

Unaccustomed drivers may be overawed by the experience and it is essential to take certain precautions. Cars must be in good working order (brakes and tyres particularly; snow tyres and chains in winter) and drivers must abide rigorously by the highway code. For instance, horns must be sounded on twisting roads with reduced visibility and along narrow roads and cars going downhill must give way to those climbing. When climbing continuously, it is advisable to watch the oil and cooling liquid levels. In addition, it is recommended to avoid driving in bad weather, getting caught by nightfall, stopping beneath a cliff (falling rocks are frequent) or leaving the car unattended in an isolated spot (danger of theft).

Tricky scenic roads – Michelin maps on a scale of 1:200 000 show very narrow roads (where passing is difficult or impossible), unusually steep ones, difficult or dangerous sections, tunnels and the altitude of major passes.

Snow cover – Maps nos 916, 919 and 989 on a scale of 1:1 000 000 show major roads which are regularly blocked by snow with their probable closing dates and those which are cleared within 24 hours. Access roads to resorts are normally cleared daily.

A Few Words of Advice

Advice given to off-piste skiers also applies to hikers and mountaineers. However, a prolonged stay above 3 000m/9 842ft calls for special precautions. Atmospheric pressure is one third lower and the heart beats faster to compensate for the lack of oxygen. It takes roughly a week to get used to it as the production of red cells in the blood is intensified so that as much oxygen can be carried as at lower altitudes.

The main dangers are the following. **Mountain sickness** or hypoxaemia (symptoms: digestive problems, breathing difficulty, headache) which can normally be treated with appropriate medicine that tourists are advised to take with them; the more serious cases (pulmonary oedema) have to be treated in hospital. **Hypothermia** is also a danger in mountain areas for people caught by a sudden change in the weather such as fog, for instance, which always brings a cold snap. **Frostbite** is less obvious as symptoms appear progressively: loss of feeling in the hands and feet, numbness and paleness of the skin. The danger lies in the wrong treatment being applied on the spot: never try to heat up the affected part of the body, by whatever means, unless you can keep it warm until the doctor arrives, as a new attack of frostbite on a partially rewarmed limb would cause even more damage.

Accidents can be avoided or their consequences lessened by following these simple rules; it is also recommended never to go hiking or mountaineering on your own, and to let someone know of your planned itinerary and when you intend to return.

Weather forecast – Up-to-date recorded information about regional weather is available to hikers (*for telephone numbers, see Tourist information*). In addition, more specific information can be obtained:

(⌖) Five-day forecast in high-mountain areas: ☎ 08 36 68 04 04 - www.meteo.fr

(⌖) Risk of avalanche: ☎ 08 36 68 10 20. www.meteo.fr offers avalanche predictions; English version at www.henrysavalanchetalk.com.

Avalanches – Whether they happen naturally or are started by passing skiers, they represent a permanent danger which must not be dismissed lightly. **Bulletins Neige et Avalanche** (BNA), posted in every resort and hiking base, warn of the risks that must be taken into consideration by anyone planning an excursion. A new more precise scale of potential risks has been devised for the benefit of those who practise off-piste skiing, cross-country skiing or snowshoeing. This is only a general guideline which needs to be supplemented with more precise information concerning the planned itinerary. In addition, it is advisable to be fairly flexible and evaluate the risks incurred in each case.

Lightning – Violent gusts of wind are the warning signs of an imminent thunderstorm, which brings with it the danger of being struck by lightning. Avoid walking along ridges, taking shelter beneath overhanging rocks or isolated trees, at the entrance of caves or hollows in the rock and near metallic fences. Do not carry large metallic objects such as an ice-axe and crampons. Do not huddle under a metallic-framed shelter. Stand more than 15 metres/yards from any high point (rock or tree) and adopt a crouching position, keeping your hands and any bare parts of your body away from the surface of the rock. Before lightning strikes, the atmosphere often becomes electrified and a sound like the humming of a swarm of bees can sometimes be heard, well known to mountain-dwellers. Finally, remember that a car provides a safe shelter during a storm as it makes an excellent Faraday cage.

Assistance – Contact the **gendarmerie** who will get their own rescue service to deal with the problem or will call on the local rescue teams.

Who pays for it? – The cost can be very high, especially if a rescue helicopter is called out, and the person rescued or his family are normally expected to pay. It is therefore advisable to take out insurance to cover such risks.

SKIING

The Alps are the ideal area for winter sports, an environment in which new ways of getting across snowfields are tested and existing techniques perfected.

For up-to-date information, contact the **Association des Stations Françaises de sports d'hiver/ Ski**

Avalanche-Risk Scale

1 – **Low:** snow cover is stable and there are only rare avalanches on very steep slopes.

2 – **Limited:** snow cover is again stable but avalanches may be started in specific areas by an excessive number of skiers or hikers.

3 – **Likely:** snow cover is only moderately stable and avalanches may be started in many places by individuals; avalanches are also likely to start naturally as for 4 on the scale.

4 – **Very likely:** snow cover is fairly unstable on all steep slopes and avalanches are very likely to occur, set off by skiers or hikers, or even spontaneously.

5 – **Extremely likely:** snow cover is very unstable following a heavy snow fall and major avalanches will occur even on gentle slopes.

France, 61 bd Haussmann, 75008 Paris, ☏01 47 42 23 32, www.ski-france.fr

Downhill skiing – This is the most popular form of skiing, available in all the Alpine resorts. The French champion Émile Allais devised its present form in 1931.

Cross-country or Nordic skiing – This type of skiing is ideal on fairly level terrain; skis are long and narrow, boots are low and fixed at the point only. Skiers either glide forward in a stride (traditional style), or skate in modern racing style; both are Olympic disciplines. There are marked tracks of various lengths in most resorts.
In addition, most resorts provide specially marked areas for cross-country skiers in the lower parts of ski slopes. This form of skiing can be practised at any age, each skier going at his own pace. The **Vercors** region is particularly suitable for cross-country skiing, with special markings, mountain refuges and shelters. Information is available from the Parc naturel régional du Vercors, www.parc-de-vercors.fr. Hard-core skiers can try the **Haute Trace des Escartons** between Saint Véran and Névache. The **Parc naturel régional du Queyras,** which combined with the **Guisane** valley boasts some of the best cross-country skiing in the south, offers similar facilities: www.pnr-queyras.com.
For more information, contact:
Hautes-Alpes Ski de Fond – 1 av. Vauban - 05100 Briançon, ☏04 92 20 15 09, www.skidefond05.com

Ski touring – This form of skiing is suitable for experienced skiers with plenty of stamina as it combines the technique of cross-country skiing for uphill sections and that of off-piste skiing for downhill sections. Skiers should be accompanied by a qualified guide, and special equipment is necessary: skis fitted with seal skins for climbing. There are several famous itineraries across the Alps: the **Grande Traversée des Alpes** (GTA) which follows footpath GR 5 from Lake Geneva to the Mediterranean.
For more information, contact the **Bureau Information Montagne/GTA** – Maison de la Montagne, 3 rue Raoul-Blanchard, 38000 Grenoble, ☏04 76 42 45 90, www.grenoble-universites.fr. Ski-touring is also popular in the Alpes de Haute-Provence Region, where there are more than 1000 km of trails in the upper Ubaye, the upper Verdon (and the *pays* d'Annot), and also in more southern regions such as the slopes of Contadour.
 Contact a guiding centre if you want to be accompanied. These are listed in the mountaineering section.

Val Thorens – one of the great French resorts

S. Sauvignier/MICHELIN

Alternative ways to ski:

Monoskiing – Requires a good sense of balance because both feet are fixed to a single ski, facing downhill. It is mostly practiced off-piste. An ancestor of snowboarding, it was abandoned for a time but is now back in force in France; it is still rare in North America: Association française de Monoski – 390 rte du Mas, 38250 Lans-en-Vercors - www.monoski-france.com

Snowshoeing –This old-fashioned winter sport has become popular again with the introduction of smaller, light-weight metal snowshoes that have opened the sport to people of all ages and abilities who want to experience untrammelled nature far from crowds (if you go very far, take a guide). It is best to begin with a lesson on how to walk lightly on the snowshoes and how to use poles; this is quite easily mastered.
Most guiding centers offer interesting snowshoe tours in nature preserves, with no previous experience required, either for a half-day or for a longer circuit with a rest stop.

Snowboarding – This very popular sport, since 1998 an Olympic event in its own right, is practised on a single board on steep slopes, often on mogul runs or where the snow is uneven. Techniques and equipment are constantly evolving. Boarders may use the same slopes as skiers, but for the more free-spirited, many resorts have "snowparks" where boarders can practice acrobatic moves.

Mogul skiing – This acrobatic form of skiing has also become an Olympic event; it consists of skiing down very bumpy runs and is a good way of getting used to off-piste skiing.

Ski-joering – Some resorts now offer this old Scandinavian means of transport: riding on skis while attached to a horse or sled dogs.

Telemark skiing – This Norweigan technique is the ancestor of modern skiing: ski boots are attached at the heel by a cable that leaves the heel free, permitting the skier to execute elegant turns by genuflecting over one ski and bringing the tail of the other up and around: Association française de télémark – FFS - 50 rue des Marquisats - BP 2451 - 74011 Annecy -☎04 50 51 40 34 - www.ffs.fr

Off-piste skiing – This is intended for very experienced skiers who ski outside marked runs at their own risk. The presence and advice of a guide or instructor with a comprehensive knowledge of dangerous areas is highly recommended. Some resorts have off-piste areas which are unmarked but patrolled.

WINTER SPORT RESORTS

See the Places to Stay map at the beginning of the guide and the table of resorts below. All the resorts mentioned offer accommodation listed in The Michelin Guide France.
The Alps boast a great variety of resorts. Beside internationally famous resorts such as Tignes, Val d'Isère, Courchevel and Chamonix, there are a great number of more modest ones which have retained their village character and attract a family clientele. Skiing resorts have changed over the past decades as skiing itself has developed. The first ones evolved from existing traditional villages or small towns, such as Morzine or Megève; the second generation of resorts, including Val d'Isère, L'Alpe-d'Huez, Les Deux-alpes, moved to high pastures in search of good skiing slopes. The post-war period saw the blossoming of planned resorts like Courchevel, Chamrousse, Tignes and the latest resorts, such as Les Arcs, Avoriaz, Les Ménuires, Val-Thorens and Flaine, all of which were designed by a single property developer.
Ski-lifts reach higher and higher, extending the resorts' skiing areas which are often linked. In some cases (L'Alpe-d'Huez, Val d'Isère, Tignes, Les

Deux-Alpes, Val-Thorens), they reach so high that the snow cover holds throughout the summer making all-year skiing possible.

Summer skiing resorts – Six resorts offer summer skiing, depending on snow conditions, as well as more traditional summer activities. Val d'Isère and Tignes have snow-making on their glaciers, so are more reliable.

- **L'Alpe-d'Huez** – June to late July on the Sarennes Glacier (3 000m/9 842ft).
- **Les Deux-Alpes** – mid-June to August on the Mont-de-Lans Glacier (3 420m/11 220ft).
- **La Plagne** – July on the Bellecôte Glacier (3 416m/11 207ft).
- **Tignes** – June to September on the Grande Motte Glacier (3 430m/11 253ft).
- **Val d'Isère** – late June to mid-August
- **Val-Thorens** – July to August on the Péclet Glacier (3 400m/11 155ft).

Dates vary according to conditions: confirm with the ski area or at http://pistehors.com before making plans.

Linked skiing areas – A number of individual resorts have joined together to form extensive ski areas. Note that the term *domaines reliés*, or linked resorts such as Portes du Soleil, means you can ski from one resort to another, while *domaine skiable* means that, while you can ski all the areas with one ticket, you may have to take a bus or car among areas.

- **Les Aravis** – St-Jean-de-Sixt, La Clusaz, Le Grand Bornand, Manigod.
- **Les 2 Alpes** – LaGrave, La Meije, Les 2Alpes, Vénoesc-Vénéon
- **Espace les Arcs** – Les Arcs, La Plagne, and Peisey-Nancroix
- **Espace Diamant** – Crest-Voland, Cohennoz et les Saises, Flument, N-D de Bellecombe
- **Espace Killy** – Tignes and Val-d'Isère.

- **Espace San Bernardo** – Séez-St-Bernard, La Rosière
- **Évasion Mont-Blanc** – Combloux, LaGiettaz, Megève, St-Gervais, St-Nicholas-de-Véroce, Les Contamines-Montjoie, Les Houches
- **Grand Domaine** – St François, Longchamp, Valmorel, Doucy-Combelouvière
- **Le Grand Massif** – Les Carroz-d'Arâches, Flaine, Morillon, Samoëns, Sixt-Fer-à-Cheval
- **Les Grandes Rousses** – Allemont, l'Alpe-d'Huez, Auris-en-Oisans, Oz-en-Oisans, Vaujany, Villard-Reculas
- **Paradiski** – La Plagne, Plagne-Montalbert, les Arcs/Bourg-St-Maurice, Peisey-Vallandry, Champagny-en-Vanoise, Montchavin-les-Coches, Villaroger
- **Les Portes du Soleil** - Abondance, Avoriaz, la Chapelle d'Abondance, Châtel, les Gets, Montriond et Morzine, St-Jean-d'Aulps; Swiss resorts: Champéry, Morgins, Torgon, Val d'illiez
- **Savoie Grand Renard** – La Féclaz, le Revard, St-François-de-Sales
- **Les Sybelles** – Les Bottières-Jarrier, St-Colomban, St-Alban-des-Villards, La Toussuire, le Corbier, St-Jean-d'Arves, St-Sorlin-d'Arves
- **Les Trois Vallées** – Les Ménuires, Courchevel, Val-Thorens, La Tania, Méribel and St-Martin-de-Belleville, Brides-les-Bains, Orelle.
- **Valée-Verte** – St-Jean-d'Aulps, Bellevaux, Hirmentaz, Les Habères
- **Valloire/Valmeinier** – Valloire, Valmeinier

Handiski

It's possible to ski even if you have a handicap. Special teams, infrastructure and equipment are available at many ski areas. Ski sleds allow people to ski seated, while those with sight or hearing difficulties can also ski, accompanied by qualified personnel. Often there are discounted lift-tickets for the handicapped and their companion; all equipment, of course, must be approved by ski technicians and by the French Fédération Hand-isport. Information about special ski instruction through Handiski is found at www.esf.net

Fédération Handisport – 42, rue Louis-Lumière - 75020 Paris -☎01 40 31 45 00 -www.handisport.org

HIKING

Hiking is the best way to explore mountain areas and discover the finest scenery. Footpaths are extensively described in this guide and three types of hike are identified. **Rambles** are, in principle, suitable for anyone, including children. **Day hikes** require more stamina and some prior training for a walking time exceeding 4hr and a difference in altitude of 700m/2 297ft. A few more demanding **itineraries for experienced hikers** are also described including extremely steep or vertiginous sections which do not however require any specialised mountaineering knowledge; these are worth the extra physical effort for the exceptional panoramas. Before leaving, always get the latest weather forecast and make sure that the length of the hike is compatible with the time of departure. In mountain areas, the estimated length of an excursion is calculated according to the difference in altitude: 300m/984ft per hour going up and 500m/1 640ft going down, excluding stops.

Leave early in the morning if you can, so that all the climbing can be done during the cool hours of the day and you stand a better chance of observing the fauna.

Whatever the type of hike, you should carry with you a map on a scale of 1:25 000 or 1:50 000, 1.5 to 3 litres of water per person, energy-building food, a hat, waterproof clothing, a pullover, sunglasses, sun cream, a first-aid kit and a plastic bag for garbage which you must carry down with you; you cannot leave garbage at the shelters. You should also wear mountain boots and carry a pair of binoculars to spot distant peaks and observe the fauna. Avoid wearing brightly coloured clothes, moving too

abruptly and being too noisy for fear of frightening the animals away.

Mountain-refuge bookings
– Refuges are now equipped with radio-telephones (numbers available at tourist offices) and booking is now compulsory during the summer season. Hikers arriving without a booking should not therefore count on finding a bed for the night.

Long-distance footpaths (GR)
– Many footpaths marked in red and white run through the Alps. Booklets or "topo-guides" published by the Fédération française de la randonée pédestre give maps, detailed itineraries, accommodation information (refuges and lodges), and useful advice (also Minitel **3615 RANDO).** The Rhône-Alpes regional tourist office distributes a guide listing the walks and hikes in the Alps.

- **GR 5** goes across the Alps from Lake Geneva to Nice, following the high Alps north to south, and crossing other footpaths on its way.
- The **TMB** (Tour du Mont Blanc) goes round the massif, entering Switzerland and Italy. Allow eight days.
- **GR 55** runs through the Parc national de la Vanoise.
- **GR 54** "Tour de l'Oisans" goes round the Parc national des Écrins and the Oisans region.
- **GR 58** enables hikers to explore the Queyras region (numerous refuges and lodges).
- **GR 56** goes through the Ubaye region.

Other footpaths run through the Préalpes.
- **GR 96** goes through the Chablais, the Aravis and the Bauges massifs.
- **GR 9, 91, 93 and 95** criss-cross the Vercors.
- **GR 93** continues across the Dévoluy and **GR 94** runs through the Buëch, Bochaine and Baronnies regions.
- **GR 6** "Alpes-Océan" links the Ubaye and Forcalquier Regions via Sisteron.

🏃 **GR 4** "Méditerranée-Océan" goes right through Haute-Provence via Entrevaux, Castellane and Moustiers-Ste-Marie.

In addition, there are numerous local footpaths offering interesting hikes or linking main itineraries. Shorter routes, known as **Sentiers de Petite Randonnée,** or **PR,** are marked in yellow.

Useful addresses – Topo-guides are published by **La Fédération française de la randonnée pédestre** –14 rue Riquet, 75019 Paris - ☎ 01 44 89 93 93 - www.ffrp.asso.fr A very comprehensive hiking guide is published by **Le Comité régional de tourisme Rhône-Alpes FFRP** – 3 hameau de Saint-Gras, rue de Joigny-73490 La Ravoire -☎ 04 79 71 00 08-www.ffrp-rhone-alpes.com In the Alps, contact **l'Association de randonnée en Savoie**, 4 rue du Château, 73000 Chambéry, ☎ 04 79 75 02 01; for the Alpes-Haute-Provence region, contact the **Association départementale des Relais et Itinéraires** (**ADRI**), 19 rue du Docteur-Honnorat, 04000 Digne-les-Bains, ☎ 04 92 31 07 01-www.alpes-hautes-provence.com/adri. For a map of shelters, contact the **Comitè départemental de randonnée pédestre des Hautes-Alpes**, 12 rue Faure-du-Serre, 05000 Gap, ☎ 04 92 53 6511, www.cdrp05.fr.st

MOUNTAINEERING

The Alps are one of the major mountaineering regions of the world. The sport, which is increasingly popular, requires **good physical condition** and **appropriate equipment**. It is essential to be accompanied by a qualified mountain guide for any expedition, even a minor one.

The best mountaineering terrain is found in the Mont-Blanc, Écrins and Vanoise massifs. Nearby resorts serve as the base for expeditions: Chamonix-Mont-Blanc, St-Gervais-les-Bains, Pralognan-la-Vanoise, Bourg-d'Oisans and Saint-Christophe (La Bérarde) and La Grave.

Discuss frankly with your guide your level of skill and your preferences (ice-climbing, rocks, frozen waterfalls, etc.). You should be aware that your guide is engaged to provide the means to climb, not the result. In other words, guides do all they can to ensure your safety, but they have no obligation to get you to the summit if they judge your abilities insufficient, or the weather conditions unfavourable. ⏱ *See the section on Safety in the Mountains, and look below for a list of useful addresses.*

Rock-climbing

The infinite variety of sites and of rock types in the Alps has made the area a rock-climbing centre. In the Maurienne region, **Aussois** is the most celebrated and has welcomed several international climbing Open competitions. The cliffs of **Presles** offer the best variety of climbing routes (some 300) and of canyons in the Vercors range.

The cliffs of the **Haute Ubaye**, the sheer rock faces of **Verdon** (notably the cliff at l'Escales) and the abrupt steps of the **Préalpes de Digne**, the sandstone of **Annot** and the rock spurs of **les Baronnies** (Orpierre) are justly renowned.

Before gaining the skill and grace of experienced climbers — and to become accustomed to heights —

The via ferrata at Les Vigneaux

J.-L. Gallo/MICHELIN

debutant climbers need to learn basic techniques from qualified instructors. Several climbing schools offer half-day and day-long lessons, as well as longer courses leading to climbs on high cliffs at altitude. For information, contact local or *départemental* tourist offices, or one of the *bureaux des guides* listed below.

Via ferrata – *Via ferrata* climbing, which is a cross between mountain-eering and hiking has become increas-ingly popular in the past few years. These rock-climbing courses (you pay a fee to use them) fitted with metal rungs and cables originated in the Dolomites during the First World War; they were planned by the Italian army and only discovered by the public in the 1950s. The first *via ferrata* courses were set up in the Briançon region at the beginning of the 1980s. Basic equipment includes a harness, a helmet and two ropes (preferably with a fall absorber) to secure yourself to the cable which runs the whole length of the course. It is impera-tive that inexperienced climbers be accompanied by a guide or join a group. Although the routes offer varying levels of difficulty, several are not suitable for children or for people with low endurance or susceptibility to altitude. Some of the more recently developed Alpine via ferrata require a high level of technical skill and equip-ment and can be classified as outright rock-climbing.

Notable via ferrata

At Chamonix, the via ferrata of the **Balcon de la Mer de Glace** glacier is for experienced climbers. In Savoie, you can climb a portion or the whole length of the longest route in France, at **Aussois-La Norma** (3 460m/11 352ft). You will find easier routes charging lower fees in **Isère**. In Gre-noble, the **Prise de la Bastille** route offers a spectacular view over the city. In the southern Alps, well-known via ferrata are found at Sisteron (the route from **Grande Fistoire to la Motte-du-Caire**), in the l'Argentière region (**Vignaux** and **les gorges de**

la Durance), at **Auron**, at Briançon (la **Croix de Toulouse**), at **Freisnières** and at Serre-Chevalier (**l'aiguillette du Lauzet**)

The departmental tourist office of the Hautes-Alpes publishes a guide to the *via ferrata,* as does the Fédéra-tion française de la montagne et de l'escalade (see below).

Ruisseling – This winter sport could be described as ice-climbing since those who practise it use rock-climb-ing techniques and equipment to climb up frozen waterfalls and moun-tain streams. Contact the guides office in Aussois and Val Cenis.

CANYONING

A good knowledge of potholing (caving), diving and rock-climbing techniques is necessary to abseil (rappel) or jump down tumultuous mountain streams and to follow their course through narrow gorges (clues) and down steep waterfalls. The magic appeal of this sport lies in the variety of the terrain, in the sunlight playing on the foaming water, or in the con-trast between the dense vegetation and the bare rocks heated by the sun. Summer is the best period to practise canyoning: the water temperature is bearable and the rivers are not so high. However, the weather forecast plays a crucial role when it comes to deciding whether to go canyoning or not, as a storm upriver can make it dangerous to go through a gorge and cause basins to fill up with alluvial sediments. In any case, it is preferable to leave early in the morning (storms often occur during the afternoon) to allow oneself time to overcome any unforeseen minor problems. A beginners' course does not exceed 2km/1.2mi and is supervised by instructors. Later on it is essential to go canyoning with a qualified instruc-tor, who can evaluate the state of a stream and has a good knowledge of local weather conditions. The main canyoning areas are the Vallée d'Abondance in **Savoie**, La Norma and Val Fréjus ("Indiana Jones" course) in the **Haute-Maurienne**, the Canyon des Écouges and Gorges du Furon in the **Vercors**, the **Ubaye Valley** between Les Thuiles and Le Lauzet, in particular the Ravin de Sauze, **the upper Var and the Cians valleys**, and, of course, the **Verdon** (Ravin du Four near Beauvezer). The Vallon du Fournel (**Briançonnais**) and the Vallon du Pas de La Tour (**Ubaye**) are best for beginners. Remember that, in spite of appearances, *clues* are no less dangerous in summer, when the river's flow is slower, than at other times. Long, narrow ravines, sometimes with no way out to higher ground, can be filled by a rush of water if a sudden cloudburst swells the river. Respect for the natural environment in the region's otherwise impassable gorges is more essential than ever.

Useful addresses – **Le Club alpin français** publishes guides and brochures: 24 rue de Laumière, 75019 Paris, ☎ 01 53 72 87 13 - www.ffcam.fr. **La Fédération française de la montagne et de l'escalade**, 8-10 quai de la Marne, 75019 Paris, ☎ 01 40 18 75 50, www.ffme.fr. The FFME publishes a *Guide des sites naturels d'escalade en France* by D. Taupin, where you will find climbing sites throughout France. Guides can be hired though local *bureaux*, which also offer lessons and outings of varying difficulty, from scrambles for children to serious climbing.

The Conseil général des Alpes-Maritimes produces guides on via ferrata, canyoning and other outdoor sports: Route de Grenoble, BP 3007, 06201 Nice Cedex 3 ☎ 04 97 18 68 65 -www.cg06.fr (look under "les guides randoxygène": www.randoxygene. org)

The tourist office of **Alpes-de-Haute-Provence** publishes a guide, *Canyoning, escalade, via ferrata*: Immeuble-François-Mitterrand BP 170 - 04005 Digne-les-Bains Cedex - ☎04 92 31 57 29 -www.alpes-hautes-provence.com

◆ **Bureau des Guides de Briançon**, Place Suze- ☎04 92 20 15 73 - www.montagne-virtuel.com.

◆ **Bureau des Guides des Écrins**, 05340 Ailefroide, ☎04 92 23 32 02, or 05290 Vallouise, ☎04 92 23 32 39 - www.guides-ecrins.com
◆ **Bureau des Guides de Serre-Chevalier**, 05240 La Salle-des-Alpes, ☎ 04 92 24 75 90, www.guides-serrechevalier.com
◆ **Bureau des Guides de l'Ubaye,** ☎04 92 81 20 76 - www.ubaye.com
◆ **Bureau des Guides de Verdon**, rue Grande, 04120 La Palud-sur-Verdon, ☎04 92 77 30 50, www.escalade-verdon.com

CYCLING AND MOUNTAIN BIKING

The Route des Cols (Galibier, Croix de Fer, Iseran, Lautaret, Izoard etc) was made famous by the Tour de France and in summer many cycle and mountain bike races take place throughout the region, in particular in the area around Vars, which plays host to the "Six jours de Vars," an annual week-long cycling event.

IGN maps with cycling itineraries are available and many lodges (*gîtes d'étape*) offer budget accommodation. Tourist offices have lists of establishments providing a rental service.

Mountain biking is extremely popular as it can be practised almost anywhere, in particular along forest roads, mule tracks and cross-country skiing tracks; some ski areas open their lifts to mountain bikes, giving access to downhill ski trails.

Look for signs referring to VTT (*vélo tout-terrain*) or FCC (Féderation française de cyclisme) trails. Some areas offer a choice of marked itineraries, such as Aussois, Bourg-St-Maurice, Parc naturel régional du Vercors, val d'Allos, Serre-Ponçon/Durance, pays du Buëch, Embrunais/Savinois, Champsaur, Val du Mercantour, Vallée de l'Ubaye, Digne-les-Bains/Pays Dignois, Verdon les Collines.

Mountain biking itineraries are available locally from the information centres of regional parks; you can also consult the website **www.sitesvtt. com**. Regional tourist offices offer brochures on cycling. For rentals, consult local tourist offices. The local train network (TER) transports bikes for free.

🚲 **Fédération française de cyclisme,** 5 rue de Rome, 93561 Rosny-sous-Bois Cedex - ☎ 01 49 35 69 24 - www.ffc.fr

🚲 **Hautes-Alpes: Comité départemental de cyclotourisme de la Savoie** – Maison des Sports - 90 rue Henri-Oreiller, 73000 Chambéry -☎04 79 85 09 09

🚲 **Comité départemental de cyclotourisme de la Haute-Savoie** – H. Saccani - 10 chemin de la Fruitière, 74960 Meythet -☎ 04 50 22 16 76

🚲 **Comité départemental de cyclotourisme de l'Isère** – M. Costantini - 7 rue de lIndustrie, 38327 Eybens Cedex -☎06 78 51 79 94 -www.cyclo38ffct.org

🚲 **Alpes-de-Haute-Provence: Comité départemental des Alpes-de-Haute-Provence**, M. Manent, 04270 Mésel, ☎ 04 92 35 58 39.

🚲 **Var: Comité Départemental de Cyclotourisme**, L'Hélianthe, rue Emile-Ollivier, 83000 Toulon, ☎ 04 94 36 04 09, www.cyclotourisme83-ffct.org

WHITE-WATER SPORTS

White-water sports are increasingly popular, particularly in the Alps which offer a dense network of rivers and streams, pleasant summer temperatures and many outdoor leisure parks where it is possible to discover and practice these activities, and where you can rent all the necessary equipment. Several of these parks are described in the green Address Books in the Sights section.

In every area, the Comité départemental de tourisme (👋 see Tourist information) has a list of the various organisations providing group activities.

Rafting – This is the easiest of all the white-water sports. It consists in going down impetuous rivers in groups of six to eight persons, aboard inflatable rubber rafts manoeuvred with paddles and controlled from the rear by an instructor/cox. The technique is simple and team spirit is the key to success. Isothermal and shockproof equipment

White-water rafting on the Haute-Isère

S. Frances/EXPLORER

Useful Terms

These will help you to understand the information on signs posted near canyoning itineraries:

- **Bassin:** basin filled with water, deep enough to swim in; if no depth is indicated, it is less than 10m/6.2mi.

- **Chenal:** area where the water flows along a large "gutter" requiring a special technique to tackle it; a small gutter is called a **goulotte.**

- **Durée parcours amont** (or **aval**): the estimated time to complete the course upstream (or downstream), allowing time to gain access + time to go through the canyon (upstream or downstream of the signs) + time to return on foot to the starting point.

- **Escalier de géant:** a succession of rocky ledges forming a flight of steps several metres high.

- **Échappatoire:** exit making it possible to shorten the course.

- **Longueur de nage:** indicates the total distance that has to be swum.

- **Marmite:** hollow filled with water into which it is possible to jump (after checking the depth).

- **Vasque:** shallow basin.

is provided by the club organising the trip. The level of difficulty is graded from I to VI (easy to virtually impossible). Beginners and amateurs who have not acquired a solid technique are advised not to attempt any difficulty rated above III. Remember to book in advance.

The Alps are the ideal area for rafting, preferably during the thaw (April to June) and in summer along rivers which maintain a constant flow. Among the rivers particularly suitable for rafting are the upper Isère (between Bourg-St-Maurice and Centron, grade III), the Doron de Bozel in the Vanoise region (between Brides-les-Bains and Moûtiers, grades IV and V), the Giffre and the Dranses de Savoie. The lower Ubaye is a popular rafting river, while the Rabioux, a tributary of the Durance, is internationally famous as a proving ground for experts.

Canoeing and kayaking – Canoes, originally from Canada, are manoeuvred with a simple paddle. They are ideal for family trips along rivers. In kayaks (of Inuit origin) on the other hand, paddlers use a double-bladed paddle. There are canoeing-kayaking

schools in white-water sports centres throughout the Alps and touring takes place on the lakes and the lower courses of most rivers, particularly the the Giffre, the Chéran, the Arly, the Doron de Bozel, the Guiers Vif et Mort, the Isère (Les Arcs) the Ubaye and the Verdon, and also on the Clarée, the Guisane, the Gyronde, the Biaisse, the Durance, the Guil, the Buëch, the Méouge, the Drac, the Souloise and the Séveraisse.

On some rivers, during summer months, canoe-kayaking is carefully regulated: be sure you're within the rules.

The Fédération française de canoë-kayak publishes an annual guide called *France canoë-kayak et sports d'eaux-vives* as well as a map, *Les Rivières de France*, of all suitable rivers: 87 quai de la Marne, BP 48, 94344 Joinville-le-Pont – ☎ 01 45 11 08 50, www.ffcanoe.asso.fr

Hydrospeed – Anyone wishing to try swimming down mountain streams must know how to swim with flippers and be in top physical condition. Swimmers wear a wet suit and a helmet and lie on a very tough streamlined float, called a "hydrospeed."

CAVING AND POTHOLING

This activity requires thorough training if participants wish to explore caves left in their natural state. However, several sites are accessible to amateurs on the condition that they are accompanied by instructors from potholing clubs.

The necessary equipment is sophisticated: reinforced suit, rock-climbing equipment, inflatable dinghy, helmet, waterproof bag, carbide and halogen lamps. The main risk comes from sudden spates which are difficult to forecast as they can be caused by storms occurring miles away.

Vercors Massif – This is one of the best areas for potholing: there are more than 1 500 caves or entrances marking the beginning of itineraries, often situated along hiking itineraries. It is therefore essential to remain cautious particularly when attempting an unplanned exploration.

The following sites offer the opportunity to spend a day discovering underground exploration: the Goule Blanche and Goule Noire, the Grotte de Bournillon, the Scialet de Malaterre (near Villard-de-Lans), the Trou qui souffle (dry cave) near Méaudre, the Grotte de la Cheminée and the Scialets d'Herbouvilly.

The **Grotte du Gournier** (above the Grotte de Choranche) is particularly good for supervised beginners; the passage allows them to practise a number of different techniques while moving horizontally through a fossil cave. Only experienced potholers may venture beyond the fossil gallery. The whole network covers a distance of 18km/11.2mi.

Savoie – There are more than 2 000 caves listed in the area; the temperature inside these caves remains constant throughout the year, around 4°C/39°F. The highest chasms are situated in the Vanoise Massif, at Pralognan and Tignes (3 000m/9 842m) whereas the Gouffre Jean-Bernard in Haute-Savoie holds the depth record (–1 600m/5 249ft).

The most extensive Alpine chasm (58km/36mi) is situated under the Alpette, in the **Chartreuse Massif.**

Fédération française de Spéléologie, 28 rue Delondine, 69002 Lyon, ☎ 04 72 56 09 63 - www.ffspeleo.fr

Maison de l'aventure, 26420 La Chapelle-en-Vercors, ☎ 04 75 48 22 38 - www.maison-aventure.com

RIDING

There are many riding centres throughout Savoie, Dauphiné and Haute-Provence and numerous touring itineraries – from one-day treks to week-long excursions – identified along the way by orange markings. In addition, tours for beginners and experienced riders are organised by the *associations régionales de tourisme équestre* (ARTE).

Le Comité national de Tourisme équestre publishes a brochure, updated annually, called *Cheval nature*

Hiking With a Pack Donkey

Rest your shoulders for a while and hire a real beast of burden for a day or up to a week. This extra member of the family can carry a 40kg/88lb pack and trots along willingly at a pace of 4kph/2.5mph, whatever the terrain. Farms providing the animals, the equipment and the necessary information for a successful tour can be found in Thorens-Glières, Les Carroz, St-Sigismond, St-Martin-en-Vercors, St-Martin-le-Vinoux, Guillaumes, Seyne-les-Alpes and Val-des-Près. A national donkey association, based in runs a website, available in English, with links to donkey fanciers internationally.

Fédération nationale "âne et randonnées," 13 montée St-Lazare, 04000 Digne-les-Bains - ☎ 04 92 34 23 11 - www.ane-et-rando.com

(4.50€ plus mailing charges), which lists all the programs for equestrian tourists as well as lodgings that welcome both horse and rider: 9 bd. Macdonald, 75019 Paris ☎01 53 26 15 50, www.ffe.com Also, consult www.tourisme-equestre.fr

ANGLING

For *départemental* angling associations, consult the green table.

Trout is the prize catch in mountain areas; it can be caught with live insects or larvae (in mountain streams with steep banks) or with artificial flies and a rod and reel in wider streams and mountain lakes. Other common fish found in Alpine streams and lakes are grayling, barbel, chub and perch. In France, fishing permits are only available to members of a local angling club; tourists must generally pay for a year's club membership, although day permits may be available in some areas. Seasons vary according to species and the type of water being fished. Any catches under the permitted size (50cm/19.7in for pike and 23cm/9.1in for trout) must be released at once.

Be aware that many rivers are damed, and that water can be released unexpectedly; many sites are unsuitable for children.

Special regulations apply to fishing in some of the large lakes. For more information, look at the website of the **Union nationale pour la pêche, www.unpf.fr,** and consult the associations listed in the green box. **In the Savoie and Haute-Savoie,** 71 fishing sites (lakes, rivers, ponds) have been listed for fishing. The largest variety of fish are found in the rivers Giffre, Arve and Ménoge, while the Fier is one of the best fishing rivers in an area known for its waterfalls and impressive scenery.

In the Isère region, the rivers Drac and Isère and their many tributaries, as well as the lakes (Laffey, the Belledonne massif, and the 7 Laux) offer excellent sport. For **the handi-capped**, 18 sites are equipped to permit access.

Lac du Bourget – White-fish angling along the shore is only allowed near harbours (Aix-les-Bains, St-Innocent) but it is possible to hire a boat; besides perch and pike, one sometimes finds salmon. With a special permit, you can fish for trout and char with a dragnet. **The pays du Buëch** offers an infinite variety of fishing in fast streams. The bridge at Serre is in the top category, where you find trout, dace and barbel. **The Parc naturel régional du Verdon** offers a map of all its fishing sites and their particularities (*Pêche nature dans le Verdon*).

USEFUL ADDRESSES

Union nationale pour la pêche: www.unpf.fr

Conseil supérieur de la pêche, Immeuble Le Péricentre, 16 av. Louison Bobet, 94132 Fontenay-sous-Bois Cedex ☎01 45 14 36 00, www.csp.environnement.gouv.fr

Fédération PPMA:

Isère: rue du Palais, 38000 Grenoble, ☎ 04 76 44 28 39 - www.federation-peche-isere.asso.fr

Haute-Savoie: Le Villaret - 2092, rte des Diaquenods, 74370 Saint-Martin-Bellevue -☎04 50 46 87 55 - www.pechehautesavoie.com

Savoie: ZI Les Contours, 73230 At-Alban-Leysse - ☎ 04 79 85 89 36.

Fédération Départementale pour la pêche:

Alpes-de-Haute-Provence: Étoiles des Alpes - Bâtiment B -traverse les Eaux Chaudes - BP 103, 04003 Dignes-les-Bains -☎04 92 32 25 40 - www.unpf.fr/04

la Drôme, 50 chemin de Laprat, 26000 Valence, ☎ 04 75 78 14 40 - www.unpfr.fr/26

Hautes-Alpes, 6 rue Cadet-de-Charance, 05000 Gap, ☎ 04 92 53 54 71 - www.unpf.fr/05.

IN THE AIR

Circling dots and darts gliding slowly and silently over the valleys are a common sight in the French Alps, as thermal updrafts and strong air currents typical of mountainous terrain provide a remarkable site for unpowered flight. Many summer resorts with easy access to nearby summits offer opportunities for paragliding, deltaplane, and "kiting," where riders skim across water, snow or land attached to a large kite. In fact, old-fashioned kite-flying has taken on new popularity as enthusiasts compete with acrobatic, combat and racing kites. Les Saisies, Signal de Bisanne and L'Alpe-d'Huez on the edge of the massif of la Chartreuse St-Hilaire are the most renowned. **Chamonix** is still one of the main paragliding centres, although access to the slopes of Mont Blanc is restricted in July and August. (École de parapente de Chamonix, www.summits.fr/chamonix-paragliding.html). The **Vercors** is also a favourite areas, as its many well-oriented valleys allow a gentle introduction to the sport. Two remarkable sites are worth mentioning: the Cornafion, near Villard-de-Lans (500m/1 640ft flights, access forbidden in May and June for the protection of the fauna); and the Moucherotte (landing in Lans-en-Vercors).

To learn the various forms of unpowered flight, it is highly recommended to take one of the many courses offered by schools under the aegis of the Fédération française de vol libre (FFVL) See below for the address, or consult Minitel, 3615 FFVL. A training course of about a week will give you the necessary skills as well as a knowledge of weather necessary to understand appropriate flying conditions. Then, you apprentice during a series of 20 flights radio-guided by an instructor on the ground.

Fédération française de vol libre, 4 rue de Suisse, 06000 Nice, ☎ 04 97 03 82 82, www.ffvl.fr

Paragliding

Fédération française de planeur ultra-léger motorisé, 96bis rue Marc-Sangnier, 94700 Maisons-Alfort Cedex, ☎ 01 49 81 74 43, www.ffplum.com

Paragliding – This descendent of parachuting, which emerged in its present form in 1985 after a long evolution, has now spread to winter sports resorts where participants are equipped with skis. Although the northern Alps, and particularly Chamonix, are renowned, Haute-Provence is also an ideal area for practising paragliding. The national gliding centre is located in Saint-Auban-sur-Durance (www.cnvv.net). and there are many schools in the area.

Deltaplane (Hang-gliding) – A rigid, triangular wing carries the pilot, who hangs in a frame and, using his body, directs flight by moving the centre of gravity relative to the aerodynamic centre of the wing. This sport has seen remarkable development over the past 35 years.

Useful addresses: **Le Comité régional de tourisme** publishes a brochure "Parapente," listing 21 sites: Rhône-Alpes Tourisme – 104 Route de Paris, 69260 Charbonnières-les-Bains -☎ 04 72 59 21 59 -www.rhonealpes-tourisme.fr

Fédération française de vol libre
– 4 rue de Suisse, 06000 Nice -☎04 97 03 82 82 - wwwffvl.fr

Calendar of Events

JANUARY

Orcières-Merlette – International week of song, piano and flute (early in month) ☎04 92 55 89 89

–Meeting of all-terrain vehicles on snow (end of month) ☎04 92 55 77 35

Puy-St-Vincent – Humour festival (2nd week of month) ☎04 92 23 35 80

Valloire – International ice-sculpture competition ☎ 04 79 59 03 96

MARCH

Courcheval – Les Musicîmes, chamber music ☎ 04 79 08 00 29

Dignes-les-Bains – Film festival ☎04 92 32 29 33

Grenoble – Spring Fair ☎04 76 39 66 00 - www.alpexpo.com

Orcières-Merlette – Jazz festival ☎ 04 92 55 89 89

Les Orres –Comic strip festival ☎04 92 44 01 61

Saint-Gervais –International humour festival ☎04 50 47 76 08

APRIL TO MAY

Aix-les-Bains – Festival des nuits romantiques, classical music ☎04 79 88 68 00

Chambéry – Festival of the first novel ☎04 79 33 42 47 - www.chambery-tourisme.com

Évian-les-Bains – Escales Musicales, classical music festival ☎04 50 26 85 00 - wwwroyalparcevian.com

Gréoux-les-Bains – Provençal spring music festival ☎04 92 78 01 08

JUNE

Annecy – International festival of animated films ☎04 50 10 09 00

Chambéry – Estivales du Château des ducs: music, dance, theatre, sculpture ☎ 04 79 70 63 55

Les Orres – International sheepdog competition ☎04 92 44 01 61

Riez – Festival of alpine pastoral traditions (*transhumance*) ☎04 92 77 99 09

Ubaye Valley –Festival of the alpine countryside (end of month): activities, music, theater, readings, exhibits. ☎08 20 20 62 10

JULY

Les Adrets – Festival de l'Arpenteur (surveyor), live performances ☎04 76 71 16 48

Aiguebelle – Summer festival of jazz, classical music, cultural events ☎04 79 36 29 24

Aix-les-Bains – Festival of Operetta ☎04 79 88 09 99 - www.aix.operettes.fr.st

Annecy – Les Noctibules, festival of street arts ☎04 50 33 44 00

Les Arcs – Academy festival of Les Arcs, chamber music ☎04 79 17 12 57

Barcelonnette –Jazz festival (last 2 weeks of month) ☎04 92 81 04 71, www.barcelonnette.com

Beauvezer – International guitar festival (end of month) ☎04 92 83 53 01

Bourget-du-Lac – Fireworks and medieval festival ☎ 04 79 25 01 99 - www.bourgetdulac.com

Die –Festival of chamber music at the Abbey of Valcroissant ☎04 75 22 03 03

Digne-les-Bains – Festival of roving theater (end of June, early July) ☎04 92 31 68 30, or 04 92 36 62 62

Esparron-de-Verdon – Provençal-Icelandic classical music festival (1st fortnight of month) ☎04 92 77 19 75

Les Gets - Festival of mechanical music (even-numbered years) ☎04 50 79 85 75

La Grave – Festival of the Music of Messiaen ☎04 76 79 90 05

Grenoble – Young European theatre ☎04 76 01 01 41 (early in month)

– Festival of short films (early in month) ☎04 76 54 43 51

Manosque – Jean Giono Days (end of month) ☎04 92 87 73 03

Montsapey – Festival of classical music ☎04 79 36 29 24

Serres – Jazz Festival (end of month) ☎04 92 67 00 67

Volonne – Medieval Festival ☎04 92 33 50 00

JULY-AUGUST

Alpe-d'Huez – Organ concerts, Thursdays at 8.45pm

Chambéry - Evenings with Rousseau ☎04 79 85 12 45 - www.chambery-tourisme.com

Combloux – Musical Hours (Mondays) ☎04 50 58 60 49

Cordon – Festival of baroque music (over 8 days the first 2 weeks of month) ☎ 04 50 58 60 49 - www.combloux.com

Guil-Durance – International Classical Music Festival with concerts at Gap, Mont-Daupin, Vars, Guillestre, Réotier, Saint-Crépin, Ceillac, l'Argentière-la-Bessée, Eygliers, Risoul ☎04 92 45 03 71

Lurs – "Lurs under the stars" with jazz and gospel music ☎04 92 79 11 65

Le Mônetier-les-Bains – International Organ Festival ☎04 92 24 98 99

La Rosière 1850 – Musifolies (last week July, 1st week August) ☎04 79 06 80 51

Saint-Disdier-en-Dévoluy –Classical and traditional music ☎04 92 58 91 91

Sisteron – Nights of the Citadel ☎04 92 67 06 00

AUGUST

Barcelonnette – Latin American and Mexican festival (2nd week of month) ☎04 92 81 04 71, www.barcelonnette.com

Briançon – Chamber Music Festival (1st fortnight of month) ☎06 33 21 27 30; Sword dance "Bacchu Ber" (16 July) ☎ 04 92 20 22 91

Colmars – Medieval Festival (mid-August)

Le Grand-Bornand – For the delight of children: European festival of children's theatre ☎04 50 02 78 00

La Côte-St-André – Hector Berlioz music festival ☎ 04 74 20 61 43

Orcières – Festival of the mountains with traditional music (2nd week of month) ☎04 92 55 89 71

Passy – Festival of books about mountains ☎04 50 58 80 52

Samoëns – Embrasement (setting on fire) du lac aux Dames ☎04 50 34 40 28 - www.samoens.com

Simiane-la-Rotonde Festival of Ancient Music, Les Riches Heures musicales de la Rotonde, (1st fortnight of month)☎04 92 75 90 14/47, www.festival-simiane.com

Val d'isère – Festival of baroque music and art in the Tarentaise ☎04 79 06 06 60

Vallouise Écrins chamber music festival ☎04 92 23 36 12

Val-Thorens – International chess festival (second week of month) ☎04 79 00 08 08 - www.valthorens.com

September

Crémieu – Les Médievales: shows and parties in medieval costume ☎04 74 90 45 13

Gréaux-les-Bains – Classical singing "Les Courants d'airs" (1st week of month) Events also at Manosque and Valensole ☎04 92 78 01 08

Manosque – Festival of literary encounters ☎04 92 72 75 81

Mont-Dauphin – Story-telling Festival ☎04 92 45 18 34

Moustier-Sainte-Marie Festival of the "Diane," traditional Provençal musical groups (31 Aug - 8 Sept) ☎04 92 74 67 84

St-Hilaire-du-Touvet – Coupe Icare: festival of films about gliding and salon of aerial sports ☎04 76 08 33 99

OCTOBER

Chambéry – Festival of comic books ☎04 79 33 95 89 - www.chamberybd.fr

NOVEMBER-DECEMBER

Château-Arnaux –Salon of painting and sculpture (mid-November to mid-December), www.odysee-fort-robert.com

TRADITIONAL FESTIVALS AND SPECIALIST FAIRS

JANUARY-FEBRUARY

Ceillac – Festival of Queyras traditions ☎04 92 45 05 74
Abriès – Winter carnival ☎04 92 46 72 26

MARCH

Vars – Week of good taste devoted to local food specialties ☎04 92 46 69 21

APRIL-MAY

Département of Alpes-de-Haute-Provence – Olive Festival: markets, tastings throughout the *département* ☎04 92 34 36 38
Banon – Cheese Festival ☎04 92 73 36 37

PENTECOST (WHITSUNDAY)

Annot – Feast of St. Fortunat

JUNE THROUGH SEPTEMBER

Gap – Arts and crafts fairs (one per month) ☎04 92 52 56 56

JULY

Annot – Fête Provençale (3rd weekend of month) ☎04 92 83 23 03 - www.annot.fr
Les Arcs – International folklore festival of the Haute Tarentaise ☎ 04 79 07 12 57
Briançon – Grand Escarton crafts fair ☎04 92 21 08 50
Ceillac – Pilgrimage to Lake Sainte-Anne (July 26)
Combloux – Festival of alpine architecture and decoration ☎04 50 58 60 49 - www.combloux.com

Forcalquier – Potters' fair (last Thursday of month) ☎04 92 77 00 61
Saint-Étienne-les-Orgues – Herbal remedies fair (14 July) ☎04 92 73 00 22
Saint-Véran – Pilgrimage to the chapel of Notre-Dame-de-Clausis (16 July)

JULY-AUGUST

Forcalquier – Crafts fairs

15 AUGUST

Bramans – Traditional 15 August celebration ☎04 79 05 03 45
Chamonix – Festival of Guides: sound and light show 14 August, blessing of ropes and ice-axes 15 August ☎04 50 53 00 88
Les Contamines-Montjoie – Pilgrimage to Notre-Dame de la Gorge (sound and light show in evening)
La Grave – Festival of guides: mass and blessing of the mountain ☎04 76 79 90 21
Guillaumes – Procession of military engineers
Pesey-Nancroix – Festival of traditional costumes ☎04 79 07 94 28 - www.peisey-vallandry.com
St-Martin-de-Belleville – Pilgrimage to Notre-Dame-de-la-Vie ☎04 79 00 08 08
Tignes – Festival of the lake ☎04 79 40 25 80 - www.tignes.net

August

Castellane – Crafts fair ☎04 92 83 61 14
Châtel – La "Belle Dimanche" festival of alpine pastures (3rd Sun of month) ☎04 50 73 22 44
La Cluaz – Reblochon cheese festival ☎04 50 32 65 00 - www.lacluaz.com
Cruis–Pottery fair (1st Sunday of month) ☎04 92 77 00 61
Digne-les-Bains – Parade of lavender floats (1st weekend of month) ☎04 92 36 62 62
–Lavender Festival (2nd fortnight of month) ☎04 92 31 05 20

Flumet – Mule fair (1st Tuesday of month) ☎04 79 31 61 08 - www.flumet-montblanc.com
– Mule team festival

Pralognan-la-Vanoise – Festival of the Alpes and guides (beginning of August) ☎04 79 08 79 08 - www.pralognan.com

La Rosière-Montvalezan, Séez-Saint-Bernard – Traditional festival of sheepherders (3rd Sunday of month) ☎04 79 41 00 15 - www.seezsaintbernard.com

St-Gervais – Guides festival ☎04 50 47 76 08

Seyne – Mule-driving competition (2nd Saturday of month) ☎04 92 35 00 42

Ugine – Festival of the mountains ☎04 79 37 56 33

Venosc – Festival of wool and natural materials ☎04 76 80 06 82 - www.venosc.com

SEPTEMBER -OCTOBER

Albenc – Fair of natural and biological products ☎ 04 76 36 50 10

Beaufort – Salon of French gastronomic products (2nd or 3rd weekend of month) ☎04 79 38 15 33 - www.areches-beaufort.com

Die – Festival of Clairette, a local sparkling white wine (beginning of month)

Gréaux-les-Bains – Fair of Christmas figurines (*santons*) during All-Saints holiday ☎04 92 78 01 08

Moustiers-Ste-Marie – Fête de Diane (31 August-8 September) ☎04 92 74 67 84

Sisteron – Regional fair (1st weekend, lasts 4 days)

NOVEMBER - DECEMBER

Autrans – International festival of mountain adventure films ☎04 76 95 77 80 - www.festival-autrans.com

Chambéry – Saveurs et terroirs: market of gourmet products ☎04 79 33 42 47

Champtercier – Fair of Christmas figurines (*santons*), 1st week of month ☎04 92 31 10 37

Esparron-de-Verdon
Village Christmas crêche (from mid-December)

Isola – Chestnut festival (1st weekend of month)

SPORTING EVENTS

JANUARY

Autran – La Foulée blanche (the white rush) cross-country ski competition ☎ 04 76 95 37 37 - www.lafouleeblanche.com

Bessans – International marathon of cross-country skiing ☎04 79 05 96 52

Champagny-en-Vanoise – Trophée Mer et Montagne ☎04 79 55 06 55

Les Houches (Chamonix) – The Kandahar, international downhill ski race ☎04 50 53 11 57 - www.chamonixsports.com

Mégève – International competition of polo on snow ☎04 50 21 27 28 - www.megeve.com

Praz-sur-Arly – Week in the air ☎04 50 21 90 57

St-François-Longchamp – Handiski-competitions (handicapped skiers) ☎04 79 59 24 18

St-Pierre-de-Chartreuse – Crossing the Chartreuse on skis ☎ 04 76 88 62 08

Serre-Chevalier – White Trail foot race on snow ☎04 92 24 98 98

Tignes –Airwaves: festival of extreme and alternative sports ☎ 04 79 40 04 40

Villard-de-Lans – Crossing the Vercors on skis ☎ 04 38 02 08 35

FEBRUARY

Les Ménuires – Trophée de l'espoir ☎ 04 79 00 73 00 - www.lesmenuires.com

MARCH

Arèches-Beaufort – Competition Pierra-Menta (high-level skiing-mountaineering competition) ☎04 79 38 37 57 - www.pierra-menta.com

APRIL

La Clusaz – Défi Foly, race on spring meltwaters ☎04 50 32 65 00

La Grave – Derby de la Meije race over ungroomed terrain, all skiing techniques ☎04 76 79 90 05 - www.derbydelameije.com

JUNE

Embrun – Rafting on the Durance River ☎04 92 43 72 72

Les Gets – La Pass'Portes, meeting of mountain bikes ☎04 50 75 80 80

AUGUST

Chamrousse – Lumberjack competition (first weekend of month) ☎04 76 89 92 65 - www.chamrousse.com

Courcheval – World cup of summer ski-jumping ☎04 79 08 00 29

St-Jean-de-Maurienne– Trans'Maurienne (mountain bike competition in the upper Arc Valley) ☎04 50 23 19 58 - www.transmaurienne.com

Val d'Isère – Salon of 4x4 vehicles and leisure ☎04 79 06 60 60

SEPTEMBER

Vercors – Transvercor, crossing the massif on mountain bikes ☎04 38 02 08 35

DECEMBER

Pays du Mont-Blanc – International ice-hockey competition ☎04 50 47 08 08

Val-Thorens – Andros Trophy (snow and ice-driving competitions - first weekend of Dec) ☎04 79 00 08 08 - www.valthorens.com

Val-Thorens – Boarderweek : International snowboarding competition and concerts (mid-Dec) ☎04 79 00 08 08

Shopping

Woodcarving and painting – The **Queyras** is undoubtedly the most famous of Alpine regions for the skill of its woodcarvers. The Maison de l'Artisanat, 05350 Ville-Vieille, ☎ 04 92 46 75 06 has a fine selection of wooden objects as well as other handicraft samples. Arvieux on the other hand is famous for its traditional toys, on sale at a local cooperative: L'Alpin chez lui, 05350 Arvieux, ☎ 04 92 46 73 86 - www.alpinchezlui.com. Wood painting is the speciality of the **Chartreuse** region, in the area of Entremont-le-Vieux.

Earthenware and santons – These are the speciality of the **Alpes-de-Haute-Provence** region. **Faïences de Moustiers** are world-famous, but there are other earthenware workshops in Barcelonnette, Reillanne and St-Michel-l'Observatoire. Fine pottery is manufactured in the nearby towns of Forcalquier and Castellane. **Santons** (human and animal figures which make up a Provençal Christmas crib) are handmade and painted in Gréoux-les-Bains, Champtercier and Manosque. Provençal cloth, from the lower Durance, south of Sisteron, is also a pleasant reminder of holidays.

Gastronomy – Cheese and wine in the north and olive oil and honey in the south are the main Alpine specialities.

Cheeses – Below are the addresses of some places where it is possible to watch cheese being made. Cheese-lovers should make time for a visit to a Savoyard dairy like the one in **St-François-de-Longchamp**, where it is possible to watch Beaufort -- the "prince of gruyère cheeses" being made in high-pasture chalets at the **Col de la Madeleine**. Among the other varieties to bear the Appelation d'Origine Controlée or AOC, at once the designation of a local product and a confirmation of quality, are **Abondance** from the val d'Abondance, **tomme de Savoie** (not to be confused with the **tome des Bauges**, which is more fruity in flavour) **bleu de Termignon** and **reblochon** from Savoie. This last is also one of the main ingredients of Savoie's most famous dish, *tartiflette,* a rich potato dish baked with onion, crème fraîche, bacon and local white wine. There are many cooperative cheese-makers you can visit; you can find their addresses through tourist offices and Chambres d'agriculture.

Wines – Two itineraries offer the opportunity of discovering and tasting wines from Savoie: the "red itinerary" starts from Chambéry and goes through the Combe de Savoie via Apremont, Montmélian and Challes-les-Eaux; the "blue itinerary" skirts the shores of the Lac du Bourget. Below are some useful addresses:
A list of cooperatives offering tastings and sales is provided by:
Comité interprofessionel des vins de Savoie – 3 rue du Château, 73000 Chambéry - ☏04 79 33 44 16 - aoc. vindesavoie@wanadoo.fr
The French shores of Lake Geneva produce a white wine called *Roussette de Savoie* which is very palatable served with fried fish; several local inns have it on their menu, particularly in Excevenex, Port de Séchex, Corzent and Amphion-les-Bains. Die is known for its sparkling *Clairette de Die,* made from a blend of Clairette and Muscat grapes. From the north come powerful liqueurs like *Chartreuse, Cherry-Rocher* and aperitifs such as *Chambéryzette* and *Vermouth. Génépi,* a gold-coloured aperitif, is distilled in the Ubaye

and can be found in Barcelonnette or in Forcalquier, which is perhaps better known for its aniseed-flavoured pastis and the *vin cuit de Noël,* a dark amber-coloured wine traditionally enjoyed at Christmas, now sold year-round in Forcalquier.

Olive oil – Production is concentrated in the Alpes-de-Haute-Provence département; the Moulin de l'Olivette, place de l'Olivette in Manosque produces and sells high-quality olive oil and suggests ways of using it. There are other mills in Oraison (Moulin Paschetta) and Peyrus (Moulin Mardaric). The Baronnies also produces high-quality olive oil.

Honey – The Haute-Provence region produces large quantities of honey from a whole variety of plants; lavender honey comes essentially from the Alpes-de-Haute-Provence *département.* Honey from Savoie (miel de Savoie) is produced between July and September; Vercors honey comes from around the regional park. There are two official seals of origin, namely "miel de lavande" and "miel toutes fleurs de Provence". The Maison du miel et de l'abeille in Riez *(see Plateau de Valensole)* offers an introduction to bee-keeping. Several bee-keepers in the area sell their product in towns like Castellane (les ruchers Apijuvence), Château-Queyras and Molines-en-Queyras.
As well as the famous exports listed above, you find some lesser-known specialities of the Alps. Look out for

A Queyras Speciality

Objects and furniture made by craftsmen from the Queyras region are not usually painted or varnished (although the wood is sometimes stained) and have to meet with five criteria to be granted the Queyras seal of origin:

– the article must be made in the region by a local craftsman;

– it must be made entirely of solid pine;

– it must be decorated with traditional carved motifs from the Queyras region;

– the parts must be joined with pegs and dovetailed and no part can be factory-turned;

– at least one fifth of the surface of the object or piece of furniture must be carved.

croquants de Queyras, little crunchy honey and almond cakes, and confiture de genièvre, a juniper conserve sold in the markets of the Ubaye. Other treats include biscuits de Savoie, rissoles aux poires (pastry filled with pears), pralines known as cloches or roseaux d'Annecy and sabayon, a sweet egg cream which takes its name and inspiration from the Italian zabaglione.

For guides to the crafts and food products of the area, contact departmental tourist offices.

Sightseeing Across the Border

SWITZERLAND

Useful Information
Bordering Lake Geneva are the cantons of Vaud and Valais and the prosperous, international city of Geneva, all within easy reach of Haute-Savoie. The Green Guide Switzerland, the Michelin Hotel and Restaurant Guide Switzerland and Michelin Map 729 provide all the information you need for a weekend break or a longer stay.

Swiss Tourist Offices
Canada: 926 The East Mall, Etobicoke, Toronto, Ontario M9B 6K1 ☎ (416) 695-2090 (English) (514) 333-9526 (French)
United Kingdom: Swiss Travel Centre, 30 Bedford St., London WC2E 9ED ☎ 00 800 100 200 30
United States: Swiss Centre, 608 Fifth Ave., New York, NY 10020-2303 ☎ (212)757 5944
Internet: www.MySwitzerland.com ☎ toll-free 011-800-100-200-30

Formalities
For a stay of less than three months, citizens of an EU member state require a valid ID card (or in the case of UK visitors, a passport). Travellers from outside the European Union must be in possession of a passport. When travelling by car, drivers should be prepared to present a driving license, international driving permit and car registration papers. Motorcyclists will require the same documents and must wear helmets when on the road. Owners of pets brought into the country will be required to prove that the animal has been vaccinated against rabies in the past year, but more than a month before their entry into Switzerland.

Excursions
Vallorcine to Émosson – Travellers may like to continue the route from Chamonix to Vallorcine as far as Martigny and then on to the Émosson Dam (see Green Guide Switzerland); the approach to the lake offers a superb view of the north face of Mont Blanc. From the resort of Châtellard-Village at the bottom of the valley, a three-stage cable car trip takes visitors to a height of 1 961m/6 335ft in 13min. The first section is the steepest in Europe, rising at a dizzying gradient of 87%. The cable car runs daily from mid-June to mid-September; a round-trip ticket costs 48 SFr. Experienced walkers can return on foot in about 2hr 30min. For further information contact the tourist office in Chamonix ☎ 04 50 53 00 24 or at the station in Martigny (Switzerland) ☎ +41 (0)27 769 11 11 - www.cff.ch

On the water – Avoid the traffic jams and cruise across Lake Geneva. The Compagnie Générale de Navigation ☎ (00 41) 848 811 848 offers regular sailings between France and Geneva, Vevey, Nyon and its headquarters in Lausanne.

ITALY

Useful Information
Italian State Tourist Office – ENIT (Ente Nazionale Italiano per il Turismo)
Canada: 175 Bloor Street, Suite 907 South Tower, Toronto, Ontario M4W 3R8 ☎ (416) 925-4882 - www.italiantourism.com
United Kingdom: 1 Princes Street, Mayfair, London W1B 2AY ☎ +44 (0) 20 7408 1254 - www.italian-touristboard.co.uk

New highway numbers!

Many stretches of the French national highway system are being transferred to the départements. As a result, the numbering of roads is being modified, a process that started in 2006 and will continue for several years. The status of many roads is still in doubt, so we could not report systematically the changes either on our maps or in our text. As a general rule, you will find the former number of a national road in the last two digits of the new départemental road: for example, N 16 becomes D 1016, and N51 becomes D951.

United States: 630 Fifth Avenue, Suite 1565, New York City, NY 10111 ☎ (212) 245-5618/4822; 12400 Wilshire Boulevard, Suite 550, Los Angeles, CA 90025 ☎ (310) 820-1898 - www.italiantourism.com

The **Green Guide Italy, The Michelin Guide Italia** and **Michelin Map 562 Italy North West** provide further in-depth information on the western Italian Alps and the north-west coast.

The Mont Blanc Tunnel

Val d'Aoste – *After the tunnel, continue on the A 5 or follow the S 26 towards Turin (* 👣 *see Massif du MONT-BLANC).* The valley of the Dora Baltea and its tributaries is surrounded by the highest peaks of the French and Swiss Alps, including the Matterhorn, Mont-Blanc, Monte Rosa, Grand Combin, Dent Hérens, Gran Paradiso and Grande Sassière. Countless excursions by car and cable car or on foot, quiet valleys, picturesque villages and above all the superb **views**★★★ make the Aosta valley one of northern Italy's most popular holiday destinations. An agreement dating back to 1948 guarantees considerable autonomy for a region where many locals still speak a Provençal dialect and official documents are written in French as well as Italian. Aosta, the capital, has preserved relics from Roman and Medieval times.

Aoste tourist office – 8, Piazza Chanoux -☎ 0165 23 66 27 - www.regione.vda.it

Via the Tunnel de Fréjus

Susa★ – *Via A 32.* Marking the intersection of the two main roads to France, the "gateway to Italy" -- and site of the 2006 Olympic games -- lies at the foot of a colossal massif, crowned by the Rocciamelone (3 538m/11 608ft). Besides its best-known landmark, the 4C **Savoy Door**★ (Porta Savoia), the town also boasts a fine **Romanesque campanile** on the south side of the Gothic **cathedral** and the elegant **Arco di Augusto**★, the oldest monument in the city (8C BC).

Further along the road to Turin, perched high on a hill, stands the Benedictine **abbey Sacra di San Michele**★★★ *(A 32 then S 25).* The great staircase leads up to the **Zodiac Door** with its decorated capitals and pilasters. The Romanesque-Gothic abbey church, built on top of the rocky eminence, has fine 16C frescoes. From the esplanade there is a lovely **view**★★★ of the Alps, the Dora Valley, the Po and Turin plains.

Susa tourist office – 39 corso Inghilterra ☎ 0039 122 62 24 47 - www.montagnedoc.net

Discounts

Significant discounts are available for senior citizens, students, young people under 25, teachers, and groups for public transport, museums and monuments and for some leisure activities such as movies (at certain times of day). Bring student or senior cards with you, and bring along some extra passport-size photos for discount travel cards.

The **International Student Travel Conference** (www.istc.org), global administrator of the International Student and Teacher Identity Cards, negotiates benefits with airlines, governments, and providers of other goods and services. The non-profit

association sells international ID cards for full-time students over age 12, young people under 25 and teachers. ⚫ *See the section on travelling by rail for discounts on public transport.*
The tourist office of Alpes-de-Haute-Province sells a "**museum passport**" giving reductions or free entry to museums and parks in the *département*.

Books

HISTORY AND CULTURE

Napoleon's Exile – Patrick Rambaud
Napoleon and the Hundred Days – Stephen Coote
First Lady of Versailles; Mary Adelaide of Savoy, Dauphine of France – Lucy Norton
Madeleine Kamman's Savoie: The Land, People and Food of the French Alps – Neil C. Kamman and Madeleine Kamman
The Red and the Black – Stendahl
Tears of Glory: The Betrayal of Vercors, 1944 – Michael Pearson

Some books by Jean Giono available in translation:
Colline
Song of the World
Joy of Man's Desiring
The Man who Planted Trees

ALPINE SPORTS

Savage Snows: The Story of Mont Blanc – Walt Unsworth
100 Hikes in the Alps – Vicky Spring and Harvey Edwards
Rock Climbing – Phillip Baxter Watts

Cycling in the French Alps – Paul Henderson
Walking in the French Alps: GR5 – Martin Collins
Freeheel skiing: Telemark and Parallel Technique – Paul Parker
Time Out Skiing and Snowboarding in Europe – Dominic Earle
A Guide to Climbing – Tony Louren
Killing Dragons – the Conquest of the Alps – Fergus Fleming
How the English made the Alps – Jim Ring

FILMS AND THE FRENCH ALPS

The Eagle with the Two Heads (1948) – Jean Cocteau; Vizille
La Bride sue le Cou (1961) – Roger Vadim; St-Nizier-du-Moucherotte

Some films by Jean Giono:
– **Crésus** (1960)
– **The Man who Planted Trees** (1987)

Murmur of the Heart (1971) – Louis Malle; Aix-les-Bains
Allons z'enfants (1980) – Yves Boisset; Curial district in Chambéry
The Woman Next Door (1981) – François Truffaut; Grenoble
Louis: Enfant Roi (1993) – Roger Planchon; Baroque chapel in the Musée Dauphinois in Grenoble
Les Marmottes (1993) – Elie Chouraqui; Chamonix
Le Parfum d'Yvonne (1994) Patrice Leconte; a passionate liaison in a luxury hotel in Evian
Rien ne vas plus (1997) – Claude Chabrol; Aix-les-Bains
Napoleon and Me (2006) – Paolo Virzi. The emperor (Daniel Auteuil) plots his return from Elba.

BASIC INFORMATION

Business Hours

Most of the larger shops are open Mondays to Saturdays from 9am to 6.30 or 7.30pm. Smaller, individual shops may close during the lunch hour. Food shops – grocers, wine merchants and bakeries – are generally open from 7am to 6.30 or 7.30pm; some open on Sunday mornings. Many food shops close between noon and 2pm and on Mondays. Bakery and pastry shops sometimes close on Wednesdays. Hypermarkets usually stay open non-stop until 9pm or later.

Electricity

The electric current is 220 volts. Circular two-pin plugs are the rule. Adapters and converters (for hairdryers, for example) should be bought before you leave home; they are on sale in most airports. If you have a rechargable device (video camera, portable computer, battery recharger), read the instructions carefully or contact the manufacturer or shop. Sometimes these items only require a plug adapter, in other cases you must use a voltage converter as well or risk ruining your device.

Mail

Main post offices open Monday to Friday 9am to 6.30 pm, Saturday 9am to noon. However, many post offices, especially smaller ones, close at lunchtime between noon and 2pm, and some may close early in the afternoon: in short, opening hours vary widely. A new system of Relais Poste is supposed to offer more flexible service in convenient locations. Stamps are also available from newsagents and bureaux de tabac. Stamp collectors should ask for *timbres de collection* in any post office.

Money

There are no restrictions on the amount of currency visitors can take into France. However visitors carrying a lot of cash are advised to complete a currency declaration form on arrival, because there are restrictions on currency export.

BANKS

Bank opening hours vary widely. Generally, they are open from 9am to noon and 2pm to a variety of afternoon closing times; branches are closed either on Monday or Saturday; if open on these days, it is often only for the morning. Banks close early on the day before a bank holiday. So, don't count on a bank being open when you need it. A passport is necessary as identification when cashing travellers' cheques in banks. Commission charges vary, and hotels usually charge more than banks for cashing cheques. One of the most economical ways to use your money in France is by using **ATM machines** to get cash directly from your bank account or to use your credit cards to get cash advances. Be sure to remember your PIN number, you will need it to use cash dispensers and to pay with your card in most shops, restaurants, etc. Code pads are numeric; use a telephone pad to translate a letter code into numbers. PIN numbers have 4 digits in France; inquire with the issuing company or bank if the code you usually use is longer. Visa and Mastercard credit networks have merged in France, so merchants take

American Express ☎ 01 47 77 72 00
Visa ☎ 0 800 90 13 87
Mastercard/Eurocard/ Cirrus/Maestro ☎ 0 800 90 13 87
Diners Club ☎ 01 49 06 17 50

both interchangeably. However, the cash advance functions have not merged, and Visa is more widely accepted for this than MasterCard ; other cards, credit and debit (Diners Club, Plus, Cirrus, etc) are also accepted in some cash machines. American Express is more often accepted in premium establishments. Most places post signs indicating the cards they accept; if you don't see such a sign, and want to pay with a card, ask before ordering or making a selection. Cards are widely accepted in shops, hypermarkets, hotels and restaurants, at tollbooths and in petrol stations. If your card is lost or stolen, call one of the following 24-hour hotlines:

Your bank's hotline will be printed on the back of your card: make a note of it. If your card is stolen, you can call a 24-hour helpline to make a report: ☎08 36 69 08 80. You must report any loss or theft of credit cards or travellers' cheques to the local police who will issue you with a certificate (useful proof to show the issuing company).

Public Holidays

Museums and other monuments may be closed or may vary their hours of admission on the following public holidays:

1 January New Year's Day (*Jour de l'An*)	
Easter Easter Day and Easter Monday (*Pâques*)	
1 May May Day	
8 May VE Day	
Thurs 40 days after Easter Ascension Day (*Ascension*)	
7th Sun-Mon after Easter Whit Sunday and Monday (*Pentecôte*)	
14 July France's National Day (*Bastille Day*)	
15 August Assumption (*Assomption*)	
1 November All Saints' Day (*Toussaint*)	
11 November Armistice Day	
25 December Christmas Day (*Noël*)	

National museums and art galleries are closed on Tuesdays; municipal museums are generally closed on Mondays. In addition to the usual school holidays at Christmas and in the spring and summer, there are long mid-term breaks (10 days to a fortnight) in February and early November.

Taxes and Tipping

There is a Value Added Tax in France (TVA) of 19.6% on almost every purchase (books and some foods are subject to a lower rate). However, non-European visitors who spend at least 175€ in any one participating store on the same day can apply for a refund of the VAT; the VAT cannot be reimbursed for items shipped. Usually, you fill out a form at the store, showing your passport. Upon leaving the country, you submit all forms to customs for approval (they may want to see the goods, so if possible don't pack them in checked luggage). The refund is usually paid directly into your bank or credit card account, or it can be sent by mail. Big department stores that cater to tourists provide special services to help you; be sure to mention that you plan to seek a refund before you pay for goods (no refund is possible for tax on services). If you are visiting two or more countries within the European Union, you submit the forms only on departure from the last EU country. The refund is worth while for those visitors who would like to buy fashions, furniture or other fairly expensive items, but remember, the minimum amount must be spent in a single shop.

People travelling to the USA cannot import plant products or fresh food, including fruit, cheeses and nuts. It is acceptable to carry tinned products or preserves.

TIPPING

Since a service charge is automatically included in the price of meals and accommodation in France, any

Notes and Coins

The euro banknotes were designed by Robert Kalinan, an Austrian artist. His designs were inspired by the theme "Ages and styles of European Architecture". Windows and gateways feature on the front of the banknotes, bridges feature on the reverse, symbolising the European spirit of openness and co-operation.
The images are stylised representations of the typical architectural style of each period, rather than specific structures.

Classical

Baroque and Rococo

Romanesque

19C iron and glass

Gothic

Renaissance

20C modern

Euro coins have one face common to all 12 countries in the European single currency area or "Eurozone" (currently Austria, Belgium, Finland, France, Germany, Greece, Ireland, Italy, Luxembourg, The Netherlands, Portugal and Spain) and a reverse side specific to each country, created by their own national artists.

Euro banknotes look the same throughout the Eurozone. All Euro banknotes and coins can be used anywhere in this area.

additional tip (pourboire) is up to the visitor, generally small change, and generally not more than 5%. Taxi drivers and hairdressers are usually tipped 10-15%.

As a rule, prices for hotels and restaurants as well as for other goods and services are significantly less expensive in the French regions than in Paris.

Telephone

Public Telephones – Most public phones in France use pre-paid phone cards *(télécartes)*, rather than coins. Some telephone booths accept credit cards (Visa, Mastercard/Eurocard). *Télécartes* (50 or 120 units) can be bought in post offices, branches of France Télécom, *bureaux de tabac* (cafés that sell cigarettes) and newsagents and can be used to make calls in France and abroad. Calls can be received at phone boxes where the blue bell sign is shown; the phone will not ring, so keep your eye on the little message screen.

National calls – French telephone numbers have 10 digits. Paris and Paris region numbers begin with 01; 02 in northwest France; 03 in northeast France; 04 in southeast France and Corsica; 05 in southwest France.

International calls – To call France from abroad, dial the country code (0033) + 9-digit number (omit the initial 0). When calling abroad from France dial 00, then dial the country code followed by the area code and number of your correspondent.

International dialling codes
(00 + code):

◆	Australia	☎ 61
◆	New Zealand	☎ 64
◆	Canada	☎ 1
◆	United Kingdom	☎ 44
◆	Eire	☎ 353
◆	United States	☎ 1

To use your **personal calling card** dial:

AT&T	☎ 0-800 99 00 11
Sprint	☎ 0-800 99 00 87
MCI	☎ 0-800 99 00 19
Canada Direct	☎ 0-800 99 00 16 or 0-800 99 02 16

Some stores sell phonecards for overseas calls that can be used from both public and private phones. These are cheaper than using a regular phone card at a public booth.

i **International Information:** US/Canada: 00 33 12 11

i **International operator:** 00 33 12 + country code

i **Local directory assistance:** 12

Emergency Numbers
Police: 17
Fire *(Pompiers)*: 18
SAMU (Paramedics): 15

Minitel – France Télécom operates a system offering directory enquiries (free of charge up to 3min), travel and entertainment reservations, and other services (cost per minute varies). These small computer-like terminals can be found in some post offices, hotels and France Télécom agencies and in many French homes. 3614 PAGES E is the code for **directory assistance in English** (turn on the unit, dial 3614, hit the connexion button when you get the tone, type in "PAGES E," and follow the instructions on the screen).

Internet – Internet use is now widespread in France and has supplanted Minitel for most purposes. E-mails are the cheapest way to communicate overseas. Many post offices have public Internet terminals and cyber cafés are opening rapidly. For an updated list of cybercafés, go to www.world66.com/netcafeguide. In major cities, France Télécom has Internet kiosks on the street. Better hotels have business centers where you can access computers, and often hotel rooms have wireless access.

French websites, especially those for tourists or offering commercial services, often are multilingual: just click on the little British or American flag on the home page.

Cellular phones in France and across Europe operate on the GSM standard, which is not widespread in the US. Those with GSM phones can often arrange with their service providers to take with them a phone equiped with an international SIM (Subscriber Information Module) card that allows them to keep their regular phone number and to be billed by their provider. This can be expensive, however, so if you plan to place calls frequently, it is cheaper to rent or buy a phone for the trip. Phone stores for purchase or rental are found at airports and around France. By consulting websites, you can research phone rentals before you go, often with delivery or airport pickup. Try www.cellularabroad.com for information as well as service offers.

Also available on the French cell phone market are *Mobicartes,* pre-paid phone cards that fit into mobile units and that can be purchased in different denominations in convenience stores.

Time

France is 1hr ahead of Greenwich Mean Time (GMT).

When it is noon in France, it is
3am in Los Angeles
6am in New York
11am in Dublin
11am in London
7pm in Perth
9pm in Sydney
11pm in Auckland
In France "am" and "pm" are not used but the 24-hour clock is widely applied.

Conversion Tables

Weights and measures

| 1 kilogram (kg) | 2.2 pounds (lb) | 2.2 pounds |
| 1 metric ton (tn) | 1.1 tons | 1.1 tons |

to convert kilograms to pounds, multiply by 2.2

| 1 litre (l) | 2.1 pints (pt) | 1.8 pints |
| 1 litre | 0.3 gallon (gal) | 0.2 gallon |

to convert litres to gallons, multiply by 0.26 (US) or 0.22 (UK)

| 1 hectare (ha) | 2.5 acres | 2.5 acres |
| 1 square kilometre (km²) | 0.4 square miles (sq mi) | 0.4 square miles |

to convert hectares to acres, multiply by 2.4

1 centimetre (cm)	0.4 inches (in)	0.4 inches
1 metre (m)	3.3 feet (ft) - 39.4 inches - 1.1 yards (yd)	
1 kilometre (km)	0.6 miles (mi)	0.6 miles

to convert metres to feet, multiply by 3.28 . kilometres to miles, multiply by 0.6

Clothing

Women							Men
	35	4	2½	40	7½	7	
	36	5	3½	41	8½	8	
	37	6	4½	42	9½	9	
Shoes	38	7	5½	43	10½	10	Shoes
	39	8	6½	44	11½	11	
	40	9	7½	45	12½	12	
	41	10	8½	46	13½	13	
	36	4	8	46	36	36	
	38	6	10	48	38	38	
Dresses &	40	8	12	50	40	40	Suits
Suits	42	12	14	52	42	42	
	44	14	16	54	44	44	
	46	16	18	56	46	48	
	36	08	30	37	14½	14.5	
	38	10	32	38	15	15	
Blouses &	40	12	34	39	15½	15½	Shirts
sweaters	42	14	36	40	15¾	15¾	
	44	16	38	41	16	16	
	46	18	40	42	16½	16½	

Sizes often vary depending on the designer. These equivalents are given for guidance only.

Speed

kph	10	30	50	70	80	90	100	110	120	130
mph	6	19	31	43	50	56	62	68	75	81

Temperature

Celsius (°C)	0°	5°	10°	15°	20°	25°	30°	40°	60°	80°	100°
Fahrenheit (°F)	32°	41°	50°	59°	68°	77°	86°	104°	140°	176°	212°

To convert Celsius into Fahrenheit, multiply °C by 9, divide by 5, and add 32.
To convert Fahrenheit into Celsius, subtract 32 from °F, multiply by 5, and divide by 9.

Haute-Savoie, village of Combloux
G. Simeone/PHOTONONSTOP

NATURE

The mountain range of the Alps – the highest in Europe – stretches along a curved line from Nice on the Mediterranean coast to Vienna in Austria covering a distance of 1 200km/750mi. The French Alps extend from Lake Geneva to the Mediterranean, a distance of 370km/230mi, and they are over 200km/125mi wide at their widest point, between the Rhône Valley and the Italian Piedmont. The highest peak, Mont Blanc, rises to 4 807m/15 771ft, but the altitude gradually decreases towards the south and the range is easily accessible through a series of deep wide valleys.

Landscapes

The region is famed for magnificent views which appear to change with every bend of the steep, winding roads. It is an area full of contrasts from the colourful shores of Lake Geneva to the glaciers of Mont Blanc, the chalk cliffs of Vercors and the dry Mediterranean landscapes of Haute-Provence.

Geologists divide the French Alps into four main areas:

– The **Préalpes,** or alpine foothills, consisting almost entirely of limestone rocks formed during the Secondary Era, except in the Chablais area.

– The **Alpine trench** *(sillon alpin)*, a depression cut through marl, lying at the foot of the central massifs.

– The **central massifs** *(massifs centraux),* consisting of very old and extremely hard crystalline rocks. The tectonic upheavals of the Tertiary Era folded the ancient land mass *(see below),* creating "needles" and high peaks, which are the highest of the whole Alpine range. From north to south, these massifs are: the Mont-Blanc, the Belledonne, the Grandes Rousses, the Écrins and the Mercantour.

– The **intra-Alpine zone,** forming the axis of the Alps. It consists of sedimentary rocks transformed and folded by the violent upheavals which took place in the area. It includes the Vanoise, the Briançonnais and the Queyras as well as the upper valleys of the Tarentaise, the Maurienne and the Ubaye.

FORMATION OF THE ALPS

Among the "younger" of the Earth's mountains, formed at roughly the same time as the Pyrenees, the Carpathians, the Caucasus and the Himalayas, the Alps are also one of the most geographically complex ranges. Long before the folding of the peaks some 65 million years ago, and the erosion by water, wind and ice which continues to this day, powerful forces were at work beneath the surface.

To explain the phenomenon of gelogical upheaval that has formed the Alps, we turn to the concept of plate tectonics, which describes the earth's crust as consisting of a number of rigid plates moving in relation to one another. The Alps are situated at the boundary of the African and European plates. During the **Paleozoic Era,** beginning 570 million years ago, a huge folding of the Earth's crust produced the Hercynian mountains, which had a crystalline structure similar to that of the Vosges and the Massif Central today, where the central massifs now stand. The luxuriant vegetation, stimulated by the hot and humid climate, produced a considerable amount of plant deposits which are the origin of several coalfields at La Mure and in the Briançonnais. Erosion followed, and after 200 million years the crystalline foundation was submerged under the sea and a layer of marine sediments such as coral thousands of metres thick was formed.

The **Mesozoic Era** began approximately 230 million years ago. Pushed and compressed by the African continent which was moving to the north, the seabed deposits of limestone and sand (which were transformed into sandstone when compressed) as well as clay (which under high pressure often flaked into shale) piled up on the ancient foundation of

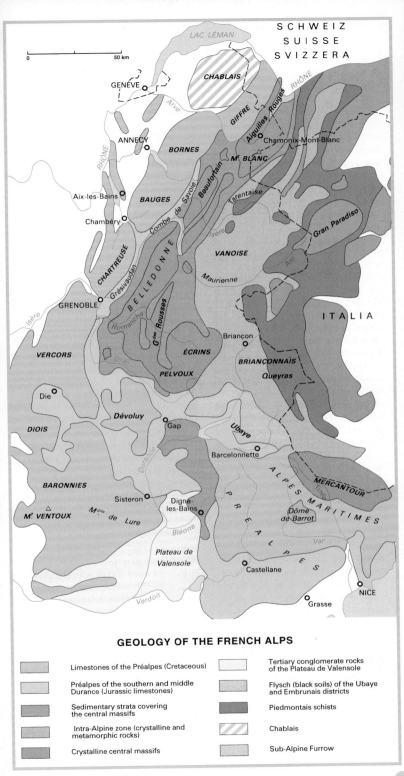

GEOLOGY OF THE FRENCH ALPS

Limestones of the Préalpes (Cretaceous)	Tertiary conglomerate rocks of the Plateau de Valensole
Préalpes of the southern and middle Durance (Jurassic limestones)	Flysch (black soils) of the Ubaye and Embrunais districts
Sedimentary strata covering the central massifs	Piedmontais schists
Intra-Alpine zone (crystalline and metamorphic rocks)	Chablais
Crystalline central massifs	Sub-Alpine Furrow

crystalline rocks. The climate was uniform; forests consisted of pines, oaks, walnut trees, eucalyptus and palm trees. Huge reptiles such as dinosaurs roamed the earth and the first birds appeared. The **Tertiary Era,** which began 65 million years ago, saw the formation of the high range of mountains as we know them. Starting about 30 million years ago, a spur of the African plate, consisting of Italy and part of the Balkans, advanced and collided with Europe, pushing up masses of schist, folding the area like putty pressed between your fingers and forming to the east the Italian Alps and the Vanoise, to the west the Chablais and to the north the Swiss Alps.

More recently, about 5 to 10 million years ago, the continuing force of the African plate pushed up the ancient crystalline foundation from under the seabed deposits of limestone, marl and clay; this layer literally came unstuck and began to slide westwards in spectacular folds, creating the Préalpes. A depression appeared between the crystalline massifs and the Préalpes, which eventually became the Alpine trench through the work of erosion. Most recently, in the last few millions of years before our era, the Dauphinois and the Savoy areas were covered by shallow inland seas, where a layer of sediment accumulated from erosion of the nearby mountains. Thus was formed the gentle, fertile countryside of the Albanais and Geneva.

A general cooling of the earth's atmosphere over the last 2.5 million years caused by the rise of the Himalaya and the Isthmus of Panama, has brought about a series of glacial periods during which the whole alpine region was covered with a huge mantle of ice. Erosion then worked relentlessly on a complete remodelling of the Alps into the mountain range it is today.

REGIONAL LANDSCAPES

These vary considerably according to the different geological structure of each area. It seems therefore logical to adopt the geologists' division of the Alps into four distinct parts preceded by what we might call the Alpine fringe.

Listed from west to east and south to north, they are: the Préalpes, the Alpine trench, the central massifs and the intra-Alpine zone.

Alpine Fringe

The Albanais, the Geneva area and the Bornes Plateau situated on the edge of the northern Alps offer landscapes of green rolling hills dominated by a few moderate mountain ranges such as the **Salève** south of Geneva and the **Mont du Chat** near the Lac du Bourget. The basins left behind by retreating glaciers have been filled in by deep lakes: the Lac d'Aiguebelette and Lac du Bourget.

Préalpes

The northern Préalpes lie just beyond the Alpine fringe along a north-south axis, forming a barrier which rarely rises above 2 500m/8 202ft. They consist of five distinct massifs carved out of limestone (except for the Chablais), separated by the cluses, (transverse valleys) of the Arve, Annecy, Chambéry and Grenoble.

Overlooking Lake Geneva and drained by the three Dranse rivers, the **Chablais** is backed by the **Giffre** with its lively winter resorts, Samoëns and Flaine.

The **Bornes** Massif, flanked by the **Chaîne des Aravis** in the east, is drained by several rivers including the Fier and extends from the valley of the Arve to the blue waters of the lake of Annecy; La Clusaz is an important ski resort.

Further south, the **Bauges** Massif, extending to the Cluse de Chambéry, offers pleasant pastoral landscapes where small ski resorts are developing. The **Chartreuse** Massif, with the Cluse d'Isère to the south, stands like an imposing limestone fortress; features include high cliffs, deep gorges, valleys with pastures and magnificent dense forests on the well-watered slopes.

The **Vercors** is the largest of the Préalpes massifs; within its impressive outer ramparts, this natural citadel offers beautiful forest and pastoral landscapes, as well as striking gorges and popular resorts such as Villard-de-Lans.

The southern Préalpes spread over a vast area along a curved line in a northwest-

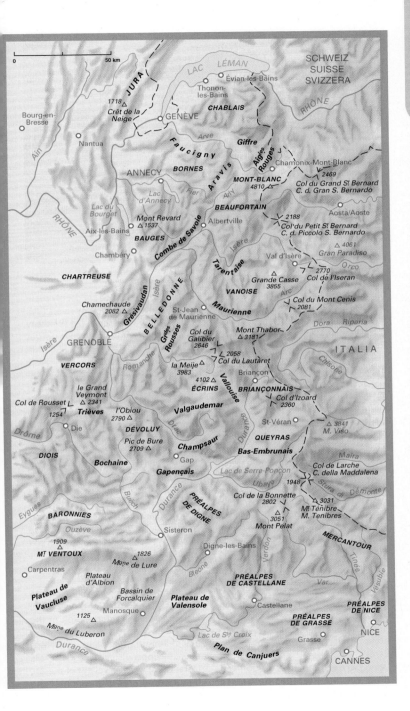

Préalpes de Digne

southeast direction. The Durance Valley divides them into two groups:

West of the river, on the Dauphiné side, is the wild and austere **Dévoluy,** with its cliffs and bare summits below which sheep and cattle graze.

The wooded **Bochaine** marks the transition between north and south whereas the **Diois** and **Baronnies** already offer typical southern landscapes where soaring limestone peaks collapse into waves of rock set in conflicting directions. To the south, the limestone massif of **Mont Ventoux** stands alone, towering 1 909m/6 263ft above the Avignon Basin.

East of the Durance, the relief becomes more intricate, without any apparent plan; the mountain ranges of the **Préalpes de Digne** and **Préalpes de Castellane** are cut crosswise by deep wild gorges, known as *clues,* guarded by picturesque towns like Sisteron, Digne and Castellane. These areas are the least populated of the Alpine region: owing to strict conservation regulations, the slopes have retained their varied vegetation, but the summits are mostly bare.

Lying between the River Verdon and River Var, the **Préalpes de Grasse** rise to an altitude varying between 1 100m/3 609ft and 1 600m/5 250ft.

The **Préalpes de Nice** are deeply cut in a north-south direction by rivers (Var, Tinée, Vésubie) which make their way to the sea through impressive gorges overlooked by villages perched high above the river beds.

Lying between the Préalpes, the **Plateau de Valensole** occupies the former delta of the River Durance filled in by an accumulation of rocks from nearby mountains. These rocks and pebbles, bound together by a kind of natural cement, form a conglomerate which has been carved by erosion into the famous **Pénitents des Mées** (👉 *see Vallée de la Moyenne DURANCE*). Further east, there are several limestone plateaux through which streams penetrate and disappear into sink-holes. Spectacular gorges have been carved out by the River Verdon and River Artuby.

Alpine Trench

In the northern Alps, the **Bassin de Sallanches** and the **Val d'Arly** form, together with the depression of the **Combe de Savoie** and **Grésivaudan,** a wide longitudinal plain into which open the upper valley of the River Isère (Tarentaise) and the valleys of the Arc (Maurienne) and of the Romanche (Oisans). Owing to the means of communication provided by this internal plain, to the fertile soil which favours rich crops (maize, tobacco, vines) and to the availability of hydroelectric power, the Alpine trench has become one of the most prosperous areas of the whole region.

In the southern Alps, a similar depression cut through marl runs along the foot of the Écrins, Briançonnais and Queyras massifs; the River Durance and its tributaries flow through this relatively flat area partly flooded by the artificial Lac de Serre-Ponçon. Some strange rock formations, carved out of ancient moraines, can be seen in this region. They stand like groups of columns and are known as **Demoiselles coiffées** (capped maidens) because they are crowned by a piece of hard rock (🔵 see Barrage et lac de SERRE-PONÇON). Between Sisteron and Manosque, the fertile Durance Valley brings Provence, its typical vegetation and orchards to the heart of the southern Alps.

La Clarée Valley

M. Blanchard/MARCO POLO

Central Massifs

This central mountain range includes **Mont-Blanc,** the **Aiguilles Rouges,** the **Beaufortain,** the **Belledonne,** the **Grandes Rousses,** the **Écrins-Pelvoux** and, in the south, the **Mercantour.** Together, these massifs, rising to over 4 000 metres/13 123ft, form the high Alps, consisting of hard crystalline rocks, which were uplifted during the Tertiary Era while their sedimentary cover was removed. Austere and impressive, they are well known among mountaineers who like to cross the glaciers and climb the needles and snow-capped peaks. The Beaufortain is the only massif to have retained its layers of schist: it offers pleasant pastoral landscapes scattered with wooden chalets. Beautiful lakes have filled in the basins left by the glaciers.

Intra-Alpine Zone

Situated between the central massifs and the Italian border, the **Vanoise** Massif and the **Briançonnais-Queyras Massif** also belong to the high Alps but they consist of a mixture of schist and metamorphic crystalline rocks. Valleys are deep and slopes are covered with pastures. Thanks to its mild, sunny climate and snow-covered slopes, the Vanoise (which has the Tarentaise and Maurienne as natural boundaries and includes the Parc national de la Vanoise) has recently acquired the highest concentration of winter resorts in the French Alps including Val-d'Isère, Tignes, Courchevel, La Plagne, Méribel-les-Allues and Les Arcs.

The Briançonnais-Queyras Massif has a more complicated relief due to the diversity of its rock structure: sandstone, limestone and schist carried over from the Italian side as a result of overthrust. Its characteristic southern light, blue skies and generous sun make this area one of the healthiest in Europe, which explains the rapid development of summer and winter tourism centred round high villages such as St-Véran (2 040m/6 693ft).

The **Gap, Embrun** and **Ubaye** districts, lying between the high Alps and the Préalpes, offer a mosaic of heights, small basins and wide valleys carved out of layers of "black soil," or flysch in the case of the Ubaye.

ALPINE RELIEF

The slow but irresistible action of glaciers, rivers, rain and frost has completely remodelled the Alps over thousands of years into the mountain range it is today.

The action of the glaciers – Around 10 000 years ago, glaciers covered the whole Alpine range and spread over the adjacent flat areas as far as the region of Lyon. Some of these "solid rivers" were huge, reaching thicknesses of 1 100m/3 609ft in the Grésivaudan for instance. They scooped out cirques with steep back walls and dug U-shaped valleys characterised by successive narrowings and widenings and a series of steps, with tributary valleys "hanging" over the main ones.

Alpine glaciers today – Since the beginning of the 20C, Alpine glaciers have been consistently receding because they are not being sufficiently renewed, and today they only cover an area of 400km/154sq mi; four fifths of them are in Savoie (Mont-Blanc and Vanoise), the remainder being in the Écrins Massif.

The Mer de Glace is a very good example of a "valley glacier." Moving downstream, we find in succession a **névé,** an expanse of snow not yet turned into ice, and a **glacial "tongue"** cut by deep crevasses. Level changes are marked by jumbled piles known as **séracs;** accumulations of debris carried down by the glacier are called **lateral moraine** when deposited on the edges, **terminal moraine** when deposited at the end and **medial moraine** when deposited between two joining glaciers. Alpine glaciers move at a speed of 70m/230ft per year.

Erosion by water – When the ice mantle disappeared, mountain streams and rivers began to smooth out the relief. Connecting gorges opened up the "bolts" and joined the floor of a "hanging" valley to that of the main valley. These valleys, wide but often closed off, like that of Chamonix for example, would be completely isolated but for audacious road construction. There are gorges of another kind, mainly in the Préalpes, which cut across the axis of the folds: they are called **cluses** (transverse valleys). They are often the only means of communication between the mountain and the lower areas. The most active mountain streams deposit debris they have been carrying when they reach the bottom of the main valley and their accumulation at the foot of the slopes forms alluvial cones which obstruct the valleys.

STREAMS AND RIVERS

The southern Alps have three distinct river networks: in the centre the Durance and its tributaries, in the east the

Pointe de l'Échelle and Lac Blanc in the Massif de la Vanoise

J.-P. Chanut/PHOTONONSTOP

Var which gathers water streaming down the Alpes Maritimes, and in the west the tributaries of the Rhône.

Mediterranean rivers are particularly interesting because they behave like real mountain streams: during the summer, they are reduced to a trickle of water owing to the absence of rain and intensive evaporation. But in spring and autumn, violent rain storms or sudden thaws fill up the river beds so suddenly that the flow of foaming water tumbles down at the speed of a galloping horse. For instance, the rate of flow of the River Var varies from 17m/600cu ft per second to 5 000m/176 575cu ft per second. The Durance, Verdon, Aigues and Ouvèze rivers are equally capricious. However, the Durance and Verdon have been harnessed by dams (Serre-Ponçon across the Durance, Castillon and Ste-Croix across the Verdon) and canals. The impressive gorges dug by these rivers (Grand Canyon du Verdon, Gorges du Cians) are one of the main attractions of Haute-Provence.

Underground streams forming mysterious hydrographic networks sometimes reappear further on; streams from the Montagne de Lure, for instance, feed the famous resurgent spring of Fontaine-de-Vaucluse (&see The Green Guide Provence: FONTAINE-DE-VAUCLUSE).

ALPINE CLIMATE

The Alpine range is divided into two distinct climatic regions: the northern Alps which are subject to west winds off the Atlantic and the southern Alps which enjoy a Mediterranean climate. The separation between these two regions follows a line drawn from west to east between the following mountain passes: Col de Rousset, Col de la Croix Haute, Col du Lautaret and Col du Galibier.

Rainfall over the **northern Alps** is abundant all year round and temperatures are low. The Préalpes and central massifs get the brunt of the rainy weather. The intra-Alpine zone, protected by these barriers, is drier and sunnier; snow remains on the slopes longer. However, many factors such as altitude, aspect and the general direction of the various ranges and valleys, contribute to create a great variety of microclimates.

Altitude – Temperatures fall rapidly as the altitude increases (roughly 0.5°C/1°F every 100m/328ft); interestingly, this phenomenon can be reversed in winter, during periods of settled weather, as cold, heavier air slips down the slopes and accumulates in the valleys and the warm air rises.

Aspect – South-facing slopes, called **"adrets,"** enjoy more sunshine than north-facing slopes called **"ubacs,"** usually covered with forests and on which snow holds better.

Relief – It has an influence on rainfall and wind direction; rain and snow fall more generously on the first heights in their path and on slopes exposed to the wind. Winds generally blow along wide valleys, particularly during the warm season when, towards midday, warm air rises from the valleys and causes clouds to form round the summits. This is a sign of continuing fine weather. Later on in the day, the process is reversed and a cold mountain breeze blows down into the valleys. Heights usually attract storms which are often violent and spectacular.

The climate enjoyed by the **southern Alps** displays typical Mediterranean features: a good deal of sunshine, dry weather, clear skies, the absence of mist or fog, rare yet abundant precipitation and the famous *mistral* wind. In winter there is a fair amount of snow and plenty of fine weather in which to enjoy it. Spring is characterised by a short rainy spell while the mistral blows hard from the southwest. Summer is hot and dry over the whole of Haute-Provence and the air filled with the delicate scent of lavender and thyme. Nearer the summits, temperatures are more moderate. In the autumn, violent storms are succeeded by sunny spells, the air is pure and the light ideal for discovering the beauty of nature.

Alpine Flora

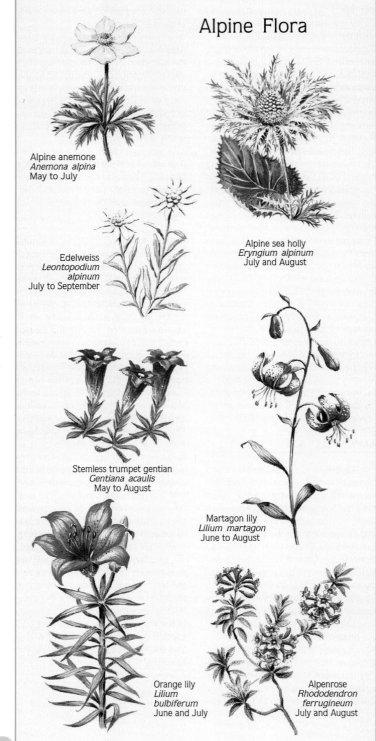

Alpine anemone
Anemona alpina
May to July

Alpine sea holly
Eryngium alpinum
July and August

Edelweiss
*Leontopodium
alpinum*
July to September

Stemless trumpet gentian
Gentiana acaulis
May to August

Martagon lily
Lilium martagon
June to August

Orange lily
*Lilium
bulbiferum*
June and July

Alpenrose
*Rhododendron
ferrugineum*
July and August

M. Janvier/ MICHELIN

Flora

In mountain areas, the pattern of vegetation is not only influenced by the climate and the type of soil, but depends also on aspect and altitude which defines a succession of vertical stages. This staging is modified by man who has done much to alter original landscapes. South-facing slopes (adrets), which offer the best conditions for settlement and agriculture, have been the most subject to deforestation, whereas northern slopes (ubacs), often uninhabited, have retained their trees which thrive in the prevailing wetter conditions; a pattern seen at its best in valleys running from east to west.

Slopes are usually farmed up to an altitude of about 1 500m/5 000ft; above this there is a belt of conifer forest. From around 2 200m/7 000ft upwards, the trees give way to Alpine pastures with their rich mixture of wild grasses and Alpine flora. Above 3 000m/10 000ft, bare rock prevails, with mosses and lichens clinging to it in places.

TREES

The Alps are famous for their vast forests of conifers. Old **fir trees** have broad crowns with flattened points looking like storks' nests. The bark is greyish; the cones, standing up like candles, break up when ripe and shed their scales. The soft needles are lined up like the teeth of a comb (hence the name *sapin pectiné*) and have a double white line on their inner surface (hence the name *sapin argenté* – silver fir). The **spruce** is the most commonly found tree on north-facing slopes. It has a pointed, spindle-shaped crest and drooping branches, and its reddish bark becomes deeply fissured with age. It has sharp needles and its hanging cones fall to the ground in one piece when ripe. The only conifer in the French Alps to shed its leaves in winter, the **larch** is commonly found growing on south-facing slopes, particularly in the *"Alpes sèches"* (dry Alps). The cones are quite small. The delicate, light-green foliage casts relatively little shade, thus favouring the growth of grass, one of the attractive features of larch woods, while the dropped needles create an acidic soil that favours rhododendrons and bushes such as blueberries. The many species of **pine** all have needles growing in tufts of two to five encased in scaly sheaths. The cones have hard rough scales. The forest pine, with its tall slender trunk, grows in considerable numbers in the southern Alps, usually on the *adrets* (sunny slopes).

Deciduous Trees

The grey-trunk beech prevails in the Préalpes up to an altitude of 800m/2 625ft. With its thick boughs it provides shade for many rare plants: Turk's-cap lily, belladonna or deadly nightshade, medicinal speedwell and many more. Among other deciduous trees, there are alders, maples, birches, service trees, willows and laburnums with their lovely clusters of yellow flowers.

MEDITERRANEAN VEGETATION

Trees and xerophilous plants (adapted to extremely dry conditions) require mild temperatures which do not fall below 4°C/39°F during the coldest month of the year.

Trees – Several varieties of oaks and pines, as well as almond trees and the typically Provençal cypresses and olive trees grow in the southern Alps, either in cultivated areas or scattered on dry, rocky moors known as *garrigues*. Such landscapes can be seen in the Durance Valley, on the southern slopes of Mont Ventoux or the Montagne de Lure and in the Baronnies and Diois areas. Further north, above 600-800m/1 968-2 625ft, forests of white oaks, forest pines and beeches prevail, particularly on north-facing slopes. Such forests often alternate with heaths where gorse, box and lavender grow.

The evergreen **holm oak** has a short, thick-set trunk with a wide-spreading dome and fine, dark green leaves. It grows on arid calcareous soil at less than 328m/1 000ft; in stunted form, it is a characteristic element of the *garrigues* (see below).

The deciduous **downy** or **white oak,** so-called because the undersides of the leaves are covered with dense short white hairs, requires more water than the evergreen oak. It is found in valleys and on the more humid mountain slopes.

The **Aleppo pine,** one of the Mediterranean species of pine trees, has a light, graceful foliage and a trunk covered with grey bark which twists as it grows.

The outline of the dark **cypress,** a coniferous evergreen, marks the Mediterranean landscape with its tapered form pointing towards the sky, while the common **almond tree** delights the eye with its lovely early spring pink blossoms.

Garrigues – This word is used to describe vast expanses of rocky limestone moors. Vegetation is sparse, consisting mostly of holm oaks, stunted downy oaks, thistles, gorse and cistus as well as lavender, thyme and rosemary interspersed with short dry grass which provides pasture for flocks of sheep.

ALPINE FLORA

The name "Alpine" is normally used to describe those plants which grow above the tree line. Because of the short growing season (July and August), these hardy and mostly small species flower early, while the disproportionate development and colouring of the flowers is the result of exposure to intense ultraviolet light. Their resistance to drought is often their main characteristic; many have woolly leaf surfaces and thick, water-retaining leaves.

Remote origins – Most Alpine plants originated elsewhere. The dandelion and the centaury are among those which came from the lower mountains and the plains but adapted to the harsher conditions at high altitude; others come from the Mediterranean area, like the pink and the narcissus, from the Arctic (buttercup, white poppy) or from Asia like the primula and even that most emblematic Alpine flower, the edelweiss. The few truly indigenous species such as columbine and valerian managed to survive the Quaternary glaciations.

Suitable sites – Mountain plants do not grow at random: some need an alkaline soil, others prefer an acid soil; some flourish on scree, in a cleft in the rock or in a bog. Each type of site has its specific plant species or combination of species – always the same – which is able to thrive in the given conditions.

Fauna

Above the tree line, at high altitudes, animals have learnt how to adapt to the special conditions of a harsh environment, in which it is only possible to survive by building up one's defences against the cold, the snow and the lack of food. Some animals are protected against the cold by their thick coat or plumage, others such as the marmot hibernate below ground, solving at the same time the problem of food shortage. The blue hare and the snow-partridge, which are the favourite game of foxes and birds of prey, make themselves inconspicuous by changing colour with the seasons. In winter, large herbivores like the ibex and the chamois make their way down to the forests in search of food and shelter. In addition to this struggle for life, these animals must contend with man's expansion into their habitat; most of the shy, rarer species seem doomed to extinction in the near future except in conservation areas within the nature parks.

Mammals – The **ibex** is a stocky wild goat with a pair of easily recognisable curved, ridged horns which can be more than a metre long; this peaceful animal enjoys basking in the sun. Males sometimes gather in flocks of more than 50. When snow begins to fall, they join up with the females who are smaller and shier. The males then fight for the females and the clatter of their horns knocking echoes throughout the mountains. The measures undertaken by the Parc national de la Vanoise to protect the species have ensured its survival.

The graceful silhouette of the nimble **chamois** can be seen high up on the steep rocky peaks capped with snow all year round. The "Alpine antelope" has a

Black grouse

Chamois

Ibex

Salamander

Tengmalm's owl

Moufflon

Bearded vulture

M. Guillou/MICHELIN

tough reddish brown coat, thicker and darker in winter, with a black line on its back. Its small head is surmounted by curved slender dark horns. This extremely strong animal jumps from one rock to the next and climbs the steepest passages; its thin, strong legs and its special hooves explain its extraordinary agility. It lives in groups of between three and 20 head, led by a male goat. A chamois can weigh as much as 50kg/110lb (half the weight of an ibex). In summer it feeds on grass, whereas in winter it goes down to the forest and nibbles at the bark of trees.

The short-eared **blue hare** lives in the very high Alpine pastures and is very difficult to observe owing to its scarcity and above all its ability to change colour with the seasons in order to blend in better with its surroundings. Pure white in winter, it thus becomes greyish in summer.

The reddish brown summer coat of the **stoat,** or weasel, becomes white in winter apart from a thin tuft of black hair at the end of its tail. This small carnivorous mammal lives among stones or near chalets.

The mascot of the Alps is the **marmot**, also known as a groundhog, which has found a congenial home in the vast parks of the area. Skiers cause it no anxiety at all, since it passes the winter season hibernating with its fellows under the snow in warm tunnels. From April to September, it enlivens alpine pastures with its whistling call.

You may need binoculars, and a stroke of luck, to catch a glimpse of a solitary **lynx,** stalking the slopes at sunset in search of birds, marmots, chamois and small deer. Virtually extinct in the region by the beginning of the 20C, this wild cat has returned to the woods of Savoie from Switzerland.

The **Corsican moufflon** is a large wild sheep, living in flocks led by the older males. Originally from Asia, but particularly well adapted to the Mediterranean climate and vegetation, it has been introduced into the Mercantour and Queyras nature parks. Males are easily identified by their thick scroll-shaped horns.

One of the most retiring creatures in the mountains is the **snow-mouse**, which can live at an altitude of 4 000m/13 123ft.

Butterflies and moths – There are more than 1 300 different species of butterflies and moths in the Alpes-de-Haute-Provence *département* alone and more than 600 species in the area around Digne (there is an exceptionally fine collection of lepidoptera in the local museum), among them some 180 butterflies which represent three quarters of the total butterfly population of France. Among the most remarkable species are the Swallowtail butterfly, the Parnassius and, smaller but also rarer, the Diana and the Proserpina, the Jason, the Vanessas and the Érèbiae (including the Scipio, currently becoming extinct) which hover over lavender fields. The destruction of the traditional environment and the development of industries in the area are responsible for numerous species becoming extinct every year.

Birds of Prey – **Golden eagles** can be seen throughout the Alps, circling above their territory, which can cover most of a valley. Breeding pairs remain together for life, rearing their young in eyries on the side of inaccessible cliff faces. Eagles prey on marmots in summer and feed off ibex carcasses when food becomes short in winter.

In winter and spring, you will hear, but probably not see, the **Tengmalm owl**, whose call is long and piercing. It is found also in Scandinavia, and is well adapted to cold and mountain forests. The reintroduction of the **bearded vulture,** which soars on wings 2.80m/9ft long from tip to tip, has been a great success story, and you can observe a colony of 60 birds in the Parc naturel régional de Verdon (see Castellane). A scavenger of carrion, it generally stays close to herds of cattle.

HISTORY

Time Line

Events in italics indicate milestones in history

THE CELTS AND THE ROMANS

6-5C BC	The Celts progressively occupy the whole Alpine region; the powerful Allobrogi settle in the area situated between the River Rhône and River Isère.
218	Hannibal crosses the Alps in spite of the Alloborgi's attempt to stop him.
125-122	The Romans conquer southern Gaul.
121	The Allobrogi finally acknowledge Roman superiority.
1C BC	During the reign of Augustus, the whole Alpine region is pacified.
End of 2C AD	The first Christian communities expand in spite of persecution.
4C	Christianity gets a firm hold on the region and bishoprics are founded.
313	*Proclamation of the edict of Milan, through which Constantine grants religious freedom to the Christians.*
476	*Fall of the Roman Empire.*

THE FRANKS AND THE KINGDOM OF BURGUNDY

534-36	The Franks seize Burgundy and invade Provence.
800	*Charlemagne becomes Emperor of the West.*
8C	Franks and Arabs devastate Provence.
987	*Hugues Capet is crowned King of France.*
10C	Provence becomes part of the kingdom of Burgundy. The Saracens are repelled.
1032	The kingdom of Burgundy is annexed by the Holy Roman Empire. At the same time, the archbishop of Vienne splits his huge territory into two: the future Savoie to the north and the future Dauphiné to the south.

SAVOIE, DAUPHINÉ AND PROVENCE

11-12C	Expansion of the three provinces. The dynasty of the Count of Savoie becomes the guardian of the Alpine passes. The ruler of Dauphiné adopts the title of "Dauphin" and the Count of Provence Raimond Bérenger V inherits the County of Forcalquier which is thereafter united with Provence. Building of abbeys and monasteries throughout the land. St Bruno founds the Carthusian Order and monastery.
1209	*Albigensian Crusade led by Simon de Montfort.*
1232	Chambéry becomes capital of Savoie
1268	The Dauphin Guigues VII marries the daughter of the Count of Savoie.
1270	*Death of King St Louis of France, who was married to the daughter of the Count of Provence.*

C. de Torquat/PIX

Seal of Amadeus VI

1337-
1453 *Hundred Years War.*
14C Savoie becomes a powerful feudal state under Amadeus VI, VII and VIII.
1349 Dauphin Humbert II, being in political and financial difficulties, negotiates the sale of Dauphiné to the King of France. It is decided that the heir to the throne of France will, from then on, bear the title of "Dauphin" (see GRE-NOBLE).
1416 Savoie becomes a dukedom.
1419 Unification of Savoie and Piedmont.
1447 Dauphin Louis II (the future King Louis XI) settles on his domains, puts an end to the feudal system and creates the Parliament of Grenoble.

ITALIAN WARS AND WARS OF RELIGION

1461-83 *Louis XI's reign. The king inherits Savoie in 1481*
1488 Crusade against Vaudois heretics in the Alpine valleys.
1489-
1564 Life of Guillaume Farel, a native of Gap, who preaches the Reformation.
1492 *Christopher Columbus discovers America.*
1494-
1559 The Italian Wars reveal the strategic importance of the Dauphiné passes.
1536 With the help of the Swiss cantons, François I invades Savoie which remains under French rule for 23 years.
1559 Treaty of Cateau-Cambrésis: Savoie is returned to the Duke of Savoie who transfers his capital from Chambéry to Turin.
1543-
1626 Life of Lesdiguières, the protestant governor of Dauphiné, who fights the Duke of Savoie.

1562-98 Fierce fighting between Catholics and Protestants: Sisteron, Castellane and Seyne are besieged; armies of the rival factions clash at Allemagne-en-Provence
1589 *Beginning of Henri IV's reign.*
1598 *End of the Wars of Religion; Edict of Nantes: Protestants obtain the freedom of worship and guaranteed strongholds.*
17C Savoie is occupied several times by French troops.
1628 Dauphiné loses its autonomy.

FROM LOUIS XIV TO THE REVOLUTION

1643-
1715 *Louis XIV's reign.*
1685 *Revocation of the Edict of Nantes: Protestants flee the country.*
1692 The Duke of Savoie invades the southern Alps. The king sends Vauban to the area in order to build fortresses and strengthen existing ones (Briançon, Mont-Dauphin, Sisteron and Colmars).
1707 Invasion of Provence by Prince Eugène of Savoie.
1713 Treaty of Utrecht: Dauphiné and Provence expand; France loses part of the Briançonnais but receives the Ubaye region in compensation.
1736 Jean-Jacques Rousseau settles in Les Charmettes near Chambéry.
1740-48 War of the Austrian Succession. Eastern Provence is invaded by Austrian and Sardinian troops; Savoie is occupied by the Spaniards, France's allies. The treaty of Aix-la-Chapelle ends the war and the Spaniards have to give up Savoie.
1774 *Beginning of the reign of Louis XVI, deposed by the revolution less than 20 years later.*
1786 Balmat and Paccard are the first Alpinists to climb Mont Blanc.

1788 Reaction in Grenoble and Vizille to the closure of the local parlements foreshadows the Revolution.

1789 *Bastille day signals the start of the French Revolution; départements are created the following year.*

1791 Dauphiné is divided into three départements: Isère, Drôme and Hautes-Alpes.

1792 French revolutionary troops occupy Savoie which becomes the "Mont-Blanc *département*."

1793 Creation of the "Alpes-Maritimes *département*" (returned to the kingdom of Sardinia in 1814).

19C

1811 The Route du Mont-Cenis is built by order of Napoleon I.

1815 By the treaty of Paris, Savoie is given back to King Victor-Emmanuel I of Sardinia. Napoleon I, returning from exile on Elba, lands in Golfe-Juan on the Mediterranean coast and crosses the southern Alps to Grenoble.

1852 *Napoleon III becomes Emperor of France.*

1858 Napoleon III meets the Italian statesman Cavour in Plombières (Vosges region): they agree that France shall help the King of Sardinia to drive the Austrians out of Italy; in exchange, France is to receive Nice and Savoie.

April 1860 A plebiscite is organised in Savoie: an overwhelming majority vote in favour of the union with France. The new province is divided into two départements: Savoie and Haute-Savoie.

1869 Aristide Bergès harnesses the first high waterfall in Lancey thus becoming the "father" of hydroelectric power.

1870 *Proclamation of the Third Republic on 4 September.*

1872 Inauguration of the Fréjus railway tunnel.

1878 Mountaineer Henri Duhamel takes to the slopes of Chamrousse on skis.

End of the 19C Acceleration of the population drift from the mountains to the towns.

20C

1924 First Winter Olympic Games held in Chamonix.

June 1940 The advancing German army is temporarily halted by the River Isère. Italian attacks are repelled by border garrisons.

1944 Fierce fighting in the Vercors: Dauphiné is one of the main strongholds of the Resistance. One of the underground fighters' most heroic feats takes place on the Plateau des Glières (*see THORENS-GLIÈRES*).

1945 The Resistance liberates the Ubaye region.

1947 The Treaty of Paris alters the Franco-Italian border in favour of France which receives the Vallée Étroite (*see Le BRIANÇONNAIS*).

1955 Cable-cars make the high peaks accessible to everyone.

1955-1967 Construction of the huge Serre-Ponçon Dam.

1962 Signing of the Accords d'Évian (Treaty of Évian, *see ÉVIAN-LES-BAINS*)

1963 Creation of the Parc national de la Vanoise, the first French national park.

1965 Inauguration of the Mont Blanc road tunnel.

1968 10th Winter Olympics held in Grenoble.

1980 Opening of the Fréjus road tunnel, over 100 years after the railway tunnel.

1992 16th Winter Olympic Games held in Albertville.

1995	Creation of the Parc naturel régional de Chartreuse.
1996	Creation of the Parc naturel régional du massif des Bauges.
1999	Fire in the Mont Blanc tunnel claims 41 lives.
2005	Fire in the Mont Fréjus tunnel; despite improved safety systems, two lives lost.
2006	Glacier Monitoring Service (WGUS) announces that three-quarters of European glaciers may be lost in next 100 years, due to climate change.

THE HOUSE OF SAVOIE

The House of Savoie was the longest reigning dynasty in Europe: it began with the feudal lord Humbert "White Hands," who became count of Savoie in 1034 and ended with the last king of Italy, Umberto II, Victor-Emmanuel III's son, who abdicated in 1946. For nine centuries, the House of Savoie ruled over Savoie when it was a county, then a duchy; it governed Piedmont from 1429 onwards, Sardinia from 1720 and finally provided Italy's monarchs from 1861 to 1946.

How counts became dukes – Their role as "gatekeepers" of the Alps gave the counts and later the dukes of Savoie exceptional power. The history of Savoie amounts to a string of successive occupations, each followed by a treaty returning it to its rightful owner.

During the Middle Ages, three of Savoie's rulers, Amadeus VI, VII and VIII, gave the region unprecedented ascendency; their court, held in Chambéry, rivalled in splendour those of the most important sovereigns of Europe. The most illustrious, **Amadeus VIII,** was the first to bear the title of Duke of Savoie and at the end of his life was elected as the last Antipope under the name of Felix V.

In the 16C, the Treaty of Cateau-Cambrésis freed Savoie from French domination which had lasted 23 years. **Duke Emmanuel-Philibert** reorganised his domains and moved his capital from Chambéry to Turin, which was less easily accessible to French monarchs. His wish to expand on the Italian side of the Alps was accomplished during the reign of Victor-Amadeus II, who gained the kingdom of Sicily by the Treaty of Utrecht, then promptly exchanged it for Sardinia and became the king of that region.

Union with France – The people of Savoie were tired of their government which they ironically called "il Buon Governo." Moreover, they were worried by Cavour's anticlerical policy and turned towards France for help. Napoleon III and Cavour met in Plombières in 1858 and decided that, in exchange for France's help against Austrian occupation, Italy would relinquish Nice and Savoie if the populations concerned agreed. This led to the plebiscite of April 1860: by 130 533 votes to 235, the people of Savoie overwhelmingly agreed to become French.

Famous Natives of the Alps

SCHOLARS AND WRITERS

Savoie, which has belonged to France for just over 100 years, was, strangely enough, the cradle of the French language; the Savoyard humanist **Guillaume Fichet** (1433-78) set up the first printing press in Paris. Almost two centuries later, in 1606, the first French Academy was founded in Annecy; one of its founders was **Saint François de Sales** (1567-1622), who inspired religious life in his native Savoie and whose works contributed to the blossoming of the French language (see ANNECY).

One of the prominent early figures of the southern Alps was another humanist **Guillaume Farel** (1489-1565), a native of the Gap area, who preached the Reformation with Calvin in Geneva. At that time, Occitan was the dominant language of the southern Alps, as indeed of the whole of southern France; although its official use was discontinued in the 16C, it continued to be spoken by the people for another three centuries.

Champtercier, in the hills above Digne, was the birthplace of Pierre Gassendi

(1592-1655), a philosopher, mathematician and scientist who rose to prominence in the 17C.

During the late 18C and early 19C, the brothers **Joseph** (1753-1821) and **Xavier** (1763-1852) **de Maistre** rejected the ideals of the French Revolution and supported absolute monarchy.

However, the most famous man of letters of the Alpine region was undoubtedly the novelist **Henri Beyle** (1783-1842), a native of Grenoble, better known by his pseudonym **Stendhal.** Besides his masterpieces, *Le Rouge et le Noir* (1830) and *La Chartreuse de Parme* (1839), he wrote numerous studies, including *De l'amour* (1822), in which he analysed love, and *Vie d'Henry Brulard* in which he depicted his childhood and adolescent years in Grenoble.

The 19C also saw the birth of the **Félibrige** movement, a revival of the Occitan language and of Provençal traditions under the leadership of **Frédéric Mistral** (1830-1914). One of his disciples, **Paul Arène** (1853-96), a native of Sisteron, wrote tales and poems both in French and Occitan. Better known was **Jean Giono** (1895-1970), born in Manosque, who celebrated Haute-Provence and its country folk in works such as *Regain* (1930) and *Jean le Bleu* (1932). His contemporary, **Alexandre Arnoux** (1884-1973), also chose Haute-Provence as the setting for most of his works *(Haute-Provence, Rhône mon fleuve).*

SOLDIERS AND POLITICIANS

Born in Grésivaudan, **Bayard** (1476-1524), known as "le chevalier sans peur et sans reproche" ("the knight who is fearless and above reproach") has gone down in history as the model soldier of his time. He had the honour of knighting King François I after the battle of Marignan in 1515.

François de Bonne de Lesdiguières (1543-1626) led the Huguenots from Dauphiné during the Wars of Religion and was given command of the armed forces of his native region by King Henri IV, which led him to fight against the Duke of Savoie. He was the last Constable of France before Richelieu abolished the title in 1627.

In 1788, two natives of Grenoble, judge **Jean-Joseph Mounier** and barrister **Antoine Barnave**, led the peaceful protest of the Assemblée de Vizille which paved the way for the French Revolution a year later. Another native of Grenoble, **Casimir Perier**, was prime minister of France in 1831-32, during the reign of King Louis-Philippe. His grandson was President of the French Republic in 1894-95.

SCIENTISTS AND INVENTORS

Among her famous sons, Savoie counts the mathematician **Gaspard Monge** (1746-1818), who devised "descriptive geometry" at the age of 19 and later helped found the École Polytechnique, and the chemist **Claude Louis Berthollet** (1748-1822), who discovered the whitening properties of chlorine, widely used in the manufacture of linen.

Dauphiné on the other hand prides itself on having had several inventors such as **Vaucanson** (1709-82), who built automata and partly mechanised the silk industry, and **Xavier Jouvin** (1800-44), who devised a system of classifying hand sizes and invented a machine for cutting gloves to these sizes.

V. d'Amboise/PIX

Stendhal

ART AND CULTURE

ABC of Architecture

Religious architecture

SISTERON – Ground plan of the Église Notre-Dame (12-15C)

The early Romanesque style from northern Italy is characterised by a chancel with three capital apsidal chapels and a single nave. The basilical plan has no transept.

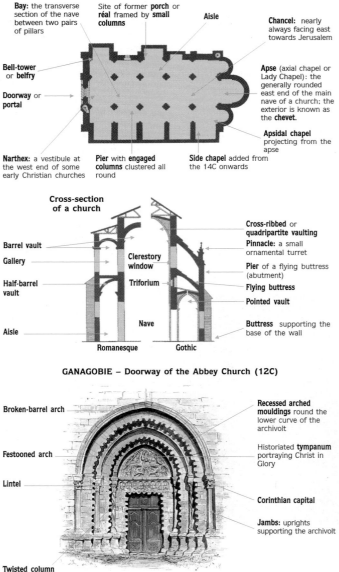

Bay: the transverse section of the nave between two pairs of pillars

Site of former **porch** or **réal** framed by **small columns**

Aisle

Chancel: nearly always facing east towards Jerusalem

Bell-tower or **belfry**

Apse (axial chapel or Lady Chapel): the generally rounded east end of the main nave of a church; the exterior is known as the **chevet.**

Doorway or portal

Apsidal chapel projecting from the apse

Narthex: a vestibule at the west end of some early Christian churches

Pier with **engaged columns** clustered all round

Side chapel added from the 14C onwards

Cross-section of a church

Barrel vault

Gallery

Half-barrel vault

Aisle

Clerestory window

Triforium

Nave

Romanesque

Cross-ribbed or **quadripartite vaulting**

Pinnacle: a small ornamental turret

Pier of a flying buttress (abutment)

Flying buttress

Pointed vault

Buttress supporting the base of the wall

Gothic

GANAGOBIE – Doorway of the Abbey Church (12C)

Broken-barrel arch

Recessed arched mouldings round the lower curve of the archivolt

Festooned arch

Historiated **tympanum** portraying Christ in Glory

Lintel

Corinthian capital

Jambs: uprights supporting the archivolt

Twisted column

R. Corbel/MICHELIN

EMBRUN – Porch (14C) of the Cathédrale Notre-Dame

This highly ornamented and elegant feature, usually found on the north side of a church, is common in northern Italy.

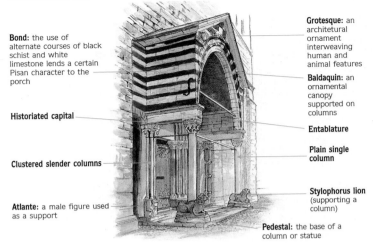

Bond: the use of alternate courses of black schist and white limestone lends a certain Pisan character to the porch

Grotesque: an architetural ornament interweaving human and animal features

Baldaquin: an ornamental canopy supported on columns

Historiated capital

Entablature

Plain single column

Clustered slender columns

Stylophorus lion (supporting a column)

Atlante: a male figure used as a support

Pedestal: the base of a column or statue

EMBRUN – Chancel and crossing of the Cathédrale Notre-Dame (12-13C)

The Romanesque parts (barrel-vaulted aisles and apse) blend harmoniously with the pointed vaulting of the Gothic nave

Corbelled **base** supporting the weight of the pipes

Stop: a set of organ pipes

Great organ case: the wooden frame encasing the mechanism

Clerestory window

Diagonal

Section of **vaulting** between ribs

Transverse arch used to reinforce the vaulting

Keystone

Gallery: a balcony providing room for members of the congregation

Triumphal arch: the large arch separating the nave from the chancel

Oven-vaulted apse

Main arch separating the nave from the aisles

Engaged column

Backing **pilaster** against which a column rests

R. Corbel/MICHELIN

ARVIEUX – Nave of Renaissance church (16C) with Baroque altarpiece

Cornice: the third or upper part of an entablature resting on a frieze

Attic: the top part of a structure designed to make it more impressive

Altarpiece

Frieze: a decorative band near the top of an interior wall below the cornice

Entablature: it comprises the architrave, the frieze and the cornice.

Corner piece: the wall section situated between the arch and its frame

Coffer: a sunken panel in a vault or ceiling

Pilaster: an engaged rectangular column

Agrafe: an ornamental element in the form of a mascaron placed on the keystone

NÉVACHE – Baroque altarpiece from the Église St-Marcellin-et-St-Antoine (15-17C)

Modillion: a small console supporting a cornice

Crowning piece

Scroll

Armature: a frame of metal bars supporting and protecting a window

Cartouche: an ornamental tablet often inscribed or decorated

Composite capital combining elements from different classical orders

Saddle-bars fixed into the masonry to maintain stained-glass panels in place

Twisted columns decorated with vine branches

Foliated scrolls: a kind of ornamentation depicting foliage

Niche: recess in a wall, usually meant to contain a statue

Altas

Altascloth

Predella: the bottom tier of an altarpiece divided into several panels

R. Corbel/MICHELIN

Palaces and Castles

GRENOBLE – Façade of the Palais de Justice (16C)

The doorway and chapel of the former palace of the Dauphiné Parliament date from the Late Gothic. The main part of the edifice bearing the Renaissance imprint contrasts with the plainer left-hand extremity which is more recent.

Triangular pediment

Corinthian pilaster

Chimney stack: a structure in which several chimneys are grouped

Table: a flat vertical surface

Mullioned window: a **mullion** is a vertical post dividing a window

Curved pediment

Coats of arms

Basket-handled arch

Pointed decorative **gable** surmounting the doorway and windows

Cornice: a horizontal projection crowning a wall

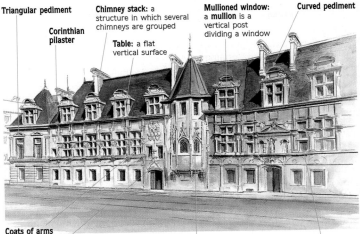

ST-GEOIRE-EN-VALDAINE – Château de Longpra (18C)

This former fortified castle, turned into a residential castle in the 18C, has very steep roofs well-suited to the hard winters of the Dauphiné region.

Dormer window

Chimney pot

Central block projecting from the rest of the building

Roof clad with **shingles**

Wrought-iron balcony

Corner stones

Fanlight: the upper part of a doorway or window

French window

Stone base of the edifice

Steps preceding the main entrance

R. Corbel/MICHELIN

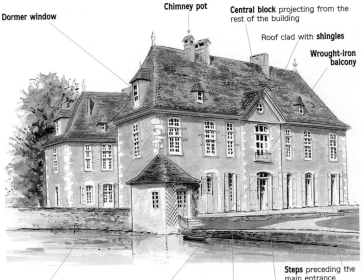

Art and Architecture

RELIGIOUS ART

Churches and chapels – In the north of the region, churches and chapels are small but solidly built on steep slopes or summits where their thick stone walls, pierced by small windows, have been braving the bad weather for centuries, their wide roof structures forming an awning to protect the most exposed façades. In Savoie, churches are surmounted by characteristic steeples swelling out into onion shapes, whereas in Dauphiné, stone spires are topped by pyramids. The names of these humble churches built by thrifty peasants are evocative: Notre-Dame-de-Tout-Secours (Our Lady of All Assistance), Notre-Dame-des-Neiges (Our Lady of the Snows).

In the south, the majority of churches date from the Romanesque period. The main features of the **Early Romanesque** style, imported from Italy, are the simple plan, massive appearance and rustic aspect of the buildings. Moderate in size, these churches were designed without a transept and with a single nave with narrow openings, surmounted by barrel vaulting or a strong timber frame and ending with an oven-vaulted apse.

The best examples of this early style, in which a minimum of decoration was used, are the Église St-Donat, the crypt of Notre-Dame-du-Dromon and of the Prieuré de Vilhosc near Sisteron. The **Late Romanesque** style flourished during the 12C and 13C, introducing a new harmony between spaces, openings and curves as well as the general use of more refined building stones. However, in spite of gaining in height, churches retained their rustic look while the influence from Lombardy and Piedmont could still be felt, particularly in the Briançonnais, Queyras, Ubaye and Embrun regions. Designed like basilicas, these churches were adorned with baldaquined porches, often supported by squatting lions as in Embrun, Guillestre, St-Véran and La Salle. The slender steeples were surmounted by four-sided pyramids. Exterior ornamentation remained sober owing to the use of hard limestone, difficult to carve. Interior decoration was also rare, with one exception however, the Monastère de Ganagobie which has a beautifully carved pediment and remarkable mosaics. On the other hand, the stylistic simplicity of the Abbaye de Boscodon bears evidence of the primitive Cistercian influence.

The Romanesque style lasted into the 13C and 14C with the building of the Église Notre-Dame in Forcalquier, of the Église St-Sauveur in Manosque and of the churches in Seyne-les-Alpes and Bayons.

The **Gothic** style had only a limited impact on the region and is best represented by the cathedrals built in Embrun and Forcalquier.

The only worthy example of the **Baroque** architectural style in the southern Alps is the Église Notre-Dame de Briançon, built between 1703 and 1718. However there is a wealth of Baroque ornamentation, such as wreathed columns, carved pulpits, organ cases, altarpieces and recessed statues all richly painted and gilt.

In the north, on the other hand, particularly in Savoie, many churches were built or decorated at the time of the Counter-Reformation (a movement which, during the 16C and 17C, tried to counteract Protestant austerity with an

Belfry of Notre-Dame-de-Bellecombe

C.Pedrotti/FOC

abundance of ornamentation, concentrating mainly on decorative altarpiece and pulpit designs). Artists mostly came from Italy. The best examples of this rich style are Notre-Dame-de-la-Gorge and the church of Champagny-en-Vanoise, and in the Maurienne and Tarentaise areas, Baroque trails *("les Chemins du Baroque")* have been specially designed to enable visitors to discover this unique heritage (◖ *see Planning Your Trip*).

Murals – Pilgrims and travellers crossing the Alps in the 14C and 15C decorated churches and chapels with bright frescoes in a naive style. These illustrated the life of Jesus (Chapelle St-Antoine in Bessans, Chapelle de Puy-Chalvin and Chapelle de Prelles, to name a few) and various saints (the most popular being Christopher, patron saint of travellers and St Sebastian, who cures the plague), as well as many episodes from the Old and New Testaments.

An equally popular theme was that contrasting the **"virtues,"** represented by beautiful young maidens, and the **"vices,"** riding various symbolical animals. In most cases, the connection is still clear to modern eyes, such as pride riding a lion, anger on the back of a leopard and laziness mounted on a donkey, but a few, such as the badger of avarice, hardly have the same powerful associations today. The corresponding punishments for these deadly sins were depicted with great realism and, for that reason, they have generally disappeared. The most common technique was tempera painting which used an emulsion of pigment mixed with egg, glue and casein. In the Alpes-Maritimes region, the name of some of the artists who painted these murals are known, for instance **Canavesio** in St-Étienne-de-Tinée, **Andrea de Cella** in Roure. From the mid 15C to the mid 16C, a Gothic school of painting, based in the Comté de Nice, produced some remarkable pictures such as the altarpiece by **Louis Bréa** which decorates the church in the tiny village of Lieuche.

Crosses and oratories – Discreet and humble, dotted along paths and on the edge of precipices, crosses and oratories represented an art form which expressed the religious fervour of mountain folk and travellers having to face a hostile natural environment. Oratories were originally mere heaps of stones known as "Montjoie," sometimes with pre-Christian origins, but they gradually became larger, were surmounted by crosses and included a recess which sheltered a small statue. Crosses were erected in the most dangerous places, in order to comfort passers-by. The most remarkable of these, which are situated in the Queyras, bear the symbols of Christ's Passion and are known as "croix de la Passion."

CASTLES AND FORTS

Feudal castles – These, or what is left of them, usually draw the visitors' attention because of the sheer beauty of their ruins standing in picturesque surroundings in isolated spots or overlooking ancient villages. Very few of them offer any real architectural interest, either through their style or state of preservation. Particularly noteworthy, however, are the Château de Simiane and its famous rotunda, dating from the 12C and 13C, the Château de Bargème, dating from the 13C, and the Château de Montmaur, dating from the 14C. Many castles, such as those of Montbrun-les-Bains and Tallard, were seriously damaged during the Wars of Religion, which were particularly violent in that area. Some castles were entirely rebuilt during the 17C and 18C, while sometimes retaining part of their former structure: such is the case of the castles of Gréoux-les-Bains, Esparron-du-Verdon and Château-Queyras.

Fortifications – Towns had, since Antiquity, been protected by walls which often had to be rebuilt or consolidated during the Middle Ages and even later, until the reign of Louis XIV, owing to constant border conflicts. Embrun has retained a 12C tower and Sisteron still boasts four 14C towers and a citadel dating from the end of the 16C. However, most of the border fortifications were built by Vauban who, from 1693 onwards, endeavoured to "enclose" Haut-Dauphiné.

Sébastien le Prestre de Vauban (1633-1707) took his inspiration from his predecessors, in particular Jean Errard (1554-1610) who is believed to have rebuilt the Sisteron fortifications and wrote a treatise on fortifications published in 1600. Having observed the numerous sieges which took place during his lifetime, Vauban was able to evolve a series of new types of fortifications, well adapted to the local terrain. In his opinion, Dauphiné was not sufficiently well protected by the natural barrier of the Alps which could be crossed at certain times of the year. He therefore studied in great detail the advantages and drawbacks of natural sites such as peaks, passes and valleys in order to choose the best position for his defences.

He protected gun-sites from enemy fire by means of armoured casings, shielded gunners and soldiers, and made an exact science of defensive features like fortified gates and broken-line walls. The results of his ingenuity can be seen in Briançon, Mont-Dauphin, Château-Queyras, Colmars and Entrevaux, fortresses which were still being used in the 19C.

Vauban was equally aware of the aesthetic aspect of his works and of its importance, making skilful use of local materials like the pink marble in Mont-Dauphin, which blend well with the landscape.

Residential chateaux – They first appeared in the 16C, when former castles were often remodelled and a Renaissance building was added to the existing structure (Allemagne-en-Provence, Château-Arnoux and Tallard).

During the 17C and 18C, the chateaux lost their military aspect, which gave way to comfort and attractive features. There are practically no constructions of this type in the area with the exception of the Château de Sauvan, designed by Jean-Baptiste Franque in 1719, which is a real gem. The Château de Malijai is another example of the classical style in the region.

Traces from the past – Most ancient villages, especially in the southern Alps, have retained a wealth of details from the main architectural styles of the past: Romanesque vaults, cellars and doorways; Gothic arches and twin openings; Renaissance lintels, carved jambs decorated with acanthus leaves, mullioned windows and elegant wrought iron; 17C pediments and bosses; 19C neo-Classical buildings and various other imitations.

TRADITIONAL ARCHITECTURE

Houses

In the Savoie and Dauphiné mountains, rural dwellings are in harmony with the harsh conditions of the natural environment: isolation, bad weather and intense cold. Houses are therefore stocky with a minimum of openings. A lot of space is set aside for storage: a wood shed, larders for cheese and charcuterie and barns for hay and grain, often situated above the living area to insulate it from the cold.

All the houses have balconies, known as *solerets,* which enable their occupants to take advantage of the slightest ray of sun; protected by overhanging roofs, these balconies are also used for drying clothes as well as wood for winter use etc.

In areas where snow is abundant, roofs are of prime importance and are always very large, overhanging all round to protect the houses and their immediate surroundings. They are either steep and smooth in order to allow the snow to slide off easily or almost flat in order to allow the snow to form a protective layer against the cold.

In forested areas, timber is the most common building material; in former days, trees were selected on north-facing slopes where they grow more slowly and their wood is therefore harder.

Villages are often situated halfway up south-facing mountain slopes with all the houses facing the sun. In flat areas and on plateaux, houses are usually grouped round the church.

In Haute-Provence on the other hand, where climatic conditions are milder in spite of strong winds and a marked contrast between summer and winter, stone and tiles are the traditional building materials. Villages are built on dry

House from the Maurienne region

rocky south-facing slopes, their houses nestling round the shaded square with the café, church and town hall nearby.

Préalpes de Savoie – In the forested areas of the Chablais, Aravis and Bauges mountains, the most traditional type of house is the wooden chalet built on a stone base with an overhanging roof covered with wood or slate and balconies all round. The living quarters for people and animals as well as the storage space are on the ground floor whereas the barn is on the upper floor.

Préalpes du Dauphiné – In the Chartreuse area, large stone-built farmhouses are surrounded by various outbuildings. In the Vercors area, on the other hand, stone-built gabled houses, two or three storeys high, have everything under one roof.

Oisans region – In this high mountain area, houses are very rustic in appearance and their rather flat roofs are covered with heavy slabs of schist, known as *lauzes,* although these are now often replaced by slates or corrugated metal. Openings are small and often arched.

Beaufortain, Tarentaise and Maurienne regions – In forested areas, houses have wooden façades and flat roofs covered with wood. Wherever scree-covered slopes predominate, houses are stone built with wooden balconies, few small openings and flat roofs covered with *lauzes,* which retain a thick layer of snow in winter. Some of these houses consist of a single room.

Briançonnais and Vallouise regions – This is an area of scattered stone-built houses: the animals' stalls are on the lower level behind a line of stone arches, the living area, entirely surrounded by wooden balconies, is on the intermediate level and the barn, directly accessible from the rear, on the upper level. The roof is usually covered with slates.

Queyras region – Built of stone and wood, the houses of this area are highly original (ⓒ *see ST-VÉRAN).* The ground floor, which includes the living area and stalls, is stone-built and surmounted by several wooden storeys used for drying and storage. The roofs, overhanging on the balconies, are covered with wood or *lauzes.*

Embrunais and Ubaye regions – This area, which marks the transition between the high mountains and Haute-Provence, offers great architectural variety. Houses are rectangular and stocky, stone built with wooden balconies; the steep four-sided roofs are covered with slates. The interior plan is simple: the kitchen and animals' stalls are at ground level, the bedroom and threshing floor above and the barn at the top of the house. In Guillestre, families would move down to the warmer ground floor to live with the animals.

R. Corbel/MICHELIN

House from the Vercors region

Haute-Provence – Village houses, often built of irregular stones and several storeys high, have a Mediterranean look about them, owing to their rounded tiles covering the roofs and forming under the eaves a decorative frieze known as a *génoise*. Isolated houses, called *granges*, are generally larger, but still fairly high, and surrounded by outbuildings. Outside walls are coated with roughcast and, inside, floors are usually covered with terracotta tiles. A dovecote can be seen nearby. Lower wooden houses with thatched and slate roofs can still be seen to the east near Mercantour.

Hilltop Villages

These hilltop villages and small towns, known as "villages perchés"(Sisteron, Forcalquier, Digne) contain an amazing number of dwellings within a relatively small area enclosed by a wall.

Their origin is thought to go back to the 9C Arab invasions. In fact, the inhabitants of the region deliberately chose to build their villages on high ground, between the vineyards (which have now disappeared) and other crops. These villages are situated high above the surrounding countryside, on the edge of plateaux or on top of rocky peaks to which they cling. Built of local stone, they almost blend with the background and look very picturesque.

The steep and twisting streets or lanes are only for pedestrians; they are paved or simply stony, interrupted now and then by flights of steps and often spanned by arches. In some cases, the ground floor of the houses consists of rows of arcades which protect passers-by from the sun and rain. Tiny shaded squares are adorned with attractive fountains and sometimes with a belfry surmounted by a wrought-iron campanile. The high, narrow houses huddle together round the church or the castle which dominates them.

Seen from above, their bright tiled roofs appear to be tangled in a confused mass. Old studded doors, bronze door knockers and carved lintels show that these were once the residences of the local nobility and wealthy middle class. Very often, these small villages are still enclosed within their walls, the fortified gate still being the only entrance.

During the 19C and 20C, villages moved down into the valleys as peasants chose to live in the middle of their land where they built their farmhouses, known as *mas* in Provence. However, places like Montbrun-les-Bains, Lurs, Banon, Bargème, Brantes, Valensole, Auvare, Simiane-la-Rotonde and St-Auban-sur-l'Ouvèze still remind visitors of the old Provençal way of life.

Dovecotes and Bories

There are many **dovecotes** in the southern Alps, particularly in the Diois, Baronnies and Forcalquier areas: pigeons were a precious source of food and their droppings were used as fertilizer for the kitchen garden. There were two basic styles: some dovecotes formed part of a larger structure including a shed and hen house on the lower level; others were separate buildings raised on pillars. The latter were subject to tax. In some cases, the holes through which the birds had access to their nests were

Manosque-St-Sauveur   Quinson   Allemagne-en-Provence

often cut in the shape of diamonds, stars or hearts.

The drystone huts known as **bories** are typical of the Forcalquier area. Their use was never clearly defined and at various times most probably served as sheep pens, tool sheds, shepherds' huts or other temporary dwellings. Whether round or square, they only have one opening, the door. They were built of 10-15cm/4-6in-thick limestone slabs, layered up into distinctive false corbelled vaulting: as the walls were built up, each stone course was laid to overhang the preceding one so that finally the small opening at the top could be closed simply by placing one slab over it. The interior was lined with earth or mortar.

Much larger than *bories* are the **jas,** similar drystone constructions covered with *lauzes* and used as sheep pens.

Campaniles

These metal structures, which can either be simple cages containing a bell, or intricate wrought-iron masterpieces, form part of the Provençal skyline. In this part of the world, campaniles were designed to withstand the assaults of the powerful mistral better than the traditional limestone belfries and today they can be seen on top of church towers, town gates and other public buildings.

Generations of craftsmen have toiled to produce elaborate wrought-iron works, onion or pyramid-shaped, spherical or cylindrical. Most remarkable are those on the tower of the Église St-Sauveur in Manosque, the clock tower in Sisteron, the church tower in Mane and that of the Chapelle St-Jean in Forcalquier, not forgetting the lace-like onion-shaped structure surmounting the Soubeyran gate in Manosque.

Sundials

In the southern Alps, from the Briançonnais to the Vallée de la Tinée, numerous buildings, houses, churches and public buildings are decorated with colourful sundials appreciated by lovers of popular art and photographers alike. Considered as a kind of homage to the sun, so omnipresent in this region, these dials, dating mostly from the 18C and 19C, were the work of travelling artists, very often natives of Piedmont like Jean-François Zarbula who travelled the length and breadth of the region for 40 years making many sundials on his way and decorating them with colourful exotic birds. The sundial makers had to be familiar not only with the art of setting up a dial, but also with the art of fresco painting. **Decorations** are often naive yet charming, dials being set within a round, square or oval frame and surrounded by motifs depicting aspects of nature such as flowers, birds, the sky, the sun or the moon. The most elaborate of these sundials include some Baroque features: *trompe-l'œil* decoration, fake marble, scrolls, shells, foliage, fake pilasters; the best example of this type of work can be seen on the towers of the Collégiale Notre-Dame in Briançon.

Mottos are equally interesting; often written in Latin, sometimes in French, they express the passing of time: 'Passers-by, remember as you go past that everything passes as I pass' (Villard-St-Pancrace); or death: 'All the hours wound, the last one kills'; or the sun: 'Without the sun I am nothing, but you, without God, are powerless' (Val-des-

Briançonnais façades

Prés). These mottos, which often make an attempt at moralising, remind us that we must make good use of our time: 'May no hour go by that you would wish to forget,' 'Mortal, do you know what my purpose is? To count the hours that you waste' (Fouillouse).

CONTEMPORARY ARCHITECTURE

During the past few years, the economic expansion of the Alps, the rapid development of the towns and the advent and growth of winter sports resorts have created a real need for public and residential buildings. Today the Alps rank as one of the most prominent French regions in the field of modern architecture.

Churches – The first modern art edifice built in the Alps was the Église Notre-Dame-de-Toute-Grâce on the Plateau d'Assy. Its completion in 1950 marked a turning point. Designed by Maurice **Novarina,** who was responsible for many buildings in the Alps, it had no revolutionary feature but, for the first time in the history of contemporary religious art, great artists were commissioned to decorate the church. Annecy, Aix-les-Bains, Grenoble and L'Alpe-d'Huez all followed the trend for modern churches and chapels.

Public buildings – Between 1964 and 1970, Grenoble was turned into a vast building site in preparation for the Winter Olympic Games. At the same time, an extensive programme of research into the technical and aesthetic aspects of modern architecture was launched. Urbanisation was not so systematic in other Alpine cities; however, there were some modern achievements such as the sports complex in Chamonix, the Maison des Arts et Loisirs (Arts and Entertainment Building) in Thonon, the Palais de Justice (Law Courts) in Annecy, the Maison de la Culture (Cultural Centre) in Chambéry, the Dôme in Albertville and Grenoble Museum to name only a few.

Winter sports resorts – Rapidly developing resorts tended to follow the general trends of modern urban architecture and serve the demand for comfort and organised entertainment, a combination which was bound to produce its share of functional, unremarkable buildings, yet some of these new creations proved highly original: for instance Avoriaz with its strange, rock-like buildings or the triple pyramid of La Plagne, both controversial but defining projects.

Traditions and Folklore

In spite of harsh living conditions, the Alps have always been densely populated, with a well-structured social life following the rhythm of the seasons and strongly attached to its traditions, each valley having its own customs, dialect and costume.

TRADITIONAL LIFE

Traditional life in the Alps was regulated in two ways: by the main events of life (birth, marriage and death) and by the impact of the seasons on the environment.

Birth – A mother's first visit after the birth of her child was to the local church to express her gratitude to God, but before the end of her confinement, tradition demanded that she eat several dozen eggs, which the child's godmother would bring to her. Children were christened very soon after being born.

Marriage – Many rituals were linked to marriage: in some areas, young maidens prayed to the local saint to provide a husband for them, in Entrevaux, girls would make a clay figure of the ideal partner. There were also all kinds of symbolic customs before a wedding: in the Embrunais area, the young man would offer his fiancée some jewellery on the Sunday preceding the ceremony. In the Hautes-Alpes region, a young man who married someone from another village had to cross a symbolic barrier, usually a ribbon or a decorated log, on the day of the wedding, whereas a young maiden in the same situation had to buy a round of drinks for the young men of her village in order to make amends for not having chosen one of them. After the wedding, the locals played a variety of tricks on the young couple throughout the wedding night.

Funerals – When a death occurred, the whole village would take turns to watch over the body while members of local brotherhoods sang the *de pro-fundis* and Miserere. A funeral banquet inevitably took place after the funeral. In high mountain areas it was impossible to bury the dead in winter because the ground was frozen, so the bodies were kept covered with snow, on the roof of the house, until the thaw came.

The seasons – In the Alps, the year was divided in two: summertime during which people worked in the fields and looked after the animals, and wintertime, when all outdoor activity ceased. Summer was a particularly busy time because the haymaking and harvesting season was short. Bread was made once a year by the whole village, the large loaves having to last a whole year; only with the introduction of the potato in the 18C was the fear of food shortages at the end of a hard winter diminished. Cattle and sheep farming were the main sources of wealth; the herds were taken from the stables to the summer pastures where they were looked after on a private or collective basis.

In winter, village folk usually stayed at home and lived on what had been stored during the summer: wood for heating, bread, dry vegetables, smoked meat, charcuterie and cheese. Men would repair their tools and make furniture and other objects such as toys, while women were busy at their spinning-wheels. Many men however left their homes to wander from region to region, selling the seeds of Alpine plants and herbs, sweeping chimneys, or finding temporary employment in the valleys as masons and builders. The Queyras and Briançonnais regions even had a reputation for "exporting" wandering schoolmasters, hired by villages for their food and lodging and a small wage. Those travellers who could read and write wore a feather in their cap, teachers of arithmetic wore two and the few who could teach Latin proudly added a third. Many of the mountain-dwellers left their homes for good and settled in the towns. Today, the men and women who remained find winter employment in the numerous sports resorts.

COSTUMES

A shawl, an embroidered bodice and belt, and an apron brightened up the long black skirt women wore, and still do on festive occasions. In St-Colomban-des-Villars, the number of blue stripes sewn onto the dress indicated the size of the dowry which a husband would receive, allowing bachelors to plan the most advantageous match. Headdresses were extremely varied and consisted of a lace or linen bonnet decorated with ribbons and worn under a felt or straw hat. Most remarkable of all was the **frontière:** worn by women from the Tarentaise area, it was richly adorned with gold and silver braid and had three points framing the face like a helmet. Gold belts and necklaces were the most popular pieces of jewellery; in some areas, women wore a **ferrure,** a gold cross and heart hanging round their neck from a black velvet ribbon, as a token from their betrothed.

Men's costumes were simpler, consisting of a loosely fitting jacket of dark ordinary cloth, a pair of black trousers, a white shirt with a touch of lace around the collar, a black tie and wide woollen belt, not forgetting a large felt hat.

LEGENDS

The mystery surrounding the mountains was the source of many legends and tales, recounted at village gatherings during the long winter evenings.

The devil of Bessans – For all his proverbial cunning, the devil was outwitted by a native of Bessans who sold his soul to him in exchange for supernatural powers. As death drew close, the man went to see the Pope in Rome and asked for his pardon. He obtained it on the condition that he would hear mass in Bessans, Milan and St. Peter's in Rome on the same day. He therefore used the powers he still had to get from one place to the next in a flash. Since then, the men of Bessans have been carving devils.

St John's fingers – In the 6C, St Thècle, a native of Valloire, dreamt that she saw St John the Baptist blessing Christ with three fingers as he baptised him. It is said that the saint's six-year search for those three fingers ended in Alexandria on the grave of St John, where they suddenly appeared. She took them back to her local diocese, a town which was later called St-Jean-de-Maurienne, where the relic is still kept.

The seven wonders of Dauphiné – These seven wonders, which are the pride of the people of Dauphiné, are sites or monuments steeped in mystery and strange myths: Mont Aiguille, known as the mount Olympus of Dauphiné, is a kind of "table mountain" dominating the Vercors, once believed by local people to be inhabited by angels and supernatural animals. Fairies were thought to live in the **Grottes de Sassenage** near Grenoble, but it was the devil who haunted the **"fontaine ardente"** near the Col de l'Arzelier. Between Grenoble and St-Nizier, a ruined keep still bears the name of **"Tour sans venin"** because, according to the legend, no snake can get near it since the lord of the castle brought back some magic earth from the crusades. Candidates for the remaining wonders include the remarkable **Pont de Claix,** built by Lesdiguières, the **Grottes de la Balme** and the **Pierre Percée,** a rock shaped like an arch.

The frontière: a traditional regional headdress

G. Biollay/DIAF

Ancient beliefs from Haute-Provence – Legend has it that fairies live in the rocks overlooking Moustiers-Ste-Marie. On the other hand, the people of Arvieux (☞ see Le QUEYRAS) were, for a long time, divided into two groups: the *"gens du Renom,"* who were thought to have gained their wealth through a deal with the devil, and the *"gens de la Belle,"* who invented all sorts of rituals to protect themselves from the former, marriage between the two groups being, of course, strictly forbidden.

FESTIVALS

Paganism and Christian belief were often combined in the many traditional feasts of the Alpine communities, where religious fervour was mixed with superstition. Nowadays, however, these events have become merry folk festivals. Most villages still celebrate the feast-day of their own patron saints as well as various events linked with work in the fields, not forgetting pilgrimages which are still popular. The religious side of these festivals consists of a procession followed by mass or a benediction. Non-religious events also form part of the festivities, among them the Provençal **bravade,** which is a kind of mock attack organised by the local youth; in Riez, it traditionally pitted the bourgeoisie, in the role of the Christians, against the craftsmen, posing as the Saracens. The curious sword dance known as **Bacchu Ber**, performed in Pont-de-Cervières every year on 16 August, features young men representing death, the stars and the rising sun. Entrevaux has its feast on Midsummer's Day, when the hero of the day, St John, is carried in effigy from the cathedral to the chapel of St-Jean-du-Désert, 12km/7.5mi out of town and back. In Annot, the winner of the archery contest is named "king for the day."

Every Provençal festival has its costumed musicians, playing the flute and the tambourin. In Moustiers-Ste-Marie, a group of musicians, known as the **Diane,** wakes the community every night around 4am with its lively music, during the nine days of the Moustiers festival.

HANDICRAFT

Woodwork

The densely forested Alps have, for centuries, produced enough wood to keep local craftsmen busy during the winter evenings, thus maintaining a strong wood-carving tradition which blossomed between the 17C and 19C, particularly in the Maurienne and Queyras areas.

These regions have retained some splendid samples of this popular art including furniture and other objects made by the local farmers out of larch or walnut wood.

Wood-carving in Maurienne – The Maurienne region was famous for its carved religious furnishings and objects: pulpits, altars, statues. Bessans was well known as early as the 17C for the skill of its craftsmen. One of them, Étienne Vincendet, who lived in the 19C, was the first craftsman to carve the famous "devils."

Chests and toys from Queyras – Wedding chests are an ancient speciality of the Queyras region. Carved out of larch with chisels and gouges, they are made up of four panels and a lid. Inside, there is often a small compartment meant for silverware and precious objects. The best samples of these chests have remarkable carvings on their front panels. Geometric motifs (rosettes) were first drawn with the help of a pair of compasses, whereas other motifs (interlacing, palmettes, hearts, foliage and arabesques) were copied from Gothic motifs or inspired by the Renaissance style and leather objects from Cordoba. The wood was carved with a knife; this took a very long time. Some chests bear a mark indicating when it was made and by whom.

The people from Queyras made numerous other pieces of furniture which testify to their considerable woodworking skills: dressers, chairs, salt-boxes, cots, kneading-troughs/cupboards as well as a wealth of objects for daily use such as spinning-wheels, lace hoops, bread seals (which enabled a housewife to distinguish her own bread baked in the communal oven), butter-boards, and boxes of all shapes and sizes.

Traditional toys, which used to be so popular, have practically disappeared except in La Chalp where, in 1919, a Swiss vicar had the good idea of encouraging the local production of wooden toys in order to slow down the drift from the land to the towns. Small characters, animals and pieces of dolls' furniture are cut out of thin planks of wood and then assembled and painted by hand in the craftsmen's homes.

Provençal furniture – In Haute-Provence, furniture is mainly made of walnut and more or less decorated according to the prosperity of the area. In addition to chests, tables and beds, there are large dresser cupboards, *crédences* and kneading-troughs.

The dresser cupboard has two double doors separated by two drawers. This massive piece of furniture is sometimes decorated with foliage, grotesque and diamond motifs. A *crédence* is a kind of sideboard with two drawers, sometimes with an added crockery shelf. The kneading-trough or bread box was the most common piece of furniture; often placed on top of a low cupboard, it was used to store food.

Moustiers earthenware

Manufacturing technique – The word faïence, which means earthenware in French, comes from the name of an Italian town, Faenza, already renowned for its earthenware production before the 15C. The earthenware tradition in Moustiers could never have developed without the town's plentiful supplies of clay, water and wood, but the turning point came in the 17C, when a monk brought back from Italy the secret process of earthenware making. Manufacture stopped altogether in 1873 and though later revived in the 1920s, now only serves the tourist trade.

There are several manufacturing stages. A kind of paste made of a mixture of clay, sand and chalk is moulded into shape then dried and fired in an oven at a temperature of about 1 000°C/1 832°F. This "terracotta," which is hard and porous, is then dipped into tin oxide, forming an enamel, and slightly fired again. The artist then paints his motifs on the object, using metal oxide colours. Another high temperature (850°C/1 562°F to 950°C/1 742°F) firing session follows. With this method, the choice of colours used is limited to those able to withstand such high temperatures. There is, however, another method, which allows the use of a wider choice of colours: the earthenware object is fired before being painted; the artist then applies the colours mixed with certain chemicals which act as a fixative, then the object is fired a second time at a lower temperature of around 400°C/752°F.

There are four main types of faïence:
– the blue monochrome earthenware (1680-1730), influenced by the Nevers and Rouen traditions,
– the Bérain decoration (early 18C) named after the artist who introduced new motifs,
– the refined polychrome decoration imported from Spain in 1738,
– the *"petit feu"* (low temperature) decoration (late 18C), with bright colours.

"Santons"

They are the symbol of Provençal handicraft. These small earthenware figures, intended to represent the villagers of Bethlehem at the time of Christ's birth, are in fact typical Provençal villagers dressed in regional costume and representing 19C village trades. There is a famous annual fair *(foire aux santons)* in the village of **Champtercier,** near Digne.

THE REGION TODAY

Economy

For hundreds of years, Alpine economy was based on agriculture and handicraft until the region witnessed two economic revolutions: the first, which happened as a result of the discovery of hydroelectric power, led to the industrialisation and urbanisation of the valleys; the second, which was the rapid development of tourism, led to drastic changes in high mountain landscapes. These two phenomena, however, saved the region from the population drift to the cities, which threatened its future prosperity.

Today, the northern Alps are already a very dynamic region with important towns such as Grenoble and Annecy, whereas the southern Alps are changing at a slower pace and still retain a strong traditional economy centred on small and medium-sized towns such as Briançon, Sisteron and Digne. The creation of large nature reserves has not only protected native plants and animals, but has contributed to the strong growth of all-season tourism.

AGRICULTURE

Forestry and cattle farming have always been the mainstays of rural life in the Alps. Farms, fewer in number, are growing larger and must share space with tourist resorts. Farming in this reduced space has become highly specialized and quality of the product has become primordial. Orchards and nut groves dot the landscape and the broad valleys of the Combe de Savoie and Grésivaudan are given over to cereals, as are the Gapençais, Embrunais, Buëch valley and Plateau de Valensole to the south. Vegetables and flowers are grown around Grenoble, in Bièvre-Valloire and in the lower Arve valley. In the valleys where dairy production is traditional, the only crop grown today is hay; In many areas, especially on the steeper slopes, farmers still make hay by hand, scything grasses and binding up bales. Coniferous forests, rapidly taking over from pastures, are exploited for pulp, lumber and specialty furniture wood.

Cattle – In mountainous regions, south-facing slopes are generally devoted to pastures and farming whereas north-facing slopes are covered with forests. For a period it seemed that the dairy industry would abandon the high Alps, but determined effort has saved this tradition. Seasonal migration of cows from the villages to high mountain pastures is now mostly by truck, although some cattle still make the trek , called "transhumance" from low prairie to mid-level pastures and finally, in June, to the high Alps. For the past 20 years, the sound of bells has once again resonated across alpine pastures, notably the Grand-Bornand and the Tarentaise regions. High-altitude chalets dot the mountains, and cheese is once again made there according to old traditions, bringing life to areas far from ski resorts that would otherwise become depopulated. The development of the big parks has

Montbéliarde   Tarentaise   Abondance

Egers/JACANA

also helped this process. High qualitiy cheese is also produced in the *fruitières* (cheese cooperatives): Reblochon from the Bormes, Vacherin from the Bauges, Beaufort from the Beaufortain, Tomme from Savoie, Bleu de Sassenage and St-Marcellin from Dauphiné.

Alpine cattle, famous for their sturdiness and ability to walk long distances, are also generous milk-producers. The most traditional breeds are the **Tarine** and the red-and-white **Abondance**, whose milk is essential to the best traditional cheeses. These breeds co-exist, however, with the high-yielding black and white **Holstein**, the blond **Aquitaine**, and particularly the **Montbéliarde** from nearly Franche-Comté. Nowadays, you will rarely see the blond **Villarde** of the Vercors, the famous "cow of all trades," that, wearing shoes like a horse, pulled a plow or a cart and fed the household with rich milk and beef. A special program has preserved this blood-line, which was nearly wiped out by the arrival of tractors and better milk-producers, but which is essential to ensuring genetic diversity.

Pig farming is developing in cheese-producing areas: by-products from cheese-making, especially Reblochon, are used to feed pigs, which explains why most cheese cooperatives keep a lot of pigs as a sideline.

Sheep – Sheep farming is one of the main economic activities of the Alpes du Sud and Haute-Provence *départements*. These specialise in the production of lambs fattened quickly and sold when they reach the age of three months. In summer, the resident population is joined by sheep (led, traditionally, by goats, with donkeys to carry the lambs) migrating from lower Provence in search of greener grass. This migration, known as **transhumance,** begins around Midsummer's Day and ends around Michaelmas at the end of September. Starting in the 19th century, the old ways were abandoned and animals were transported to the higher pastures by train and, later, by truck. Unfortunately, they adapted badly to the brusque transition from the plain

to the mountain and many died. A law introduced in 1972 encouraged transhumance, but with well-organized rest stops and water sources. The old trails are no longer used however and, to the delight of tourists, sheep (and some goats and donkeys) trot along national roads. Transhumance inspires many festivals, where the traditional Provençal shepherd skills are celebrated.

Sheep from Haute-Provence do not migrate since they can roam freely over vast areas during the warm season and take shelter in large sheds known as *jas* when winter approaches.

Forestry – In recent years, the policy of reforestation, which is intensive in some areas, has been helped by the restrained use of high pastures and the discontinuation of mowing at high altitude. In fact, forests now cover more than a third of all usable land, and even half in the Préalpes and the northern Alps. They are essentially made up of conifers (fir trees and spruce), and of deciduous trees at low altitude; more than half the forested areas belong to municipalities or private owners. The rest belongs to the state and is administered by the Office National des Forêts (Forestry Commission).

Even though the northern Préalpes boast some splendid specimens of beech, which thrive in humid countries, forests of conifers predominate as in the rest of the Alpine region. Spruce is the most common conifer of the Salève, Faucigny, Aravis and Bauges areas, whereas fir trees grow most happily in the Chartreuse, Vercors, Beaufortain, Maurienne, and Grésivaudan, as well as in the Diois and Préalpes de Digne; in the high mountain areas of the southern Alps, such as the Briançonnais, Queyras, Embrunais, Ubaye and Mercantour areas, there are mixed forests of fir trees, spruce and larch.

Many Alpine areas owe their prosperity to their forests; some have retained the traditional practice of *"affouage,"* which consists in allotting a certain quantity of wood to each household within the precinct of a given municipality. Forestry development has become easier through the improvement of forest tracks and the use of chain saws as well as towlines when access is particularly difficult. Wood is essentially used as timber or sold to sawmills and paper mills. Quantities are indicated in cubic metres. One cubic metre (35.3cu ft) of spruce can be converted into 800m/957sq yd of paper or 24 000 ordinary newspaper pages. Whole areas of Haute-Provence have been reforested since the middle of the 19C and forests, which are now protected, are not used for industrial purposes.

Lavender and lavandin – The delicate scent of lavender is characteristic of Haute-Provence. At the beginning of this century, the picking of the flowers of this wild plant, which grows at an altitude of between 600m/1 968ft and 1 400m/4 593ft on the southern slopes of Mont Ventoux and the Montagne de Lure, represented an extra income. Then, when it became necessary to replace cereal crops, lavender was cultivated on the plateaux and high slopes. Well adapted to the climate and calcareous soils of Provence, this plant helped many farmers to survive when they were about to give up. Land which had not been ploughed for 20 years was suddenly covered with numerous green bushes with mauve flowers giving off a delightful fragrance in July.

Later on, *lavandin,* a more productive but less fragrant hybrid, was cultivated on the lower slopes and in the valleys between 400m/1 312ft and 700m/2 297ft.

Superb fields of *lavandin* can be spotted on the Plateau de Valensole and along the road from Digne to Gréoux-les-Bains. 🕯 *See also Route de la lavande in the section Themed Itineraries*

The harvest takes place from July to September according to the region: most of the picking is now mechanised but the inaccessible or closely planted older fields are still picked by hand. After drying for two to three days, the picked lavender is sent to a distillery equipped with a traditional still.

Each complete operation lasts 30min: 1 000kg/2 205lb of picked lavender are needed to produce 5-10kg/11-22lb of lavender essence or 25-40kg/55-88lb of *lavandin* essence. Lavender essence is reserved for the perfume and cosmetic industries, whereas *lavandin* essence is used to give a pleasant smell to detergents and cleaning products. Lavender flowers can also be dried and placed in scent bags.

The annual production for the whole of Provence varies from 30t to 40t of lavender essence and from 800t to 900t of *lavandin* essence. Production reached its height in the 1920s, and is today under pressure from synthetic products and imports.

Olive trees and olive oil – Olive groves traditionally mark the northern boundaries of the Mediterranean region. The production of olive oil, which represents more than two thirds of the national output, comes mainly from the Alpes-de-Haute-Provence and the Luberon area. Following the hard winter of 1956, when almost a quarter of the olive trees growing in the Baronnies area died, olive groves were renewed with hardier species. There are many varieties and the flavour of the fruit varies accordingly; the type of soil and picking time are also very important; tradition holds that several varieties should grow in the same olive grove. The harvest begins as early as the end of August, depending on the area. Olives are picked by hand when they are intended to be eaten whole or, for processing at the mill, gathered with a rake that is run through the branches; formerly, they were shaken into nets. Olives from Nyons *(tanches)* were the first to have been granted an AOC (Appellation d'Origine Contrôlée) seal of origin; other varieties now have this rating. Olive oils from the Baronnies (Nyons) and Alpes-de-Haute-Provence (Digne, Les Mées) are considered among the best. 🕯 *See also the "Routes de l'Oliver" from the Themed Itineraries section.*

Truffles – The truffle, or *rabasse* in Provençal, is an edible, subterranean fungus which develops from the mycelium, a network of filaments invisible to the naked eye. They live symbiotically with the root of the downy oak, known in Provence as the white oak. These small stunted oaks are planted in fields called *truffières*. The most productive of these are situated below 500m/1 640ft, but there are a few up to an altitude of 1 000m/3 281ft. The Vaucluse *département* is the main producing area of the Mediterranean region, followed by the Luberon, Riez and Forcalquier areas as well as the upper valley of the River Var. Truffles, known as the "black gold" of Haute-Provence, are harvested from mid-October to mid-March, when they are ripe and odorous. Pigs are traditionally used to sniff out truffles, but they are being replaced by dogs, easier to train and less greedy. Once the animal has found a truffle (sometimes buried as deep as 25cm/10in), it is carefully dug up by hand. A white variety of truffle, which is harvested between May and mid-July mainly in the upper valley of the River Var, is used as a flavouring in cooking. This variety, three times less expensive than its cousin, is known as a *truffe blanche de St Jean* or by its Provençal name, *mayenque*.

HYDROELECTRIC POWER AND INDUSTRY

In the French Alps, industries were at first intended to satisfy local needs, but then they undertook to work for the rest of the country and even for the export trade. This led to the development of clock factories in Cluses, of several silk factories, subsidiaries of the textile industries in Lyon, of paper mills in Dauphiné, supplied with wood from the forests of the Chartreuse and the Vercors, of cement factories in the Préalpes, of glove factories in Grenoble and of steel foundries in Ugine.

Hydroelectric power – Known as *houille blanche* (literally white coal), this was the fuel which drove Alpine industry forward. During the late 1860s, a factory owner of the Grésivaudan region, called Amable Matussière, who wished to increase the driving power of his mills, called on two engineers, Fredet and **Aristide Bergès.** The latter deserves credit for having harnessed the first 200m/656ft waterfall at Lancey in 1869. At first, the power of the turbines was used mechanically, but by 1870 the invention of the dynamo by Gramme, followed by the building of the first power lines on an industrial scale (the first line dates from 1883), made the new power stations switch to the production of electricity.

The Alpine relief lends itself to the production of hydroelectricity: the combination of high mountain ranges and deep valleys creates numerous waterfalls. Engineers began by using waterfalls with a low rate of flow, situated high above the main valleys. They then tapped the main valley rivers, which had a much higher rate of flow, thus creating a concentration of industries along these valleys (valley of the River Isère, known as Tarentaise, Arc Valley, known as Maurienne, Romanche Valley). During the 1950s, engineers conceived complex projects embracing whole massifs and involving water storage. The flow of water, channelled through miles of tunnels and sometimes diverted from the natural river basin, is collected in huge reservoirs like that formed by the Tignes and Roselend dams or ducted into neighbouring, more deeply cleft valleys (Isère-Arc by-pass). Today virtually all possible hydrorelectric sites are being exploited.

Most of the turbines are linked to the EDF (Électricité de France) network. The region produces 25 billion Kwh. of electricity, of which 50% is exported elsewhere in France; nuclear energy also supplies the local grid. At the same time, research is underway for other renewable sources of electricity, such as solar power, as well as on means of energy conservation.

There are basically four main types of dam. **Gravity dams** withstand water pressure by their weight alone. They are triangular in section with an almost vertical upstream face and a back sloping at about 50°; examples include Chambon and Bissorte. **Arch dams,** graceful and economic in design, have a curved structure with its convex side upstream which transfers the pressure of water laterally to the steep sides of the gorge, as at Tignes, le Sautet, St-Pierre and Monteynard. **Buttressed dams** are used when the width of the dam does not allow the use of an arch; they are a combination of gravity and arch dams and can be seen at Girotte, Plan d'Amont and Roselend. **Riprap dykes**, which simply close off a glacial dam and are barely visible, are found at La Sassière, Mont-Cenis and Grand-Maison.

Industry and water power – Electro-metallurgy and **electrochemistry** were the two industries which benefited most from the use of hydroelectricity. They settled near the power stations built by the industrialists themselves, but the cost of transport of raw materials is a major handicap in the mountains. In the face of stiff world competition for steel and aluminum, industry has become highly specialized: Ugine-Savoie exports 75% of its steel production, while at Saint-Jean-de-Maurienne, where most factories have closed, Péchiney maintains a research centre for aluminum. The future belongs to specialised industries; firms now choose to settle in cluses (transverse valleys) near large, well-located towns such as Annecy, Chambéry and Grenoble, with Grenoble's reputation for high-tech engineering training often tipping the scale. **Mechanical engineering** and **electrical engineering** have become vital aspects of the industrial landscape of the Alps, while the traditional clock industry is still going strong in Annemasse.

Food and Drink in the Alps

Alpine cuisine owes more to the quality and freshness of local produce than to the complexity of its recipes. Cheese from the rich Alpine pastures, fish from the lakes and rivers, mushrooms from the forests, crayfish from the mountain streams, game (thrush patés from Provence are delicious!), potatoes and fruit form the basis of most Alpine dishes, served with wine from Savoie or Provence. As for Provençal cuisine, its main characteristic is the generous use of garlic and olive oil, the latter replacing the butter so liberally used in the north.

REGIONAL PRODUCE

Fish – Fish from the lakes and mountain streams are a must in any gastronomic menu: arctic char, pike and trout are prepared in many different ways: meunière (dipped in flour and slowly fried in butter), poached, in butter sauce or braised.

Meat – Beef from Dauphiné is particularly famous; it is delicious served *en daube* (stewed) with herbs from Provence. Lamb from the Sisteron area is said to be more tender and savoury than anywhere else and there is a whole range of charcuterie available, such as ham cured with herbs and spices from the Mont Ventoux region, known as **jambon aux aromates de Ventoux.** Rabbit is appreciated by gourmets, particularly **lapin en cabessol,** stuffed and cooked in a white wine sauce.

Cheeses – Made from cow's, ewe's or goat's milk, cheeses vary a great deal according to the manufacturing process. Alpine pastures of the Beaufortain and Tarentaise areas produce **Beaufort,** one of the tastiest kinds of Gruyère, whereas **Reblochon,** an Alpine farmhouse cheese, is a speciality of the Aravis. Among the wide selection of Tommes – the name means "cheese" in Savoyard dialect – available in the northern Alps, **"Tomme de Savoie"** is the best known. **Tome des Bauges** – always written with a single "m" – is also deservedly famous. The small **Saint-Marcellin** is the most popular cheese of the lower Dauphiné area. Originally made from pure goat's milk, it is now processed from mixed goat's and cow's milk. **Bleu de Sassenage** includes ewe's milk as well. Several regional dishes are based on these tasty cheeses, one of the most famous being the **fondue savoyarde,** which successfully combines Gruyère cheese with the local dry white wine.
In the southern Alps, **Picodon** from the Diois area is a sharp goat's cheese matured for at least three months, while **Banon** is a rustic, strong-tasting cheese from the Montagne de Lure.

Herbs – Either growing wild or cultivated on sunny slopes, herbs are essential ingredients of Alpine cuisine, especially in Haute-Provence. The general term *"herbes de Provence"* includes **savory** *(sarriette)* used in the making of goat's and ewe's milk cheeses, **thyme** *(thym)* used to flavour vegetables and grilled meat or fish, **basil** *(basilic),* **sage** *(sauge),* **wild thyme** *(serpolet),* **rosemary** *(romarin)* which helps the digestion, **tarragon** *(estragon),*

juniper berries *(genièvre)*, used in the preparation of game dishes, **marjoram** *(marjolaine)* and **fennel** *(fenouil)*. The secret of tasty cooking lies in the subtle combination of these herbs.

SPECIALITIES AND RECIPES

Gratins – The universally known **gratin dauphinois** is a delicious mixture of sliced potatoes and milk; **gratin savoyard,** topped with Tomme de Savoie is a similar dish in which milk is replaced by broth. Few people know, however, that there are numerous other kinds of gratins made with pumpkin, courgette, spinach, beans, millet and crayfish tails, this last being an outstanding delicacy.

Tarte au Beaufort – This tart is filled with fresh cream mixed with Beaufort cheese and served hot.

Toasts savoyards – This delicious snack is made from creamy Reblochon mixed with peeled walnuts and spread on toasted rye bread.

Tartiflette – Cut a whole Reblochon cheese in thin slices, having first removed the rind. In a flat dish, arrange alternate layers of sliced potatoes and Reblochon; add chopped garlic, herbs, salt and pepper. Cook in the oven for 30min, adding fresh cream 5min before the time is up. Serve with smoked charcuterie and a dry white wine from Savoie. To make a **pela,** two halves of Reblochon, rind side up, are allowed to melt into a mixture of diced potato, onion and bacon.

Tourte de veau – This pie from the Ubaye region is filled with pieces of shoulder of veal marinated in onion and garlic and covered with bone jelly. It can be eaten hot or cold.

Raïoles – A favourite dish to the north of Annot, these "ravioli" from Haute-Provence are stuffed with a paste made from dried walnuts and saffron and served with spinach and pumpkin.

Aïoli – This is a rich mayonnaise made with olive oil and flavoured with plenty of crushed garlic, intended to be served with hors-d'œuvre, poached fish and various other dishes.

Fougasse – This kind of flat bread dough cooked in olive oil and topped with crushed anchovies is sold in most baker's shops in Haute-Provence and served as a snack or hors-d'œuvre. Its big brother, the **pompe à huile,** was traditionally served on Christmas Eve with liqueur wine.

Raclette and fondue – These simple dishes are linked in most people's minds with alpine chalets and dinner after a hard day's skiing. Raclette, which is basically cheese melted at the table and served with baked potatoes, pickles and viande de Grisons (thin strips of dried beef) or other *charcouterie*, depends totally on the quality of the cheese. As for fondue, it doesn't deserve its monotone reputation. Every household has its secret recipe, with comté, emmenthal, beaufort or vacherin cheese added to give texture, and garlic rubbed on the pot or a few spoonfuls of Kirch added for colour.

Farcement –Lately, this very traditional dish has made a notable comeback. Basically a brillant answer to the slim choice of ingredients available to alpine cooks, farcement consists of old potatoes from the end of the winter, bacon and dried fruit melded together to form a bread-like main course.

Desserts – In Savoie, strawberries, raspberries and bilberries are used to make delicious tarts; **gâteau de Savoie,** on the other hand, is a light sponge cake unlike the rich **walnut cake** from the Grenoble region.
Fruit is abundant in the southern Alps, particularly in the Durance Valley. Plums are the most popular filling of the traditional tart, known as *tourte,* which rounds off many family meals.

Thirteen desserts – Traditionally served for Christmas, in honour of Christ and the 12 apostles, these desserts include raisins, dried figs, several kinds of nuts, apples, pears, nougat (made from honey), prunes stuffed with marzipan, melons and dry cakes flavoured with orange blossom.

Lou Pastelou – This speciality of Haute-Provence, a heavy pie made with chopped walnuts and sugar, originally became popular as a way of using up the little nut pieces left over from oil pressing.

WINES AND LIQUEURS

Vines have been growing in Savoie since Roman times and wine-growing is today one of the most dynamic activities of the region; this is a remarkable feat considering the drawbacks of the local climate. In fact vines grow in areas enjoying a microclimate (south-facing slopes up to an altitude of 500m/1 640ft or on lake shores) and where the soil is well drained and stony (moraines). There are several types of local vines; one of these, the **Mondeuse,** with its delicate strawberry, blackcurrant and bilberry bouquet, produces one of the best red wines of the region, which matures very well. According to a local saying, "September makes the wine", for this month is generally mild, sunny and dry. The area produces light, dry white wines, which must be drunk while they are still young.

White wines from **Seyssel** and **Crépy** (on the shores of Lake Geneva), both A.O.C. (Appellation d'Origine Contrôlée, guaranteeing the quality) are fruity and go well with fish; they are at their best when they are between two and four years old.

The label "Vins de Savoie" includes several wines from the Massif des Bauges; Abymes, St-Badolph, Chignin, Apremont, Cruet, Azye, an extra dry sparkling wine from the banks of the Arve, as well as reds from Chautagne on the Lac du Bourget, and Arbin, where the *mondeuse* grows.

Wines designated "Roussette de Savoie" are light, dry whites with a fruity taste; Frangy and Marestel are two names you may see.

The wine production of Haute-Provence has considerably declined and there are now fewer quality wines. However, two A.O.C. *(see above)* wines are among the most palatable: Côtes du Ventoux from the Bédoin area (*see The Green Guide Provence)* and Côte du Lubéron, from the mountainous area of the Luberon *(see The Green Guide Provence).* On the southern border of Haute-Provence, there are some excellent rosé wines, and to the north of the region, the famous Clairette de Die is one of the great French sparkling wines, made from a mixture of *clairette* and muscat grapes by the same method as Champagne.

Among the **liqueurs** produced in the northern and southern Alps, Chartreuse, known as the "elixir of life" is undoubtedly the most famous; its formula, dating from the 16C, includes the essence of 130 different plants to which are added alcohol distilled from wine and honey. Others include gentian liqueur, marc brandy from Savoie, "Origan du Comtat", made from herbs from the slopes of Mont Ventoux, and above all absinthe, based on wormwood, a medicinal plant well known in the Alps. The success of the liqueur, which goes back to the 19C, is principally due to its digestive and tonic properties; it is said to cure mountain sickness. White, green or brown depending on the ingredients used, the liqueur is between 30° and 40° proof. In order that it may retain its green colour, the bottles used are protected from daylight by a casing. Local distillers each have their own recipe; however, they generally abide by the "rule of forty": 40 sprigs of wormwood are left to macerate for 40 days in one litre of marc brandy to which are added 40 lumps of sugar. The bottle is exposed to daylight every day for 40min.

Chartreuse Distillery, Voiron

Mont Blanc Summit
P. Greboval/ MICHELIN

ABONDANCE★

POPULATION 1 294
MICHELIN MAP 328 N3
LOCAL MAP SEE THONON-LES-BAINS

The massive buildings of the Abbaye d'Abondance bear witness to the past vitality of one of the most important monasteries in the Alps. The village, which developed in the Val d'Abondance below the abbey, is a winter sports centre as well as a pleasant summer and health resort producing an excellent cheese similar to **Tomme de Savoie.** *74360 Abondance – July to Aug: daily 9am-noon, 2-6pm (closed afternoons Sun and public holidays); rest of year: daily 9am-noon, 2-5pm closed Sun and public holidays except Patrimoine holiday - ☎ 04 50 73 02 90*

▶ **Orient Yourself:** Situated at the intersection of the Dranse and Malève valleys, Abondance is 30km/18.75mi south of Évian between Morzine and Lake Geneva (Lac Léman). The easiest route is by D22 through the Gavot area towards Châtel.

Don't Miss: The abbey has remarkable 15C frescos; and you must of course taste the celebrated local cheese.

Organizing your time: You will need an hour each to see the Abbey and La Chapelle-d'Abondance; if you decide to take one of the suggested hikes, add another three to four hours.

Especially for Kids: In the summer, the abbey organizes a tour aimed at families, "On the Trail of Giacomo," as well as workshops for children.

Also See: Nearby sights: AVORIAZ, CHÂTEL, EVIAN-LES-BAINS, MORZINE, THONON-LES-BAINS, YVOIRE

Abbey★

During the Middle Ages, the Abbaye d'Abondance had a major religious and cultural impact on the northern Alps under the rule of the Augustinian order. A branch of the Cistercian order took over in 1607 and remained here until 1761.

Frescoes in the abbey cloisters

J. Sierpinski/SCOPE

Cloisters

 ♿ 🕐 *July to Aug: daily 10am-noon, 2-5.30pm; May-June and Sept-Oct: daily except Tue 10am-noon, 2-5pm; 20 Dec to April: daily except Sat 10am-noon, 2-5pm. Guided tours (1hr) 10am-3pm.* 🕐 *Closed from mid-Oct to mid-Dec, 1 Jan and 25 Dec. 2€, children under 12 years no charge -* ☎ *04 50 81 60 54.*

There are only two galleries left, dating from the 14C. The Porte de la Vierge (the Virgin Mary's door), which gave access to the church, is richly decorated, although badly damaged, with a Virgin and Child on the tympanum and graceful statues on either side. Surprisingly fresh, sometimes naive, the **frescoes**★★ decorating the cloisters depict scenes from the life of Christ and of the Virgin Mary; they are believed to have been painted by Giacomo Jacquerio of Piedmont between 1410 and 1420. *The Wedding at Cana* is particularly remarkable with a wealth of details of daily life in Savoie in the 15C.

Church

🕐 *Daily 10am-noon, 1-6pm, no charge -* ☎ *04 50 81 60 54. No charge.*

The five bays of the 13C nave and the aisles were destroyed by successive fires. Two bays were rebuilt in 1900, the remainder of the church is original. The chancel paintings by Vicario date from 1846. Note the fine 15C abbot's seat.

Museum of Religious Art

🕐 *Guided tours with the cloister and church. 2€ (children under 12 years no charge)* ☎ *04 50 81 60 54.*

Part of the abbey buildings house an important collection of religious vestments, paintings, statues, silver and gold plate and 15C manuscripts. The chapter-house has been reconstructed.

Maison du Val

Plaine d'Offaz – 🕐 *Daily except Sat-Sun 10am-noon, 2-6pm* 🕐*closed 15 Oct-20 Dec and public holidays in May and June. 3.50 to 4.50€*

This permanent exhibit in a local house demonstrates how history, geography and pastoral traditions are all reflected in the making of the celebrated Abondance cheese. Afterwards, you can sample some with a glass of Savoie wine or apple cider.

For coin categories see the Legend on the cover flap.

WHERE TO STAY

⌂**Chambre d'hôte Champfleury** – 74360 Richebourg - 3km/2mi NE of Abondance towards Châtel on D 22 – ☎ 04 50 73 03 00 -champslfeury-2wanadoo.fr- ✉ - 5rms- ⌂⌂half-pension. At the heart of the Abondance valley, this chalet typical of the Savoie region offers renovated south-facing rooms with a balcony or north-facing with a terrace.

Excursion

Les Plagnes

5.5km/3.4mi southeast. Cross the Dranse d'Abondance and turn left before a saw-mill towards Charmy-l'Adroit and Les Plagnes.

The road reveals the bottom of the valley dotted with large chalets and dominated by the Pic de la Corne and the Roc de Tavaneuse. Beyond a hamlet called Sur-la-Ravine, it dips into the forested upper Malève Valley and reaches Les Plagnes de Charmy, within sight of the Pointe de Chavache, in front of a lake framed by wooded slopes.

🏊 La Chapelle-d'Abondance

🏠 74360 Abondance – 🕐 *July to Aug: daily 8.30am-12.30pm, 4-7pm; Dec-Apr daily 8.30am-12.30pm, 2-6.30pm; rest of year: Mon to Fri 9am-noon, 2-5pm -* ☎04 50 73 51 41 - www.valdabondance.com

6km/3.7mi northeast on D 22. At the foot of the Mont de Grange and the Cornettes de Bises, this is a charming family resort where the typical regional houses, with wooden façades and carved openwork balustrades, are reminiscent of Swiss chalets across the border. The 18C church, decorated in Baroque style, has an elegant onion-shaped spire. The **Maison des Soeurs**, formerly a girls' school run by nuns, now houses the tourist office and temporary exhibits.

There are fine cross-country tracks towards Châtel and Abondance.

Hikes

▶ *Start from La Chapelle d'Abondance; both climbs are relatively easy*

Les Cornettes de Bises
Allow 3hr. It is advisable to carry identity papers since the itinerary skirts the Swiss border. From the village centre, walk north to the Chalets de Chevenne, then continue to climb alongside the stream to the Col de Vernaz on the Swiss border. Follow the ridge to the Chalets de la Callaz, then start the last climb to the summit (alt 2 432m/7 979ft).

The splendid **panorama**★★★ extends over the whole lake and the Alps from Mont Blanc to the Bernese Oberland.

Mont de Grange
Allow 3hr 30min. Cross the Dranse and walk south along the path leading to the Chalets du Follière.

The Alpine flora is particularly varied and chamois can be seen on the rocks high above the valley. The ascent starts at the end of the Chemine coomb; from the summit (alt 2 433m/7 982ft) there is a striking **view**★★ of the Val d'Abondance and the shores of Lake Geneva. You may spot some chamois on the rocks above the valley.

Beyond La Chapelle-d'Abondance, the peaks, pastures and forests of the vast Châtel Basin offer some of the best landscapes in the Haut Chablais.

Nature trail "On the Trail of the Chamois"
Allow 3h. Change in altitude 380m/1 247ft. Leave from the Plan des Feux at La Chapelle-d'Abondance, route of Crêt Bénit. Signposts guide you along the easy path up to the chalets of Pertuis.

ABRIÈS★

POPULATION 354
MICHELIN MAP 334 J4 LOCAL MAP SEE LE QUEYRAS

One of the oldest resorts in Haut-Queyras, this village is, depending on the season, the starting point of excursions, hikes, climbing or cross-country skiing expeditions in the peaks along the Italian border and in the nature reserve of the Guil valley. Abriès also draws visitors to its colourful market, held every Wednesday.  *Le Bourg, 05460 Abriès –* 🕐 *Daily 9am-noon, 3-7pm -* ☎ *04 92 46 72 26, www.abries.ristolas.queyras.com*

▶ **Orient Yourself:** To find Abriès, located deep in the Queyras region, follow D 947 up to the very end of the Guil Valley. In season, a shuttle bus (paying) travels between Château-Queyras and La Monta.

🕓 **Organizing Your Time:** Calculate two hours to tour the village, and another half-day if you plan to walk up to Valpreveyre and to ride the chair-lift up to La Collete de Gilly.

🄺🄸🄳🅂 **Especially for Kids:** At Ristolas, visit the Maison de la Nature.

🕯 **Also See:** Nearby sights: BRIANÇON, BRIANÇONNAIS, CEILLAC, GUILLESTRE, MOLINES-EN-QUEYRAS, MONT-DAUPHIN, Le QUEYRAS, SAINT-VÉRAN, VARS

Visit

The village has been devastated throughout history by floods and fires. The flood of 1728 carried off the cemetary, the church porch and the stone lions, found swimming in the floodwaters. No wonder the sundial bears the inscription: *Il est plus tard que vous ne croyez,* "It is later than you think."

Trail of the inscribed stones

🐾 This interesting trail, lined with inscribed stones illustrating the history of Abriès, is complemented by a brochure published by the Parc naturel régional du Queyras, on sale (4.50 €) at the tourist office.

The hamlet of Valpreveyre

🐾 **Valpreveyre**, now abandoned, can be reached by following the Bouchet mountain stream and turning right at Le Roux *(6km/3.7mi on the D441)*; the road is rough but offers beautiful views of neighbouring peaks, as well as charming, well-preserved old houses.

🄺🄸🄳🅂 Maison de la nature

🕓 *July to Aug and school holidays: 2-7pm; Mon-Fri 2-6pm, Wed 9am-noon. 3€, children 12-18 years 1€ -* ☎ *04 92 46 86 29/ 88 20*
Located in an old farmhouse, this ecologically themed exhibit, in partnership with the national park of Queyras, highlights the natural heritage of the upper Guil : geology, botany and animals, and the role of humans in this ecosystem.

Maison du costume d'autrefois

🕓 *July to Aug: Mon 3-9pm, Tue-Sat 10am- noon, 3-7pm; 15 Dec- 15 Apr , Mon-Fri 10am-noon, 3-7pm; rest of year: Wed-Sat 2-6pm and by appointment. 3€, children 1.50€ -* ☎ *04 92 46 87 32* Located in the basement of a former presbytery, this museum displays traditional costumes of the Queyras region.

🚶Hikes

Walk to La Colette de Gilly★

Alt 2 467m/8 094ft) 🚠 *Take the Gilly chair-lift on the way out of Abriès towards Ristolas* 🕓 *July-Aug: daily 9.10am-12.15pm, 1.30-5pm. 5€ -* ☎ *04 92 46 78 08.*
🚶 From the station (2 150m/7 054ft), a path (with red and white markings of trail GR 58) climbs steeply to La Colette de Gilly *(45min)* then on to the Gilly Peak (2 467m/8 094ft, another *15min*), offering **panoramic views**★ of the Tête du Pelvas, Bric Bouchet, Grand Queyron, Pic Ségure and Pic du Fond de Peynin.

Hiking round the Bric Bouchet (2 997m/9 833ft) via Italy★★
About 8hr, the trail is signposted; one night in the Lago Verde (Italy) mountain refuge; bring along identity papers.

🚶 Marked itinerary with possible alternatives from Abriès or Valpreveyre. Here are two of them: the shorter and more demanding one, suitable for long-distance skiing in winter, leads to the border pass of Valpreveyre with close views of the Bric Bouchet; then on to the Lago Verde refuge where the two alternatives meet. The longer one offers better views of the various landscapes from Valpreveyre through the hamlet of Le Roux to the border pass of **Abriès** or **St-Martin** (2 657m/8 717ft) during an easy 4hr walk. Superb **view**★★ of the **Val Germanisca** (Italy) and the Bric Bouchet Summit. The Lago Verde refuge (2 583m/8 474ft) is an hour further on, along the well-marked path. The **Grand Queyron** Peak (3 060m/10 039ft) stands out to the north. From the refuge, **Prali** and its ethnological museum can be reached in 2hr 30min. ▶ *Continue along the path until it reaches a resurfaced road. Turn left here and follow the track along the river which leads to the first houses of Pomieri.* There is a way back from Prali through the Col de la Croix or the Col d'Urine (🕯 *see above*) over two or three days, with overnight stops in Villanova or at the Jervis refuge (at Col de la Croix).

Col de la Croix and Col d'Urine via Ciabot del Pra (Italy)★★
Two days' walk and a night spent in the Jervis refuge; carry identity papers.

🚶 From La Monta, a 2hr walk to the Col de la Croix; follow path GR 58 C; note the old border stone with a fleur-de-lis on the French side. The Jervis refuge is a 1hr 30min walk further on; the footpath goes down to Ciabot del Pra. Continue northwards to reach the **Col d'Urine** in about 3hr. The imposing **Tête du Pelvas** (2 929m/9 610ft) towers over the pass and the small valley which prolongs it to the west and leads to the valley of Valpreveyre *(2hr walk from the pass).* ▶ *Trail GR 58B takes you back to Abriès in 30min.*

AIX-LES-BAINS♨♨

POPULATION 25 732
MICHELIN MAP 333 I3
LOCAL MAP SEE LAC DU BOURGET

This well-known spa, which specialises in the treatment of rheumatism and respiratory ailments, is also one of the best-appointed tourist centres in the Alps, with lively streets, splendid palace hotels near the baths and attractive lake shores. 🛈 *place Maurice-Mollard – 73100 Aix-les-Bains –* 🕐*July to Aug: daily 9am-6.30pm; Apr to May and Sept: 9am-noon, 2-6pm, Sun 10am-6.30pm; Oct and Feb to Mar: daily except Sun and public holidays 9am-noon, 2-5.30pm -* ☎ *04 79 88 68 00 - www.aixlesbains.com*

▶ **Orient Yourself:** Aix-les-Bains lies at the foot of Mont Revard, on the eastern shore of Lac du Bourget. Follow A 41 and A 43, 10km/6.25mi from Chambéry.

🅿 **Parking:** The town hall parking lot is located at the heart of the town, near spas, gardens and pedestrian malls.

😊 **Don't Miss:** After touring the town, stop by the Faure museum for the bronze sculptures by Rodin.

🕐 **Organizing Your Time:** Try to spend an evening in town, strolling along the lakeside.

🧒 **Especially for Kids:** Children will enjoy the aquarium of the lac du Bourget.

🕯 **Also See:** Nearby Sights: ANNECY, Lac d'ANNECY, L'ALBANAIS, Les BAUGES, Lac du BOURGET, CHAMBÉRY

Address Book

For coin categories see the Legend on the cover flap.

EATING OUT

Brasserie de la Poste – *32 av. Victoria -* ☎ *04 79 35 00 65 - closed Sun evening and Mon.* This family-run establishment has won a loyal local clientele. The terrace opens on the street and the principal dining room is enlivened by models of boats. Daily menu written on a slate in traditional style.

Les Platanes – *At the Petit-Port -* ☎ *04 79 61 40 54 - www.jazzaupetit-port.com - closed Nov- Jan.* Near the lake, a paradise for jazz-lovers. Patrons can dine to the rhythm of mini-concerts on Fridays and Saturdays, enjoying lake fish and fresh frogs' legs. There is a pleasant terrace in the shade of plane trees.

Auberge du Pont Rouge – *151 av. du Grand-Port -* ☎ *04 79 63 43 90 - closed 1-12 Aug, Sun evening, Mon and noon in winter, Mon evening and Wed evening.* Leave the city centre for this discrete residence with a dining room prettily renovated in contemporary style and a shaded terrace. Specialities from soutwest France and lake fish.

WHERE TO STAY

Hôtel La Croix du Sud – *3 r. du Dr-Duvernay -* ☎ *04 79 35 05 87 - www.hotel-lacroixdusud.com - closed Nov-Mar - 16rms.* This little pink building in the bend of a quiet street in the town centre draws people taking the waters. The modestly furnished rooms, with plaster mouldings and marble chimney-pieces, are spotlessly clean and Madame la Patronne waits on guests hand and foot. A garden courtyard adds charm.

Hôtel Beaulieu – *29 av. Charles-de-Gaulle -* ☎ *04 79 35 01 02 - www.hotel-beaulieu.fr - closed 2 Nov-1 Apr -31rms -* restaurant. A century-old façade behind which are equally old rooms, but well kept and colourfully furnished. Some have been renovated. Pleasant terrace in a shadey garden, and a dining room in a sun-room.

Hôtel Palais des Fleurs – *17 r. Isa-line -* ☎ *04 79 88 35 08 - www.hotelpal-aisdesfleurs.com - closed 10 Nov-31 Jan -* P *- 42rms-* restaurant. Whether you are here to see the sights, take the waters or attend a seminar, this quiet hotel in a residential neighbourhood offers a fitness centre and a heated swimming pool, open all year round.

Hôtel Astoria – *Pl. des Thermes -* ☎ *04 79 35 12 28 - www.hotelastoria.fr - closed 25 Nov -9 Jan - 134rms -* restaurant. This superbly restored Belle Époque mansion opposite the Baths gives an impression of the former splendours of Aix-les-Bains. The splendid atrium opens onto six floors of rooms which are spacious and comfortable, as well as the restaurant with its mezzanine and the magnificent lounges. Menu for hotel guests only.

Hôtel Le Manoir – *37 r. Georges-1er -* ☎ *04 79 61 44 00 - www.hotel-lemanoir.com - closed 18-28 Dec -* P *- 73rms -* restaurant. This manor house on the hillside above Aix-les-Bains occupies a quiet location amid a delightful garden with trees and flowering plants. The terrace is ideal for surveying the charm of the scene from the moment the sun rises. Inside, the decor is rustic in style. Indoor swimming pool.

ON THE TOWN

Casino "Grand Cercle" – *200 r. du Casino -* ☎ *04 79 35 16 16 - www.casinograndcercle.com - dailySun-Thur 11am-3am, Fri-Sat and public holidays 11am-4am.* This jewel of 19C thermal spa architecture has preserved its opulent interior design, including the Italian theatre and the Salviati room with its magnificent ceilings adorned with mosaics. Roulette, blackjack, stud poker, boule and 175 slot machines. irish pub, piano-bar, restaurants, disco-thèque and tea-dancing.

SHOPPING

Les Artisonales – *Quai Jean-Baptiste-Charcot - May to Sept: Wed 5-10pm* Local crafts and farm products are sold at this weekly evening market: charcuterie, cheese, leather goods, objects and utensils in wood.

J-P Savioz – *37 av. du Grand-Port -* ☎ *04 79 35 40 02 - Daily except Mon 9.30am-12.30pm, 3pm-7pm, Tue 3-7pm, closed*

15 Sept-1 Oct and Sun afternoon in July-Aug. For 20 years, M. Savioz has created pastries, ice-cream, and chocolates; in 1993, he won a world chocolate-making championship. As for Mme Savioz, she is the French dragée-making champion. **La Royale** – 2 r. Albert-1er - ☎04 79 35 08 84 - daily except Sun afternoon 9am-12.30pm, 2.30-7pm - closed 1-15 Feb and 1-15 July. Chocolate is the specialty of this shop and the variety is dazzling. As well, the almond and fruit bars are exceptional.

AFTERNOON TEA
Salon de Thé du Grand Hôtel du Parc – 28 r. de Chambéry - ☎04 79 61 29 11 - info@grand-hotel-du-parc.com - Open daily except Mon 1-6pm - closed 20 Dec-15 Feb. This tea room in the circa-1817 Grand Hotel is much appreciated by locals as well as visiting spa clients. Lovely ceiling with caissons, old mirrors, beautiful china, good silver, 12 sorts of tea served "à l'anglaise" as well as delectible pastries, ice-cream and home-made sherbet.

LEISURE
Swimming beaches – Aix-les-Bains has 3 beaches, one of which is managed by the city and has a nautical sports centre with a range of activities. The two other beaches, Aix-Memars and Aix-Rowing, have lifeguards in season as well as restaurants nearby. Or, you can choose to bring a picnic.

Cruises on the lake – Compagnie des bateaux du lac du Bourget et du haut-Rhône - le Grand-Port - ☎04 79 63 45 00 - www.gwel.com - Boat tours starting at 12€; cruise with meal from 29.70€. You can enjoy a one-hour cruise or the entire day on lac du Bourget, the canal of Savières and the Haut-Rhône, with or without meals on board. Also, you or your company can organize cruises with cocktails, tastings, or seminars.

A Bit of History

Taking the waters: a fashionable pastime – Aix's health-giving waters have been famous for almost 2 000 years. The Romans excelled in the art of hydropathy and the baths were at once a social club, a casino and a fitness club. The name of the town comes from *Aquae Gratianae*, "the waters of Emperor Gratianus."

During the Middle Ages, the baths were severely neglected. Taking the waters became fashionable again in the 16C, but the first real establishment dating from the 18C was only equipped with showers. The treatment offered became more sophisticated in the 19C with the introduction of the steam bath and shower-massage, a technique brought back from Egypt by Napoleon's doctors, which is still the great speciality of the spa.

The splendour of Aix-les-Bains at the turn of the century – The expansion of the spa town, which began in 1860, reached its peak during the Belle Époque. Luxury hotels were built in order to attract the aristocracy and the crowned heads of Europe: the "Victoria," for instance, welcomed Queen Victoria on three occasions, whereas the Splendide and the Excelsior counted among their guests a maharajah from India, the emperor of Brazil and Empress Elizabeth ("Sissi") of Austria-Hungary. Most of the buildings in the spa town were designed by an architect from Lyon, Jules Pin the Elder (1850-1934), whose masterpiece was undoubtedly the Château de la Roche du Roi.

After the Second World War, most of these magnificent hotels could not adapt to the new type of clientele and had to close down for economic reasons; some of them were turned into apartments.

The Spa Town

The life of the spa town is concentrated round the baths, the municipal park with its vast open-air theatre, the Palais de Savoie and the new casino, as well as along the lake with its beach and marinas. Rue de Genève, rue du Casino and adjacent streets form the shopping centre of the town.

Treatment

The baths – the **Pellegrini** (1832) and the **Chevalley** (2000) – are open all year round and are supplied by two hot springs, the sulphur spring and the alum spring; the massage-shower is still the best-known treatment, and the pools are designed for treatment of rheumatism and recovery from injuries. Cold water from the St-Simon spring is used for drinking.

To the south, the **Établissement thermal de Marlioz** (Marlioz baths), situated in a peaceful shaded park, treats disorders of the respiratory system. Queen Victoria enjoyed splashing about here.

Walking Tour

The Lake Shore

▷ *Follow avenue du Grand-Port and leave Aix by V on the town plan, heading towards Culoz. At the port, turn left onto Boulevard Robert-Barrier.*

Grand Port

The Compagnie des bateaux du lac du Bourget et du haut-Rhône offers both short and day-long cruises around the area. ♨ See the Leisure section of the green Address Book for details.

Esplanade du bord du lac★

This vast open space (10ha/25 acres) is equipped with children's games and is suitable for picnics. A shaded alleyway skirting the Lac du Bourget calls for pleasant walks within sight of the Hautecombe Abbey and the steep slopes of the Dent du Chat.

Petit Port

This is a fishing port and a marina. 🔲 An aquarium, **La Maison du lac du Bourget** (♨ *July and Aug: daily 10am-6pm; May to June and Sept: daily 2-5pm, Sat-Sun 10.30am-5pm; rest of year: daily except Tue 2.30-7pm (last entrance 1hr before closing)* ♨ *Closed Dec and Jan. 5.5€, children 4-12 years 4.70€.* ☎ *04 79 61 08 22 - www. aquarium-lacdubourget.com.),* containing around 50 fresh water species in their natural environment, is housed in the Centre of Hydrobiological Studies. The **beach** is just beyond.

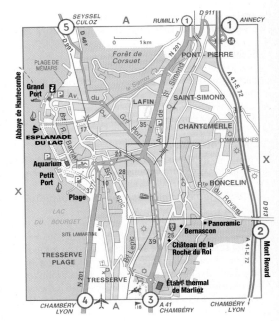

The Roman Town★

▶ *Begin at the Tourist Information Office*

Arc de Campanus

Erected by a member of the "Pompeia" family, this arch stood 9m/30ft high in the centre of the Roman town. The remains of the **Roman baths** can only give a rough idea of their former splendour (24 different kinds of marble were used to decorate them).

Temple de Diane

This remarkable rectangular Roman monument, its stones set in place without mortar, now houses the **Musée Lapidaire** (⏾ *See Sights, below*). Note the classic Italianate façade on the former **Grand Hôtel** (1853) on the corner, once one of the most prestigious addresses in town.

Casino Grand Cercle★

West of the town hall, across place du Revard.

Despite a series of renovation projects, this stylish casino still symbolises the golden age of Aix's high society. The main building dates from 1849, but it is the elegantly decorated gaming rooms, opened in 1883, which are particularly worth a visit. The finest of these is the grand **Salle des Jeux**★, with allegorical figures intricately depicted by Antonio Salviati on a vast, brightly coloured mosaic ceiling. Sarah Bernhardt was one of the many great performers to appear at the casino's **theatre,** decorated in Belle-Époque style.

Casino d' Aix-les-Bains

Mosaic in the Salle de Jeux

▶ *Turn left into rue Casino, then left again on to rue Victoria and follow rue du Temple to St Swithun's church.*

St Swithun

Built in 1869, thanks to donations from the English community, this Anglican church bears witness to the resort's British connections and the lasting popularity of "taking the cure."

▶ *Turn right into rue de Genève, then follow rue Dacquin to the left.*

Église Notre-Dame

Twelve 17C paintings representing the Apostles are displayed in the chancel of this Byzantine-style church, opened in 1900, when the resort was at its height.

▶ *Return to the Thermes nationaux and head uphill along rue Georges I.*

The Corniche

For the hotel developers of the Belle-Époque, this area, overlooking the town, was the most sought-after of all. Visitors strolling through streets can still admire the façades of some of the prestigious symbols of a bygone era: the **Splendide,** the **Royal** and the **Panoramic;** returning towards the convention centre you pass by the **Bernascon**. Above, on the corniche road is the fairytale **Château de la Roche du Roi** on the way to the Établissement thermal de Marlioz.

AIX-LES-BAINS

Alsace-Lorraine Av. d'	BY		
Anglais Bd des	CY		
Annecy Av. d'	CY		
Bains R. des	CZ	2	
Barrier Bd R.	AX		
Berthollet Bd	CZ	3	
Boucher Sq. A.	CY	5	
Carnot Pl.	CZ	6	
Casino R. du	CZ	8	
Chambéry R. de	CZ	9	
Chantemerle Bd de	CYZ		
Charcot Bd J.	AX	10	
Clemenceau Pl.	BY	12	
Colonne R. E.	BZ		
Côtes Bd des	CYZ		
Dacquin R.	CZ	13	
Davat R.	CZ	15	
Fleurs Av. des	CZ	16	

Garibaldi Bd	AX	17	
Garrod R. Sir-A.	CZ	18	
Gaulle Av. de	CZ	19	
Genève R. de	CYZ		
Georges-1er R.	CZ	21	
Grand Port Av. du	AX BY		
Hôpitaux Carrefour des	BY		
Italie Av. d'	BY		
Jacotot R.	BZ		
Lamartine R.	CZ	22	
Lattre-de-Tassigny Av. Mar.-de	AX BY	23	
Lepic Bd	AX BZ		
Liberté Av. de la	BZ		
Liège R. de	CZ	24	
Marlioz Av. de	AX	25	
Mollard Pl. M.	CZ	26	
Monard R. S.	CZ	27	
Paris Bd de	CY		
Petit Port Av. du	AX BYZ	28	

Pierpont-Morgan Bd	BY	29	
Président-Wilson Bd du	BZ		
Près-Riants R.	BY	30	
Près-Riants Carrefour des	BY		
République R.	CY	32	
Revard Pl. du	CZ	33	
Roche-du-Roi Bd de la	CZ	34	
Roosevelt Av. F.	AX	35	
Rops Av. D.	AX	37	
Russie Bd de	AX	39	
Seyssel R. C.-de	CZ	40	
Solms Av. M.-de	BCZ		
St-Simond Av. de	AX BCY		
Temple R. du	CZ	43	
Temple-de-Diane Sq.	CZ	45	
Tresserve Av. de	BCZ		
Vaugelas R.	CY		
Verdun Av. de	BZ	46	
Victor-Hugo R.	CZ		
Victoria Av.	CZ	47	

Abbaye de Hautecombe	AX	
Aquarium	AX	
Arc de Campanus	CZ	B
Casino Grand Cercle	CZ	
Château de la Roche du Roi	AX	
Église Notre-Dame	CZ	
Église St-Swithun	CZ	

Esplanade du Lac	AX	
Établissement thermal de Marlioz	AX	
Grand Port	AX	
Hôtel Beauregard	CZ	
Hôtel Bernascon	AX	
Hôtel de Ville	CZ	H
Hôtel Panoramic	AX	
Hôtel Royal	CZ	

Hôtel Splendide	CZ	
Mont Revard	AX	
Musée d'Archéologie et de Préhistoire	CZ	M
Musée Faure	CY	
Petit Port	AX	
Plage	AX	
Temple de Diane	CZ	K
Thermes nationaux	CZ	

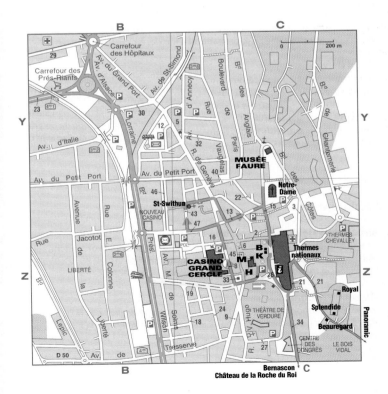

Sights

Musée Faure ★

Daily except Tues and public holidays (except Pentecost Mon) 10am–noon, 1.30–6pm Closed 22 Dec– 3 Jan. 4€, children under 16 years no charge - ☎ 04 79 61 06 57.

In 1942, Dr Faure bequeathed to the town a rare collection of paintings and sculptures including a large number of works by the Impressionists and their predecessors, Corot, Jongkind and Boudin. Note in particular *Mauve Dancers* by Degas, the *Seine at Argenteuil* by Sisley, *Ferryboat in Bonnières* by Cézanne and works by Vuillard and Pissarro.

The collection of sculptures is also rich in works by Carpeaux and Rodin, including a series of bronze, marble and terracotta sculptures forming part of his project entitled *The Doorway to Hell,* inspired by Dante's *Divine Comedy.* The last floor houses furniture and objects recreating Lamartine's surroundings in the Perrier boarding house, which is no longer there.

Thermes nationaux and caves

May–Oct: guided tours (1hr) daily except Sun and Mon at 3pm Closed public holidays. 4€, children under 12 years no charge. ☎ 04 79 35 38 50.

Inaugurated in 1783, renovated and enlarged during the 19C, the baths were completed by the Nouveaux Thermes in 1934, modernised in 1972; these are open to visitors. A vast room in the basement contains the **Roman remains** of a *caldarium* (hot bath) and of a circular pool. A 98m/322ft-long gallery gives access to the **caves** where one of the sulphur springs can be seen.

Musée lapidaire

Access through the Tourist Information Centre. Can be seen only during the tourist office's Aix-Gallo-romaine tours, organized every alternate Thur. 5€ - ☎04 79 88 68 00 Stone fragments, ceramics, glassware and coins dating from the Gallo-Roman period. Remarkable male bust, probably of a Roman emperor.

Hôtel de ville

This restored château, once home to the Marquis of Seyssel, lends a Savoyard look to the spa district. The elegant **staircase ★** was built during the early Renaissance period, with stones from the Roman monuments.

In 1816, Aix-les-Bains was the setting of one of the most famous love stories in French literature, between the Romantic poet Alphonse de Lamartine and Julie Charles who died a year later and inspired the moving lines of Le Lac.

Excursions

Lac du Bourget ★★ – *See Lac du BOURGET.*

Abbaye royale de Hautecombe ★★

A regular **ferry service** (*see the Address Book)* links the Grand Port and the abbey which can also be reached by driving round the lake (*see Lac du BOURGET:* 1 *Round tour of the lake).*

Circuit de la Chambotte ★★

36km/22.4mi – about 2hr 30min. Leave Aix by R on the town plan and N 201. Turn left at La Biolle along D 991B; turn left in St-Germain and left again at La Chambotte past a small chapel.

View from the Restaurant de la Chambotte★★
Splendid **view** over the Lac du Bourget and the mountains lining its shores; in the distance, one can see the Allevard, Grande-Chartreuse and southern Jura massifs.

▶ *Return to La Chambotte and follow D 991B to Chaudieu.*

This road offers good bird's-eye views of the northern extremity of the lake and of the Marais de Chautagne (Chautagne marshland).

▶ *From Chaudieu, return to Aix by the lakeside road described under Lac du BOUR-GET.*

Mont Revard★★★
Alt 1 537m/5 043ft. Drive along the road to Le Revard until you reach the former cable-car station. The **panorama**★★★ is splendid: to the west, there is an aerial view of the Lac du Bourget, the Dent du Chat, the Rhône like a shiny ribbon in the distance and Aix-les-Bains in the foreground; to the east, there is a fine vista of Mont Blanc behind a series of forested heights.
Beyond the Col de la Cluse, the **view**★ embraces the whole verdant Albanais depression and the heights of the southern Jura in the distance. Further down, the Lac du Bourget comes into view.
Pleasant rural landscapes unfold between Trévignin and Aix-les-Bains *(reached by D 913).*

L'ALBANAIS★
MICHELIN MAP 333 I/J6

This rich agricultural region of gently rolling green hills once specialised in tobacco-growing and remains economically robust. The countryside unfolds along winding roads and down the many rivers that delight anglers; the three biggest lakes in the Haute Savoie as well as the Parc naturel régional des Bauges are found nearby.  *4 place de l'Hôtel-de-Ville - 74150 Rumilly* ◷ *July to Aug: Mon-Fri 9am-12.30pm, 2.30-6.30pm, Sat 9am-12.30pm; Jan to June and Sept to Dec: Mon-Fri 8.30am-noon, 2-6pm, Sat 8.30am-noon* ◷*closed 25 Dec to 1 Jan -* ☎*04 50 64 58 32 - www.ot-albanais74.fr*

▶ **Orient Yourself:** The Albanais depression lies between the Lac du Bourget and the Lac d'Annecy and is framed by the Gros Foug, Revard and Semnoz mountains. It gives access to the Jura mountains via Bellgarde, and to Switzerland via Geneva.
◉ **Don't Miss:** The excursion to the Vallée du Fier is pleasant; you will also enjoy the Musée de l'Albanais.
🄺🄸🄳🅂 **Especially for Kids:** There is a recreation park around a pond in Rumilly.
◔ **Also See:** Nearby Sights: AIX-LES-BAINS, ANNECY, Lac d'ANNECY, Les BAUGES, Lac du BOURGET, CHAMBÉRY, THORENS-GLIÈRES

Excursions

Vallée du Chéran *– 40km/25mi – allow half a day*

Rumilly
Guided tours – ◷ *July to Aug: only by appointment at the tourist office*

This former stronghold at the confluence of two mountain streams is the capital of the Albanais region, a lively market town and industrial centre. The old town, nestling round the "Halle aux Blés" (corn exchange, rebuilt in 1869), includes a few interesting 16C and 17C buildings, in particular around **place de l'Hôtel-de-Ville** with its graceful fountain. Also worth visiting are the **Église Ste-Agathe** (1837) with its Tuscan-style façade and 12C bell tower, and the part-13C **Chapelle Notre-Dame-de-l'Aumône** (🕐 *2-6pm* - ☎*04 50 64 58 32*) on the bank of the Chéran.

The **Musée de l'Albanais** (*avenue Gantin* – ♿🕐 *July to Aug: daily except Tue 10am-noon, 3-7pm (Mon 6pm); June and Sept: daily except Tue 9-11am, 2-6pm (Mon 5pm)* 🕐*closed the rest of the year. No charge.* ☎ *04 50 01 19 53*), housed in a former tobacco factory, deals with local history from the 17C onwards.

▶ *Leave Rumilly by D 3 going south.*

Alby-sur-Chéran ★

🛈 *Musée de la Cordonnerie - 74540 Alby-sur-Chéran* 🕐 *July to Aug: Mon-Sat 8.30am-12.30pm, 2.30-6.30pm, guided tours on request; June and first 2 weeks of Sept: Mon-Sat 8:30am-noon, 2-6pm* 🕐 *closed the rest of the year -* ☎*04 50 68 39 44.*

This picturesque village was an important shoemaking centre housing no fewer than 300 craftsmen in the 19C. The charming triangular **place du Trophée**★, situated in the old part of Alby, is surrounded by medieval arcaded workshops, which have been tastefully restored. The **Musée de la Cordonnerie** (🕐 *July to Aug: daily except Sun 10am-12.30pm, 2.30-6.30pm; June and first 2 weeks of Sept: daily except Mon and Sun: 10am-noon, 2-6pm.* 🕐 *Closed public holidays. No charge.* ☎ *04 50 68 39 44 - www.mairie-alby-sur-cheran.fr*)**,** located inside the town hall, is devoted to the shoemaking industry. The Église Notre-Dame-de-Plainpalais (1960) designed by Maurice Novarina has a remarkable stained-glass wall.

From the bridge over the Chéran is a lovely **view**★ of the village and its surroundings.

▶ *Leave Alby by D 3 towards Le Châtelard.*

Place du Trophée in Alby-sur-Chéran

The road offers fine views of the Chéran. Beyond Cusy, where the route bears left, the Bauges Massif bars the horizon to the south. Another left turn leads to the **Pont de l'Abîme** (℮ see Les BAUGES) which spans the Chéran, 94m/308ft above the river bed in a spectacular **setting**★ including, to the northeast, the imposing rocky peaks of the **Tours St-Jacques.**

You can drive on to the Vallon de Bellevaux along D 911 (℮ see Les BAUGES). Alternatively, drive north on the D 5 to Gruffy after crossing the Chéran.

Musée de la Nature
In Gruffy at the Guevin farm as you enter the village. 🚶🕐 *July to Aug: 2-6pm; mid-Mar to 30 June and Sept to 15 Nov: daily except Mon and Sat 2-6pm* 🕐 *Closed 1 Nov and 15 Nov-15 Mar. 3.90€, children 6-16 years 2.50€ -* ☎ *04 50 77 58 60 - www.musee-nature.com*
The museum gives a good idea of traditional life in Savoie by means of the reconstruction of a 19C farm, a mountain chalet and the cheesemaking process.

Continue towards Viuz-la-Chiésaz; the dark silhouette of the **Crêt de Châtillon** (1 699m/5 574ft), the highest peak of the Semnoz mountain, towers over the village. Roads D 141, D 241 and D 41 lead to the summit (℮ see Lac d'ANNECY: Excursion ③).

Address Book

EATING OUT

MODERATE
⊖⊖**Rôtisserie du Fier** – *In the Val du Fier - 74910 Seyssel - 3km/2mi S of Seyssel on D 991 and D 14 -* ☎ *04 50 59 21 64 - closed Tue and Wed during the school holidays in Feb and autumn (around 1st Nov).* This romantic location makes the ideal setting for the simple, wholesome and excellent cooking using mainly fresh ingredients. On sunny days, tables are set in the garden along the tree-lined river bank.

WHERE TO STAY

BUDGET
⊖**Camping Le Chéran** – *74540 Cusy - 7.5km/5mi S of Alby-sur-Chéran on D 63 and D 3 -* ☎ *04 50 52 52 06 - open Apr-Sept - reservations recommended - 26 pitches– catering available on site.* For those who love peace and solitude, this campsite is the answer; at the end of a steep and narrow track, it occupies a beautiful unspoiled natural setting on the river bank. It is well kept and offers friendly service and a small restaurant with local fare.

MODERATE
⊖⊖**Gîte rural du Château de Lupigny** – *74150 Boussy - 7km/4mi N of Alby-sur-Chéran towards Rumilly on D 31 -* ☎ *04 50 01 12 01 -* 🍴 *- 1 gîte 1/7 persons: weekly rates.* At the tip of a rocky pinnacle stands a fortified building that once served as a watchtower. Guests can choose to stay in the gîte or the comfortable guest room. Anyone with an eye for fine architecture should take a moment to admire the 15C spiral staircase.

⊖⊖**Chambre d'hôte La Ferme sur les Bois** – *Le Biolley - 74150 Vaulx - 10km/6mi NE of Rumilly on D 3 -* ☎ *04 50 60 54 50 - http://perso.wanadoo. fr/annecy-attelage - closed 1 Nov-Easter -* 🍴 *- 4rms - restaurant* ⊖⊖. This former farmhouse has been completely renovated and now features fine rooms with colourful rustic furnishings. Guests can enjoy the comfort of sitting round the open fire in the evenings. Weather permitting, there are trips around the estate in a horse-drawn cart.

SPORT AND LEISURE
A particularly exciting experience is **canoeing in the Chéran gorge** down as far as Rumilly. Book during season at the Club Alpes-Sports-Nature-Takamaka, 17 Faubourg Ste-Claire, 74000 Annecy, ☎ 04 50 45 60 61.

▷ *Drive west along D 38 to Marcellaz-Albanais before returning to Rumilly by D 16.*

Val du Fier ★ *42km/26mi – allow 2 hr*

▷ *Leave Rumilly by D 31 across the Pont Édouard-André towards Lornay.*

At first the road follows the Fier, then crosses it before reaching the hilltop village of **Clermont**.

Château de Clermont

🕐 *July to Aug: guided tour (1hr, last admission 1h before closing) 2-7pm; May and Sept: Sat-Sun 4-7pm* 🕐 *closed the rest of the year. 5€, children under 12 years no charge - ☎ 04 50 69 63 15.*

Built straight onto the rock at the end of the 16C, this palace in Italian Renaissance style consists of three 2-storey wings★, an imposing gateway and two square towers. The gallery on the south wing offers a fine view across the Albanais.

▷ *Return to St-André along D 31 and turn right just before the factory.*

Val du Fier ★

This is a typical transverse valley hidden under greenery, seen at its best in the late-afternoon light. The road goes through several narrow defiles including two tunnels. Just before the last tunnel, a path on the left leads to a gate barring the entrance to the **Voie romaine du Val du Fier** (Val du Fier Roman road), part of the road which, in the 1C AD, linked the Albanais region and the Rhône Valley.

▷ *Return to Rumilly via Val-de-Fier and Vallières.*

From Vallières you can make an interesting detour to **Lagnat-Vaulx** *(follow D 14 to Hauteville and D 3 to Vaulx)* and stroll through the wooded **Jardins secrets** *(♿🕐 guided tours (1hr15min - last admission 1hr before closing): mid-June to early Sept: 1.30-7pm; Apr to mid-June: Sat-Sun and public holidays 1.30-7pm; Sept to mid-Oct: Sun 1.30-6pm. 7€, children 6-16 years: 4€ - ☎ 04 50 60 53 18 - www.jardins-secrets.com)*, a pleasant succession of small gardens with fountains, pergolas and patios, which feel more Andalucian than alpine.

ALBERTVILLE

POPULATION 17 340

MICHELIN MAP 333 L3 – LOCAL MAP SEE BEAUFORT

Lying at the entrance of the Arly Valley, Albertville is the converging point of several scenic roads leading to the Beaufortain and Tarentaise areas. Conflans, perched on a rocky spur overlooking the confluence of the River Isère and River Arly, was the economic centre until eclipsed by its former satellite in the 18C; the old town is well worth visiting. 🛈 *Place de l'Europe – 73204 – ☎ 04 79 32 04 22 - www.albertville.com* 🕐 *July to Aug: daily except Sun and public holidays 9am-6.30pm; Sept to June: daily except Sun and public holidays 9am-noon, 2-6pm. Guided tours of the town (2hr) June-15 Sept – Contact the tourist office. 5€, children 2.50€*

▷ **Orient Yourself:** At 50km/31.25mi from Chambéry on the A430, Albertville sits on the route for Mont-Blanc and the Tarentaise.

Don't Miss: Try to visit Conflans in the evening, when the medieval atmosphere is strongest.

Organizing Your Time: You need an hour to stroll about Conflans, and another for a fast look at the Olympic installations. Taking one of the suggested excursions would add about 2hrs.

Especially for Kids: The nature trail at Pointières will intrigue children.

Also See: Nearby Sights: ANNECY, Lac d'ANNECY, Massif des ARAVIS, Les BAUGES, BEAUFORT, La Vallée des BELLEVILLE, Route de la MADELEINE, MEGÈVE, La TARENTAISE

Sights

The Olympic City

In 1992, Albertville hosted the opening and closing ceremonies of the 16th Winter Olympic Games while events took place in nearby resorts. It was the third time since 1924 that the games had been held in the French Alps.

Olympic venues

The venue where the opening and closing ceremonies were staged is now a sports and leisure park where major events are held.

The **Halle olympique** (Olympic stadium) is a training centre for the French ice-hockey team as well as a public ice-skating rink and a venue for the European Ice-skating Championship. The climbing wall, open to the public, is one of the biggest in Europe.

The **Anneau de vitesse** (speed-skating rink) has become a sports stadium hosting regional competitions.

The **Maison des 16es Jeux olympiques** (16th Olympic Games Centre – *July to Aug: 9h30-7pm, Sun and public holidays 2-7pm; Sept to June: daily except Sun and public holidays 9.30am-12.30pm, 2-6pm. 3€, children under 16 years no charge - ☏ 04 79 37 75 71*) houses an exhibition devoted to the 1992 Olympic Games.

Le Dôme

Designed by Jean-Jacques Moisseau, this new cultural centre stands on place de l'Europe and comprises a theatre, a multimedia reference library and a cinema with a panoramic screen.

Conflans ★

▶ *Drive north across the pont des Adoubes and up the montée Adolphe-Hugues; leave the car in the car park on the right; continue on foot as indicated below.*

Château Manuel de Locatel

Closed for repairs. This 16C castle overlooks the new town of Albertville. The 17C ceiling painted by an Italian artist is remarkable.

Porte de Savoie

Before going through the gate, admire the lovely **view**★ of the building dominated by the slender Tour Ramus and of the charming 18C fountain.

Conflans

Rue Gabriel-Pérouse

This is the former "Grande-Rue" (High Street), lined with medieval workshops still occupied by craftsmen whose shops are advertised by signs in wrought iron.

▶ *Turn left to go up to the church.*

Church

This hall-church is in authentic 18C style; the nave, which consists of four bays, is prolonged by a chancel with a flat east end. The carved **pulpit,** dating from 1718, is remarkable; note also the baptismal font and the retable over the high altar.

Return to rue Gabriel-Pérouse, which leads to the Grande Place.

Grande Place★

A lovely 18C fountain decorates the centre of this picturesque square, lined on one side with a 14C brick building, known as the Maison rouge, and culminating in an art gallery.

Maison Rouge

🕐 *Mid-June to mid-Sept: daily 10am-7pm; mid-Sept to mid-June: daily 2-6pm* 🕐 *Closed 1 Jan, 1 May and 24, 25 and 31 Dec. 2.50€, children no charge -* ☎ *04 79 37 86 86.* This striking building in the style of the neighboring Piedmont, has sheltered both monks and soldiers and now houses the **musée d'Art et d'Histoire**. Exhibits include archeological finds from Gilly-sur-Isère, reconstruc-

For coin categories, see the Legend on the cover flap.

EATING OUT

🍽**Le Ligismond** – *17 Pl de Conflans -* ☎ *04 79 37 71 29 - closed during 1 week in spring, 1-15 Nov, and Christmas holiday.* This comfortable, quiet restaurant located in the heart of the old town has a lovely terrace under a flower-laden pergola. Traditional fare.

WHERE TO STAY

🛏**Chambre d'Hôte la Grange aux Loups** – *Le Villaret, 73720 Wueige, 8km/5mi NE of Albertville, towards Beaufortain, turn left towards Césarches-le-Villaret, then right at Le Villaret (col de la Forclaz) -* ☎ *04 79 38 08 32 - www.grangeauxloups.com - closed Oct-Nov - - 5rms: - restaurant.* This farm dating from 1792, many times renovated, surrounded by acres of forest and pasture, offers calm, clean air and natural surroundings. There is an adventure trail in the forest for an athletic work-out. Large rooms, many wood-paneled. Lovely view of Mont-Blanc from the lounge.

tions of Savoyard homes, local religious statues, regional furniture, traditional tools, costumes and old skis.

La Grande Roche
This terraced area, under the Sarrasine tower (12C) and shaded by ancient lime trees, overlooks the confluence of the River Isère and River Arly, offering fine views of the Combe de Savoie depression with the rocky peaks of the Chartreuse Massif in the distance.
The **Porte Tarine** has kept watch over the town and the route de la Tarentaise since the 14C.

Excursion

Route du Fort du Mont★★ *29km/18mi – about 1hr 30min*

▷ *From the Porte de Savoie in Conflans, drive along D 105. (Snow may block this steeply rising road between December and April).*

The road climbs continuously, soon offering a panoramic view of the Doron and Arly valleys with the pyramid-like Mont Charvin in the distance to the north.
Higher up, a wide bend forms a good **belvedere** over the Basse Tarentaise Valley which narrows between Feissons and Aigueblanche.
Continue past the Fort du Mont to the second hairpin bend at les Croix (two chalets stand nearby – alt 1 120m/3 675ft). There are fine **views**★★ of pastures in the foreground, the Combe de Savoie, through which flows the River Isère, and the Mont Blanc Massif.

▷ *Return by the forest road on the left towards Molliessoulaz. From Molliessoulaz, a path leads down into the Doron Valley and joins up with D 925 which takes you back to Albertville.*

🚶 Kids A bit before **Pointières**, starting near the chapel, there is an interesting and very easy nature trail (1hr30min) which illustrates how people lived in the mountains before they started leaving for jobs in the towns.

Route du Col de Tamié *40km/25mi – allow 2hr*

From Albertville to Faverges
▷ *D 104 towards Faverges.* The Col de Tamié between the Massif des Bauges and the Dent de Cons links the area around Annecy to the Combe de Savoie and the Tarentaise. The road winds upwards towards the Col de Ramaz and a view of the Combe de Savoie. *Turn onto the first road on the right; follow the sign for "Plateau des Teppes."*

Plateau des Teppes★
🚶 Beyond la Ramaz there is a fine view of the Abbaye de Tamié. ▷*Park the car on the second bend and continue on foot along the path to your right (15min there and back).* Climb to the top of a small rise beyond the wood for a delightful **view**★ of Albertville.

▷ *Return to the Col de Ramaz and continue towards Col de Tamié.*

Below the Fort de Tamié, a fine, extended **view**★ opens up just before the pass: Abbeville at the confluence of the Arly and the Isère. A nature trail has been opened inside the walls of the fort. (⚊🕐 *June to mid-Sept: 10am-7pm. 2.50€ - ☎04 79 31 37 50 - www.fordetamie.com)*

▶*The abbey comes into view immediately on the other side of the Col de Tamié.*

Abbaye de Tamié

⚊*Only the church is open to the public; an audiovisuel presentation describing monastery life is offered in the building at the parking lot entrance.* Founded in 1132 and rebuilt at the end of the 17C, the abbey stood empty for 70 years until, in 1861, a Cistercian community settled here. The monks make a famous cheese, known simply as Tamié.

▶Continue towards Faverges. The road runs around part of the Sambuy, which can be reached by ⚊chair-lift from Vargnoz. (⚊*See Lac d'ANNECY,* 2)

Faverges – (⚊*see Lac d'ANNECY,* 1)

ALLEVARD ⚓

POPULATION 3 081
MICHELIN MAP 333 J5
LOCAL MAPS SEE BELOW AND LE GRÉSIVAUDAN

Allevard, lying in the green Bréda Valley, at an altitude of 475m/1 558ft, is the starting point for numerous excursions. The jagged ridges of the Allevard Massif (highest peak: Puy Gris, 2 908m/9 541ft), which are covered with snow for the greatest part of the year, give the whole area a genuine Alpine atmosphere. The vast forests of conifers covering the lower slopes from 1 500m/4 921ft are the main attraction of mountain resorts of the upper Bréda Valley such as Le Curtillard. 🔲 *place de la Résistance – 38580 Allevard* 🕐 *Daily except Sun and public holidays 9am-noon, 2-6pm; Sun and public holidays 9am-noon* 🕐*closed 1 May -* ☎ *04 76 45 10 11 - www.allevard-les-bains.com*

▶ **Orient Yourself:** Allevard is midway between Grenoble and Chambéry. Leave A 41 at exit 23, follow D29, then D 525 to the resort.

☺ **Don't Miss:** Spend time hiking around the upper Bréda valley.

🕐 **Organizing Your Time:** The area offers excellent hiking excursions, ranging from 1hr (Chartreuse St-Hugon) to a demanding day-long hike to the Lacs des Sept-Laux.

Kids **Especially for Kids:** The "Pierrot Gourmand" festival of children's films offers amusing workshops, exhibits and talks. The tourist office will provide dates.

⚊ **Also See:** Nearby Sights: Les BAUGES, CHAMBÉRY, Massif de CHAMROUSSE, Massif de la CHARTREUSE, Le GRÉSIVAUDAN, ST-PIERRE-DE-CHARTREUSE

A Bit of History

The **Chaîne de Belledonne,** which forms part of the central massifs (⚊*see Introduction: Formation of the Alps),* overlooks the Isère Valley from Allevard to the Croix de Chamrousse towering above Grenoble. Its highest point is the Rocher Blanc (2 928m/9 606ft), and it only includes two small glaciers.

Allevard established itself as a local iron smelting centre as early as the 13C, and although the industry has long since moved on, a museum, a themed walk and the remains of the smelting-houses are reminders of the town's metalworking past.

It was after an earthquake in 1791 that the Allevardins discovered the local "black water" and its curative properties: the natural traces of carbon and sulphur compounds aid the treatment of respiratory complaints. The baths, a striking architectural mix of the classical and the oriental, are the centre of a popular spa resort.

Excursions

1 **Route du Collet d'Allevard** ★★

10km/6.2mi – about 30min – T see local map

▶ *Leave Allevard by D 525^A to Fond-de-France. Turn left after 1.4km/0.9mi onto D 109.*

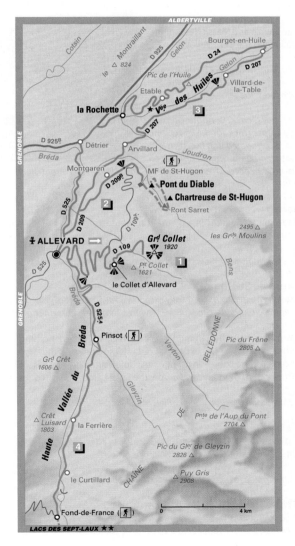

Hairpin bends afford a series of glimpses of Allevard and its immediate surroundings, of the Veyton and Gleyzin valleys separated by the Pic de Gleyzin and finally of the upper Bréda Valley. As the road reaches the 🚠 winter sports resort of **Le Collet d'Allevard** (1 450m/4 757ft), it reveals a vast panoramic view embracing the Vercors, Chartreuse and Bauges massifs as well as the Grésivaudan, Chambéry and Combe de Savoie depressions. ⬤ The view is even better 3km/1.9mi further on from the summit of **Grand Collet** (1 920m/6 299ft), which can be reached by chair-lift.

2 Chartreuse de St-Hugon

8.5km/5.3mi, then 1hr there and back on foot – ⬤ see local map

▶ *Leave Allevard by D 525 north, turn right onto D 209 then right again after the bridge across the Buisson.*

The road gives panoramic views of the Combe de Savoie and Massif des Bauges before following the Bens Valley.

▶ *After 6.5km/4mi, ignore D 109 on your right and park the car near the St-Hugon forest lodge*

⬛ *1hr there and back. Continue on foot along the forest track for 1.5km/0.9mi then, near a corrugated iron hut, turn left onto a path leading down to Pont Sarret (boots may be needed after a thaw or heavy rain).*

In the Buddhist centre at Chartreuse de St-Hugon

Pont Sarret
This bridge spans the Bens in a pleasant forest setting with the foaming torrent below.

▶ *Cross the bridge and follow the path uphill on the opposite bank of the Bens.*

Chartreuse de St-Hugon
🕐 *July to Aug: guided tours (1hr) daily except Wed at 4pm; rest of year: Sun and public holidays 4pm* 🕐 *Closed Dec to Mar. 3€, children under 14 years no charge - ☎ 04 79 25 78 00.*
A "chartreuse" is a Carthusian monastery in an isolated spot; nothing remains of this one founded in the 12C except a 17C building with a Gothic-style pediment surmounted by a wrought-iron fan light, occupied since 1982 by a Buddhist centre, the most important of its kind in Europe; the Dalai Lama has visited several times.

▶ *Continue along the path and bear left at the fork.*

Pont du Diable
The engraved stone on this 200-year-old bridge used to mark the border between France and Savoie, then part of the Italian Piedmont.

▶ *Cross the bridge to rejoin the road and return to the lodge on the right.*

3 Vallée des Huiles ⋆

50km/31mi round tour – about 2hr 30min – ⬤ see local map

▶ *Leave Allevard by D 525 north then bear right on D 925 towards Albertville.*

La Rochette
The cardboard factories of this industrial town and tourist centre are among the largest in Europe.

▶ *Drive east towards Étable for 1km/0.6mi and turn right.*

The road climbs through the upper Gelon Valley, known as the Vallée des Huiles, along the cultivated slope of the valley which contrasts with the forested slope opposite. Upstream from Étable stands the solitary Pic de l'Huile which gave its name to the whole valley; "Huile" is derived from a local form of the word *aiguille*, or needle, and refers to the rocky spur at the end of the valley.

▶ *Continue on the D 24 towards to Bourget-en-Huile and turn left along D 207 towards Allevard.*

After crossing the Gelon, the road winds along the forested slope of the valley. Just beyond Villard there is a fine view of the basin of La Rochette and the lower Bréda Valley leading to the Grésivaudan. Woods give way to pastures dotted with walnuts and chestnuts as one approaches the lovely village of Arvillard.

▶ *Return to Allevard along D 209.*

Hike

4 **Haute Vallée du Bréda**

17km/10.6mi – about 30min – 🕐 *see local map*

▶ *Follow D 525A to Fond-de-France.*

This excursion through restful landscapes is popular with tourists taking the waters in Allevard. **Fond-de-France** (alt 1 089m/3 573ft) is the ideal starting point for mountain hikes.

Hike to the Lacs des Sept-Laux★★
Leave the car in Fond-de-France in front of the Sept-Laux hotel. This trip is suitable for experienced hikers: 3hr 45min climb; 1 150m/3 773ft difference in altitude; it is advisable to wear mountain boots.
🚶 Most of the walk is through woodland (follow the yellow and then yellow and red markings). At the halfway mark, take the less demanding Sentier des deux Ruisseaux track. Beyond the Lac Noir *(2hr 30min walk)* the hike is easier and quite pleasant, as the path skirts several **glacial lakes: Lac Carré, Lac de la Motte, Lac de Cottepens** and **Lac du Cos**★★. *Walk along the Lac de Cottepens towards the Col des Sept-Laux; bear left where you see yellow, white and red markings on a rock.* A steep path, not easy to spot, leads through pastureland and rocky terrain up to a mound overlooking the small Lac Blanc and affording a stunning **panorama**★★★ of the Sept-Laux, of the Eau d'Olle Valley and of numerous peaks and ridges all around. Walkers with energy to spare can follow the path along the edge of the pasture for a further 10min to a mountain lake.

L'ALPE-D'HUEZ ✳ ✳

MICHELIN MAP 333 J7
LOCAL MAP SEE BASSIN DU BOURG-D'OISANS

L'Alpe-d'Huez, lying at an altitude of 1 860m/6 102ft, more than 1 000m/3 281ft above the Bourg-d'Oisans Valley, is one of the most attractive winter sports resorts in the French Alps. In summer, L'Alpe-d'Huez is the starting point of fascinating **hikes** and mountaineering expeditions in the Massif des Grandes Rousses, and the end of one of the most famously gruelling climbs of the Tour de France cycle race, with 21 numbered hairpin bends leading up to the top. The resort comprises numerous large chalet-style hotels close to the swimming-pool and the summer pastures. *place Paganon – 38750 Alpe-d'Huez Dec to Apr: 8.45 am-7pm; July to Aug: 9am-7pm; May-June: weekdays only, closed public holidays, 9am-12.30pm, 4.30-6pm – ☎ 04 76 80 35 41 - www.alpedhuez.com*

▶ **Orient Yourself:** This famous resort is 65km/40.6mi east of Grenoble, via N 85, then N 91 and D211

Don't Miss: The view of Mont-Blanc is spectacular

Organizing Your Time: To watch the Tour de France, plan well ahead.

Kids Especially for Kids: The ice cave enchants children.

Also See: Nearby Sights: Le BOURG-D'OISANS, Massif de CHAMROUSSE, Route de la CROIX-DE-FER, Route du GALIBIER, La GRAVE, L'OISANS, Le VALBONNAIS

Route de Villars-Reculas ★

4km/2.5mi along D 211B – local map see Bassin du BOURG-D'OISANS. This steep road offers bird's-eye views of the Bassin du Bourg-d'Oisans below. The village has retained its charm, with houses of stone surmounted by wooden barns forming a picturesque sight.

Address Book

For coin categories, see the Legend on the cover flap.

EATING OUT

You will find restaurants not only in the resort area, but also on the mountain, open even in summer. Try **Le Génépri** with its alpine menu, **Le Passe Montagne** with its family atmosphere, or the high-altitude **La Cabane du Poutat** with its selection of regional specialities.

WHERE TO STAY

The resort has some 32 000 beds available, with a wide range of prices. Contact the tourist office or reservation service; lodging in the valley is cheaper.

Hôtel Dôme – Pl. du Cognet - 38750 L'Alpe-d'Huez - ☎ 04 76 80 32 11 - www.dome-alpedhuez.com - closed 21 Apr-30 Jun and Sept-14 Dec - ⏚ - 21rms - restaurant. This hotel occupies two storeys of a residential building near the slalom racecourse. Functional rooms, dining decorated in wood and stone. Shopping arcade on ground floor.

Hôtel Au Chamois d'Or – Rd-pt des Pistes - 38750 L'Alpe-d'Huez - ☎ 04 76 80 31 32 - www.chamoisdor-alpedhuez.com - closed 21 Apr-19 Dec - ⏚ - 43rms - restaurant. This imposing wooden chalet is located at the highest point of the resort, overlooking the Pic du lac Blanc and Grandes Rousses slopes. South-facing terrace with a view of the Oisans glaciers, lounge with alpine touches. Pretty rooms with local decor.

TRANSPORT

Free shuttle buses connect the whole resort. In summer, there is a special Visalp pass available.

The Resort

🎿 Ski area

L'Alpe-d'Huez (1 120-3 330m/ 3 675-10 925ft) is the most important ski resort in Dauphiné. Linked to the resorts of Auris, Oz, Vaujany and Villard-Reculas, it now has 121 Alpine ski runs totalling 245 km/28mi, including a beginner area, a snowpark, night skiing, summer skiing on the Sarennes Glacier and Nordic skiing. Summers, mountain biking or hiking are popular; ski lifts transport you up the mountain.

Sights

Musée d'Huez et de l'Oisans

Route de la Poste. 🕐 *July to Aug and Dec to Apr: daily except Sat 10am-noon, 3-7pm;* 🕐 *Closed the rest of year. 2€, children under 16 years no charge -* ☎ *21 76 11 21 74.*
This municipal museum displays objects discovered since 1977 on the **Brandes** archaeological site (near the airfield), where remains of a 13C-14C silver mine were unearthed. There are also exhibits concerning traditional life in the Oisans area, local fauna and flora, and the development of the resort.

Centre Notre-Dame-des-Neiges

🕐 *Guided tour Tue 5.30pm -*☎*04 76 11 21 74 - www.notredamedesneiges-alpedhuez. asso.fr*
The modern rotunda-like building (1970) houses a meeting centre and serves as a parish church and a concert venue. Thirteen decorative windows represent scenes from St Mark's Gospel. The Kleuker organ (1978) is particularly noteworthy.

Hikes

Pic du Lac Blanc★★★

🚡 *Access is by means of two successive gondola rides followed by a cable car ride.* 🕐*July to Aug: gondola departures starting 7.45am (30min), the cablecar leaves starting at 8.15am (every 6min). 13€.* ☎ *04 76 80 30 30.*
Alt 3 323m/10 902ft. As you come out of the cable-car *(viewing table)*, there is a sweeping **view,** from left to right, of Les Deux-Alpes, Lac Lauvitel, Mont Ventoux (in the distance), L'Alpe-d'Huez (below), Le Taillefer, as well as the Belledonne and Chartreuse massifs. *Climb on to a mound (viewing table).* The **panoramic view**★★ is even wider, with Pic Bayle in the foreground and, in the distance, the heights of the Maurienne and the peaks of the Vanoise and Écrins massifs.
The **Dôme des Petites Rousses**★★ can be reached from Lac Blanc (🚶1hr there and back.)

La Grande Sure★ (or Le Signal)

Alt 2 114m/6 936ft. 🚶 *Access by the Le Signal chairlift in winter and on foot (*🚶*2hr there and back) in summer.*
Extensive **views** of the Grandes Rousses range, the Oisans region, the Taillefer Mountain and the Belledonne range.

Lac Besson★

6.5km/4mi by the road leading to Col de Poutran in the north. The road winds through pastures, reaches Col de Poutran and L'Alpe-d'Huez basin and, beyond, a high plateau dotted with glacial lakes. From Lac Besson, the most picturesque of these lakes, it is possible to climb on foot up to a ridge which reveals **Lac Noir** below in wild surroundings. A path (30min there and back) goes round the lake, offering more impressive views.

ANNECY★★★

CONURBATION 136 815
MICHELIN MAP 328 J5
LOCAL MAPS SEE LAC D'ANNECY AND MASSIF DES ARAVIS

Annecy lies on the shores of the Lac d'Annecy, water and mountains blending admirably to form one of the most remarkable landscapes in the French Alps, equally unforgettable in summer and winter: there is a fine overall view from the height crowned by the castle and overlooking the town. If the shores of the lake, the River Thiou and the Vassé canal have earned it the nickname of "the Venice of Savoie," the colourful streets of Old Annecy have a Piedmontese air, a charming combination which perhaps explains why the Annéciens seem to understand the art of living well. *Centre Bonlieu, 1 rue J.-Jaurès – 74000 Annecy Mid-May to mid-Sept: daily 9am-6.30pm, Jan to Mar and mid-Oct to Dec: daily except Sun 9am-12.30, 13.45-6pm closed 1 May, 1 Nov, 11 Nov, 25 Dec, 1 Jan - ☎ 04 50 45 00 33 - www.annecytourisme.com and www.lac-annecy.com. Guided tours of the town (2hrs) 5.30€, children under 12 years no charge – Contact the tourist office.*

▸ **Orient Yourself:** Chambéry is 50km/31.25mi to the southwest, and Geneva 61km/38mi to the north.

🅿 **Parking:** There are 8 parking lots in the town centre, where it is pointless to try to drive. The Bonlieu lot, centrally located, is often full. Try the lot at the train station, which is near pedestrian streets.

👁 **Don't Miss:** Be sure to see the Palais de l'Ile, the Château-Musée, and take a lake tour for splendid views and wonderful air.

🕐 **Organizing Your Time:** You should try to spend a morning in the old city, while markets are open; the afternoon and evening can be spent around the lake.

Especially for Kids: Take children to the Observatory, an ecological exhibit at the Château-Musée; to the beach at Albigny; and to see La Turbine, the science centre at Cran Gevrier.

👍 **Also See:** Nearby sights: L'ALBANAIS, ALBERTVILLE, AIX-LES-BAINS, Lac d'ANNECY, Massif des ARAVIS, Les BAUGES, Lac du BOURGET, CHAMBÉRY, La CLUSAZ, La ROCHE-SUR-FORON, THORENS-GLIÈRES

A Bit of History

Beginnings – The site was occupied as far back as prehistoric times (a lake settlement stood where the harbour is now situated). The town, which owes its name to a Roman villa, Villa Aniciaca, developed round its castle from the 12C onwards under the name of Annecy-le-Neuf, to distinguish it from the neighbouring Gallo-Roman city of Annecy-le-Vieux. It gained importance in the 16C when it replaced Geneva as the regional capital.

Humanist and spiritual father – The outstanding religious and literary figure of Annecy is **François de Sales** (1567-1622). Born in the nearby Château de Sales (*see THORENS-GLIÈRES*), he studied law before being ordained in Annecy at the age of 26. His reputation as a gifted preacher and a vigorous denouncer of Calvinism soon spread all over France; de Sales was created bishop of Geneva but could not hope to hold sway in the heartland of the Reformation and based himelf in Annecy. In 1608, François de Sales published his *Introduction à la vie dévote* (Introduction to a Life of Piety). His belief that man could live a pious life without withdrawing from the secular world met with such success that forty editions were sold in the author's lifetime. Having perceived the usefulness of a congregation devoted to the poor

Address Book

For coin categories, see the Legend on the cover flap.

EATING OUT

Auberge la Ferme des Ferrières – *800 rte des Burnets - 74370 Ferrières - 7km/4.4mi NW of Annecy by N 201 and D172, towards Burnets - ☎04 50 22 04 00 - letondal.m@numero.fr - closed Wed in summer; Mon-Thur in winter.* All the ingredients come from the family farm: pigeons, chickens, ducks, rabbits, fruits and vegetables. On offer are also cheese-based Savoyard specialties. Rustic dining room, terrace with view.

Le Fréti – *12 r. Ste-Claire - ☎ 04 50 51 29 52 - www.le-freti.com - closed for lunch except Sun.* This establishment at the heart of the old town is above the arcades and the family-run cheese-making business, from which issue mouth-watering specialities and the scent of raclettes, fondues and tartiflettes to tempt food-lovers. Simple decor. Summer terrace.

Le Bilboquet – *14 fg Ste-Claire – ☎04 50 45 21 68 - closed 1-15 July, Sun except evenings in July-Aug, and Mon.* This address in the "Venise savoyarde" has an intriguingly angled façade. The interior, welcoming and quiet, has stone walls. A cuisine based on the season and the market.

Brasserie St-Maurice – *7 r. Collège-Chapuisien - ☎ 04 50 51 24 49 - www.stmau.com - closed Sun and Mon.* This house dates from 1675 and now houses a restaurant. Practically as soon as the sun has risen, regulars and tourists settle themselves on the terrace. The dining room is on the first floor and features stone and wood-panelled decor. Cuisine is contemporary with Provençal overtones.

Auberge de Savoie – *1 pl. St-François-de-Sales - ☎ 04 50 45 03 05 - closed 18 Apr-3 Mar, 28 Aug-5 Sept, 24 Oct-1 Nov, Tue except in July-Aug and Wed.* The windows of this inn overlook a charming paved square opposite the Palais de l'Isle. The sophistication of the contemporary decor in the old inn building is complemented by a menu specialising in fish and seafood.

L'Atelier Gourmand – *2 r. St-Maurice - ☎ 04 50 51 19 71 - closed 6-14 Jan, Sun evening, Tue lunch and Mon.* Visitors here can feast their eyes as well as their palate. The owner, a painter in his day, puts up an impressive performance as chef, producing mouth-watering French cuisine. The tastefully decorated dining room is hung with Italian inspired paintings.

WHERE TO STAY

Chambre d'hôte Au Gîte Savoisien – *98 rte de Corbier - 74650 Chavanod - 6km/4mi SE of Annecy on D 16 towards Rumilly, village du Corbier - ☎ 04 50 69 02 95 - www.gite-savoisien.com - ⌷ - reservation required - 4rms - ⌷restaurant.* This old farm on the slopes above Annecy in the heart of a small village offers simple and comfortable rooms, three of them air-conditioned. In summer, guests can relax in the garden with a view of the mountains, or play a game of pétanque. A gîte is also available.

Hôtel Kyriad Centre – *1 fg des Balmettes - ☎ 04 50 45 04 12 - www.annecy-hotel-kyriad.com - 24rms.* This modern hotel at the entrance to the pedestrian district occupies a 16C building. The rooms, decorated in blue and yellow, are pleasant. Good service. Public parking nearby.

Hôtel Les Terrasses – *15 r. L.-Chaumontel - ☎ 04 50 57 08 98 - www.hotel-les-terraces-annecy.com - ⌷ - ⌷restaurant.* This new hotel is located in a quiet district near the train station. Bright rooms furnished in pale wood. The restaurant offers a single menu which is changed every day. On fine days, patrons can eat on the terrace in the sun and relax in the garden. Prices are very reasonable out of season.

Chambre d'hôte Le Jardin du Château – *1 pl du Château - ☎ 04 50 45 72 28 - jardinduchateau@wanadoo.fr - ⌷ - 8rms.* This friendly address is well-located in the heart of the old city. All the rooms have a kitchenette and several have balconies. Terrace with a view of Annecy, pretty garden, small snackbar.

ON THE TOWN

Au Fidèle Berger– *2 r. Royale -☎ 04 50 45 00 32 - Daily except Sun and Mon 9.15am-7pm, closed 2 wks in Nov and puvblic holidays*. This comfortable *salon de thé* attracts a chic clientele to sample its home-baked pastries and sip cups of tea or coffee. The display window attracts the public with its tantalising chocolate fountain.

BHV (Brasserie de l'Hôtel de Ville) – *pl de l'Hôtel-de-Ville - ☎ 04 50 45 00 81 - daily 11am-2am*. This popular address is on the edge of the old town opposite the landing stage. Local residents and tourists compete for seats on the terrace, while night owls jostle shoulders during the lively evening events held at the end of the week.

Café des Arts – *4 passage de l'Isle - ☎ 04 50 51 56 40 - summer: daily 10am-2am; rest of year: 10am-1am, closed Sun evening from Oct to Apr*. This café with its slightly retro charm is located in the courtyard of the former prison, providing an oasis of calm at the heart of the old town. There are cartoon strips available to read, exhibits and a pleasant terrace in summer.

L'Auberge du Lac – *Le port - 74290 Veyrier-du-Lac - ☎ 04 50 60 10 15 - www. bord-du-lac.com - daily from 8am - closed Nov-Feb*. This well-named watering hole boasts a magnificent terrace at the water's edge, opposite a stunning backdrop. Pontoon boat.

SHOPPING

Several shops, particularly in the rues Ste-Claire and Royale sell evocatively named sweets such as the "Roseau du Lac" (the lake reed), a coffee-filled chocolate; the "Cloche d'Annecy" (the bell of Annecy) and the "Savoyarde", chocolate filled with nuts. For other food specialties, simply wander the streets of the old city. On the rue Ste-Claire, stop at **Le Freti**, No. 12, for local cheese.

Market – Tuesday, Friday and Sunday morning, the rue de la République and the rue Ste-Claire fill with colourful stalls. Producers sell their best cheese on Tuesday. The Sunday market is considered one of the finest in France.

La Fermette – *8 r. Pont-Morens, vielle-ville - ☎04 50 45 01 62 - 9am-7pm -closed Mon-Wed in Jan and Nov*. Charming boutique for all sorts of regional products: honey, preserves, candies, wines, génépri, charcuterie, cheese, crafts, etc. Try hot cheese sandwiches made of, for example, reblochon or raclette cheese.

Meyer le Chocolatier d'Annecy – *4 pl St-François -☎04 50 45 12 08 -daily except Sun and Mon 9am-12.30pm, 2-7pm* People make special trips from all over the Savoie to taste the celebrated chocolates filled with coffee, nuts, liqueurs...

SPORT

Bathing in the lake – There are 3 excellent, supervised beaches with clear, clean water at a temperature that becomes quite bearable in summer. The **Plage des Marquisats** is near the city centre, and you can recline on the grass. The **Plage de l'Impérial**, near the celebrated hotel, charges a fee in summer. The **Plage d'Albigny** is on Annecy-le-Vieux.

LOCAL FESTIVALS

Festival international du film d'animation – ☎ *04 50 10 09 00 - www. annecy.org*. This well-known festival, held in June, brings animated films from around the world for a competition lasting a week.

Fête du Lac – Held on the first Saturday of August. The lake is lit up with an enormous fireworks display.

Venetian carnaval – *End of Feb, early Mar*. Masks, extravagant costumes: during two days the old city of Annecy rivals Venice in gaiety.

and the sick, he met Jeanne de Chantal, the ancestor of Madame de Sévigné, who later founded the first Convent of the Visitation of the Virgin. François de Sales was canonised in 1665 and **Jeanne de Chantal** in 1767. Their relics are kept in the basilica of the Visitation.

Jean-Jacques the proselyte (1728) – At the age of 16, **Jean-Jacques Rousseau,** ill-treated by his employer, fled from his home town, Geneva, to Annecy; there he was dazzled and disarmed by **Madame de Warens,** who had been asked to convert him to Catholicism. Her task was easy for he was 'sure that a religion preached by such a missionary could not fail to lead him to Paradise'. Readers of the *Confessions* can see the place where they first met in the Ancien Palais Épiscopal.

Les Bords du Lac★★ *2hr*

Leave the car in the car park of Centre Bonlieu or on place de l'Hôtel-de-ville. From Quai Eustache-Chappuis on the Canal du Vassé or place de la Libération head towards avenue d'Albigny.

Centre Bonlieu
This cultural centre, designed in 1981 by Maurice Novarina and Jacques Lévy, houses the Maison du Tourisme, the library, the theatre and several shops.

Avenue d'Albigny
This royal avenue, lined with hundred-year-old plane trees, crosses the common where the townspeople used to watch important events, such as military maneuvres. The concrete and glass law courts (1978), designed by Maurice Novarina, stand to the left. The enormous **Préfecture** building, constructed after the Savoie region was annexed to France (1860), is in neo-Louis XIII style.

▶ *Walk across the Champ de Mars to the viewing table by the lake.*

There is an extensive **view**★ of the Grand Lac framed by mountains, with Mont Veyrier and the Crêt du Maure in the foreground.

Parc de l'Impérial
Follow ② on the map. Shaded by beautiful trees, this pleasant park (2ha/ 5 acres) at the east end of Avenue d'Abigny takes its name from a former luxury hotel, now the conference centre and a casino. The park includes a beach and the largest sports centre on the lake as well as an aviary.

▶ *Return to the town along the lake shore.*

Pont des Amours
The bridge spans the Canal du Vassé, offering lovely views of the shaded canal one way, dotted with small crafts, and of the wooded Île des Cygnes the other way.

Jardins de l'Europe★
These gardens, which used to form an island, were joined to the town and laid out as an arboretum with a variety of species from Europe, America and Asia including several huge **sequoias** and a ginkgo biloba, also called "maidenhair tree." From the harbour along the Thiou there are interesting views of the massive castle.

▶ *Walk to place de l'Hôtel-de-ville and continue on foot through Old Annecy.*

Old Annecy★★ *1hr 30min –* 🕐 *see plan*

The old part of town has been largely pedestrianised and renovated during the last few decades. Note the arcaded houses and Italian-style wells. A colourful market *(wide choice of regional cheeses)*, held on Tuesday, Friday and Sunday mornings, brings life to rue de la République and rue Ste-Claire.

▶ *Start from place de l'Hôtel-de-ville and walk across quai E.-Chappuis.*

Église St-Maurice

The church was built in the 15C with a large overhanging roof in typical regional style. Inside, the vast Gothic nave, traditional in churches with a Dominican connection, is flanked with side chapels built by aristocratic families or guilds, whose arms and emblems are displayed. The town's tailors, for example, marked their chapel, the second on the right, with a pair of scissors. Note in particular a 16C fresco of the Assumption near the pulpit and, in the chancel, a fine **Deposition**★ by Pieter Pourbus the Elder and a remarkable **mural painting** in *grisaille* dating from 1458.

▶ *Walk towards the river past the Église St-François.*

Église St-François de Sales

St François de Sales and St Jeanne de Chantal were originally buried in this Baroque-fronted 17C church which once belonged to the order they founded; grilles in the transepts still mark the places where they were originally laid to rest. The Église St-François is now the parish church of the Italian community.

▶ *Cross the bridge over the River Thiou, which is the natural outlet of the lake.*

The old town

Pont sur le Thiou

The picturesque **Palais de l'Isle**★★ standing in the middle of the river offers the most famous **view**★★ of Old Annecy.

▶ *Continue along rue Perrière.*

Rue Perrière

The houses are built over a row of arcades.

▶ *Turn right, then right again and cross the Thiou once more.*

From the bridge, enjoy a lovely view of the houses lining the river bank. The entrance of the Palais de l'Isle is on the right.

Palais de l'Isle★★

🕐 *Same hours as the Château-Musée. 3.20€, combined ticket 6€. No charge first Sun of month, Oct to May -* ☎ *04 50 33 87 30.*

This monument has become a local emblem. Built on an island in the 12C, when Annecy was little more than a market town, the palace was used in turn as the Count of Geneva's residence, the mint, the law courts and a fearsome prison, which

ANNECY						
			Jean-Jacques-Rousseau R.	DY 55	République R.	DY 83
Chambéry Av. de	DY	23	Lac R. du	EY 57	Royale R.	DY 85
Chappuis Q. Eustache	EY	26	Libération Pl. de la	EY 61	Ste-Claire Fg et R.	DY 91
Filaterie R.	EY	43	Pâquier R. du	EY 71	St-François-de-Sales R.	DY 89
Grenette R.	EY	51	Perrière R.	EY 75	St-François-de-Sales Pl.	EY 87
Hôtel-de-Ville Pl. de l'	EY	53	Pont-Morens R. du	EY 76	Tour-la-Reine Ch.	EY 95
			Poste R. de la	DY 78		

Église St-Maurice	EY	E	Palais de l'Île (Musée de		Pont sur le Thiou	EY N
Maison Lambert	EY	F	l'histoire d'Annecy)	EY M²	Théâtre	EY T

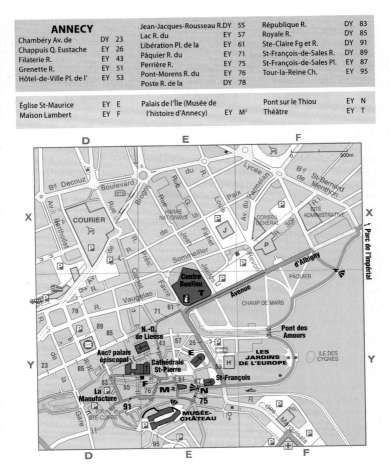

it remained until 1870, resuming that grim role for a time during the Second World War.

It now houses a centre for urban architecture and the **Musée de l'Histoire d'Annecy,** illustrating the town's prestigious past and the history of Savoie; the courtroom, jailers' quarters, prison cells and former chapel are open to visitors.

▷ *Turn left along quai de l'Isle, cross the Pont Morens and turn right.*

Rue Ste-Claire ★
The high street of Old Annecy is lined with arcaded houses. The 16C mansion at **no 18** has a particular link to the bishopric of St François de Sales. Thirty years before Richelieu's Académie Française was inaugurated, de Sales became the co-founder of the Académie Florimontane, a literary institution intended to promote the public good, influence opinion and spread the cult of beauty. The society still meets to this day.

On the corner of rue de la République stands a former convent of St Clare which became known as the **"Manufacture"** when it was turned into a spinning mill in 1805. The whole area has been tastefully renovated and pedestrianised; the lively placette Ste-Claire and place Volland contrast with the peaceful quai des Clarisses.

▷ *Turn back at the Porte Ste-Claire and walk along rue de la République to rue Jean-Jacques-Rousseau.*

Ancien palais épiscopal
It was built in 1784, on the site of Madame de Warens' house; a bust of Rousseau stands in the courtyard. St François de Sales wrote his famous *Introduction à la vie dévote* (Introduction to a Life of Piety) in the 16C **Maison Lambert,** at no 15 rue Jean-Jacques-Rousseau.

Cathédrale St-Pierre
Built in the 16C with a Renaissance façade and a Gothic interior, it became the episcopal seat of Bishop François de Sales when he was evicted from Geneva by the Calvinists; however, it was raised officially to a cathedral only in 1822. Jean-Jacques Rousseau sang in the choir and played the flute in the cathedral. The organ is splendid and free concerts are offered in summer (🕐 *July to Aug: 6.30pm Wed*)

▷ *Turn left onto rue Filaterie lined with imposing arcades.*

Revival of the Ecosystem of the Lac d'Annecy

In spite of the many mountain streams which flow into it, the fairly shallow lake (30-45m/98-148ft deep) had lost most of its bird population by the end of the 1960s as pollution from hotels along the shores and from motor boats had upset its fragile ecosystem. The local municipalities clubbed together to build an impressive network of underwater drainpipes leading to an ultra-modern filtering plant.

This action, combined with collective awareness of the dangers of pollution, led to the lake waters becoming pure again. Char and trout have come back and swans are nesting in the reeds once more.

The **Réserve naturelle du Bout-du-Lac,** situated at the western end of the lake, shelters reptiles, ducks, swans and beavers.

Continuing past the Église Notre-Dame-de-Liesse with its tower which leans slightly, one reaches rue du Pâquier, also lined with arcades; the 17C Hôtel de Sales, decorated with sculptures illustrating the Seasons, is at no 12.

▶ *Turn right onto quai E.-Chappuis to return to place de l'Hôtel-de-ville.*

Musée-Château d'Annecy★

🕐 *June to Sept: daily 10.30am to 6pm; Oct to May: daily except Tue 10am-noon, 2-5pm.* 🕐 *closed public holidays. 4.70€, children under 12 years no charge; no charge first Sun of month, Nov to May -* ☎ *04 50 33 87 30.*

▶ *Access by car via chemin de la Tour la Reine, or on foot, up the castle ramp or the steep hill starting to rise from rue Ste-Claire.*

This handsomely restored former residence of the lords of Geneva, from a junior branch of the House of Savoie, dates from the 12C to the 16C. The castle was damaged by fire several times, abandoned in the 17C then used as a garrison before being restored with the help of public funds. There is a fine view of the clustered roofs of the old town and its four church steeples and, beyond them, the modern town.

To the right of the entrance stands the massive 12C Tour de la Reine, with 4m/13ft-thick walls; this is the oldest part of the castle. From the centre of the courtyard, one faces the austere living quarters of the Logis Vieux (14C-15C), with its stair turret and deep well; to the left is the early Renaissance façade of the Logis Nemours (16C) and to the right the late-16C **Logis Neuf,** which housed the garrison of the castle. At the end of the courtyard are the recently restored 15C Logis and **Tour Perrière,** which house the Kids**Observatoire régional des lacs alpins** (As for Château-Musée. Combined ticket)**,** illustrating the various aspects of mountain lakes including the effects of pollution on the fauna and displaying archaeological finds. In the **Salle des fresques,** on the top level, fragments of 15C murals give a good idea of what the medieval castle was like.

From the terrace, there is a good overall view of Old Annecy and of the modern town beyond.

The Logis Vieux and the Logis Nemours house an interesting **museum of regional art** on three floors linked by a spiral staircase. Note the remarkable fireplaces facing each other in the vast kitchen, the splendid guardroom with its rows of columns and the great hall. There are collections of contemporary art, carved glass and popular art including pottery, earthenware, glassware and furniture.

Additional Sights

Conservatoire d'Art et d'Histoire de la Haute-Savoie

🕐 *July to Sept: daily except Sun 10.30am-6pm* 🕐 *closed public holidays. No charge.* ☎ *04 50 51 02 33.*

This art and history museum, situated just south of the castle, is housed in a fine 17C building in Sardinian style. The collections include numerous paintings and engravings depicting landscapes of Haute-Savoie, as well as 18C and 19C paintings.

In the chapel, the Cité de l'image en mouvement (CITIA) has an **exhibit of animated films**; for more than 20 years, Annecy has hosted an annual festival of animation. 🕐 *June to Sept: daily 10.30am-6pm; Apr to May and Oct to Dec: weekdays, Sat and 1st Sun of month 10am-noon, 2-7pm* 🕐 *closed Tue and public holidays.*

Basilique de la Visitation

 🕐 *Daily 8am–noon, 2-6pm (July to Aug: 5pm); guided tours by appointment.* ☎ 04 50 45 22 76.

The church of the Couvent de la Visitation stands on the slopes of Crêt du Maure, affording a vast open vista of Annecy and the western Préalpes. The richly decorated interior of the 1930 building with its sturdy grey-marble pillars attracts many pilgrims, particularly for the feast-day of St François on 24 January and in August. The relics of St François de Sales and St Jeanne de Chantal are displayed at the end of the aisles; the stained-glass windows illustrate the life of the patron saints of Annecy as does the small **museum** adjoining the church on the right. The church has a peal of 37 bells.

La Turbine

SW of Annecy - place Chorus, Cran Gevrier   🕐 Kids *Daily 2-6pm, closed Mon.* ☎ 04 50 08 17 00 - www.laturbine-crangevrier.com.

This is an educational centre for scientific, technical and industrial subjects relevent to the Haute-Savoie, aimed at the general public, with workshops for children.

Lake cruises★★★

🕐 *Apr to Oct: several types of boat trips with commentaries (1hr). 10.80€. May to mid Sept: boat trips among ports (2hrs). 13.30€. Lunch trips and dinner-dances on board the MS Libellule, enquire for times and reservations: Compagnie des Bateaux du Lac d'Annecy -* ☎ *04 50 51 08 40 - www.annecy-croisieres.com.*

The **Compagnie des bateaux d'Annecy** organises lake tours, leaving from the pier on the Thiou with stops in Veyrier, Menthon, Duingt, St-Jorioz and Sévrier. The *Libellule,* a panoramic boat with a capacity of 600 passengers, offers lunch-cruise and dinner-show combinations. Contact also **Bateaux Dupraz**, with launches leaving from the quai Napoléon III - ☎04 50 52 42 99 - www.bateauxdupraz.com, or **Vedettes Toe**, from the Pont des Amours - ☎04 50 52 42 99.

Excursion

Gorges du Fier and Château de Montrottier★

20km/12.4mi – about 2hr 30min.

▶ *Leave Annecy by N 508; 3km further on, beyond the motorway underpass, turn left on D 14. Turn left again past the Église de Lovagny along D 64 and drive down a steep hill.*

Gorges du Fier★★

🕐*Mid-June to mid-Sept: 9.15am-5pm; mid-Mar to mid-June and mid-Sept to mid-Oct: 9.15-6pm, last visit 40min before closing. 4.90€, children 7-15 years 2.60€ -* ☎ *04 50 46 23 07 - www.gorgedufier.com.*

Visitors can walk along galleries clinging to the sheer walls of the gorge; sunlight plays through the foliage which forms an arched roof over the narrow defile. Beyond the exit and a cluster of beeches, there is a belvedere on a rocky promontory which affords a good view of the

The Gorges du Fier

G. Sommer/EXPLORER

"Mer de Rochers" (sea of rocks), an impressive heap of boulders piled on top of one another.

▷ *Drive back to the D 116 junction and turn left then right up the path leading to the Château de Montrottier.*

Château de Montrottier★

🕐 *Guided tour (1hr15min) June to Aug: 2-7pm; mid-Mar to May and Sept to mid Oct: daily except Tue 2-6pm (last visit 1hr before closing). 7€, children 7-15 years 4.50€ - ☎ 04 50 46 23 02 - www.chateaudemontrottier.com*

The castle stands on an isolated mound between the Fier and its former bed, known as the "Grande Fosse." Built between the 13C and the 16C, it is a fine specimen of Savoyard military architecture; a 36m/118ft-tall round keep towers over it. The castle houses important **collections**★ bequeathed in 1916 by the former owner to the Académie Florimontane: weaponry, earthenware, porcelain, ceramics, ivory from the Far East, antique furniture, statuettes and four 16C bronze reliefs by Peter and Hans Vischer of Nuremberg.

In fine weather, it is worth climbing the 86 steps up to the crenellated walk at the top of the castle; a panoramic view of nearby peaks stretches away to Mont Blanc in the distance.

▷ *Go back to D 116 and turn right towards Corbier.*

The road runs along the cliff for a short while then rapidly leads down to the river and crosses it. After a steep climb through a small wood, one is rewarded by a magnificent view of the castle and the valley below.

▷ *In Corbier, take D 16 to the left towards Annecy.*

Les Ponts de la Caille

4km/2.5mi south of Cruseilles. From Annecy, take the N 201 towards Cruseilles.
The two very different bridges spanning side by side the gorge of the Usses, 150m/492ft above the river bed, form a fascinating **picture**★, much admired in Savoie.

Pont Charles-Albert

This suspension bridge, commissioned in 1838 by Charles-Albert de Sardaigne, is now used only for foot traffic. (*Do not attempt if you fear heights.*)

Pont moderne

The "new" bridge, inaugurated in 1928, consists of a single arch with a 138m/453ft span, one of the largest non-reinforced concrete arches of its kind.

LAC D'ANNECY★★★

MICHELIN MAP 89 FOLD 14 OR 244 FOLDS 18 AND 19 – LOCAL MAP OPPOSITE

The Lac d'Annecy is the jewel of the Savoie region. The snow-capped peaks of the Tournette (2 351m/7 713ft), the pointed needles of the Dents de Lanfon or the elegant curves of the Montagne d'Entrevernes towering above its deep blue waters form one of the most attractive Alpine landscapes, discovered barely 100 years ago by artists and writers. A tour of the lake by boat or car enables one to appreciate the full beauty of this impressive lake setting. *Rte d'Albertville - 74320 Sévrier - July to Aug: Mon-Sat 9.30am- 12.30pm, 2.30-6.30pm; rest of year, telephone for information - ☎04 50 52 40 56 - www.visit-lacannecy.fr.*

▶ **Orient Yourself:** Some 15km/9.4mi long and girded by a road that hugs the shore and offers many opportunities to stop and gaze, the Lac d'Annecy is smaller than the Lac du Bourget. The lake view opens slowly if you come from Albertville on N 508 through Faverges. There are more spectacular views from the Col de Bluffy (D 909) to the SE and the Col de Leschaux (N 912) to the south.

☺ **Don't Miss:** The view from the Col de la Forclaz is worth the climb up.

🕐 **Organizing Your Time:** Make time around mid-day to pause at one of the many beaches around the lake, where the water is extraordinarily clear.

Kids Especially for Kids: The musée de la Cloche at Sevrier, nature observation at the Réserve du Bout-du-Lac, and the animal park at Semnoz will delight children.

⏱ **Also See:** Nearby sights: L'ALBANAIS, ALBERTVILLE, AIX-LES-BAINS, ANNECY, Massif des ARAVIS, Les BAUGES, Lac du BOURGET, CHAMBÉRY, La CLUSAZ, La ROCHE-SUR-FORON, THORENS-GLIÈRES

A Bit of History

The lake – The picturesque vistas afforded by the lake are largely due to its twisting contours. The Lac d'Annecy consists of two depressions originally separated at the straits overlooked by Duingt Castle. Smaller (2 800ha/6 919 acres) and less deep (40m/131ft on average) than the Lac du Bourget, it is fed by several streams and a powerful underwater spring, the **Boubioz,** located 250m offshore from La Puya. The main outlet of the lake is the Thiou which flows through old Annecy and into the Fier.

The steep wooded slopes of the Petit Lac in the south offer a more austere aspect than the more accessible shores of the Grand Lac in the north, dotted with villages and hamlets surrounded by clusters of trees; in former times, vineyards flourished here. A state-of-the-art purification plant near Annecy ensures pure water for fish and swans. Pollan (a kind of whitefish) is often found on local menus, but gourmets prefer arctic char, trout, perch and carp.

Excursions

☐1 The West Shore from Annecy to Faverges★★
38km/23.6mi – about 1hr 30min – ⏱ see local map

This itinerary, which runs in an almost straight line from Annecy to Faverges, makes a delightful **day trip★★**. The drive along the shore and through the Parc régional des Bauges from Sévrier to Faverges offers lovely views of the lake, of the heights of the Tournette and of the jagged peaks of the Dents de Lanfon. A cycle track runs above, along part of the same route, between Letraz and Chaparon.

▶ *Leave Annecy by N 508, ③ on the town plan.*

The road skirts the promontory of La Puya, offering good views of Mont Veyrier in the foreground and the Parmelan, Tournette and Dents de Lanfon beyond.

Sévrier

This resort, protected by the wooded slopes of the Semnoz, consists of hamlets lying on the very edge of the lake, overlooked by a church remarkably situated on a promontory. There is a lovely old priory whose gardens are open to the public.

Écomusée du Costume savoyard

Opposite the church 🚳🕐 *mid-June to mid-Sept: weekdays 10am–noon, Sun and public holidays 2.30–6.30pm; May to mid-June and last 2 weeks of Sept: daily except Sat 2–6pm* 🕐 *closed Oct–Apr. 3.70€ - ☎04 50 52 41 05 - www.echo-de-nos-montagnes.com.*
Housed in a former girls school, this is a lovingly assembled exhibit of costumes, lace, embroidery and shawls as well as object of daily use from the 19C, and a collection of Savoie crosses whose design is unique to each village.

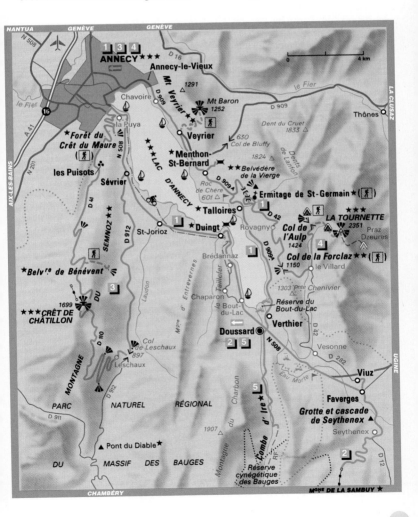

Address Book

For coin categories, see the Legend on the cover flap.
🕯 *See also the Address Book for Annecy*

EATING OUT

🍽🍽**Le Poisson Rouge**– *20 prom des Seines, les Avollions - 74320 Sévrier - along the lake, toward Albertville - ☎04 50 52 40 48 - closed Jan and Feb.* On the shores of the lake, a restaurant accessible on foot, on roller-blades (along the bicycle path), by boat (private pontoon), or by car- 🅿 The shaded terrace has a great view of the Dents de Lanfon. A popular place.

🍽🍽**Restaurant l'Arpège** – *823 rte d'Albertville - 74320 Sévrier - A 41 exit Annecy-Sud, towards the lake - ☎ 04 50 19 07 35 - www.hotel-de-chuguet. com -* 🍽🍽*hotel 25rms -* Seen from the outside, this place appears boring, but inside it's anything but. Panoramic view of the lake, spacious terrace, daily menu created by the chef. Don't pass up a good thing!

🍽🍽**Bistrot du Port** – *At the port - 74320 Sévrier - ☎ 04 50 52 45 00 - www. bistrot-du-port.com - closed end of Nov to 15 Feb, Tue-Wed in Oct-Nov and Mon.* A special holiday feeling imbues this pleasant restaurant decorated with a nautical theme. Sit in the heated veranda in winter or on the terrace in summer to admire the view while enjoying lake fish and grilled meats.

🍽🍽🍽**Au Gay Séjour** – *74210 Faverges - ☎ 04 50 44 52 52 - www.hotel-gay-sejour.com - closed 14 July-31 Aug, Sun evening and Mon, except public holidays.* This family chalet offers the chance of an enjoyable and peaceful break. Decor and facilities are simple, very well kept and clean. Local cooking is served in a small neat dining room with a pleasant view from the windows. Warm welcome guaranteed.

🍽🍽🍽**Chappet** – *1850 rte d'Annecy, Bout-du-Lac - 74210 Doussard - ☎04 50 44 30 19 - www.hotel-chappet.com - open Mar-Sept, closed Thur evening, Sun evening, and Mon, except July-Aug.* Honest local cuisine featuring lake fish served on a shaded terrace in summer and in an elegant and spacious dining room the rest of the year. If you wish to stay a bit longer, there are also comfortable guestrooms upstairs.

WHERE TO STAY

🍽**Hôtel le clos Marcel** – *Allée de la Plage - 74410 Duingt - ☎04 50 68 67 47 - www.closmarcel.com - closed 28 Sept-27 Apr - 15rms -* 🍽*restaurant.* All the rooms face the water with a view of the mountains opposite. Peaceful garden on the lake. Private pontoon boat. Dining room with a panoramic view and a terrace overlooking the lake.

🍽**Hôtel Residel** – *20 chemin des Aires - 74320 Sévrier - ☎04 50 52 67 50 - www. hotel-residel-annecy.com -* 🅿*-21rms.* These two chalet-style buildings, located near N 508, have undergone extensive renovation. All the rooms have a terrace or a balcony and face the lake. Studios and apartments all have kitchenettes. Warm welcome.

🍽**Chambre d'hôte Le Corti** – *30 imp. des Hirondelles – near the town hall - 74210 Doussard - ☎ 04 50 44 34 76 - closed Oct-Jan -* 🍴 *- 3rms.* Having walked round the lake or gone on a mountain ramble, guests here will be delighted to rest in the peace and quiet of one of the small rooms with sloping ceilings in this country house or in the gîte. There is one small snag: the bathrooms are on the landing. The garden has a small vegetable patch.

🍽🍽**Hôtel Beauregard** – *691 rte d'Albertville - 74320 Sévrier - ☎04 50 52 40 59 - www.hotel-beauregard. com - closed 17 Nov-15 Jan -* 🅿 *-45rms -* 🍽*restaurant.* An imposing residence

The view from Col de la Forclaz

A. de Valroger/MICHELIN

where the rooms, functional and clean, face either the lake or the road. Family-style accomodation in the new wing. Restaurant with a rotunda offers a view of the lake. Traditional cuisine.

◯◯**Hôtel La Châtaigneraie** – *74210 Lathuile - 4km/2.5mi S of Duingt on N 508 then secondary road towards Lathuile - ☎ 04 50 44 30 67 - www.hotelchataigne-raie.com - open 15 Apr-15 Oct, closed Sun evening and Mon except May-Sept. -* P *- 25rms -* ◯◯*restaurant.* Ideal for taking the air at the foot of the mountains. A swimming pool, tennis court and shaded garden. Tidy, well-equipped rooms. The cuisine features local produce and is served on the terrace in summer months. Attentive service.

◯◯**Gîte de Pontgibaud** – *255 Rte de Saury - 74210 Lathuile - ☎04 50 32 96 76 - www.gite-camping-annecy.com - closed 1st 2 weeks Nov - 5rms -* ◯◯*restaurant.* This large farm offers a remarkable view over the lake, which the rooms overlook. There are also duplex apartments ideal for families. The terrace, surrounded by greenery, invites relaxation after a meal.

SPORTS

Nearly all the lake's beaches have water-sports facilities for sailing, canoe-kayaking, scuba diving and waterskiing.

Musée de la Cloche★

N 508, on the way out of Sévrier. Kids ♿ ⏲ *July to Aug: daily 10am-12.30pm, 2-6.30pm; May, June and Sept: 10am-noon, 2.30-5.30, Sun and public holidays 2.30-5.30pm; Oct to Apr: daily except Sun 10am-noon, 2.30-5.30pm, Sun and public holidays 2.40-5.30pm* ⏲ *closed 25 Dec and 1 Jan. Last admission 1hr before closing. 4.90€, children 6-18 years 4€.* ⏲ *Visit to the metalworks from mid-Apr to mid Oct: afternoons on Fri, Sun and public holidays; daily in Aug. 2€ - ☎04 50 52 47 11 - www.paccard.fr*

This museum, the work of the **Paccard bell-foundry,** explains the manufacturing process and traces the history of this ancient craft through a collection of bells dating from the 14C to the 19C; other exhibits include tuning forks, which were of prime importance in the making of peals. The "Savoyarde" now in the Sacré-Cœur Basilica in Paris, the "Jeanne d'Arc" in Rouen Cathedral and the mighty 42t "World Peace Bell," cast for the millennium celebrations in Newport, Kentucky, were all made in Annecy.

Between Sévrier and Duingt the road turns away inland at **St-Joriaz**. Along the beach there is a path past the rushes, where there is a famous prehistoric (3 000BC) lake dwelling; some 700 pilings remain just under the water surface. The **Château de Duingt** is linked to the shore by a drawbridge.

Duingt★

Situated at the narrowest part of the lake which marks the separation between the Grand Lac and the Petit Lac, this pleasant summer resort has retained its rustic Savoyard character. The **castle** (⊶ *not open to the public*) has been keeping watch on the narrows from a tiny wooded island since the 11C. It was restored in the 17C and 19C and, like the Château d'Héré just south of Duingt, it once belonged to the De Sales family. Further on, the road skirts the steep and more austere shores of the Petit Lac.

Doussard

Kids ⏲ *Information at Réserve office at Le Grimpillon, Talloires: unacccompanied visits and guided tours July to Aug - ☎04 50 64 44 03 - www.asters.asso.fr.* The Réserve naturelle du Bout-du-Lac maintains a nature trail which leads into the rushes and a 15C tower from which you can observe birds and a beaver colony. The picturesque village of Doussard was often painted by 19C landscape artists.

▶ *At Doussard, follow the road leading through the Combe d'Ire for 6km/3.7mi.*

Combe d'Ire★

This deep wooded furrow overlooked by the Montagne de Charbon, through which runs a rushing stream, used to be one of the wildest and most mysterious Alpine valleys; the last bear was killed in 1893. It is now part of the **Réserve cynégétique des Bauges** (Les Bauges game reserve), rich in chamois, roe-deer, black grouse, rock-partridge, marmots and moufflons.

▷ *Rejoin N 508 and turn right to Faverges.*

The road goes through the marshy valley of the River Eau Morte, offering closer views of the Bauges Massif and the jagged crest of its highest peak, the Arcalod (2 217m/7 274ft).

Faverges

Situated at an important crossroads, between the Chaîne des Aravis and the Massif des Bauges, this large village is overlooked by the 13C round keep of its castle; traditional industries include prefabricated wooden chalets, machine tooling, household appliances and the well-known pens and cigarette lighters of Tissot-Dupont.

2 ROUTE DE LA FORCLAZ★★★

FROM FAVERGES TO ANNECY *40km/25mi – about 1hr 45min – see local map*

The road climbs up through the fine Alpine valley of Montmin, beneath the escarpments of the Tournette, to the Col de la Forclaz and its beautiful view of the lake.

Grottes and Cascade de Seythenex

2km/1.2mi south of Faverges then right; path signposted "Grottes de Seythenex." ⏱ *guided tours (40min) July to Aug: 9.30am-6pm; May to June and first 2 weeks of Sept: weekdays 10am-5.30pm. 2.90€, children 1.75€ - ☎ 04 50 44 55 97 - www.cascade.fr* Several footbridges lead to the top of the waterfall which drops 30m/98ft through a narrow crack into a picturesque wooded vale. It is possible to walk along the former underground river bed which testifies to the power of water erosion. An exhibit shows how craftsmen use water power in their workshops, sawmills and nut-oil mills.

▷ *Turn right at Seythenex and follow the road to Vargnoz.*

Montagne de la Sambuy★

The **Seythenex chair-lift** (⏱ *Mid-June to early Sept: 10am-5pm (every 20min); mid-Dec to Jan: 9am-4.30pm; Feb to Mar 9am-7pm. 5.40€ return - ☎04 50 44 44 45)* leads to the Favre refuge (alt 1 820m/5 971ft) affording a fine **view** of the Belledonne range to the south, the Aravis Massif and Lac d'Annecy to the north, the Mont-Blanc Massif to the northeast and the Vanoise glaciers to the southeast.

▷ *Return to Faverges and drive north along D 12.*

Viuz

This hamlet is within sight of the snow-capped summit of Mont Blanc. Next to the church and its 12C Romanesque apse, a small **Musée archéologique** (⏱ *July to Aug: daily 2.30-6.30pm; Sept to June: daily except Sat-Sun 2.30-6.30pm; guided tours (1hr) on request* ⏱ *Closed public holidays except 14 July and 15 Aug. 2.90€, children 1.75€ - ☎04 50 32 45 99 - www.viuz.sav.org)* houses a collection of Gallo-Roman objects found locally, including a remarkable cauldron of the 3C, an amber necklace and numerous Roman coins.

▷ *Continue on D 282 to Vesonne. The gradient reaches 13% on certain stretches; please drive with extra care and concentration.*

The climb from Vesonne to Montmin reveals panoramic views of the Massif des Bauges to the south, including some of its highest summits, the Belle Étoile, the Dent de Cons, Sambuy and Arcalod, and of the Tournette to the north.

Montmin

Set in pastoral surroundings, this attractive resort is the ideal starting point for mountain expeditions, such as the ascent of the Tournette.
From Le Villard, the road climbs to the Col de la Forclaz through pastures and picturesque hamlets.

Col de la Forclaz★★

Alt 1 150m/3 772ft. From the belvedere on the left there is a bird's-eye view of the Lac d'Annecy; note the shallow bank just off Duingt, occupied by lake-dwellings in prehistoric times, which casts a yellowish shadow on the deep blue waters of the lake.

▷ *Follow a path on the right, which goes up to a small café, known as La Pricaz, then turn left to reach the belvedere (15min there and back).*

Fine panoramic view of the summits of the Bauges Massif, rising to the peak of the Arcalod. If this spectacular view makes you want to take to the air, certified hang-gliding and deltaplaning instructors will take you on an unforgettable two-person flight. *For more information, contact the centre at Montmin - ☎ 04 50 02 99 62.*
The steep drop from the Col de la Forclaz to Rovagny reveals more beautiful views of the Bauges, the Semnoz, the curve of the Grand Lac and Annecy nestling on its shores.
Further on, the Ermitage de St-Germain overlooks a narrow wooded valley.

Ermitage de St-Germain★

From D 42, 15min there and back up a steep footpath starting on the left of the first tunnel (on the way down).
This is a centre of local pilgrimage, particularly on Whit (Pentecost) Monday; otherwise, the place is a charming and quiet retreat. According to tradition, St Germain, the first abbot of the Abbaye de Talloires, retired to a grotto in the small escarpment overlooking the road. The splendid **landscape** formed by the chapel and its ancient lime tree with Talloires Bay, the Duingt narrows and the Bauges mountain range in the background also attracted St François de Sales (see ANNECY), who planned to retire here.
There is a wider **panorama** of the Grand Lac and the surrounding mountains from the **Belvédère de la Vierge**★ (*15min there and back along a steep footpath skirting the cemetery).* Go back to the tunnel entrance and start walking along the second path on the left: the view of Talloires Bay is magnificent.

Talloires

One of the area's best-loved resorts, with a beach and water sports centre, Talloires lies in beautiful **surroundings**★★, with the harbour nestling inside a rounded bay, sheltered by the cliffs of the Roc de Chère opposite the wooded promontory of Duingt Castle.

▷ *Past the junction with the direct road to Annecy, D 909A, the Château de Menthon comes into view, higher up on the right.*

Fr. Isler/MICHELIN

Talloires

Menthon-St-Bernard★

This is a pleasant family resort on the shores of the Lac d'Annecy. The **Château de Menthon**★ *(2km/1.2mi climb by D 969 starting from the church –* ⏱ *Guided tour (1hr) July to Aug: noon-6pm; May to June and Sept: Fri, Sat-Sun and public holidays 2-6pm* ⏱ *closed Oct - Apr. 6.50€, chlldren 6-15 years 3.50€; costumed tours Sat-Sun and public holidays from May to Sept 7.50€, children 6-15 years 4.50€ -* ☏*04 50 60 12 05 - www.chateau-de-menthon.com)* was the birthplace of St Bernard de Menthon, who founded the Grand-St-Bernard hospice. The present 13C and 15C château, crowned with turrets, has the picture-perfect look of a fairytale castle. Don't miss the beautiful **view**★ of the lake from the terrace.

🚶The **Roc de Chère**★ *(2hr there and back on foot)*, a wooded promontory separating Menthon-St-Bernard and Talloires, shelters a **nature reserve** *(office of the Réserves naturelles, Le Grimpillon, Talloires* ☏*04 50 64 44 03 - www.asters-asso.fr)*covering 68ha/168 acres with interesting species of Mediterranean and Northern flora. The **view** extends across the Petit Lac to the Tournette and the Bauges mountain range, with Duingt Castle in the foreground.

Veyrier

There is a lovely view of the Grand Lac from the garden behind the town hall (opposite the church); the view stretches from south east to north east, from the glaciers of the Vanoise to the peaks of the Salève and Voirons.

Mont Veyrier★★

🚶*1km/0.6mi, then 5hr there and back on foot. Leave Veyrier by the Route du Mont Veyrier, turn left into the Route de la Combe. Leave the car at the end of the road and follow the Sentier du Col des Contrebandiers which leads to the summit of Mont Baron.* From the viewing table, there is a bird's-eye **view** of the Lac d'Annecy, framed by mountains on all sides. In fine weather, the view extends southeast to the glaciers of the Vanoise Massif and northeast as far as Lake Geneva.

From Chavoire onwards, the road widens, affording a good overall view of Annecy overlooked by the Basilique de la Visitation and the castle.

③ The Semnoz★★

ROUND TOUR FROM ANNECY *52km/32mi – about 2hr –* 🕐*see local map*
The Semnoz is a picturesque wooded ridge stretching from the Crêt du Maure, a
forested area ideal for walking, to the Crêt de Châtillon, its highest peak.

*The road leading to the summit can be blocked by snow from November to May, but it
is usually cleared by late spring.*

Annecy★★★ – 🕐*See ANNECY.*

▶ *D 41 from Annecy rises quickly towards the Crêt de Châtillon.*

Forêt du Crêt du Maure★
This vast wooded area, which is to a large extent the result of 19C reforestation,
is criss-crossed by footpaths leading to numerous belvederes.

▶ *From the Semnoz road, follow a path which starts at the second hairpin bend after
entering the forest, by a reservoir.*

The Chalet Super-Panorama offers one of the loveliest **views**★★ of the lake.
Kids A bit further on D 41, the pens of the **animal park of la Grande Jeanne** hold
marmots, deer and reindeer, to the delight of children.

Les Puisots
The old hamlet, burnt down in 1944 (memorial), was replaced by the chalets of a
centre aéré (outdoor centre) for children and a public park.
The road goes through the forest, offering a few glimpses of the Albanais depression.

▶ *Follow the forest road leading to the Belvédère de Bénévent. Leave the car in a bend
on the left and follow a footpath on the right.*

Belvédère de Bénévent★
View of the Tournette and the Duingt narrows. The peaks of Le Beaufortain are just
visible on the horizon between the Tournette and the Dent de Cons. At the cross-
country skiing area is an **alpine garden** you can tour (FRAPNA - ☎04 50 67 37 34)

▶ *Return to D 41.*

The landscape changes to stony pastures dotted with blue gentians in early summer. The climb becomes more pronounced and, after a right bend, a vast mountain
panorama opens out in front of your eyes.

Crêt de Châtillon★★★
*15min there and back on foot. Leave the car at the end of the road and walk up
through pastureland to the summit where a tall cross and a viewing table stand.*
The **panoramic view** embraces some famous summits of the western Alps: Haut-
Faucigny, Mont Blanc, Vanoise, Écrins, Aiguilles d'Arves and Viso massifs.
The road goes down to the Col de Leschaux through a pine forest and continues in
a series of hairpin bends along the steep slopes of the Semnoz, offering fine views
of the surrounding mountains.

▶ *From the Col de Leschaux, return to Annecy by D 912 and N 508 via Sévrier.*

Hikes

Belvédère de la Tournette

FROM ANNECY – HIKE FROM THE CHALET DE L'AULP *35km/22mi – allow 2hr –* see local map

▷ *Leave Annecy by ③ on the town plan, follow D 909 to Menthon-St-Bernard then D 42 towards the Col de la Forclaz.*

Route du Col de l'Aulp

3.5km/2.2mi from Le Villard – This forest road goes past Le Villard then climbs between steep wooded slopes, revealing the chalk cliffs of the Tournette on the right. The road gives way to a track which leads to the Col de l'Aulp (1 424m/4 672ft) just below the Tournette: from the mound situated behind the chalet, there is a lovely **view** of part of the Lac d'Annecy.

The road continues to the Chalet-Buvette de l'Aulp (1 424m/4 672ft) at the foot of the Tournette. There is a particularly good view of the lake from a little rise beyond the kiosk.

▷ *A stony, badly maintained road provides the only other access to the Chalet-Buvette de l'Aulp. From here, the only way up is on foot.*

From the Chalet de l'Aulp to the Refuge de la Tournette

2hr there and back on foot; difference in altitude 350m/1 148ft. You will need a good pair of binoculars to watch the ibexes roaming around.

A marked path rises to the east of the pass then skirts the limestone cliffs overlooking the Cirque du Casset. From the viewing table near the Refuge de la Tournette (alt 1 774m/5 820ft), there is a splendid **panorama**★★ of the western shore of the lake overlooked by the Semnoz. Climbing to the summit of the Tournette requires good experience of hiking through rocky terrain; however, no special equipment is necessary as there are handrails and ladders along the way. One of the finest **panoramas**★★★ of the northern Alps unfolds from the summit (alt 2 351m/7 713ft).

ANNOT★

POPULATION 988
MICHELIN MAP 334 I9

This small town, lying on the banks of the River Vaire, 700m/2 297ft above sea level, is the oldest settlement in the valley, developing as a stopping point on the Roman road which linked Digne and Nice along the line of today's N-202. Annot is surrounded by picturesque rocks, known as **grès d'Annot**. These sandstone formations, which were sculpted by erosion into strange shapes and natural arches, make for interesting walks around the town and earned Annot the nickname "the painters' paradise." *Bd Saint-Pierre, BP 54 – 04240 Annot - ☎ 04 92 83 23 03, www.annot.com*

▷ **Orient Yourself:** The old Roman road, now N 202, is 2km /1.25mi to the south of Annot, by D 908. It leads to the lac de Castillon and, 17km/10.6mi further, to Saint-Julien-du-Verdon. By following N 202 7km/4.4 mi eastwards, you can link up with D 902, which crosses the gorges of Dalius.

▷ **Don't Miss:** The reddish colour of the grès d'Annot rocks contrasts spectacularly with the lush vegetation.

🕐 **Organizing Your Time:** Give yourself a good hour to tour the village, and another three hours to wander among the rocks.

👢 **Also See:** Nearby Sights: BEUIL, CASTELLANE, Gorges du CIANS, CLUES DE HAUTE-PROVENCE, COLMARS, Val d'ENTRAUNES, ENTREVAUX, Route NAPOLÉON, PUGET-THÉNIERS, VILLARS-SUR-VAR, ST-JULIEN-DU-VERDON

Old Town ★

The old town looks quaint with its steep twisting lanes, its arcades, its arched alleyways and its leaning houses. The **Cours Provençal** is the centre of activity, a typical southern avenue lined with splendid old plane trees. For a good overall view, walk along rue Basse then **Grande-Rue** leading through a fortified gate to the church. On the way, note the 16C-18C carved doorways and the **Maison des Arcades**, a fine 17C mansion; its ground floor houses the **Musée Regain**, which has a collection of prehistoric objects found in the Méaiiles cave as well as a geology exhibit (🕐 *Jul-Aug: daily except Wed. No charge -* ☎*04 92 83 23 03*).

The Romanesque **church** has an unusual raised east end designed as a defensive tower, a lovely Renaissance steeple with statues of the four Evangelists, as well as a 17C aisle and adjoining chapel. Walk under a gateway onto rue des Vallasses where there is a wash-house opposite the Tour du Peintre (Artist's Tower). Rue Notre-Dame on the left leads back to Grande-Rue; a detour to the right along rue Capone leads to a communal oven.

For coin categories, see the Lengend on the cover flap.

WHERE TO STAY AND EATING OUT

⊜⊜**Hôtel de L'Avenue** – Av de la Gare - ☎*04 92 83 22 07 - hot.avenue@ wanadoo.fr - closed 2 Nov-31 Mar - 11rms -* ⊜⊜*restaurant*. This house with its green shutters has well-kept rooms in pastel colours. The terrace on the small street is shaded by trees. The cuisine is regional, the dining room contemporary.

Chapelle Notre-Dame de Vers-la-Ville

👣 *20min there and back on foot. From the Cours, follow the street to the right of the fountain then the chemin de Vers-la-Ville.* The path is lined with the Stations of the Cross. The 12C chapel is surrounded by rocks piled on one another, contributing to a good overall **view** of the village and its mountain setting.

Les Grès d'Annot ★

🚶 *3 hrs. Pick up the topoguide at the tourist office; you may be able to finish only part of the hike. From the chapel, take the signposted path "Chambre du roi."* These rock formations are a paradise for amateur and professional climbers alike. Others will be content to take a leisurely walk to the **Rochers de la gare** along a trail marked "Chemin des Grès" and to watch serious climbers handle the cliffs. The vegetation seems to bind the rocks together and sometimes literally grows out of the blocks, which have been given appropriate names: you may be able to make out the camel, the stem, the zodiac, the face and the king's bedroom. It is worth walking as far as the Arches de Portettes.

The Whitsun (Pentecost) parade, known as the Bravade, for which the townspeople dress in uniforms of Napoleon's grenadiers, commemorates the return of local troops from defeat at the hands of the British and Prussians at Waterloo. In the years of the Restoration that followed, the songs and regalia of the procession came to symbolise the old soldiers' resentment of Louis XVIII and Charles X and their nostalgia for their exiled emperor.

Excursion

Route du Col de la Colle St-Michel

FROM ANNOT TO COLMARS *46km/29mi – around 1hr*

▶ *Head north from Annot by D 908*

Le Fugeret

The village lies in a green depression on the left bank of the Vaire. Note the charming 18C humpback bridge spanning the stream with its single 14m/46ft arch. The slopes of the valley offer a landscape of scattered sandstone rocks and clumps of walnut, chestnut and pine trees, as well as lavender fields.

Méailles★

This hilltop village is built on a limestone ridge overlooking the left bank of the Vaire. The small church has Gothic features and contains an interesting altarpiece depicting *The Virgin and Child* (early 16C) as well as several 17C paintings.

On the way down, there is a marked contrast between the forested slopes and the barren limestone layer overlooking the **valley of the Vaire** dotted with picturesque villages; the Digne-Nice railway line is a showpiece of civil engineering skills.

▶ *Beyond the pass, turn left onto D 32 towards Peyresq.*

Peyresq

This old shepherds' village lies in a very picturesque **setting**★ overlooking the source of the Vaire and was restored by a group of Belgian students to house an international cultural and artistic university centre; it has retained a 15C mansion and a 13C Romanesque church.

▶ *Return to the D 908*

Col de la Colle St-Michel

Alt 1 431m/4 695ft. The pass offers a soothing landscape of green pastures. In winter, it is a cross-country skiing centre with 50km/31mi of tracks available. An easy crossing of the Colle-Saint-Michel links the valley of the Var to the valley of **upper Verdon**. (see COLMARS)

Hike

Grotte de Méailles

▶ *From Méailles, drive towards La Combe and, in the first major bend on the right, park the car in the lot. Wear non-slip shoes and carry several torches. Allow 4hr there and back for a short exploration of the cave entrance. Visitors are asked not to break stalactites or frighten bats.*

From the parking area, a well-marked path leads north across a ravine then climbs in a landscape of scrub dotted with cairns. The two entrances of the cave are situated beyond the ridge, about 10m/11yd apart. The main gallery slopes gently down 150m/164yd to a stream and a vast chamber partitioned by numerous concretions. There are other chambers further on, but some are difficult to negotiate and beginners should stop here.

MASSIF DES ARAVIS ★★

MICHELIN MAP 333 L/M 2/3

The natural boundaries of the Massif des Aravis, which forms part of the western Préalpes, are the Lac d'Annecy Basin, the valleys of the River Arly and River Arve and the Bornes depression. The rocky Chaîne du Bargy and Massif du Jallouvre form the horizon to the north and the mighty barrier of the **Chaîne des Aravis** stretches between the Val d'Arly and Vallée de Thônes (highest peak: Pointe Percée at 2 752m/9 029ft), continued to the north by the **Chaîne du Reposoir.** 🚩 *74450 Le Grand-Bornand* 🕐 *July to Aug: 9am-noon, 2-7pm; Sept to Nov and May to June: daily 9am-noon, 2-7pm, Sun and public holidays 9am-noon; Dec to Apr: Mon-Fri 9am-noon, 2-6.30pm, Sat 9am-noon, 2-7pm -* ☎*04 50 02 78 00 - www.legrandbornand.com*

▶ **Orient Yourself:** You may leave either from Annecy (28km/17.5mi by D 16, then D 909) or from Menthon-St-Bernard along a superb road (D 909).

☻ **Don't Miss:** The chartreuse du Reposoir is an enchanting place, while the view as you cross the Col des Aravis is spectacular.

🕐 **Organizing Your Time:** Take the route toward the Col d'Aravis at the end of the afternoon for the best lighting of the celebrated view of Mont-Blanc.

Kids **Especially for Kids:** During the second half of August, Le Grand-Bornand holds a festival of children's theatre, "Au bonheur des Mômes" ("Fun for Kids").

👌 **Also See:** Nearby sights: ALBERTVILLE, ANNECY, Lac d'ANNECY, BEAUFORT, La CLUSAZ, CLUSES, Les CONTAMINES-MONTJOIE, Route des GRANDES ALPES, MEGÈVE, La ROCHE-SUR-FORON, ST-GERVAIS-LES-BAINS, Bassin de SALLANCHES, THORENS-GLIÈRES

Reblochon country – The Vallée de Thônes, lying at the heart of the Aravis region, has been the home of Reblochon cheese since the 13C. After maturing in the high Alpine pastures, this strong creamy cheese made from the unpasteurised milk of Abondance, Tarentaise and Holstein cows is sold in the market towns of Thônes and Le Grand-Bornand.

A Bit of History

Like the other massifs of the Préalpes, the Chartreuse, Bauges and Vercors, the Massif des Aravis is surrounded by high limestone peaks. Two powerful streams, the Fier and the Borne, cut through the massif by way of long and narrow gorges such as the **Défilé de Dingy** (Fier), the **Défilé des Étroits** and **Gorge des Éveaux** (Borne). Between the Fier and the Borne, the **Parmelan** (alt 1 832m/6 010ft), whose high cliffs stretch across the Annecy landscape, is a favourite of mountain hikers. in January, you should look out for the famous dog-sled race known as the "Grand Pia."

Excursions

1 Route de La Clusaz

FROM ANNECY TO LA CLUSAZ *41km/25.5mi – about 1hr –* 👌*see local map*
The road rises above the lake then goes through the wooded valleys of the River Fier and River Nom, beneath the towering cliffs of the Parmelan Massif. Between Veyrier and the Col de Bluffy there are open views of the Grand Lac and, in the distance, of the Sambuy and Charbon mountains

Annecy★★★ – *See ANNECY.*

▶ *Leave Annecy by D 909 to La Clusaz.*

At first the wide road follows the contour of the lake, revealing the Semnoz and Entrevernes mountains on the opposite shore.

Veyrier – *See Lac d'ANNECY, 2.*

From the Col de Bluffy to the bridge at Alex, the road leads down into the Fier Valley and through the Défilé de Dingy. Further upstream, you can see the **Cascade de Morette** (waterfall) on the opposite slope.

Cimetière des Glières

The cemetery, situated on the right of the road, contains the graves of 105 Resistance fighters of the Plateau des Glières (*see THORENS-GLIÈRES*). An inscription relates the different stages of the operation.

The **Musée de la Résistance en Haute-Savoie** (*June to mid-Sept: 10am-12.30pm, 2-6.30pm, last admission 30min before closing. Guided tour (2hrs) by appointment. No charge.* ☎ *04 50 51 87 00*), housed in a reconstructed 18C chalet on the right of the cemetery, illustrates in detail the successive episodes of the fierce fighting that took place on the plateau. There is also a memorial to those deported during the Second World War.

Thônes★

Nestling below the cliffs of the Roche de Thônes, at the confluence of the River Fier and River Nom, this market town is the ideal starting point for mountain excursions. The Forêt du Mont is the favourite haunt of ramblers and the slopes of Mont Lachat attract amateur botanists looking for edelweiss.

The 17C **church** stands on the main square lined with old arcaded houses. The elegant onion-shaped steeple surmounted by a slender spire (42m/138ft) and the interior decoration are in typical Baroque style. Note the high-altar **retable**★ (1721), the carved figurines of the 17C altarpiece to the left of the chancel and the woodwork including 18C stalls.

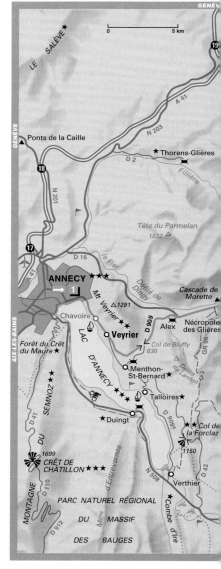

The first floor of the **musée du pays de Thônes**★ (July to Aug: daily except Sun 10am-noon, 3-7pm; Sept to June: Mon-Sat (closed Mon and Wed mornings) 9am-noon, 1.30-5.30pm, guided tours (1hr) in July-Aug Closed Sun and public holidays except 14 July and 15 Aug. 2.70€, children 1€ - ℡04 50 02 97 76) is devoted to the history of the area, which remained loyal to the King during the revolution. The second floor covers local arts and crafts; exhibits include a 15C *Pietà*.

Until the beginning of the 20C, there were many water-mills and sawmills along the Mainant Valley. The Étouvières sawmill has found a new role as an **Écomusée du Bois et de la Forêt** devoted to timber working in the Thônes region.

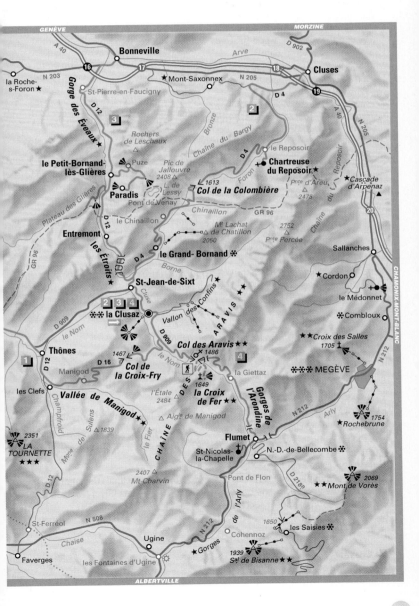

Address Book

For coin categories, see the Legend on the cover flap.

EATING OUT

Croix St-Maurice – *Pl de l'Église - 74450 Le Grand-Bornand -* ☎ *04 50 02 20 05 - www.hotel-lacroixstmaurice.com - 1-20 Oct.* Traditional chalet in the heart of the capital of Reblochon cheese. Panoramic view of the church with the Aravis mountains in the background. The guestrooms, often wood-paneled, are kept freshly up-to-date.

La Ferme de Lormay – *Lieu-dit "Lormay" - 74450 Grand-Bornand - 7km/4mi from Le Grand-Bornand towards the Bouchet valley and Route des Troncs -* ☎ *04 50 02 24 29 - closed 20 Apr-20 Jun, 10 Sept-20 Dec and Tue -* . Do not miss a stopover in this farm at the "back of beyond," built in 1786. There is a friendly welcome. Sausages and hams hang drying above the hearth. Meals are generous and authentic.

WHERE TO STAY

Chambre d'hôte La Passerelle *– Near the church - 74450 St-Jean-de-Sixt -* ☎ *04 50 02 24 33 - www.gites-chaletla-passerelle.com-* *- 5rms.* Close to the ski runs of La Clusaz and le Grand-Bornand, this new chalet, tucked behind the church, opens onto a large field with a view of the Mont de l'Étale in the background. The rooms are comfortable, well lit and have wood panelling.

Hôtel La Vieille Ferme *– Station de l'Étale - 74230 Manigod - 10km/6mi NE of Manigod towards the Croix Fry and Merdassier passes (on D 160) -* ☎ *04 50 02 41 49 - www.la-vieille-ferme-manigod. com - closed mid- Apr-1 June, 30 Oct-20 Dec and Wed out of season -* ▢ *- 6rms -* *restaurant.* At the heart of the summer pastures, this old mountain farm is located at the foot of the ski slopes in winter. Rooms are modern and appealing, while the restaurant, with its wooden fittings, is more typical of the region. There is a fabulous view of Mont Charin and La Tournette from the terrace.

3km/1/9mi west of the town centre – ⚙🕐 *July to Aug: daily except Sat 10am-noon, 2.30-7.30; Apr-June and Sept-Oct: Wed and Sun 2.30-5.30. 3.50€, no charge on the Patrimoine holiday. In July-Aug, ticket combined with nature trail (2hr30min) 5.60€ -* ☎*04 50 32 18 10 - www.ecomuseedubois.com*

▶ *Drive south on D 12 then take the first left (D 16).*

The road follows the **Vallée de Manigod**★★, the name given to the upper Fier Valley. The slopes are planted with fir trees and orchards and dotted with old chalets.

Les clefs

The church built on a wooded height overlooking the Fier forms a charming picture beneath the steep cliffs of the Tournette.
The road rises further still, to Col de la Croix-Fry.

Col de la Croix-Fry

The pass is equipped with ski lifts. The vast **panorama**★ includes the whole Aravis range. On the way down, the transverse valleys of La Clusaz (River Nom) and Les Étroits (River Borne) appear successively.

▶ *D 909 leads to La Clusaz.*

La Clusaz★★ – 🐾*See La CLUSAZ.*

☑ Route de La Colombière

FROM LA CLUSAZ TO CLUSES *40km/25mi – about 1hr 30min –* 🕒*see local map The Col de Colombière is blocked by snow from late November to late May.* Linking the Thônes and Arve valleys, this route offers a succession of contrasting landscapes from the austere upper valley of the River Chinaillon to the delightful Vallée du Reposoir beyond the Col de la Colombière.
North of La Clusaz, the road follows the wooded valley of the River Nom.

St-Jean-de-Sixt
This peaceful resort lies on the edge of the Nom and Borne valleys, at the heart of the Aravis Massif.

▶ *Follow D 4 towards Le Grand-Bornand.*

Le Grand-Bornand ✳
The pleasant, sunny home town of Reblochon cheese (market on Wednesdays) is also a winter sports resort, with an annexe at Le Chinaillon (6km/3.7mi higher up), and a good place to start excursions to Pointe Percée via Le Bouchet.
The road continues up to Pont de Venay, past Le Chinaillon, in a series of hairpin bends offering fine **views** of the Tournette and the high peaks of the Aravis range.

Le Chinaillon
The ski resort and old village is close to the ski slopes of Mont Lachat de Châtillon. Beyond the Pont de Venay, the landscape becomes wilder as the rocky escarpments of the Jallouvre Massif replace the Alpine pastures.

Col de la Colombière
Alt 1 613m/5 292ft. The view extends to the northeast towards the limestone heights of the Faucigny, Les Dents Blanches and Les Avoudrues. On the way down to Le Reposoir, the green summits and rocky peaks of the Chaîne du Reposoir come into view and the roofs of the Chartreuse du Reposoir can be seen in the foreground, below the village.

▶ *From Le Reposoir, take a narrow road to the Chartreuse.*

Chartreuse du Reposoir ✳
This Carthusian monastery (or *chartreuse*) was founded in 1151 and restored in the 17C. Abandoned by the order of St Bruno in 1904, it is now home to a community of Carmelite nuns.
From Le Reposoir to Cluses, the road overlooks the wooded gorge of the Foron before reaching the orchards of the Arve Valley and Cluses.

Cluses – 🕒 See CLUSES

☑ Vallée du Borne

FROM LA CLUSAZ TO BONNEVILLE *40km/25mi – about 1hr 15min –* 🕒*see local map*
This pleasant itinerary follows the Borne Valley through two picturesque gorges.

St-Jean-de-Sixt – 🕒 See ☑ above.

Défilé des Étroits ✳
The River Borne cuts crosswise through the limestone range to form this narrow gorge which the road follows beneath impressive cliffs.

Entremont

As the valley widens, the village comes into view amid lush meadows. In the church, there is an interesting **treasury** (⏱*Guided tour (2hrs) by appointment.* ☏ *04 50 03 51 90 or 04 50 03 52 68)*, in particular a gilt wood reliquary dating from the 12C.
The road continues through a pleasant pastoral landscape with the Jallouvre Massif looming in the distance (highest peak, 2 408m/7 900ft).

Le Petit-Bornand-les-Glières

This small summer resort, set in restful surroundings, is the ideal starting point for a trip to the Plateau des Glières *(2km/1.2mi south of the village, at Essert, a forest road leads to the plateau)*.

▷ *Take the signposted road to the left of the town hall.*

Route de Paradis

The breathtaking climb up the steep slopes of the Jallouvre offers bird's-eye views of the lower and upper Borne Valley *(for the best views, stop at Puze and again at a crossroads, 2.5km/1.5mi further on)*.
🔍The road ends at the Paradis ski centre with stunning **views**⋆ of the Rochers de Leschaux and the funnel-shaped chasm below.

▷ *Return to Le Petit-Bornand and continue on D 12 towards Bonneville.*

Gorge des Éveaux⋆

The road follows the Borne through another transverse valley which narrows considerably, the stream running below at the bottom of the gorge.

▷ *The road crosses the Borne in St-Pierre-en-Faucigny and reaches the River Arve in Bonneville.*

Bonneville – ⏱*See La ROCHE-SUR-THORON,* 3.

High pasture on the Col d'Aravis

Fr. Isler/MICHELIN

④ Route des Aravis *(can be obstructed by snow from December to April).*

FROM LA CLUSAZ TO FLUMET *19km/11.8mi – about 1hr –* 🌀 *see local map*
This is one of the best-known itineraries in the Savoie Alps, due to the view of Mont Blanc from the Col des Aravis The road climbs in a succession of hairpin bends, beneath the escarpments of the Étale. Mont Blanc suddenly appears as you reach the pass, particularly impressive in the late afternoon sunlight.

Col des Aravis★★
Alt 1 498m/4 915ft. The chapel of St Ann stands amid pastures overlooked by the impressive cliffs of the Étale, with the Porte des Aravis on the opposite side. The **view** finally extends over the whole Massif du Mont-Blanc, from Aiguille Verte in the north to Mont Tondu in the south, with the Tête du Torraz in the foreground.

La Croix de Fer★★
2hr there and back on foot. Follow the path (chemin du Chalet du Curé) starting from the restaurant and leading to the Croix de Fer.
🔲 The **panorama** is even more impressive here than from the pass, extending beyond Mont Blanc south to the Vanoise glaciers.

Gorges de l'Arondine
On the way down from the pass, the road goes through deeply cut gorges, where slate used to be extracted at the beginning of the 20C.

Flumet
🔖This large village, situated at the confluence of the River Arly and River Arondine and at the intersection of the Val d'Arly, Col des Saisies and Col des Aravis roads, is very busy in season. It is a pleasant summer resort offering walks through forested areas on the road to Notre-Dame-de-Bellecombe. It is also a lively winter resort linked to the nearby village of **St-Nicolas-la-Chapelle.**
The bridge which spans the Arly 60m/197ft above the river bed opens the way to the picturesque village of Notre-Dame-de-Bellecombe.

LES ARCS

MICHELIN MAP 89 FOLD 4 OR 244 FOLD 21
LOCAL MAP SEE MASSIF DE LA VANOISE

This ski centre, one of the most important in the Alps, includes the pedestrian-only resorts of Arc 1600, Arc 1800, Arc 1950 and Arc 2000. In addition, Arc 1800 is linked by ski runs in winter and by road in summer to Vallandry and **Villaro-ger**, situated in a forested area on the edge of the Parc national de la Vanoise. Arc 2000 is famous for its **Kilomètre lancé** (speed-skiing) competitions requiring a special ski-suit, helmet and extra-long skis. The track, which has a 77% gradient, was used for the 1992 Winter Olympic Games, when the speed of 229.299kph/142.5mph was reached (the record is 251.4kph/402.2mph). 🏠 *Place de la Gare - 73700 Bourg-St-Maurice* 🕐 *July to Aug: Mon-Sat 9am-12.30pm, 2-7pm, Sun and public holidays 9am-12.30pm, 2-6.30pm; mid-Dec to April: daily 9am-12.30pm, 2-9pm; May to June: Mon-Sat 9am-noon, 2-6pm, Sun 9am-12.30pm -* ☎ *04 79 41 55 55 - www.lesarcs.com*

▶ **Orient Yourself:** Leave Bourg St-Maurice by N 90 towards the northeast; then take D 119 to the right. Arc 1600 is 12km/7.5 mi on, or you can take the Arc-en-ciel cable car in season; Arc 1800, Arc 1950 and Arc 2000 are further on.

Don't Miss: If you find the atmosphere of the ski resorts too busy, explore the surrounding countryside, which is still wild and untrammeled.

Especially for Kids: Arc 1600 is the most family-oriented centre.

Also See: Nearby Sights: BEAUFORT, BOURG-ST-MAURICE, CHAMPAGNY-EN-VANOISE, COURCHEVEL, Route des GRANDES ALPES, La PLAGNE, La TARENTAISE, TIGNES, VAL-D'ISÈRE, MASSIF de la VANOISE

The Resorts

The three older resorts are modern and functional, but their architectural style blends reasonably well with the landscape owing to the extensive use of wood. The newest, Arc 1950, marks a departure. The Arcs are linked by a free shuttle service.

Arc 1600 (or Arc Pierre Blanche)

Access is by the **Arc-en-ciel** funicular; *7min, starting point behind the Bourg-St-Maurice train station –* July to Aug: *7.30am-7.30pm (departure every 30min);* Jan to Apr: 8.30am-9.30pm (departure *every 20 min);* closed May to June and Sept to Dec. In summer: 7€ return. In winter: 10€ return - ☏ 04 79 07 12 57. This resort is known for its traditional family atmosphere and for its spruce trees. There is a lovely **view**★ of Bourg-St-Maurice, the Beaufortain and Mont Blanc.

WHERE TO STAY

The four Arc resorts, plus Bourg St-Maurice and surrounding villages offer a wide variety of lodging: apartments, studios, chalets or hotels, and even camping and caravan sites. Contact the tourist office or central reservation service, open all year.

TRANSPORT

From Bourg St-Maurice, the funicular takes you to Arc 1600, connected by free shuttle service to the other Arcs.

Arc 1800

South of Arc 1600, this resort occupies a fine position overlooking the Isère Valley and offering **panoramic views**★ of the Beaufortain, Mont-Blanc and Bellecôte massifs as well as the Haute Tarentaise Valley. It is also the most compact of the four centres.

Arc 1950

This small new village, opened in 2003, is a direct contrast to the others; abandoning the austere style of the 1970s, the architects chose wood, slate and bright colors in a modern interpretation of traditional taste. The atmosphere is relaxed with an emphasis on amusement and comfort. A cabriolet (small, open cablecar) connects the resort to Arc 2000.

Arc 2000

More recent and remote than Arcs 1600 and 1800 and 1950, this high-mountain resort, lying just beneath the Aiguille Rouge with a remarkable view★ of the Rosière and Mont-Blanc, attracts advanced skiers.

Ski area

It is on the whole not so vast as that of Les Trois Vallées, but extremely varied. The ski slopes of Arc 1600 and Arc 1800 offer few difficult passages except in the Deux Têtes area. Skiing above Arc 2000, on the other hand, is more than satisfying for advanced skiers: the Dou de l'Homme chair-lift, Grand Col ski lift and Aiguille Rouge cable car give access to 10 black runs which are technically very demanding. The area of **Paradski**, which includes les Arcs, la Plagne and Peisey-Vallandry, is accessible by the Vanoise Express.

Peisey-Vallandry★ is also made up of three resorts: Nancroix, a favourite with Nordic skiers, Plan Peisey, best known for its downhill runs, at the foot of the

Aiguille Grive and the newer Vallandry. The area is linked to Les Arcs, La Plagne, the Espace Killy and les Trois Vallées.

Hikes

The beautiful panoramas more than make up for the unattractive aspect of the ski area in summer.

Aiguille Rouge★★★
Alt 3 227m/10 587ft. *From the main square in Arc 2000, a path leads to the Dou de l'Homme chairlift, followed by the Aiguille Rouge cable car. Mountain boots and sunglasses are recommended.* 🕐 *July to Aug: daily 9am-5.30pm (5min trip, continuous)* 🕐 *closed May to June and Sept to Dec. Price not available -* ☎ *04 79 07 12 57.*
Enjoy the stunning close-up view of Mont Pourri and, further away, of the Sommet de Bellecôte and Les Trois Vallées. You can spot in the distance the Belledonne and Lauzière ranges as well as the Aravis Massif to the west, the Mont Blanc Massif to the north and the summits marking the Italian and Swiss borders to the east.

▸ *Take the cable car back and either go down by chairlift, or head downhill on foot to the lovely* **Lac Marlou** *(be sure to ask the pisteurs about the risk of avalanches).*

Télécabine le Transarc★★
Access from Arc 1800. 🕐 *July to end of Aug: 9.15am-5pm (10min, continuous).* 🕐 *closed May to June and Sept to Dec. Price not available -* ☎ *04 79 07 12 57.* The gondola passes over the Col du Grand Renard and reaches the foot of the Aiguille Grive at an altitude of 2 600m/8 530ft. There are good views of the Aiguille Rouge, Mont Pourri, Grande Motte de Tignes and the impressive ridge of Bellecôte, as well as the Mont Blanc and Beaufortain massifs to the north.
Numerous possibilities of hikes of varying levels of difficulty. Some itineraries are described below.

Aiguille Grive★★★
Alt 2 732m/8 963ft.
🚶 *Experienced hikers, who do not suffer from vertigo, can reach the summit in about 30min up very steep slopes. The ascent should only be attempted in dry weather.*
From the viewing table, there is a stunning **view**★★★ of the Vanoise Massif.

Refuge du Mont Pourri★★ *(3hr).*
🚶 A relatively untaxing round tour on the edge of the Parc de la Vanoise, via Col de la Chal, Mont Pourri mountain refuge and the Lac des Moutons.
It is also possible to take a trip to the Aiguille Rouge from the highest point reached by the Transarc gondola. The walk by the Col de Chal to the Aiguille Rouge cablecar takes under 1hr; take the cable car up and down the Aiguille Rouge, then continue on foot to Lac Marlou and return to the arrival platform of the Transarc gondola.

Télésiège de la Cachette★
Alt 2 160m/7 087ft. *Access from Arc 1600 (Arc Pierre Blanche).* 🕐 *July to Aug: 9am-5pm (5min, continuous).* 🕐 *closed May to June and Sept to Dec. Price not available.* ☎ *04 79 07 12 57.* Fine views of the Isère Valley, Bourg-St-Maurice and Mont Blanc.

Hike to L'Arpette★★
From the top of the la Cachette chairlift, go right to join a path which climbs alongside the Arpette chairlift and leads to the Col des Frettes. Once there, take a path to the left which leads to L'Arpette (alt 2 413m/7 917ft), a hang-gliding and paragliding take-off point. Splendid **views**★★ of La Plagne, Les Arcs and the main peaks of the Haute Tarentaise.

ARGENTIÈRE✳✳✳

MICHELIN MAP 328 O5 – 8KM/5MI NORTH OF CHAMONIX
LOCAL MAP SEE MASSIF DU MONT-BLANC

Argentière is the highest (1 252m/4 108ft) resort in the Chamonix Valley; with its annexes of Montroc-le-Planet and Le Tour, it forms an excellent holiday and mountaineering centre offering a wide choice of expeditions to the Massif du Mont-Blanc and Massif des Aiguilles Rouges. The relatively gentle slopes of the upper Arve Valley provide pleasant walks through a fringe of larch woods.

The Argentière Glacier is hardly visible from the village; note, however, the morainal debris forming a bulge round the rock surface once covered by the top end of the glacier and, higher up, the vertical walls of the U-shaped valley which the Ice Age glacier would have filled completely.

A legend in the French Alps, Armand Charlet (1900-75), a native of Argentière, was held to be the king of mountain guides until the early 1960s. He set a record, which has never been equalled, by climbing the Aiguille Verte (4 121m/13 520ft) more than 100 times. 🛈 *24 Rte du Village - 74400 Argentière* 🕑 *July to Aug: daily 8.30am-12.30pm, 2.30-7pm; winter season and off-season: telephone for hours - ☎04 50 54 02 14 - www.chamonix.com*

▶ **Orient Yourself:** Argentière is 8km/5mi northeast of Chamonix on N 506.
🚠 **Don't Miss:** Many ski-lifts, including the cable-car to Grands-Montets, stay open all summer. The views from the top are spectacular.
👣 **Also See:** Adjacent Sights: Chamonix-Mont-Blanc, Les CONTAMINES-MONTJOIE, Les HOUCHES, Massif du MONT-BLANC, MEGÈVE, SAINT-GERVAIS-LES BAINS, Bassin de SALLANCHES

Loïc Johan/EXLORER

Argentière Glacier

The Resort

🎿 Ski area

The Grands-Montets ski slopes, for the most part ungroomed, are among the finest and most famous in Europe. Argentière is a real paradise for experienced skiers: their length, their gradient, the quality of the snow and the splendid landscapes account for their popularity, but the runs rarely seem overcrowded. The Point de Vue black run, which starts from the Aiguille des Grands-Montets and stretches over 5.2km/3.2mi, is an exceptional downhill run offering unforgettable views of the Argentière Glacier, Aiguille Verte and Aiguille du Chardonnet. The Chamois run along the Combe de la Pendant is also worth mentioning. These runs are only suitable for experienced skiers. Others will find easier runs along the Bochard and Marmottons chairlifts. 🏔 As for hikers, a special trail linking the Plan Joran and Pendant plateaux is at their sole disposal. From the Logan cable-car, there are many hikes mapped out.

WHERE TO STAY

⊜⊜🛏**Hôtel Arveyron** – *Rte du Bouchet - 6km/3.75mi SW of Argentière on N 506 - ☎ 04 50 53 18 29 - www.hotel-arveyron.com - open 11 June-19 Sept and 22 Dec-15 Apr - 🅿 - 30rms - ⊜⊜restaurant.* Relax in the garden underneath cherry trees and admire the view of Mont-Blanc. The comfortable rooms are paneled in wood and the dining room offers well-prepared regional family fare. Good quality for price.

⊜⊜🛏**Hôtel Beausoleil** – *74400 Le Lavancher, 2km/1.25mi SW of Argentière on N 506, then a B road - ☎ 04 50 54 00 78 - www.hotelbeausoleil-chamonix.com closed 9-14 May and 20 Sept-20 Dec.* 🅿 *- 17rms - ⊜⊜ restaurant.* Conveniently close to town, this typical family chalet with an alpine garden gives you an opportunity to stroll on grass or snow, according to the season. The atmosphere invites total repose. Tennis court. The cuisine is classic traditional mountain fare.

Hikes

If you plan to ride several lifts in the Mont-Blanc area, it is a good idea to look into the Mont Blanc Multipass, which gives access all lifts run by the Compagnie du Mont-Blanc over a period of from 1 to 14 days. The pass can be purchased at any company lift ticket office - ☎ 04 50 53 22 75 - www.compagniedumontblanc.com

🚡 Aiguille des Grands-Montets ★★

Alt 3 295m/10 810ft
Access by the Lognan and Grands-Montets cable-cars (🕐 Late June to early Sept: Argentière to Lognan: 7.30am-17pm; Lognan-Grands-Montets: 7.45am-4.45pm. Argentière-Lognan: 12€ return, juniors 12-15 years 10.20€, children 4-11 years 8.40€; Argentière to Les Grands-Montets: 24€ return, juniors 20.40€, children 16.80€, family pass 72€; for rest of year, telephone or consult website. - ☎ 04 50 54 00 71 - www.compagniedumontblanc.com) About 2hr 30min return. From the last platform, climb to the viewing table (120 steep steps).

The **panorama**★★★ is breathtaking. The view extends to the Argentière Glacier over which tower the Aiguille du Chardonnet and Aiguille d'Argentière to the north, Mont Dolent to the east, Aiguille Verte and Les Drus to the south, with the Aiguille du Midi, Mont Blanc and Dôme du Goûter further away. Slightly to the west, there is a fine view of the Chamonix Valley as far as Les Houches with the Aravis range in the distance.

Hikes to the Col de Balme★

🦅🚶Le Tour

3km/1.8mi northeast of Argentière. This pleasant village lies just below the Tour Glacier which, in summer, reveals many crumbling seracs *(for general information on glaciers see Introduction: Alpine relief)*. The resort is the starting point for easy hikes to the Col de Balme during the warm season and, in winter, the ski area is ideal for beginners and intermediate skiers owing to its gentle slopes, the quality of its snow and the amount of sunshine.

🚠Col de Balme★★

Alt 2 204m/7 231ft. *Access all year round by the* **Col de Balme gondola** *(🕐 Mid-July to mid-Aug: 8.30am-5.15pm; mid-June to mid-July and end-Aug to mid-Sept: 9am-4.45pm; for rest of year, telephone or consult website. 14€ return for 2 stages, juniors 12-15 years 11.90€, children 4-11 years 9.80€, family 42 € - ☎ 04 50 54 00 58 - compagniedumont-blanc.com). Allow 10min to walk from the lift to the pass.*

The **view**★★ extends northeast to the Swiss Alps and southwest to the Chamonix Valley surrounded by the Aiguille Verte, Mont Blanc and the Aiguilles Rouges massif. Food and drink is available in several places. At the beginning of July, when the herds go up to the high pastures, bovine tempers fray in the rush to the green grass on the other side …

Aiguillette des Posettes★

Alt 2 201m/7 221ft. *Hiking enthusiasts can prolong the excursion to the Col de Balme by coming down via the Tour du Mont-Blanc – Col des Posettes alternative, climbing alongside the Aiguillette ski lift. From the top of the ski lift, there is a 10min ascent to the summit.*

A fine **view** can be had of the Col de Balme, the Aiguille du Tour and glacier of the same name, Argentière and Grands-Montets, the Aiguille Verte, Aiguilles Rouges and Émosson Dam.

Réserve naturelle des Aiguilles-Rouges★★★

3km/1.8mi north of Argentière on N 506. This nature reserve, situated between Argentière and Vallorcine and covering an area of 3 300ha/8 155 acres at an altitude of 1 200m/3 937ft to 2 995m/9 826ft, offers a selection of high-altitude mountain landscapes within sight of the magnificent Massif du Mont-Blanc.

The **chalet d'accueil** (☎ 04 50 54 08 06 - www.asters.asso.fr. - or contact tourist office) situated on the Col des Montets (alt 1 471m/4 826ft), presents exhibits about the fauna, flora and geology of the cristalline massifs. The laboratory downstairs has taxidermy displays. An **ecological discovery trail,** which follows the old stagecoach route from Chamonix to Martigny, shows you the remarkable diversity of high-altitude flora and fauna *(guide for sale at the chalet)* over a distance of 2km/1.2mi. The nature reserve is inhabited by ibexes, chamois, blue hares and black salamanders. In addition, there are beautiful views of the Tour and Argentière glaciers.

L'ARGENTIÈRE-LA-BESSÉE

POPULATION 2 312
MICHELIN MAP 334 H4 LOCAL MAP SEE LE BRIANÇONNAIS

This industrial centre, which owes its name to ancient silver-lead mines, lies at the confluence of the River Gyronde and the River Durance. In summer, sports enthusiasts make straight for its nearby canyoning and rock-climbing sites.

23 rue de la République - 05120 L'Argentière-la-Bessée ⏱ *July to Aug: daily 9am-noon, 3-7pm, Sun 9am-noon; rest of year: daily except Sun and Mon 9.30-noon, 3-6pm -* ☎ *04 92 23 03 11 or 0810 00 11 12 - www.paysdesecrins.com*

▶ **Orient Yourself:** L'Argentière is the gateway to the Vallouise region. The old town of L'Argentière-l'Église, 2km/1.25mi from N 94, is especially picturesque.
☺ **Don't Miss:** A tour of the silver mine iw worthwhile, even if you have to make an appointment.
⏱ **Organizing Your Time:** Give yourself 2hrs to visit the silver-mining exhibits.
↻ **Also See:** Nearby Sights: BRIANÇON, Le BRIANÇONNAIS, CEILLAC, EMBRUN, Vallée de FREISSINIÈRES, Route des GRANDES ALPES, GUILLESTRE, MONT-DAUPHIN, MONTGENÈVRE, Le QUEYRAS, SERRE-CHEVALIER, La VALLOUISE, VARS

L'Argentière-Église

The old district of L'Argentière-Église, 2km/1.25mi from N 94, has retained its rustic character. Arriving from Briançon, turn right, cross the Durance then turn left towards the industrial zone and drive beyond the railway line.

Chapelle St-Jean
⏱ *Tours for at least 8 people by request at the cultural service -* ☎ *04 92 23 04 48*
This chapel, one of the few Romanesque buildings (12C) in the Hautes-Alpes region, was founded by the Knights Hospitallers on the road to Italy. Note the carved capitals decorated with plant motifs and geometric patterns.

Church
Same conditions as for the Chapelle St-Jean.
It dates from the 15C; the exterior is decorated with **murals** (1516) depicting the vices and the virtues (↻ *See ABC of ARCHITECTURE*), while the door is adorned with a splendid 16C wrought-iron bolt representing a chimera's head.

Additional Sights

Musée des Mines d'argent
♿⏱ *Mid-June to mid-Sept: 9am-noon, 2-6pm; April to mid-June: daily except Sat-Sun 9am-noon, 2-6pm; rest of year by request. 1.50€ -* ☎ *04 92 23 02 94.*
In what was once the farmhouse of the Château St Jean, this museum retraces the evolution of silver mining which used to be the most important economic activity of the valley.

Vallon du Fournel★
▶*Leave L'Argentière on D 423 up the narrow Fournel Valley (access not allowed in winter). Walking shoes recommended.*

Drive up to L'Eychaillon from where there is a fine view of the Gorges du Fournel and the ruins of the medieval castle. Leave the car and walk down the miners' path to the bottom of the gorge. Silver mining had its heyday in the 19C, when up to 500 miners were employed. The mines closed down in 1908.

Anciennes mines d'argent

Guided tour (2hrs30min - appointment required, minimum age 6 years old) mid-June to mid-Sept: 9am-noon, 2-6pm;Apr to mid-June and mid-Sept to Oct: daily except Sat-Sun and during snowfalls 9am-noon, 2-6pm. 7€, children 5€ - ☎ 04 92 23 02 94. In summer, a shuttle bus runs between the museum and the mine site.
Archeological finds have revealed mining activity in the area going back to the 12C *(The mines can be cold and the pathways uneven in places; warm clothing and sturdy shoes recommended.)*

Réserve biologique des Deslioures

Apr-Oct: unaccompanied visits. No charge. ☎ 0 892 700 7 65.
One of the aims of this nature reserve, which forms part of the Parc national des Écrins, is the preservation of a thistle-like plant known as **Alpine sea holly**.

Mountaineering Activities

Via Ferrata des Vigneaux★

Situated at the end of the village of Vigneaux, on D 4 to Prelles; rock-climbing enthusiasts are advised to refer to the Planning Your Trip chapter. This is the most popular "via ferrata" in the Briançonnais region; it is less crowded in the early morning or late afternoon. There are two courses to choose from on the Falaise de la Balme, which is almost 200m/656ft high. Spectators will need binoculars to track the climbers to the top.

Canyon du Fournel

Follow D 423 towards the silver mines. The canyoning course is situated upriver from the rock-climbing school (leave the car there). Note that the Canyon is located below a hydroelectric station. Follow the instructions posted at the start of the course and listen for the warning siren that signals the opening of the dam. The canyon is fully equipped and the site is one of the most popular among those wishing to be introduced to **canyoning.** However, those who wish to do the course unaccompanied when the water level is low are advised to ask about meteorological conditions at the guides' office in Argentière.

AURON

POPULATION 220
MICHELIN MAP 341 C2

This former hamlet, once the granary of St-Étienne-de-Tinée, has become a lively summer resort and winter sports centre. Auron is only an hour away from Nice, so its sunny skies, sleigh rides and attractive ski runs draw visitors from along the Côte d'Azur. The village is named after a 6C bishop of Gap called Aurigius, who became a saint; according to legend, he was being chased by highway robbers on his way back from Rome, when his horse saved him by jumping in one single leap from the River Tinée to Auron 500m/1 640ft above. *La Grange-Cossa, avenue de Malhira - 06660 Auron Mon-Sat 9am-noon, 2-5.30pm- ☎04 93 23 02 66, www.auron.com*

▶ **Orient Yourself:** Auron, wonderfully situated at 1 600m/5 249 ft, lies on a plateau under the towering peak of Los Donnas 2 474m/8 117ft. To get there, you go through the valley of the Tinée.

🖱 **Don't Miss:** The view from the foot of Los Donnas.

🕐 **Organizing Your Time:** The Pinatelle cable car climbs daily to the Auron ski area (*see below*).

📷 **Especially for Kids:** The Auron ski area merits the P'tits Montagnards designation, meaning it is especially congenial for families and children.

🖐 **Also See:** Adjacent Sights: BEUIL, Route de la BONNETTE, ISOLA 2000, SAINT-ÉTIENNE-DE-TINÉE, VAL D'ENTRAUNES, Vallée de la TINÉE

ON THE TOWN

Via ferrata of Auron – *Information about prices at the tourist office.* Seven separate sections are open for climbing, 3-4 hours total. All the thrill of contact with the rock: in several passages your hands and feet grip the rock face, while you are held secure by the cables. Supreme thrill: the longest suspended footbridge in France (46m/151 feet).

Sights

Chapelle St-Érige

🕐 *Tours by appointment 9am-6.30pm;* ☎ *04 93 23 02 66. The key is available at the Tourist Office. Identity papers are required as a guarantee.*

This Romanesque chapel dedicated to Aurigius has a single nave with a double apse, which is covered with a larch framework carved with notched motifs. The rich **decoration**★ painted in tempera dates from 1451.

Between the two apses, a recess surmounted by a canopy is covered with paintings illustrating the life of Mary Magdalene. In one image, covered only by her long, flowing golden hair, she is borne up to heaven by two angels. On the canopy she is depicted in a meadow, preaching to a congregation of Provençal farmers. An older fresco showing the angel Gabriel, part of an Annunciation scene, is believed to date from the 13C. On the left-hand wall, a huge St Christopher holds Jesus as a child.

From outside, there is a fine **view**★ of the mountains all round.

St Denis; fresco in the Chapelle St-Érige, Auron

Las Donnas★★

🚠 A **cable car** (🕐 *July to Aug: 9.15am-12.15pm, 2-4.45pm; Dec to Apr: 9am-4.45pm, 5.60€ return -* ☎*04 93 23 00 02)* in two sections takes visitors up to 2 256m/7 402ft in 7min, close to the summit of Las Donnas. Panoramic view of the upper Tinée Valley and summits on the Franco-Italian border.

AUSSOIS✳

POPULATION 628
MICHELIN MAP 333 N6
LOCAL MAP SEE LA MAURIENNE OR MASSIF DE LA VANOISE

Set in **fine surroundings**★ at an altitude of 1 500m/4 921ft, beneath the towering summits of the Rateau d'Aussois and Dent Parrachée, this charming old village of Aussois lies on the doorstep of the Parc national de la Vanoise (*see Massif de la VANOISE*). Aussois enjoys a remarkable amount of sunshine and offers numerous hikes and mountain bike trails for summer visitors.

▶ **Orient Yourself:** Aussois is 7.5km/4.7mi east of Modane in the Haute Maurienne. Take A 43 to Modane, then D 215

- **Don't Miss:** The Forts of l'Esseillon, clinging to a rock face, are stunning.
- **Organizing Your Time:** Every Sunday during the summer, there is a pleasant accompanied walk for visitors. No charge.
- **Especially for Kids:** There are donkey rides, with two easy climbs on via ferrata for children over 5 years old.
- **Also See:** Nearby sights: BESSANS, BONNEVAL-SUR-ARC, Route du GALIBIER, Route des GRANDES ALPES, Route de l'ISERAN, La HAUTE MAURIENNE, MODANE, Route du MONT-CENIS, ST-JEAN-DE-MAURIENNE, VAL-D'ISÈRE, Massif de la VANOISE

The Resort

In summer

Many walks and hikes are possible, for all levels of skill and conditioning. In a radius of 10km/6.25mi around Aussois, more than 500 climbing routes are available including the via ferrata du Diable★, considered one of the most beautiful in France. At l'Esseillon, there are hundreds of miles of mountain biking trails.

Ski area

The south-facing ski area, which reaches an altitude of 2 750m/9 022ft and has reliable equipment, is popular with intermediate skiers and family parties. Snow conditions on the slopes situated above 2 000m/6 562ft are usually good until April. For cross-country skiers, there are 35km/21.7mi of trails available between Aussois and Sardières.

The 17C **church** still has its original rood beam and Gothic fonts instead of a stoup

Walks and Hikes

Télésiège le Grand Jeu★

The chairlift reaches 2 150m/7 054ft. Views across the Arc Valley towards the summits of Longe-Côte, the Aiguille de Scolette and the Pointe de la Norma with the massif du Thabor in the distance. Climb alongside the Eterlou chairlift for more panoramic views: Rateau d'Aussois, artificial lakes of the Plan d'Amont and Plan d'Aval. From there, the Plan Sec mountain refuge is accessible in dry weather. In winter it is possible to reach the foot of Dent Parrachée by the Bellecôte chairlift: **views**★★ of the Haute Maurienne northern slopes, with Grande Ruine and the Meije to the southwest.

Walk to Fond d'Aussois★★

6km/3.7mi drive from the Maison d'Aussois. The route leads to the Plan d'Aval Dam *(stop to admire the view at the first car park)*, then along an unsurfaced road to the Plan d'Amont Dam. *Park the car and continue on foot. 3hr 30min there and back.*

The footpath skirts the lake shore then leads to the Fond d'Aussois refuge. View of the glacial cirque beneath Dent Parrachée.

Hike to the Col d'Aussois★★★

Access from the Fond d'Aussois refuge – 4hr there and back. Difference in altitude: 700m/2 297ft – Should only be attempted in dry weather and not before the end of July. Mountain boots are essential.

For superb views all round, experienced hikers can climb to the **Pointe de l'Observatoire** (3 015m/9 892ft).

AVORIAZ✳✳

POPULATION 5 016
MICHELIN MAP 328 N3 – 14KM/8.7MI EAST OF MORZINE
LOCAL MAP SEE THONON-LES-BAINS
ACCESSIBLE BY CABLE-CAR FROM A STATION 4.5KM/2.8MI FROM MORZINE

Created out of alpine pastures in 1966, Avoriaz is a modern resort situated at an altitude of 1 800m/5 906ft. Its original and uniform architectural style – buildings clad with wood, looking like huge rocks – blends well with the surroundings. Private motor vehicles are banned from the centre and replaced by sleighs. *Place centrale - 74110 Avoriaz* 🕐 *July to Aug: 9am-7pm; mid-Dec to Apr: 8.30am-7pm; school holidays: Sat-Sun 9am-7.30pm –* ☎ *04 50 74 02 11 - www.avoriaz.com*

▶ **Orient Yourself:** In the northeast corner of Haute-Savoie, close to the Swiss border, Avoriaz is 14km/8.75 east of Morzine on D 338, a winding road covered in snow late in the year. It is also possible to take the cable car from 4.5km/2.8mi below Morzine.

🅿 **Parking:** Leave your car in one of the lots; the resort itself is pedestrian.

🕰 **Don't Miss:** The tourist office organizes tours of the resort, to help you appreciate the unusual architecture.

Kids Especially for Kids: The ski school of former champion Annie Famose welcomes children.

🕯 **Also See:** Nearby Sights: ABONDANCE, CHÂTEL, CLUSES, ÉVIAN-LES-BAINS, Les GETS, MORZINE, SAMOËNS, SIXT-FER-À-CHEVAL, THONON-LES-BAINS, YVOIRE

The "Brasilia of the Alps"

The striking modern architecture of Avoriaz couldn't fail to catch the imagination of the public and the press, who soon dubbed the new town "Brasilia des Neiges" drawing a parallel with Brazil's state-of-the-art capital. The irregular contours of the first hotel, Les Dromonts, were designed to blend in with the rugged landscape, and subsequent developers followed architect Jaques Labro's lead with jutting façades overlaid with sequoia. Even if the look isn't to everyone's taste, the resort's facilities have made it a firm favourite with skiers.

Avoriaz

P. Jacques/FOC

The Resort

Summer activities

Avoriaz is developing summer activities notably a golf course with gorgeous sur-roundings, mountain-biking trails accessible by the ski-lifts, and spas.

Ski area

Avoriaz enjoys excellent snow condi-tions and a favourable position at the heart of the vast Portes du Soleil ski area, which includes 12 French and Swiss win-ter resorts between Lake Geneva and Mont Blanc with an impressive total of 650km/404mi of ski runs. However, in order to take full advantage of the area, you must arrive when the snow is plentiful at low altitudes (all the resorts, except Avoriaz, are barely above 1 000m/3 281ft).

The Avoriaz ski slopes are ideal for intermediate skiing; the ski runs lead-ing to Les Lindarets offer pleasant ski-ing through the forest. Advanced skiers can take the Combe chairlift which gives access to four black runs, including the Combe-du-Machon. There are also ski lifts to the Châtel and Morzine areas and, in Switzerland, to the resorts of Cham-péry and Les Crosets.

The **Festival du film de demain** (Fes-tival of Films of Tomorrow), following the Festival du Fantastique (Supernatu-ral Film Festival) created in 1973, takes place every year in January and attracts enthusiasts from all over the world.

For coin categories see the Legend on the cover flap.

EATING OUT

Le Bistro – *Pl. Centrale, near the tourist office* - ☎ *04 50 74 14 08 - closed May, June, Sept-Nov .* Why not travel here by sleigh? Seated around a large friendly table, or in a more peaceful corner, guests can sample specialities such as fondue or stone-grilled meats. At lunchtime, take your pick from the hors d'œuvre buffet and roasts.

WHERE TO STAY

Hôtel de la Falaise *– Quartier de la Falaise -* ☎ *04 50 74 26 00 - avb@pierreetvacances. com - closed 22 Apr-22 Dec - 30rms half-board.* All the rooms have south-facing balconies. Food is served at the La Chapka restaurant, tastefully decorated in the local style, with carved wooden furniture, benches covered in red velvet etc.

Excursion

In summer, it is well worth exploring the surrounding area along D 338 to Morzine. After 1km/0.6mi, the **Chapelle d'Avoriaz,** designed by Maurice Novarina, appears on the right and there is a fine view of the Lac d'Avoriaz. The road then overlooks the Vallon des Ardoisières with the snow-capped Hautforts Summit (2 466m/8 090ft) in the distance.

After running for a while along a ledge covered with pastures and dotted in summer with colourful pansies and gentians, the road reaches the resort of **Super-Morzine** (view of Mont Blanc) then runs down towards Morzine.

BARCELONNETTE ★

POPULATION 2 819
LOCAL MAP L'UBAYE

Barcelonnette lies at the heart of the Ubaye Valley amid orchards and lush meadows. This little Mediterranean-style town is one of the administrative centres of the Alpes-de-Haute-Provence. ▯ *place Frédéric-Mistral, 04400 Barcelonnette* ◉*July-Aug 9am-noon, 2-6pm -* ☎ *04 92 81 04 71, www.barcelonnette.com*

- ▶ **Orient Yourself:** The easiest way into the town, situated deep in the mountains, is by the D 900 out of Gap, 69 km/43mi to the west, and Serre-Ponçon. The other routes wind over very high passes that are closed in winter.
- ▯ **Parking:** There are several parking lots just outside the town centre, which is closed to traffic.
- ◉ **Don't Miss:** The lively Place Manuel has great charm, and Musée de la Vallée is housed in the villa La Sapinière.
- ◉ **Organizing Your Time:** Count at least an hour to stroll through the city, and another hour to visit the Musée de la Vallée
- ▦ **Especially for Kids:** La Maison du Rafting organizes activities just for children.
- ◔ **Also See:** Nearby Sights: Route de la BONNETTE, COLMARS, PRA-LOUP, Le SAUZE, Lac de SERRE-PONÇON, Route des GRANDES ALPES, L'UBAYE, VAL d'ALLOS

A Bit of History

A troubled past – Founded in 1231 by the count of Barcelona and Provence under the name of Barcelone, the town, and the Ubaye region with it, first belonged to the House of Savoie then to France in 1713, when it was exchanged for part of Dauphiné under the Treaty of Utrecht. Soon afterwards, the townspeople asked to join the Parlement de Provence and the town took the name of Barcelonnette.

Walking Tour

Place Manuel

~•~ This vast open space at the heart of the grid-like former bastide (walled town in southern France) is surrounded by colourful buildings and pavement cafés full of holidaymakers, with almost daily concerts. Note the **fountain** with a medallion of JA Manuel Manuel (1775-1827), a distinguished political figure from Barcelonnette, by David d'Angers and the **Tour Cardinalis** (15C), the former bell-tower of a Dominican convent which once stood here.

Villa la Sapinière

Housed in one of the most splendid Mexican villas, the **Musée de la Vallée** ★ (10 avenue de la Libération ⏱ July to Aug: 10am-noon, 2.30-7pm (last admission 1hr before closing); June and Sept: daily except Sun and Mon 3-7pm; school holidays: daily except Sun and Mon, 2.30-6pm; rest of year: Wed-Sat 2.30-6pm ⏱ Closed 1 Jan and 25 Dec 3.30€, children under 10 years no charge - ☎ 04 92 81 27 15) illustrates the history of the Ubaye Valley including an exhibit of Iron-Age burial rites, the charter of the town dating from 1231 and various objects connected with agriculture and handicrafts in the 19C.

In season, the ground floor houses the **Maison du Parc national du Mercantour** (⏱ July to Aug: 10am-noon, 3-7pm; last half of June and first half of Sept: 3-7pm ⏱ closed the rest of the year. No charge - ☎ 04 92 81 21 31) where information about guided **themed hikes** is available. (⏱July and Aug and during winter and spring school holidays. Contact the Park office for details on how to reserve.)

Cemetery

Situated at the end of allée des Rosiers, it houses a fascinating array of funeral monuments erected by the emigrants after their return: temples, mausoleums, chapels in stone and Carrara marble were, for the most part, the work of Italian artists.

Address Book

For coin categories see the Legend on the cover flap.

EATING OUT

Le Gaudissart – Pl. Aimé-Gassier - ☎ 04 92 81 00 45 - closed Mon out of season. This brasserie is often crowded at noon. The daily special and regular menu offer excellent quality for price. Pleasant renovated dining room and a terrace under a pergola. The parking lot just opposite is very practical.

Adélita – Rue Émile-Donnadieu - ☎ 04 92 81 16 12 - adelita2@wanadoo.fr - closed Jan and at noon, except July-Aug. The Mexican atmosphere of Barcelonnette invites thoughts of guacamole, enchiladas and other spicey dishes, all found at the Adélita. The wood-paneled dining room is a bit small, but the cooking is authentic and the service friendly.

WHERE TO STAY

Chambre d'hôte Le Bosquet – 2 av. Mme Watton-de-Ferry - ☎ 04 92 81 41 28, lebosquet@wanadoo.fr - closed end of Oct to 20 Dec. - 4 rms - 🍽. This agreeable house offers large rooms furnished with lovely old furniture, as well as a ping-pong table and a terrace with a barbecue.

Hôtel Azteca – 3 r. F.-Arnaud - ☎ 04 92 81 46 36, hotelazteca@wanadoo.fr- closed 14 Nov -6 Dec - 🅿 - 27rms.

The Azteca is furnished and fitted with items from Mexico, in memory of people from this area who emigrated there in 1820. Whether in the old villa or the recently built annexe, all rooms that have a balcony face the mountains; a peaceful stay is guaranteed.

ON THE TOWN

Place Manuel – Pl. Manuel – This lively square, surrounded by numerous bars with terraces, has a small bandstand on which local groups frequently perform, to friendly encouragement.

SHOPPING

Market – Pl Amié-Gassier - Wed and Sat 8am-1pm. You can learn a lot about local products and sample them as well at the morning market, where stalls offer milk and cheese products from the Ubaye, alpine liqueurs, génépri, charcuterie, preserves and honey.

SPORT

Maison du Rafting – Four à Chaux-Pont du Martinet, 04340 Méolans-Revel - ☎ 04 92 85 53 99, www.river.fr - open daily 9am-10pm - closed Oct-Mar. The centre has an annexe at Barcelonnette and a base camp at Méloans. It offers guides for a range of both mountain and river sports. On site are camping, snack bar, small lake, mountain biking...

Excursions

Église de St-Pons ★

2km/1.2mi west by the D 9 or the D 900. The interesting church, which formed part of a Benedictine monastery, has retained some Romanesque features (west doorway, chancel and apse). The two doorways are remarkable; their arches are decorated with mouldings and supported by columns with a frieze at the top. Note in particular the naive style of the frieze on the 12C west doorway. The 15C **south doorway**★ is more richly decorated; the themes illustrated are all connected with death since this door used to give access to the cemetery. On the left embrasure are a Crucifixion and a figure resurrected from a tomb; beneath the arch is an image of the Magi.

Le Sauze and Super-Sauze ✻

immeuble La Perce-Neige, 04400 Le Sauze ☎ 04 92 81 05 61, www.sauze.com 5km/3.1mi southeast.
Situated at an altitude of 1 400m/4 593ft, Le Sauze is one of the oldest winter sports resorts in the Alps, dating from the 1930s and linked to the recent Super-Sauze (alt 1 700m/5 577ft) by road (5km/3.1mi) and **cable-car** (⏱ *summer months: 9am-12.30 p.m., last ride up 12.15pm, last round-trip 12h, 2-6pm, last ride up 5.40pm, last round trip 5pm; round-trip adult 5€, children under 12 years, 4 €, one-way 3.90€ and 3€*). There is a wide choice of summer hikes and mountain expeditions to the nearby Chapeau de Gendarme and Pain de Sucre.
The two resorts are known for their family atmosphere, their sunshine and the gentle gradient of their slopes, offering numerous cross-country skiing and snowshoeing possibilities. A snowpark offers challenges to boarders and freesyle skiers.

Pra-Loup ✻

8.5km/5.3mi southwest. ⏱ *See PRA-LOUP*

The "Barcelonnettes" in Mexico

It all started in Jausiers (*9km/5.6mi northeast of Barcelonnette*) in 1805, when two brothers, Jacques and Marc-Antoine Arnaud decided to leave the family business and try their luck in America. In Mexico, Marc-Antoine opened a fabric store known as "El cajon de ropas de las Siete Puertas" (a craft centre in Barcelonnette now bears the same name). The success of the business was such that by 1893 there were more than 100 fabric stores in Mexico owned by natives of the Ubaye region. Some tried their hand at other businesses (paper, breweries and finance, including the London and Mexico Bank which was empowered to print money!).

The 1910 Mexican revolution followed by the First World War put an end to the flow of emigrants which, however, started again in 1930 and finally stopped in 1950. Most of the emigrants were country folk who, except for the Arnaud brothers, eventually returned to their native country and built sumptuous villas to mark their success in the New World.

Set amid spacious parks, these opulent houses built between 1880 and 1930 testify to the spectacular success of their owners. Architectural styles vary considerably and denote various influences; Italian, Tyrolean, Baroque, but certainly not Mexican. There are two fine examples along avenue des Trois-Frères-Arnaud and avenue Antoine-Signoret and several along avenue de la Libération. One of the last to be built was the Villa Bleue (1931), avenue Porfirio-Diaz, which is decorated with an impressive monochrome stained glass depicting the owner's Mexican textile factories.

Hikes

Chapeau du Gendarme★★

(4hr 30min there and back)

 From the Raquette car park in Super-Sauze a marked path follows the ski runs then goes through the woods to a stream *(where hikers are advised to fill up with water; there is no water further up)*. The path continues alongside the stream before heading due west to a ridge. Follow the ridge towards the southwest, leaving the ruins of a sheepfold to your left, then go round a rock spur and join up with another trail at Collet du Quieron. Continue south towards the east face of the **Chapeau de Gendarme**★★ and take the steep, right-hand fork to the Col de Gyp, where there is a fine **view**★ of the Vallée de Bachelard. At the summit (2 685m/8 809ft), a splendid **view**★★ takes in the Barcelonnette Basin and the **Gorges du Bachelard**.

Vallon du Riou Bourdoux★

3hr hike from the Le Tréou car park. From Barcelonnette, follow D 900 towards Gap then turn right onto D 609 to La Frâche. Pass the aerodrome and, leaving the access road to La Frâche on your left, cross the Riou Bourdoux and continue along the forest road. The road runs past devices designed to hold back the black mud from which the torrent takes its name. The unpredictable character of the Riou Bourdoux led to the building of some of the biggest dams in Europe at that time. Completed in 1880, after 14 years of construction, these feats of engineering minimised the devastating effects of the floods and retained the alluvial deposits.

Stop by the Tréou forest lodge and follow the **marked nature trail** (*guidebook on sale at tourist office*). The walk leads past panels explaining how the torrent was tamed. In a small coppice are the ruins of the village of Cervière, abandoned in the 19C; the cemetery cross stands as a reminder of this once important centre.

Col de la Pare★

4hr 30min there and back from Les Dalis car park; difference in altitude 800m/2 625ft. For the section to Le Tréou see above.

To the right, the trail marked "Col de la Pare" leads through a forest of larch and pine trees to a cottage, the gîte de la Pare (45min). Beyond the cottage, a path goes up to an altitude of 2 000m/6 562ft, above which there is no vegetation, and continues along the scree-covered slopes to the Col de la Pare (2 655m/8 711ft), overlooked by the Grande Épervière (2 884m/9 462ft), with the impressive Grand Bérard (3 048m/10 000ft) further away to the north. There is a fine **view**★ of the Barcelonnette Basin and of the surrounding mountains.

BARGÈME★

POPULAT ION 115
MICHELIN MAP 340 O3

In a beautiful **setting**★ a few miles northeast of Comps-sur-Artuby, this hilltop village is the highest municipality of the Var département (1 097m/3 599ft). The church, the ruined walls and the towers of the castle can be seen from a long way off. In the last few years, the village has regained its old-world charm through a programme of extensive restoration work. *Mairie - 83840 Bargème ⓒ Mon, Tue, Thur and Sat 2-5pm - ☎ 04 94 50 21 94*

▸ **Orient Yourself:** Bargème is located 9km/5.6mi NE of Comps-sur-Artuby, in the Parc naturel régional du Verdon.

🅿 **Parking:** Motor vehicles are banned from the village.
🕐 **Organizing Your Time:** Give yourself one hour to stroll around the village.
🗻 **Also See:** Nearby sights: CASTELLANE, MOUSTIERS-STE-MARIE, Route NAPOLEON, ST-JULIEN-DE-VERDON, Lac de STE-CROIX, Grand Canyon du VERDON

A Walk Through the Village

🐌 Walk through the "Porte de Garde," one of the two 14C fortified gates still standing. The narrow streets, linked by alleyways and arched passages, are lined with old houses brightened up by colourful hollyhocks.

Église Saint-Nicholas
🕐 *July to Aug: guided tours at 2.30pm, 3.30pm, 4.30pm, 5.30pm; last half of June and first half of Sept: on request to the Association des amis du vieux Bargème -* ☎ *04 94 50 23 00*
The stone-built 11C Romanesque church has an oven-vaulted apse. Note in particular the **Retable de saint Sébastien**★, an altarpiece in carved wood.

Castle
Dating from the 13C, it comprised four round towers, a square keep and a main courtyard. Although the building is in ruins, its layout is revealed by the remaining stairs, chimneys and windows.
From the castle, the **view**★ extends to the Malay and Lachens mountains and, beyond, to the Préalpes de Grasse, Canjuers Plateau and Maures Massif.

Chapelle Notre-Dame-des-Sept-Douleurs
Facing the castle, this small building, in typical local style with awning and wooden railings, was built during the Wars of Religion to atone for the murder of young nobleman Antoine de Pontevès, stabbed at the church altar during mass in the blood-feud that had claimed the lives of his father and grandfather.

LES BAUGES★

MICHELIN MAP 89 FOLDS 15 AND 16 OR 244 FOLD 18

The Massif des Bauges stands like a powerful citadel between the Annecy and Chambéry valleys. In spite of its impressive outer defences (Dent du Nivolet towering above Chambéry, Mont Revard above Aix-les-Bains and the Montagne du Charbon above the Lac d'Annecy), the centre of the range, through which flows the Chéran, offers gently modelled Alpine landscapes and forested slopes.
🗎 *73630 Le Châtelard* 🕐 *Daily except Sun 9am-noon, 2-6pm* 🕐*closed 1 and 8 May, 1 and 11 Nov.*

▶ **Orient Yourself:** Wherever you choose to leave from, you will have to follow winding mountain roads over imposing natural barriers: the Croix du Nivolet, Mont Revard or the Montagne du Charbon.
🗻 **Don't Miss:** The wilderness of the valley of Bellevaux; and taste the famous tome des Bauges.
🕐 **Organizing Your Time:** The road network forms an X: be prepared to backtrack from time-to-time.
Kids **Especially for Kids:** Some farmers have workshops for children. Check at the Maison du Parc.

Also See: Adjacent Sights: AIX-LES-BAINS, L'ALBANAIS, ALBERTVILLE, ALLEVARD, ANNECY, Lac d'ANNECY, Lac du BOURGET, CHAMBÉRY, Massif de la CHARTREUSE, Le GRÉSIVAUDAN

Highlight

Maison du Parc ◷ Daily except Sat-Sun and public holidays 8am-noon, 1.30-5.30pm - ☎04 79 54 86 40 - www.pnr-massif-bauges.fr The **Réserve nationale des Bauges,** created in 1950, stretches over 5 500ha/13 591 acres and is home to 600 chamois and 300 moufflons. Since 1995, the **Parc naturel régional du massif des Bauges** is responsible for conservation and development of facilities within an area covering over 80 000ha/197 684 acres from the Lac d'Annecy in the north, Val d'Isère in the east, the cluses (transverse valleys) of Chambéry to the south and the hills of the Albanais to the west. Within the park, small, well-defined areas still bear the economic and cultural imprint of the religious orders which, in times past, were focal points of economic life. Until the end of the 19C, villages rang with the sound of nails being formed on anvils, an important economic activity. Another important industry was production of wooden dishes out of beech, maple and wild cherry wood.

The **Réserve cygétique des Bauges** (National Game and Wildlife Preserve of the Bauges) in the upper valley of the river Chéran contains more than 1 000 chamois as well as numerous moufflons, roe-deer and black grouse. ⊞Fifteen nature trails taking from 3 to 7 hours to cover bring you closer to the wildlife - ☎04 50 52 22 56, or 04 79 54 84 28.

Excursions

① A Tour of the Two Lakes

FROM CHAMBÉRY TO ANNECY *68km/42.3mi – about 2hr – ◷see local map*

▷ *From Chambéry take N 6 towards Albertville then, at the intersection of N 512 and N 6, turn onto the N 512 and then immediately afterwards onto the D 11 towards "Curienne."*

Beyond Leysse, there is a clear view of the Chambéry Valley and the Combe de Savoie-Grésivaudan meeting at right angles with the jagged silhouette of the Allevard Massif in the background.

▷ *From Le Boyat, follow the lane to Montmerlet. Continue on foot (45min return).*

Mont-St-Michel★

☞Head uphill on the path to the right. There is a choice of several itineraries, some easier than others; the most pleasant of them, beginning on the right as you go

---

Nature Notes

Notice how the predominant tree species varies according to the aspect of the slopes. Oaks and boxtrees flourish on the dry, rocky hillsides while fir trees prefer the moisture of the valleys. You may also come across a variety of Mediterranean maple, which thrives in hot, dry weather.

From Le Boyat to the Col des Prés, the view extends north to the Mont de Margeriaz and south to the Chambéry Basin overlooked by Mont Granier. The pastures around the **Col des Prés** (alt 1 135m/3 724ft) are dotted with buttercups and daffodils.

For coin categories, see the Legend on the cover flap.

WHERE TO STAY

◎◎**Chambre d'hôte La Grangerie** – *Les Ginets - 73340 Aillon-le-Jeune - 2km/1.25mi from the resort, towards Les Ginets -* ☎ *04 79 54 80 1964 71 - www.lagrangerie.com -* ⚞ *- 4rms -* ◎◎ *restaurant.* On a winding road above the village, this converted old farm has views of the Bauges massif. The proprietor is a mountain guide who offers a warm welcome and can take you on walks. In winter, you can ski directly to the runs.

◎◎**Hôtel le Chamois** – *At the resort, at the foot of the ski runs - 73340 Aillon-le-Jeune -* ☎ *04 79 54 60 67 - www.lechamois.com -* ⓟ *- 4rms -* ◎◎ *restaurant.* A few steps from the ski hill or hiking trails, depending on the season, this modern building offers balconies on most rooms, which are well-equipped. The TV room opens directly onto the dining room, which specializes in Savoie specialties such as raclette, tartiflette and others.

into the wood, leads to the Chapelle du Mont St-Michel. From the top, there is a bird's-eye **view** of the Chambéry Valley, of the town and of Challes below, with the snow-capped peaks of the Belledonne range in the distance. The Lac du Bourget is partly visible to the northwest, with the Mont du Chat towering above.

🎿Aillon-le-Jeune

Situated at the relatively low altitude of 1 000m/3 281ft, this winter sports resort has spread its chalets all over the valley.

The road then follows the Aillon Valley with the grass-covered Grand Colombier (2 043m/6 703ft) and the more arid Dent de Rossanaz (1 891m/6 204ft) on the right. Beyond Le Cimeteret, the **Lescheraines** Basin comes into view: Le Châtelard village (see below) lies on the opposite bank of the Chéran backed by the Charbon Massif with the Pécloz summit (2 197m/7 208ft) in the distance.

Pont du Diable

Follow the road to the Col de Leschaux for 600m/656yd; leave the car near two chalets facing each other and follow the marked path on the right; it goes round a private house to reach the wood and the bridge (15min there and back on foot).

A small bridge spans the foaming Bellecombe mountain stream. This place is the main starting point of hikes in the area.

Between **Col de Leschaux** and Sévrier, there are fine **vistas**★ of the "Grand" Lac d'Annecy, overlooked by the Château de Menthon and framed by Mont Veyrier, the Dents de Lanfon and the Tournette, and lower down, of the picturesque Roc de Chère facing the Château de Duingt at the narrowest part of the lake.

Sévrier – 🕭*See Lac d'ANNECY,* **1**.

2km/1.2mi before reaching Annecy, the road comes close to the lake as it goes round the Puya promontory.

2 From the Pont de l'Abîme to the Pont Royal

FROM AIX-LES-BAINS TO CHAMBÉRY *104km/65mi – around 3hr –* 🕭*see local map*

Pont de l'Abîme★

The bridge spans the gorge through which flows the Chéran, 94m/103yd above the river bed (*abîme* means abyss). A spectacular **view**★ includes the peaks of the **Tours St-Jacques.**

From the Pont de l'Abîme to La Charniaz, D 911 follows the narrow Chéran Valley, affording views of the Montagne du Charbon and then, just before La Charniaz, of the summits enclosing the upper Chéran Valley. The road then goes through the Lescheraines Basin, where several routes intersect.

Le Châtelard

The village, its central street lined by old houses with wooden shutters and a 19C church, lies on either side of a wooded ridge once crowned by a castle, which separates the wide and open Lescheraines Basin from the more austere upper Chéran Valley. The administrative centre of the Parc naturel régional du massif des Bauges is here.

Beyond Le Châtelard, landscapes are definitely more Alpine with the impressive silhouette of the Dent de Pleuven (1 771m/5 810ft) towering over the valley and the Arcalod (2 217m/7 274ft) looming in the distance.

▷ *On reaching École, turn onto the Route de Jarsy at the church then follow the forest road through the Vallon de Bellevaux.*

Vallon de Bellevaux★

Turn right immediately after a bridge over the Chéran and continue to follow the stream through its wooded upper valley, one of the narrowest in the Alps. About 1.5km/0.9mi after the roundabout, the road leads to the meadows of Orgeval. An interesting nature-path with yearly exhibits borders the Chéran.

▷ *Turn back at the end of the road.*

Chapelle Notre-Dame de Bellevaux

On the way back, leave the car on the car park of the Office National des Forêts then take the narrow path on the left to a plantation of young trees. A small oratory marks the place where the Bellevaux monastery once stood. Further up, in a clearing, stands the Chapelle Notre-Dame de Bellevaux, known as the Sainte Fontaine, an old place of popular pilgrimage on Whit (Pentecost) Monday. There is a refreshing spring nearby.

Hike to Dent d'Arclusaz★

Allow an entire day: 2hr 30min there, 3hr back plus breaks. Not recommended in poor weather conditions. Remember to take sufficient water for a day's walking, as there are no sources of drinking water along the route. Follow the marked path from the Col du Frêne. From the **Col du Frêne** and on the way down to St-Pierre-d'Albigny there are splendid **vistas**★ of the Combe de Savoie, through which flows the River Isère.

Château de Miolans★

July to Aug: daily 10am-7pm; May to June and Sept: daily 10am-noon, 1.30-6.30pm, Sun 1.30-7pm; April: Sat-Sun, public holidays 1.30-7pm, first 2 weeks Nov: 1.30-7pm. 6€, children 3€ - ☎ 04 79 28 57 04.

The castle occupies a commanding **position**★★ on an isolated rock spur overlooking the Combe de Savoie; it is one of the finest examples of medieval

Château de Miolans

Fr. Isler/MICHELIN

military architecture in the Savoie region. From 923 to 1523 the castle was the seat of the lords of Miolans before it was inherited by the dukes of Savoie and converted into a state prison (1559-1792).

▶ 🚗 *Leave the car in the car park, 100m/110yd out of Miolans village, and enter the castle through the gates; allow 1hr.*

Fine panoramic **view★** extending to the Chartreuse and Belledonne ranges.
The square **keep,** flanked by four turrets, is the most characteristic part of the castle. From the top of the **Tour St-Pierre** there is an even more breathtaking **view★★** – you may be able to make out Mont Blanc in the distance. In the garden, narrow steps lead down to the secret dungeons known as **oubliettes;** equally interesting is the **Souterrain de défense★**, a kind of underground watch-path with loopholes covering the access ramp to the castle.

▶ *Narrow twisting lanes link the Château de Miolans to the Pont Royal. Return to Chambéry by the A 43 motorway.*

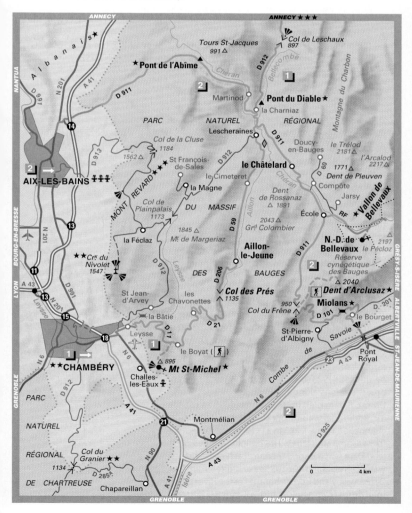

BEAUFORT★★

POPULATION 1 985
MICHELIN MAP 333 D6

Set in pleasant meadows which provide rich grazing for its dairy herds, the village of Beaufort is best known for the cheese that bears its name. The smooth contours of the slopes favour cross-country ski runs and several winter sports resorts have developed in the area, namely Arêches, Les Saisies, Val-Joly and Queige-Molliessoulaz. *Grande-Rue - 73270 Beaufort July-Aug: Mon-Sat 8.30am-7pm, Sun and public holidays 9am-noon, 2.30-6.30pm; May to June and Sept to mid-Dec: 9am-noon, 2-6pm; Dec to Apr: Mon-Sat 8.30-noon, 2-5.30pm. Open Sun during school holidays - ☎04 79 38 37 57 - www.areches-beaufort.com*

▶ **Orient Yourself:** The village is 19km/12mi east of Albertville on D 925. It is linked with Arêches to form the ski resort of Arêches-Beaufort. As for the Beaufortrain, it is spectacular but assessible only by tortuous roads.

⊙ **Don't Miss:** The desolate country around the Roselend dam contrasts with the somber forests that surround it.

⛄ **Also See:** Nearby Sights: ALBERTVILLE, Massif des ARAVIS, Les ARCS, BOURG-ST-MAURICE, Route des GRANDES ALPES, MEGÈVE, La TARENTAISE

Highlight

Beaufortain★★

Bounded by the Val d'Arly, Val Montjoie and Tarentaise, the Beaufortain forms part of the central massif in the same way as the Massif du Mont-Blanc, but barely rises to 3 000m/9 843ft (Aiguille du Grand Fond: alt 2 889m/9 478ft) and displays neither glaciers nor peaks with sharp outlines, apart from the Pierra Menta monolith. On the other hand, the Beaufortain offers visitors an unbroken belt of forest (lower Doron Valley) and pastoral landscapes likely to appeal to those who prefer mountains of medium height.

Searching for water power

The Beaufortain region is an intensively exploited source of water power. The **Lac de la Girotte** *(2hr 30min there and back on foot from the Belleville power station to the end of the road running through the Hauteluce Valley),* the first reservoir to be utilised (1923), helped supply water to seven power stations along the River Dorinet and River Doron. A dam built in 1946-48 doubled its capacity. Additional water from the Tré-la-Tête glacier, channelled to the lake via a tunnel, compensated for seasonal shortages. The building of the Roselend Dam was a daring technical achievement; its water comes along 40km/25mi of tunnels from the Doron Valley and from tributaries of the River Isère, then drops from a height of 1 200m/3 937ft to the

Bathie power station in the Basse Tarentaise region, providing 982 million kWh of electricity. St-Guérin and La Gittaz are nearby reservoirs.

Sights

Between Villard and Beaufort, the valley widens below the impressive Montagne d'Outray, guarded by the ruined **Château de Beaufort.** Beyond Beaufort, you can see the V-shaped gorge known as Défilé d'Entreroches. The **church** offers a typical example of Savoyard decoration, with its rood beam, altars in carved gilded wood and a remarkable pulpit dating from 1722.

Nearby Sights

Signal de Bisanne★★
▶In Villard-sur-Doron, take the road signposted "Signal de Bisanne" (13km/8mi).The twisting road overlooks the Doron Valley. From the top (1 939m/6 362ft), the splendid **panorama** extends all around to the Combe de Savoie, the Aravis mountains, the Beaufortain and Mont Blanc massifs. *Also accessible from Les Saisies, ⓒ see ②*.

Défilé d'Entreroches
▶Leave Beaufort by the D 295. Park the car 1km/0.6mi beyond Beaufort, near the first bridge over the Doron. The raging mountain torrent has carved interesting rock formations in this gorge.

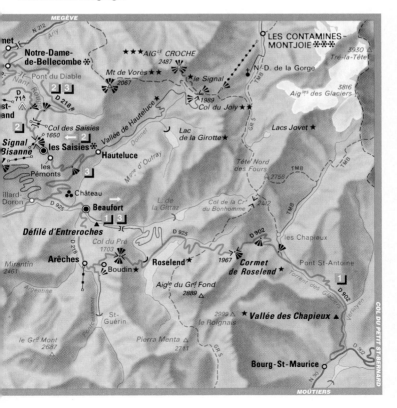

1 Route du Cormet de Roselend★★

FROM BEAUFORT TO BOURG-ST-MAURICE *45km/28mi – about 3hrs*
– see local map

▶ *Leave Beaufort by the D 218 heading south towards Arèches.*

Arêches
Surrounded by gentle slopes ideal for skiing, Arêches is one of prettiest winter resorts of the Beaufortain region. The huge houses, notably that of the Société de Mines (1645), recall the mines and quarries that abounded from the 15C to the early 20C.

▶ *The Route du Col du Pré continues to the left, passing the village of Boudin.*

Boudin★
From the road leading to the St-Guérin Dam, there is a fine overall view of this characteristic Alpine village with its large chalets rising in tiers, its little church and its communal bread oven. Since it came under heritage protection in 1943, nothing seems to have changed.

Barrage de Roselend★
The buttressed dam rests against a natural arch blocking the gorge of the River Doron. The **artificial lake**★ and its austere surroundings come into view on the way down

The Lac de Roselend

from the Col du Pré. Past a belvedere, the road follows the top of the dam then skirts the lake which flooded the village of Roselend (the chapel is a copy of the old church) and begins its final climb. The view extends westwards to Mont Mirantin and Grand Mont (2 687m/8 816ft), two of the best-known summits of the Beaufortain.

Cormet de Roselend★

This depression, stretching over several kilometres, links the Roselend and Chapieux valleys at an altitude of more than 1 900m/6 234ft, in a landscape of remote treeless pastures, dotted with rocks and a few rustic shelters. From the small mound on the right, surmounted by a cross, there is a wide **view**★ of the surrounding summits towering over the Chapieux Valley, including the Aiguille du Grand Fond (2 889m/9 478ft), the highest of them all.

The drive down from Cormet offers a glimpse of the Aiguille des Glaciers (3 816m/12 520ft), the most southern peak of the Mont Blanc Massif. Road D 902 continues past the village of Les Chapieux, partly destroyed in 1944, towards Bourg-St-Maurice.

Vallée des Chapieux★

Two mountain streams, the Versoyen and the Torrent des Glaciers, meet here. Beyond Bonneval, the road follows the deep forested valley of the Versoyen until it reaches a rock spur crowned with a ruined tower. There are fine views of the Haute Tarentaise just before the road veers to the right towards Bourg-St-Maurice.

2 Route des Saisies★

FROM FLUMET TO BEAUFORT *41km/25.5mi – about 1hr 30min – see local map*

Flumet – *See Massif des ARAVIS 4.*

The road starts climbing through a forest of fir trees; view of the Aiguille Verte and Mont Blanc just before the last hairpin bend.

Notre-Dame-de-Bellecombe

This is the most popular and the most developed of the Val d'Arly ski resorts.

▸ *Turn right onto D 71 (liable to be blocked by snow from late November to April).*

Crest-Voland

This typical Savoyard village is a peaceful summer and winter resort; linked by ski lifts to the nearby resort of Les Saisies under the name of Espace Cristal, it offers a wide choice of skiing, including cross-country skiing. It is well known to advanced skiers for its treacherous black run nicknamed "the kamikaze." There are numerous trails for summer hiking, in particular to Le Cernix, Cohennoz or Les Saisies, and in winter you can showshoe through the surrounding snowfields.

▶ *Return to Notre-Dame-de-Bellecombe.*

The next part of the journey to the Col des Saisies offers wide vistas of the Aravis mountains extending to Pointe Percée, their highest peak (2 752m/9 029ft).

Les Saisies ☀

This winter sports resort in pastoral surroundings was founded in 1963 near the **Col des Saisies** (alt 1 633m/5 358ft) on Alpine pastureland belonging to nearby villages. All the cross-country skiing events of the 1992 Winter Olympics took place in Les Saisies, today the main Alpine centre for that sport. It is also the home town of **Frank Piccard** who was a double Olympic champion in Calgary in 1988.
From the pass and from **Les Pémonts** village, there are wide **views** ★ of the Beaufortain mountains.
The road then runs along the green **Vallée de Hauteluce** ★.

Hauteluce

This sunny summer and winter resort offers visitors the lovely picture of the graceful onion-shaped spire of the church **St-Jacques-d'Assyrie** in the foreground and Mont Blanc in the distance, seen through the Col du Joly in the upper part of the valley.
The **écomusée** (🕒 *July to Aug: Mon-Sat 10am-noon, 3-7pm. No charge -* ☎ *04 79 38 80 31)*, situated at the heart of the village, organises exhibits on traditional life and development projects concerning the Beaufortain region.
Before reaching Beaufort, note the ruined castle perched on a wooded height.

3 The Arly and Doron Gorges

FROM BEAUFORT *72km*

▶ *Leave Beaufort by the D 925 and follow the D 218 towards Hauteluce.*

The drive over the Col des Saisies to **Notre-Dame-de-Bellecombe** includes some fine views of the Massif des Aravis. Just after Notre-Dame de Bellecombe, the wide-reaching view takes in the Arly valley.

Notre-Dame-de-Bellecombe – 🍂 *see* 2 *above*

Flumet – 🍂 *see Massif des ARAVIS* 4

Beyond Flumet and the Pont de Flon, lies the Arondine basin through which the tributary flows before joining the Arly. The prettiest view is that of **St-Nicholas-la-Chapelle** with its attractive onion spire and the picturesque landscape around it.

▶ *Turn right onto the D 109 at the Pont de Flon.*

Between the bridge and Le Château, the road climbs the steep, terraced slopes of Héry, with impressive views of the Gorges d'Arly and the little village of Cohennoz on the opposite side. Just before the road turns sharply to the north there is a place to park and a viewpoint★. The Dent de Cons rises above the factory chimneys of the

Beaufort Cheese

It takes 10l/2.2gal of milk from cows of the Tarine and Abondance breeds, processed through 10 different stages, to make 1kg/2.2lb of cheese. Copper vats with a capacity of 4 000l of milk can produce eight rounds of Beaufort.

The first stage is called **emprésurage,** during which rennet is added to the heated milk; the curd is then allowed to harden and the cheese is constantly heated and mixed. During the fourth stage, it is poured into moulds known as **cloches de soutirage** from which rounds of cheese later emerge pressed between wooden hoops and covered with linen. **Pressage** and **retournement** give the cheese a denser and firmer aspect. **Saumurage** comes next, causing the crust to form. The long maturing process can then start: over six months, the 4Okg/88lb rounds of cheese are salted, rubbed with linen and turned over twice a week in damp cellars kept at a constant temperature of 10°C/50°F.

Ugine valley, and in the far distance, beyond the Combe de Savoie, the snow-capped peaks of the Massif d'Allevard are visible until late in the year.

Ugine

The old town, its houses clustered around the church, looks down towards the steelworks at **Les Fontaines-d'Ugine.**

▶ *Drive back to the Gorges d'Arly and turn right onto the D 67 towards Queige and the Col de Forclaz.*

The road winds its way uphill giving views of the Arly valley and the end of the Massif d'Aravis to the west.

Housed in the 13C Château de Crest-Crechel, the **Musée des Arts et Traditions populaires du Val d'Arly** (*⊙Guided tour (1hr30min) mid-June to mid Sept: daily except Tue 2-6pm. 4€, children under 12 years no charge*) displays furniture, tools and costumes from the region.

The road continues past the ruined fortresses of Barrioz and Cornillon to **Queige,** a village on the right bank of the River Doron, which the road follows to Beaufort. The road between Venthon and Villard runs through forest, although the Roche Pourrie and the summit of the Mirantin (2 461m) are visible near Queige power station.

LA VALLÉE DES BELLEVILLE✲✲✲

MICHELIN MAP 333 M5
LOCAL MAP SEE MASSIF DE LA VANOISE

St-Martin-de-Belleville became an important tourist centre with the creation of the Les Menuires (1964) and Val-Thorens (1972) resorts. Its vast and splendid **ski area** forms the main part of **Les Trois Vallées**✲✲✲ (*⌖see Massif de la VANOISE*). Besides its 120 marked ski runs, the valley has retained large areas in their natural state, which make it one of the most attractive areas in Europe for off-piste skiing. In summer, the valley is ideal for **walking** and **hiking** (180km/112mi of footpaths and trails). Furthermore, the many traditional villages in the area and the 36 churches and chapels, most of them Baroque, cannot fail to attract visitors who appreciate the cultural aspect of tourism. **Les chemins du Baroque** (a circuit of Baroque churches and buildings, *⌖see Planning Your Trip*) will guide you around the artistic heritage of the valley. ▪ – *Imm. l'Épervière - 93440 St-Martin-de-Belleville*

July to Aug: 9am-noon, 2-7pm; Dec to Apr: 9am-7pm; rest of year except Sat-Sun: 8.30am-noon, 13.30-6pm - ☎04 79 00 20 00 - www.st-martin-belleville.com

▶ **Orient Yourself:** This huge area covering 23 000ha/56 835 acres (Bella Villa means large estate in Latin) lies between the Tarentaise and the Maurienne on the eastern edge of the Massif de la Vanoise.

Don't Miss: The panoramic view from the Cime Caron is exceptional.

Organizing Your Time: A guided tour of 22 hamlets and villages in the valley of Belleville is a practical way to see the area (contact the tourist office).

Especially for Kids: The bureau des guides at Les Menuires offers climbing courses for children.

Also See: Nearby Sights: ALBERTVILLE, BOURG-ST-MAURICE, CHAMPAGNY-EN-VANOISE, COURCHEVEL, Route de la MADELEINE, MÉRIBEL, LA PLAGNE, PRALO-GNAN-LA-VANOISE, La TARENTAISE, Massif de la VANOISE

Villages of the Lower Valley

The deep valley is dotted with clumps of deciduous trees.

St-Jean-de-Belleville

Rebuilt in 1928 after a major fire, the village has retained a richly decorated church which has two remarkable altarpieces: a Baroque one by Todesco and another over the high altar in early Empire style (early 19C). From St-Jean, there is an interesting detour through the **Nant Brun Valley.**

St-Martin-de-Belleville

Alt 1 400m/4 593ft. This charming old village has gentle sunny slopes linked by chair-lift to those of Méribel and Les Menuires. In summer numerous hikes are possible in the surrounding area as well as concerts in the churches.

The stocky **Église St-Martin** (*Guided tours on request at tourism office - ☎04 79 00 20 00*) surmounted by a Lombard-style steeple, is characteristic of 17C-18C hall-churches. 1km/0.6mi south, along the road to Les Menuires, stands the **Chapelle Notre-Dame-de-Vie** (*guided tours on request at tourism office each Wed during*

Notre-Dame-de-Vie, St-Martin-de-Belleville

S. Sauvignier/MICHELIN

winter and summer seasons - ☎04 79 00 20 00). This 17C edifice, crowned with a cupola and surmounted by a slender steeple, is an important place of pilgrimage (15 August and first Sunday in September) set in pastoral surroundings. Its remarkable **altarpiece**★, dedicated to the Virgin Mary, was carved in arolla pine by J.-M. Molino. A profusion of decoration includes the paintings of the Trinity and the Blessed Virgin which adorn the cupola, attributed to the school of Nicolas Oudéard.

Salins-les-Thermes via D 96★

Narrow road safe in summer and dry weather only. This itinerary offers picturesque views of the villages.

Address Book

For coin categories, see the Legend on the cover flap.

EATING OUT

◡◡**Bar de la Marine** – *73440 Val-Thorens* - ☎ *04 79 00 03 12* - *alexmegard@ aol.com* - *closed May-Nov.* A curious name for a restaurant located on the high mountain slopes! At the summit of the chairlift Cascade, skiers will find excellent pot-au-feu and other robust dishes.

◡◡**Le Sherpa** – *73440 Val-Thorens* - ☎ *04 79 00 00 70* - *www.lesherpa.com* - *closed 6 May-26 Nov.* This hotel-restaurant built in the 1970s lies slightly out of the town centre and is very peaceful. The cuisine is traditional in a warm ambiance. Comfortable guestrooms overlook the mountains through French windows. The atmosphere is friendly and ideal for families.

◡◡**Le Bellevillois** – *Place de lÉglise* - *73440 Val-Thorens* - ☎ *04 79 00 04 33* - *www.levalthorens.com* - *closed 14 Apr-20 Dec.* Walls painted with frescos of rural life, tile floors and rustic furniture, the pleasant ambiance of the restaurant at the hotel Val-Thorens lends itself to fine food and company, with a small orchestra playing during dinner.

◡◡◡**La Bouitte** – *In St-Marcel* - *73440 St-Martin-de-Belleville - 2km/1mi SE of St-Martin-de-Belleville on a second-ary road* - ☎ *04 79 08 96 77* - *www. la-bouitte.com* - *open July-Aug and 15 Dec-1 May, closed Mon in summer.* If you're starting to feel a little peckish, take off your skis and treat yourself to a bite to eat on the terrace of this chalet-restaurant. Charming dining room with rustic style decor.

WHERE TO STAY

◡◡ **Hotel le Lachenal** – *In the village* - *73440 St-Martin-de-Belleville* - ☎*04 79 08 96 29* - *lechenal@aol.com* - *closed May-June and Sept-mid-Dec* - *3rms* - ◡*restaurant* - Tucked behind the church in the heart of the village, this small 17C building has a doll-house aspect. Its 3 rooms are a tad cute but comfortable. Typical Savoyard menu, served on the terrace or in the wood-paneled dining room.

◡◡◡**Le Val Thorens** *73440 Val-Thorens* - ☎ *04 79 00 04 33* - *www. levalthorens.com* - *closed 25 Apr-4 Dec* - *80rms* - ◡◡ *half-pension at restau-rant.* Located at the centre of the resort this large hotel has has a 1980s-style wood-panelled façade. It offers opulent comfort without ostentation, and draws a loyal clientele of regulars. Its three restaurants include Le Bellevillois, listed above, and La Fondue.

◡◡◡**L'Ours Blanc** – *At Reberty* - *73440 Les Menuires - 1.5km/1mi SE of Les Menuires* - ☎ *04 79 00 61 66* - *www. hotel-ours-blanc.com* - *open 4 Dec-17 Apr* - 🅿 - *49rms* - ◡◡◡ *restaurant.* This large chalet in a village above Les Menuires enjoys a magnificent site: the windows of all the guestrooms overlook the ski runs and snow-capped moun-tains. Besides the view, the modern rooms offer modern comfort and the profound quiet of the high Alps.

Winter Resorts of the Upper Valley

Beyond the Chapelle Notre-Dame-de-Vie, the slopes become smooth and moderately steep; Les Menuires can be seen in the distance, with Pointe de la Masse and Cime de Caron *(both accessible by cable-car)* towering over the resort.

Les Menuires ✲✲

BP 22 - 73440 Les Menuires ⊙ July-Aug: daily 9am-12.30pm, 2-7pm; Dec-Apr: 9am-7pm; rest of year: Mon-Thur 8.30am-noon, 1.30-6pm, Fri until 5pm - ☎04 79 00 73 00 - www.lesmenuires.com

This modern resort consists of seven sites spread over 2km/1.2mi at an altitude varying between 1 780m/5 840ft and 1 950m/6 365ft. The two main sites (La Croisette and Les Bruyères) are practical and pleasant at the same time; the skiing area is nearby and there is a large shopping centre. Recent landscaping and tree-planting projects, and a return to a more rural style of architecture, have succeeded in softening the resort's functional edges.

Ski area

Enjoying a fair amount of sunshine, Les Menuires is appreciated by advanced skiers for its demanding ski runs (the Pylônes, Léo Lacroix and Rocher Noir). The off-piste area is easily accessible and skiing facilities are extended over the whole ski area of Les Trois Vallées. There are some 30km/18.6mi of cross-country skiing tracks, which are particularly fine between Le Bettaix and Le Châtelard.

In winter, guided excursions are available for ski-trekking enthusiasts, and in summer you can choose among a wide variety of activities.

Mont de la Chambre ★★

Alt 2 850m/9 350ft. *From La Croisette, take the gondola then walk up to the summit, which is only a few minutes away.* The fine panorama includes Mont Blanc, the Vallée de Méribel, the Val-Thorens and Vanoise glaciers.

It is possible to walk back to Les Ménuires *(2hr)*.

Val-Thorens ✲✲✲

Maison de Val-Thorens - 73440 Val-Thorens ⊙ Summer: daily 9am-12.15pm, 2-7pm; winter: daily 8.30am-7pm; rest of year: daily 9am-12.15pm, 2-6pm - ☎04 79 00 08 08 - www.valthorens.com

In winter, the car-free village has parking available outside with shuttle services to the centre. The highest ski resort in Europe, set in magnificent surroundings, it is overlooked by the Aiguille de Péclet (3 561m/11 683ft) and bounded by three glaciers marking the limits of the Parc national de la Vanoise. The barren landscape does not entice hikers but attracts rock-climbers instead.

Ski area

Situated between 1 800m/5 905ft and 3 300m/10 827ft and covered with snow from November to May, Val-Thorens is a skiers' paradise: snowfields all round, crisp mountain air, breathtaking views of the Mont Blanc, Vanoise and Écrins massifs, famous ski runs including the Combe de Caron and access in 20min to the ski areas of Mont de la Chambre and Mont Vallon de Méribel. The Orelle gondola takes skiers from the Maurienne Valley up to the Val-Thorens ski area in 20min. In summer, several intermediate and expert runs are open on the Glacier de Péclet.

Cime de Caron ★★★

Alt 3 198m/10 492ft. *Access by the **Caïrn and Caron gondolas** followed by the **Caron cable car** (⊙ Summer: Tue, Wed, Thur 10am-4pm; winter: 9am-5pm. 9€, children 5-13 years 5.70€ – minimum 2hr there and back) - ☎04 79 00 08 08*

Val-Thorens, Europe's highest winter sports resort

The summit can be reached from the arrival point in 5min. The extraordinary **pano-rama**★★★ unfolding from the viewing table embraces practically the whole of the French Alps, in particular the imposing summits of the **Mont Blanc, Vanoise, Queyras** and **Écrins** massifs to the northeast and south, the **Belledonne** and **Aravis** ranges to the west and northwest with the Jura mountains on the horizon.

Glacier de Péclet★
Access by **Funitel** *(twin-cable cable car –* 🕐 *Dec to May: 9am-5pm (8min, continuous) 9€, children 5-13 years old 5.70€ -* ☎ *04 79 00 08 08)* Close-up view of the glacier and the Cime de Caron. Advanced skiers can, in summer and autumn, take the 3 300m chairlift to the summit *(use caution at the summit)* from which there is a splendid **panorama**★★★ of the Mont Blanc and Vanoise massifs.

Hikes

A map of the local footpaths is available from the tourist office. The various summits in the surrounding area can all be spotted from the Cime de Caron and Pointe de la Masse viewing tables; it is well worth making the ascents at the beginning of a stay to take in an overall view of the region.

🚶There are pleasant walks for inexperienced hikers to the **Lac du Lou** *(2hr 30min there and back from Les Bruyères)* and **Hameau de la Gitte**★ *(1hr 45min there and back from Villaranger).* The following hikes are suitable for experienced hikers. Note that, in an effort to preserve the natural habitat of the 250 ibexes and 400 chamois, tourist infrastructure in the area has been kept to a minimum; maintained hiking paths are a rarity, and even these must be followed without the usual signs and markings.

La Croix Jean-Claude★★★
4hr 30min. Difference in altitude: about 600m/1 968ft.
Just before Béranger, take a path on the right to the hamlet of Les Dogettes; turn right towards two small mountains (the Fleurettes); continue to the spring and beyond to the ridge separating the Belleville and Allues valleys; turn left to Croix Jean-Claude and Dos de Crêt Voland (2 092m/6 864ft).
🚶 Magnificent **view**★★ of the Belleville villages, Méribel, the Vanoise, La Plagne and Mont Blanc. The path reaches the Roc de la Lune *(signposted "Col de la Lune").* The walk down to Béranger offers fine views of the villages.

Crève Tête★★★

Alt 2 342m/7 684ft. Take a small road starting in a bend preceding Fontaine-le-Puits; it leads to the Col de la Coche and to the dam of the same name (alt 1 400m/4 593ft). A rough road on the left leads directly to the Pas de Pierre Larron. If you do not wish to take it, park your car at the end of the dam and walk along the Darbellaz path to the Pas de Pierre Larron in 1hr 30min.

🚶 From the **Pas de Pierre Larron,** the **view**★ extends to the valley of the River Isère and Mont Blanc. Go to the refuge on the left. A steeper and more demanding path leads to the summit *(2hr)* offering superb **views**★★★ *(🕯️see VALMOREL).*

Pointe de la Masse and tour of the lakes★★

Take the gondola to La Masse. From the first section, allow 5hr for the whole itinerary. 🚶 *Less experienced hikers are advised to skip the ascent of the Masse (in this case allow 3hr 30min). The tour includes Lac Longet, the Pointe de la Masse, Lac Noir, Lac Crintallia and Le Teurre.* From the viewing table at the top of La Masse (2 804m/9 200ft), there is a splendid **panorama**★★ of the Écrins, Grandes Rousses, Belledonne ranges, Mont Blanc, the Vanoise and the Vallée des Encombres immediately below.

Vallée des Encombres

The village of **Le Châtelard,** near St-Martin, lies at the entrance to this secluded 14km/8.7mi-long valley. Tourist facilities have been limited in order to preserve the exceptionally rich alpine fauna. There are fine guided hikes *(ask at La Compagnie des Guides at Les Menuires - ☎04 79 01 04 15 - www.guides-belleville.com)* to the **Petit Col des Encombres**★★ (alt 2 342m/7 684ft) and the **Grand Perron des Encombres**★★★ (alt 2 825m/9 268ft) offering impressive views of the Maurienne Valley and Écrins Massif.

BESSANS ✳

POPULATION 311
MICHELIN MAP 333 O6 – LOCAL MAP SEE LA MAURIENNE

Bessans lies in a small valley enclosed by high summits, at the heart of the traditional Maurienne region. Some of the land belonging to the municipality forms apart of the Parc national de la Vanoise *(🕯️ see Introduction: Nature parks and reserves)*. The old village was largely destroyed by fire in 1944. However, a strong sense of tradition still survives (the local costume is still worn on festive occasions) and a reputation for decorative woodcarving, a speciality of the area since Renaissance times. Today, the village specializes in the famous **diables de Bessans,** rooted in local legend *(🕯️see Introduction;Traditions and Folklore).* 🚹 *Rue Maison-Morte - 73480 Bessans* 🕐 *Mid-June to mid-Sept: 9am-noon, 2-7pm; Sept to mid-Dec and Mar to mid-June: daily except Sun and public holidays 9am-noon, 2-5.30pm, Sat 9am-noon; mid-Dec to April: 9am-noon, 2 (Sun 3.30)-6.30pm - ☎04 79 05 96 52 - www.bessans.com*

▶ **Orient Yourself:** Bessans is located 36km/24.44mi from Modane, by N 6, then D 902

🔄 **Don't Miss:** The paintings in the St-Antoine chapel are exceptional.

🕐 **Organizing Your Time:** A wonderful nature trail links Bessans to Bonneval-sur-Arc in 2hr30min

🔥 **Also See:** Nearby Sights: AUSSOIS, BONNEVAL-SUR-ARC, Route des GRANDES ALPES, Route de l'ISERAN, La Haute MAURIENNE, MODANE, Route du MONT-CENIS, TIGNES, VAL D'ISÈRE, Massif de la VANOISE

Ski Resort

⛷Ski area
The resort offers more than 80km/49.7mi of marked cross-country trails. Its superb snow coverage at a moderate altitude of 1 700m/5 577ft offers fine ski treks during the greater part of the season.

Sights

Church
🕐 *Daily except Mon and Sun morning 10am-noon, 3.30-6.30pm For guided tour (July to Aug), ask at the Tourist Office - ☎04 79 05 96 52*
It contains many 17C statues and an altarpiece by Clappier, one of the famous sculptors from Bessans. There is also a very expressive Crucifixion and a remarkable **Ecce Homo.**

Chapelle St-Antoine★★
🕐 *Same conditions as for church, above. Access through the cemetery, opposite the side door of the church.* Built in the 14C and restored in the 19C, the building is decorated outside with murals in poor condition, depicting the virtues and the vices. Inside, the **paintings**★ illustrating the life of Jesus Christ are believed to date from the 15C. The chapel also contains statues carved by local sculptors between the 17C and the 19C including several representations of Christ at the time of the Passion and St Anthony with his bell (hermits used bells in the past to frighten evil spirits away). The Renaissance coffered ceiling, decorated with stars, dates from 1526.

SATAN AS A SOUVENIR?

For an unusual souvenir, try the shop in rue St-Esprit (of all places), where the devil makes work for idle hands. Handcrafted figures combine fine workmanship and diabolical inspiration!…Contact Georges Personnaz and his son Fabrice, ☎ 04 79 05 95 49 - chapoteur@wanadoo.fr

The devil's in the detail: a finely carved souvenir from the village

Vallée d'Avérole★★

At the time of the Renaissance, Italian artists came through this valley, dotted with chapels and pastoral villages, characteristic of the Haute Maurienne (La Goula, Vincendières, Avérole). Leave your car in the car park located 0.5km/0.3mi before Vincendières and continue on foot to Avérole *(45min there and back)*: view of the Pointe de Charbonnel (south) and the Albaron (north).

Refuge d'Avérole★★
Alt 2 210m/7 250ft. *Easy hike from Avérole, the only steep climb coming at the very end (2hr 15min there and back); difference in altitude: 200m/656ft.*
Beautiful mountain setting with glaciers, waterfalls and the Bessanese summit (3 592m/11 785ft) in the foreground.

BEUIL★

POPULATION 334
MICHELIN MAP 115 FOLD 4, 81 FOLD 9 OR 245 FOLD 24

Clinging to a steep, south-facing slope of the upper valley of the River Cians and overlooked by Mont Mounier (2 817m/9 242ft), Beuil owes much to its charming setting★. An elegant church steeple, surrounded by snowfields or a lilac haze of lavender, stands at the centre of this pleasant summer and winter resort, best explored on a mountain hike, a rafting excursion, a skiing trip, or a stroll through narrow, medieval streets with their allure of Provence. *Quartier du Passaire, 06470 Beuil-les-Launes–* *Daily: 9am-noon, 2-6pm, Sun and public holidays: 10am-noon, 2-5pm* *04 93 02 32 58, www.beuil.com*

▶ **Orient Yourself:** Beuil is located between the valleys of Entraunes and of La Tinée; the town of Guillaumes is 20km/12.5mi to the west, Saint-Sauveur-de-la-Tinée is 24km/15mi to the east.

Don't Miss: Scenic hiking and cross-country skiing trails.

Organizing Your Time: Take an hour to walk around the town.

Especially for Kids: The ski area of Valberg, linked to Beuil, has the designation P'tits Montagnards, meaning it has facilities for children.

Also See: Nearby Sights: ANNOT, AURON, BARCELONNETTE, Route de la BONETTE, Gorges du CIANS, Val d'ENTRAUNES, ENTREVAUX, Route des GRANDES ALPES, ISOLA 2000, PUGET-THÉNIERS, ST-ÉTIENNE-DE-TINÉE, VILLARS-SUR-VAR.

The Resort

Ski area

Lovers of winter sports have been meeting in Beuil-les-Launes, the oldest resort in the Mediterranean Alps, since 1910 and the architecture keeps its turn-of-the-century style. Ski runs with generous snow cover please beginners as well as black-run experts and cross-country skiers.

Despite being only an hour from the coast, Valberg (*see below*) also enjoys good snow conditions on slopes from 1 500-2 011m/4 921-6 598ft. Linked to Beuil, it offers 50 ski runs and a snow park for snow-boarders; major investments have been made in snow-making and in upgrading lifts. Cross-country skiers have 25km/16mi of trails at their disposal, and a groomed trail 10km/6.25mi long is reserved for snowshoes. Finally, you can whirl around an ice-skating rink.

Sights

Church

10am-5pm

Rebuilt in the 17C, it has retained a 15C Romanesque bell-tower and some fine **paintings★**: on the right there is an Adoration of the Magi by an artist from the Veronese School and, further along, fragments of an altarpiece (St. Lucia) and a predella. The high-altar retable in Primitive style has 16 panels and, on the left, there is a predella illustrating Christ rising from the tomb as well as the panel of an altarpiece depicting St Catherine of Sienna.

WHERE TO STAY

Hôtel L'Escapade – *On the D 28 in the direction of the Gorges du Cians - 04 93 02 31 27, hotel-escapade@wanadoo.fr - closed 22 Mar-2 Apr and Oct-Dec - 11rms- restaurant.* You will appreciate this mountain hotel's simple accommodation and will meet local people in the bar.

Chapelle des Pénitents-Blancs
🕐 *Visit by appointment at the Mairie, ☎ 04 93 05 50 13*

This Renaissance chapel was built with stones from Grimaldi Castle, once the seat of a powerful dynasty whose territorial claims to the area from the 14C to the 17C set them in constant conflict with the treacherous dukes of Savoie. The façade decorated in *trompe-l'œil* was recently restored by the fresco artist Guy Ceppa.

Excursions

Route du Col de Valberg★

20km/12.4mi west along D 28 – about 45min, not including walks.

This road links the **Gorges du Cians** ★★★ (👁 *see Gorges du CIANS)* and the **Gorges de Daluis** ★★ (👁 *see VAL D'ENTRUANES)* via the Valberg Pass.

🏂🎿 Valberg ☀
🛈 *Place du Quartier, BP 8, 06470 Valberg, ☎ 04 93 23 24 25, www.valberg.com*
Lying amid larch forests and green pastures, Valberg is a sunny summer and winter resort created in 1935 at an altitude of 1 669m/5 476ft. It is only 80km/50mi away from the Mediterranean coast and is the starting point for round tours of the Gorges du Cians and Gorges du Daluis as well as hikes to Mont Mounier (alt 2 817m/9 242ft). Behind the simple façade of the mountain church, the **Chapelle Notre-Dame-des-Neiges,** is a more elaborate **interior**★, a fine example of modern religious art. The coffered ceiling, like the upturned hull of a boat, combines depictions of the Virgin Mary with brightly coloured images of skiers and alpine flowers.

Croix de Valberg (Croix de Sapet)
🚶 *1h45min there and back on foot. Follow the footpath marked Les Oursons, which begins at the end of the village in the direction of Guillaumes, and continue up past the Lac du Senateur; you can also take the Croix du Sapet pedestrian lift (3.60€, 4.10€ with bicycle, under 12 years old 2.60€ and 3.60€)* The cross made of wooden skis is lit at night. Cross-country ski and hiking trails start from here. The **panorama**★★ reaches from the Grand Coyer to Mont Pelat , and from Mont Mounier to the Mercantour. On the way down from the Col de Valberg to Guillaumes, the road offers a succession of picturesque **views**. The forested north-facing slope makes a striking contrast with the vineyards, orchards and wheat fields on the cultivated southern side.

▷ *Follow the D 28 to Guillaumes or take the D 29 via Péone, some 8km/5mi away*

Péone★
The tall houses of this ancient village nestle at the foot of the dolomitic peaks which are one of the natural attractions of the pretty surroundings. Several Catalan families settled here in the 13C and the inhabitants have kept the nickname "Catalans." The maze of narrow streets and stepped lanes takes one past beautiful doorways, windows and trompe-l'œil façades to the charming place Thomas-Guérin with its sundial and carved doorways. The Promenade des Demoiselles leads to the **Cheminées de calcaire**★, striking rock formations which resemble petrified flames.

Guillaumes – 👁 *See Val d'ENTRAUNES.*

Route du Col de la Couillole★

Col de la Couillole

1 678m/5 505ft. Extended view on either side of the pass. This is a popular vantage point for fans of the Monte-Carlo Rally. The road winds up to the pass, within sight of the Gorges du Cians and the village of Beuil, amid spruce and larch woods.

Roubion★

Le Village, 06420 Roubion - ☎ 04 93 02 10 30 - www. roubion.com
This village, perched on top of a red-schist ridge, at an altitude of 1 300m/4 265ft, is reached by a winding road overlooking the raging torrent of the Vionène river in a striking countryside★ where green trees contrast with red schist. It has retained part of its 12C fortifications, some old houses, a belfry carved out of rock and the 18C Fontaine du Mouton on the village square.

From the main square, a **tunnel** through the rock takes you to the trail (9km/5.6mi) to **Vignols,** a pretty mountain village with well-preserved farmhouses. To the right of the **church**, which has an interesting chapel with lively, colourful interior painting, follow a little passageway to a fine **viewpoint** looking down into the Vionène valley; a narrow, lavender-dotted street leads back to the entrance to the village.

Chapelle St-Sébastien★

Right towards St-Sauveur-de-Tinée, then right again down a small road leading down the hill. (⊙ Guided tour by appointment at the tourist office 10am-5pm - ☎ 04 93 02 10 30.) Situated below the village, this rustic 16C chapel is decorated with murals: symbolic images of the virtues and vices and 12 panels relating the legend of St Sebastian with captions in Old Provençal. Outside, there is a representation of St Michael slaying the dragon.

▶ *Turn left onto the D 130 towards Roure*

Roure★

Mairie, Place André-Ségur, 06420 Roure ☎ 04 93 02 00 70
Lying at the heart of a beautiful mountain setting, this ancient village has retained a wealth of interesting 17C and 18C domestic architecture. The houses are partly built of red schist and their roofs are covered with red-schist slabs (lauzes). Some of them still have walls made of roughly hewn larch trunks.

The Return of the "Bone Breaker"

The **bearded vulture,** the largest Alpine bird with an impressive 2.80m/9ft wing span, is typical of Europe's endangered species. Decimated throughout the Alpine region during the 19C, it survived in the Pyrenees and in Corsica. This vulture has a strange lifestyle: it flies over almost inaccessible high pastures and feeds on dead chamois and ewes, ripping off large bones from their carcasses and dropping them from a great height onto the rocks below in order to break them, hence its nickname. In 1993, the Parc national du Mercantour and the Parco Naturale delle Alpi Marittime joined forces to attempt the reintroduction of the bearded vulture into the area. The operation was highly successful. Young birds (90 days old) are placed in caves and usually fly away 30 days later. However, it takes eight years for the vultures to be fully grown and they have a life expectancy of 40 years.

To date, five bearded vultures have been reintroduced into the southern Alps and a total of 70 into the whole Alpine range stretching from Austria to France, as part of a unique international programme.

The Baroque **church** (🕐 10am-5pm, ☎ 04 93 02 00 70), rebuilt in the 18C, contains some fine works of art: the 16C **St-Laurent altarpiece**★, richly coloured in green and red against a gold background, is framed by twisted columns and surmounted by a representation of the Entombment.

The **Chapelle St-Bernard-et-St-Sébastien**★ (🕐 9am-6pm, by request at the Auberge Le Robur or at the Mairie, ☎ 04 93 02 00 70) is decorated with remarkably well-preserved naive frescoes by Andrea de Cella depicting the life of St Bernard of Menthon and of St Sebastian, famous for his healing powers against plague and cholera. The friezes separating the panels date from the Renaissance.

The nearby **Arboretum** planted in 1988 by botanist Marcel Kroenlein has brought together specimens of mountain trees from around the world.

▷ *Return to D 30*

The road runs down to the Tinée Valley and the village of St-Sauveur in a series of tight hairpin bends, through a landscape of schist and patchy forest, its wild beauty enhanced by the contrasting colours of the rocks.

St-Sauveur-sur-Tinée – 👁 *see Vallée de la TINÉE, Excursions*

ROUTE DE LA BONETTE★★

MICHELIN MAP 334 I6

This road stretches from the Ubaye Valley to Nice via the Vallée de la Tinée covering a distance of some 150km/93mi. Several military constructions along the route are a reminder of its long-standing strategic importance. The present road, built in 1963-64, goes through part of the Parc national du Mercantour and over the Col de la Bonette, which makes it the highest road in France.

▷ **Orient Yourself:** When clear of the snow that blocks passage from November through June, the second-highest road in Europe brings Barcelonnette to within 149km/93 miles of Nice.

📷 **Don't Miss:** The 18 viewing tables explain the main features of the extraordinary countryside between the Casernes de Restefond and St-Étienne-de-Tinée.

🕐 **Organizing Your Time:** Give yourself half a day, counting stops at the La Bonnette peak and the old military camp at les Fourches.

👁 **Also See:** Nearby Sights: AURON, BARCELONNETTE, BEUIL, ISOLA 2000, PRA-LOUP, ST-ÉTIENNE-LA-TINÉE, Vallée de la TINÉE, L'UBAYE, VAL D'ALLOS

Excursions

Cime de la Bonette★★★

BARCELONNETTE TO ST-ÉTIENNE-DE-TINÉE *64km/40mi – about 3hr*
This twisting road is blocked by snow from November to the end of June.

Barcelonnette★ – 👁 *See BARCELONNETTE.*

▷ *From Barcelonnette, follow D 900 towards Italy.*

Y. Bontoux

View of the Pas de la Cavale from the Col des Fourches

Jausiers – 🕭 *See L'UBAYE.*

▶ *Coming out of Jausiers, turn right towards Nice.*

On the left, the road passes the little valley of Abriès and climbs towards **Le Restefond** in a series of hairpin bends offering lovely views of the Ubaye Valley. Between the Casernes de Restefond, a complex fortified by Maginot in 1931, and St-Étienne-de-Tinée, 18 viewing tables explain the main features of the landscape.
The road continues to climb past the **Col de la Bonette** (2 715m/8 907ft) to an altitude of 2 802m/9 193ft before skirting round the foot of the Cime de la Bonette, one of the highest altitudes reached by a European road.

Cime de la Bonette★★★
Alt 2 862m/9 390ft. 🕭 *From the highest point of the road, 30min there and back on foot. Viewing table.* The breathtaking **panorama** embraces most of the mountain ranges of the southern Alps: the Queyras (Font Sancte), Monte Viso and the Ubaye (Brec de Chambeyron and Tête de Moïse) to the north, the Pelvoux to the northwest; then the upper Verdon (Grande Séolane and Mont Pelat) and the southern Alps to the west, the Préalpes de Digne to the south and the Corborant and Argentera to the east. A special viewing table explains the formation of the Alps.
On its way down, the road reaches the ruins of the **Camp des Fourches,** a large encampment occupied until the end of the Second World War by a battalion of chasseurs alpins (mountain troops). 🕭 From there, a path leads in 15min to the Col des Fourches which affords a superb **view**★ of the vast cirque of Salso Moreno, close to the Italian border *(viewing table with explanations of local geology).*

🚶 Hike to Pas de la Cavale★★ Hike to the Lacs de Vens★★★ – 🕭 *See ST-ÉTIENNE-DE-TINÉE.*

Only 3km/1.8mi beyond Le Pra, you see the Cens waterfall on the left. As the road runs down into the valley, the short grass of the high pastures yields to a larch forest.

▶ *At Pont-Haut, turn right onto D 63 to St-Dalmas.*

St-Dalmas-le-Selvage★

06660 Saint-Dalmas-le-Selvage ☉ *daily except Sunday 9am-noon, 2-5pm -* ☎*/fax 04 93 02 46 40*

St-Dalmas, situated at the top of the upper Tinée Valley, is the highest village of the Alpes-Maritimes département. The tall, Lombard-style steeple of the village **church** (☉ *by appointment with tourist office)*, built in neo-Romanesque style and covered with larch shingles, stands out against the splendid wild setting of the Jalorgues Valley. The west front is decorated with *trompe-l'œil* **paintings:** one of these depicts St Dalmas, a 3C martyr who preached the gospel in the Alps. Inside, notice the fine 16C altarpiece and several interesting paintings.

The narrow streets are lined with stocky houses built of dark schist, covered with shingles and adorned with numerous sundials.

There is an interesting 3hr walk, *le sentier de découverte*, sketched out by the tourist office to explore village life in former days; a guidebook is available for 5€.

Col de la Moutière★

12km northwest along a narrow road. The road offers bird's-eye views of the village and goes through a splendid larch wood, known as the Bois de Sestrière. Beyond the refuge of the same name, the road enters the central zone of the Parc national du Mercantour. You can observe colonies of marmots near the pass below the Cime de la Bonette.

▶ *From St-Dalmas, return to D 2205 and turn right to St-Étienne-de-Tinée.*

The road follows a stream through an impressive gorge.

St-Étienne-de-Tinée★ – ☋*See ST-ÉTIENNE-DE-TINÉE.*

BONNEVAL-SUR-ARC★★

POPULATION 216
LOCAL MAPS SEE ROUTE DE L'ISERAN AND LA MAURIENNE

Bonneval has retained the charming character of its old village. In summer, it is an excursion centre offering many itineraries within the Parc national de la Vanoise as well as a mountaineering centre organising fascinating expeditions to the border massifs of the Levanna, Ciamarella and Albaron. *73480 Bonneville-sur-Arc* ☉ *Daily 9am-noon, 2-6.30pm (Sun 6pm)* ☉ *Closed Sun and public holidays out of season –* ☎ *04 79 05 95 95 - www-bonneval.sur-arc.com*

▶ **Orient Yourself:** Situated beneath the Col de l'Iseran, in the imposing cirque where the River Arc has its source, Bonneval is the highest municipality in the Maurienne region.

Don't Miss: Be sure to stop at the hameau de l'Écot.

Especially for Kids: The trout-fishing trail along the Arc will amuse children.

Also See: Nearby Sights: AUSSIOS, BESSANS, Route des GRANDES ALPES, Route de l'ISERAN, La Haute MAURIENNE, MODANE, Route du MONT-CENIS, TIGNES, VAL-D'ISÈRE, Massif de la VANOISE

The Resort and Old Village

⚓Ski area

Most of the tourist facilities are in the hamlet of Tralenta, 500m/0.3mi from the village. Ten ski lifts serve an area of moderate size but good quality. You can practice winter sports from December to May between 1 800m/5 905ft and 3 000m/9 843ft on some of the best snow in the French Alps. Beginners and intermediate skiers enjoy the Moulinet ski lift, close to the Vallonet Glacier. Advanced skiers take the 3 000 ski lift to the foot of **Pointe d'Andagne** from where there is a magnificent **view**★★ of the Haute Maurienne (Bessans below, Pointe de Ronce on the left and the rocky ridges of the Vanoise on the right) with the Meije and Aiguilles d'Arves in the background. In summer, skiers make for the **Glacier du Grand Pissaillas,** reached from the Col de l'Iseran.

Bonneval-sur-Arc

The Old Village★★

Bonneval has preserved the character of its old streets and houses by burying electric and telephone cables and banning individual television aerials and satellite dishes, as well as cars which are kept outside the village.

You can walk safely and undisturbed through the narrow streets lined with stone houses, covered with rust-coloured *lauzes* (slabs of schist) and adorned with wooden balconies where dry cow-dung, still used as fuel because wood is scarce, is sometimes stored.

At the heart of the village, a large old chalet known as **La Grande Maison** houses a butcher's and a baker's.

L'Écot

This hamlet, which lies in imposing and austere surroundings, more than 2 000m/6 562ft up, has retained its old stone houses and 12C Chapelle Ste-Marguerite. Once extremely remote, it is today a favourite tourist destination. (*It is best to leave your car in the lot outside Bonneval-sur-Arc and to walk to l'Écot.*)

🚶Hikes

Bonneval is the ideal starting point for **walks** and **hikes** through the Parc national de la Vanoise and the conservation area of **Les Évettes** which offer hikers 120km/74.6mi of marked footpaths.

Refuge du Criou★

Alt 2 050m/6 727ft. ⚓Access: in winter by the Vallonet chairlift, in summer on foot *in 30min.* View of the seracs of the Glacier du Vallonet and Glacier des Sources de l'Arc and of the Col de l'Iseran road.

Address Book

For coin categories, see the Legend on the cover flap.

EATING OUT

Practical note – The 3 zones of the village, Vieux village, Pré Catin and Tralenta, offer a large choice ranging from snackbars near the ski hill to pizzerias, crêperies and traditional Savoyard restaurants. Altogether, you will find a dozen places to eat in the area.

⊜⊜**Le glacier des Evettes** – *Au vieux village -* ☎ 04 79 05 94 06 *- www.evettes. fr.st -19rms* Functioning as restaurant, hotel, bar and newsstand, this address also offers a varied menu, with salads to complement traditional fare. The hotel has accommodation for families.

WHERE TO STAY

⊜⊜**Hôtel La Bergerie** – ☎ 04 79 05 94 97 *- closed 28 Apr-11 Jun and 23 Sept-17 Dec -* 🅿 *-* ⊜*restaurant.* The main attraction of this 1970s building is its site, opposite the ski slopes, with peace and quiet guaranteed. On the menu, local dishes predominate. The rooms are comfortable and fitted out in wood.

⊜⊜**Hôtel à la Pastourelle** – ☎ 04 79 05 81 56 *- www.pastourelle.com - closed 1-6 June and school holidays around 1 Nov - 12rms-* ⊜*restaurant.* This hotel/restaurant with its stone slab roof and stone walls blends in perfectly with the old village. The rooms are painted in typical local style and are very cosy. The restaurant-crêperie is welcoming. Note the stone walls and small vault in the dining room.

Le Carro Refuge★★
Alt 2 760m/9 055ft. *From L'Écot, 3hr 15min on the way up (steep climb); 2hr on the way down. You can also take the scenic path from the Pont de l'Oulietta (alt 2 480m/8 136ft) on the Col de l'Iseran road; this itinerary is long (4hr), but easy and extremely rewarding.*
🔺 Fine **views**★★ of the Albaron and of the Sources de l'Arc, Évettes and Vallonet glaciers. From the refuge, you can admire the Lac Noir and the Lac Blanc.

Les Évettes Refuge★★
Alt 2 615m/8 579ft. *From L'Écot, 1hr 45min on the way up, 1hr on the way down.*
🔺 The steep climb affords views of L'Écot and Bonneval. From the refuge, the **panorama**★★ is splendid: the Glacier des Évettes and the Albaron are reflected in the still waters of the Lacs des Pareis. The Glacier du Grand Méan and Glacier du Mulinet can be seen beyond the refuge. You can also make a detour to the **Cascade de la Reculaz**★ *(1hr there and back).* When you reach the waterfall, cross the little bridge and go to the left past the waterfall. The view is quite impressive *(but not suitable for anyone liable to feel dizzy).*

Walk to the Chalets de la Duis★
From L'Écot: 2hr there and back. Very easy walk.
This would be a good family outing along a broad path in an idyllic setting of green pastures overlooked by fine glaciers.

LE BOURG-D'OISANS★

POPULATION 2 984
MICHELIN MAP 333 J7
LOCAL MAPS SEE BASSIN DU BOURG-D'OISANS AND L'OISANS

Le Bourg-d'Oisans ("Le Bourg" for short) is the modest capital of the Oisans region and one of the most successful tourist resorts in Dauphiné. Its position at the junction of a number of valleys has always made it a natural meeting point and fairs, markets and numerous shops ensure that it remains lively all year round. Some local names testify that, during the Middle Ages, a group of Saracens colonised the area. *quai Girard – 38520 Le Bourg-d'Oisans ⏰ July to Aug: Mon-Sat 9am-7pm, Sun and public holidays 10am-noon, 3-6pm; mid-Dec to April: Mon-Sat 8.30am-noon, 2.30-6pm, Sun and public holidays 8.30-11.30am; rest of year: Mon-Sat 9am-noon, 2-6pm - ☎ 04 76 80 03 25 - www.bourgdoisans.com*

▶ **Orient Yourself:** Bourg is located 52km/32.5mi east of Grenoble through the Gorges de la Romanche (N 91).
🕐 **Organizing Your Time:** From the village of Bourg six valleys open up.
Kids Especially for Kids: Nature trails "Écureuil" (squirrel) and "La Grenouille" (the frog) are designed for children.
👜 **Also See:** Nearby Sights: L'ALPE-D'HUEZ, Les DEUX-ALPES, Massif de CHAMROUSSE, Route de la CROIX-DE-FER, Route du GALIBIER, La GRAVE, Lacs de LAFFREY, L'OISANS, Le VALBONNAIS, VIZILLE

Sights

Musée des Minéraux et de la Faune des Alpes★
⏰ *July to Aug: 10am-6.30pm; Sept to June: 2-6pm.* ⏰ *Closed Nov, 1 Jan and 25 Dec. 4.60€, children 6-18 years 2€ - ☎ 54 76 80 27 04 - www.musee-bourgdoisans.com.* Housed in one of the aisles of the church, the museum displays a permanent collection of minerals particularly rich in quartz, as well as excellent temporary exhibits. Alpine fauna are also represented and a palaeontology section has a collection of fossils dating back to the time of the Alpine geological upheavals.

🚶 *45min there and back on foot along the shaded alleyway beyond the church.* From the platform built at the highest point of the walk, you have a fairly clear view of the Bassin du Bourg-d'Oisans, of the Grandes Rousses mountain range and of the first peaks rising south of the River Vénéon.

Cascade de Sarennes★
🚶 *1km/0.6mi to the northeast, then 15min there and back on foot. Leave Le Bourg on the road to Briançon; 800m/0.5mi further on, turn left onto D 211 towards L'Alped'Huez and park the car just before the bridge over the Sarennes; continue on foot along the path on the right.* The triple waterfall of this tributary of the Romanche is very impressive in springtime.

Excursions

Corniches du Bassin d'Oisans

1 FROM LE BOURG-D'OISANS TO L'ALPE-D'HUEZ
14km/8.7mi – about 30min – 👜 see local map

From Le Bourg-d'Oisans, follow the Briançon road then turn left to L'Alpe-d'Huez. The road climbs in a series of hairpin bends, affording lovely vistas of the Romanche and Vénéon valleys and, in the distance, the Rochail Massif and Villard-Notre-Dame Glacier. Just before the attractive old village of **Huez,** perched on the hillside, there is a good view of the remote upper Sarennes Valley. As the road reaches L'Alpe-d'Huez, the Meije suddenly appears above the vast white-capped Mont-de-Lans Glacier. The narrow road, cut into the cliff face, makes for one of the most impressive drives in the French Alps

L'Alpe-d'Huez✳✳ – *See L'ALPE-D'HUEZ.*

② FROM LE BOURG-D'OISANS TO THE VALBONNAIS

29km/18mi – about 1hr – see local map
This interesting itinerary links the Bourg-d'Oisans Basin and the Valbonnais via the Col d'Ornon, following the course of the River Lignarre and River Malsanne.

▷ *From Le Bourg-d'Oisans take N 91 towards Grenoble. Turn left at La Paute onto D 526.*

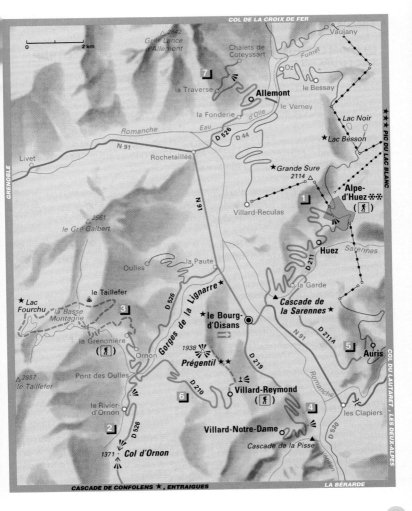

Gorges de la Lignarre★

The river has dug its way through schist (slate used to be quarried here). From Le Rivier, there is a fine view of the Belledonne and Grandes Rousses ranges to the north.

Col d'Ornon

Alt 1 367m/4 485ft. The pass crosses a barren stony landscape. The road follows the narrow valley of the rushing River Malsanne.

▷ *At Le Périer, turn left towards the Cascade de Confolens. Leave the car at the entrance to the Parc national des Écrins and continue on foot.*

Cascade de Confolens★

2hr there and back.

🚶 The path on the left leads to the 70m/230ft-high waterfall, set in lovely surroundings.

On the way down to Entraigues, there are fine **views**★ of Mont Aiguille to the southwest, across the River Drac.

Entraigues – 🌐 See Le VALBONNAIS, Excursions

③ FROM LE BOURG-D'OISANS TO THE REFUGE DE TAILLEFER AND LAC FOURCHU★

14km/8.7mi drive then 3hr on foot – difference in altitude: 800m/2 625ft

▷ *From Le Bourg d'Oisans take N 91 to Grenoble; at La Paute turn left onto D 526 (see drive ② above). At Pont-des-Oulles, turn right to Ornon and La Grenonière.*

🚶 Beyond the Parc des Écrins information panel *(on a bend)* the road is unsurfaced. Park here and continue on this road for 200m/219yd, take a path on the right which leads to La Basse-Montagne, a 20min walk.

▷ *From La Basse-Montagne, allow 2hr for experienced hikers. Leave the stream on your left and follow the path (red markings) through the woods. After 1hr the path, meandering through pastures, reaches the Taillefer refuge.*

From the ledge (2 000m/6 562ft) there is a fine view of the Taillefer Massif and the Lignarre Valley, while behind the building you can see L'Alpe-d'Huez and the Grandes Rousses Massif.

▷ *Continue westwards to reach the Lac Fourchu in 45min along an easier path.*

In spring and summer, the peaceful shores of the lake (2 060m/6 759ft) are dotted with wild flowers, rhododendron bushes, clusters of houseleek and columbine. There is a succession of small lakes lower down.

▷ *You can go straight back via the Lac de la Vache and La Basse-Montagne.*

Petites Routes Des "Villages-Terrasses"★★

These itineraries leading to villages perched on heights overlooking the Bassin du Bourg-d'Oisans follow very narrow cliff roads where vehicles can only pass one another at specified points. With the exception of drive ⑦ they all require experience of driving on mountain roads and must not be attempted by beginners.

4 Route de Villard-Notre-Dame ★★
From Le Bourg-d'Oisans, 9km/5.6mi – about 1hr. The road has a 10% gradient and must be avoided during or after a rainy period; dangerous gulley across the road at the start.

This road offers fine views of mountain scenes and of a remote village at the end. The best view is on a bend, 8km/5mi from Le Bourg-d'Oisans, and includes the lower Vénéon Valley with the Aiguille du Plat-de-la-Selle in the distance and a succession of waterfalls in the foreground.

5 Route d'Auris
From La Garde (on the way to L'Alpe-d'Huez), 8km – about 45min. Follow D 211A towards Le Freney.

This itinerary is interesting for its bird's-eye views of the Bassin du Bourg-d'Oisans (sheer drop of some 500m/1 640ft).

6 Route de Villard-Reymond ★
From Le Bourg-d'Oisans, drive north along N 91, turn left onto D 526 to Pont-des-Oulles then left onto D 210 for 8km/5mi.

The road runs upriver along a tributary of the Lignarre. ◄ From the terraced village of **Villard-Reymond**, walk to the cross at the Col de Saulude *(15min there and back)* and admire the **view**★ of the village of Auris, of L'Alpe-d'Huez and the Belledonne range.

Prégentil ★★
1hr 30min there and back on foot from Villard-Reymond (northwest).

From the summit (alt 1 938m/6 358ft), there is a sweeping view of the high mountains surrounding the Bassin du Bourg-d'Oisans.

7 Route de la Traverse d'Allemont ★
From Le Bourg-d'Oisans, take N 91 towards Grenoble, turn right onto D 526 to La Fonderie d'Allemont. 6.5km/4mi – about 30min.

From there, take D 43 to Allemont, turn left onto Route de la Traverse; shortly before this hamlet, turn right onto a forest road; after 6km/3.7mi, leave the car beyond a bend (parking); ◄ *walk 100m/109yd along the path which starts at the bend.*

From that point, there is a splendid **view**★ of the patchwork of fields in the northern, well-cultivated part of the Bassin du Bourg-d'Oisans and of the mountains that surround it.

▶ *Return to the car and drive for another 200m/219yd.*

On the right, there is a **panorama**★★ of Le Bessey village and the Dôme des Petites Rousses as well as the Col de la Croix-de-Fer and Lac Noir, with the Belledonne and Taillefer massifs forming the horizon to the north and south.

▶ *Drive on for another 300m/328yd.*

There is a clear view of the Grandes Rousses massif and the Combe d'Olle.

LAC DU BOURGET★★

MICHELIN MAP 333 H/I 3/4

Enclosed within its impressive mountain setting, the Lac du Bourget has been the most famous French lake ever since the Romantic poets, headed by Lamartine, celebrated the changing colour of its waters and the wild beauty of its steep shores. 🗺 *Place du Gén.-Sevez - 73370 Le Bourget-du-Lac* 🕐 *July to Aug: Mon-Sat 9am-noon, 2-6pm, Sun 9am-noon; rest of year: Mon-Sat 9am-noon, 2-6pm -* ☎ *04 79 25 01 99 - www.bourgetdulac.com*

▶ **Orient Yourself:** The lake is between the Mont du Chat and La Chambotte, 3km/1.9mi south of the Rhône River and 13km/8.1mi north of Chambéry.

😊 **Don't Miss:** Stop to see at least one of the many panoramic viewpoints on the lake.

🕐 **Organizing Your Time:** Ferries cross the lake daily, between Aix-les-Bains and the abbey of Hautecombe.

👣 **Also See:** Nearby Sights: AIX-LES-BAINS, L'ALBANAIS, ANNECY, Lac d'ANNECY, Les BAUGES, CHAMBÉRY, Massif de la CHARTREUSE

A Bit of History

The Lac du Bourget is the largest (4 500ha/11 120 acres) natural lake in France and also the deepest (145m/476ft). Unlike the Lac d'Annecy, it has never been known to freeze in winter. Windstorms can be extremely violent. Like Lake Geneva, it has been part of an ongoing clean-up project in recent years and the waters abound in fish. The lake used to extend northwards to the Grand Colombier Mountain and was supplied directly by the Rhône. Today, it is separated from the river by the Chautagne marsh; it is however still linked to the Rhône by the 3km/1.8mi-long Savières Canal.

La Chambotte offers the most impressive view of the lake.

Excursions

1 Round tour of the Lake★★

STARTING FROM AIX-LES-BAINS
87km/54mi – about 3hr 30min

The road overlooking the western shore of the lake clings to the steep slopes of the Mont du Chat and the Mont de la Charvaz, offering superb vistas.

On the east side, the road runs close to the lake at the foot of the cliffs of the Mont de Corsuet, revealing the changing moods of the lake.

▶ *Leave Aix by ④ on the town plan, N 201 towards Chambéry.*

The road, skirting the foot of Tresserve hill, a sought-after residential area, follows the low-lying shore, quite busy until Terre-Nue.

Le Bourget-du-Lac

This lakeside town, once linked by steamers to Lyon via the Canal de Savières and the Rhône, is now an expanding holiday resort with a harbour and a beach along the Lac du Bourget.

Address Book

For coin categories, see the Legend on the cover flap.

EATING OUT

🍽**Les Oliviers** – *In Brison village - 73100 Brison-St-Innocent - 6km/4mi N of Aix-les-Bains on D 48 and D 991 - ☎ 04 79 54 21 81 - www.restaurant-les-oliviers. com - closed 15 Jan-15 Feb*. This house facing the lake has a newly renovated dining room, heated by an open fire in winter. The chef offers contemporary cuisine and some regional dishes using fresh local products, according to the season. Shaded terrace in summer.

🍽**Auberge de Savières** – *73310 Chanaz - ☎ 04 79 54 56 16 - www. savieres.com - closed 18 Dec-15 Mar, Tue evening and Wed except from 12 July-1 Sept*. Some people moor their boats opposite this inn after a trip along the Savières canal. Or you might like to cruise in one of the restaurant's own boats, before sitting down to family recipes by the side of the canal.

🍽**Le Bouchon d'Hélène**– *Résidence Van-Gogh - Technolac - 73370 Le Bour-get-du-Lac - ☎ 04 79 25 00 69 - closed 2-10 Jan, 15-30 Aug, Sat lunch and Sun evening*. The decor of this restaurant, enlivened with paintings and vases of flowers, is based on simplicity. If you want a quiet table, reserve on the mez-zanine. The cuisine is based on fresh products, and a slate announces the daily specials.

🍽🍽**La Grange à Sel** – *La Croix Verte - 73370 Le Bourget-du-Lac - ☎ 04 79 25 - www.lagrangeasel.com - closed Jan, Sun evening and Wed*. This old salt storage barn has a vine growing over its façade, a tree-lined terrace and a flower garden. Inside, old stones and beams are left bare, there is an open fire and small lounges. The chef will delight you with his carefully chosen specialties.

🍽🍽🍽**Auberge Lamartine** – *Rte du Tunnel-du-Chat - 73370 Le Bourget-du-Lac - 3.5km/2mi N of Le Bourget on N 504 - ☎ 04 79 25 01 03 - www.lamartine-marin.com - closed mid Dec-mid Jan, Tue lunchtime Sept-May, Sun evening and Mon except public holidays*. Let your gaze drift across the water as you savour a meal full of subtlety and character. This well-reputed establish-ment has a dining room on two levels overlooking the Lac du Bourget. Warm decor with discreet furnishings and soft lighting.

🍽🍽**Atmosphères** – *618 Rte des Tournelles - 73370 Le Bourget-du-Lac - 2.5km/1.25mi NO of Le Bourget on D 42 - ☎ 04 79 25 01 29 - www.atmospheres-hotel.com - closed 15 Feb-1 Mar, 27 Oct-11 Nov, Tue and Wed - 🛏4rms*. This quiet little chalet in the midst of greenery has a remarkable view of the mountains. The dining room has been renovated and, on nice days, the terrace is popular. Cuisine follows produce available in local markets. Simple guestrooms.

WHERE TO STAY

🛏**Chambre d'hôte Montagnole** – *516 chemin de Boissy - 73420 Viviers-du-Lac - ☎ 04 79 35 31 26 - 🍴 - 3rms*. This villa offers simple but comfortable and well-equipped rooms: two have kitchens. Added advantages include a little garden and a pretty view over the cliffs of Revard.

🛏🛏**Hotel le Clos du Lac** – *85 Rte du Bourget-du-Lac - 73420 Viviers-sur-Lac - ☎04 79 54 40 07 - resaviviers@monal-isahotels.com - 🅿 - *Forty identical, air-conditioned rooms in this chain hotel are managed by friendly, competent staff. In the back, a garden with a large green lawn invites a moment of leisure in the sunshine.

🛏🛏🛏🛏**Ombremont** – *Rte du Tunnel-du-Chat - 73370 Le Bourget-du-Lac - 2km/1mi N of Le Bourget on N 504 - ☎ 04 79 25 00 23 - www.hotel-ombre-mont.com - closed Nov- mid- May - 🅿 - 12rms*. Set in a wooded park with flower beds, this majestic residence dating from the 1930s overlooks the lake. Most of the pretty, individually decorated rooms have idyllic views over the lake. Lovely swimming pool and sauna.

Built on an ancient religious site, the **church** (🕐 *Free access all year: 10am-6pm; for guided tours contact the tourist office -* ☎*04 79 25 01 99*) was rebuilt in the 13C and remodelled in the 15C and 19C. Inside, the **frieze**★ running round the walls of the apse is a 13C masterpiece. Note also the 15C font.

The **Château-Prieuré** (🕐 *July to Aug: for guided tours (1hr30min) contact the tourist office -* ☎*04 79 25 01 99. 4€, children 2€*) adjacent to the church (*entry through the arched doorway*) was built in the 11C by St. Odilon, abbot of Cluny, then remodelled in the 13C and 15C. The tour includes the refectory, the kitchen, the chapel from which a staircase leads to an oratory opening on to the chancel of the church, and the library with its ceiling lined with Cordoba leather. The 15C cloisters consist of two superposed galleries; the Gothic vaulting is particularly impressive on the lower level. The attractive gardens, illuminated in season, are decorated with fountains and yew trees trimmed to look like chess pieces

Château Thomas II
Near the mouth of the Leysse. 🕐 *July to Aug: for guided tours contact the tourist office -* ☎ *04 79 25 01 99*. The hunting lodge of the Dukes of Savoie was the scene of diplomatic and dynastic intrigue until the 15C.

▷ *Continue along N 504; at the second intersection signposted Bourdeau, turn left onto D 914 signposted Abbaye de Hautecombe, Col du Chat.*

The road rises above the lake towards the Col du Chat; from the second hairpin bend, there is a fine **panorama**★ of the Chambéry depression separating the Bauges (Mont Revard) and the Chartreuse (Mont Granier) massifs, with the indented Massif d'Allevard in the distance.

Chapelle Notre-Dame-de-l'Étoile
15min there and back on foot. The signposted path starts on a bend of D 914. From the platform in front of the church, there is a fine overall **view**★ of the lake and its frame of mountains including the Grand Colombier, the Semnoz and Mont Revard. After crossing a fertile plain, just beyond Petit-Villard, the road dips into a valley with massive oak trees. After the fork in the road at Ontex, with the Jura looming in the distance, you swing into the valley of St-Pierre-de-Curtille. The road descends towards the north end of the lake, where the Château de Châtillon stands on a wooded promontory, a perfect example of the sort of view celebrated by the Romantic poet Alphonse de Lamartine (1790-1869), who is so closely associated with this area.

▷ *Turn right onto D 18 to the Abbaye royale de Hautecombe.*

Abbaye royale de Hautecombe★★
The abbey stands on a promontory jutting out into the lake. It is the burial place of many members of the House of Savoie including **Béatrix de Savoie** (1198-1266)**,** whose ambitions for her four daughters were more than fulfilled when three of them became queens (of England, France and the Two-Sicilies) and the fourth one, empress of Germany. The last king of Italy, **Umberto II,** was buried in Hautecombe in 1983. During the 19C, the **church** (🕐 *Tour with audio (30min) daily except Tue 10-11.45am, 2-5pm (in winter, 4.30pm), free access only on Good Friday* 🕐*closed 25 Dec and Ash Wednesday*) was entirely restored in neo-Gothic style by artists from Piedmont, which explains the profusion of ornamentation. The 16C former doorway, situated on the left-hand side, is in striking contrast with the highly decorated façade. The interior is also profusely adorned: there are paintings by Gonin and Vacca over the vaulting as well as 300 statues★★ in marble, stone or gilded wood and low-relief sculptures decorating the funeral monuments of the princes of Savoie. Some statues, carved out of Carrara marble, are remarkable, in particular a **Pietà**★ by Benoît Cac-

ciatori. Among the restored paintings from the 14C to the 16C is an Annunciation by Defendente Ferrari.

Near the landing-stage, the **grange batelière** (water barn), built by Cistercian monks in the 12C, was designed to store goods reaching the abbey by boat; the barrel-vaulted lower part comprises a wet dock and a dry dock.

▶ *Return to D 914 as far as Quinfieux and take D 210 to the left towards Chanaz.*

Chanaz★

Situated on the banks of the Canal de Savières, a once busy commercial route, this lively old border town found a new purpose when the canal was opened to pleasure boats. There is an interesting oil-mill still producing walnut oil. The 17C **Maison de Boignes,** easily identified by its two entrances, is now the town hall.

Musée Gallo-Romain

In the Chapelle Notre-Dame-de-la-Miséricorde. ⏲ *July to Aug: 2.30-6.30 pm; Apr-Oct: Fri, Sat, Sun and Mon 2.30-5.30pm (Sun 6.30pm) - ☎04 79 52 11 84 . 3€, children under 10 years no charge.* A 5C pottery workshop, excavated at Portout between 1976 and 1987, contributed to this rich collection of glazed ceramics, articles of daily use, money and jewelry. This was probably a major production centre, exporting down the river system.

At **Portout** (⌂ *see below*) you can visit a recon-structed workshop: ⏲ *July to Aug: guided tour and activities 2.30 and 5.30pm; Apr-Oct, free access. Contact M. Rat-taire - ☎04 79 62 02 03*

▶ *From Chanaz, drive along D 18 towards Aix-les-Bains.*

Canal de Savières

This 4km/2.4mi canal connects the waters of the Lac du Bourget to the Rhône and acts as a "safety valve" when, after the spring thaw or the heavy autumn rains, the flow is reversed and the river overflows into the lake. A major trade route until the 19C, the canal was also the easi-est way for the dukes of Savoie to travel from Chambéry to Lyon.

The road crosses the Canal de Savières at Por-tout, then runs through marshland to Chaudieu.

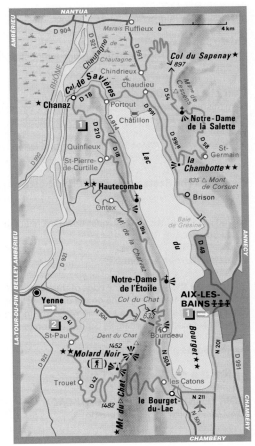

The Canal de Savières

▶ *Turn left onto D 991 then right at Chindrieux towards the Col de Sapenay.*

The narrow twisting road affords impressive views of the Lac du Bourget, the Abbaye de Hautecombe and the Dent du Chat summit, with the Rhône Valley to the north, guarded by the impressive Grand Colombier.

Col du Sapenay★
Alt 897m/2 943ft. The road goes through a mountain landscape of fir trees and pastures.

Chapelle Notre-Dame de la Salette
From this high point in the Montagne de Cessens, where the monks of Hautecombe first settled, the view★ extends over the Albanais depression to the east.

▶ *At St-Germain, turn onto D 991B, then turn left in La Chambotte past a small chapel.*

View from the Restaurant de la Chambotte★★ – 🕭 See AIX-LES-BAINS: Excursions.

Beyond La Chambotte, the road goes down to Chaudieu, offering fine views of the Lac du Bourget.

▶ *In Chaudieu turn left onto D 991.*

From then on, the road skirts the edge of the lake; good views of the Dent du Chat and the Abbaye de Hautecombe on the opposite shore. Just beyond **Brison-les-Oliviers,** a fishing village with a strong wine-growing tradition, the road runs close to the shores of the lovely Baie de Grésine and on to Aix-les-Bains.

Aix-les-Bains♨♨ – 🕭 See AIX-LES-BAINS.

② Route du Mont du Chat

FROM YENNE TO LE BOURGET-DU-LAC
34km/21mi – about 2hr – see local map

Yenne

The small capital of the Bugey Savoyard region occupies a favourable position at the entrance of the Défilé de Pierre-Châtel, through which the Rhône forces its way out of the Alps.

The west doorway of the 12C-15C **church** has retained some fine Romanesque capitals; inside, the **stalls**★ dating from the 15C are delicately carved with Flamboyant motifs and decorated with the twinned royal arms of France and Savoie. The sacristy contains a fine Christian tombstone from the 6C.

The town centre offers pleasant walks through its streets lined with old houses.

▶ *From Yenne take D 41 (which branches off D 921 to the left); from St-Paul continue south on D 41 past Trouet, then turn left onto D 42 to the Lac du Bourget.*

Mont du Chat★

A television relay pylon (alt 1 504m/4 934ft) stands some 50m/55yd south of the pass. Fine **view** of Aix-les-Bains and the lake from the platform below (1 470m/4 823ft).

Molard Noir★★

1hr there and back on foot from Mont du Chat.

🔲 Follow the ridge to the north, through the woods; from the clifftop on the west side, a fine stretch of the Rhône Valley can be seen from the Défilé de Pierre-Châtel north to the Grand Colombier. The top of Molard Noir (alt 1 452m/4 764ft, viewing tables) offers a vast **panorama** of Mont Revard and, beyond, of Aiguilles de Chamonix, Mont Blanc, the Vanoise Massif, the Belledonne range and Mont Granier.

On the east side, the road meanders through the woods.

▶ *Continue on D 42 to Le Bourget-du-Lac.*

BOURG-ST-MAURICE

POPULATION 6 747
MICHELIN MAP 333 N4
LOCAL MAPS SEE LE BEAUFORTAIN AND MASSIF DE LA VANOISE

Bourg-St-Maurice is situated at the heart of the Haute Tarentaise region and occupies a commanding position at the intersection of the upper Isère Valley, the Chapieux Valley and the road leading to Italy via the Col du Petit-St-Bernard. For this reason, "Le Bourg," as the locals call it, is the ideal starting point for driving tours in the area. 🛈 *place de la Gare – 73700 Bourg-St-Maurice* 🕐 *July to Aug: Mon-Sat 9am-12.30pm, 2-7pm, Sun and public holidays 9am-12.30pm, 2-6.30pm; mid-Dec to April: 9am-12.30pm, 2-7pm; May to June: Mon-Sat 9am-noon, 2-6pm, Sun 9am-12.30pm -* ☎ *04 79 07 12 57 - www.lesarcs.com*

▶ **Orient Yourself:** Bourg-St-Maurice is 55km/34.4mi southeast of Albertville on N 90, or you can pass by Beaufortain or la Maurienne.

😊 **Don't Miss:** Try to see the frescos in the Chapelle de Vulmix

🧒 **Especially for Kids:** Two festivals entertain children: the Edelweiss festival in July, and the humour festival in August

⌚ **Also See:** Nearby Sights: Les ARCS, BEAUFORT, La Vallée des BELLEVILLE, Route des GRANDES ALPES, Route de l'ISERAN, La PLAGNE, La TARENTAISE, TIGNES, VAL-D'ISÈRE, Massif de la VANOISE

Museum

Musée des Minéraux et Faune de l'Alpe

Avenue du Maréchal-Leclerc. ⏰ *July to Aug: Tue-Sat 10am-noon, 3-7pm, Sun and Mon 3-7pm; Sept to June: on request. 4€, children under 8 years no charge -* ☎ *04 79 07 12 74.*

Fine crystals, with an exhibit showing where they are found and how they are cut. There is also an exhibit of alpine animals.

Excursions

Chapelle de Vulmix

4km/2.5mi south on D 86. This simple chapel, restored in the 17C, contains splendid 15C **frescoes**★ depicting the life of St Grat, known as the protector of crops; the legend begins on the south wall.

Hauteville-Gondon

4km/2.5mi from Bourg-St-Maurice, drive along D 90 towards Aime then follow D 220.

Église St-Martin de Tours

⏰ *Guided tours on request at the tourist office -* ☎ *04 79 07 04 92 or 04 79 60 59 00* Built in the 17C, the church is richly decorated in Baroque style, with several 18C altarpieces including the fine polychrome retable over the high altar framing an illustration of the legend of St Martin.

The altar of Église St-Martin, Hauteville-Gondon

Les Arcs ★★★

Take N 90 from the northeast exit of Bourg-St-Maurice and turn right almost immediately onto D 119. Arc 1600: 12km/7.5mi (or funicular during the season), Arc 1800: 15km/9.3mi, Arc 2000: 26km/16.2mi. There is also a new resort, Arc 1950. (⬧ *see Les ARCS).*

For coin categories, see the Legend on the cover flap.

WHERE TO STAY

⬧**Hôtel de la Petite Auberge** – *Le Reverset -* ☎ *04 79 07 05 86 - closed May, Oct-Nov, Sun evening and Mon -* 🅿 *- 12rms -* ⬧*restaurant.* In a little courtyard off the road, this simple inn offers clean and comfortable rooms, and the restaurant serves traditional fare in perfect taste. Shaded terrace in summer.

The **"Fête des Edelweiss"** (⬧*see Calendar of events*), which takes place in July, is an international folk festival showing off the picturesque costumes of the Tarentaise and Aosta valleys - ☎*04 79 07 12 57 - www.lesarcs.com*

Besides skiing, Les Arcs offers other sports including swimming, gym, climbing, tennis and golf; there is also expert instruction. Ask for the multi-sport card at the sports club.

Route du Petit-St-Bernard★★

31km/19.3mi – about 1hr 15min – 🔖 *local map see Massif de la VANOISE*
This former international trade and military route today has a major tourist appeal as part of the famous "Tour du Mont Blanc." The road leading to the pass on the French side, built during the reign of Napoleon III, has a 5% gradient as it climbs above the Isère Valley from 904m/2 966ft (at Séez) to 2 188m/7 178ft.
The pass is usually blocked by snow from the end of October to the end of May.

▷ *From Bourg-St-Maurice, take N 90 towards Val d'Isère and Italy.*

Séez

This ancient village, situated on the old Roman road, was named Séez because it stood close to the sixth milestone between Lyon and Milan. It grew prosperous in the 19C through its woollen-cloth industry, an activity which has recently picked up again after a long period of decline. The Baroque **Église St-Pierre** (🕐 *July to Aug: Wed-Sat 10am-noon, 3-6pm (7pm Thur); last 2 weeks of June and first 2 weeks of Sept: Tue-Sat 5-8pm; Christmas and Feb school holidays: Thur 3-7pm - ☎ 04 79 41 00 15*), contains a splendid altarpiece by Fodéré, a local artist, and the 15C recumbent figure of a knight in armour to the left of the entrance.

Espace baroque Tarentaise

Rue St-Pierre 🕐 *July to Aug: Mon-Sat 9.30-noon, 2-6.30pm; last 2 weeks of June and first 2 weeks of Sept: Mon-Fri 2.30-6pm; school holidays (except Easter): Tue-Fri 3-6pm; rest of year: Tue and Thur 3-8pm. 3€ - ☎ 04 79 40 10 38*
This museum offers, on three storeys, a working forge, a collection of jewelry from the Savoie and an educational exhibit on Baroque art in the region, particularly church art. (🔖 *see Chemins du Baroque in Planning your Trip*)

▷ *Bear left as you leave Séez.*

The road climbs in a series of impressive hairpin bends with Mont Pourri towering above to the south, offering views of the Moyenne Tarentaise to the southeast, and then of the upper Isère Valley towards the snow-capped peaks which divide the Haute-Tarentaise from the Haute-Maurienne.

🦮 La Rosière 1850✳

▷ *20km/12.5mi from Bourg St-Maurice by N 90, towards the Col du Petit-St-Bernard, or by D 84 past picturesque villages.*
🏠 *La Rosière-Bourg, 73700 La Rosière 1850* 🕐 *July to Aug and Christmas holidays: 8.30am-7pm; rest of year: Mon-Fri 9am-noon, 2-6pm* 🕐 *closed public holidays - ☎04 79 06 80 51 - www.larosiere.net.* This pleasant resort situated, as the name suggests, at an altitude of 1 850m/6 070ft, overlooks the Tarentaise from a commanding position. Its ski slopes, part of the **Espace San Bernardo**, offer good snow coverage and plenty of sunshine within a vast international skiing area linked to the Italian resort of La Thuile. The Roc Noir, Traversette and Belvédère summits, the ski runs of San Bernardo and La Tour, afford splendid **views**★ of Mont Blanc and a panoramic **viewpoint** over the Rocher de Bellevarde, the dam at Tignes and Mont Pourri (3 779m/12 398).
In summer, La Rosière is a peaceful holiday resort offering a wide choice of excursions. There are kennels breeding the famous St Bernard dogs nearby.

Col du Petit-St-Bernard★

Fierce fighting during the Second World War caused great damage to the hospice believed to have been founded by **St Bernard de Menthon** (923-1008), whose statue stands in front of the buildings. The institution provided shelter for travellers facing terrible snowstorms. Further on stands the Colonne de Joux, originally surmounted by a statue of Jupiter (Jovis), which, so the story goes, was torn down by St Bernard himself. A statue of the saint, commissioned by a benefactor of the hospice, replaced it at the end of the 19C.

The **view**★ to the right of the Hotel de Lancebranlette extends to Mont Ouille, with the Italian slope of Mont Blanc to the right.

The **Jardin botanique La Chanousia** (🕐*July to Aug, and Sept depending on snowfall: 9am-7pm - ☎04 79 07 43 32*), is a late 19C botanical garden founded by the Canon Chanoux to preserve Alpine natural surroundings. Neglected after the Second World War, it has been replanted and now contains about 1 000 species of Alpine plants.

Hikes

Lancebranlette★★★

4hr there and back on foot by a mountain path which is often in poor condition at the beginning of summer. Mountain boots are recommended. Detailed information is available at the Chalet de Lancebranlette.

🚶 From the chalet, climb the northwest slope of the pass towards an indented crest on the left. An isolated building halfway up the slope is a useful landmark to aim for. Once you reach a vast cirque in a landscape of screes and pastures, keep going left to join the path which winds all the way up to the summit (2 928m/9 606ft). Vast **panorama** including the Italian side of Mont Blanc (viewing table).

Hike to Lac de la Plagne★★

Start from Rosuel – 2hr 30min on the way up. Difference in altitude: 650m/2 133ft.

🚶 Follow footpath GR 5 as far as the bridge over the Ponturin, then continue along the left side of the river. A path on the right bank leads down to the lake in 1 hr 45 min. From there, it is possible to rejoin GR 5 which leads to the Col du Palet (about 4hr return).

BRIANÇON★★

POPULATION 10 737
MICHELIN MAP 334 H3
LOCAL MAP SEE LE BRIANÇONNAIS

Europe's highest town (1 321m/4 334ft) occupies a strategic position at the intersection of the Guisane, Durance, Cerveyrette and Clarée valleys, close to the Montgenèvre Pass leading to Italy. This explains the number of strongholds surrounding the town. The old fortified town or **Ville Haute,** surrounded by a ring of forts planned by Vauban, Louis XIV's military engineer, has retained its steep, narrow streets, but the forbidding setting which once deterred enemies now draws tourists and skiers. Briançon, which has had a military skiing school since 1904, forms part of the winter sports complex of **Serre-Chevalier** (🕐 *see SERRE-CHEVALIER*). 🚹 *1 Place du Temple – 05100 –* 🕐 *Daily 9am-noon, 2-6pm, Sundays and holidays variable - ☎ 04 92 21 08 50 - www.ot-briancon.fr. Guided tours of the town (2hrs) –* 🕐 *July to Aug: daily 10am and 3pm; June and Sept: Wed, Fri, Sat 2.30, 4.90€ . Contact the "Service du Patrimoine" (Heritage Dept.) -* ☎ *04 92 20 29 49 - www.vpah.culture.fr*

▸ **Orient Yourself:** To get to Briançon, take the N 91 from the Col du Lautaret, or the N 94 from Gap. Follow the roadsign "Briançon-Vauban" to find the old town, entered through the Dauphine and Pignerol gates.

🅿 **Parking:** You can park on the Champ-de-Mars.

🚫 **Don't Miss:** The upper town, with its charming streets and its battlements offers wide views over the town and the surrounding mountains. The outlook from behind the Collégiale Notre-Dame is also worthwhile; climb a bit more to an even better view from the Croix de Toulouse.

🕓 **Organizing Your Time:** Give yourself two hours to visit the upper town.

Kids **Especially for Kids:** Both the Maison du Parc national des Ecrins and the Parc sur la Schappe (see below) have exhibits for children.

◔ **Also See:** Nearby Sights: ABRIÈS, L'ARGENTIÈRE-LA-BESSÉE, Le BRIANÇONNAIS, CEILLAC, Vallée de FREISSINIÈRES, Route du GALIBIER, Route des GRANDES ALPES, La GRAVE, GUILLESTRE, MOLINES-EN-QUEYRAS, MONT-DAUPHIN, MONT-GENÈVRE, L'OISANS, Le QUEYRAS, ST-VÉRAN, SERRE-CHEVALIER, La VALLOUISE, VARS

Address Book

For coin categories, see the Legend on the cover flap.

EATING OUT

🍽️🍺 **Le Rustique** – *36 r. du Pont-d'Asfeld - ☎ 04 92 21 00 10 - closed 15 Jun-4 July, 15 Nov-4 Dec*. This pretty house with its coloured façade is as rustic as its name suggests. Inside the dining room is white with a vaulted ceiling and old wooden floor and adorned with traditional farming implements and an old sleigh. Local specialities include the famous fondue.

🍽️🍺 **Le Péché Gourmand** – *2 rte de Gap - ☎ 04 92 21 33 21 - closed spring and Christmas holidays, Sun evening and Mon*. Is it a sin to love food? While reflecting on this, in this old house on the banks of the Guisane, enjoy the sophisticated, authentic cuisine.

Menus Vauban – Five local restaurants have put forgotten dishes from the age of Louis XIV back on the dinner table. Look for Vauban's name at: **Hôtel de la Chausee, Passé Simple, Écrins, La Caponnière,** and **La Maison de Catherine**.

WHERE TO STAY

🍽️ **La Riolette** – *38 rue du Mélezin, 05100 Villard-St-Pancrace - ☎ 04 92 20 58 68, grec_rhc@club-internet.fr - closed 4 Nov-22 Dec - ⚡ - 5 rms - 🍽️ restaurant*. These simple rooms overlooking Briançon offer the calm of the countryside, only a few minutes from downtown. The restaurant of this big family house features products directly from the owners' farm.

🍽️🍺 **La Chausee** – *4 rue Centrale - ☎ 04 92 21 10 37 - hotel.de.la.chausee@wanadoo.fr - closed 19 Apr-11 May and 3-26 Oct - 13 rooms - 🍽️ restaurant*.

This lower-town hotel has been in the family for five generations. Rooms are simple but spacious, some with balconies. The restaurant is decorated in chalet-style and the cuisine accents local specialties: tartiflette, fondue, raclette…

ON THE TOWN

🎭 To keep abreast of the lively cultural and nightlife of Briançon, pick up the monthly guide B. Mag at the tourist office.

SPORTS AND LEISURE

Parc 1326 Briançon – *37 rue Bermont-Bonnet - ☎ 04 92 20 04 04 - www.vert-marine.com* A large, grassy amusement park with swimming pools, a waterpark with toboggans, whitewater, etc., miniature golf, skating rink, tennis courts, jogging track and more.

Kids **Parc sur la Schappe** – *☎ 04 92 46 16 91 🕓 June to Aug: daily 9am-10pm; Sept to May: 9am to 7pm*. On the former site of a silk factory, this outdoor recreation park offers nature trails, a lake, Jungle Park games, etc., adapted for children as young as 4 years. There is also a snack bar.

Bureau des Guides de Briançon – *Parc Chancel - ☎ 04 92 20 15 73 - bgb05@club-internet.fr – Jul-Aug: daily 9.30am-7pm; Sept-Jun 5pm-7pm*. For the past 25 years, a team of keen mountaineers has done its utmost to ensure that visitors enjoy the mountains in complete security, in all seasons: rock-climbing, mountaineering, canyoning, hiking and paragliding are on offer in the summer; excursions on skis, snowshoes and off-piste are on the menu in winter. A festival organized the first Sunday of August recognizes their exploits.

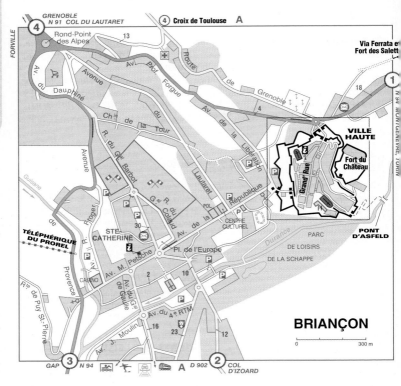

BRIANÇON

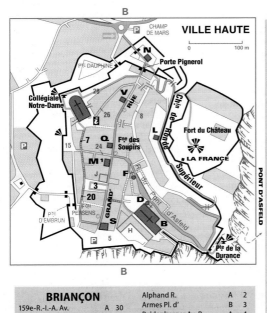

VILLE HAUTE

Barbot R. du Gén.	A	
Blanchard Pl. Médecin Gén.	B	5
Carlhan R. du Cdt	B	7
Castres R. de	B	8
Centrale R.	A	10
Colaud R. du Gén.	A	
Col-d'Isoard Av.	A	12
Dauphiné Av. du	A	
Daurelle Av. A.	A	13
Eberlé Pl. du Gén.	B	15
Europe Pl. de l'	A	
Forger Av. R.	A	
Forgue Av. Prof.	A	
Gaulle Av. Gén.-de	A	16
Grand'Rue	B	
Grenoble Rte de	A	
Italie Rte d'	A	18
Lautaret Av. du	A	
Libération Av. de la	A	
Mercerie R. de la	B	20
Moulin R. J.	A	
Pasteur R.	A	23
Petsche Av. M.	A	
Pont d'Asfeld R. du	B	
Porte-Méane R.	B	24
Provence Av. de	A	
Puy St-Pierre Rte de	A	
République Av. de la	A	
Temple R. du	B	26
Tour Chemin de la	A	
Vauban Av.	B	28

BRIANÇON			Alphand R.	A	2
159e-R.-I.-A. Av.	A	30	Armes Pl. d'	B	3
4e-R.-T.-M. Av. du	A		Baldenberger Av. P.	A	4

A Bit of History

The capital of the Briançonnais region – In accordance with the **Grande Charte** granted to them in 1343 and later confirmed by the kings of France, 52 municipalities of the Briançonnais region, situated on either side of the border with Italy, formed a kind of free state with Briançon as their capital. One of the privileges of the *Escartons*, as they were known, was to fix and levy their own taxes. Thirty-two of these municipalities became Italian under the Treaty of Utrecht signed in 1713.

A military town – The rock, which towers over the Durance, was fortified in turn by the Celts and the Romans and again during the Middle Ages. The fortifications were strengthened in 1590 by the Huguenot commander Lesdiguières, and a second wall was erected in 1690. However, after a fire destroyed most of the town in 1692, Louis XIV asked Vauban to rebuild the fortifications as war had broken out between France and Savoie. Vauban undertook the building of a ring of forts which was completed almost 200 years later. After Napoleon's defeat at Waterloo in 1815, Briançon was besieged by allied forces but held out until peace was signed under the Treaty of Paris several months later.

Ville Haute★★ *1hr 30min – Car park on the Champ de Mars*

▷ *Signs on each steet explain their names, while guideposts are placed before principal buildings and historic sights.*

The walled city is accessible through four gates: Porte Pignerol to the north, Porte d'Embrun to the southwest, Porte de la Durance to the east and Porte Dauphine (recently opened to ease the flow of traffic).
It is divided into four districts by the intersection of Grand-Rue and rue Porte-Méane, which leads into rue du Pont-d'Asfeld: Quartier du Temple grouped round the Collégiale Notre-Dame, Quartier Mercerie with place d'Armes in its centre, which was the commercial and administrative district, the residential district of the Grand Caire to the northeast, and Quartier de Roche which was centred on the various monasteries including the Récollets and Pénitents. Two steep streets running through the town, known as *gargouilles,* have a fast-flowing stream in the middle, which provided a ready supply of water for fighting fires. There is a good view of the old town from the upper battlements.

Porte Pignerol

As was usual in the 18C, the gate comprises several separate defences. The outer gate, rebuilt in the 19C, bears an inscription recalling the 1815 siege. The guardhouse, known as "D'Artagnan," stands in front of the line of defense: the drawbridge, a gate reinforced by a portcullis and another gate decorated with a splendid frontispiece. The building to the right of this gate houses the Service du Patrimoine. A vaulted passage gives access to the walled town. Exhibitions devoted to "Three hundred years of military architecture" are held in the building adjacent to Porte Pignerol.

▷ *Follow the road to the left of the gate*

Chapelle des Pénitents	B	D	Fontaine des Soupirs	B		Musée de la Mesure	
Chapelle des Récollets	B	F	Fort des Salettes	A		du Temps	B M¹
Chemin de ronde supérieur	B		Fort du Château	B		Pont d'Asfeld	A
Cloche de Som de Serre	B	L	la France (statue			Porte de Pignerol	B
Collégiale Notre-Dame	B		de Bourdelle)	B		Porte de la Durance	B
Corps de garde dit			Maison des Têtes	B	V	Téléphérique du Prorel	A
" d'Artagnan "	B	N	Maison du Parc national des			Via Ferrata de la	
Croix de Toulouse	A		Écrins	B	S	Croix de Toulouse	A
Église des Cordeliers	B	B	Maison Jean Prat	B	Q		

Chemin de ronde supérieur★

This upper line of defence overlooks the roofs of the walled city with the towers of the Collégiale Notre-Dame rising above. It skirts the **Fort du château** (◷ *July to Aug: 10am-6pm; from May to Oct, guided tour (about 2hrs) available at the Service du Patrimoine - ☎ 04 92 20 29 49 - www.briancon.com/vah 5.15€, children under 12 years old, no charge.*) in front of which towers a 9m/30ft-high statue of "France"a by Bourdelle, originally intended to stand on the spot where American troops first set foot on French soil during the First World War and rescued from store-room obscurity in 1933. The **Som de Serre bell,** used in the past to sound the alarm, hangs in the small tower to on the left.

The Porte d'Embrun and Briançon's formidable defences

▶ *Continue along the road which leads down to the town.*

The terrace of the **Porte de la Durance** offers a charming **view**★ of the Durance valley and the bridge.

Pont-d'Asfeld★

This single-arched bridge spanning the Durance 56m/184ft above the river bed was built in 1729-31 by military engineers headed by Asfeld, Vauban's successor, in order to link the town with the Fort des Trois Têtes.

▶ *Turn onto the rue du Pont-d'Asfeld.*

It leads to the "religious" district. Look first for the fine restored steeple of the **Chapelle des Pénitents,** badly damaged by fire in 1988 and, for the most part, sadly neglected since; a little further on stands the **Chapelle des Récollets**, which only French Boy Scouts may visit.

▶ *Turn left onto the Grande Gargouille.*

Grande Gargouille or Grand-Rue★

This is the main shopping street of the walled town, very lively in summer on either side of its fast-flowing central stream. Going down the street, note the **Fontaine des Soupirs** (Fountain of Sighs, paid for as a fine by two merchants) under an arch on your right and the beautiful doorway of no 64, dating from 1714. The **Fontaine François I,** named after the French king who made a present to the town of the elephants' heads decorating the fountain, stands under an archway on a street corner. The **Maison de Jean Prat,** at no 37 across the street, has a fine Renaissance front decorated with masks and statues (St John the Evangelist with two angels). The **Maison des Têtes** at no 13 was decorated at the turn of the century with figures in regional costume representing the owner's family.

At no 47 stands the **Musée de la Mesure du Temps** (♿ ◷ *July-Aug: daily 10.30am-6.30pm, rest of the year by appointment - ☎ 04 92 21 07 93. 4.50€, children 2 €*), the converted stable in which a private collection of over 200 clocks and other timepieces is on permanent display. The water clocks even allow you to hear time passing drop by drop.

Place d'Armes

Its brightly coloured façades and pavement cafés give this former market square linking the Grande Gargouille and Petite Gargouille a southern atmosphere; it is decorated with two **sundials.** The left-hand one, painted in the 18C on the front of the former prison, bears the simple inscription "Life slips by like a shadow," whereas the right-hand one, which adorns the 19C law courts bears the more elaborate inscription 'From sunrise to sunset, this fleeting shadow rules simultaneously over the work of Themis (the goddess of justice) and of Mars (the god of war)'. The central well, dug on the orders of Vauban, stood the city in good stead during the siege of 1815. A street to the left leads to the former Cordelier monastery (now the town hall) and to its church, the **église des Cordeliers** (🕐 *guided tours by appointment with the Service du Patrimoine -* ☎*04 92 20 29 49),* which has painted murals inside and an imposing façade decorated with Lombard arcading.

▶ *Return to the Grande Gargouille*

Maison du Parc national des Écrins [Kids]
Place Médecin-Gén.-Blanchard ♿ 🕐 *July to Aug: daily 10am-noon, 3-7pm; Sept through June: daily except Sat-Sun 2-6pm* 🕐 *Closed holidays except 14 July and 15 Aug. No charge -* ☎ *04 92 21 42 15, or 04 92 21 08 49.*
The National Park office is based in an imaginatively converted 18C military hospital, where a permanent exhibition presents the flora and fauna of the area and the history of skiing in agreeably unstuffy style.

▶ *Head towards the Porte d'Embrun and turn right onto the Petite Gargouille (rue de la Mercerie).*

Petite Gargouille ★
A narrow street of tall, rather austere façades, offset by some fine decorative ironwork on the doors.

Collégiale Notre-Dame
Built during the early 18C to a plan reworked by Vauban, this imposing edifice has a remarkable façade flanked by two high towers decorated with sundials. The left-hand one, dating from 1719, is in Baroque style; it is one of the finest painted sundials in the Alps. The stone lions placed in front of the doorway belonged to a church demolished in 1692, and now provide tourists with a much-needed spot to rest their legs. The **viewing table** situated behind the church offers a good view of the three tiers of fortifications built in to the terrain, of the modern town below, of the Fort des Salettes to the north with the Croix de Toulouse above it, of the mountains framing the Briançon Basin and of the Montgenèvre Pass to the east.

Croix de Toulouse ★★   *8.5km/5.3mi – about 1hr*

Leave Briançon by ④ on the town plan (Route de Grenoble) and turn left onto D 232T towards the Croix de Toulouse. The narrow road rises through pine trees in a series of hairpin bends. Carry on along the unsurfaced part and leave the car near a block-house.
🚶 It is also possible to reach the Croix de Toulouse on foot *(2hr there and back)* from the Fort des Salettes. A well-marked path runs along the cliffside offering fine views.
The Croix de Toulouse (alt 1 962m/6 437ft) is a rock spur situated at the end of a ridge separating the Guisane and Clarée valleys and towering over Briançon. From the viewing table, the **view** extends on one side to the walled town, with its ring of forts and the Durance Valley in the distance, and takes in the whole Guisane Valley up to the Col du Lautaret on the other side.

Round tour via Puy-St-André and Puy-St-Pierre
15km/9.3mi – about 1hr

▶ *From Briançon, drive southwest towards Puy-St-Pierre on the road between ③ and ④ on the town plan.*

The small road rises quickly above the Durance Valley. Beyond the village of **Puy-St André,** it affords interesting **views** of the Condamine and Écrins massifs.

🚶 *Park the car below Puy-Chalvin and continue on foot.*

Puy-Chalvin
The 16C **Chapelle Ste-Lucie** (🕐 *July toAug: Mon and Thur 5-6.30pm by appointment at the town hall of Puy-Saint-André -* ☎ *04 92 20 24 26*) standing in the heart of this hamlet is covered with murals inside and outside. The front is decorated with panels, separated by interlaced motifs, illustrating scenes from the Passion and representing various saints. Inside, the paintings in naive style depict scenes from the life of Christ.

▶ *Return to Puy-St-André and turn left to drive to Puy-St-Pierre along D 335.*

Puy-St-Pierre
Almost completely destroyed during the Second World War, this hamlet has retained a church standing on the edge of a cliff and offering a splendid **panorama**★★ of Briançon and the Durance Valley. At night, the floodlit church can be seen clearly from the Ste-Catherine district in Briançon.
🚶 *A 15min walk upwards.* The history of irrigation and the techniques of modern hydro-engineering are revealed in the open-air **Musée de Plein Air sur les Canaux d'Irrigation**, near the "Serre che soleil" path.

▶ *Continue along D 335 then D 35 to return to Briançon.*

Hikes

Fort des Salettes★

From the Champ de Mars – 45min there and back on foot – along the chemin des Salettes. 🕐 July to Aug: daily except Sat, 10am-6pm, guided tours (about 2hrs) by appointment with the Service du Patrimoine from May to Oct - ☎ *04 02 20 29 49 - wwww.briancon. com/vah, 5.15€, children under 12 years no charge.*
🏯 Designed by Vauban in 1692, the fort was not built until a year after his death in 1707 and was remodelled during the 19C. It was intended to guard the access to Briançon from Montgenèvre and Italy. Its small keep standing in the middle of a courtyard is surrounded by bastions linked to it by underground passages.
From the platform in front of the fort, there is an interesting **view**★ of the walled town and its ring of forts.

Le Prorel★
Start from the cable-car station in the Ste-Catherine district. The journey is in two sections and it is possible to do part of the journey or take a one-way ticket only. Be prepared to face strong, cold winds blowing continuously at the top. 🕐 July to Aug: 9.45am-7.30pm, 20min total ride. 9.50€ return, both sections - ☎ *04 92 25 55 03.*
On the way up, there are superb views of the summit (2 566m/8 419ft). 🚶 There are numerous possibilities for fine walks to the surrounding heights offering magnificent **panoramic views**★★. You can go back down towards Chantemerle or Puy-St-Pierre (via the Chapelle Notre-Dame-des-Neiges).

Chapelle Notre-Dame-des-Neiges

Alt 2 292m/7 520ft. *15min on foot; marked path.* This small chapel decorated with ex-votos can be reached from the cable-car station; it offers a fine view of the Serre-Chevalier Valley.

You can return to Briançon along the marked path running through the high pastures (about 2hr 30min).

Via ferrata at the Croix de Toulouse

The path leading to the foot of the cliff starts between two cafés opposite the Champ de Mars car park (*15min walk*). The course ends just east of the Croix de Toulouse and it is possible to go back along the chemin des Salettes. (*4 hrs return, altitude difference 400m/1 312 ft*) Ask at the **Bureau des Guides** (*Parc Chancel, July to Aug: daily 9.30am-7pm; Sept to June: daily 5-7pm - ☎ 04 92 20 15 73, bgb0@club-internet. fr*) for further information.

LE BRIANÇONNAIS★★

MICHELIN MAP 77 FOLDS 7, 8 AND 18, 189 FOLDS 8 AND 9 OR 244 FOLDS 42 AND 43

The geography of the Briançonnais is marked by striking contrasts which Vauban described in the following terms: "The area includes mountains reaching for the sky and valleys sinking to incredible depths." In the centre of the area lies Briançon at the intersection of four valleys. During the Middle Ages, the communities of these valleys formed a kind of federation under the terms of the Grande Charte (*see BRIANÇON*). The large stone-built houses, decorated with arcades and columns, testify to the fact that the inhabitants were relatively well off. The region is well known for its southern mountain climate, clear skies, unmistakable light, and good snow coverage which encouraged the early development of important ski resorts such as Montgenèvre and Serre-Chevalier.

▶ **Orient Yourself:** Great efforts are made to clear the passes of Lautaret and de Montgenèvre of snow during the winter, but drivers heading for the Izoard or the valley of the Clarée may encounter snowdrifts from October through June.

🔅 **Don't Miss:** The valleys of the Guisane and the Clarée, especially the route to Izoard, are spectacular, but the rest of the countryside is also impressive.

🕐 **Organizing Your Time:** Give yourself two or three days in the Briançonnais.

🔅 **Also See:** Nearby Sights: ABRIÈS, L'ARGENTIÈRE-La-BESSÉE, BRIANÇON, CEILLAC, Vallée des FREISSINIÈRES, Route du GALIBIER, Route des GRANDES ALPES, La GRAVE, GUILLESTRE, MOLINES-EN-QUEYRAS, MONT-DAUPHIN, MONTGENÈVRE, L'OISANS, ST-VERAN, SERRE-CHEVALIER, La VALLOUISE, VARS

Excursions

1 Vallée de la Guisane★

FROM COL DE LAUTARET TO BRIANÇON *32km/20mi – about 1hr.*

This wide valley, linking the *départements* of Isère and Hautes-Alpes, has acquired a high reputation for cross-country skiing, ski-trekking and alpine skiing at the **Serre-Chevalier** winter sports complex. *See SERRE-CHEVALIER*

Col du Lautaret★★– 🕐 *See L'OISANS* [2] *and SERRE-CHEVALIER: HIKES.*

The imposing mass of the Meije glaciers comes into view soon after the Col du Lautaret. The road goes through a wide valley, relatively arid except for the larch forest covering the north-facing slope *(ubac)*. On the way down from the pass, road N 91 skirts the barren slopes of the **Grand Galibier** (alt 3 229m/10 594ft). The pyramid-shaped Grand Pic de Rochebrune can be seen in the distance, down the valley beyond Briançon. The valley then widens and villages begin to appear.

Le Casset

The elegant steeple rises above the steep roofs of this hamlet dwarfed by the mighty Glacier du Casset. The Parc national des Écrins information centre is open in summer, 🕐 daily except Tuesday, 2.30-7pm. (🕐 *See SERRE-CHEVALIER: HIKES*).

Le Monêtier-les-Bains★ – 🕐 *See SERRE-CHEVALIER.*

▷ *In Villeneuve, turn left onto the road leading to La Salle-les-Alpes.*

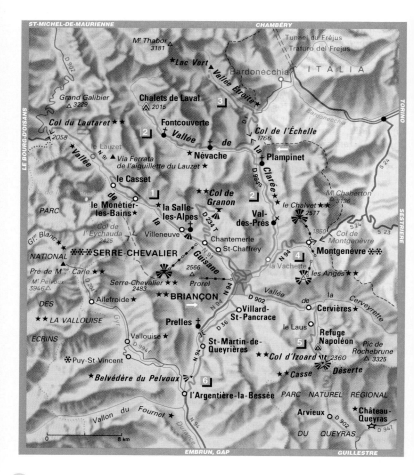

La Salle-les-Alpes ★

The road rising just above Chapelle Ste-Lucie leads to the centre of the old town and one of the most beautiful churches in the Briançonnais. **L'Église St-Marcellin**★ (🕓 *tours by appointment -* ☎ *04 92 25 54 02)* has a Romanesque bell-tower (13C-14C) from an earlier building, an elegant, canopied south porch and a late Gothic nave with quadripartite vaulting. A gilded chancel altarpiece, which dates from the 17C and depicts the Virgin and Child, is framed by Baroque ornamentation including twisted columns and recesses. The lectern and pulpit are the work of local artists. On a terrace stands the **Chapelle St-Barthélemy**★ (🕓 *same conditions as church)*; frescoes represent episodes from the lives of the saints, and there is an attractive **view**★ of the valley

▷ *In Chantemerle, take D 234T up to the Col de Granon, 12km/7.5mi away. The road climbs up the arid slopes overlooking the left bank of the River Guisane, offering broad views of the Briançonnais mountains and Écrins Massif.*

Col de Granon★★

🔭 *Leave the car beyond the barracks and climb to a viewing table on the right.* From here (2 404m/ 7 887ft), the **panorama** unfolds in front of your eyes, including the Briançon mountains and the Massif des Écrins

▷ *Go back along D 234T and take a detour through the old village of St-Chaffrey before rejoining N 91.*

Briançon★★ – 🕓*See BRIANÇON.*

② Vallée de la Clarée★★

FROM BRIANÇON TO THE CHALETS DE LAVAL *30km/18.6mi – about 2hr, not including walks – see local map.* 🚉 *La Vachette, 05100 Val-des-Prés* 🕓 *Tue-Sat 9am-noon, 2-5pm -* ☎ *04 92 20 02 20 - www.ot-claree.com*

This picturesque valley owes its name to the clear waters of the mountain stream running through it. Being unsuitable for ski lifts, the area has retained its lovely villages with houses covered with larch shingles and decorated with sundials. Landscapes change as one drives up the long and narrow valley, fresh and wooded at first, then more open and populated beyond Plampinet, when it suddenly veers to the left. The upper part again becomes narrower as the Clarée cascades down through the austere landscape formed by a vast glacial cirque on Mont Thabor.

Briançon★★ – 🕓*See BRIANÇON – tour of the town: 1hr 30min*

▷ *Leave Briançon by* ①️ *on the town plan, (N 94 towards Montgenèvre). At la Vachette turn left onto the D 994 and into the Vallée de la Clarée.*

The road overlooks the narrow valley of the River Durance and the Pont d'Asfeld with the Chalvet Summit towering above the Clarée Valley.

▷ *In La Vachette, bear left along D 994G, which goes up the Clarée Valley.*

Shortly beyond La Vachette, the road reaches the confluence of the River Durance and River Clarée. The mighty river of the southern Alps looks very disappointing compared to its tributary, the Clarée, which the road follows from that point.

Val-des-Prés

Lovely village with typical houses resting on an arcaded base. The **church** has an imposing square bell-tower with two tiers of Romanesque arcading and a large portico in characteristic regional style.

The road follows the Clarée among pine trees through one of the most attractive parts of the valley.

Plampinet

Situated at the top of the village, the **Église St-Sébastien** (🕐 *On request from the tourist office -* ☎ *04 92 20 02 20, or the Service du Patrimoine -* ☎ *04 92 22 30 18*) is a solid building, characteristic of mountain architecture, decorated with a fine sundial. The **murals**★, dating from 1530, which are probably the work of an artist from Piedmont, are remarkable for their lively details and warm colours.

The **Chapelle Notre-Dame-des-Grâces** (🕐 *Same conditions as for the church*) has also retained a set of 16C murals★, slightly older than those of the church, illustrating the virtues and the vices.

The valley becomes more open beyond Plampinet. The road leading to the Vallée Étroite *(see below)* starts on the right between Plampinet and Névache.

Névache★

🅘 *Ville Haute 05100 Névache in season* 🕐 *daily 9am-6pm -* ☎ *04 92 21 38 19.*

The church of the *"ville haute,"* **L'Église St-Marcellin et St-Antoine**★ (🕐 *July to Aug: 10am-5pm; Sept-June: Sat-Sun 10am-5pm, Wed and Fri 2-7pm, guided tours on request to the Service du Patrimoine -* ☎ *04 92 22 30 18 or at the tourist office, 3.50€.*) was built in 1490 to make good a vow made on pilgrimage by Charles VIII. A representation of the Annunciation decorates the tympanum of the west doorway; the wooden doors are beautifully carved with interlaced Gothic motifs.

Inside, there is a fine Baroque **altarpiece** decorated with 15 statues. The **treasury**, includes an 11C copper pyx inlaid with enamel.

Beyond Névache, note the picturesque shingle roofs of the Chalets de Fontcouverte (1 857m/6 093ft) and its lovely **chapel**. The Cascade de Fontcouverte is nearby.

Chalets de Laval

The road ends at the Chalet de Laval (alt 2 015m/6 611ft), the starting point for several mountain excursions such as the ascent of Mont Thabor.

Hike to Lac de Laramont and Lac du Serpent★

▸ *From the chalets at Fontcouverte continue on the D 301 to La Fruitière. Difference in altitude: 500m/1 640ft to Lac de Laramont, 700m/2 297ft to Lac du Serpent*

🅧 The path continues past the refuge of Ricou and joins GR 57, which leads to Lac Laramon (2 359m/7 740ft). From the shores of the lake, a fine **panorama**★★ includes the Massif des Écrins. Lac du Serpent (2 448m/8 031ft) lies due east.

③ Vallée Étroite★

17 km/10.6mi – about 2hr

▸ *The road leading to the Vallée Étroite, which crosses to the Italian side, is open only from mid-June to mid-November, and only to private cars (no buses). Between Plampinet and Névache, turn right onto D 1 towards the Col de l'Échelle.*

Col de l'Échelle

Alt 1 766m/5 794ft. This is the lowest border pass in the western Alps. On the Italian side, the road goes down steeply towards the Bardonecchia Valley, with views of the Vallée Étroite and Mont Thabor.

Vallée Étroite★

This valley, which was Italian territory from the Treaty of Utrecht in 1713 until 1947, still retains its signposting in Italian.

Lac Vert★

🏃 *1hr there and back on foot. Leave the car at the CAF refuge and continue along the road until you reach the signpost "Lago Verde." Follow the path.*
The small lake suddenly appears framed by larch trees; its colour is due to the profusion of green algae that it contains and its clear, icy water.

4 Route de Montgenèvre

FROM BRIANÇON TO MONTGENÈVRE *12km/7.5mi – about 30min*

▷ *Leave Briançon by ① on the town plan, N 94.*

The road overlooks the deep valley of the River Durance. Leaving the Clarée Valley road to its right, the N 94 rises rapidly, offering glimpses of the Briançon Basin and the Clarée Valley. As Montgenèvre gets nearer, pine trees give way to the larches of the Forest of Sestrière.

Montgenèvre★ ★ – 👣 *See MONTGENÈVRE.*

5 Route du Col de L'Izoard★★

FROM BRIANÇON TO CHÂTEAU-QUEYRAS *38km/24mi – allow 2hrs*

The Col d'Izoard is often obstructed by snow from October to June.

Briançon★★ – 👣 *See BRIANÇON*

▷ *Between Briançon and Cervières, the itinerary follows the cliff road through the Gorges de la Cerveyrette.*

Cervières

This village, damaged during the Second World War, has nevertheless retained a 15C church and a few traditional houses including the 18C **Maison Faure-Vincent -Dubois**★ (🕐 *on request to Mme Favrichon - ☎ 04 92 21 07 59).*

▷ From Cervières, a 10km/6.2mi-long road, partly surfaced, runs through the pastoral **Vallée de la Cerveyrette**.

Drive out of Cervières, stop the car and turn round to see the top of the Barre des Écrins (alt 4 102m/13 458ft) through the lower Cerveyrette Valley.
As the road winds up past **Le Laus** towards the pass along the River Izoard, the **Pic de Rochebrune,** one of the familiar silhouettes of the Briançonnais's landscapes, appears on the left.

The **Refuge Napoléon** was erected in 1858 with funds bequeathed by Napoleon (👣 *see ROUTE NAPOLÉON)* in return for the warm welcome given him after his escape from Elba.

Col d'Izoard★★

Alt 2 360m/7 743ft. This is the highest point of the Route des Grandes Alpes south of the Col du Galibier. There is a memorial dedicated to Alpine forces who contributed to the construction of many mountain roads. A small **museum** (🕐 *July to Aug: 2-6pm*

- ☎ *04 92 45 06 23)*, situated at the pass itself, is devoted to the **Tour de France** cycle race which goes across the Col d'Izoard.

 Go up (15min there and back on foot) to the viewing panels overlooking the road. The superb **panorama** includes, to the north, the Briançonnais mountains with Mont Thabor in the background, and, to the south, the heights of the Queyras region, the Pic des Houerts, Pic de la Font Sancte and Chambeyron Massif.

Casse Déserte

Casse Déserte★★

The ragged spires, towering over the Col de l'Izoard road, are due to a local geological phenomenon causing layers of ground limestone and gypsum to be bonded into a yellowish conglomerate, known as *cargneule*. The hardest blocks of this conglomerate are less eroded than the rest and form groups of "needles."

Arvieux – 👣 *See Le QUEYRAS.*

The site of Château-Queyras comes into view upon reaching the Guil Valley.

Château-Queyras★ – 👣 *See CHÂTEAU-QUEYRAS.*

⑥ Haute Durance

FROM BRIANÇON TO L'ARGENTIÈRE-LA-BESSÉE *17km/10.6mi – about 1hr*

▶ *Leave Briançon by ③ on the town plan (N 94), then turn left and cross the Durance towards Villard-St-Pancrace.*

Villard-St-Pancrace

Note the fine houses in typical Briançonnais style. The 15C church has two beautiful south doorways with triple arches resting on slender columns. The artist's signature (1542 J Ristolani) is on the left-hand jamb of the right-hand doorway. A sundial bears the Latin inscription: 'They (the hours) all wound, the last one kills'.

Next to the church stands the 17C **Chapelle des Pénitents**, and on a hilltop the **Chapelle St-Pancrace** (🕐 *Contact the Mairie - ☎ 04 92 21 05 27)*, with 15C murals.

▶ *Drive through the village of Villard-St-Pancrace then along D 36 to rejoin N 94.*

Prelles

The **Chapelle St-Jacques** *(Key at the Mairie - ☎ 04 92 21 04 06 or from M. Bortino - ☎ 04 92 21 05 03.)*, situated in the high street, has retained 15C **murals**★; in the chancel, there is a Christ in Glory with the 12 apostles lined up beneath. Scenes of pilgrims on their way to Santiago de Compostela are on the left-hand wall of the nave.

▶ *Rejoin N 94 and drive south.*

Between Prelles and Queyrières, the road clings to the cliffside above the gorge through which flows the River Durance.

St-Martin-de-Queyrières

The church standing on the roadside is typical of the Embrun region.

Queyrières

This village, backing onto a rock, is characteristic of the Briançonnais area.

Belvédère du Pelvoux★

A viewing table placed near the road helps to locate the main summits of the Écrins Massif, which can be seen through the valley of the lower Vallouise.

L'Argentière-la-Bessée – ♿ *See L'ARGENTIÈRE-LA-BESSÉE.*

PAYS DU BUËCH

MICHELIN MAP 334 C5/6

Much travelled but little explored, this depression of the Préalpes du Sud opens the way to the main Alpine winter route *(N 75)* and to the railway line from Grenoble to Marseille via the Col de la Croix Haute. The area enjoys a Mediterranean climate, although pastures and fir forests still predominate as far south as St-Julien-en-Beauchêne; the Col de la Croix-Haute marks a sort of climatic boundary, where the green north gives way to the dry bare landscape of the Southern Alps. The area is also known as "la Bochaine."

- ▶ **Orient Yourself:** Between Grenoble and Sisteron, N 75 passes villages with a distinctly Provençal character, among fields and orchards on the flanks of bare and wild mountains. The Buëch river is a tributary of the Durance. The Pays de Buëch is located northeast of Dévoluy, southwest of the Baronnies.
- Thermal updrafts make Aspres a centre for soaring sports: look up at the sky to watch the silent, graceful flight of gliders and deltaplanes.
- ○ **Organizing Your Time:** Count on a half day to see the area, including stops.
- ▲ **Also See:** Nearby Sights: BUIS-LES-BARONNIES, Le CHAMPSAUR, DIE, Le DÉVOLUY, GAP, MONTMAUR, Route NAPOLÉON, SISTERON, Le TRIÈVES

Vallée du Buëch

From Lus-la-Croix-Haute to Serres *43km/27mi – about 2hr*

Lus-la-Croix-Haute
Lying at the centre of a wide Alpine basin through which flows the Buëch, at an altitude of 1 150m/3 773ft, Lus-la-Croix-Haute is the highest resort of the Pays du Buëch, with six ski runs.

- ▶ *From the Grande-Place in Lus, drive east along D 505.*

Vallon de la Jarjatte ★
The road follows the upper Buëch Valley, with forested slopes on either side.
On approaching La Jarjatte, where there are 20km/12.5mi of cross-country ski trails, there are impressive **views**★★ of the indented silhouettes of the Aiguilles framed by the Vachères (2 400m/7 874ft) and Tête de Garnesier (2 368m/8 769ft). The head of the valley forms a cirque in a setting of dark escarpments towering over a dense fir forest.

- ▶ *Return to N 75.*

The road follows each bank of the Buëch in turn. The wide river bed is overlooked by the jagged peaks of the Diois, known as *"serres"*; the wooded slopes of Montagne Durbonas can be seen on the left as the road reaches the village of **St-Julien-en-Beauchêne**.
Beyond St-Julien, the landscape becomes more arid, and deep gullies run down the mountain slopes, with a few pines and oaks dotted about; rocky peaks are now and then surmounted by ruined castles such as the 12C fortress of La Rochette.

For coin categories, see the Legend on the cover flap.

EATING OUT
◖◗ **La Sérafine** – *Les Parois - 05400 Veynes - 2km/1mi E of Veynes on the Gap road then a B road* - ☎ *04 92 58 06 00 - closed Mon and Tue – reservations required.* This 18C stone building at the centre of a hamlet provides a home-from-home. Before the fire or on the terrace, guests will appreciate the Alsatian cooking, with ingredients fresh from the market, and the fine wine cellar.

Veynes

Avenue Cdt-Dumont, 05400 Veynes, ⏱ *Mon-Fri 9am-noon, 2.30-5.30pm, Sat 10am-noon -* ☎ *04 92 57 27 43.*

Owing to its position on the main Gap-Die route, this former stronghold suffered much at the hands of the Huguenots and of the duke of Savoie's troups. From 1894 onwards, it gradually became a major railway junction with lines to Grenoble, Marseille, Briançon and Valence, as well as an industrial centre; the town's **Écomusée** (♿ ⏱ *June to Sept: Wed-Sat 3-7pm; Apr: Wed-Sat 2-6pm; Christmas, Feb and All Souls holidays: Wed-Sat 2-6pm -* ☎ *04 92 58 00 49 - www.ecomusée-cheminot, 3.50€, children 1.50€*) recalls the life and work of the railwaymen. Today, Veynes has turned to tourism instead; known for its colourful façades and sunny enough for some homes to be heated by solar power, the town is the perfect place to start hikes and pony-treks through the south Buëch region. The Base nautique des Isles (water sports park) provides plenty of summer activities.

Aspres-sur-Buëch

Route de Grenoble, 051040 Aspres-sur-Buëch, ⏱ *July to mid-Sept: Tue-Sat 9am-noon, 3-6pm; rest of year Tue-Sat 9am-noon,* ☎ *04 92 58 68 88*

This lively town lies at the intersection of N 75 and D 993/D 994 linking Die and Gap, and in a picturesque mountain setting (good overall **view** from the former castle mound crowned with a war memorial).

The **church** has an interesting Romanesque doorway bearing statues of Christ between Mary and St John the Baptist (unfortunately mutilated).

Beyond the Pont de la Barque, at the confluence of the Buëch and Petit Buëch, a narrowing of the valley hides the village of Serres.

Serres★

Place du Lac, 05700 Serres, ⏱ *Daily except Sat-Sun10am-12.30pm, 2-5.30, Sat 9.30-noon -* ☎ *04 92 67 00 67.*

There is a parking lot near the river, next to the tourist office.

The picturesque old village, an attractive maze of narrow lanes and covered passageways, clings to a pointed rock above the River Buëch. From the parking lot, turn left up the rue Varanfrain to the arcaded square, **placette de la Fontaine**. Walk up to the old high street where the **town hall** stands, a former residence of the ducal family Lesdiguières (17C porch and fine 16C vaulting inside). *Turn back and walk eastwards along the high street, now* **rue Henri-Peuzin**.

Snow in Provence? Serres in the winter sun.

E. Baret

Sundials in the Pays du Buëch

This tour through the valleys of the Buëch region leads to the discovery of an interesting collection of sundials showing the diversity of local pictorial art during the 18C and 19C. In **St-Julien-en-Beauchêne**, the Durbon forest lodge (a former Carthusian monastery) is decorated with two 18C sundials. In **Aspres-sur-Buëch**, a contemporary sundial, made according to traditional techniques, adorns the town hall. At the **Col de Cabre**, near La Beaume, a sundial has been carved in the rock at the western exit of the tunnel. The primary school in **Serres** also has its sundial, showing the sun's trajectory and the position of the equinox (see *Planning Your Trip*).

Note on the right the bell-tower surmounted by a wrought iron belfry and several carved doorways along the street, in particular **no 56**. Pause to admire the **Maison de Lesdiguières**✶ (no 39) with a fine Renaissance façade dashed with galena crystals to make it sparkle at sunset. The Romanesque church was remodelled in the 14C; the south side is the most interesting with its six **funerary recesses** and two beautifully carved doors. Opposite the church, a passageway leads to the former **Jewish quarter** notable for its high-fronted houses, sometimes six storeys tall and backing on to the square. In 1576 Serres became the property of the **Duc de Lesdiguières** and a safe haven for Huguenots (Protestants), no doubt reassured by the new ducal armouries established in the town. On the death of Henri IV, however, the Wars of Religion flared up once again. Richelieu ordered the destruction of the citadel in 1633 and the Huguenots were either converted to Catholicism or driven into exile.

Hikes

Montagne de Céüse✶
This table mountain offers interesting hikes from different starting points.
🥾 *From Veynes: take D 20 towards Châteauneuf d'Oze heading north, then turn left at the intersection onto the forest road leading to the Col des Guérins.*
Footpath GR 94 skirts the east side of the isolated mountain to reach Manteyer on the northeast slope.
🥾 *From the Céüse 2000 resort: take the track which starts opposite Hôtel Gaillard, climb as far as the ledge, then follow the steep course of the Marseillais ski lift to the top. Go up towards the Torrent chairlift until you reach a signpost.* A path leads to the Pic de Céüse which reveals a splendid **view**✶✶ of the Massif de Bure and Massif des Écrins to the north and of the Ubaye to the east. It is possible to return via the west side, skirting the top of the rock-climbing course, going down through the Vallon d'Aiguebelle and then following the signs.

Plateau de Bure✶✶ – 🕑 *See MONTMAUR, Hike*

BUIS-LES-BARONNIES ★

POPULATION 2 226
MICHELIN MAP 332 E8
LOCAL MAP SEE LES BARONNIES

Between the ridge of Les Baronnies and the distant silhouette of Mont Ventoux, this little town on the Ouvèze looks south in more ways than one. Vines, olives, apricots and almonds flourish in the valley and fields of lavender (◔ see Introduction) supply many family-run distilleries. The clink of pastis glasses on the café terrace and the click of boules announce your arrival in the south. Some 80% of France's lime blossom tea – tilleul or tilhotou to the locals - comes from this area; on the first Wednesday in July, traders gather along the river bank for the **Foire au Tilleul** ★, the largest market of its kind in Europe. ▯ *14 bd Michel-Esserie, BP 18, 26170 Buis-les-Baronnies* ◔ *Daily except Sun 9am-noon, 2-5.30pm -* ☎ *04 75 28 04 59 - www.buislesbaronnies.com.*

▶ **Orient Yourself:** Located at the far end of the Gorges d'Umbrieux, Buis stands away from the Rhone Valley, just the place to avoid passing armies and the mistral, while remaining easy to reach. The A 7 is 60km/37.5mi to the west.

◔ **Organizing Your Time:** The Old Town is well worth an hour or two on foot; an excursion around the countryside will take about 3 hours.

◔ **Also See:** Nearby sights: Pays du BUËCH, MONTBRUN-LES-BAINS, Route NAPOLÉON, SISTERON

ᕙ Walking Tour

The Old Town ★ 1hr

Esplanade
This alleyway, shaded by plane trees, runs along the Ouvèze, where the town walls once stood; it is a typical Provençal *cours* (avenue), particularly lively on market days (*Wednesday mornings*). Across the river, the Rocher St-Julien, a popular challenge for rock-climbers, rises to a height of 767m/2 516ft.

The Place du Marché

B. Kaufmann/MICHELIN

Place du Marché

This "square," looking more like a wide street, is lined with slightly pointed stone arcades dating from the 15C.

Rue de la Conche

The shopping street has retained a few fine doorways.

▶ *Turn left onto rue de la Commune.*

Former Dominican monastery

The recently restored 16C building has been turned into holiday accommodation. Note the staircase and the cloisters.

▶ *Walk past a gate on the left and through a vaulted passageway called rue de la Cour-du-Roi-Dauphin.*

Church

🕐 *8am-noon - ☎ 04 75 28 02 50.*
Burnt down during the Wars of Religion and rebuilt in the 17C, it contains wood carvings and stalls from the former Dominican church.

▶ *Walk along the left side of the church.*

Former Ursuline convent

Founded in the 17C, it is now a cultural centre. The only original feature left is the fine Renaissance doorway of the former chapel, which today houses the library.

▶ *Walk past the east end of the church to avenue Aristide-Briand and return to the Esplanade, then go to the embankment on the right bank of the river.*

Maison des Plantes Aromatiques

♿ 🕐 *July to Aug: daily 9am-12.30pm, 3-7pm, Sun and public holidays 10am-12.30pm, 3-6pm; June and Sept: 9am-noon, 4-6pm, Sun and holidays 10am-12.30pm, 2.30-5.30pm; Oct to May: 9am-noon, 2-5.30pm, Sun and holidays 10am-12.30pm, 14.30-5.30pm.* 🕐 *closed 25 Dec to 1 Jan, Sun in Dec, Jan and Feb - ☎ 04 75 28 04 59 - www.maisondesplan-*

tes.com The garden includes an astonishingly varied collection of aromatic plants and medicinal herbs, while the museum offers exhibits and programs to educate the public. There is also a boutique selling herbal products.

The **Tour de Saffre** (12C) is the only part of the town walls still standing.

Along the Ouvèze

Pierrelongue
▶ *7 km/4.4mi to the south on the D 5*
Perched on a rocky knoll overlooking the village, the ugly **church,** built at the end of the 19C by an obstinant curé, looks totally out of place in this attractive setting.

Mollans-sur-Ouvèze
▶ *9 km/5.6mi south on the D 5*
This small "border" town is the gateway to the Baronnies region; the passage from Provence to the Dauphiné is symbolised by the dolphin on the elegant 18C fountain. The bridge across the Ouvèze links the *basse ville,* with its 18C covered wash-house, and the *haute ville* with its belfry crowning an old round tower; opposite stands a small chapel projecting over the Ouvèze. From there, a walk through the narrow streets of the "high town" leads to the church and a large square keep, all that remains of the castle.

Entrechaux
▶ *Located at the junction of the D 54 and the D13*
This village, formerly the possession of the Bishops of Viason, is overlooked by the ruins of its castle, which include a 20m/66ft-high keep.

Excursions

☐1 Les Baronnies du Buis ★

ROUND TOUR FROM BUIS-LES-BARONNIES *97km/60.6mi – allow 3hr – see local map*
This relatively low range (1 757m/5 764ft) of the Préalpes du Sud stretches from west to east, its limestone ridge being separated by the upper valleys of the River Eygues and River Ouvèze. Mountain streams have cut deep furrows in the hillsides, sculpting a barren landscape, characteristic of the area, while orchards and vineyards cover the lower slopes. This is the country of lime trees, whose leaves compose the tilleul infusion, of lavender, olives and herbal medicines.

▶ *From Buis-les-Baronnies drive northeast along D 546.*

The road follows the Ouvèze amid olive groves and goes through the picturesque **Gorges d'Ubrieux.**

▶ *Turn left onto D 108 and drive up to the Col d'Ey.*

Olive trees, pines and broom grow on south-facing slopes. Fine views of the Ouvèze Valley, Buis-les-Baronnies, Saint-Julien and Mont Ventoux.

Col d'Ey

Alt 718m/2 356ft. From the pass, flanked by the Montagne de Montlaud to the east and the Montagne de Linceuil to the west, the view extends to the Ennuye Valley and the Montagne de Buisseron.

▷ *Take D 528 left towards Rochebrune.*

Rochebrune

The village stretches over a rock spur; its only street leads to a round tower (all that remains of the 13C castle) and to the 12C church remodelled in the 15C. Fine **view** of the Ennuye Valley.

▷ *Return to D 108 and turn left.*

Ste-Jalle

The **old town**★ has retained part of its walls and two of its gates. One of these is surmounted by the Chapelle des Pénitents (17C). The **castle** consists of a massive square keep (12C-13C), a round tower with Renaissance windows, and living quarters (17C-18C) looking more like a large house.

The size of its bell-tower spoils the otherwise fine proportions of the 12C Roman-esque church of **Notre-Dame-de-Beauvert**. The unusual carved **doorway** has a tympanum depicting a rooster and three figures of a farmer, a lord and a troubadour representing the different social classes. A large transept separates the barrel-vaulted nave from the three semicircular apsidal chapels. The oven-vaulted axial chapel is decorated with very simple arcading.

▷ *Follow the River Ennuye along D 64 then turn right onto D 94 after Curnier.*

The road runs through the pleasant valley of the River Eygues, planted with vines and with peach, cherry and olive trees.

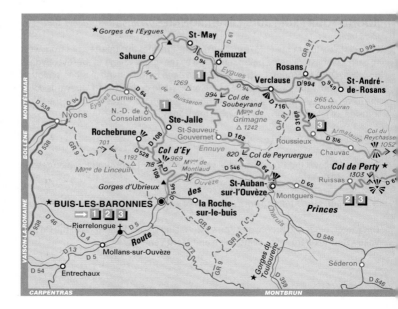

Sahune

The old village lies on the left bank of the Eygues. Beyond Sahune, the road makes its way through the deep **Gorges de l'Eygues**★; note the regular layers of the rock face and the foaming waterfall on the left.

St-May

This village is perched on a promontory overlooking the gorge. Beyond St-May, the Eygues flows between brightly coloured limestone cliffs.

▷ *Turn right onto D 162.*

> ### SHOW TIME
>
> **Le Canard en bois** – *Le Village - 26510 Montréal-les-Sources - 5km/3mi E of Sahure on D 205 -* ☎ *04 75 27 42 04 – Fri or Sat every fortnight, telephone to confirm dates.* This cabaret in a woodland setting is dedicated to French chanson, theatre and acoustic music. At the end of performances, proprietor Marcel Moratal serves liberal quantities of wine and patrons strike up discussions with each other and with the performers.

The road rises through orchards to the **Col de Soubeyrand** (alt 994m/3 261ft) set among fir trees. On the way down from the pass, firs give way to oaks and the view extends to Mont Ventoux.

▷ *Go through St-Sauveur-Gouvernet and turn left onto D 64, then right onto D 546.*

② **Route des Princes d'Orange**

BUIS-LES-BARONNIES TO EYGUIANS *63km/39mi – allow 3hr –see local map*
From the 14C to the 18C, this road gained strategic importance as a link between the Principality of Orange and Orpierre; both were territories of the house of Orange-Nassau, whose descendants are now the Dutch royal family.
On leaving Buis-les-Baronnies, the D 546 crosses the **Gorges d'Ubrieux.**

St-Auban-sur-l'Ouvèze

Built on a rocky promontory at the confluence of the River Ouvèze and River Charuis, this old village has retained part of its former defences. From place Péquin, at the top of the village, there is a fine view of the surrounding area dotted with many farms. There is a wide choice of hikes in and around a beautiful chestnut grove. The area's economic life is centred around medicinal herbs (tilleul, sage and camomile) as well as aromatic plants.

▷ *Beyond St-Auban, follow D 65 via the Col de Perty.*

The road goes through Montguers (note the charming isolated chapel on the plateau) then rises in a series of hairpin bends through a wild landscape, offering **views** of the whole Baronnies area.

Col de Perty★★

Alt 1 303m/4 275ft. A path to the right leads to the viewing table *(10min return on foot).* Splendid panorama of the Durance Valley and the southern Alps to the east, of the Ouvèze Valley and the Mont-Ventoux Massif to the west.

The road continues along the Céans Valley.

Orpierre ★

This mountain village at the bottom of the Céans Valley became the seat of a barony belonging to the prince of Orange in the 13C, rising in prominence as a Protestant centre under the house of Nassau before declining after the Revocation of the Edict of Nantes and being ceded to the French crown in 1713. For all its political changes, Orpierre has retained its pleasant **old centre**★ with some fine Renaissance door-ways along the **Grand-Rue** and the narrow passages, known as *"drailles,"* linking its picturesque old streets.

The cliffs overlooking the village offer many marked and suitably equipped itinerar-ies for rock-climbing enthusiasts (Quiquillon★, Falaise de Quatre heures, Cascade de Belleric - level 5 to 6a).

Beyond Orpierre and several gorges, the Céans Valley suddenly widens as the river joins the Buëch and the Blaisance.

Lagrand

Of the important monastery which flourished here in medieval times, only the **church** (🕐 *July to Sept: daily 8am to 5pm; other months, on request at the Mairie except Sat-Sun - ☎ 04 92 66 25 35*) remains; this well-preserved Romanesque building has a large nave, covered with broken barrel vaulting, ending with a pentagonal apse set in a rectangular east end. Inside, the only decorations are floral motifs carved on the capitals. Note the gilded wood tabernacle in a recess on the right-hand side.

The west doorway has been heavily restored. The south side used to open onto the cloister and the monastery buildings. Note the funeral recesses near the base.

The town hall at the entrance of the old village is a fine 18C building characteristic of Provençal country houses of that period.

Eyguians

It is here that the Route des Princes d'Orange reaches the Buëch Valley.

③ Le Pays de Rosans

FROM BUIS-LES-BARONNIES TO ST-ANDRÉ-DE-ROSANS *95km – around 3hr*

⚑ *For Buis-les-Baronnies to Orpierre see* ② *above*

▶ *From Orpierre, drive west along D 30 then turn right onto D 130.*

The road follows the St-Cyrice Valley, then goes through a forest as it climbs to the Col du Reychasset; beyond the pass, there is a fine **view** of the Armalauze Valley.

▶ *Take D 316 on the left, then D 316B through Chauvac and Roussieux .*

Good **views** of the pyramid-shaped Coustouran Summit (965m/3 166ft).

▶ *Take the D 116 to Verclause.*

Verclause

This old fortified village was a fief of the Dauphin in the 13C. The ruins of its castle and chapel stand on a promontory offering a lovely **view**★ of the Eygues Valley and the Montagne de la Clavelière.

▶ *Turn right on to the D 94 and D 994.*

Rosans

(Guided tours in season; ask at the Écomusée - ☎92 66 66 66.) The most westerly village in the Hautes-Alpes has a true Provençal atmosphere. Its narrow streets wind round the hill in a spiral to the imposing 13C keep.

St-André-de-Rosans

One of the most important Cluniac monasteries in Haute-Provence was founded here in the 10C; it was destroyed during the Wars of Religion, leaving behind the ruins of a vast 12C **church,** including the walls of the nave and an apsidal chapel with traces of a rich decoration inspired by Antique art.

CASTELLANE ★

POPULATION 1 508
MICHELIN MAP 334 H9
LOCAL MAPS SEE GRAND CANYON DU VERDON

This tourist centre, located at the intersection of the Route Napoléon and the Route du Haut-Verdon, close to the famous canyon, lies at the foot of a 184m/604ft-high limestone cliff in one of the most striking **settings** ★ of the Haute-Provence region. First, an ancient fort, then a Roman town, **Petra Castellana** occupied the top of the cliff; in the 15C, the town was moved to the valley below and surrounded with fortifications, the remains of which are still visible today. ▯ *rue Nationale – 04120 Castellane,* ◷ *July to Aug: daily 9am-12.30pm, 4-7pm, Sun 9am-12.30; Apr to June and Sept to Oct: daily except Sun 9am-noon, 2-6pm; Nov to Mar: daily except Sat-Sun 9am-noon, 2-6pm -* ☎ *04 92 83 61 14*

▶ **Orient Yourself:** Nestled in the mountains along the N 85, the famous Route Napoleon, halfway between Digne-les-Bains and Grasse, Castellane extends out from the Place Marcel-Sauvaire, centre of local life.

🅿 **Parking:** There are free parking lots at both ends of the village. You must pay to park on the Place Marcel-Sauvaire, however.

◷ **Organizing Your Time:** If you have a few days, Castellane is a good base from which to tour the mountainous countryside.

The history of Castellane is described on signboards around the town centre.

CASTELLANE	
Blondeau R. du Lt	2
Église Pl. de l'	3
Fontaine R. de la	4
Liberté Pl. de la	5
Mazeau R. du	6
Mitan R. du	7
Nationale R.	8
République Bd de la	9
Roc Pont du	10
Sauvaire Pl. M.	14
St-Michel Bd	12
St-Victor R.	13
Tesson R. du	15

Fontaine aux Lions	B
Musée ethnologique (Ancienne sous-préfecture)	M

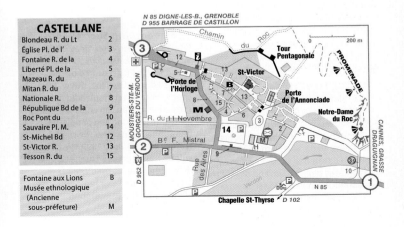

Kids **Especially for Kids:** Children will enjoy the Musée Sirènes et Fossiles as well as the Base de Loisirs Sirocco, where they can swim and paddle canoes.

Also See: Nearby Sights: ANNOT, BARGÈME, CLUES DE HAUTE-PROVENCE, DIGNE-LES-BAINS, ENTREVAUX, MOUSTIERS-STE-MARIE, Route NAPOLÉON, RIEZ, ST-JULIEN-DU-VERDON, Lac de STE-CROIX, Plateau de VALENSOLE, Grand Canyon du VERDON

Sights

Place Marcel-Sauvaire

This central square, a useful central parking spot, is decorated with arcades and a fountain and lined with hotels, cafés, shops and administrative buildings. A market is held here every Wednesday and Saturday.

In rue Nationale nearby, no. 34, which welcomed Napoleon on his way back from Elba in March 1815, houses a small ethnological museum, the **Musée des Arts et Traditions Populaires** (*July to Sept: daily except Mon 10am-noon, 3-6pm; May, June and Oct: daily except Sun and Mon 10am-noon, 3-6pm. 2€ - ☎ 04 92 83 71 80.*).

Address Book

For coin categories, see the Legend on the cover flap

EATING OUT

La Main à la Pâte – *5 R. de la Fontaine* - ☎ *04 92 83 61 16 - closed Dec to Feb.* Salads and pizzas feature prominently on the menu of this establishment in a narrow street in the old town. There is a relaxed atmosphere in the two dining rooms with their warm Provençal decor.

Auberge du Teillon – *04120 La Garde, 6km/4mi SE of Castellane on N 85* - ☎ *04 92 83 60 88 - aubergeteillon@club-internet.fr - closed 18 Nov-10 Mar, Sun evening and Mon from Sept to June and Tue lunch in July and Aug.* If you miss this inn beside the Route Napoléon, do a U-turn! The menus are truly mouth-watering and the regional fare sophisticated and imaginative. Some rooms available.

WHERE TO STAY

Nouvel Hôtel du Commerce – *Pl. de l'Église* - ☎ *04 92 83 61 00 - accueil@hotel-fradet.com, closed Nov to Feb* - P *- 35rms - restaurant.* The rooms in this hotel on the village square have been renovated to stress function over charm. The dining room and terrace are pleasant, and be sure to sample the Provençal-inspired cuisine.

ON THE TOWN

Le Glacier – *Pl. de la Fontaine* - ☎ *04 92 83 62 88 – Open daily 7.30am-2am.* Winter or summer, this welcoming bar is always buzzing. In fine weather, you will have to fight for your place on the terrace on a small square. At the first sign of a nip in the air, people flock to the concerts. Good selection of beer and ice cream.

Place Marcel-Sauvaire – *Pl. Marcel-Sauvaire* – This is a must for those who decide to stop in Castellane. There are parking spaces in the shade, a big advantage in hot weather, and one or two bars where visitors can quench their thirst.

SPORT

Kids **Base de Loisirs Sirocco** – *Lac de Castillon - le Cheiron* - ☎ *04 92 83 72 97 June through Aug: daily 9am-7pm, closed Sept to May.* Located on the artificial lake at Castillon, this water sports centre is set in splendid natural surroundings. You can enjoy seimming, canoeing, kayaking and peddle-boating, and can picnic near the snack bar.

Nature hikes – Since 1999, the bearded vulture has reappeared in the Gorges du Verdon. The tourist office has organized guided tours where you can observe this impressive raptor.

Fortifications

Several sections of the walls built in 1359 are still standing: the **Tour Pentagonale** and two complete gates, the **Tour de l'Horloge** surmounted by a wrought-iron campanile (near the Tourist Information Centre) and the **Porte de l'Annonciade**. There is a good overall view of the walls and Tour Pentagonale from chemin du Roc, off boulevard St-Michel.

Old town

Situated north of place Marcel-Sauvaire, the old town includes some picturesque twisting lanes and a lovely **Fontaine aux Lions** along rue du Mitan.

Église St-Victor

To visit, ask at the tourist office.
This 12C Romanesque church has a remarkable Lombard tower with rough-hewn stones, originally part of the old city walls, at its corners and wide openings with rounded arches. Inside, the

Porte de l'Horloge and Notre-Dame-du-Roc

quadripartite vaulting and the oven-vaulted apse are characteristic of the transition between the Romanesque and Gothic styles. The walnut decoration of the chancel and the baldaquin surmounting the high altar date from the 18C.

Musée Sirènes et Fossiles

May to Sept: daily except Tue and Sun afternoon, 10am-noon, 3-6pm. 4€ (children 2.50€) - ☎ 04 92 83 19 23.
Between the town hall and the post office stands a museum run by the Réserve Géologique de Haute-Provence and devoted to manatees or sea cows, the aquatic mammals of the order *Sirenia* which once inspired sailor's tales of mermaids.

Walks

Vallée des Sirènes fossiles

Take the N 85 from Digne. After 6km park the car at Col de Lèques, on the right after the campsite. A half-hour walk through woodland and lavender leads to the "valley of the sea cows," where a unique collection of over a hundred Sirenia fossil remains is now protected by a museum.

Chapelle Notre-Dame-du-Roc

1hr there and back on foot.
Pleasant **walk**★ offering a fine overall view of Castellane nestling at the foot of its rock. A path starting behind the church joins up with a wider one; turn right. This path, which passes the ruined feudal village of Petra Castellana, rises

---

WHAT TO BRING BACK

Ruchers Apijouvence – *Le Cheiron* ☎ 04 92 83 61 43, jeanclaude. meurant@free.fr, July to Aug, tours at 3.30pm; sales all year from 9am. Three generations of the same family work in this bee-keeping enterprise that sells no fewer than 155 kinds of honey.

Éden Senteurs – *Rte des Gorges-du-Verdon,* ☎ 04 92 83 69 02, from Easter to 1 Nov: 9.30am-12.30pm, 2.30-6pm, July-Aug: 9h30am-8pm. This soap-making and perfume shop specializes in the local lavender.

rapidly over the roofs of the town and the crenellated Tour Pentagonale. Some ruined walls on the left are all that remain of the feudal village.

The chapel, surmounted by a tall statue of the Virgin Mary, dates from 1703; it stands on top of the cliff, 180m/590ft above the bed of the River Verdon and is a popular place of pilgrimage (note the large number of ex-votos).

From the terrace, the **view**★★ extends over the town, the 17C bridge spanning the river, the Castellane Basin surrounded by mountains and the beginning of the Gorges du Verdon.

Excursions

Chapelle St-Thyrse★

7km/4.3mi south on D 102 towards Robion; take great care because of the narrowness of the access road.

The picturesque road rises from the gorge to the plateau where the restored 12C Romanesque **chapel** stands in a remarkable **setting**★. The interior is decorated with blind arcading in the oven-vaulted apse and along the north and west walls of the nave.

The 3-tiered steeple is characteristic of early Romanesque style.

Grand Canyon du Verdon★★★ – 👁 *See Grand Canyon du VERDON.*

Lacs de Castillon et Chaudanne★ – 👁 *See ST-JULIEN-DU-VERDON.*

CEILLAC✷

POPULATION 276
MICHELIN MAP 334 I4
LOCAL MAP SEE LE QUEYRAS

Located at an altitude of 1 650m/5 413ft, at the confluence of two mountain streams, this lovely village has survived fire, flood and the demands of modern life and retained its unspoilt, traditional character. One of the most attractive winter sports resorts in the Hautes-Alpes *département*, Ceillac is a perfect starting point for walks along the GR 5 and GR 58. Anglers, mountain-bikers and paragliders will be in their element. Others come for the climbing, riding or just to admire the beautiful **countryside**★. ▯ *Place Philippe-Lamour, 05600 Ceillac,* 🕙 *15 June to Sept and 15 Dec through Mar: daily 9am-noon, 2-6pm; rest of year: daily except Sat-Sun and holidays 9am-noon, 2-6pm -* ☎ *04 92 45 05 74*

▸ **Orient Yourself:** Ceillac is 14km/8.75mi from Guillestre. The D 60 crosses the valley of the Cristillan, with its erosion-scarred slopes, to arrive at a splendid plateau.

👁 **Don't Miss:** Be sure to take the walk through larch forests to the deep blue lac St-Anne.

🕙 **Organizing Your Time:** Give yourself a day to see Ceillac and to tour the surrounding country

👁 **Also See:** Nearby Sights: L'ARGENTIÈRE-LA-BESSÉE, BRIANÇON, Le BRIANÇON-NAIS, EMBRUN, Vallée de FREISSINIÈRES, GUILLESTRE, MOLINES-EN-QUEYRAS, MONT-DAUPHIN, Le QUEYRAS, ST-VÉRAN, Lac de SERRE-PONÇON, VARS

The Resort

The Alpine **ski area** is not extensive but has several good points in its favour: beautiful surroundings, good snow coverage (owing to the altitude, a north-facing aspect and good upkeep of the slopes), a reasonable gradient (800m/2 625ft) and variety. The ski area offers 12 alpine trails and some 45km/28mi of cross-country trails. There is ski-trekking towards Col Girardin and the Cristillan Valley as well as three groomed paths for walking and 25km/15.6mi of snowshoeing trails.

WHERE TO STAY AND EATING OUT

Hôtel La Cascade – *2km/1mi SE of Ceillac, at the foot of Mélezet - ☎ 04 92 45 05 92 - info@hotel-la-cascade.com- closed 14 Apr-31 May and 8 Sept-19 Dec - P - 23rms- restaurant.* The bright and simple rooms of this mountain inn look over unspoilt nature, stretching far away and encompassing forest, Alpine meadows, lakes and mountain summits. Local specialties on the menu.

Église St-Sébastien★

The chancel contains 16C murals with, in the centre, Christ inside a mandorla. next to the church, the **Chapelle des Pénitents** (*July to Aug: daily except Sat-Sun 5-7pm - ☎04 92 45 05 74*), now a museum of religious art, contains statues, altarpieces, sacred receptacles and paintings, as well as a small exhibit on the flood of 1957.

Hikes

Dogs must always be kept on a lead for the protection of cattle and wildlife.

Vallon du Mélezet★

It is possible to drive upstream for 5km/3mi.
This picturesque valley, dotted with tastefully restored hamlets, has forested slopes rising above 2 000m/6 562ft, the towering Font Sancte (3 387m/11 112ft) on the right and a waterfall known as the **Cascade de la Pisse.**

Lac Ste-Anne★★

Alt 2 415m/7 923ft. 2hr 15min there and back on foot. Park the car at the end of the Vallon du Mélezet road (1 967m/6 453ft).
Pleasant hike through a fine larch forest and across pastures. The deep blue-green waters of the Lac Ste-Anne are held in place by a moraine deposited by a former glacier. The reflection of the Pic de la Font Sancte adds to the beauty of the landscape. A small chapel stands by the lake (pilgrimage on 26 July).

CÉRESTE✳

POPULATION 1 036
MICHELIN MAP 334 B9

This little village in sun-bleached stone, a maze of pleasant streets behind the remains of its old medieval walls, lies between the pays d'Apt and the pays de Forcalquier. In May, fields of spring flowers make the drive down from the Prieuré de Carluc through the Vallon du Nid d'Amour even more charming.
Place de la République, 04280 Céreste, June to Sept: daily except Wed and Sat-Sun 9.30am-12.30pm, 2-6pm, Wed 9.30am-6pm, Sat-Sun 10am-noon; Oct to May: Mon and Fri 10am-noon, 2-4.30pm,Wed, Thu and Sat 10am-noon. ☎ 04 92 79 09 84 - www. cereste.fr

▶ **Orient Yourself:** Located on N 100, 23km/ 14.4mi southeast of Forcalquier in the valley of the Encrème, Céreste straddles the frontiers of the Apt and Forcalquier regions.

🕐 **Organizing Your Time:** Give yourself a half day to explore the village and tour the surrounding area.

Also See: Nearby Sights: Vallée de la Moyenne DURANCE, FORCALQUIER, Monastère de GANAGOBIE, GRÉOUX-LES-BAINS, MANE, MANOSQUE, Plateau de VALENSOLE

Sights

Upper town

After strolling through the rue de la Bourgade, walk up to the church. The broad façade and the elegant wrought-iron decoration around the bell are both typically Provençal; the lawned courtyard lends a further southern note.

Lower town

This is the prettiest part of the village. Just off the narrow, typically Provençal streets are medieval and 17C houses, the communal bread oven and the village fountain. The village square once led up to the door of an ancient church, now converted into a barn; the arched Romanesque porch still survives. Follow the avenue du Pont-Romain, to where a charming arched bridge, said to be Roman (but probably not) crosses the Encrème river.

Nid d'Amour

Below the village on the banks of the Encrème, this "love-nest" is actually a vaulted stone wash-house fed by two natural springs: cool and refreshing on hot summer days. *Beware of falling rocks.*

Excursions

🐾 *Dogs must always be kept on a leash for the protection of cattle and wildlife; there are beavers living in the Encrème and its tributaries.*

Tour d'Embarbe

Follow the road to Apt for 2km/1.2mi, then turn left just before the river. This forbidding stone tower has kept watch over the road since the 12C. Its massive 2m/6.56ft thick walls are broken only by the narrowest arrow slits off a spiral staircase.

Prieuré de Carluc

Follow the N 100 towards Forcalquier for 5km/3mi, then follow the signposted road to the left. 🕐 *Temporarily closed, although guided tours are available through the tourist office -* ☎ *04 92 79 09 84*

Only ruins remain of this 12C monastery, affiliated to the abbey of Montmajeur, which would have once have dominated the hollow known as the Ravin de Cure. One of the three churches at the site has survived, thanks largely to its nave carved into the face of the cliff. The animal and plant motifs on the capitals are still visible, as are a caryatid, straining under the weight, and a pair of well-fattened doves. To the left is a mysterious gallery, also hollowed out of the rock, which would have led through to a second church. The traces of tombs indicate that this was once a place of burial and of veneration, made all the more sacred by the presence of saintly relics.

Vallée de l'Encrème

The Encrème and its tributaries support a protected population of beavers. Branches bitten to a point are the sign that Europe's largest rodents have been hard at work: their dams across the river have submerged openings but remain dry inside.

CHAMBÉRY★★

POPULATION 55 786
MICHELIN MAP 333 I4
LOCAL MAPS SEE P 247 AND LES BAUGES

Captured by François I, then retaken by the Duchy a generation later, Chambéry has always mirrored the changing fortunes of France and Savoie. The town was until the 16C the capital of a sovereign state and remains the centre of the Savoyard heartland, its well-restored old centre having regained something of its past splendour. ⛱ *24 boulevard de la Colonne, 73000 Chambéry* 🕐 *July to Aug: Mon-Sat 9am-6pm, Sun and public holidays 9.30am-12.30pm; last 2 weeks of June and first 2 weeks Sept: Mon-Sat except public holidays 9am-noon, 1.30-8pm, Sun 9.20am-12.30pm - ☎ 04 79 33 42 47 - www.chambéry-tourisme.com Guided tours of the town – Contact the guides' office, 6 Place du Château* 🕐 *May to Sept: tours (1hr30min) at 4pm. 5€, children 3.5€ - ☎04 79 28 68 73.*

▶ **Orient Yourself:** Located south of the Lac du Bourget, in the depression between the Bauges and Chartreuse massifs, Chambéry is close to the three principal alpine parks: Parc national de la Vanoise, Parc naturel régional de Chartreuse and Parc naturel régional du massif des Bauges.

🔎 **Don't Miss:** The Italian paintings at the Musée des Beaux-Arts are splendid.

🕐 **Organizing Your Time:** The château, still a government building, and the Sainte-Chapelle are accessible only on guided tours.

🧒 **Especially for Kids:** The many trompe-l'oeil decorations on public buildings will intrigue children; for an outing, there is the nearby Lac d'Aiguebelette.

⚲ **Also See:** Nearby Sights: AIX-LES-BAINS, L'ALBANAIS, ALLEVARD, ANNECY, Lac d'ANNECY, Les BAUGES, Lac du BOURGET, Massif de la CHARTREUSE, GRENOBLE, Le GRÉSIVAUDAN, St-PIERRE-DE-CHARTREUSE

A Bit of History

The capital of Savoie – Chambéry became the capital of the counts of Savoie in 1232. At that time, it was only a large village defended by a fortress. The expansion of the town is due to the prosperity of the House of Savoie and to the efforts of the **three Amédées. Amédée VI (Count of Savoie, 1343-83)** was known as "the Green Count" because of the colours he wore when taking part in tournaments. He extended his domains towards Switzerland and Italy and took part in a crusade against the Turks. Because his armour was always covered with blood during battle, **Amédée VII (Count of Savoie, 1383-91)** was called "the Red Count." **Amédée VIII (Duke of Savoie, 1391-1434),** the "Duke-pope," was made duke by the emperor of the Holy Roman Empire and acquired the Geneva and Piedmont provinces. He retired to the castle-monastery of Ripaille, then played the role of anti-pope for 10 years during the Great Schism before returning to his monastery as a simple monk.

Savoie then went into decline until its prestige and influence were restored by **Emmanuel-Philibert** who made Turin the capital of Savoie, Chambéry remaining the seat of justice. Chambery's most famous son of the 19C was **Benoît de Boigne**

Address Book

For coin categories, see the Legend on the cover flap.

EATING OUT

BUDGET

Le Sans-Bruit – *2 r. de Lans - ☎ 04 79 33 36 50 - closed Sun- non-smoking only.* This restaurant has no menu, but only a list of Savoyard specialties and cheese dishes, as well as a daily noontime special. A colourful bistrot ambiance.

Aux Piétons – *30 pl. Monge - ☎ 04 79 85 03 81.* At the gates of the old town, several small rooms have been done up to look like old streets with paving on the floor, a pavement and guardrails. Terrace. Occasional "café théâtre" show on the first floor. Friendly atmosphere.

Le Café Chabert – *41 r. Basse-du-Château - ☎ 04 79 33 20 35 - alroboma4@aol.com - closed 23 Dec-3 Jan, evenings except in July-Aug and Mon.* As you walk through the town, take a stroll down the 14C rue Basse du Château. In summer the tables spill onto the pedestrian street. Menus changed daily offer good value for money.

Auberge Bessannaise – *28 pl Monge - ☎ 04 79 33 40 37 - closed Thur evening in winter and Mon.* Easily recognized by its terrace and flower-boxes outside a traditional house, this restaurant specializes in traditional dishes such as fondue, *foie gras maison*, beefsteak and fish from Lac du Bourget. Choose the best-lighted dining room.

WHERE TO STAY

Hôtel Curial – *371 r. de la République - ☎04 79 60 26 00 - www.curial.antaeus.fr - P -149rms.* This is a very practical location close to the town centre and near the Curial quarter. Rooms, furnished in beech, house from one to six people, and kitchenettes are available.

Art Hôtel – *154 r. du Sommeiller - exit 16 La Cassine - ☎ 04 79 62 37 26 - www.arthotel-chambery.com - P - 36rms.* This hotel is near the train station and a stone's throw from the old town and its shopping districts. It offers contemporary comfort and is fully sound-proofed. The breakfast buffet gets the day off to a good start.

Hôtel des Princes – *4 r. Boigne - ☎ 04 79 33 45 36 - hoteldesprinces@wanadoo.fr - 45rms.* This small hotel is well located at the entrance to the old town, and has been renovated throughout. It offers a warm welcome and has a friendly atmosphere and fresh decor. Good value for money.

Hôtel Mercure – *183 pl. de la Gare - ☎ 04 79 62 10 11 - www.accorhotels.com - 81rms.* This hotel opposite the station is easy to get to and functional. Its rooms are spacious and fitted with sound-proofing and air-conditioning. The original architecture of the façade distinguishes it from other hotels in this chain.

ON THE TOWN

Le Fidèle Berger – *15 rue de Boigne - ☎ 04 79 33 06 37 - Daily except Mon 8am-7pm, Sun 8am-12.15pm - closed 7-31 Aug.* Since 1832, the years have passed here with no discernable effect: the luxurious decor, magnificent counter in wood and marble, old furniture, wood paneling... In the tearoom, you will enjoy delicious pastries of chocolate or fresh fruit.

La Régence – *20 r. d'Italie - ☎ 04 79 33 36 77 - daily except Mon 8am-12.30pm, 2.30-7pm, Sun 8am-12.30pm.* This chocolate shop and tearoom is renowned for its specialties, notably its "Flocons de neige des Alpes" (Alpine snowflakes).

SHOPPING

Confiserie Mazet – *2 pl Porte-Reine - ☎ 04 79 33 07 35 - Daily except Sun 8.30am-12.30pm, 2-7pm, Sun 8am-12.30pm, Mon 2-6.30pm, closed public holidays.* This shop is over 180 years old, as is its most renowned specialty, the Mazet, a fruit-flavoured acid drop. The Ducs de Savoie and the Tomme de Savoie with bilberries are among the 70 kinds of chocolate and candies made on site.

Local tipples – Chambéryzette, a dry vermouth, is flavoured with wild strawberries, while "vermouth de Chambéry," created by the Maison Dolin in 1821, is made by steeping a mixture of herbs in dry white wine. "Le Bonal," concocted in the 19th century by a monk, is composed of grapejuice and roots of the gentian flower; it is thought to bring comfort before dinner.

SPORTS AND LEISURE

Base d'aviron du lac d'Aiguebelette

– Bouvent, 73470 Novalaise - ☎04 79 36 06 34 - www.aviron-lac-aiguebelette.com - open all year by reservation - 16€/hr: book of five sessions: 55€/person. Shel-tered from the wind, and thus deserted by windsurfers, the lake offers an ideal site for rowers. After learning proper technique in a rowing bassin, you can try your skills on this pretty natural lake, where motorboats are banned.

Swimming beaches – Leaving Lépin-le-Lac, the road leads to the port and a public beach on the eastern shore of Aiguebelette, north of the town. There are also several beaches along the western shores.

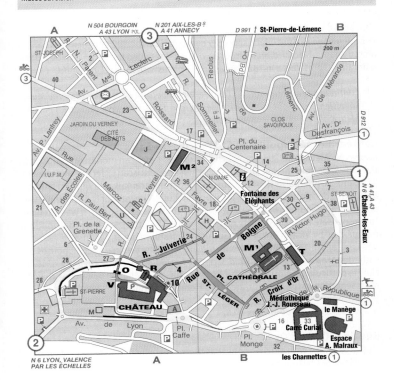

(1751-1830), a rich merchant's son whose picaresque adventures saw him enlist in the French guard corps before joining a Greek regiment and then seeing service with the Egyptian and Indian armies. A maharajah who recognised his military talents named him governor of a vast territory on the subcontinent. After the prince's death, the by now fabulously wealthy General de Boigne returned to Europe, married in London and settled in Chambéry, where his public works and charitable projects earned him the nickname *"le munificent"* ("the generous one"). Made president of the *département* by Napoleon and an aide-de-camp by Louis XVIII, he ended his days as a count, elevated to the nobility by the King of Sardinia.

Old Town★★ *4hr walk including a tour of the castle*

A **small train** (◷ *May to Sept: guided tour (45min, every hr) 10am-7pm. 6€, children 3€ - ☎ 04 79 33 42 47)* takes tourists round the pedestrianised historic centre during the summer season. Many blind walls are decorated with impressive *trompe-l'œil* paintings by local artists; particularly fine examples can be found at the covered market and on the corner of the Théâtre Charles-Dullin.

▶ ☞ *Start from the Fontaine des Éléphants and follow the itinerary marked on the plan.*

Fontaine des Éléphants
Chambéry's most famous monument was erected in 1838 to celebrate **Général Comte de Boigne** (1751-1830), a great benefactor of the town. The elephants are a reminder of the time he spent in India.

▶ *Follow boulevard du Théâtre.*

Théâtre Charles-Dullin
Rebuilt following a fire which seriously damaged it in the 19C, the theatre is named after the famous actor-director from Savoie. It has retained the original stage curtain painted by Louis Vacca in 1824, depicting *Orpheus' visit to the Underworld.*

▶ *Continue along boulevard du Théâtre, which becomes rue Ducis after the Musée Savoisien. Turn right onto the rue de la Croix-d'Or and right again down passage Métropole, which leads to the cathedral.*

Cathédrale métropolitaine St-François-de-Sales★
Known as "Métropole," the former church of the Franciscan monastery founded in the 13C, dates from the 15C and the 16C, when the Franciscan order was at its height. It became a cathedral in 1817. The late-15C west front is remarkable with its Flamboyant-Gothic decoration and early-17C wooden doors. The interior is surprisingly vast and the single vaulting over the aisle and side chapel is noteworthy; it was intended to compensate for the instability of the terrain. In 1835, the church was decorated in *trompe-l'œil* by Vicario in the neo-Gothic style fashionable at the time.
The base of the 13C steeple, the only remainder of the original church, houses the cathedral **treasury** (◷ *May to mid-Sept: Sat 3-5.30pm, no charge - ☎04 79 70 58 15).* Note in particular an ivory **diptych**★ from the 10C, a 13C enamel pyx, a carved-wood representation of the Nativity and a 15C Flemish painting.

▶ *Walk back to rue de la Croix-d'Or.*

Rue de la Croix-d'Or
This street, lined with old mansions, was the most aristocratic avenue in Chambéry. The **Hôtel de Châteauneuf** at no 18 was built by an ironmaster in the 17C (remark-

able **wrought-iron work**⋆ in the courtyard). The **Hôtel des Marches et de Bellegarde** at no 13 opposite, has a lovely façade dating from 1788. Napoleon stayed here in 1805; Pope Pius VII had been imprisoned here on the Emperor's orders the year before. Walk along the driveway to admire the staircase.

Place St-Léger⋆

This vast oblong area was rebuilt and pedestrianised at the end of the 1970s. It was paved with pink porphyry, adorned with fountains and lamp-posts and its façades were restored and painted in warm colours; lined with numerous pavement cafés, it is the ideal place to stop for a drink.

Rue Basse-du-Château⋆

Picturesque footbridge-gallery and old workshops; note in particular the 15C shop at no 56 and the little 16C tower on the Hôtel du Chabod (no 76). The street leads to the castle

Place du Château

Overlooked by the castle, the square is framed by the fine 18C Hôtel de Montfalcon, an Italian-style palace, and the 17C **Hôtel Favre de Marnix**. A statue of the brothers **Joseph-Marie and Xavier Maistre** (⚲ see Introduction: Famous natives of the Alps) stands in the centre.

Château⋆

The château can only be seen on a tour; contact the Bureau du Patrimoine, opposite the statue of the Maistre brothers. ⏱ *July to Aug: guided tours (1hr15min) Mon-Fri at 10.30am, 2.30pm, 3.30pm, 4.30pm, Sun and 15 Aug at 2.30pm, 3.30pm, 4.30pm; May to June and Sept: Mon-Fri at 2.30pm; Oct to Apr: Sat-Sun and public and school holidays 2.30pm.* ⏱ *Closed 1 Jan and 25 Dec. 4€, children 2.5€.* ☎ *04 79 33 42 47.*

This former residence of the counts and dukes of Savoie and occasional home to the kings of Sardinia was rebuilt in the 14C-15C and partly destroyed by two fires in the 18C, after which a royal palace - now the Préfecture - was built.

▷ *Follow the ramp which passes beneath the former Porterie (lodge) and leads to the courtyard surrounded by the Sainte-Chapelle and the préfecture.*

Tour Trésorerie

14C. Local history and family tree of the House of Savoie.

Salles basses

14C. A monumental staircase leads to these barrel-vaulted rooms with 3m/10ft-thick walls, used as a chapel and a crypt and later as an arsenal.

Sainte-Chapelle⋆

The east end of the 15C Flamboyant-Gothic chapel is surrounded by a watch-path. The Baroque façade dates from the 17C. The building was named Sainte-Chapelle when the Holy Shroud was deposited inside in 1502 (later transferred to Turin; a replica is exhibited). The 16C stained-glass windows are remarkable. There are traces of *trompel'œil* frescoes (1836) by the Piedmontese

Italian influences: the arcades in rue Boigne

Fr. Isler/MICHELIN

artist Vicario. The large tapestry showing the arms of Savoyard towns was made in only two weeks to celebrate the union of Savoie and France.

Numerous historic weddings were celebrated inside, including that of Charlotte of Savoie and Louis XI (1423-1483) and Alphonse de Lamartine (1790-1869) and his English wife, Miss Marianne-Elisa Birch.

A **peal of 70 bells** (🕐 *May to Sept: guided tours (1hr) 2.50€; contact the tourist office - ☎ 04 79 33 42 47; international bell-ringers meeting in July and concerts the first and third Sat of the month at 5.30pm*), made by the Paccard bell-foundry in Sévrier (🔎 *see Lac d'ANNECY*), was placed inside the Tour Yolande in 1993.

▶ *Near the* **Tour Demi-Ronde**, *go down the steps leading to place Maché.*

Go through the 15C Flamboyant archway of the **Portail St-Dominique**, part of a Dominican monastery re-erected here in 1892.

▶ *From place Maché, start back towards the castle and turn left onto rue Juiverie.*

Rue Juiverie

Bankers and money changers used to live in this street, recently pedestrianised. Look inside the courtyard of no 60.

▶ *Continue along the narrow rue de Lans leading to place de l'Hôtel-de-Ville.*

Walk along the covered passage on the right (nos 5 and 6 place de l'Hôtel-de-Ville), one of the many **"allées"** in the old town.

Rue de Boigne

Designed by Général de Boigne and lined with arcades as is customary across the Alps, its orderly yet lively atmosphere makes this one of the town's most characteristic streets. It leads back to the Fontaine des Éléphants.

Quartier Curial

Most of the buildings in this important military district, dating from the Napoleonic period, were restored when the army left in the 1970s.

Carré Curial

The courtyard is open to the public. These former barracks, built in 1802 and modelled on the Hôtel des Invalides in Paris, have retained their original plan and have been refitted to house shops and offices.

Espace André-Malraux

Designed by the Swiss architect Mario Botta, this cultural centre containing a 900-seat theatre, audio-visual rooms and exhibition areas, stands next to the Carré Curial.

Centre de congrès "le Manège"

The former riding school of the Sard *carabinieri* is a harmonious blend of traditional military architecture and modern design. A transparent peristyle has been added.

Médiathèque Jean-Jacques-Rousseau

Designed by Aurelio Galfetti (1993), the building is crowned by a panoramic glass roof. Its unusual shape – and Arthur Rimbaud's poem *"Bâteau-Ivre"* – gave rise to its local nickname, the *"Bâteau-Livre"* or *"Book-boat."*

Sights

Musée savoisien★
🕐 *Open daily except Tues 10am-noon, 2-6pm. 3€, no charge first Sun of month - guided tours (1hr) by appointment* 🕐 *closed public holidays -* ☎ *04 79 33 44 48.*
The museum is housed in a former Franciscan monastery, later the archbishop's residence; the 13C, 15C and 17C buildings, surrounding vast cloisters, contain a large collection of prehistoric and Gallo-Roman exhibits on the ground floor. The upstairs galleries are devoted to religious (mainly medieval) art and coins from Savoie. A fine collection of Primitive Savoyard paintings is being restored. There is also a set of non-religious late-13C murals. The ethnographical section displays an excellent collection of objects illustrating traditional crafts, agriculture, daily life and popular art. The role of the Savoie region during the Second World War is also explained.

Musée des Beaux-Arts★
🕐 *Open daily except Tues 10am-noon, 2-6pm. 3€, children under 18 years no charge. No charge first Sun of month* 🕐 *closed public holidays -* ☎ *04 79 33 75 03.*
Temporary exhibitions are held on the ground floor, in the vaulted room where the people of Chambéry voted for union with France, and on the first floor. The second floor is devoted to Italian painting: works by Primitive Sienese artists (altarpiece by Bartolo di Fredi), Renaissance paintings *(Portrait of a Young Man,* attributed to Paolo Uccello) and works from the 17C and the 18C (Florentine and Neapolitan schools in particular). The 19C is represented by two major trends, neo-Classicism and Realism. Still-life painting, northern schools and regional painting are also represented.

Église St-Pierre-de-Lémenc
To the north of the town. 🕐 *Sat 5-6pm, Sun 9.30-10.30am -* ☎ *04 79 33 35 53.*
The church stands on the site of an ancient Roman settlement; the priory to which it belonged was one of the liveliest religious centres in medieval times. The small rotunda is a remainder of the first church; once believed to be a Carolingian baptistry, it has now been identified as a reliquary chapel from the 11C.
The chancel of the **crypt**★ was built in the 15C as a base for the Gothic church above. It contains a Deposition of the same period, mutilated during the Revolution.

Around Chambéry

Les Charmettes
2km/1.2mi south. Leave Chambéry along rue Michaud. At the first major junction out of town, follow D 4 then drive straight on along the narrow surfaced alleyway leading to Les Charmettes. Stop by the former chapel below the house. 🕐 *Apr to Sept: daily except Tue 10am-noon, 2-8pm; Oct to Mar: daily except Tue 10am-noon, 2-4.30pm* 🕐 *Closed public holidays. No charge. July to Aug: Rousseau evenings, costumed tours on Wed and Fri -* ☎ *04 79 33 39 44.*
The country house of Madame de Warens, who converted the Calvinist Jean-Jacques Rousseau to Catholicism, now belongs to the town of Chambéry. The charming De Warens captivated the young philosopher who described his stay here from 1736 to 1742 as "a time of happiness and innocence" in his *Confessions*. The careful restoration has preserved the 18C furnishings: on the ground floor, the dining room has *trompe-l'œil* decoration and the music room recalls Rousseau's musical career. On the first floor are the rooms occupied by Rousseau and Madame de Warens preceded by an oratory.
The terraced garden, containing plants which were popular in the 18C, overlooks the Chambéry Valley with the Dent du Nivolet in the distance.

Challes-les-Eaux ♯

6km/3.6mi southeast. From Chambéry, drive east along avenue Dr-Desfrançois, N 512, which veers southeast and joins N 6.

This little spa town specialises in the treatment of gynaecological and respiratory diseases. The spring waters are cold and contain a high concentration of sulphur. The casino and the baths, in mid-19C style, are pleasantly situated in a shaded park east of N 6. The former 17C castle is now a hotel.

Mont St-Michel ★

9.5km/6mi east, then 1hr there and back on foot. Drive 1km south of Challes along N 6, turn left then left again onto D 21; at the Boyat junction, turn left then left again towards Montmerlet; leave the car near the hamlet (parking lot) and take the footpath on the right.

There is a choice of several itineraries; as you go into the wood, the footpath on the right leads to the Chapelle du Mont St-Michel. Note how tree species vary according to the aspect of the slopes. From the top, there is a bird's-eye **view** of the Chambéry depression, of the town and of Challes below, with the snow-capped peaks of the Belledonne range in the distance. The Lac du Bourget is partly visible to the north-west, with the Mont du Chat towering above.

Lac d'Aiguebelette ★

The lake is easily accessible from Lyon via the Lyon-Chambéry motorway. This attractive triangular expanse of water dotted with two islets (a chapel stands on one of them), covers an area of 550ha/1 359 acres; its unpolluted waters are 71m/233ft deep in parts. The steep and forested eastern shore contrasts with the more accessible western and southern shores where leisure activities are concentrated: fishing, swimming, boating and pedalo rides. Marked footpaths offer interesting hikes in the surrounding area.

Lac d'Aiguebelette

Montmélian

This ancient, rapidly expanding little town, a centre of local viticulture, surrounds its rocky knoll, on which one of the most powerful strongholds in Europe once stood, dismantled in 1706 on the orders of Louis XIV. The top of the rock *(accessible by a ramp signposted "le fort")* is now occupied by a platform which offers a lovely **panorama** ★★ of the Isère Valley and of the Alps as far as Mont Blanc. Another rock to the northwest has been nicknamed "La Savoyarde" because its silhouette suggests a woman's head wearing the regional headdress (♿ *see Introduction: Traditions and folklore*). One reminder of Montmélian's past as a fortified town is the **Pont Cuénot,** whose ten arches have spanned the Isère since the 17C; for many years the only way to enter the town was by the bridge. Although the **Maison du Gouverneur** was remodelled in the 18C, it is not difficult to make out its Renaissance origins.

Combe de Savoie

Combe de Savoie is the name given to the northern section of the *sillon alpin* (Alpine trench), which includes the Isère Valley between Albertville and the Chambéry depression. Unlike the Grésivaudan to the south, it is an area exclusively devoted to agriculture. Villages, occupying sunny positions at the foot of the Bauges mountains between Montmélian and Mercury, are either lost among orchards or surrounded by fields of maize and tobacco or by famous vineyards; this is the main wine-growing

For coin categories, see the Legend on the cover flap.

EATING OUT

◖◖◖▥**La Combe "Chez Michelon"** – *73610 La Combe - 4km/2.5mi N d'Aiguebelette on D 41 - ☎ 04 79 36 05 02 - chezmichelon@aol.com - closed 1 Nov-6 Dec, Mon evening and Tue*. This restaurant stands in splendid isolation between the mountains and the forest, with its large bay windows overlooking the Lac d'Aiguebelette. In summer, meals are served on the terrace in the shade of centuries-old chestnut trees. This is a good family address, without fuss or pretension, that also offers one or two rooms.

WHERE TO STAY

◖ **Hôtel l'Or du Temps** – *814 Rte de Plainpalais - 73230 St-Alban-Leysse - ☎04 79 85 51 28 - www.or-du-temps.com - closed 1-8 Jan and 7-28 Aug - ▣ -19rms*. Outside the town, this renovated former farm has a pretty terrace facing the Massif des Bauges. Modern rooms with brightly coloured furniture, welcoming dining room with rustic touches such as stone floors and an old stone manger. Traditional menu.

area in Savoie. The best overall view of the Combe de Savoie can be enjoyed from the Rocher de Montmélian. Moreover, the roads leading to the Fort du Mont, Col du Frêne and Col de Tamié offer bird's-eye views of the depression. The most impressive sight in the area is the "eyrie" at Miolans (◔*see Les BAUGES, ❷*)

Hike

Croix de Nivolet★★
48km/30mi – allow 2hr

▸ *Leave Chambéry by the D 912 heading east, then follow signs to "Massif des Bauges"*

Between Villaret and St-Jean-d'Arvey the road rises steeply beneath the cliffs of two mountains, Mont Peney and the Dent de Nivolet, crowned by a monumental cross which is illuminated at night. After a glimpse of the Château de la Bâthie and, on the other side, the wooded gorges of the Bout-du-Monde, literally the End of the World, a series of tight bends leads to an impressive view of the Chambéry valley and Mont Granier. From St-Jean-d'Arvey to Plainpalais, the road runs along the top of the Leysse valley, until the river vanishes into a fissure in the rock just after Les Déserts. Ahead are the escarpments of Mont de Margeriaz.

🎿La Féclaz
This important centre of cross-country skiing is popular with the inhabitants of Lyon and Chambéry.
2hr there and back on foot; park the car at the start of the chairlift.
🚶 Follow the yellow-marked footpath *(no 2)* to the Chalet du Sire and continue through the woods. From the top of the Dent de Nivolet there is a superb **view**★★ of the Lac du Bourget and of the mountain ranges as far as Mont Blanc in the east.

Excursion

Route de l'Épine★ *85km/53mi – allow one day*
Roads between Chambéry and the Lac d'Aiguebelette are busy on Sundays during the holiday season. The Col de l'Épine is blocked by snow from November to April.

▶ *Leave Chambéry by the N 6, then turn right onto D 916.*

Panorama★★

Between St-Sulpice and the pass, the road offers glimpses of Mont Revard with its cable-car station, and of the Dent du Nivolet surmounted by a huge cross; beneath them lie Aix-les-Bains, its lake and the city of Chambéry. The parapet on the last bend before the pass makes a good viewpoint.

Col de l'Épine

Alt 987m/3 238ft. The pass may take its name from a thorn believed to be from Christ's crown of thorns, which was venerated in Nances Castle nearby. Beyond the pass, the cliff road offers bird's-eye views of the Lac d'Aiguebelette overlooked by the sparsely forested escarpments of Mont Grelle, with the Chartreuse summits in the background and the Vercors cliffs still further away.

▶ *Leave Novalaise by the D 916 to the west.*

The road follows the line of the massif to Col de la Crusille (573m/1 880ft), then runs parallel to a small tributary of the Rhône as far as **St-Genix-sur-Guiers,** once on the border between Savoie and France. Convenient motorway connections to Lyon and Chambéry have boosted its growth as a popular holiday town.

▶ *Continue west on the D 914 for 3km/1.9mi.*

Aoste

This busy market town with a thriving food-processing industry controlled, in Roman times, the traffic between the main city of Vienne (south of Lyon) to Italy via the Petit-St-Bernard Pass. Aoste, named after Emperor Augustus, owed its importance to its production of pottery and ceramics, some of which have been found as far away as Germany and the British Isles; the well displayed exhibits of the **Musée archéologique** (🐾🕐 *Feb to Nov: daily except Tue 2-6pm* 🕐 *closed Dec to Jan and public holidays. 3.60€, children under 12 years no charge* -☎*04 76 32 58 27*) illustrate life in Aoste under the Romans. Note in particular a

Musée d'Aoste

Roman glass from the workshops at Aoste

"crossroads altar" surmounted by a roof with four recesses intended for the deities of travel. Social life in the Gallo-Roman city is also explained, covering religious rituals (the goddess of Abundance is particularly attractive), domestic life (reconstruction of a kitchen) and crafts (model of potters' workshops and a rich collection of **ceramics★**). Walk south across N 516 towards the retirement home; a remarkably well-preserved **pottery kiln** lies under a concrete awning and behind glass, about 10m/11yd left of the entrance.

▶ *Return to St-Genix-sur-Guiers and turn onto the D 916 to Le-Pont-de-Beauvoisin.*

The road now heads upstream along the course of the Guiers, a tributary of the Rhône which once formed the Franco-savoyard frontier and now marks the boundary of the *département* of Isère.

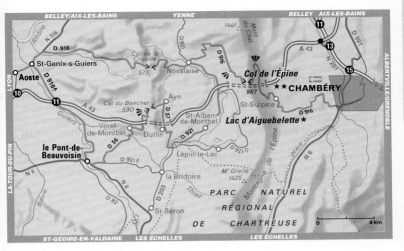

Le Pont-de-Beauvoisin

This small town is at the centre of an important tobacco-growing area and also manufactures furniture. From the border **bridge** spanning the Guiers, there is a pleasant view of the river lined with fine old houses over which towers the steeple of the Église des Carmes.

▷ *Take the D 36 north towards Dullin.*

The prospect from the road, which runs right along the edge of the slope, stretches as far as the Petit Bugey. The **view**★ to the left just as the road enters the Col du Banchet is the best of many between Vérel-de-Montbel and Ayn.

▷ *From Ayn take the D 37 towards Lac d'Aiguebelette.*

The road leads to the plateau around Dullin which is planted with tobacco, nut trees and cereal crops, before running alongside the western shore of the Lac d'Aiguebelette between St-Alban-de-Montbel and Novalaise.

▷ *From Novalaise follow the road back to Chambéry.*

CHAMONIX-MONT-BLANC✳✳✳

POPULATION 9 830
MICHELIN MAP 328 O5
LOCAL MAP SEE MASSIF DU MONT-BLANC AND P 257

Already the French mountaineering capital thanks to its Compagnie des Guides, Chamonix has also become one of the best equipped ski resorts in the Alps. The development of the town as a skiing destination began when the first Winter Olympic Games were held here in 1924. Today, the Chamonix Valley offers a mixture of architectural styles and incessant traffic throughout the high season. Hardly beautiful in itself, its main attraction lies in its magnificent landscapes, lively atmosphere and numerous opportunities to practice sports and enjoy cultural events. 🛈 *place Triangle de l'Amitié, BP 25 – 74400 Chamonix-Mont-Blanc* 🕐 *July to Aug: 8.30am-7.30pm (20-21 Aug, 7pm); Sept to mid-Dec: Mon-Sat 8.30am-12.30pm, 2-6.30pm; rest of year, telephone for hours -* ☎ *04 50 53 00 24 - www.chamonix.com*

▶ **Orient Yourself:** Chamonix is 101km/63mi east of Annecy by A 41 and A 40.

🖎 **Don't Miss:** The cable-car up the Aiguille-du-Midi is a major attraction, and the Musée Alpin offers interesting exhibits about local life and traditions.

🕑 **Organizing Your Time:** Chamonix is very crowded in July-August and during school holidays; try to come some other time. At all times, reserve your rides up the Aiguille-du-Midi and Montenvers, and be sure to check the weather.

▣ **Especially for Kids:** Children between 4 and 15 years old benefit from reduced fares on the lifts; there are also family passes.

⚲ **Also See:** Nearby Sights: ARGENTIÈRE, Les CONTAMINES-MONTJOIE, Les HOUCHES, MEGÈVE, Massif du MONT-BLANC, ST-GERVAIS-LES-BAINS, Bassin des SALLANCHES

The Resort

Rue du Dr-Paccard, extended by rue Joseph-Vallot, is the town's main artery. The short rue de l'Église, perpendicular to it, leads to the church at the heart of the old town and to the **Maison de la Montagne**, which houses the offices of the Compagnie des Guides. In the opposite direction, avenue Michel-Croz leads past the **statue** of Docteur Michel Gabriel Paccard (⚲*see Massif du MONT-BLANC*) to the station and the newer districts of Chamonix lying on the left bank of the Arve.

The controversial concrete buildings of the Bouchet sports centre and of place du Mont-Blanc stand on this side of the river.

A **bronze sculpture** by Salmson, depicting the naturalist Horace Bénédict de Saussure (1740-99) and the mountain guide Jacques Balmat (1762-1834) admiring Mont Blanc (⚲*see Massif du MONT-BLANC*), decorates the widened Pont de Cour.

Musée alpin

89 av Michel-Croz 🕑 *Daily 2-7pm; during school holidays: 10am-noon, 2-7pm; guided tours Wed 2.30pm* 🕑 *Closed in May, from mid-Oct to mid-Dec, 25 Dec, 1 Jan. 5€, children under 12 years no charge. (Ticket combined with Espace Tairraz) -* ☎ *04 50 53 25 93.*
This museum illustrates the history of the Chamonix Valley, daily life in the 19C, the conquest of Alpine summits, scientific experiments and early skiing in the valley.

Espace Tairras

Rocade du Dr. Payot 🕑 *School holidays: 10am-noon, 2-7pm; rest of year: 2-7pm* 🕑 *closed May to mid-June. 5€, children 12-18years 1.50€ -* ☎*0450 55 53 93.* The space is

---

The Compagnie des Guides

Founded in 1821 to improve safety on Mont Blanc, the Compagnie originally comprised 34 guides, all natives of Chamonix. Today, 200 highly trained professionals not only take you up the mountain, they lead hikes and treks, run a program for juniors and operate schools in all aspects of mountaineering. Winter tours include skiing, ski-touring, snow-shoeing and heli-skiing, as well as climbing. Popular excursions include the TMB (Tour of Mont Blanc with overnight stops in refuges) and the ascent of Mont Blanc in small groups (10hr hard-going trek). In winter, skiing down the Vallée Blanche with a guide is an unforgettable memory for any experienced skier. Charges for excursions are available at the Compagnie's offices in Chamonix (☎ 04 50 53 00 88 - www.chamonix-guides.com), in Argentière and in Les Houches.

The *fête des guides* on 15 August gathers mountain lovers for a charitable cause.

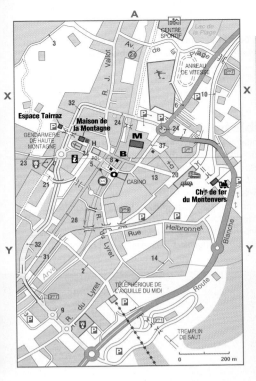

CHAMONIX

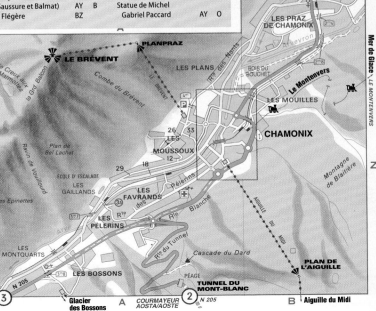

shared by the 🎨 **Musée des Cristaux**, with remarkable examples of crystal from Mont-Blanc and around the world, and to temporary exhibits about the regional heritage.

Excursions

Viewpoints accessible by cable car
The following excursions to nearby peaks involve cable-car journeys. A Multipass sold by the Compagnie du Mont-Blanc is often the cheapest solution if you plan to take several lifts. Be sure to reserve places in advance, particularly in high season.

🚡 Aiguille du Midi cable-car★★★
Minimum 2hr there and back by cable-car. 🕐 *1-8 July and 22-31 August: 7.30am-5.30pm; 9 July to 21 Aug: 7.10am-5.30pm; Sept: 8.10am-5.30pm; rest of year telephone for hours and prices. Trip in two stages: Chamonix-Plan de l'Aiguille and Plan de l'Aiguille-Aiguille du Midi. (departures every 10-30min). Adults 36€ return; juniors 12-15 years 30.60€; children 4-11 years*

The Mer de Glace

25.20€; not recommended for under 4s - ☎ 04 50 53 30 80 - www.compagniedumontblanc. com. You can book in summer by calling ☎ 08 36 68 00 67 (reservations: 2€)
The Aiguille du Midi cable-car, suspended part of the time 500m/1 640ft above ground, and the gondola form the most thrilling attraction in the French Alps.

🚠 Plan de l'Aiguille★★
Cablecar to Plan de l'Aiguille only: adults 16€ return; juniors 12-15 years 13.60€; children 4-11 years 11.20€. Alt 2 310m/7 579ft. This midway stop, situated at the foot of the jagged Aiguilles de Chamonix, is the starting point for easy walks. Good view of the upper parts of the Mont-Blanc Massif.

Aiguille du Midi★★★
Piton Nord: alt 3 800m/12 467ft. The upper station is separated from the highest point – Piton Central – by an abyss spanned by a footbridge. From the viewing platform, there is a bird's-eye **view** of the Chamonix Valley 2 800m/9 186ft below. The indented Aiguilles de Chamonix appear slightly lower and you can see the Aiguille Verte, Grandes Jorasses and Aiguille du Géant overlooking the snowfields of the Col

J.-L. Gallo/MICHELIN

du Géant. For a 360-degree video preview, go to www.compagniedumontblanc. com, select Aiguille du Midi and click on "panorama."

Piton Central (accessible by lift – ⏱ verify times at ticket booth or by telephone. 3€. ☎ 04 50 53 30 80.): alt 3 842m/12 605ft. There is a totally clear view of the snow-capped peaks of Mont Blanc and of the dark rock face of the Aiguilles. Mont Rose and Mont Cervin can be seen in the distance.

⌂Venture through the galleries dug at the base of the Piton Nord: one of them leads to a platform facing Mont Blanc; the other – used by skiers intending to ski down the **Vallée Blanche** *(Combined ticket Chamonix-Pointe Helbronner adults 54 € return; juniors 12-15 years 45.90€; children 4-11 years 37.80€)* – to the gondola station *(Aiguille du Midi to Pointe Helbronner,⌂ see Massif du MONT-BLANC).*

Le Brévent★★★

⌂*Minimum 1hr30 min there and back by gondola (to Planpraz, 20 min)) then by cable-car (Planpraz-Brévent 20 min) ⏱ Mid-July to Aug: 8am-5.45pm; mid-June to mid-July and Sept: 9am-5pm; rest of year, consult schedules. Adults 20€ return; juniors 12-15 years 17€; children 4-11 years 14 € - ☎ 04 50 53 22 75 - www.compagniedumontblanc.* Alt 2 526m/8 287ft.

Planpraz★★ relay station (Alt 2 062m/6 765ft) offers a splendid view of the Aiguilles de Chamonix. From the Brévent summit *(viewing table),* the **panorama** extends over the whole French side of the Mont-Blanc Massif, including the Aiguille du Midi and the Chamonix Valley.

La Flégère★

⌂*Cable-car LesPraz-La Flegère (15min) plus l'Index chairlift (20min) ⏱ mid-July to Aug: 7.40am-5.30pm; mid-June to mid-July and first 2 weeks Sept: 8.40am-4.30pm; rest of year, inquire for hours) Adults 18€ return; juniors 12-15 years 15.30€; children 4-11 years 12.50€ - ☎ 04 50 53 18 58 - www.compagniedumontblanc.com.*

Alt 1 894m/6 168ft. From the viewing table at LesPraz, there is an impressive **view** of the Aiguille Verte and the Grandes Jorasses summits closing off the Mer de Glace depression. It is possible to stop here, or to continue up by chairlift.

From the top of **l'Index**★★, (2 385m/7 825ft) the **view** embraces the whole Mont Blanc Massif from the Aiguille du Tour to the Aiguille du Goûter.

Mer de Glace via the Montenvers mountain railway★★★

Minimum 2 hrs there and back; change in altitude 900m/2953 ft ⏱ July to Aug: (departure every 30min) 8am (mid-July to Mid-Aug 7am)-6.30pm; May to June and Sept, first week July and last week Aug: 8.30am-5.30pm; mid-Dec to April: 10am-4.30pm ⏱ closed 3 weeks in Oct. Hours may change due to weather. 22.50€, children 15.80€ - ☎ 04 50 53 12 54 - www.compagniedumontblanc.com.

The Montenvers Rack-Railway

This picturesque train, which enables non-mountaineers to experience the feel of high mountains and glaciers, gets its name from the viewpoint at the end of the line. In a mere 5km/3mi, there is a drop of 870m/2 854ft between the upper and lower stations.

The service ran in summer from 1908 onwards, the train being pulled by a Swiss steam engine which negotiated slopes with a 20% gradient with the help of a rack; the ascent lasted approximately 1hr at an average speed of 6kph/3.7mph. Since 1993, the line has been modernised with protection against avalanches and more powerful engines are now used, so that the service runs all year round and trains have a top speed of 20kph/12.4mph.

Lowest altitude of the glacier: 1 700m/5 577ft.

🚶 From the upper station at the top of the **Montenvers** (alt 1 913m/6 276ft), there is the famous **panorama**★★★, a natural wonder comprising the **Mer de Glace** and two impressive "needles," **Aiguille du Dru** and **Aiguille Verte** with the **Grandes Jorasses** in the background. *Viewing table in front of the Hôtel du Montenvers.*
At the summit, you can visit the **Galerie des Cristaux**, **Le Musée de la Faune Alpine** and the **Grand Hôtel-Restaurant du Montenvers** (1840), which has a museum with exhibits explaining the history of the site.

Before Leaving

🐾 Take warm clothing with you as the weather is unpredictable at high altitude;

🐾 Even when going on easy hikes, wear mountain boots and sunglasses;

🐾 Several cable-car rides involve a sudden huge change in altitude; do not rush to the top when you arrive, but take it easy: one ought to be able to hold a conversation whilst climbing;

🐾 The less daring will find that midway cable-car stations offer interesting viewpoints;

🐾 Food and drink are available at the Planpraz and Brévent stations and there are restaurants at the Aiguille du Midi, Brévent and Flégère top stations;

🐾 Dogs are not usually allowed, particularly when the itinerary goes through a nature reserve.

Advice concerning excursions to the **Aiguille du Midi** and the **Vallée Blanche**:

🐾 During peak periods, departure times are fixed and passengers are given a numbered boarding card: it is imperative to abide by these regulations.

On arrival at the Piton Nord, it is advisable to go over the footbridge in order to gain access to the Piton Central and Mont Blanc terrace which ought to be seen first. The Piton Nord can be visited before returning to Chamonix. Access to the Helbronner gondola is via the Vallée Blanche gallery, on the left after the footbridge. The ice tunnel is reserved for suitably equipped mountaineers.

The Chamonix Valley can undoubtedly boast the most remarkable **ski area** in Haute-Savoie, for it offers some of the finest runs to be found anywhere, combining length, gradient and unsurpassed mountain scenery. In order to make the most of this incomparable ski area without encountering long queues at the lifts, it is advisable to avoid school holidays and weekends.
The ski area spreads over several massifs linked by shuttle services: the Brévent and Aiguille du Midi to Chamonix, the Flégère to Les Praz, the Grands-Montets to Argentière and the Balme to Le Tour. Snow cover is usually excellent above 1 900m/6 234ft (on the second section of each massif), but is often insufficient to allow skiers to ski right down to the bottom of the valley (return by cable-car is provided for). Experienced skiers favour such runs as the **Charles Bozon**, the Combe de la Charlanon and Col Cornu (Brévent area), the Pylônes and Pic Janvier (Flégère area) and above all the second section of the **Grands-Montets**★★★ (👁 see ARGENTIÈRE). Off-piste itineraries, to be ventured only with a guide, are exceptional, in particular the famous **Vallée Blanche**★★★ (20km/12.4mi downhill run with a 2 800m/9 186ft drop from Aiguille du Midi). Inexperienced skiers feel particularly at ease in the Balme area, where slopes are moderate and snow plentiful. There are also some fairly easy runs in Planpraz and La Flégère. Note that the **Compagnie du Mont Blanc** sells a variety of ski passes depending on your skills and schedule; consult the website. In summer, the Aiguille du Midi cable car enables enthusiasts to ski down the glacial valley known as the Vallée Blanche. Cross-country skiing is practised between Chamonix and Argentière, at the bottom of the valley.

Address Book

For coin categories, see the Legend on the cover flap.

EATING OUT

Le Panoramic – *Summit of Le Brévent – by gondola and cable car -* ☎ *04 50 53 44 11 - closed 20 Apr-15 Jun, 1 Oct-15 Dec and evenings.* Sitting on the terrace, you feel suspended in mid-air... There is a breathtaking view of Mont-Blanc, the Aiguille du Midi and the Bossons glacier. The menu features local cuisine, with tea and coffee breaks in the sunshine; life as it should be!

Le Dru – *25 rue Ravenel-le-Rouge -* ☎ *04 50 53 33 06 - boncristian@wanadoo.fr* The painted façade of this midtown chalet draws the eye. Comfortable decor including wood, old peasant tools and a collection of oil lamps. Try the fondue or the substantial "Trio du Dru" with three hearty cheese dishes.

La Bergerie – *232 av. Michel-Croz -* ☎ *04 50 53 45 04 - www.labergerie-chamonix.com - closed 2 weeks in May - reservations advisable.* The decor features traditional local farming equipment. Hearty grills prepared over an open wood fire. Regional dishes are also on offer, and there is a peaceful shady terrace for summer days.

La Calèche – *18 r. du Dr-Paccard -* ☎ *04 50 55 94 68 - www.restaurant-caleche.com - closed 15 Nov-1 Dec.* This restaurant at the heart of the resort resembles a museum or bric-à-brac fair, with a variety of antique and old-fashioned articles, copper pots, bells and old skis displayed all around the dining room. The waiting staff wear traditional local costume, and a folk group puts on a show once a week.

L'Impossible – *9 chemin du Cry -* ☎ *04 50 53 20 36 - closed Nov, Tue evening in May-Jun and Sept-Oct, and lunchtime - 15.09/26.22€.* This typical local farm dating from 1754 has preserved its original character with beamed ceiling and the traditional fireplace under the roof truss on the first floor. The proprietor uses this to prepare his local specialities and grilled meats.

Le 3842 – *At the summit of Aiguille du Midi – by cable car -* ☎ *04 50 55 82 23 - closed Oct-May.* After travelling up in the cable-car and negotiating a series of galleries and footbridges, patrons sit down to dine at 3 842m/12 600ft above sea level. In these extreme conditions, the dining room necessarily has narrow windows, but you're eating more or less on the rooftop of Europe!

Maison Carrier – *Rte du Bouchet -* ☎ *04 50 53 00 03 - www.hameaualbert.fr - closed 5-20 June, mid-Nov-mid-Dec, Tue lunchtime and Mon except July- Aug and public holidays* Treat yourself to a feast in this local restaurant on the premises of Hameau Albert 1. One of the dining rooms is an authentic farm room dating from 1794. The cooking is typical of the rural mountain region, and traditional meat dishes are grilled over a large central open fireplace.

WHERE TO STAY

Good to know – To make a selection among the more than 68 hotels and 4 000 rooms of all sorts found in Chamonix and the surrounding area, consult the reservation centre at the tourist office. Local hoteliers also compile a booklet listing accomodation.

Camping La Mer de Glace – *At Les Praz-de-Chamonix - 2.5km/1.5mi NE of Chamonix on N 506 -* ☎ *04 50 53 44 03 - campongmdg@wanadoo.fr - open 29 Apr-2 Oct - 🚫 - 150 pitches.* This is indisputably the best campsite in the valley. The various buildings, designed as chalets, blend harmoniously into an unspoiled natural setting. There is no entertainment, so as not to disturb the peace and quiet of the valley. Simple clean accommodation.

Chambre d'Hôte Chalet Beauregard – *182 rue Mollard -* ☎ *04 50 55 86 30/ 06 30 52 63 97 - www.chalet-beauregard.com- closed 3 weeks in May and 15 Oct -Nov - 🚫 - 7rms and 1 loft.* This Savoyard chalet surrounded by a small garden carries the right name: the view of Mont-Blanc and the Aiguille du Midi is magnificent. Rooms are austere but comfortable, often with a balcony. Pleasant breakfast room.

Chambre d'hôte La Girandole – *46 chemin de la Persévérance*

- 1.5km/1mi NW of town centre towards Le Brévent cable-car and the Route des Moussoux - ☎ 04 50 53 37 58 - www.lagirandole.free.fr - closed 15 May-17 June and Nov-Dec - ⊟ - 3rms. A journey more resembling a treasure hunt brings you to this typical local chalet off the beaten track. It sits in a remarkable landscape, and the windows of its fine timber-panelled lounge overlook Mont-Blanc, the Aiguille du Midi and the Aiguille Verte. Warm welcome.

⊜⊟**Hôtel Faucigny** – 118 Pl de l'Église - ☎ 04 50 53 01 17 - www.hotelfaucigny-chamonix.com - closed 15 Apr-16 May, 28 My-16 June, 30 Sept-27 Oct and 4 Nov-21 Dec - 20rms. A central location and reasonable prices are the major advantages of this renovated hotel. Some first-floor rooms have a view of Mont-Blanc; those on the second floor are under the mansard roof.

⊜⊜⊟**Hôtel Aiguille du Midi** – 479 chemin Napoléon - 74400 Bossons - 3.5km/2mi SW of Chamonix on N 506 - ☎ 04 50 53 00 65 - www.hotel-aiguilledu-midi.com - open 20 May-20 Sept and 20 Dec-17 Apr - 🅿 - 40rms - ⊜⊟restaurant. The façade of this Savoyard house is decorated with pretty Tyrolean frescos. The rooms are a bit tired, but the place has many advantages: pleasant garden, swimming pool, tennis court and gym. Good classic cuisine.

⊜⊜⊟**Hôtel Le Cantou**– 9 Ch Pierre-Belle, 74400 Les Bossons - ☎ 04 50 55 85 77 - www.hotelcantou.com - 🅿 -17rms. This is a charming chalet with flower boxes, where you should choose rooms on the second floor, newer and more spacious, some with a mezzanine allowing more bed space. Patio next to the swimming pool.

⊜⊜⊜⊟**Hôtel du Prairon**– at Prairon, alt. 1 860m/6 102ft -by gondola - 74170 St-Gervais-les-Bains - ☎ 04 50 53 05 094 40 07 - www.prairon.com - open 26 June-5 Sept and 18 Dec-mid-Apr - 12rms - ⊜⊜⊟restaurant. At the summit of Prairon, the calmest night you will ever spend, high on the mountain. The panoramic view is astonishing, from the Aravis to Mont-Blanc. The restaurant offers simple cooking, and the rooms have alpine decor.

ON THE TOWN

Bar du Plan de l'Aiguille – Le Plan de l'Aiguille - ☎ 06 65 64 27 53 - plan-delaiguille@free.fr - Apr-Nov: access by the Aiguille du Midi cable car. This modest bar at the foot of the Aiguille du Midi, in a magnificent site 2 317m/7 436ft above sea level makes a pleasant place to stop for rambling enthusiasts.

L'M – R. Joseph-Vallot - ☎ 04 50 53 58 30 - www.chamonixhotels.com - Daily 9am-11pm. One of Chamonix's finest terraces with picture-postcard views. Glass in hand, admire the Aiguilles de l'M, de Charmoz, de Blaitière, du Plan and du Midi.

SHOPPING

L'Alpage des Aiguilles – 91 rue Joseph-Vallot - ☎ 04 50 53 14 21 - www.aplesgourmet.com - Daily 9am-8pm - closed 2 May-15 June and 1 Oct- 15 Dec. This boutique is a marvel, bursting with regional produce: sausages, hams, remarkable cheese such as the strong-flavoured summer Beaufort... To accompany this rich fare, choose a bottle from the well-stocked cellar.

Le Refuge Payot – 255 rue du Dr-Paccard - ☎ 04 50 53 18 71 or 04 50 53 16 86 - www.refugepayot.com – open daily 8.15am-8pm. This boutique is well stocked with local specialities of all kinds: charcuterie (bilberry sausage), cheeses (Fromage d'Abondance), jams (milk jam), wines from Savoie, confectionery and ready-cooked local dishes to take away.

Les P'tits Gourmands – 168 rue du Dr-Paccard - ☎04 50 53 01 59 - open daily 7am-7.45pm. The propietors have successfully merged three sorts of boutique: pastry shop, chocolate shop and tearoom. The chocolate cake, the almond-blueberry confection, the fruit tarts and the excellent home-made chocolate will make it hard for you to leave.

PUBLIC TRANSPORT

Le Mulet – A free shuttle bus runs continuously around the centre of Chamonix. You won't regret leaving your car in the parking lot.

The **Carte d'Hote**, given you at your hotel, gives you free access to all public transport and reductions on many public services.

It is possible to visit an **ice cave** (🕐 *Closed from Oct to mid-Dec*) freshly dug every year through the Mer de Glace. A **gondola** (*combined ticket for train, gondola, ice cave 22.50€ adult, 15.80€ children*) leads to it from the Montenvers upper station. In summer, you can take a footpath starting to the right of the station. The site of the cave changes every year because of the glacier's movement.

Crossing the Mont Blanc Massif★★★

– 1 day there and back – 👣*see Massif du MONT-BLANC,* 5.
Hikers with high-altitude mountain experience can climb the Mer de Glace along the Balcon de la Mer de Glace via ferrata. *(Contact the Guides de Chamonix office).*

Walks and Hikes

There are many hikes possible along 200km/125mi of marked footpaths. A *Carte des Promenades d'été en montagne* is published by the Chamonix tourist office.

Short tour of Mont Blanc★★★
4-day round tour – 👣*see Massif du MONT-BLANC.*

Lac Blanc★★
Alt 2 352m/7 717ft. *From Les Praz, take the cable car to La Flégère then the gondola to L'Index. 1hr 15min on foot to the lake. Walk back directly to La Flégère in 1hr. Mountain boots essential (for crossing névés and walking along the stony path).*
🔼Sweeping view from left to right of the Tour Glacier, Aiguille du Chardonnet, Aiguille d'Argentière and glacier of the same name, Grands-Montets, Aiguille Verte, Mer de Glace, Grandes Jorasses, Aiguille du Géant, Aiguille du Midi and Mont Blanc.

Walk from La Flégère to Planpraz★★
Take a bus to Les Praz, then the cable car to La Flégère. From there, about 2hr on foot to Planpraz. Take the gondola back to Chamonix.
🔼This relatively easy walk is part of the Grand Balcon Sud itinerary linking the Col des Montets and Les Houches; it offers uninterrupted views of the Mont-Blanc Massif.

Hike from the Plan de l'Aiguille to the Montenvers★
about 2hr 15min on foot.
🔼Overall views of the valley, from Les Houches to Argentière, and Aiguilles Rouges in particular. Towards the end, take the path on the left leading to the Mer de Glace.

CHAMPAGNY-EN-VANOISE❄❄

MICHELIN MAP 333 N
LOCAL MAP SEE MASSIF DE LA VANOISE

This unpretentious village, situated at an altitude of 1 250m/4 101ft, beneath the impressive **Grand Bec** (3 403m/11 165ft) and opposite Courchevel, has retained its traditional character in spite of its recent expansion as a tourist resort. 🅻 *Le Centre - 73830 Champagny-en-Vanoise* 🕐 *July to Aug: 9am-noon, 2-7pm, Sat 9am-noon, 1-7pm, Sun and public holidays 9am-noon, 3-7pm; rest of year: Mon-Fri 9am-noon, 2-6pm* 🕐 *closed 1 and 8 May and first week of Nov -* ☎ *04 79 55 06 55 -www.champagny.com*

▶ **Orient Yourself:** Take A 430 to Albertville, then by N 90 towards Courcheval.
😊 **Don't Miss:** Walk along the easy nature trail in Champagny-le-Haut.

🕐 **Organizing Your Time:** This is ideal country for hikes, and you may also see ibex, partticulary in the spring when they venture close to villages.

🕯 **Also See:** Nearby Sights: Les ARCS, La Vallée des BELLEVILLE, COURCHEVEL, MÉRIBEL, La PLAGNE, PRALOGNAN-LA-VANOISE, La TARENTAISE, Massif de la VANOISE

The Resort

🎿🏂The pleasant and sunny **ski area,** linked to that of La Plagne and of Paradski by gondola and chairlift, offers runs for skiers from beginners to experts. When snow cover is adequate, the **Mont de la Guerre red run,** with its 1 250m/4 101ft drop, offers splendid views of the Courchevel and Pralognan snowfields. Champagny-le-Haut also has fine cross-country skiing trails.

For coin categories, see the Legend on the cover flap.

WHERE TO STAY

🛏🛏🛏**Hôtel L'Ancolie** – *Le Crey* - ☎ *04 79 55 05 00 - www.hotel-ancolie.com - closed 15 Apr-25 Jun and 6 Sept-19 Dec 31rms -* 🛏🛏 *restaurant.* This chalet above the resort has an outdoor swimming pool and a terrace overlooking the Vanoise slopes. Spacious rooms decorated in cherry wood. Simple local cuisine.

Baroque Church

🕐 *july-Aug: daily except Mon 3-6pm; guided tours Monday 5pm. 5€. -* ☎*04 79 55 06 55 or at the FACIM office -* ☎*04 79 60 59 00.*
Erected at the top of a mound in 1250 and rebuilt in 1648, the church contains a remarkable **altarpiece**★ (1710) dedicated to the Virgin Mary, by Jacques Clérant, a sculptor from Chambéry. The altar front representing the Christ child surrounded by angels is in similar style.

Excursions

Télécabine de Champagny★

🕐 *Mid-July to mid-Aug: daily except Fri and Sat 9am-12.45pm, 2-5.30pm; rest of year contact tourist office. 7€, children under 10 no charge.* ☎ *04 79 55 06 55.*
Alt 1 968m/6 457ft. The gondola journey reveals the Péclet, Polset and Grand-bec peaks and the Vanoise glaciers. From the terrace of the restaurant (closed in summer) at the top of the Borselliers ski lift (alt 2 109m/6 919ft, viewing table), the **view**★ extends to the Grande Casse, Aiguille de l'Épena, Grande Glière, Pointe de Méribel and Les Trois Vallées.

Champagny-le-Haut★★

The narrow road, hewn out of the rock, overlooks the Gorges de Champagny and leads into the austere basin of Champagny-le-Haut. Note the **Cascade de la Chiserette** on the left, just before the village of the same name. Beyond Chiserette, there is a view of the Grande Motte Glacier with the Grande Casse Peak on the right.
🔳 The Porte du Parc du Bois information centre is the starting point of a ♿ 👶 **nature trail** that explains features of the landscape *(1hr 30min walk on flat ground).*

Hikes

From La Plagne, the main paths lead to Mont Jovet, la Grande Rochette and the Col de la Chiaupe, connected by cable car to the Bellecôte glacier. The most beautiful walks, however, start above Champagny-le-Haut in the parc de la Vanoise.
🔳 Begin early at Laisonnay-d'en-Bas (1 559m/5 115ft): from there, trails lead to the **Col du Palet**★★ *(7hr 30min there and back,* 🕯*see TIGNES),* **Col de la Grassaz** *(7hr thereand back)* and **Col du Plan Séry** *(5hr 30min there and back).* Hikers are rewarded with views of the Grand Bec, Grande Motte and Grande Casse summits.

LE CHAMPSAUR★

MICHELIN MAP 77 FOLDS 16 AND 17, 89 FOLD 20, 244 FOLDS 40 AND 41
OR 245 FOLDS 7 AND 8

The Champsaur is the area surrounding the upper Drac Valley upriver from Corps. Lying at altitudes often higher than 1 000m/3 281ft – similar to those of the Chamonix Valley – this region offers rural landscapes of a kind quite unknown in the northern Alps. The most impressive bird's eye views are from the Col du Noyer when coming from Dévoluy. Several winter sports resorts have developed in the Champsaur area: Orcières-Merlette, Ancelle, St-Michel-de-Chaillol, St-Léger-les-Mélèzes and Laye. *Maison du Tourisme Champsaur-Valgaudemar, Les Barraques Mon-Fri 8.30am-noon, 1.30-6pm ☎ 04 92 49 09 35, www.champsaur-valgaudemar.com.*

La Maison de la Vallée (Parc des Écrins) , 05260 Pont-du-Fossé, July to Aug: 3-7pm, rest of the year: Tue-Fri 9am-noon, 2-5pm; Welcome Centre at Prapic, June and Sept: daily except Sat 2-7pm; July to Aug: 10am-12.30pm, 2-5.45pm - ☎ 04 92 55 95 44

▶ **Orient Yourself:** The Route Napoleon (N 85) crosses Le Champsaur between Grenoble and Gap. Take the D 944 for 6km/3.75mi to reach the Col de Manse, starting point for excursion ①

◉ **Don't Miss:** Admire the splendid countryside along the Drac Noir and the Drac Blanc, as well as the medieval streets of St-Bonnet-en-Champsaur

◐ **Organizing Your Time:** It will take you a day to make all three excursions. Give yourself two days if you want to take advantage of the many hiking paths.

Kids Especially for Kids: Seven "ecomusée" sites in the region offer educational exhibits; the Base de Loisirs near St-Bonnet has swimming and other water sports; at Laye, there is a Jungle Park with activities for the whole family.

Ⓒ **Also See:** Nearby Sights: Pays du BUËCH, Le DÉVOLUY, GAP, Lacs de LAFFREY, MONTMAUR, Route NAPOLEON, Lac de SERRE-PONÇON, Le VALBONNAIS, Le VALGAUDEMAR

Excursions

① Drac Noir★

FROM COL DE MANSE TO ORCIÈRES *66km/41mi – about 2hr 30min (not including tours from Orcières-Merlette)*

Col de Manse

The pass links the Gap Basin and Drac Valley in a landscape of high pastures. You pass a Refuge Napoléon (Ⓒ *see Le BRIANÇONNAIS,* ⑤*).*

▶ *Follow D 13 towards Ancelle.*

The road offers a pleasant drive through pastures, with lovely glimpses of the upper Drac Valley, and then through larch woods down to the bottom of the valley.

For coin categories, see the Legend on the cover flap.

WHERE TO STAY

⊖ **Chambre d'hote La Combe Fleurie** – *Rte de Chaillol 055500 St-Bonnet -* ☎ *04 92 50 53 97 -* ⌷ *- 6rms,* ⊖ *restaurant.* Comfortable, sunny rooms in a new building near the town centre. Generous breakfast; pleasant dining room with fireplace for winter. Local farm produce and good pastries.

▶ *In Pont-du-Fossé, turn right onto D 944 then turn left in Pont-de-Corbière.* 🅑 *Pont-du-Fossé, 05260 St-Jean-St-Nicholas, ⏱ daily except Mon, telephone for schedule - ☎ 04 92 55 95 71, www.pont-du-fossé.fr*

The old mill in Pont-du-Fossé has been converted into the **Musée des Arts et Traditions du Champsaur**★ (⏱ *July to Aug: daily except Sat-Sun 3-6pm; rest of year, guided tour on request,* ⏱ *closed holidays. ; 4€ - ☎ 04 92 51 91 19, or 04 92 55 91 04*), displaying tools and other objects from traditional rural life. Opposite the museum, cast a look at the painted ceilings of the **chapelle des Patarons**, a Catholic sect opposed to the 1811 concordat between Napoleon and Pope Pius VII.

Between the Pont de Corbière and Orcières the road follows the course of the Drac Noir. Larches and firs grow along the northern slopes of the valley, which becomes increasingly mountainous.

Orcières

This south-facing village is the starting point of pleasant forest walks.

On the way out towards Prapic, note how the walls of the houses in Montcheny are adorned with *"pétètes,"* decorative little heads which are unique to the Champsaur.

🚠 **Orcières-Merlette** ✷

🅘 *05170 Orcières* ⏱ *July to Aug and mid-Dec to April: 8.30am-6.30pm; rest of year: daily except Sun 8.45am-12.30pm, 3.30-7.30pm -* ☎ *04 92 55 89 89*

5km/3mi from Orcières. Orcières-Merlette occupies a promontory overlooking the village of Orcières at the heart of the Champsaur Valley, between the Oisans and Dévoluy regions, in an austere high-mountain setting. Created in 1962 at an altitude of 1 860m/6 102ft, it has become one of the best equipped ski resorts of the Hautes-Alpes. There is an outdoor leisure centre along the Drac for summer holidaying, and the **Parc national des Écrins** offers numerous hikes.

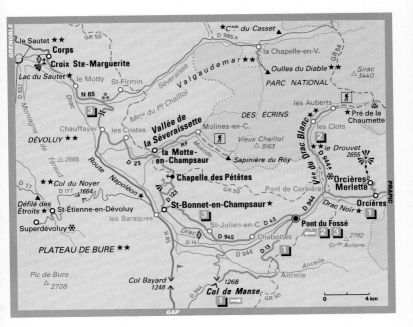

Ski area

Spread over three distinct areas (Drouvet, Lac des Estaris and Méollion), the resort has two big lifts, at Drouvet and Roche-Rousse, 54 alpine trails and a futuristic glass-enclosed **palais des sports** with a swimming pool, ice-skating rink, fitness club and bowling alley. Snowboarders can try out their jumps in the snowpark.

At 1 350m/4 429ft, the cross-country ski area of Orcières offers 50km/31.25mi of trails. When snow cover is good, cross-country skiers can follow 100km/66mi of tracks linking the valleys along the Champsaur promentory. At 1 850m/6 070ft, the Roche Rousse area offers 4km/2.5mi of trails for ski-skating enthusiasts. There are also 25km/15.6mi of groomed trails for walking. The station has the designation "P'tits Montagnards," meaning facilities for children.

In summer, there is a "Base de Loisirs" along the river, with swimming, water sports, horseback riding,

For coin categories, see the Legend on the cover flap.

WHERE TO STAY AND EAT

Chambre d'hôte Les Chemins Verts – *05500 Buissard - 1km/0.5mi E of St-Julien-de-Champsaur on D 15 -* ☎ *04 92 50 57 57 - www.leschemins-verts.com - - 4rms:* ☐ *restaurant* This charming restored farmhouse stands at 1 200m/3 936ft with a view of the Drac valley. White-walled rooms, pleasant lounge, panoramic terrace and warm welcome. Gîte available.

La Crémaillère – *4 rte de la Motte 05500 St-Bonnet -* ☎ *04 92 50 00 60 - 21 rms -* ☐☐ *restaurant.* At the entrance to the Parc national des Écrins, this chalet-style inn sits in a pleasant garden. The renovated rooms are best. The cooking is simple and local, the dining room eclectic.

▶ *From Orcières-Merlette you can take a diversion via Drouvet and walk from there to the Grand Lac des Estaris*

Drouvet★★

Alt 2 655m/8 711ft. *Gondola ride in two sections.* (🕐 *July to Aug: 8.50am-12.30pm,1.40-7pm (15min to the top). 8€, children 6.10€ -* ☎ *04 92 55 89 80)*
Panoramic view★★ of the southern peaks of the Écrins Massif to the north, the Vieux Chaillol and Gap region to the west, the resort of Merlette in the foreground to the south, the Pic de la Font Sancte in the distance to the east. There are two mountain-bike descents from the summit.

Grand Lac des Estaris★

Alt 2 558m/8 392ft. *1hr on foot from the Drouvet Summit along a stony path. Mountain boots recommended.*
Beautiful mountain lake. The journey back to Merlette takes 1hr 30min without stopping. There are several lakes along the way.
Experienced hikers can continue from the Lac des Estaris to the Col de Freissinières, or the **Col de Prelles★★**, from where there is a beautiful view of the Pelvoux Massif and Ailefroide summit *(45min climb in each case).*

▶ *Follow the road to Prapic from Orcières-Merlette.*

Prapic

This hamlet, situated at the bottom of the valley in a splendid mountain setting, has retained its heritage of traditional houses; **musée de la Casse** (🕐 *June to Oct: 9am-6pm -* ☎ *04 92 55 89 89.)* contains a reconstructed interior with furniture, clothes, tools and even newspapers. There are numerous opportunities for drives and walks.

Poet's grave

🚶 *1hr there and back; easy walk.* This walk through a lovely dale leads to a rock beneath which is the grave of a local poet, Joseph Reymond (1847-1918).

2 **Drac Blanc**★★

FROM PONT DU FOSSÉ TO CHAMPOLÉON AND LES AUBERTS

▷ *12km/7.5mi from Pont-du-Fosse to Auberts. From Pont-de-Corbière (after Pont-du-Fossé) turn left onto the D 944A to Champoleon.*

The Drac Blanc is notorious for its flash floods; one in 1928 carried away the entire vilage of Auberts. The Vallée du Drac Blanc, also known as the Drac de Champoléon Valley, is remarkably wild and desolate.

Walk to the Pré de la Chaumette refuge★

🚶 *3hr there and back via the Tour du Vieux Chaillol GR trail. Difference in altitude: 320m/1 050ft. Start from the car park at the end of the road, near Les Auberts bridge. Follow the footpath starting just before the second bridge. This very pleasant walk is suitable for everyone.* The path follows the valley planted with beeches and larches, beneath wild cliffs and waterfalls, before reaching the Pré de la Chaumette where the refuge is located.

It is possible to return to the car park via the path on the other bank.

3 **The Lower Drac**

FROM PONT-DU-FOSSÉ TO CORPS *60km – allow 2hr – see local map*

Between Pont-du-Fossé and St-Bonnet *(via D 43, D 945 and D 215)*, the road follows the Drac which meanders along its stony bed.

St-Bonnet-en-Champsaur ★

🛈 *Place Grenette 05500 St-Bonnet* 🕐 *summer: Mon-Sat 9am-noon, 2-6pm; rest of the year telephone for times-* ☎ *04 92 50 02 57 - www.saint-bonnet-en-champsaur.net*
This small town, which in 1543 was the birthplace of the Duc de **Lesdiguières,** has retained its medieval appearance and narrow streets; a Monday market brings

B. Kaufmann/MICHELIN

From peaceful meander to furious torrent: the Drac is known for its devastating flash-floods

crowds. A few art craftworkers have settled in the town. There is a 16C covered market in place Grenette, site of the tourism office.

▶ *From St-Bonnet, follow D 23 towards Bénévent, turn right at the D 123, then left at the signpost "Cimetière."*

A small road leads to a chapel surrounded by its cemetery and to the Trois Croix viewpoint offering a wide **panorama**★ of the St-Bonnet Valley overlooked by the Dévoluy.

▶ *Continue until you reach L'Auberie.*

Chapelle des Pétètes

The name means "dolls' chapel." The façade has numerous small recesses sheltering naive statuettes sculpted between 1730 and 1741 by Jacques Pascal, the carpenter who also carved the cross in front of the porch. No one can be sure whether Pascal himself invented this local art form or whether the distinctive figures with roughly shaped bodies, expressive faces and wrought-iron eyes are part of a much older tradition. Inside, the leather-covered altar comes from the chapel of Lesdiguières' former castle.

La Motte-en-Champsaur

Picturesque village with fine stone houses covered with roof shingles.

▶ *Take the forest road leading to Molines-en-Champsaur along the Séveraissette.*

Vallée de la Séveraissette

The little road follows the green, narrow valley to the tiny village of Molines at the entrance of the Parc national des Écrins, at the foot of the Vieux Chaillol cliffs. An exhibit on the history of Moline is displayed in a house at the village entrance.

▶ *Return to La Motte-en-Champsaur and turn right on D 23 to Chauffayer and N 85.*

Between Chauffayer and Le Motty, the Route Napoléon makes a detour into the lower Séveraisse Valley guarded by the ruined 15C **Château de St-Firmin**. In the distance looms the pyramid-shaped **Pic d'Olan** (alt 3 564m/11 693ft).
Beyond Le Motty, there are bird's-eye views of the artificial Lac du Sautet, which blends well with its mountain setting.

Croix-Ste-Marguerite

Lovely view of the Lac du Sautet and Obiou Summit.

Corps – ⓒ *See Le DÉVOLUY,* 2.

MASSIF DE CHAMROUSSE ★★

MICHELIN MAP 333 I7

The summits of the Chamrousse Massif, which are the last important heights at the southwest tip of the Belledonne range, are the favourite haunt of skiers from Grenoble. The area has been so extensively equipped with access roads and a large-capacity cable car to the Croix de Chamrousse viewpoint that the former Olympic venue has become a sought-after tourist centre in summer as well as in winter. In the valley below, the spa town of Uriage and the nearby village of St-Martin are pleasant holiday resorts. *42 place de Belledonne - 38410 Chamrousse July to Aug: 9am-noon, 2-6pm; Sept to mid-Dec and May to June: daily except Sat-Sun and public holidays 9am-noon, 1.45-5pm; mid-Dec to Apr: 9am-noon, 1.45-6pm closed 1 and 8 May, Ascension, Pentecost, 1 and 11 Nov. - ☎ 04 76 89 92 65 - www.chamrousse.com*

▶ **Orient Yourself:** The resort is 30km/18.75mi from Grenoble.
- **Don't Miss:** Take the short excursion to the Croix de Chamrousse.
- **Organizing Your Time:** The Maison de la Montagne organized a dawn excursion to view wild animals.
- **Also See:** Nearby Sights: ALLEVARD, L'ALPE-D'HUEZ, Le BOURG-D'OISANS, Massif de la CHARTREUSE, Route de la CROIX-DE-FER, GRENOBLE, Le GRÉSIVAUDAN, Lacs de LAFFREY, Route NAPOLÉON, ST-PIERRE-DE-CHARTREUSE, Le TRIÈVES, Le VALBONNAIS, Le VERCORS, VILLARD-DE-LANS, VIZILLE

The Spa Town and The Ski Resort

Uriage-les-Bains

Known for its waters since the 1820s, Uriage-les-Bains lies in a green, sheltered valley, at the foot of the Belledonne mountain range. The baths, the casino, hotels and villas are scattered over a 200ha/494-acre park. The isotonic waters, containing sodium chloride and sulphur, are used in the treatment of skin diseases, chronic rheumatism as well as ear, nose and throat complaints.

Chamrousse ★

This large ski centre above the Grenoble plain is actually made up of two sites, **Recoin de Chamrousse** (1 650m/5 413ft) and **Roche-Béranger** (1 750m/5 741ft). Originally a popular destination for visitors to the spa, who travelled up to enjoy the pure mountain air, Chamrousse became more widely known as a venue in the 1968 Winter Olympics.

Tour *39km/24.2mi – see also local map Le GRÉSIVAUDAN*

This tour runs in a curve from Chamrousse to the Uriage spa.
D 111 climbs steeply into the **Forêt de Prémol** ★, where deciduous trees are gradually replaced by firs and spruce. In spite of the abundant vegetation, it is possible to catch glimpses of the Vercors and Chartreuse Massifs.

Ancienne chartreuse de Prémol

The only remaining building of this former Carthusian monastery has been turned into a forest lodge. The vast clearing is the ideal place for a pause.

Beyond the Col Luitel, the road continues to climb in a series of hairpin bends, reaching its highest point at the Highways Department chalet, where the snowploughs are kept and which controls the various means of access to Roche-Béranger.

Réserve naturelle du lac Luitel ★

From Uriage-les-Bains follow D 111 towards Chamrousse and turn right onto the forest road signposted "Col du Luitel." The road skirts the lake before reaching the beginning of the nature trails. Car park near the Information Centre. ◷ *Welcome Centre open July-Aug: 3-6pm. Reserve open all year, guided tours (2hrs) available. 4€, children 2€. - ☎04 76 86 39 76. Dogs forbidden.* This nature reserve, the oldest in France, covers 18ha/44 acres of peat bog, a unique ecosystem which developed in a depression of glacial origin.

Marked footpaths and platforms on duckboards enable visitors to observe peat bog vegetation. The "lawns" on the lake shores are in fact carpets of moss floating on water. Pine trees take root in the peat but as soon as they reach a height of 3m/10ft they topple over into the lake. The flora includes rare species such as carnivorous plants (sundew, bladderwort, butterwort) and orchids.

Croix de Chamrousse ★★

Alt 2 257m/7 405ft. *1hr there and back including a cable-car ride.* ◷ *July to Aug: (7min, every 30min): daily 9am-1pm, 2-6pm; rest of year, telephone for hours. 7€ return - ☎04 76 59 09 09.*

⬛ The upper cable-car station, close to a television relay, is only a few steps away from the base of the cross, a splendid viewpoint affording a vast **panorama** ★★ *(viewing panels)*: the Drac Valley, Grenoble Basin and Grésivaudan depression over which tower the Chartreuse and Bauges massifs. In fine weather, the view extends as far as the Cévennes range.

Road D 111 continues beyond Chamrousse on its way down through the St-Martin forest, offering **glimpses** ★ of the Vercors Massif and Grenoble. Just as the road leaves the forest, there is a fine **view** ★ of the Uriage valley

The road then goes down into the valley past the 13C-14C castle, which once belonged to the Bayard family, and reaches **Uriage.**

MASSIF DE LA CHARTREUSE ★★
MICHELIN MAP 333 H5

The Grande Chartreuse is a famous monastery; it is also the well-defined mountain range known simply as the Chartreuse, where the monks of the order of St Bruno have built their retreat, cut off from the world by narrow gorges, striking limestone summits and impenetrable forests. From a geological point of view, the Chartreuse Massif contains three of the most extensive networks of underground galleries and caves in the Alps: the Alpe (nearly 30 access points for a 50km/31mi network), Dent de Crolles (60km/37.3mi network, well known to potholers) and Granier. A great many bones of prehistoric bears, which you can view in their own museum, have given this site a new scientific value.

▷ **Orient Yourself:** Between Grenoble and Chambéry, the Chartreuse is in easy drive from either city. You have a splendid view of the massif driving from Grenoble towards St-Pierre-de-Chartreuse, or from Chambéry over the Col du Granier.

☺ **Don't Miss:** Stop at the Belvédère du Charmant Som, and at the church of St-Hugues en Chartreuse.

🕐 **Organizing Your Time:** The region is at its prettiest, with green slopes and brightly coloured flowers in the springtime (May-June)

Kids Especially for Kids: The Musée de l'Ours des Cavernes (Museum of the Cave Bears) at Entremont-le-Vieux should hold children's attention.

Also See: Nearby Sights: ALLEVARD, Les BAUGES, Lac du BOURGET, CHAMBÉRY, Massif de CHAMROUSSE, GRENOBLE, Le GRÉSIVAUDAN, Lacs de LAFFREY, Route NAPOLÉON, ST-PIERRE-DE-CHARTREUSE, Le VERCORS, VILLARD-DE-LANS, VIZILLE

A Bit of History

A geological wonder – Cretaceous limestone was the basic ingredient of the geological formation of the Chartreuse Massif; 200-300m/656-984ft thick on average, it folded and split alternately. Tall cliffs cut through its thickness show thin layers of marl forming horizontal grassy outcrops, or **sangles,** suspended above vertical drops.

Parc natural régional de Chartreuse – Founded in 1995 and covering a total of 63 000ha/155 676 acres, the park includes 46 municipalities from the Isère and Savoie *départements*. Within its boundaries areas of biological importance are protected from development, waterways are managed and the environment of the high plateaux is preserved with a view to having these areas designated as nature reserves. The park is also responsible for projects such as the marking of five cultural hiking tours and the promotion of "gentle tourism" based on activities such as hiking, free-flying and rock-climbing.

Address Book

For coin categories, see the Legend on the cover flap.

EATING OUT

Le Dagobert – Pl de l'Église - 38700 Le Sappey-en-Chartreuse - ☎04 76 88 80 26 - www.le-dagobert.com - closed 15-30 Nov, Sun evening and Wed. Once past the small wine bar, you will find a rustic dining room with fireplace. In fine weather, a pleasant terrace. Traditional cuisine.

Guichard – 3 av des Frères Hardy - 38500 Voiron - ☎04 76 05 29 88 - closed 15-30 Aug, Sun evening and Mon out of season. Even at the foot of the Chartreuse massif, you can find seafood, served in a dining room with typical oceanside decor.

WHERE TO STAY

Chambre d'hôte Le Gîte du Chant de l'Eau – Mollard-Giroud, near the town hall - 38700 Le Sappey-en-Chartreuse - ☎ 04 76 88 83 16 - http://gitechantedeleau.free.fr - 5rms - evening meal. This converted barn restored in traditional style, has a large well-lit living room. One charming

feature is that books and binoculars are put at guests' disposal for discovering the surrounding countryside. Meals are prepared from the farm's own produce.

Auberge du Cucheron – 38380 St-Pierre-de-Chartreuse - 3.5km/2mi N of St-Pierre-de-Chartreuse on D 512 - ☎ 04 76 88 62 06 - aubergeducucheron@wanadoo.fr - closed 1 week in spring, 21 Oct-7 Nov, 25 Dec, Sun evening and Tue and Wed. Reservations advised - 6rms - restaurant. This inn inspires nostalgia for past days. The young couple who have taken it over have given new life to a lovely site. Traditional cuisine and Alpine specialties.

Hôtel des Skieurs – R. Giroudon - 38700 Le Sappey-en-Chartreuse - ☎ 04 76 88 82 76 - hotelskieurs@wanadoo.fr - closed mid-Dec to mid-Jan, spring holidays, Sun evening and Mon - P - 12rms - restaurant. From here you can go on a ramble, sightsee in the region or stretch out in the sun by the pool. Small, practical rooms, some with balconies, dining room with fireplace and terrace.

High rainfall and intense sunshine have helped to create a great variety of natural environments including vast forests, damp areas and pastureland. Each supports its own flora and fauna; as well as the eagle owl, the park's emblem, the Chartreuse is home to the black grouse, the pygmy owl and the rare Tengmalm's owl, while golden eagles and peregrine falcons can be seen near the numerous cliffs.

Excurions

① Col de Porte and Route du Désert★★

FROM GRENOBLE *79km/49.1mi – about 4hr – ♿ see local map*

Head north from Grenoble via La Tronche, then follow the D 512.
The road from La Tronche to the Col de Vence climbs in hairpin bends along the slopes of Mont St-Eynard (alt 1 379m/4 524ft), offering bird's-eye views of the Grésivaudan depression and Grenoble with remarkable **vistas**★★ of the Belledonne range, the Taillefer, Thabor and Obiou summits as well as part of the Vercors.

Le Sappey-en-Chartreuse
This friendly, high altitude resort nestles in a sunny basin with forested slopes, overlooked by the imposing Chamechaude Peak. The small **church**, recently restored, has eight contemporary (2002) stained glass windows by the artist Arcabas (Jean-Marie Pirot-Arcabas).

Le Marais des Sagnes
This stretch of high-altitude wetlands composes a remarkably varied ecosystem where grow orchids, rushes and willows. A well-marked nature trail takes you around the marsh (*Contact the tourist office in Sappey -* ☎*04 76 88 84 05*
From Sappey to the Col de Porte, the road follows the Sappey and Sarcenas valleys with the indented Casque de Néron in the background.

Col de Porte
This important pass is overlooked by the tilted limestone shelf of Chamechaude, looking like a huge lectern.

▶ *At the Col de Porte, take D 57D on the left towards Charmant Som.*

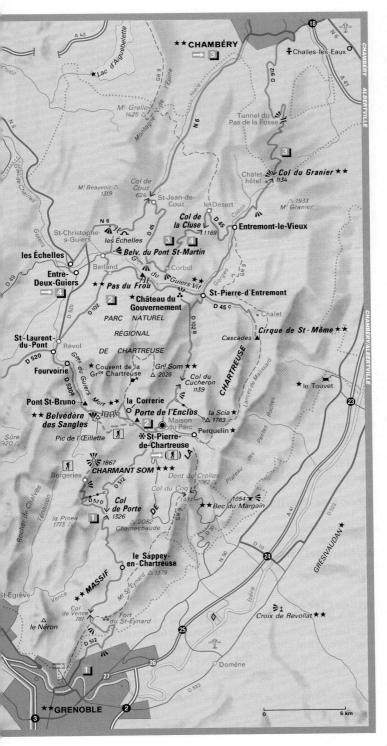

View from the summit of the Charmant Som with the Grand Som to the left and Mont Blanc in the distance

Charmant Som★★★

The road rises steeply *(14% maximum)* through a forest scarred with rocky ridges, which becomes thinner before giving way to pastures. Stop on the edge of the Charmant Som Plateau (alt 1 654m/5 427ft) and take a look at the **panorama**.

▷ *Leave the car at Bergeries and continue on foot. 1hr there and back.*

From the summit (alt 1 867m/6 125ft), there is an interesting **panorama**. Walk to the edge of the escarpment in order to get an overall view of the **setting**★ of the Grande Chartreuse Monastery.

▷ *Return to the Col de Porte. Continue with particular care as this route is often used by timber trucks.*

The road meanders through the woods and across clearings, offering closer views of the extremity of the Chamechaude shelf.

St-Pierre-de-Chartreuse✳ – See ST-PIERRE-DE-CHARTREUSE.

▷ *Turn back and follow the "Route du Désert" (D 520B, to St-Laurent-du-Pont).*

Belvédère des Sangles★★
4km/2.4mi on foot from the Valombré bridge. See ② below and ST-PIERRE-DE-CHARTREUSE.

Porte de l'Enclos

The valley seems completely enclosed by high cliffs. This was the upstream entrance of the "Désert" and the beginning of the wooded **Gorges du Guiers Mort**★★ overlooked by long limestone ridges. This is the famous **Route du Désert** which, in the 16C, bordered the grounds of the Carthusian monastery. The area was celebrated by Chateaubriand, Lamartine and Alexandre Dumas *père*.

▷ *At the St-Pierre bridge, take the road on the right to La Correrie (one way only).*

La Correrie

In a clearing with a view of the Charmant Som, this annexe of the monastery housed the lay brothers of the order and also served as the monks' infirmary. The **Musée de la Grande Chartreuse**★ (⏱ *Easter to Sept: 9.30am-6.30pm; May: 9.30am-noon, 2-6.30pm; Apr and Oct: 10am-noon, 2-6pm (last admission 1hr before closing)* ⏱ *closed rest of year. 4€, children 2€ - ☎04 76 88 60 45 - www.musée-grande-chartreuse.fr)* introduces the history of the order and the life of the monks with an audio-visual show. Be sure to see the reconstructions of the cloisters and a monk's cell.

Couvent de la Grande Chartreuse

Founded in 1084, this monastery was destroyed and rebuilt many times; an avalanche buried the original building in 1132, only for fires to damage its replacement. The present buildings date from 1676 and cannot be visited as la Grande Chartreuse is still the mother house of the Carthusian order. The monks have been forced to leave on two occasions; during the Revolution and then in 1903, only returning after the outbreak of the Second World War. The distillery which produces the famous green or yellow Chartreuse liqueur is now in Voiron (see below).

▷   *Return to the Route du Désert.*

The road goes downhill through three successive tunnels; note the strange limestone needle, known as the **Pic de l'Œillette,** standing 40m/131ft high on the roadside.

Pont St-Bruno

This imposing bridge has a single arch spanning the Guiers Mort 42m/138ft above the river bed.

▷   *Leave the car on the left bank and walk down (15min there and back) to the old bridge once used by the Carthusian monks.*

The mountain stream disappears into potholes and flows under a boulder stuck in the gorge and forming a natural bridge *(viewpoint; keep a close watch on children).*

Fourvoirie

This place name *(forata via)* is a reminder that, at the beginning of the 16C, the Carthusian monks hewed a passage through the rock which later became a road. Guarded by a fortified gate, now gone, it marked the downstream entrance of the Grande Chartreuse estate.

The Carthusian Order

In 1084, the bishop of Grenoble had a vision warning him of the arrival of seven travellers who wished to lead a solitary life. He took them to the "Désert" de Chartreuse where **St Bruno** founded the order of the same name. In the 12C, one of his successors laid down the Carthusian rule which has never been altered since. The order developed and included up to 200 monasteries at the time of the Renaissance. Today their number is reduced to just 17 throughout the world plus five convents of Carthusian nuns.

Carthusian monks and nuns observe vows of solitude and silence, dividing their days between work and prayer. Their cells open onto the cloisters. They meet only three times a day in church, share the Sunday meal and take a walk together through the woods once a week.

St-Laurent-du-Pont

This lively tourist centre was formerly know as St-Laurent-du-Désert. A historic walk (2hrs) leaves from the parking lot of the tourist office. At the **Tourbière de l'Herretang** (40ha/99acres), a peat bog located between St-Joseph-la-Rivière and St-Laurent-du-Pont, a signposted nature walk takes you around (*Contact the tourist office - ☎04 76 06 22 55*).

Défilé du Grand Crossey

This wooded transverse valley is hemmed in by high limestone cliffs. The eastern end of the gorge, where the steep slopes of the Sûre rise to almost 1 500m/4 921ft, is particularly striking at sunset.

Voiron

This busy trading centre, situated on the edge of the Chartreuse Massif, is known for its high-technology industry and has produced since 1905 the famous Rossignol skis. It is also the centre for fabrication of spirits such as the Chartreuse liqueur.

Église St-Bruno

The majestic steeple of this neo-Gothic church is visible for miles around and would not disgrace a cathedral. This local landmark was designed by Eugène Viollet-le-Duc in 1864.

Chartreuse cellars⋆

10 Bd Edgar-Kofler ◷ *guided tours Apr to Oct: 9-11.30am, 2-6.30pm (July and Aug: 9am-6.30pm); Nov to Mar: daily except Sat-Sun and public holidays: 9-11.30am, 2-5.30pm* ◷ *closed Jan, 1 May, 11 Nov and 25 Dec. No charge - ☎ 04 76 05 81 77 - www.chartreuse.fr*

The formula of the elixir of life was given to the Carthusian monks in 1605; from this elixir (71° proof), which is still made today, they later created the Chartreuse Verte (55° proof), the Chartreuse Jaune (40° proof), a Génépi (absinthe, 40° proof), the Eau de noix des Pères Chartreux (23° proof) and fruit liqueurs (21° proof): raspberry, bilberry, wild blackberry and blackcurrant. The distilling and maturing take place in Voiron, as a visit to the cellars reveals, but the selection and preparation involving 130 different plants remain a secret. There are exhibitions and slide shows as well as a video made by the monks themselves, about the various stages needed to produce the famous **Chartreuse** liqueur.

▶ *Between Voiron and Grenoble the N 75 follows the course of the Isère, running along the southern boundary of the park.*

② The Heart of the Chartreuse Massif⋆⋆

FROM ST-PIERRE-DE-CHARTREUSE *50km/31.1mi – allow 4hr – see local map*

St-Pierre-de-Chartreuse⋆ – *See ST-PIERRE-DE-CHARTREUSE.*

▶ *From St-Pierre-de-Chartreuse follow the Route du Désert (D 520) towards St-Laurent.*

The section from St-Pierre-de-Chartreuse to St-Laurent is described in ① above.

Belvédère des Sangles⋆⋆

4km/2.4mi on foot. Leave the car beyond the bridge on the Guiers Mort, then cross back and take the Valombré Forest road.

It leads to the lovely **Prairie de Valombré** which offers the nicest **view**⋆ of the Grande Chartreuse Monastery, framed by the escarpments of the Grand Som on the right and the forested ridges of the Aliénard on the left.

The road ends at a roundabout. From there, a path climbs up to the **viewpoint** overlooking the wooded gorge of the Guiers Mort.

▶ *Leave St-Laurent by D 520 as far as Le Révol, then follow D 102.*

The road rises to a small plateau occupied by the village of Berland.

▶ *Take a small road to the north.*

Belvédère du pont St-Martin

5min there and back on foot. Beyond St-Christophe-sur-Guiers, just before the bridge over road D 46, a path on the right follows the left bank of the Guiers Vif and leads to a viewpoint 30m/98ft above the stream, which affords a lovely view of the gorge.

▶ *It is possible to come back along the footpath which crosses the old bridge.*

Between Berland and St-Pierre-d'Entremont, the road follows the impressive Gorges du Guiers Vif⋆⋆ with two striking narrow sections, one of which is the "Frou."

Pas du Frou⋆⋆

This overhang, clinging to the 150m/492ft-high cliff, is the most spectacular section of road in the Chartreuse. "Frou" means awful, frightening in local dialect *(viewpoint)*.

St-Pierre-d'Entremont

History has divided the town into two administrative parts: 459 villagers live in the Isère *département* and 295 in Savoie because the Guiers river running through the centre used to mark the border between France and Savoie. The village is also a good starting point for walks in the area.

A short detour leads to the **Château du Gouvernement**⋆ *(3km/1.8mi). Head south towards the Col du Cucheron, turn right just before a bridge onto D 102B then take a sharp right again 1.5km/0.9mi further on.* The ruins of the castle stand on a grassy height which offers a lovely **view**⋆ over St-Pierre-d'Entremont and the surrounding area.

▶ *Return to St-Pierre-d'Entremont and continue along D 45E to the Cirque de St-Même chalet.*

Cirque de St-Même⋆⋆

The Guiers Vif springs out of a limestone cliff rising to 400m/1 312ft and forms two splendid waterfalls.

▶ *Return to St-Pierre-d'Entremont and drive south on D 102.*

This road forms part of the main route from Chambéry to Grenoble which avoids the Guiers gorges. Driving along this stretch is less demanding, and the landscape takes on a gentler character. The crests of the Lances de Malissard appear on the approach to the Col du Cucheron, and on the way down the peaks of Chamchaude and the Col de Porte come into view.

St-Pierre-de-Chartreuse✳ – ☕ *see ST-PIERRE-DE-CHARTREUSE*

③ Route des Trois Cols★★

FROM CHAMBÉRY TO COL DE LA CLUSE OVER COL DE COUZ AND COL DU GRANIER

54km/33.6mi – about 2hr

Leave Chambéry by Route des Échelles (N 6) heading towards Col de Couz; the road soon enters the Park. Turn left at Col du Couz and head left through St-Jean-de-Couz, then follow the D 45.

Beyond Col des Égaux the road runs above Les Échelles basin, then above the Gorges du Guiers Vif. Excellent **view**★ of the Pas du Frou *(see* ② *above)*.

Outside Corbel, by a wayside cross, there is a good view of the Guiers Vif valley as it opens out; on the opposite side are the hamlets of La Ruchère. Corbel stands at the entrance to another very picturesque valley, out of which the D 45 climbs steeply.

Col de la Cluse

1 169m/3 835ft. This pass, often pleasantly cool compared to the sunny Entremonts Valley, is the ideal place for a short pause.

▶ *Head down in the direction of Le Désert to Entremont-le-Vieux.*

Entremont-le-Vieux

Musée de l'ours des cavernes ♿ 🧒 ⏰ *July to Aug: daily 10am-12.30pm, 2.30-6.30pm; Jan: Sun 2.30-6.30; Feb-Apr and Oct: Sat-Sun 2.30-6.30pm; May to June: 2.30-6.30pm, Sat-Sun 10am-12.30pm, 2.30-6.30pm; Sept: 2.30-6.30pm; school holidays: 2.30-6.30pm ⏰ closed Nov to mid-Dec, 25 Dec and 1 Jan. 4.40€, children 7-16 years 2.50€ - ☎05 79 26 29 87 - www.musée-ours-cavernes.com*

The discovery in 1998 of remains of hibernating *Ursus spelaeus,* or cave bears, in the Grotte de Balme at Collomb launched intense research into the physiology, habits and living conditions of this ice-age beast. The museum, in the form of a cave, offers lively exhibits.

The route follows the Gorges d'Entremont, hardly wide enough at times for the road and the Cozon mountain stream. Beyond Entremont-le-Vieux the D 912 leads to the Col du Granier with the mighty Mont Granier above it.

Col du Granier★★

Alt 1 134m/3 729ft. This pass, over which tower the impressive cliffs of Mont Granier (alt 1 933m/6 342ft), opens the way to the Chartreuse Massif from Chambéry.

In 1248 a massive landslide buried many villages, killing 5 000 people and forming a huge pile of rocks at the foot of the mountain. Today, the **Abymes de Myans** is an area covered with vines and dotted with small lakes.

From the terrace of the chalet-style hotel, there are open **vistas**★★ of the Combe de Savoie, the Bauges Massif, Belledonne range and Mont Blanc in the distance.

On the way down from the pass to Chambéry, there is a **sweeping view**★★ of the Chambéry depression and the Lac du Bourget from the exit of the Pas de la Fosse tunnel.

④ Route du Col de la Cluse★★

FROM LES ÉCHELLES TO COL DE LA CLUSE *30km/18.6mi – allow 2hr*
Les Échelles-entre-Deux-Guiers

This lively tourist centre was formed by combining Les Échelles in Savoie with the neighbouring village of Entre-Deux-Guiers, lying across the Guiers Vif in the Isère *département*. In the 13C Béatrix de Savoie, countess of Provence, settled here, living in the building which is now the town hall. The village's mountain stream, once the

Vines at the foot of Mont Granier

Franco-Savoyard border, joins the Guiers Mort downstream from Les Échelles to form the River Guiers which flows through the impressive wooded Gorges de Chailles.

▶ *Follow the N 6 for 4km/2.5mi towards Chambéry*

Grottes des Échelles

Leave the car at the Auberge du Tunnel, near the eastern (Chambéry side) exit of the Échelles tunnel. ◷*Guided tours of the Sarde tunnel and the caves (1hr15min) second week July to thrd week Aug: 10am-7pm (tours every 30min, last tour starts 5.30pm); Easter to first week July, fourth week Aug to Oct: Sat 2.45 and 4.30, Sun and public holidays 11.30am, 1.45pm, 3.15pm,4.45pm. 6P, children 7-16 years 4P, under 7 years no charge. July to Aug: flaming torchlight tours on Thur -* ☎ *04 79 65 75 08.*

The two caves have historic connections with the **Route royale Sarde** and with the legendary smuggler **Mandrin** (1724-55); the public enemy no 1 of his day is reputed to have used the lower cave as a hideout. The gorge separating them is a caved-in natural tunnel which used to be the only through way between the Couz Valley and the Échelles Basin. The steepness of the Roman road was eased in medieval times by a succession of steps (or *échelles* in French), which were levelled in the 17C to allow vehicles through (monument near the lower cave). Napoleon had the tunnel dug; it was completed in 1813.

The **upper cave** consists of a corridor splitting into two; the left-hand gallery leads to several chambers linked by narrow, strangely eroded corridors. A 220m/240yd-long footbridge clinging to the rock face runs along halfway up the lower cave known as **Grand Goulet**★. From the south exit, there is a lovely **view**★ of Chartreuse Valley overlooked by the Grand Som and Sûre summits.

▶ *Continue along the N 6 to Chambéry; the route is described in D above.*

CHÂTEL✳✳

POPULATION 1 190
MICHELIN MAP 328 O3

The most popular, and at 1 235m/4 052ft also the highest Chablais ski resort owes much to a beautiful setting✳. The massive rock face of the Cornettes de Bises (2 432m/7 979ft) towers on the horizon across the Swiss border; to the southeast lies the Dranse valley, with wooded hills on one side and the Cascade de l'Essert on the other. The vast snowfields of Portes du Soleil are within easy reach and in summer the forests and fields are perfect for walks. ⓘ *74390 Chatel* ⓘ *July to Aug: daily 9am-12.30pm, 2-7pm, Sat 9am-7pm; mid-Dec to mid-May: 8.30am-1pm, 2-7pm, Sat 8.30am-7pm; rest of year: Mon-Sat 9am-noon, 2-6pm. Open mornings of public holidays -* ☎*04 50 73 22 44 - www.chatel.com*

▸ **Orient Yourself:** Chatel is near the Swiss border, and 11km/7mi from Abondance

▸ **Don't Miss:** Village festivals are colourful and fun.

▸ **Also See:** Nearby Sights: ABONDANCE, AVORIAZ, ÉVIAN-LES-BAINS, MORZINE, THONON-LES-BAINS, YVOIRE

⟫The Ski Resort

The pistes of Super-Chatel extend over the Morcan and Linga massifs, which are linked by a shuttle service and form part of the Franco-Swiss **Portes du Soleil**✳✳, an area boasting over 650km/404mi of pistes. Torgon and Morgins are accessible from Morclan; more experienced skiers may prefer the massif de Linga with the Les Renards black run and easy connections to the slopes of Avoriaz by the Col de Bassachaux.

Excursions

Whether exploring by car or on foot, the countless routes through the countryside around Châtel may leave you spoiled for choice: over 300km of paths link the twelve Portes du Soleil resorts.

Pic de Morclan✳✳
Access by the **Super-Châtel gondola** (ⓘ *July to Aug: gondola 9am-4.45pm, Morclan chairlift 9.30am-4.15pm. 8.50€ return for both parts (day passes available for hikers and paragliders -* ☎ *04 50 73 34 24) up to an altitude of 1 650m/5 413ft. The summit is reached by chairlift or on foot; allow 1hr 30min there and back on foot.* 🚶 From the summit (alt 1 970m/6 463ft) the **panorama** includes the Cornettes de Bises and Mont de Grange to the west and the Diablerets and jagged Dents du Midi on the Swiss side. It is possible to

WHERE TO STAY
🛌 **Camping l'Oustalet** – *Loy - 2km/1.25mi SW by the Rte du col de Bassachaux, along the Dranse -* ☎ *04 50 73 21 96 - www.oustalet.com - open 22 Dec-Apr and 20 June-3 Sept - 100 pitches.* This campsite also rents a chalet and mobile homes. Nearby supermarket, but no food service.

EATING OUT
🍽 **Restaurant de Loy** – ☎ *04 50 73 32 29 - open July-Aug and 22 Dec-15 Apr.* Facing the golf course, wood-paneled interior with bright table-runners, simple Savoyard cuisine.

walk along the ridge to the Pointe des Ombrieux or to the Swiss **Lac du Goleit** *(from the La Conche cable-car station).*

Tête du Linga★★
Alt 2 127m/6 978ft. Skiers have access by the Linga 1 cable car and Linga 2 chairlift. On arrival, go to the top of the Combes chairlift and climb to the summit in a few minutes. Splendid panorama of Morgins below, overlooked by the Dents du Midi.

Pas de Morgins★
Alt 1 371m/4 4981ft. The small lake lying at the heart of this forested area forms a picturesque landscape with the jagged heights of the Dents du Midi (Swiss Alps) in the background.

GORGES DU CIANS★★★

MICHELIN MAP 341 C4

The gorges of the Cians, a tributary of the River Var, are among the most beautiful in the Alps. In order to negotiate a drop of 1 600m/5 249ft over a distance of only 25km/15.5mi, the Cians has hewn its way through a narrow cleft, sculpting the rocks in the process. The superb sheer cliffs vary in appearance according to the terrain, the lower gorge being cut through limestone and the upper gorge through red schist. ▯ *see Beuil*

▸ **Orient Yourself:** Like those of Daluis to the west, the gorges du Cians cut a southern swathe between Beuil and the valley of the Var

🕐 **Organizing Your Time:** It will take you half a day to complete the excursion.

🖢 **Also See:** Nearby Sights: ANNOT, AURON, BEUIL, CLUES DE HAUTE-PROVENCE, Val d'ENTRAUNES, ENTREVAUX, Route des GRANDES ALPES, ISOLA 2000, PUGET-THENIERS, ST-ÉTIENNE-LA-TINÉE, Vallée de la TINÉE, VILLARS-SUR-VAR

Excursion

From Touët-sur-Var to Beuil *38km/23.6mi – about 2hr*

Touët-sur-Var★
🅿 *Park at the bottom of the village and climb the stairs on rue Armand-Faillères.*Tall and narrow houses, backing onto the rocky slope, line the partly roofed-over streets of this picturesque village overlooking the Var Valley. Nearly all the houses have a south-facing galleried loft, known as the *soleilloir,*

Touët-sur-Var

E. Baret/MICHELIN

used for drying figs. The recently restored 17C parish **church** is decorated with numerous paintings and altarpieces. It is curiously built over an arch spanning a mountain stream, which is visible through a small opening in the floor of the nave.

▷ *From Touët, drive west along N 202.*

The chapel on the left-hand side of road, Notre-Dame-du-Cians, dates from the 12C.

▷ *Turn right onto D 28.*

Gorges inférieures du Cians★★
Water oozes from every crack in the spiky rock face. The road winds its way through the tortuous gorge.

▷ *Turn right onto D 128, which rises sharply; caution is recommended.*

Lieuche
Black schist forms the impressive **setting**★ of this tiny mountain village.
The unassuming **church** houses the **Retable de l'Annonciation**★, one of Louis Bréa's earliest works, set in carved and gilded wood panelling (17C). From the church terrace there is an overall **view**★ of the Gorges du Cians, overlooked by the Dôme de Barrot, and part of the Var Valley.

▷ *Return to D 28, turn right then 1km/0.6mi further on left onto D 228.*

The road climbs above the Cians Valley, revealing an impressive landscape.

Rigaud
This hilltop village overlooking the Cians Valley nestles below the ruins of its medieval Templar fortress in a very attractive **setting**★; there is a fine panoramic view from a spot near place de la Mairie.
The fortified parish church, decorated in Baroque style, houses several 17C paintings including a Deposition over the high altar, a panelled naive painting dating from 1626 *(on the left)* and a Virgin with Child.

▷ *Return to D 28 and turn left.*

Gorges supérieures du Cians★★★
At the entrance of the gorge, 1.6km/1mi beyond Pra-d'Astier, the road overlooks the confluence of the Cians and the Pierlas, 100m/328ft below, and rises progressively following the mountain stream which drops down to the valley in a series of steps. The steep bright-red rocky slopes, alternately jagged and smooth, contrast with the scanty dark green vegetation. The narrowest passages, known as the **Petite Clue**★★ and the **Grande Clue**★★, where the road has been hewn out of the rock, are the most picturesque. A tunnel bypasses the Grande Clue which can only be seen on foot *(park before the tunnel)*. The cliff faces are only 1m/3.28ft apart at their narrowest point
Beuil in its striking **setting**★ suddenly appears on a bend.

Beuil★ – 🕭 *See BEUIL.*

To the west between Guillaumes and Daluis, the Var has carved out another, almost parallel, valley through the red schist: the Gorges de Daluis (🕭 *see Val d'ENTRAUNES, Excursions)*.

CLUES DE HAUTE-PROVENCE★★

MICHELIN MAP 341 C4

Only 40km/25mi from the busy coast, rushing rivers have cut their way across the mountains, forming narrow *clues*, the transverse valleys which are typical of this region. In the heart of this mountain mosaic lie hidden villages, each more delightful than the last, set in neat terraced fields or surrounded by untouched nature. *Rue Alziary, 06910 Roquesteron - ☎ 04 99 05 92 92*

▶ **Orient Yourself:** The region, located south of Puget-Théniers, is a study in contrasts: sometimes carved into tidy cultivated terraces, sometimes wild and forested.

🔹 **Don't Miss:** Be sure to take in the panoramic view from the ancient fortress of Sigale, as well as the view from the Bleine pass over the ravine of la Faye

🕐 **Organizing Your Time:** Give yourself three hours for the excursions.

🔹 **Also See:** Nearby Sights: ANNOT, CASTELLANE, Gorges du CIANS, ENTREVAUX, Route NAPOLÉON, PUGET-THÉNIERS, ST-JULIEN-DU-VERDON, Vallée de la TINÉE, GRAND CANYON DU VERDON, VILLARS-SUR-VAR

Excursions

1 Clue du Riolan★

FROM PUGET-THÉNIERS TO ROQUESTERON *23km/14.3mi – about 1hr*

Puget-Théniers★ – 🔹 *See PUGET-THÉNIERS.*

▶ *Cross the River Var and follow D 2211A.*

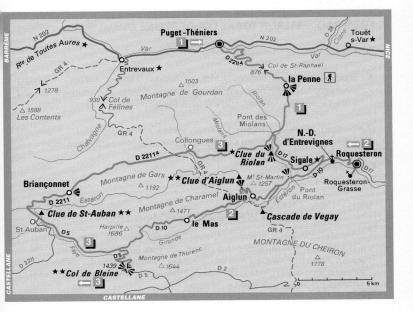

The road rises in wide hairpin bends above Puget-Théniers to the Col de St-Raphaël; beautiful view of Roudoule and the Mercantour region beyond.

La Penne

A square keep overlooks the village clinging to a rocky ridge. 👣 (*30min return*) Walk up through the pretty streets to a viewpoint and admire the view of the Vallée du Miolan and Montagne du Cheiron.

▷ *At Pont des Miolans, take D 17 on the left towards Sigale.*

Clue du Riolan★

This is an impressive gap cut across the mountain range by a tributary of the Esteron. The overhanging road offers a fine **view** of the gorge and the mountain.

Sigale★

The village stands in a picturesque **setting**★ on top of an escarpment overlooking the confluence of the Riolan and the Esteron, above terraced orchards. A viewing point gives a fine panorama of the surrounding peaks. This former stronghold has retained two fortified gates, several Gothic houses and a 16C fountain. The 19C clock tower crowning an isolated rock is surmounted by a wrought-iron campanile.

Notre-Dame-d'Entrevignes

This 12C **chapel**, situated on the right-hand side of the road to Roquestron, was rebuilt in the 15C and decorated in the 16C with murals illustrating the life of Our Lady, including a pregnant Mary (*visit on request at the Mairie -* ☎ *04 93 05 83 52*)

Roquesteron

The River Esteron marked the border between France and Savoie until 1860, when Savoie became part of France. This is the reason why there are two municipalities, Roquesteron in the north and Roquesteron-Grasse in the south, where the 12C fortified Romanesque **church** stands on top of the rocky knoll.

② Clue d'Aiglun★

FROM ROQUESTERON TO THE COL DE BLEINE *33km/20.5mi – about 1hr*

Roquesteron – 👣 *See above.*

▷ *Between the D 17 junction and Le Mas, the road is very uneven and narrow: passing other vehicles is often tricky and you are recommended to drive cautiously. Beyond Notre-Dame-d'Entrevignes, follow D 10 on the left.*

The bridge over the Riolan offers a lovely **view**★ of the gorge and the splendid emerald-green stream flowing among rocks and disappearing into potholes.

Cascade de Végay

It consists of a succession of fine waterfalls.

How Were the "Clues" Formed?

In the Mesozoic era, an inland sea formed in the area where the Alps now stand, and a layer of fine calcic deposits covered its bed. 60 million years later, the upheaval which formed the Alps brought these layers of rock to the surface. The surrounding rock was eroded and rivers dug deep paths, which, over the course of millions of years, became the clues of today.

▷ *Continue on the D 10 through Aiglun*

Aiglun
This picturesque hilltop village celebrated by Frédéric Mistral, clings to the steep slope of the gorge overlooked by the Cheiron Mountain.

Clue d'Aiglun★★
The road, which crosses the Esteron as it comes out of the gorge, offers a striking view of the most secluded *clue* in the area: only a few metres wide, between 200-400m/656-1 312ft deep and 2km/1.2mi long, it looks like a gully separating the Charamel and St-Martin mountains.

Le Mas
This village, built on the edge of a beak-shaped limestone spur, has a 13C Romanesque **church**. The D 10 meanders along the hillside.

▷ *Follow the D 5 on the left as it climbs up the forested slopes to the Col de Bleine.*

Col de Bleine★★
Alt 1 439m/4 721ft. Magnificent **view** of the deep Faye Valley, the Harpille Peak (alt 1 686m/5 532ft), the ridge of the Charamel Mountain and the Grandes Alpes du Sud in the distance.

③ Clue de St-Auban ★★

FROM THE COL DE BLEINE TO THE PONT DES MIOLANS *36km/22.4mi* – *about 1hr*

Col de Bleine★★ – ⏚ *See Clue d'Aiglun.*

▷ *5km/3.6mi beyond the pass, keep left on D 5 which runs along the Faye and joins D 2211.*

Clue de St-Auban★★
The Esteron, a tributary of the River Var, goes through this impressive gorge with vertical sides hollowed out in places and forming huge caves; the river bed is scattered with boulders marked by deep potholes carved out by spring floods.

Briançonnet
This tiny village lies in a strange setting, beneath a huge rock. The houses were built with stones from an earlier Roman settlement as the **inscriptions** set in their walls testify. There is a wide **view**★ of the Alpine summits from the cemetery adjacent to the east end of the church.

Beyond Briançonnet, the **view** embraces the Montagne de Gars and the Montagne de Charamel on either side of the River Esteron. Soon after Collongues, the Clue d'Aiglun can be seen on the right; further on, the Clue de Riolan appears like a deep gash in the landscape. From the Pont des Miolans, it is possible to return to Puget-Théniers along D 2211A.

LA CLUSAZ✳✳

POPULATION 1 845
MICHELIN MAP 328 L5
LOCAL MAP SEE MASSIF DES ARAVIS

The most important resort in the Aravis Massif owes its name to the deep gorge or *clue* **through which flows the Nom, situated downstream from the village. Its large number of pistes and other sports facilities offer something for every taste, in every season.** *161 Place de l'Église, 74220 La Clusaz May to mid-Sept: Mon-Sat 9am-1pm, 2-7pm; Sun 9am-12.30pm, 2-6.30pm; Jan to Apr: daily 9am-12.30pm, 2-6.30pm, Sat-Sun, Christmas holidays and Feb: 9am-7pm; rest of year: daily except Sun 9am-noon, 2-6pm - ☎04 50 32 65 00 - www.laclusaz.com*

▶ **Orient Yourself:** La Clusaz is 28km/17.5mi east of Annecy on D909.
Don't Miss: Take a detour through the valley of Confins.
Organizing Your Time: The festival of reblochon cheese falls in mid-August.
Kids Especially for Kids: Children over 10 years old can participate in water adventures.
Also See: Nearby Sights: ANNOT, Lac d'ANNECY, Massif des ARAVIS, CLUSES, Route des GRANDES ALPES, MEGÈVE, La ROCHE-SUR-FORON, THORENS-GLIÈRES

The Resort

La Clusaz has been a winter sports destination since the 1920s, and today amateurs of all forms of skiing appreciate the considerable differences in altitude offered by the resort's four neighbouring massifs. The Manigod and Étale massifs offer several runs for intermediate skiers as well as a wide choice of facilities. The Aiguille and de Balme Massifs offer advanced skiers black runs such as the Vraille and several red runs. There is also a snowpark as well as ungroomed trails.

Cross-country skiers have at their disposal 70km/43.5mi of trails, including 16 loops.

The ski area is linked to that of Le Grand-Bornand, both areas having a common ski pass under the name of "Aravis".

Excursions

Vallée de Manigod✳✳ – *See Massif des ARAVIS:* 1.

Vallon des Confins✳
5.5km/3.4mi. Turn left in the wide bend on the way out of La Clusaz towards the Col des Aravis and follow the Chemin du Fernuy. The road runs along the bottom of the valley then rises rapidly to the Col des Confins, a depression hollowed out by glacial erosion and lying just below the escarpments of the Aravis mountains. Continue along this road beyond the chapel in order to get a clearer view of the Vallon du Bouchet.

Address Book

For coin categories, see the Legend on the cover flap.

EATING OUT

Les Airelles– *33 Pl de l'Église - ☎ 04 50 02 40 51 - www.clusaz.com - closed 24 Apr-22 May and 13 Nov-10 Dec -14rms* . This establishment is located a stone's throw from the church and offers a pause that is both friendly and satisfying. Dining room decorated in carved wood and warmed by a large fireplace. Traditional Savoyard cuisine. Pretty wood-paneled guestrooms.

Beauregard – *Bossonnet - ☎ 04 50 32 68 00 - www.hotel-beauregard. fr* Situated between the ski hill and the village centre, this is a small village of comfortable, well-equiped chalets. The dining room, decorated in pale wood, has a pleasant Alpine decor and a terrace facing directly south. Traditional cuisine.

Alp'Hôtel – *192 Rte du Col-des-Aravis - ☎ 04 50 02 40 06 - alphotel@ clusaz.com - closed 24 Apr-29 May, 25 Sept-30 Nov - 15rms.* A multistorey chalet situated at the centre of Clusaz, with a spacious restaurant panelled in wood. Traditional menu with regional specialties. Tearoom. The rooms, furnished in cherry-wood, pin or wicker, all have balconies. The lounge has a nice open fireplace.

WHERE TO STAY

Hôtel Christiana – *☎ 04 50 02 60 60 - www.hotelchristiana.fr - closed 11 Apr-3 July and 11 Sept-19 Dec* P *- 28rms: - restaurant.* A typical local residence houses a well-kept family-run establishment. Some guestrooms have been renovated and some have terraces. Traditional menu and local specialties served in a comfortable dining room.

Hôtel les Sapins – *105 chemin Riffroids - ☎ 04 50 63 33 33 - www. clusaz.com - closed 11 Apr-13 June and 11 Sept-16 Dec -* P *- 24rms - restaurant.* Facing the Aravis mountain chain, this chalet has renovated rooms in the

La Clusaz

H. Le Gac/MICHELIN

Alpine style, withh pale wood and bright colours. The walls of the lounge are line with red velvet. The dining room opens onto the ski runs, and the menu tends towards local cheese dishes, fondue and tartiflette.

LEISURE

La fête du Reblochon – The smooth, mild local cheese is celebrated in mid-August, with tastings and lively activities. - ☎04 50 32 65 00

SHOPPING

The celebrated reblochon cheese, made from cow's milk, comes in several varieties. The type called "fermier," with a green trademark, is produced and cured on a farm. The "laitier" variety, with a red trademark, also called "fruitier" is made from the milk of several different herds. The "tomme blanche des Aravis" is a sort of reblochon that is not cured, and must be consumed hours after it is made.

CLUSES

POPULATION 17 711
MICHELIN MAP 328 M4

Cluses made its name in the 18C as an important watchmaking centre, and the precision crafting of metal components, which once served this industry, has now taken over as the town's main export. Not that the mountain town is just about business; as a cultural centre it is the ideal starting point for exploring historic Faucigny.

▶ **Orient Yourself:** Cluses, 62km/39mi from Annecy on A41, then A40, is the centre of a dense cluster of small cities and industrial zones.
🕐 **Organizing Your Time:** The winding Route de Giffre demands patience and prudence.
Especially for Kids: The Musée paysan at Viuz-en-Sallaz is a pleasant stop.
Also See: Nearby Sights: Massif des ARAVIS, AVORIAZ, La CLUSAZ, Les GETS, Route des GRANDES ALPES, Les HOUCHES, MEGÈVE, MORZINE, La ROCHE-SUR-FORON, ST-GERVAIS-LES-BAINS, Bassin des SALLANCHES, SAMOËNS, SIXT-FER-A-CHEVAL

A Bit of History

A Brief History of Timepieces – The painstaking craft of watch- and clock-making has been a local tradition since the 18C, when Clusiens returning from Germany offered their new-found skills to the watchmakers of Geneva. The town's reputation grew, and in an attempt to gain an advantage over their Swiss competitiors, a school of watchmaking, the Ecole nationale d'horlogerie, was founded in Cluses in 1848, continuing its work until 1989.

Sights

Only the **church** and the 1674 single-span bridge **(Vieux pont)** have survived from the old Cluses, which was destroyed by fire in 1844. Turin was the inspiration for the new town's grid system, and an Italian style is apparent in its squares and wide, arcaded avenues.

Musée de l'Horlogerie et du Décolletage (Espace Carpano et Pons)
100 Place du 11 November 1945 🕐 *July to Aug: 10am-noon, 1.30-6pm (Sun 5.30pm); Sept to June: daily except Sun 1.30pm-6pm (Sat 5.30pm) Last admission 1hr before closing* 🕐 *closed public holidays except 14 July and 15 Aug. 5.50€, children under 7 years no charge - ☎04 50 89 13 02.*
This illustrates the technical evolution of time-measuring instruments and includes exhibits such as Louis XIV's one-handed watch, one of Voltaire's desk clocks, marine chronometers, large watch mechanisms and watchmaking tools.

Church
Closed except during services. This former monastery chapel dates from the 15C and 17C. It contains a monumental 16C **stoup**★ bearing the benefactor's family arms and surmounted by a stone cross. Notice also the 18C Calvary in the chancel and several painted statues of the same period in the nave. A tabernacle in the Chapelle du St-Sacrament on the right represents the story of the Multiplication of the Loaves and Fishes.

Excursions

Le Faucigny★★

This region, which, until the 14C, was a bone of contention between the Dauphins (rulers of Dauphiné) and the counts of Savoie, gets its name from Faucigny Castle whose ruins still stand on a rocky spur overlooking the Arve Valley between Bonneville and Contamine-sur-Arve. The most interesting area from a touristic point of view includes the Arve Valley from Bonneville to Sallanches and the valley of the River Giffre, a tributary of the Arve, which leads to the heart of the Faucigny limestone heights.

☐ La Cluse de l'Arve

FROM CLUSES TO FLAINE *28km/17.4mi*

From Cluses, drive south along N 205 towards Chamonix.

The road follows the narrow passage between the Chaîne du Reposoir (Pointe d'Areu on the west bank) and the Chaîne des Fiz (Croix de Fer, Tête du Colonney and Aiguilles de Varan on the east bank) through which the Arve flows; the narrowest part lies between Cluses and Magland where the A 40 motorway and N 205 run alongside the railway line.

▶ *At Balme, turn left onto D 6 towards Arâches.*

The road clings to the cliffside; a sudden widening makes it possible to stop the car *(beware of falling rocks)* and admire the long corridor through which the Arve makes its way from Sallanches to Cluses, with Mont Joly barring the horizon.

🎿Arâches

Small ski resort in a pleasant wooded setting.

Les Carroz-d'Arâches

Ski resort situated on the edge of a plateau overlooking the Cluse de l'Arve. 2km/1.2mi further on, there is a clear view of the nearby Croix de Fer and Grandes Platières summits, with the narrow valley below. The road rises to 1 843m/6 047ft then goes down towards Flaine nestling inside a small basin.

🎿Flaine★★

This attractive modern resort lies in a secluded mountain valley at an altitude of 1 600m/5 249ft.

In summer and winter time, life in the car-free resort concentrates round the Forum, decorated with a polychrome geometric sculpture by Vasarely. Not far from this stands a painted sculpture entitled *Woman's Head,* which is the monumental version (12m/39ft) of an 80cm/32in model made by Picasso in 1957. The homogeneous concrete architecture is the work of Marcel Breuer, a former member of the Bauhaus School, who contributed to the UNESCO building in Paris and to the Whitney Museum of American Art in New York.

The resort makes use of a vast area, known as "Le Grand Massif", linked to the resorts of Carroz, Morillon, Samoëns and Sixt *(area pass)*. In addition, a remarkable 13km run links Flaine to the latter. Some of the resort's equipment is reserved for snowboarding enthusiasts.

The **Téléphérique des Grandes Platières** (🕐 *July to Aug: 9am-12.45, 2-5pm; Dec to Apr: 9am-4.45pm (12 minutes, continuous operation. 11.30€ return - ☎04 50 90 40 00)* gives access to the **Désert de Platé** overlooked by the Mont Blanc Massif, from the Aiguille Verte to the Aiguille de Bionnassay.

② **Route des Gets**

FROM CLUSES TO MORZINE VIA LES GETS *43km/26.7mi. Itinerary in reverse order, ◔ see MORZINE, ②.*

③ **Route de Mont-Saxonnex**

FROM CLUSES TO LA-ROCHE-SUR-FORON *36km/22.5mi – allow 1hr 30min.*

▷ *Leave Cluses by the D 4 heading south. Itinerary in reverse order from LA-ROCHE-SUR-FORON.*

④ **The Route du Giffre**

FROM CLUSES TO SAMOËNS

▷ *21 km/13mi. Leave Cluses by D 902, heading north towards Taninges.*

Immediately after Taninges, the view embraces the huge escarpments of the Rochers du Criou towering over Samoëns and flanked by the Avoudrues Massif, while Mont Buet can be seen in the distance.

▷ *The D 907 leads to Samoëns.*

⑤ **The lower Vallée du Giffre**

FROM CLUSES TO ST-JEOIRE

▷ *38km/23mi. Leave Cluses and head north towards Taninges, then take the D 4 on the left to St-Jeoire.*

From Marignier the road follows the fast-flowing Giffre.
Cross the river, ignoring the D 26 on the right, and head into the village.

La Môle viewpoint★

☺ *The road rises steeply; to be avoided after rainfall.* At the north exit, head towards Ossat and follow the road that leads up to the viewpoint, offering a wonderful view of the Giffre valley and the Arve. Mont Saxonnex is visible to the south.

▷ *Follow D 306 until the Giffre joins the Risse.*

St-Jeoire

Pleasant holiday resort at the heart of a wooded valley overlooked by the medieval château de Beauregard (⚷ *closed to public*).

The D 907 overlooks the confluence of the River Giffre and River Risse and gives a view of the massif du Reposoir and the Chaîne du Bargy, then goes through a wooded gorge to reach the Mieussy Basin within sight of the snow-capped Mont Buet.

An interesting stop is the **Musée Paysan** at **Viuz-en-Sallaz**. Some 2 500 objects used daily by Savoyard peasants from 1860 to 1950 are on display. ⏲ *July to Aug: 2-6pm; Sept to June: first Sun of month 2-6pm* ⏲ *closed public holidays. 4.40€, children 3.2€. Educational show using museum objects Wed and Fri at 4pm.* - ☎04 50 36 89 18

Mieussy

This village is one of the finest sights along the way. The onion-shaped spire of the **church** rises into the sky, enhanced by the delightful landscape with its many shades of green.

The Étroit Denté, a short gorge cut through an obstruction of glacial origin, opens into the middle valley of the River Giffre, which widens beyond Taninges.

Taninges – *See MORZINE,* 2
Itinerary from Taninges to Cluses, see MORZINE, 2

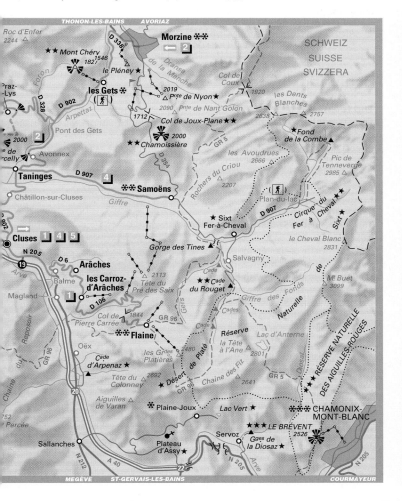

COLMARS★

POPULATION 378
MICHELIN MAP 334 H7

At the centre of the Haute Vallée du Verdon, the splendid wooded mountain setting of this small walled town, guarded by two forts, makes it a pleasant summer resort (alt 1 250m/4 101ft) and a good cross-country skiing centre in winter. Behind the town walls its pretty streets have kept an almost medieval feel, but in fact their origins are much older: the town took its name from a temple built on a hill to celebrate the Roman god, Mars (collis Martis). *Ancienne Auberge Fleurie, 04370 Colmars-les-Alpes Daily except Monday, telephone for times - ☎ 04 92 83 41 92*

▶ **Orient Yourself:** Colmars is reached by D 908, passing through the Val d'Allos, 44 km/27.5mi south of Barcelonnette.

▣ **Parking:** Parking lots are located outside the village ramparts.

◔ **Organizing Your Time:** Give yourself a half day to tour the old village and fortress and to walk to the waterfall on the Lance river.

◔ **Also See:** Nearby Sights: ANNOT, BARCELONNETTE, Val d'ENTRAUNES, PRA-LOUP, ST-JULIEN-DU-VERDON, VAL D'ALLOS

Exploring Colmars

Old town★★

Once through the Porte de Savoie or the Porte de France, visitors will appreciate the southern atmosphere pervading the city, as they wander through the narrow streets linked by tiny squares adorned with fountains. The tall houses are built to reach above the town ramparts so the open attics, known as "soleillados," are exposed to the sun; straw for animals is spread out to dry, as is the family laundry on washing day.

The walls

The original **Église St-Martin** (◔ *Daily except Mon 9am-noon, 3-6.30pm)* was built on the site of the temple of Mars in the 8C; its replacement, a 16C-17C church in Gothic style with Romanesque features, has only one side aisle, built into the town's wall. Colmars was first fortified in the 14C and acquired strategic importance as a border town when Savoie annexed Allos. In 1528, François I strengthened the walls by adding small square towers which can still be seen today in spite of successive fires. The duke of Savoie's declaration of war against France in 1690 brought the French army to the gates of Colmars, but the town narrowly survived the siege which followed. Plans drawn up by Vauban, Louis XIV's military engineer, led to the construction of the forts linked to the town by caponnières or covered

The fortress watchtower

E. Baret/MICHELIN

For coin categories, see the Legend on the cover flap.

WHERE TO STAY

◒◒ **Les Transhumances** – *Les Espiniers* - ☏ *04 92 83 44 39, http://perso.wanadoo. fr/lestranshumances -* ⬚ *reservations required -* ◒◒ *restaurant.* You have to climb a steep, narrow road to reach this farm on the heights overlooking Colmar, but the alpine views and calm are worth the effort. The rooms in the old barn and the dining room with exposed beams and mangers offer authentic charm.

WHAT TO BRING BACK

Maison de produits du pays du haut Verdon – *Rte de Colmars- 04370 Beauvezer - ☏ 04 92 83 58 57 - school holidays: 10am-12.30pm, 2.30-7pm; rest of year: Fri-Sun 10am-12.30pm, 14.30-19h.* Some 23 craftspeople from the region have taken over this former woolen mill to offer for sale a wide variety of local products: apéritifs, cloth, pottery, cheese, prepared foods from local recipes. In summer, there are opportunities to meet local producers of farm products.

passages, and to the fortification of the town gates. Visitors can now walk along half the length of the ramparts which were recently restored, much to the disappointment of the locals who are no longer allowed to hang out their washing on this prime drying spot!

Maison musée

🕐 *July to Aug: daily 10am-noon, 3.30-6.30pm - 3€, children under 10 years no charge*
By examining faithful recreations of rooms such as a kitchen or a bourgeois salon, you will appreciate how people lived in the upper Verdon in olden times. The exhibit continues into the upper parapet, where exhibits of past customs are displayed in the towers: the mock-fights known as the *bravade*, agriculture, woodworking, etc.

Fort de Savoie ★

🕐 *July to Aug: unaccompanied visit 2.30-7pm, guided tours (1hr) Mon, Wed, Sat on request. 4€, children 1.50€.*
Built in 1693-95 at the same time as the Fort de France, this fort comprises two successive enclosures; inside the second one, there are four vaulted rooms which used to house the garrison and where exhibits are now held. Stairs lead to a round tower and to the vast armoury; note the remarkable roof structure made out of larch wood. The fort is the venue for a folk festival at the end of July and for a series of "medieval days" in the second week of August.

Cascade de la Lance

🔄 *40min there and back. Follow the road which starts opposite the church.* A pleasant path leads through pinewoods to the foot of a cliff, then slips through a narrow gorge to reach the waterfall noisily splashing on the rock face.

Excursion

Haute Vallée du Verdon ★ *36km/22.4mi – allow 45min*

▸ *Leave Colmars by the D 908 heading south. At the approach to Beauvezer turn left towards Villars-Heyssier and continue to the car park.*

Gorges de St-Pierre ★

🚶 *1hr 30min on foot there and back.* A marked path leads to the gorge carved by a tributary of the Verdon. The path climbs along the steep sides, offering impressive views of the grey schist and white and ochre limestone lining the gorge.

After **Beauvezer,** a small summer resort in a pleasant, verdant setting, the road follows the bottom of the valley, overlooked in the east by the imposing Grand Coyer (2 693m/8 835ft).

The road, dug deep into the rocky slope, winds upwards from St-Michel-Peyresq. Beyond the Pont de Villaron, D 955 runs between arid mountains where lavender alternates with isolated clumps of trees. The river then flows through a long and narrow transverse valley which opens out into the small St-André-des-Alpes Basin.

St-André-des-Alpes

Place Marcel-Pastorelli - 04170 Saint-André-des-Alpes ⊙ Daily except Mon, telephone for times - ☎ 04 92 83 41 92

This village lies at the confluence of the River Issole and River Verdon and at the crossroads of several tourist routes, in a pleasant setting of orchards and lavender fields. It is a fine base for excursions in the surrounding area.

Downstream of St-André, the Lac de Castillon lies at the centre of a scrubland area.

Lac de Castillon – 👓 *see ST-JULIEN-DU-VERDON, Excursions*

Haute vallée du Var

*30 km/19mi from Colmar to St-Martin-d'Entraunes, about 1hr
– 👓 see VAL D'ENTRAUNES*

Route over the Pass of La Colle-Saint-Michel ★
46km/29mi from Annot to Colmars, about 1hr – 👓 see ANNOT.

LES CONTAMINES-
MONTJOIE ✳ ✳ ✳

POPULATION 1 129
MICHELIN MAP 328 N6
LOCAL MAP SEE MASSIF DU MONT-BLANC

Located at an altitude of 1 164m/3 819ft, at the foot of Mont Joly and the snow-capped Dômes de Miage, Les Contamines is one of the most pleasant and restful holiday resorts in the Mont Blanc Massif. The 18C church with painted façade and overhanging roof is particularly charming. *▯ 8 rue Notre-Dame-de-la-Gorge - 74170 Les Contamines-Montjoie ⊙ All year: daily 9am-noon, 2-6pm ⊙ closed Sat-Sun and public holidays Sept to mid-Dec and mid-Apr to June - ☎04 50 47 01 58 - www. lescontamines.com*

- ▸ **Orient Yourself:** Les Contamines is 16km/10mi from St-Gervais-les-Bains by D 902.
- **Don't Miss:** Notre-Dame-de-la-Gorge is found in a lovely wooded valley.
- **Organizing Your Time:** The area is known for excellent hiking trails.
- **Especially for Kids:** The Base de Loisirs du Pontet will please children.
- **Also See:** Nearby Sights: ARGENTIÈRE, CHAMONIX-MONT-BLANC, Les HOUCHES, MEGÈVE, Massif du MONT-BLANC, SAINT-GERVAIS-LES-BAINS, SALLANCHES

Summer and Winter Sports

The Contamine-Hauteluce ski resort is part of the Évasion ski area providing some 120km/75mi of downhill runs with good snow cover, attracting families looking for moderately difficult ski runs and beautiful scenery such as that of Les Contamines just beneath Mont Blanc. Cross-country skiers can enjoy 26km/16.25mi of trails.

In summer, the resort is an exceptionally fine **hiking and mountaineering centre.** Major ascents usually start from the Hôtellerie de Tré-la-Tête *(4hr 30min there and back from Cugnon)*, built just below the glacier which feeds the Lac de la Girotte. Hikers will encounter some of the most attractive footpaths in the Alps.

In addition, you can take part in various sports and cultural activities and enjoy the **Base de loisirs du Pontet,** a leisure park surrounding a small lake.

Hikes

Le Signal★
Alt 1 850m/6 070ft. *Accessible via the Gorge and Signal gondolas.* ⏱ *Gorge gondola: July to Aug: 8.45am-5.30pm; Signal gondola: 9am-12.15pm, 1.30-5pm (20min continuous) 10.40€ return -* ☎ *04 50 47 02 05.*
Splendid view of the Dômes de Miage and Tré-la-Tête Massif as well as of the Chaîne des Fiz further north.

Walk to the Col du Joly★★
Alt 1 989m/6 526ft. *30min easy climb from Le Signal.*
🚶 Superb panorama of the Mont Blanc Massif, the Hauteluce Valley and Lac de la Girotte with the Aravis mountains further away to the northwest.

Hike to the Aiguille Croche★★★
Alt 2 487m/8 159ft. *1hr 30min on foot from the Col du Joly. As the path is very steep, mountain boots are strongly recommended.*
🚶 Your efforts are rewarded by a wide and beautiful **panorama★★★**, one of the finest in the Alps, which encompasses, in a clockwise direction, the Aiguilles de Chamonix, Aiguille Verte, Aiguille du Midi, Aiguille de Bionassay, Mont Blanc, Mont Pourri, the Grande Motte and Grande Casse glaciers, Pierra Menta, the Écrins massif, the Meije, the Mont de Lans and Étendard glaciers, the vast Aravis range, Megève and its mountain airfield.

From Aiguille Croche to Mont Joly along the crest path★★★
Experienced hikers, using a map and leaving early in the morning to make the ascent of the Aiguille Croche, will be able to carry on to Mont Joly (about 2hr).
🚶 From the path, which is narrow but does not often run along the cliff edge, a succession of splendid views unfold. From Mont Joly *(viewing table, ⏱ for details see MEGÈVE)*, allow another 2hr to return to Les Contamines. *Turn round towards the Tête de la Combaz and take the path on the left which leads rapidly down to the bottom of the valley. Turn right in Colombaz*

Notre-Dame-de-la-Gorge – a small classic of the Savoyard Baroque

Fr. Isler/MICHELIN

onto the surfaced road then left 200m/218yd further on. The path leads to L'Étape from where a gondola takes you down to La Gorge. It is also possible to go back on foot.

Lacs Jovet★
Alt 2 174m/7 133ft. *Difference in altitude: about 1 000m/3 281ft. 5hr on foot there and back from Notre-Dame-de-la-Gorge.*

This well-marked itinerary, part of the Round Tour of Mont Blanc, goes through the Réserve naturelle des Contamines. Splendid light reflections on the lakes surrounded by Mont Jovet, Mont Tondu, Col du Bonhomme and Aiguilles de la Pennaz.

COURCHEVEL★★★
MICHELIN MAP 333 M5
LOCAL MAP SEE MASSIF DE LA VANOISE

Courchevel is undoubtedly one of the major and most prestigious winter sports resorts in the world. Founded in 1946 by the Conseil général de la Savoie (regional council), it played a leading role in the development of the Trois Vallées★★★ complex (*see Massif de la VANOISE*). **Émile Allais, who was the downhill world champion in 1937, was the first to introduce to French resorts the idea of grooming ski runs. Après-ski activities are just as exciting: art exhibitions, classical and jazz concerts, an impressive number of luxury shops, sports centres, fitness clubs, and famous nightclubs. However, Courchevel also owes its reputation to the quality of its hotels and gastronomic restaurants, unrivalled in mountain areas. Even in summer, when Courchevel changes radically and becomes a peaceful resort, this diversity sets it apart.** *Le Coeur de Courcheval - BP 37, 73120 Courcheval* *July to Aug: 9am-12.30pm, 2-7pm; Dec to May: 9am-7pm; rest of year: Mon-Fri 9am-noon, 2-6pm* *closed public holidays -* *79 08 00 29 - www.courcheval.com*

▶ **Orient Yourself:** The drive is 50km/31.25mi from Albertville to Courcheval, partly on D 91 with its spectacular panoramic views.

Don't Miss: The cable-car trip up the Saulire is a high point of any visit.

Organizing Your Time: The "forfait de loisir" pass gives access to many resort activities.

Also See: Nearby Sights: Les ARCS, La Vallée de BELLEVILLE, CHAMPAGNY-EN-VANOISE, Route de la MADELEINE, MÉRIBEL, PRALOGNAN-LA-VANOISE, La TARENTAISE, Massif de la VANOISE

The Resorts

The Trois Vallées, composed of Courcheval, Méribel, Les Menuires, Val Thorens and several smaller resorts, is the largest linked ski resort in the world, incorporating 200 lifts on a single pass and 600km/375mi of ski runs.

At Courcheval, snow cover is guaranteed from early December to May, owing to the north-facing aspect of the slopes and an impressive array of more than 500 snow-cannons. The resort's ski schools employ some 700 instructors and rank among the best in Europe. There are excellent runs for beginners along the lower sections of the Courcheval 1850 ski lifts (Verdon, Jardin Alpin). Advanced skiers prefer the great Saulire corridor and the Courcheval 1350 area. As for cross-country skiers, they can explore the elaborate network of 130km/81.25mi of trails linked across the Trois Vallées area.

The Courcheval area includes four resorts situated at altitudes ranging from 1 300m/4 265ft to 1 850m/6 070ft on the slopes of the Vallée de St-Bon, among pastures and wooded areas, in a vast open landscape framed by impressive mountains.

Le Praz 1300

Alt 1 300m/4 265ft. The 90m/295ft and 120m/394ft ski jumps used during the 1992 Olympic Games are close to the old village. A picturesque 7km/4.3mi-long forest road leads to the recent resort of **La Tania** and to Méribel.

Courchevel 1550

Family resort situated on a promontory near woodlands.

Moriond -Courchevel 1650

Sunny resort where urban-style architecture contrasts with traditional chalets.

Courchevel 1850

With its elaborate ski lift system, Courchevel 1850 is the main resort of the complex as well as the liveliest and most popular. There is an impressive **panorama**★ of Mont Jovet, the Sommet de Bellecôte and the Grand Bec peaks. After April, tourist activities move up to 1850 while the other areas slip into summer doldrums.

Viewpoints Accessible by Gondola

La Saulire★★★

🕓 July to Aug: Mon-Thur and every other Fri 9.30am-12.30pm, 1.30-4.40pm (Sun and public holidays 4.45pm) 🕓 closed Sat. 9.20€ return, both sections, children 5-13 years 4.60€; 6€ return for only one section, children 5-13 years 3€ - ☎04 79 08 04 09 - www. s3v.com Access from Courchevel 1850 by the Verdon gondola and the Saulire cable car. The well-equipped summit links the Courchevel and Méribel valleys and is the starting point of a dozen famous runs. Non-skiers can take a gondola to Méribel or Mottaret and a cable-car to Courchevel.

From the top platform (alt 2 690m/8 825ft), the view embraces the Aiguille du Fruit (alt 3 050m/10 007ft) in the foreground, the Vanoise Massif and glaciers further away, the Péclet-Polset Massif to the south, the Sommet de Bellecôte and Mont Pourri to the north with Mont Blanc on the horizon.

Y. Bontoux

Lac Merlet

Address Book

For coin categories, see the Legend on the cover flap.

EATING OUT

La Fromagerie – *R. des Tovets - 73120 Courcheval 1850 - ☎ 04 79 08 27 47 - open July-Aug and Dec-Apr*. This small restaurant at the entrance to the resort offers regional specialities for cheese-lovers. There is a smiling welcome in a simple, well kept setting. You should sample: tarte au Beaufort and chicken roasted with thyme and served with a Gratin de Crozets (type of pasta).

La Cloche – *Pl. du Rocher - 73120 Courcheval 1850 - ☎ 04 79 08 31 30 -tournier.freres@wanadoo.fr- closed Sat-Sun in May-June and Sept-Nov*. There is an appealingly warm atmosphere in this dining room in which tradition is revived. The decor is typical of mountain establishments, with pastel colours combined with rough old wooden floorboards and chairs covered with embroidered, appliquéed fabric and lamps from the 1930s. Sunny terrace.

Le Genepi – *R. Park-City - 73120 Courcheval 1850 - ☎ 04 79 08 08 63 - Le-genepi@wanadoo.fr - closed May-Aug and Sat-Sun in Sept-Nov*. The lounge bar is pleasantly decorated and warmed by a fireplace, and the dining room is friendly, with regional cuisine made from local produce.

La Saulire – *Pl. du Rocher - 73120 Courcheval 1850 - ☎ 04 79 08 07 52 - www.lasaulire.fr - closed May, June and Mon in Sept-Nov*. This very central restaurant serves classic cuisine and is almost as famous as the proprie-tor who opened it over 25 years ago. The dining rooms on two levels are all wood-panelled and decorated with old advertisement posters on the theme of the mountains. Lunch on the terrace.

La Via Ferrata – *Immeuble Porte de Courcheval, 73120 Courcheval 1850 - ☎04 79 08 02 07 - closed May-Nov and noon* In season, this charming Italian restaurant is one of the most fashionable of the resort. The setting, with pale wood, vaulting, stone pillars, fireplace and can-dles on the table, is especially successful. Generous menu and efficient service.

WHERE TO STAY

Courcheval is notoriously fashionable and expensive, but you can find reason-able accommodation through the Centrale de Reservation at the tourist office. See also the Address Books for Vallée des Belleville and for Méribel.

Les Peupliers – *73120 Le Praz - ☎ 04 79 08 41 47 - www.lespeupliers. com - open 25 June-15 Sept and Dec-Apr - 🅿 - 33rms - restaurant*. Tradition is a fine thing... This hotel opposite a small lake and the Olympic ski-jump has passed from father to son since 1938. The open fireplace, warm wood-panelling, the gym, rooms generally with a balcony… all these add up to a comfortable place to stay with a loyal clientèle of regulars.

ON THE TOWN

Le Panoramic – *La Saulire - 73120 Courcheval 1850 - ☎ 04 79 08 00 88 - Open daily 9am-4.45pm from mid-Dec to Apr, access by La Saulire cable-car*. Open only during the winter season, this bar-res-taurant at high altitude (2 700m/8 860ft) offers a fantastic view of some of the highest peaks in the Alps from its terrace.

LEISURE

Forfait Loisir– If you plan a longer stay in Courcheval, you might consider purchasing from the tourist office a pass, called the *forfait loisir*, which gives you access to the swimming pool, skat-ing rink, tennis courts, all the lifts in the Trois Vallées area and other attractions. Cost for 5 days is 32€ for adults, 25€ for children under 15 years; for 7 days, 42€ for adults, and 33€ for children.

Music festival – In late July through August, the Académie Musicale de Courcheval offers a series of concerts in connection with its summer music camps. Contact www.festivalmusicalp. com or the tourist office.

Bureau des Guides de Courcheval – If you are attracted by white water sports, the Courcheval area has many sites for adventure. Contact the Bureau at - ☎06 23 92 46 12 - www.guides-courcheval.com

Angling – In the Courcheval vicinity are 5 lakes at high altitude, as well as Lac de Praz and Lac de la Rosière where you will find trout and salmon. The Vallée de Bozel has fast-flowing streams. You can rent equipment, while permits can often be purchased on site.

The upper terrace of the Pierres Plates restaurant *(viewing table)*, close to the Méribel gondola station, offers a bird's-eye view of the Allues Valley with, in the distance, the northern part of the Écrins Massif (Mont-de-Lans Glacier and Meije) the Grandes Rousses Massif and the Belledonne range.

Sommet de la Saulire (television relay)
Alt 2 738m/8 983ft. *1hr there and back on foot.*
🔲 This excursion is recommended in summer to tourists familiar with mountain conditions and not likely to feel dizzy. The summit can be reached from the cable-car station, along a wide, 300m/328yd-long path and then a shorter steep lane on the right. Splendid panorama including the Meije, and the Écrins and Vanoise massifs.

Télécabine des Chenus★★
Access from Courchevel 1850 🕐 *July to Aug: daily except Sat and every other Fri 9.30am-12.30pm, 1.30-4.40pm (10min, continuous). 6€ -* ☎*04 79 08 04 09* From the upper gondola station, you can view the Rocher de la Loze and, further away, the Croix de Verdon, the Saulire, Aiguille du Fruit and the Vanoise. Skiers can reach the **Col de la Loze**★★ (alt 2 305m/7 562ft) for a fine view of the Allues Valley.

Hikes

Courchevel is an ideal **hiking centre**. A map of the area's network of footpaths is available from the tourist office.

Petit Mont Blanc★★
Alt 2 677m/8 783ft. *Allow 3hr 30min on the way up and 2hr 15min on the way down. Start from Le Belvédère (Courchevel 1650) or from the top of Mont Bel-Air.*
🔲 Walk across the Vallée des Avals then up to the summit via the Col de Saulces. Very fine **panorama** of the Pralognan Valley framed by the Grande Casse, the Vanoise glaciers and the Pointe de l'Échelle.

Lacs Merlet★★
Alt 2 449m/8 035ft. *Ascent: 2hr; start from Mont Bel-air.*
🔲 The position of the lakes at the foot of the Aiguille du Fruit forms a splendid **setting**★★. Go to the upper lake, the deepest of the Vanoise lakes (30m/98ft) and walk along the right-hand shore to the end. The Vanoise glaciers and the Aiguille du Rateau are reflected in the waters, on which drifting ice can be seen almost all year round.

Walk to La Rosière
Access by car along an unsurfaced forest road starting between Courchevel 1650 and Le Belvédère.
🔲Lovely little lake overlooked by the Dent de Villard. Nature trail introducing a few rare species including columbine and lady's slipper. Continue along the waterfall path.

Via ferrata de la Croix de Verdon★
Access by the Verdon gondola and the Saulire cable-car. This is a remarkable **viewpoint**★ (alt 2 739m/8 986ft), reached by a climbing route fitted with safety cables and ladder rungs; ideal for thrill-seekers (🕐*see Planning Your Trip).*

ROUTE DE LA CROIX DE FER ★★★

MICHELIN MAP 77 FOLDS 6 AND 7 OR 244 FOLDS 29 AND 30

One of the finest drives through the Alps leads through charming, traditional villages not yet overtaken by the pace of modern life, and some stunning landscapes; highlights include the Défilé de Maupas, the Gorges de l'Arvan and a fine view of the three Aiguilles d'Arves from the Col de la Croix de Fer.

▶ **Orient Yourself:** This itinerary, and the alternative route which branches off halfway, link the Romanche Valley, known as l'Oisans, to the Arc Valley, also called La Maurienne, and the vallée de l'eau d'Oile to the Arvan and Glandon Valleys.

🔊 **Don't Miss:** Stop to see the Aiguille d'Arves from the Col de la Croix-de-Fer.

🕐 **Organizing Your Time:** From the Col de Glandon, you can descend to the Vallée des Villard by the D 927, up to La Chambre.

Kids **Especially for Kids:** The Maison de la Faune at Vaujany and the Maison du Bouquetin (ibex) at Le Rivier -d'Allemont will interest children who like animals.

⚑ **Also See:** Nearby Sights: L'ALPE-D'HUEZ, Le BOURG-D'OISANS, Massif de CHAMROUSSE, Route du GALIBIER, Route de la MADELEINE, ST-JEAN-DE-MAURIENNE

Excursions

From Rochetaillée to St-Jean de Maurienne ★★

96km/59.7mi – about 4hr. The road is blocked by snow from November to May between Le Rivier-d'Allemond and the Combe d'Olle.

It is possible to make a round tour of some of the great Alpine passes (**Circuit des Grands Cols ★★★**) by extending this itinerary with two more described in this guide: the Route du Galibier (⚑ *see Route du GALIBIER)* and the Col du Lautaret to Le Bourg-d'Oisans (⚑ *see L'OISANS,* ⓶).

Between Rochetaillée and Le Verney, the D 526 follows the green lower Olle Valley, known as the Jardin de l'Oisans.

▶ *Drive along the left bank of the artificial lake and follow signposts to "Centrale de Grand'Maison et Hydrelec".*

As you cross the narrow Flumet Valley, you will get a glimpse of the Cascade de la Fare with the Grandes Rousses summits in the background.

Hydrelec ★
The Grand'Maison power station and Oz factory are not open to the public. Leave the car in the visitors' car park area at the entrance of the power station and walk down the path on the right to Hydrelec. ♿🕐 *Mid-June to mid-Sept: Mon-Fri 10am-6pm, Sat-Sun 2-6pm; school holidays: daily 2-6pm; rest of year: Sat-Sun and public holidays 2-6pm; closed 1 Jan, 1 May and 25 Dec. No charge -* ☎ *04 76 80 78 00.*

The reconstructions and equipment displayed on two levels illustrate the history of hydroelectric power from Chinese waterwheels and the Versailles fountains to modern turbines.

▶ *Return to D 526 and follow D 43A on the right towards Vaujany.*

Vaujany ★
This south-facing village lies in a lovely **setting** ★ on the slopes of the Rissiou, facing the Grandes Rousses. From the end of the village, there is a splendid view of the **Cascade de la Fare** ★ and its spectacular 1 000m/3 281ft drop.

Vaujany is linked by cable car to the Dôme des Rousses (2 805m/9 203ft), via the Alpettes station. From there, it is possible to reach L'Alpe-d'Huez (1 860m/6 102ft).

Maison de la Faune

🕐 *July to Aug and Christmas holidays to April: 10am-noon, 2-7pm. No charge.* Trained docents conduct tours and explain the habits of Alpine animals, with the help of interactive exhibits. Vaujany is linked by cable-car to the Dome des Rousses (2 805m/9 203ft) via La Gare des Alpettes. From here, you can cut over to l'Alpe d'Huez (1 860m/6 102ft)

A road, starting near the cemetery, leads to the Collet de Vaujany.

WHERE TO STAY

Chambre d'Hôte Soneige – *Pourchery - 38114 Vaujany - 15km/9.5mi NE of Bourg-d'Oisans -* ☎ *04 76 79 88 18 - www.solneige.com - closed mid- Apr to mid-May and Oct-Nov - 6rms -* 🍽🍽 *meal.* This chalet and a little house have been extensively renovated. The comfortable, attractive rooms have either a balcony or terrace. Dining room and lounge in vaulted former stable. Garden and Jacuzzi.

Collet de Vaujany★★

Extended view of the west side of the Grandes Rousses, with the Pic de l'Étendard and Lac Blanc.

▶ *Return to Le Verney and turn right onto D 526.*

The road rises above the stream and crosses many tributaries coming down from the Belledonne mountains. The valley becomes narrower and densely forested.

Le Rivier-d'Allemont

Kids **Maison du Bouquetin** 🕐 *July-Aug: daily 11am-12.30pm, 3-6pm; June, Sept and Oct: Sat-Sun 11am-12.30pm. 3-6pm -* ☎ *04 76 79 96 35.* Exhibits at this small museum describe the habitat, social life and survival of the ibex, the animal most symbolic of the Alps. There are films, games and walks on the mountain.

Défilé de Maupas★

Beyond Le Rivier-d'Allemond, the road makes its way through this deep gorge cluttered with fallen rocks. One of the mountain streams rushing down from the Sept-Laux Massif forms a beautiful waterfall, the Cascade des Sept-Laux, which can be seen from the road.

Combe d'Olle★★

This pasture-covered valley running between huge hilltops was the site chosen by EDF (the French Electricity Board) for the **Barrage de Grand'Maison** on the Eau d'Olle: the dam, its 220ha/544-acre lake and its power stations are linked by a 7km/4.2mi gallery to the lower reservoir (75ha/185 acres) and to the Verney Dam power station in order to insure a production of electricity of a mixed type known as "energy transfer."

▶ *At this point the itinerary divides: the alternative route over the Col du Glandon is described at the end of this section.*

Beyond the Combe d'Olle, keep to the right along D 926. The road is blocked by snow between the Combe d'Olle and St-Sorlin-d'Arves from November to May.

Col de la Croix de Fer★★

Alt 2 068m/6 785ft. *15min there and back on foot.* Climb onto the rocky knoll bearing a commemorative pyramid south of the pass, and turn towards the east for a fine **view** of the Aiguilles d'Arves.

Hike to the Étendard refuge ★★★

Allow 3hr 15min there and back on foot from the pass.

After climbing for 1hr 50min, you suddenly glimpse the refuge lower down on the shores of Lake Bramant, overlooked by the Pic de l'Étendard (3 464m/11 365ft). The Belledonne range, stretching across the horizon to the west, is particularly spectacular at sunset and there is a magnificent **view**★★ of the Vanoise Massif to the northeast with the Mont Blanc Massif in the distance.

The refuge can be reached in 10min. Experienced hikers can walk to the foot of the **St-Sorlin Glacier,** beyond lakes Bramant, Blanc and Tournant *(allow 1 day).*

Between the Col de la Croix de Fer and St-Sorlin the road offers open views of the upper Arvan Valley, with its vast sloping pastures dotted with hamlets against a background of high peaks and glaciers. The Pic de l'Étendard's glacier, the Glacier du St-Sorlin, is also visible.

St-Sorlin d'Arves

New buildings connected with the nearby ski area somewhat spoil the traditional character of this village.

▷ *In Malcrozet, turn left onto D 80 which climbs towards St-Jean-d'Arves.*

St-Jean-d'Arves

The church cemetery outside the village overlooks the upper Arvan Valley, offering an extended **view**★ of the snowy peaks of the Grandes Rousses, including the Pic de l'Étendard and the Cimes de la Cochette.

About 2km/1.2mi beyond St-Jean-d'Arves as you go into a bend, note the narrow Entraigues Valley on the right, and further on, as you come out of the tunnel, admire the lovely **picture**★ formed by the hamlet of Montrond with the Aiguilles d'Arves in the background. The road also offers impressive glimpses of the **Gorges de l'Arvan**★ which cuts deep through the schist.

▷ *The road joins D 926 just before a tunnel; turn left.*

Combe Genin ★

The late-afternoon light plays on the schist lining the sides of this imposing scree-covered corridor.

▷ *Turn back along D 926 to Belleville and take D 80 on the left.*

The road crosses the Arvan and climbs above the treeline to the village of Le Mollard with views of the lower Arvan Valley and Combe Genin.

St-Jean-d'Arves and the Massif du Col de la Croix de Fer

S. Sauvignier/MICHELIN

Col du Mollard★

There are very attractive **views**★ of the Aiguilles d'Arves and Vanoise summits from the highest point of the road (alt 1 683m/5 522ft).

As you drive west out of Albiez-le-Vieux, the thrilling descent into the Arvan Valley begins, offering breathtaking bird's-eye views. The journey down is less impressive beyond Gevoudaz as the road makes its way to St-Jean-de-Maurienne.

St-Jean-de-Maurienne – 🕭 See ST-JEAN-DE-MAURIENNE.

Col du Glandon★ 22km/13.7mi – allow 1hr 30min

This is the most direct route from Le Bourg-d'Oisans or Vizille to the Arc Valley. The road runs through the Glandon Valley, also known as the Vallée des Villards.

▶ *Bear left along D 927 after the Combe d'Olle. The road is blocked by snow upstream from St-Colomban-des-Villards from November to early June.*

Col du Glandon★

Alt 1 924m/6 312ft. *250m/273yd from the Chalet-Hôtel du Glandon.* The pass, with the colourful rock formations of the Aiguilles d'Argentière above, offers a splendid vista of Mont Blanc through the Col de la Madeleine to the northeast. The upper Glandon Valley affords austere landscapes of meagre pastures and rocky slopes brightened by clumps of red rhododendrons in early summer.

Col de la Croix de Fer and Aiguilles de l'Argentière

LES DEUX-ALPES ✳ ✳

MICHELIN MAP 333 J7

In the heart of the Oisans region, the passion for skiing continues all year round. The twin resorts of L'Alpe-de-Mont-de-Lans and L'Alpe-de-Venosc, known as "Les Deux-Alpes," spread their modern residential buildings on a vast saddle covered with pastures, which connects the Romanche and Vénéon valleys at an altitude of 1 600m/5 249ft. The resort itself reaches an elevation of 3 600 m/11 811 ft, making it the highest in Isère. *4 Place Deux-Alpes - 38860 Les Deux-Alpes mid-June to Aug and Dec to Apr: 8am-7pm; Sept to Nov and May to mid-June: Mon-Fri 9am-noon, 2-6pm closed 8 and 25 May - ☎04 76 79 22 00 - www.les2alpes.com*

▶ **Orient Yourself:** The resort is 75km/47mi from Grenoble by D 213, which branches onto N 91 just after the Lac du Chambon.

Don't Miss: The Mont-de-Lans glacier, reached by cable-car, is a superb sight.

Especially for Kids: Youngsters will enjoy the ice cave (Grotte de Glace) and the Maison de la Montagne.

Also See: Nearby Sights: L'ALPE D'HUEZ, Le BOURG D'OISANS, Route du GALIBIER, La GRAVE, L'OISANS, Le VALBONNAIS

The Resort

Ski area

Good skiers aim for the steep first section and the Tête Moute Summit. Less experienced skiers prefer the gentle slopes, the excellent snow and magnificent panoramas of the Mont-de-Lans Glacier, the largest European glacier suitable for skiing: equipped with a dozen ski lifts, it offers many green and blue runs between 2 800m/9 186ft and 3 568m/11 706ft, the highest altitude of any groomed ski run in France. This enables intermediate-level skiers to experience the thrill of a 2 000m/6 562ft difference in height on the way back to the resort. The Girose Glacier, belonging to the ski area of La Grave (*see La GRAVE*), is easily accessible *(by tracked vehicle in winter)* from the Dôme de la Lauze Summit; together they form one of the largest **summer ski** areas. Paragliding sites, a skating rink and a heated open-air pool provide plenty of activity off the slopes; walkers can head for the old village of Venosc *(Télécabine du Super-Venosc, see L'OISANS, 1)*, the La Fée refuge and Le Sapey.

Chapelle St-Benoît

This modern chapel, traditionally built in undressed stone, contains a few original sculptures including the Stations of the Cross.

Maison de la Montagne

Av de la Muzelle - Deux-Alpes 1650 July to Aug, Dec to Apr and first week Nov: 10am-noon, 3-7pm - ☎04 76 79 53 15
This nature centre offers an introduction to mountain animal life using multimedia exhibits and animal models. There is also a section devoted to montain climbing.

Viewpoints

Glacier du Mont-de-Lans ✳✳✳

2hr there and back to the Dôme du Puy Salié and half a day to the Dôme de Lauze. Climbing boots, sunglasses and binoculars recommended. Mid-June to Aug: 7.15am-5pm; first week Nov and Dec to Apr: 9.15am-4.15pm closed rest of year. 13.90€ return - ☎04 76 79 75 01.

Access by the Jandri Express cable-car from the resort centre, near the tourist office. There is a cable-car change at 2 600m/8 530ft; the next one takes you up to 3 200m/10 499ft. Fine **view** of the Vercors and Oisans areas.

A diagonal lift and funicular railway then lead to the Dôme du Puy Salié (3 421m/11 224ft). Magnificent **view**★★ of the Écrins Massif. Go to the ski lift arrival point to get a panoramic view of the Vercors, the Belledonne range, the Grandes Rousses Massif (L'Alpe-d'Huez resort and Pic du Lac Blanc), the Mont-Blanc Massif, the indented Aiguilles d'Arves and the Vanoise. Mont Ventoux can also be seen in fine weather conditions.

Skiers can take the ski lift to La Lauze and admire the splendid **panorama**★★★ of the Rateau Summit, the Écrins and Soreiller massifs and, further away to the northeast, of the Péclet, Grande Casse and Mont Pourri summits.

Address Book

For coin categories, see the Legend on the cover flap.

EATING OUT

La Petite Marmite– *70 av Muzelle - 38860 Les Deux-Alpes - ☎ 04 76 80 50 02 - lapetitemarmite@aol.com - closed 30 Apr-16 June.* A popular restaurant with a terrrace under a pergola. Friendly and efficient service goes with a delicious regional cuisine and several house specialties worth trying.

Bel'Auberge – *1 r. de la Chapelle - 38860 Les Deux-Alpes - ☎ 04 76 79 57 90 - belauberge@wanadoo.fr - open July-Aug and Dec-Apr.* This chalet-inn with finely carved woodwork offers classic rustic cuisine as well as fondues and raclettes. The proprietor, a ski instructor, takes good care of patrons.

Le Panoramic – *Summit of Jandri 2 or Jandri Express 1 cable cars - 38860 Les Deux-Alpes - ☎ 04 76 79 06 75 - closed 3 May-28 Nov and evenings.* At 2 600m/8 530ft this chalet is certainly on top of things! On skis or on foot, enjoy mountain cooking at the restaurant or toasted sandwiches in the self-service café. The view of the Vercors range reaching as far as Mont Blanc is breathtaking

WHERE TO STAY

Chambre d'hôte Le Chalet – *3 r. de l'Oisans - 38860 Les Deux-Alpes - ☎ 04 76 80 51 85 - closed 2 May-15 June and Sept-Nov - 7rms.* This large 1960s chalet at the heart of the resort offers peace and quiet in nicely kept if not altogether

inspired rooms. Good value for money. Pleasant garden in summer.

Les Mélèzes – *17 rue des Vikings - 38860 Les Deux-Alpes - ☎ 04 76 80 50 50 - hotellesmelezes@aol.com - closed 29 Apr-19 Dec - 32rms - restaurant.* Skiers will love this hotel at the foot of the ski slopes! For those who prefer a more leisurely holiday, there is a terrace, or you can choose a room with a balcony from which to watch the more energetic types. The restaurant has an Apine menu on Tues evening.

Hôtel La Belle Étoile – *111 av. de la Muzelle - 38860 Les Deux-Alpes - ☎ 04 76 80 51 19 -www.labelletoile. com - closed 5 Sept-26 Nov - 29rms, demi-pension.* This hotel near the ski slopes has much in its favour: a spa bath to relax in after skiing (or you can lounge by the fireplace!) and in summer a swimming pool, tennis court and garden. Outstanding view of La Muzelle.

LEISURE

Pass-Pieton – In July-Aug, the Pass-Pieton, at 50€, gives you access over 6 days to all ski lifts, 2 visits to the swimming pool, 1 visit to the skating rink and 1 entry to the ice cave.

Bureau des Guides – *Maison des 2 Alpes - ☎ 04 76 11 36 29.* Programs for hiking, climbing and white water sports all summer long, as well as winter sports.

Ski d'été – You can ski all summer on the Mantel and Giroise glaciers. Children under 5 and adults over 72, no charge.

Grotte de glace

🖼 🕐 *Mid-June to Aug: 7.15am-7pm; first week Nov and Dec to Apr: 9.15am-4pm* 🕐 *closed rest of year. 22.20€ (access to 3,200m/10,498ft and access to ice cave) -* ☎04 76 79 75 01 - www.2alpes.com

Several caves, dug through thick ice, are decorated with ice sculptures.

Croisière Blanche★

🕐 *Access during hours of Jandri Express. It is advisable to get bookings from the tourist office during the season. Departure from the cable car station. 28€ (includes 30min climb by cable-car from Deux-Alpes, ride in Croisière, visit to ice cave) -* ☎ *04 76 79 75 01.* Visitors on foot can reach the **Dôme de la Lauze** by tracked minibus. This excursion offers a unique experience in a high-mountain environment.

Belvédère des Cimes★

Alt 2 100m/6 890ft. *Access via the Cimes chairlift; it leaves from the outskirts of the resort, on the Mont-de-Lans side.*

This viewpoint, situated on the northeast slope of Pied Moutet, offers a fine view of the Romanche Valley and Bourg-d'Oisans Basin.

Belvédère de la Croix★

From the cross standing on top of a grassy knoll, on the way out of the resort on the Alpe-de-Venosc side, one looks down a sheer drop to the bottom of the Vénéon Valley with jackdaws whirling above. The pointed Aiguille de Venosc stands across the river and the **Roche de la Muzelle** (alt 3 459m/11 348ft), with its characteristic suspended glacier, towers above the whole landscape.

LE DÉVOLUY★★

MICHELIN MAP 334 D4

This massif, which forms part of the southern Préalpes, offers desolate and sometimes magnificent landscapes. Barren limestone escarpments dominated by the highest peak, the Obiou (nearly 3 000m/9 843ft), surround a central valley through which flow the Ribière and the Béoux. The Dévoluy is riddled with sink-holes known as **"chourums,"** also called "scialets" in the Vercors Massif, which are sometimes filled with ice, as in the case of Chourum Martin, south of St-Disdier. Roads crossing the Dévoluy, particularly the Col du Noyer, run through treeless landscapes, devoid of fertile soil and streams, scorched by the sun and overlooked by jagged peaks with scree-covered slopes. 🗊 *05250 St-Étienne-en-Dévoluy* 🕐 *July to Aug and Jan to Apr: 9am-noon, 2-6pm; rest of year: Mon-Sat 9am-noon, 2-5pm -* ☎ *04 76 30 03 85 - www.ledevoluy.com*

- ▶ **Orient Yourself:** If you enter the Dévoluy valley by the gorge of the Souloise River, ignore the overwhelming urge to gaze up the steep walls: keep your eyes on the road! Remember that the car coming up hill has priority, unless there is a place for it to pull over.
- 🚗 **Don't Miss:** Be sure to see the dam on the Sautet with the lake behind it; the mountain passes of the Noyer and Rioupes; the impressive gorges of the Souloise and the Étroits.
- 🕐 **Organizing Your Time:** The two proposed excurions, the round tour of the Cols and the circuit around the lac du Sautet, will take you a day.
- 👣 **Also See:** Nearby Sights: Pays du BUËCH, Le CHAMPSAUR, GAP, Lacs de LAFFREY, MONTMAUR, Route NAPOLÉON, L'OISANS, Lac de SERRE-PONÇON, Le TRIÈVES, Le VALBONNAIS, Le VALGAUDEMAR

Excursions

1 Round tour via the Col du Festre and Col du Noyer ⋆

STARTING FROM CORPS *81km/50.3mi – about 3hr 30min*

Corps – ⚫ *See* 2 .

▷ *From Corps, drive west along D 537. Stop just before the bridge at Lac du Sautet.*

It is worth taking a few moments by the shore to admire the Perle de Dévoluy and the reflections of the surrounding mountains.

▷ *Continue along the D 537 which now turns to the south.*

Try to catch a glimpse of the impressive Obiou, briefly visible to the west beyond Trièves and the Drac Valley.

Défilé de la Souloise ⋆
The road runs between splendid limestone escarpments.

St-Disdier
🚶 *Park in the village centre and walk to the church, a 20-min climb.* An isolated 13C church known as **La Mère-Église,** literally "the mother church," is set on the slopes overlooking the village to the east; the insignia of the Templars – the sun, the moon and the Maltese cross – are in evidence inside. A music festival is held here every summer (⚫ *July to Aug: Wed, Fri, Sun at 3pm).*

Col du Festre
Alt 1 441m/4 728ft. Fine views from this pass below the desolate heights of the Montagne d'Aurouze. The road then runs down towards Montmaur along the Béaux Valley (⚫ *see MONTMAUR).*

▷ *Turn back and take D 17 on the right.*

Col de Rioupes ⋆
This pass offers splendid **views** of a vast ring of barren mountains: Crêtes des Aiguilles, Grand-Ferrand, Obiou and Montagne de Féraud separated by the Col du Noyer from the Montagne d'Aurouze which is riddled with sink-holes.

Défilé des Étroits ⋆
Stop the car between the two bridges which D 17 crosses. The road overlooks the River Souloise which has carved a 40-60m/131-197ft deep

B. Kaufmann/MICHELIN

St-Étienne-en-Dévoluy and the Col de Rabou, the southern boundary of the Dévoluy massif

passage (only 2m/7ft wide in parts) through the rock. The via ferrata is guaranteed to set the pulse racing.

The Souloise Valley suddenly widens as the road reaches St-Étienne-en-Dévoluy.

St-Étienne-en-Dévoluy

This green oasis in the barren Dévoluy landscape was once virtually self-sufficient, cut off from the rest of the world until, after 15 long years of work, the connecting road was opened in 1872.

Superdévoluy *

This ski resort at an altitude of 1 500m/4 921ft is interesting from an architectural point of view: all the buildings are grouped to form a 2-tiered ensemble extending along the slopes of the Montagne d'Aurouze with rows of wooden balconies all facing southwest. The **ski area** between 1 500m-2 510m/4 921ft-8 235ft includes a variety of ski runs down the northern slopes of the Sommarel and the Pic Ponçon, totalling 100km/62.5mi. The link with the La Joue-du-Loup ski area is accessible to intermediate skiers; those with more experience prefer the Pierra, Sommarel and Mur red runs. Cross-country skiers have access to 35/22mi of marked trails, comprising 11 circuits. Superdévoluy is also the place to try your hand at something new, be it slalom, boarder cross, snowscooting (a cross between snowboarding and BMX biking) or even a dog-sled ride. There are 31km/19.4mi of marked trails for walkers.

Col du Noyer ★★

▶ *The pass is closed from early November to mid-May.*

Both sides of the pass (alt 1 664m/5 459ft – *viewing table 100m/109yd southwest of the former Refuge Napoléon*), offer beautiful contrasting **landscapes:** the barren ridges of the Dévoluy on one side and, on the other, the broad Drac Valley (Bas-Champsaur) chequered with various crops and framed by the heights of the Vieux-Chaillol Massif and the Gapençais mountains, with the high summits and glaciers of the Écrins Massif in the distance.

▶ *The road running down towards the River Drac is a test of your driving skills, particularly for the first 5km/3mi. At La Fare-en-Champsaur it joins the Route Napoléon (N 85) which leads back to Corps. Remember the Highway Code rule for narrow mountain roads, which states that unless a car heading uphill is able to pull over into a passing place, drivers travelling downhill should give way to it.*

② Round tour of Lac du Sautet★★

STARTING FROM CORPS *35km/21.7mi – about 2hr*

Corps

Overlooking the Lac du Sautet, the capital of the **Beaumont** region (middle Drac Valley between Corps and the confluence of the Bonne) is a lively summer resort along the famous Route Napoléon (👆 *see ROUTE NAPOLÉON*) and a convenient meeting place for pilgrims on their way to Notre-Dame de la Salette. The Obiou towers over the delightful valley **landscape**★★.

▷ *Follow N 85 south towards Gap and, as you leave Corps, turn right past the petrol station. ➥ Walk the last 91m/100yd, as it is impossible to turn round further on, 15 min there and back.*

The small **Chapelle St-Roch** overlooking the lake, has some interesting modern stained-glass windows.

▷ *Rejoin N 85, which runs above the lake. At Le Motty turn right towards Ambel along D 217.*

The road rises above the south bank of the lake and soon offers views of the Obiou, the Vercors Massif, Corps and the heights of Notre-Dame de la Salette *(beware of falling rocks)*.
Beyond Ambel, the road runs above the lower Souloise Valley which forms the other arm of the lake; the Grand-Ferrand soars straight ahead. The road then runs down to the bottom of the valley; from the bridge over the Souloise there is a view of the Petites Gillardes, resurgent springs from underground water courses which are fed by the chourums or sink-holes of the upper plateaux.

▷ *1km/0.6mi beyond the bridge, turn right onto D 537.*

Past Pellafol, there is a fine view on the right of the promontory crowned by the village of Ambel.

Pont du Sautet ★

The D 537 crosses the River Drac over this bridge, a daring piece of engineering with a single reinforced-concrete arch spanning 86m/282ft, at a height of 160m/525ft above the water

Barrage du Sautet ★★

➥ *Just after the bridge, there is a tourist kiosk, where you can walk down stairs to view the vault close-up.* This elegant curved dam, 126m/413ft high, has created a reservoir capable of containing 115 million m3/93 231cu ft of water. The hydroelectric power station further downstream was partly built underground.

For coin categories, see the Legend on the front cover flap.

WHERE TO STAY

🛏 **Le Napoléon** –*Place Napoléon 38970 Corps* ☎ *04 76 30 00 42, hotel-napoleon@wanadoo.fr - closed 12 Mar-30 Apr and 16 Oct- 9 Feb.* Located in a large building at the foot of the village, this hotel offers brightly painted rooms with locally made furniture. Pretty breakfast room.

🛏🛏 **Auberge La Neyrette** – *05250 St-Disdier -* ☎ *04 92 58 81 17 - info@laneyrette.com - closed 13-30 Apr and 8 Nov-17 Dec -* 🅿 *- 12rms -* 🍽 *restaurant.* Refurbished rooms in a quiet natural setting where guests are lulled to sleep by the murmuring of the wind. An ideal location for exploration on foot or on skis. In fine weather, you can arrange to go trout fishing. On the subject of trout, this inn by the river offers it as an option on all its menus.

The Weeping Virgin

In 1846, two local children described how the Virgin Mary appeared to them in the form of a weeping woman and spoke to them at length in regional dialect and in French. After a five-year investigation, the Catholic church acknowledged the statements of the children; a basilica was built and today the sanctuary welcomes over 150 000 pilgrims a year.

An alternative route from Corps *15km/8.7mi – 1hr*

Between Corps and the village of La Salette, the road follows the deep, fresh green valley of the Sezia. The road rises rapidly from the village to Notre-Dame de la Salette within sight of the imposing Obiou Peak (2 793m/9 163ft).

🅿 *Large car park available near the basilica.*

Notre-Dame de la Salette★

The **basilica** (🕐 *8am-7pm, when no services taking place -* ☎ *04 76 30 00 11)* stands at an altitude of 1 770m/5 807ft, surrounded by pastures and in a striking mountain **setting**★★. It is the venue of many pilgrimages, particularly on 19 September, the anniversary of the apparition of Our Lady in 1846 to two local children.

Behind the basilica, walk round a mound surmounted by a cross to enjoy a panoramic **view**★ of the Oisans, Dévoluy and Beaumont regions. 🚶 Hikers can continue to **Mont Gargas** *(Alt 2 207m/7 241ft. 2hr there and back on foot. Climb northwards along marked paths to the Col de l'Éterpat then follow the ridge line to the left).* Vast **panorama**★★ of the Obiou and of the heights south of the Oisans.

Hikes

The Superdévoluy tourist office has published a walking map showing 23 recommended itineraries, plus two topographical maps, one for mountain biking.

Plateau de Bure★★

From Superdévoluy; 4hr there and back, difference in altitude: 550m/1 804ft.

🚶 At first sight, the giant metal dishes of the Institut de radioastronomie millimétrique, or IRAM (⊶ *not open to the public)*, make this radio observatory look more like a sci-fi film set. These parabolic antennae have been listening to the cosmos since 1990, searching the spectrum on a frequency between radio waves and infrared radiation. It may seem an inhospitable place – high winds gust around the summit and temperatures have been known to fall as low as -20°C – but the altitude and dry mountain air make it ideal for observation. At the end of July, Superdévoluy plays host to a festival of astronomy which attracts stargazers from France and beyond. Join the GR 94B above Superdévoluy. Head out of the larch wood, cross the valley and follow a stony path. This leads to an area of level ground with a spring. After a series of curves the path leads to a narrow passage with a rope to hold on to (⊛ *extra care is needed here).* This is Pic Ponson, the most north-westerly point of the plateau.

DIE ★

POPULATION 4 451
MICHELIN MAP 332 F5

Die lies hidden in the hills of the sunny Diois valley, to which it gave its name, overlooked by the shiny escarpments of the Glandasse range south of the Vercors Massif. The easiest way to get to Die is along the Drôme Valley, but a far more interesting route leads over the Col de la Chaudière, Col du Rousset or Col de Menée and down through vineyards, orchards and fields of lavender. 🗊
Rue des Jardins - 26150 Die 🕐 *July to Aug: Mon-Sat 9am-7pm, Sun and public holidays 9.30am-12.30pm; Apr to June and Sept: Mon-Sat 9am-noon, 2-6pm, Sun and public holidays 9.30am-12.30pm; rest of year Mon-Sat 9am-noon, 2-6pm -* ☎ *04 75 22 03 03 - www.diois-tourisme.com*

▶ **Orient Yourself:** Situated in the heart of a vast and fertile valley and surrounded by mountains, Die is built on a slight slope. Take the prettiest routes down from the North and East: D 520, D 120, or D 539. Continuing on after completing excursion ③, you will return into the upper Buëch valley (🐾 pays de Buëch).

🅿 **Parking:** Leave your car near the ramparts to tour the old town on foot.

🎐 **Don't Miss:** If you can, time your visit to see the Fête de la Transhumance in June or the Fête de la Clairette (a local sparkling white wine) in September.

🕐 **Organizing Your Time:** You will need a half day to visit the town, and a day and a half to complete the excursions described below.

Kids **Especially for Kids:** The Jardin des Découvertes near Die on the road to Gap consists of greenhouses filled with plants and free-flying butterflies.

🐾 **Also See:** Nearby Sights: Pays du BUËCH, Le VERCORS

Address Book

For coin categories, see the Legend on the cover flap.

WHERE TO EAT AND WHERE TO STAY

⊜ **Hôtel St-Domingue** – *44 rue Camille-Buffardel -* ☎ *04 75 22 03 08 - 20 rms:* ⊜ *restaurant.* This simple and comfortable establishment is on a busy village street. A warm welcome in the rustic dining room, where there are three menus featuring traditional fare.

⊜ **Camping La Pinède** – *1.7km/1mi W of Die on D 93 -* ☎ *04 75 22 17 77 - info@ camping-pinede.com - open 23 Apr-10 Sept.- reservations recommended - 110 pitches – catering available on site.* Pitch your tent between the forest and the mountains, in this well shaded site beneath the pine trees. There are also chalets on the mountain side overlooking the camp site like a small village. Swimming pool with splash basin and tiled terrace. Tennis court and children's play area.

⊜ **Camping L'Hirondelle** – *26410 Menglon - 13km/8mi SE of Die on D 93 as far as Pont-de-Quart then D 539. D 214 and D 140 -* ☎ *04 75 21 82 08 - contact@ campinghirondelle.com - open 25 Mar- 17 Sept – reservation required - 100 pitches – catering available on site.* This campsite on the south Vercors slope offers peace and quiet, spacious pitches between shade and sunshine, and a salt-water swimming pool. Visitors can spend their time exploring and being sporty in the midst of a spacious natural setting.

⊜ **Relais de Chamarges** – *Av de la Clairette -* ☎ *04 75 22 00 95 - closed Dec-Jan, Sun evening and Mon out of season except public holidays -* 🅿 *- 11rms: -* ⊜⊜ *restaurant.* This small homelike hotel is at the exit to the town, near the road. The rooms are furnished plainly but are spotlessly clean. Shaded terrace to the front and garden to the rear of the house, facing the countryside.

A Bit of History

Die had, by the 2C AD, become an important Gallo-Roman city on the main route from Milan to Vienne. Many visitors were attracted by the cult of Cybele, the mother of the gods, involving the sacrifice of a bull and a ram, as the sacrificial altars exhibited in the museum testify.

During the 3C AD, Die was surrounded by walls and became a Christian city in which the bishop always played an important role, as in the granting of the town's first charter in 1217; the only one of his successors unwise enough to try revoking these municipal freedoms was murdered by a furious mob in front of his own cathedral. In the 16C, the Reformation had a major impact on Die, whose churches were all destroyed, but Louis XIV later reinstated the bishopric.

Today, Die is a small administrative and commercial centre, its most popular export being the **"Clairette de Die"** a sweet, sparkling white wine made from Clairette and Muscat, two famous grape varieties. The drinks traditionally flow in June to celebrate the transhumance, when the flocks are herded up to the summer pastures, and for a festival of East-West culture in the same month.

Around the Town

Roman Ramparts
Although its towers have long since disappeared, the 3C enclosure, stretching over 2km/1.2mi, is still visible on the northeast side of the town. It is possible to walk along the 3m/10ft-thick walls, built with undressed stone and ancient reclaimed masonry, from the tourist office to the Porte St-Marcel. Gallo-Roman objects found on location are now exhibited in the museum.

Porte St-Marcel
The vaulting of this Roman arched garteway is decorated with interlacing and rosettes; the friezes illustrate chariot racing and the prosperity of the *pax Romana* symbolized by a tamed lion and dancing.

Cathedral
The massive bell-tower is surmounted by a wrought-iron campanile. The south wall and Romanesque porch tower belonged to the original 12C-13C church. Note the capitals of the doorways, which illustrate biblical scenes, including Cain and Abel and Abraham and Isaac on the north side and fighting scenes with mythical beasts to the south and west. Partly destroyed during the Wars of Religion, this church was rebuilt and refurbished in the 17C; particularly noteworthy are the pulpit, the woodwork decorating the chancel, the stalls and the high altar.

Also worth seeing is the Renaissance façade of the **Maison du chanoine Faure de Vercors** in rue St-Vincent, next to the cathedral, and the Jesuit chapel, now a Protestant church.

Sights

Hôtel de ville

The building housing the town hall and the law courts is the former bishop's palace, which has retained the 11C **Chapelle St-Nicolas** (🕐 *Guided tours (30 min) at 2pm Tues and 11.30am Friday. 2€ - ☎ 04 75 22 03 03).* It is paved with a remarkable 12C **mosaic**★ representing the universe, with the North Star in the centre, surrounded by the four rivers of the Garden of Eden, and the cardinal points in the corners. The walls of the chapel are decorated with medieval frescoes and 18C hand-painted wallpaper.

Museum of History and Archeology

🕐 *July to Aug: daily except Sun 2.30-5.30pm; Apr to June and Sept to Oct: Wed and Sat 2.30-5.30pm; Sept: Tue and Sat 3.30-6.30pm, Thur 6-8pm; May: Sat 3.30-6.30pm.* 🕐 *Closed public holidays. 3 €, children no charge - ☎ 04 75 22 40 05.* Housed in a late-18C mansion, this museum contains interesting local archaeological collections, particularly rich in Gallo-Roman exhibits: sacrificial altars, a 4C Christian sarcophagus etc. One room is devoted to popular art and customs and another one to Romanesque sculptures from the cathedral.

Excursions

Kids Jardin des découvertes ★

At 3km/2mi from Die, on the road to Gap ♿🕐 *July to Aug: 10am-6pm; May to June: 10am-noon, 2-7pm. 6€, children 3.80€ - ☎ 04 75 22 17 90 - www.jardin-decouvertes. com* In a vast greenhouse, exotic plants grow without soil; protected from wind and weather, hundreds of gorgeous butterflies, including some very large ones, flutter about in liberty; educational panels explain their life cycles.

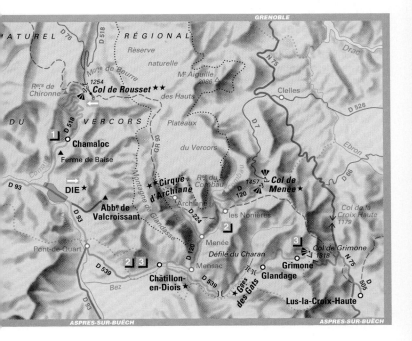

Abbaye de Valcroissant

After 6km/3.7mi along D 93 to Sisteron, take the road on the left. ⏱ *July to Aug: guided tours (1hr) Mon, Wed, Fri at 5pm; May: Fri at 5pm; June and Sept: Wed at 5pm; rest of year, on request. 3€ -* ☎ *04 75 22 12 70.*

The road goes upstream through a gorge and reaches a cirque below the cliffs of the Vercors Massif. In 1188, Cistercian monks founded an abbey in this remote place. The church and refectory can only be seen from the outside.

Pontaix

10km/6.2mi west along D 93 towards Crest. This old wine-growing village, backing onto a knoll crowned by a 13C castle, forms the most attractive site★ of the middle Drôme Valley. The castle keep stands 70m/230ft above the river. Some houses date back to the 15C and the Protestant church contains 15C and 17C paintings.

Le Claps

20km/12.4mi southeast along D 93, just beyond Luc-en-Diois. This pile of rocks is the result of a huge landslide which occurred in the 15C. It formed two natural dams and two lakes which have now dried up. The pile of rocks nearer the railway viaduct is the most impressive. Higher up, at a place known as the **Saut de la Drôme,** the river rushes through a small artificial tunnel and splashes onto the rocks; it is worth stopping for a moment when the river is in spate.

The Beauty of the Diois ★★

Life in the Diois is sustained by the Drôme and its tributaries, including the Bez, the Rif and the Boulc, which cut through an otherwise dry landscape to water the lush valleys. A drive through the narrow gorges leads past clusters of houses, perched high on the hillsides, sometimes at an altitude of over 1 000m/3 281ft. These little villages, their squares shaded by plane trees and their houses decorated with pink and white oleander in typical Provençal style, offer tourists a welcome break between two breathtaking excursions through such impressive landscapes as the Cirque d'Archiane.

1 Le Rousset

FROM THE COL DE ROUSSET TO DIE *22km/13.7mi – 1hr*
This route leading from the Vercors to the Diois region illustrates the striking contrast which exists between the northern and southern Alps.

Col de Rousset★★

Alt 1 254m/4 114ft. ⚐ *See Le VERCORS,* 4.

Chamaloc

The mellow-stone houses, roofed with curved tiles, contribute to the Provençal appearance of the village. Between Chamaloc and Die, the **Ferme de Baise** has been turned into the Maison du Parc naturel régional du Vercors and offers visitors an interesting nature trail.

2 Route de Menée ★★

FROM DIE TO THE COL DE MENÉE *45km/28mi – about 2hr. The pass is usually blocked by snow from December to March.* ⚠ *Beware of falling rocks.*

▷ *From Die, follow D 93 towards Gap.*

The road runs through the Die Basin, among vineyards overlooked by the limestone cliffs of the Glandasse Mountain.

▶ *In Pont-de-Quart, turn left onto D 539.*

Châtillon-en-Diois⋆

🛈 *Square Jean-Giono - 26410 Château-en-Disos* 🕐 *July to Aug: 9am-noon, 3-7pm; rest of year, telephone for times-* ☎ *04 75 21 10 07*

Built around a castle that is now gone, the village has retained its medieval character. An intricate network of streets, narrow lanes and covered passages, known as *viols* in local dialect, surrounds place Reviron overlooked by the clock tower. Cool fountains, flowers, and tiled roofs brighten the grey-limestone buildings.

▶ *Turn left onto D 120 towards the Col de Menée. In Menée, take D 224 to Archiane.*

Cirque d'Archiane ⋆⋆

The upper end of the Archiane Valley is barred by escarpments forming a splendid amphitheatre split in two by a huge promontory known as the "Jardin du Roi." The area is ideal for mountaineering and hiking to the high plateaux of the Vercors Massif *(GR 93)*.

Beyond Les Nonières, the road rises in a succession of hairpin bends; the barren landscape, dotted with clusters of lavender and overlooked by the impressive Rocher de Combau, gradually gives way to pine woods and pastures.

Col de Menée⋆

The road goes through a tunnel (alt 1 402m/4 600ft), beneath the pass (alt 1 457m/4 780ft). From the southern end of the tunnel, the view extends to the Montagne de Glandasse on the horizon, whereas from the northern end, there is a fine **panorama** of the isolated Mont Aiguille.

③ Villages of Yesteryear⋆

FROM CHÂTILLON-EN-DIOIS TO LUS-LA-CROIX-HAUTE *45km/28mi – about 1hr 30min*

From Die to Châtillon-en-Diois – 👣 *See* ② *above.*

Châtillon-en-Diois – 👣 *see above*

▶ *Leave Châtillon-en-Diois along D 539.*

The Cirque d'Archiane

Gorges des Gats★

Prior to the building of the road in 1865, travellers had to cross several fords in order to go up this extremely narrow gorge (only a few metres wide in places) with more than 100m/328ft-high cliffs on either side. Further on, four tunnels negotiate the **Défilé du Charan**.

Glandage and Grimone

The closely grouped houses of these hamlets with large steep roofs, well adapted to heavy snows, give an idea of the hardships of life at high altitude a few generations ago. A group of young people has given new life to these more or less abandoned villages. The church at Glandage is worth a visit.

Beyond Glandage, the southern vegetation gives way to oaks and Austrian pines. Beyond the **Col de Grimone** (alt 1 318m/4 324ft), the view extends southeast to the Montagne de Garnesier and Crête des Aiguilles.

▶ *Drive south on N 75.*

Lus-la-Croix-Haute – ⓒ *See Pays du BUËCH.*

④ Gorges d'Omblèze★

FROM DIE *48km/23mi – 2hr 30min*

▶ *Leave Die by the D 93 towards Crest then turn right onto D 129 to Ste-Croix.*

Ste-Croix

Built on a narrow ridge between the River Drôme and River Sure, the village is over-looked by 13C ruins. In an original spirit of compromise, the **church** is divided into two parts to accommodate both Catholic services (in the transept and apse) and Protestant services (in the nave).

🚶 *(1h 30min)* The old monastery (ⓒ open in season) includes a garden of medicinal and aromatic herbs. A botanic trail winds through the park.

▶ *Turn left onto D 172.*

The narrow twisting road leads through oak and pine woods to the **Col de la Croix** (alt 745m/2 444ft), then down the Sépie Valley to Beaufort-sur-Gervanne.

Beaufort-sur-Gervanne

The way into Beaufort offers a spectacular view which includes what remains of the fortifications now turned into a pleasant walk. The recently rebuilt church has retained an arcaded bell-tower.

▶ *Follow D 70 to Plan-de-Baix.*

Plan-de-Baix

Built on a hillside, the village is overlooked by limestone cliffs (Rochers du Vellan), once the site of a Roman settlement. There is a domed 12C church.

The 13C-14C **Château de Montrond** towers over the Gervanne Valley.

From Plan-de-Baix, it is possible to drive north to Léoncel and the Col de la Bataille via the Col de Bacchus (ⓒ *see Le VERCORS: Route du Col de la Bataille).*

At first D 578 follows the deep Gervanne Valley, high above the river bed, then it runs down the slopes, planted with box trees and pines, towards the entrance of the gorge guarded by a towering rock.

Chute de la Druise

Turn right in Le Moulin-la-Pipe towards Ansage and drive for 1km/0.6mi to the car park.
1hr there and back on foot; wear strong walking shoes and beware of falling rocks.
A marked path leads to the top of the waterfall; from there, another steep and stony path leads down to the bottom.

The **Gorges d'Omblèze**, lined by impressive limestone cliffs, start beyond Le Moulin-la-Pipe. The Petite and the Grande Cascades de la Pissoire fall by the roadside; la Grande Cascade often dries up in summer. Now and then, there are glimpses of the Col de la Bataille to the north.

DIGNE-LES-BAINS

POPULATION 16 064

MICHELIN MAP 81 FOLD 17 OR 245 FOLD 21

LOCAL MAPS SEE PRÉALPES DE DIGNE AND ROUTE NAPOLÉON

On the Route Napoléon, in a beautiful mountain setting, this town by the banks of the River Bléone is a sought-after spa resort and tourist centre. This important Gallo-Roman settlement and medieval bishopric is today the main administrative town of the Alpes-de-Haute-Provence *département*. It is also a lively commercial town, which centralises the regional production of fruit and lavender; a procession of flower-covered floats takes place every year in August and a lavender fair is held in September.

The town's waters have been famous since antiquity, but the spa activities had dwindled over the centuries until a new building, situated 3km/1.8mi southeast of the centre, was inaugurated in 1982; the number of people taking the waters has been growing steadily ever since. The most famous son of Digne was **Pierre Gassendi** (1592-1655), the philosopher, mathematician, astronomer and physicist who greatly admired Galileo and pioneered the study of astronomical phenomena through a telescope.

The engineer **Alphonse Beau de Rochas** (1815-93) was born in the town. He worked on a telegraphic link between France and England in the 1850s and later suggested the construction of a metal tunnel under the Channel. The explorer and writer **Alexandra David-Néel** (1868-1969), who, in 1924, was the first European woman to enter the capital of Tibet, settled in Digne in 1927 and bequeathed her house and her collections to the town. *Place du Tampinet, 04000 Digne-les-Bains July to Sept: daily 8.45am-12.30pm, 1.30-6.30pm, Sun and public holidays 10am-noon; rest of year daily except Sun and public holidays 8.45am-noon, 2-6pm - 04 92 36 62 62 - www.ot-dignelesbains.fr. Guided tours of town Mar to Oct: Fri afternoon, no charge, sign up at tourist office.*

▶ **Orient Yourself:** Digne is located at the junction of three valleys on the N 85 (the Route Napoléon), 39km/24.4mi southeast of Sisteron and 52km/32.5mi northwest of Castellane.

🅿 **Parking:** Parking lots in the town centre are all paying.

Don't Miss: See the Alexandra David-Néel Museum in the house where she lived between her two trips to Tibet. The Gassendi museum is also worth a visit.

🕐 **Organizing Your Time:** Count on a half-day to tour the town and visit at least one of the several museums.

Kids Especially for Kids: The Réserve géplogique de Haute Provence has an interesting nature trail and, for fun, visit the outdoor sports park Les Ferréols.

Also See: Nearby Sights: CASTELLANE, Préalpes de DIGNE, Vallée de la Moyenne DURANCE, Monastère de GANAGOBIE, Route NAPOLÉON, SISTERON, Plateau de VALENSOLE

Walking Tour

Old town

A network of twisting lanes and stairs surrounds the mound crowned by the Église St-Jérôme with its characteristic campanile. It is possible to reach the cathedral by walking up the picturesque Montée St-Charles, which starts on the right of rue de l'Hubac. Pedestrian shopping streets at the foot of the mound have been renovated and the buildings painted in pleasant pastel colours.

The wide boulevard Gassendi, shaded by plane trees, and place Charles-de-Gaulle are the liveliest parts of the town. Works in Carrara marble from an international **sculpture exhibit** organised in Digne between 1983 and 1991 decorate public spaces. A *list of the works displayed is available at the tourist office.*

Grande Fontaine

The 19C fountain situated at the end of boulevard Gassendi consists of two Doric porticoes perpendicular to one another and limestone concretions covered with moss.

Jardin botanique des Cordeliers

Place de Cordeliers ⛄🕒 *July to Aug: daily except Sat-Sun 9am-noon, 3-7pm; April to June and Sept to Oct: daily except Sat-Sun 9am-noon, 2-6pm. No charge -* ☎ *04 92 31 59 59* This pretty medieval garden in the courtyard of the former Cordeliers convent has been planted with aromatic and medicinal herbs and vegetables.

Sights

Musée Gassendi ★

64 bd Gassendi ⛄🕒 *April to Sept: daily except Tues 11am-7pm; Oct to Mar: daily except public holidays 1.30-5.30pm. 4€, children no charge -* ☎ *04 92 31 45 29.*

Founded in 1889 and housed in the former hospice, it is both a natural history and fine arts museum.

Artworks displayed include paintings by 19C Provençal artists: Martin, Mayan, Guindon, Ponson, Nardi and watercolours by Paul Martin, the founder of the museum. The stock of older works is rich in Italian paintings: the major work is the Virgin with a Missal by the 17C Roman artist, **Carlo Maratta**. The Venetian School is represented by *The Allegory of Vice and Virtue* by **Francesco Ruschi**. The Flemish and Dutch schools are illustrated by two portraits by **Frans Pourbus** (1569-1622) and **Van Ravesteyn**. A large collection of 19C scientific instruments is displayed, as a reminder of the town's association with the astronomer **Pierre Gassendi** (1592-1655), enlightened partisan of Copernicus and Galileo, who was born near Digne. Among the remarkable exhibits is the **astronomical clock**, which tells both the solar and standard times and gives useful geographical information. It was patented in 1865 after 22 years of research and development.

Musée d'Art religieux

Place des Récollets 🕒 *July to Sept: 10am-6pm. No charge -* ☎ *04 92 36 75 00.*

This museum, housed in the Chapelle des Pénitents, displays a permanent collection of religious art, presents temporary exhibitions on the subject and shows video films on a range of other topics.

Musée de la Seconde Guerre mondiale

Place Paradis &. ☉ July to Aug: daily except Sat-Sun 2-6pm; May to June and Sept to Oct: Wed 2-5pm ☉ closed public holidays. No charge - ☎ *04 92 31 28 95.*
This small museum is appropriately housed in a former air-raid shelter; exhibits include documents and objects from the period of the Second World War showing the strategic importance of Digne and the damage suffered by the town.

Near the town centre

Cathédrale Notre-Dame-du-Bourg★

Access by ① on the town plan. ☉ July to Aug: 3-6pm; rest of year guided tours (1hr 30min) on request. No charge - ☎ *04 92 32 06 48.*
This vast Provençal Romanesque church, built of blue schist between 1200 and 1330, has an elegant Lombard doorway surmounted by a large rose window and with crouching lions in front of it. This cathedral was used as a model for other religious architecture in the region (⌖ *see SEYNE),* but was badly damaged in the late 15C, after which orders were given to begin work on a new church, the Église St-Jérome. Excavations beneath the bell-tower have revealed construction from the 1stC AD, and traces of the vast original church, dating from the 5C AD.
There is a faded 14C mural on the inside of the west front depicting the Trinity, and large **painted medallions** in other parts of the church. The nave **murals**, dating from the 15C and 16C, illustrate the Last Judgement *(on the right)*, the Garden of Eden, Hell, the Virtues and the Vices.

DIGNE-LES-BAINS		Gaulle Pl. Ch.-de	B	6	Grande Fontaine	B	B
11-Novembre 1918 Rd-Pt du	A 17	Hubac R. de l'	A	7	Musée d'Art religieux	B	M¹
Ancienne Mairie R. de l'	B 8	Mitan Pl. du	B	10	Musée de la Seconde		
Arès Cours des	B 2	Payan R. du Col.	A	12	Guerre mondiale	B	M³
Capitoul R.	B 3	Pied-de-Ville R.	A	13			
Dr-Romieu R. du	B 4	Saint-Charles Montée	A	14			
Gassendi Bd	AB	Tribunal Cours du	B	15			

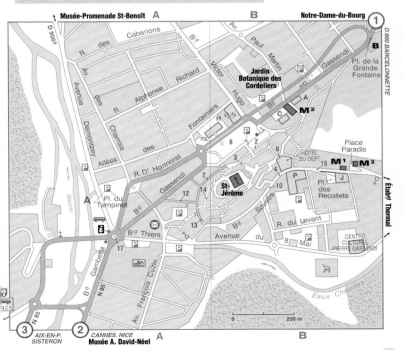

321

The blown and stained glass is the work of Canadian-born artist David Rabinowitch (1943-).

Musée Alexandra-David-Néel ★

Access by ② on the town plan. Along the road to Nice, left just after the Total petrol station, 27 avenue Maréchal-Juin 🕐 *All year: guided tours (2hrs) at 10am, 2pm, 3.30pm, 5pm. No charge -* ☎ *04 92 31 32 38 - www.alexandra-david-neel.org.*

In 1924, Alexandra David-Néel spent months disguised as a Tibetan beggar in order to cross the Himalayas and reach Tibet and its capital Lhasa, the Forbidden City. On her return, she wrote her most famous book, *Voyage d'une Parisienne à Lhassa*, translated into English as *My Journey to Lhasa*.

Address Book

For coin categories, see the Legend on the front cover flap.

EATING OUT

🍴 **Brasserie Le France** – *54 bd Gassendi -* ☎ *04 92 31 03 70 - closed Mon except in Aug.* This brasserie offers a good range of meat and fish dishes in a relaxed setting. At the first sign of sun, patrons leave the banquettes in the dining room to sit on the terrace beneath the plane trees.

🍴 **L'Étable** – *1 r. de l'Hubac -* ☎ *04 92 36 10 20 - closed 2 wks in May, 3 wks in Nov, Sun evening and Mon except 15 July-15 Sept*. A welcome address in this narrow, boutique-lined street in the old town. The dining room, decorated with a manger, has pretty blue and yellow tablecloths and curtains. The Provençal cuisine uses the best ingredients.

WHERE TO STAY

🏨 **Hôtel Julia** – *Pl Pied-de-Ville -* ☎ *04 92 32 22 96, www.aples-hebergement.com - closed Dec-Feb - 18rms:* 🍴 *restaurant.* This little hotel is on a small square with a fountain. The rooms, in rustic style, are clean and light-filled, and breakfast under the lime tree is delightful.

🏨🍴 **Hôtel Villa Gaïa** – *2km/1mi SW of Digne-les-Bains on N 85 -* ☎ *04 92 31 21 60 - hotel.gaia@wanadoo.fr- closed 22 Oct-14 Apr -* 🅿 *- 10rms -* 🍴🍴 *restaurant.* A family atmosphere pervades this bourgeois residence in a large park with huge old trees. Let yourself be pampered and make the most of its perfect peace and quiet. Tastefully furnished rooms, library, lounge and terrace. Evening meal only, reserved for hotel guests.

THERMAL WATERS

Société Thermale– *29 av. des Thermes, 3km/2mi from Digne-* ☎ *04 92 32 32 92 - www.eurothermes.com - open daily except Sun 8am-1pm, 4-6pm, Sat 8am-1pm, closed Dec to mid-Feb.* The sulphurous waters of Digne spring from a source some 850m/ 2 78 ft deep. They are reputed to clear the respiratory tract, calm rheumatism and contribute to general health and beauty.

SHOPPING

The Digne region abounds in craftspeople; the tourist office regularly updates its brochure listing their addresses. In the village of **Champtercier**, you can observe the making of *santons*, small figurines for Christmas crêches that are a specialty of the area.

Market – Esplanade Charles-de-Gaulle, Wed and Sun. This typically Provençal market covers the entire esplanade, offering local produce.

Rue de l'Hubac and rue Pied de la Ville – *R. de l'Hubac and rue Pied de la Ville* – These two arteries lined with clothes boutiques and food stores are the main shopping streets in the old town. Boutique-workshops display the work of craftspeople (faïence, wood).

LEISURE AND SPORT

Kids **Les Ferréols** – *Plan d'eau des Ferréols -* ☎ *04 92 32 42 02 - May-June and Sept: Sat-Sun; July-Aug: daily 11am-7pm - closed Oct-Apr.* This recreation centre comprises a lake, a miniature golf course, a rock-climbing practice wall, boules courts and a volleyball court.

In 1927, David-Néel fell under the spell of the Alpes-de-Haute-Provence region and bought a house in Digne which she called Samten-Dzong (the fortress of meditation). She lived in it between her long travels throughout Asia and filled it with souvenirs from the East; she wrote many books about her unique experiences and bequeathed her house and collections to the town of Digne. A camp-table, camera and Tibetan boots in the hallway are reminders of her travels; lamps, wooden figures and religious wall hangings decorate a small Buddhist temple. There is a boutique where you can purchase Tibetan handicrafts.

▶ *Follow avenue Demontzey and quai St-Benoît towards Barles, cross the River Bléone and turn left immediately after the bridge; follow the signs to the car park.*

Musée-Promenade de la Réserve géologique de Haute-Provence

Parc St-Benoît 🕐 *Apr to Oct: 9am-noon, 2-5.30pm (Fri: 4.30pm); Nov to Mar: daily except Sat-Sun 9am-noon, 2-5.30pm (Fri: 4.30pm).* 🕐 *closed 25 Dec-1 Jan and public holidays from Nov to Mar. 4.60€, children 2.75€ -* ☎ *04 92 36 70 70.*

The centre is accessible on foot from the parking lot by three marked paths: the *sentier d'Eau* (Water path) winds through an art exhibit; the Cairns path was created in 1998 by A. Goldworthy, a specialist in land art; the *sentier des Remparts* branches off along the medieval walls. The museum, lodged in an old house in the St-Benoît park, overlooking Digne, stands on tufa, a sort of rock formed as a deposit from a petrifying waterfall★.

In the **geological museum**, the region's rich geological history is described through film and multimedia, 3-D models and hundreds of fossils including a model of a 4.5m/15ft-long ichthyosaurus (the original fossil is still *in situ;* 👤 *see Préalpes de DIGNE,* 1). The aquarium contains nautili and limuli, which are considered living fossils.

Excursion

St-Michel-de-Cousson★

▶ *11km/6.8mi. Leave Digne by the D 20 leading to Entrages.*

As the road passes near the present-day spa, the ruins of the Roman baths can be seen below on the right; the road then continues towards the Col de Corobin across a typical landscape of parallel ravines dug by erosion through mountains of black marl known as **robines**. Turn right onto D 120 towards **Entrages**, a charming village overlooking the Eaux-Chaudes Valley. Go through the village and park the car in front of the heavily restored 17C church.

A signpost marks the beginning of the path leading to the Cousson's twin summits *(2hr easy walk; turn left at the Pas d'Entrages);* from the top of the ridge, there is a lovely view of Entrages.

The **Chapelle Saint-Michel-de-Cousson** stands on top of the cliff above the Asse Valley. Covered with *lauzes* (slabs of schist), it is plainly decorated apart from the fragment of a Merovingian sarcophagus placed above the doorway.

A pilgrimage takes place every year on Whit Monday (Pentecost). There is a splendid overall view★ of the Asse Valley, of the Clue de Chabrières to the south and of the Bléone Valley further west. The astronomer Pierre Gassendi used to study the skies from this vantage-point.

▶ *It is possible to continue along the path to the main Cousson Summit (1 516m/4 974ft); walk round to the left of it to return to the Pas d'Entrages.*

PRÉALPES DE DIGNE

MICHELIN MAP 334 E/F/G 7/8

Although the ancient road from Sisteron to Nice once linked the southern Préalpes de Digne to the Roman towns of the Midi, these Provençal mountains lying between the River Durance and River Verdon are the least populated and most desolate in the Alps region. Gradually left bare as a result of erosion, they were replanted with Austrian pines, larches and forest pines which help to retain the soil they grow on. There are, however, some pastures and cultivated basins. Mountain streams have cut deep into the limestone ridges, creating remote clues (gorges) which testify to the amazingly complex geology of the southern Préalpes. 🛈 *Contact the tourist office in Digne.*

▶ **Orient Yourself:** From Digne, you venture into the Préalpes on winding roads: the D 900A to the north and the D 20 to the south.

🕐 **Organizing Your Time:** The Vallée du Bès will take you half a day to see. If you add excursions ② and ③, you will have a well-filled day.

ⓖ **Also See:** Nearby Sights: CASTELLANE, DIGNE-LES-BAINS, Vallée de la Moyenne DURANCE, Monastère de GANAGOBIE, Route NAPOLÉON, Lac de SERRE-PONÇON, SEYNE, SISTERON, Plateau de VALENSOLE

Highlights

Réserve géologique de Haute-Provence – Founded in 1984, this geological reserve includes 47 municipalities surrounding the town of Digne and covers an area of 1 900km2/734mi2.

The protected territory, the largest of its kind in Europe, offers geologists and laymen unique study opportunities, enabling them to follow the evolution of the earth over 300 million years, in particular the succession of upheavals which shaped the region's mountains. The strata of transverse valleys -- Verdaches, Chabrières and Péroué -- for instance, are like an open book of local geology. Looking at the rough, often barren landscape today, it is hard to believe that the reserve lies in what was a vast "Alpine sea" during the Secondary Era, a natural habitat for fish, molluscs and coral.

Sedimentary deposits were laid during each era. The amount varied considerably, but the density was amazing. Plant deposits inform us about the flora of the Primary Era. Relics of the Secondary Era, characterised by a rich marine life, include the skeleton of a large reptile and numerous ammonite fossils, while the Tertiary Era preserved for us the footprints left by birds combing the shores of the Alpine sea.

Eighteen sites protected for their exceptional scientific value are scattered over the whole area; some are open to the public. During the summer months, you can participate in a day-long nature study tour led by a qualified mountain *accompagnateur*. (*Information: Association Empreinte -* ☎ *04 92 32 50 26*).

Excursions

① VALLÉE DU BÈS ★

ROUND TOUR STARTING FROM DIGNE *95km/59mi – 3hr on foot excluding visits.*

Digne-les-Bains ‡ ‡ – ⓖ See DIGNE-LES-BAINS.

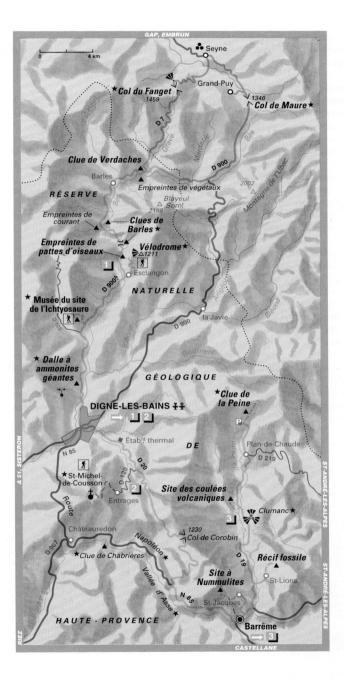

> *Drive north out of Digne-les-Bains along D 900A, which runs through the Bléone Valley.*

Dalle à ammonites géantes★

1km/0.6mi from Digne, on the left of the road.
This tilted black-limestone slab bears the imprint of 1 553 ammonites, some of them 70cm/28in in diameter, which lived here 200 million years ago.

Musée du site de l'Ichtyosaure★

> *After driving 8km/5mi north of Digne along D 900A towards Barles, park the car in the marked car park and continue on foot along the path at the end of the car park. Access: 1hr there on foot, plus return; walking shoes and water supplies are essential.*

The path runs along the left bank through a pretty oak wood, past the little waterfalls of the Bélier gorge. The path then climbs the opposite hillside in a series of turns to the Col du Jas. On reaching this broad plateau, turn left and head down to the excavation site where the fossil lies under glass protection.

Ichthyosaurus, a 4.5m/15ft-long, fish-like reptile, swam in the sea which covered the whole region 180 million years ago. Its fossilized skeleton, in remarkable condition, has been left in situ under glass. A fresco shows the natural environment of this contemporary of the dinosaurs.

Site du "Vélodrome"

> *8km/5mi from the intersection of D 900A and D 103. Leave the car before the bridge over D 900A. Follow the path signposted "Serre d'Esclangon." About 2hr there on foot, plus return.*

The itinerary goes across an area where the reddish soil contrasts with the black pines growing on it. Keep going left until you breast the first rise and proceed towards the ruins of the village of Esclangon; turn right and aim for the Serre d'Esclangon Summit.

The panorama unfolding to the west reveals one of the finest geological phenomena in the Alps, known as the **"Vélodrome"**★. This huge fan-shaped natural feature is the result, over a period of 16 million years, of the folding of layers of sandstone within a basin subjected to intense compression from the surrounding mountains. Constant erosion gradually dug the Bès Valley and gave the landscape its present appearance.

The Vélodrome

Prints of bird feet (Empreintes de pattes d'oiseaux)

▶ *10km/6.2mi from Digne-les-Bains; the site is signposted and it is possible to park on the left-hand side of D 900A.* ⌁ *About 10 min there and back.*

Twenty million years ago, the sea had not yet retreated from the area and birds resembling plovers pecked away at what they could find in the damp sand of the beach. Their footprints are clearly visible in several places and a cast with an explanatory panel is exhibited at the roadside.

Various other geological imprints *(signposted and with explanatory panels)*, which can be seen on the way to Barles, illustrate the exceptional geological diversity of the region.

Clues de Barles★

The road just gets through these two gorges squeezed alongside the mountain stream. The second gorge is the most impressive: a rocky knoll, obstructing the valley at the end of an extremely narrow passage, outlines its deeply indented silhouette against the sky.

The **imprints of water currents** visible further on are evidence of what life was like 300 million years ago, when the region enjoyed a tropical climate.

As you leave Barles, it is worthwhile to stop at the **Maison de la géologie** which has temporary exhibits.

Clue de Verdaches

It is covered with rich green vegetation.

Col de Maure★

Alt 1 346m/4 416ft. The pass links the valleys of the River Blanche and River Bès. In summer, these tributaries of the River Durance are reduced to a mere trickle and the arid appearance of their valleys is striking.

⌁ The small ski resort of **Grand Puy** close to the pass, in a setting of larch woods and pastures, is a winter annexe of Seyne, situated lower down in the valley.

Seyne – ⌁ *See SEYNE.*

▶ *From Seyne, drive south along D 7.*

The road goes through a green valley, then a small forested massif before reaching the pass.

Col du Fanget★

Alt 1 459m/4 787ft. There is a fine **view** to the north with the Blanche Valley in the foreground, flanked on the right by the Dormillouse Summit (2 505m/8 219ft) and Montagne de la Blanche, with the Parpaillon Massif and Gapençais mountains in the distance. ⌁ Le Fanget offers some 16km/10mi of cross-country ski trails and groomed trails for snowshoers.

▶ *The narrow road joins D 900A near the Clue de Verdaches.*

② Route du Col de Corobin★

FROM DIGNE TO BARRÊME *32km along D 20 and N 85 – 1hr*

▶ *From Digne, drive along D 20 towards Entrages (⌁ see DIGNE-LES-BAINS: Excursions).*

On the left, there is an ancient farm with a dovecote on either side, where Napoleon is said to have stopped for a meal on his way back from Elba. Further on, the road runs through the Cousson forest, then climbs over the Col de Corobin to join N 85 leading southeast to Barrême.

Barrême is situated at the confluence of the three small Asse valleys: the Asse de Moriez (east), Asse de Blieux (southeast) and Asse de Clumanc (north). Downstream from Barrême, the river is simply called Asse as it flows towards the impressive **Clues de Chabrières**★ (⟳ *see ROUTE NAPOLÉON*).

③ Asse de Clumanc

▶ **FROM BARRÊME TO PLAN-DE-CHAUDE** *18km/11.2mi along D 19*
The road closely follows the River Asse de Clumanc from Barrême to Plan-de-Chaude. The valley contains a wealth of fossil-bearing layers which provide an invaluable insight into successive geological upheavals. The sites are listed and marked with explanatory panels.

Fossil nummulites at St-Jacques
A path leads in 10min to a site close to the village of St-Jacques, where 40 million-year-old fossils can be seen in limestone strata. *The site can also be reached from Barrême by following the "Voie impériale" footpath (1hr).*

Fossil reef of St-Lions (Récif fossile de St-Lions)
Walking shoes recommended. Car park at the entrance to the town.
A path leads through brushwood in 30min to a site consisting of a coral reef which used to rest on shingle in this shallow part of the Alpine sea 35 million years ago. Sea urchins and oysters are recognisable in the strata; they were subsequently buried under a layer of clay.

Clumanc
The village houses covered with *lauzes* are spread out along the mountain stream. The Romanesque Église Notre-Dame houses an interesting tabernacle in gilt wood.
A path starting north of the village leads in 10min to the **panorama**★ of the castle ruins. The hillside illustrates a period in the formation of the Alps with a mixture of marl and conglomerate rocks, successively folded and eroded.

Volcanic lava flow (Site des coulées volcaniques)
▶ *Drive to the intersection with D 219, leave the car in the car park in front of the post office and follow the marked footpath for 15min.*
This is the only evidence of volcanic activity in the area: following a volcanic eruption which occurred 35 million years ago, lava and ashes settled at the bottom of the Alpine sea and were carried to this place.

Clue de la Peine★
Leave the car in the parking area near some houses. Follow the path signposted "Clue de la Peine" for 20min.
The stream has cut through layers of limestone deposited during the Secondary Era, which were folded into vertical ribbons 60 million years later during the geologic upheaval which formed the Alps, leaving a steep gorge.

▶ *Follow the same itinerary to return to Barrême, or turn left at Plan-de-Chaude on D 219 to Notre-Dame-d'Entraigues, Lambruisse and St-André-des-Alpes.*

VALLÉE DE LA MOYENNE DURANCE★

MICHELIN MAP 81 FOLDS 5, 6, 15 AND 16, 114 FOLD 5 OR 245 FOLDS 20 AND 33
LOCAL MAP SEE P 331

The River Durance, which is the last main tributary of the Rhône as it makes its way to the sea, has its source near Briançon and flows along a 324km/201mi course before joining the Rhône. Frédéric Mistral, the famous Provençal poet, used to say: "The mistral (a strong wind blowing down the Rhône Valley), Parliament and the Durance are the curses of Provence." The most unpredictable major river of the southern Alps certainly proved a real threat to local people and, for a long time, defied all attempts to harness it. Since the 1960s, however, the river has become one of the great economic assets of the region, a vital source of urban water supply and hydroelectricity.

South of Sisteron, the Durance enters the Mediterranean Basin. Here, the river bed is less steep and almost 1km/0.6mi wide, the valley broadens and the river flows between stony banks; its rate of flow is regulated by a network of dams and canals built along its course or that of its tributaries. As a result, new ecosystems have been able to flourish in the river valley, for instance wooded areas favourable to the development of animal life including colonies of beavers. *La Ferme de Font-Robert - 04160 Château-Arnaud-St-Auban July to Aug: daily 10am-7pm; rest of year: 9am-noon, 2-6pm closed Sat-Sun and public holidays, except July to Aug - ☎ 04 92 64 02 62 - www.la-moyenne-durance.fr*

▶ **Orient Yourself:** This alluvial corridor, some 100km/62.5mi wide, borders on the east the escarpments of the Valensole plateau, and on the west the wooded spurs of the Lure and Luberon mountains. At Volonne, you can rejoin the Route Napoléon and continue through the Forcalquier and Mane regions.

◉ **Don't Miss:** Admire the view of the entire region from the chapelle St-Jean; the "village perché" of Montfort; the romanesque church of St-Donnat; and the spectacular rocks at Mées.

◷ **Organizing Your Time:** The circuit along the Durance takes 3 hours.

Kids At St-Auban, there is a lake with a waterslide.

◔ **Also See:** Nearby Sights: CÉRESTE, DIGNE-LES-BAINS, Préalpes de DIGNE, FORCALQUIER, Monastère de GANAGOBIE, GRÉOUX-LES-BAINS, MANE, MANOSQUE, Route NAPOLÉON, RIEZ, SISTERON, Plateau de VALENSOLE.

Excursions

1 The Valley

FROM SISTERON TO MANOSQUE *74km/46mi – about 3hr*

Sisteron★★ – ◔ *See SISTERON.*

▶ *Leave Sisteron by ② on the town plan and drive along N 85.*

The road follows the Durance harnessed by the Salignac Dam, passes the mouth of the Jabron winding between the river and the steep edge of the Montagne de Lure and skirts the Lac de l'Escale Dam as it reaches Château-Arnoux.

Château-Arnoux-Saint-Auban

The national gliding centre is nearby and the Festival de Jazz des Alpes-de-Haute-Provence takes place in the town; things are especially lively during the Sunday markets. The square 16C **castle**, flanked by round and square towers, is now the town hall and overlooks a garden, arboretum and a keep-fit trail.

▷ *2km/1.2mi further on, along N 96, turn right along the road signposted "Route touristique de St-Jean."*

Belvédère de la chapelle St-Jean★

🚶 *15min there and back on foot. Leave the car at the top of the hill (car park near the chapel) and climb along the footpath to a viewing table.*

There is a fine **panoramic** view from west to east of the Montagne de Lure, the Durance Valley, Sisteron, the Lac de l'Escale Dam and the Rochers des Mées.

▷ *Return to N 96 and continue south.*

Montfort

This hilltop "village perché" in a charming **site**★ overlooking the Durance is extremely picturesque with its stepped streets, lined with charming old houses, climbing up to the restored 16C castle; there is a fine view of the Durance Valley and Valensole Plateau.

Address Book

For coin categories, see the Legend on the cover flap.

EATING OUT

🍴 **Au Goût du Jour** – *04160 Château-Arnoux-St-Auban -* ☎ *04 92 64 48 48 - goutdujour@bonneetape.com - closed 3 Jan-11 Feb, 22 Nov-7 Dec.* This restaurant is the annex of the Bonne Étape, which is well reputed for the quality of its food. It offers a simpler menu at a lower price chalked up on a slate. The food caters to modern tastes, as the restaurant's name suggests. Pretty dining room in Provençal colours.

🍴 **L'Oustaou de la Foun** – *04160 Château-Arnoux-St-Auban - 1.5km/1mi N of Château-Arnoux-St-Auban on N 85 -* ☎ *04 92 62 65 30, loustaoudelafoun@wanadoo.fr - closed 1-9 Jan, 22-30 June, 1st week of Nov, Sun evening and Mon.* This tree-shaded former farm just off the highway was once a postal station. Inside, regional cuisine is served in a vaulted dining room with colorful paintings, or in a room opening into a garden.

WHERE TO STAY

🛏 **Chambre d'hôte Campagne du Barri** – *04190 Les Mées - 2km/1.25 mi NE of Les Mées on D 4, towards Digne -* ☎ *04 92 34 36 93 - www.guideweb.com.provence/bb/campagne-barri – reservations required in winter - 6rms -* 🍴 *restaurant.* This comfortable 18C house has retained traces of its history: the wallpaper in the lounge dates from 1794, and the image on the pediment is a tribute to the French Republic. Pretty rooms with a good view of the mountains and the village.

🛏 **Hôtel Villiard** – *04600 St-Auban - 3.5km/2mi SW of Château-Arnoux-St-Auban on N 96 -* ☎ *04 92 64 17 42 - hotel.villiard@wanadoo.fr - closed 15 Dec-15 Jan -* 🅿 *- 18rms -* 🍴 *restaurant.* A small hotel with a garden where tables are set out in good weather. The renovated rooms are in Provençal style, well sound-proofed and impeccably kept. Good traditional cuisine.

🛏 **Auberge de l'Abbaye** – *04230 Cruis, 16km/10mi SW of Château-Arnoux-St-Auban by D 951 and D 101 -* ☎ *04 92 77 01 93 - auberge-abbaye-cruis@wanadoo.fr - closed 3 Jan-15 Feb - 9 rms -* 🍴 *restaurant.* A good place to know in this picturesque village on the flank of the Lure mountain. Rustic interiors, rooms very well-kept and simple dining room. When weather permits, tables are set out on the terrace facing the town square. A charming atmosphere.

▶ *2km/1.2mi further on, turn right onto D 101.*

The road follows a wooded vale towards St-Donat.

Église St-Donat★
Built in the 11C on the site where St Donat, the religious recluse, had settled in the 6C, the long-neglected church is one of the rare specimens of early Romanesque style in Provence *(restoration work in progress)*.
This vast basilica was intended to contain a great number of pilgrims; three large doors ensured a steady flow of visitors.

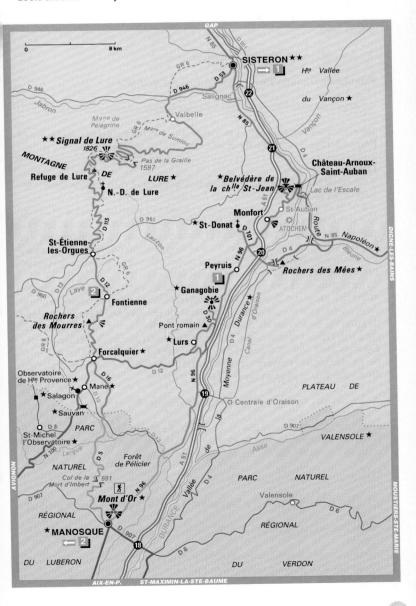

▷ *Rejoin N 96 and cross it to take D 4A across the River Durance.*

Rochers des Mées★

These 100m/328ft-high conglomerate rocks, towering over the village of Les Mées and eroded into strange shapes, are known as the **"Pénitents des Mées"** and make a particularly striking sight when illuminated at night.

▷ *Turn left and follow D 101. Return to N 96 and drive towards Manosque.*

Peyruis

The old part of the village, once guarded by a drawbridge, is still standing. The 16C church has a six-sided bell-tower, built in tufa, with gargoyles in the shape of a lion's head.

▷ *Turn right onto D 30 6km/3.7mi beyond Peyruis.*

Prieuré de Ganagobie★ – 👆 See Prieuré de GANAGOBIE.

▷ *Return towards N 96 but take the little road for Lurs just before joining it.*

The road follows an ancient Roman road and crosses the Buès over a single-arched **Roman bridge** dating from the 2C AD.

Lurs★

🅸 Place de la Fontaine, 04700 Lurs 🕐 July to Aug: Mon, Tue, Thur, Sat 9am-noon, 1.30-5.30pm; Apr to June and Sept: Mon and Thur 9am-noon, 1.30-5.30pm, Sat 9am-noon - ☎ 04 92 79 10 20. This village occupies a remarkable **position**★ on top of a rocky spur overlooking the Durance and the area around Forcalquier. Once a medieval stronghold belonging to the bishops of Forcalquier, it was gradually deserted and became derelict until it was "revived" by a group of graphic designers and is today the summer rendezvous of the printing profession through the **Rencontres internationales de Lurs** and a centre of graphic arts.

Go through the clock gate surmounted by a campanile, past the church with its interesting bell tower and along the winding streets lined with bay-windowed houses; there are traces of the old fortifications. Note the **chancellerie des compagnons de Lure,** the rustic open-air theatre, the restored **priory**, now a cultural centre, and the partly rebuilt bishops' castle. Walk round the latter along the **Promenade des Évêques**, lined with 15 oratories dating from 1864, to the Chapelle Notre-Dame-de-Vie offering fine **views** of the Durance and Préalpes de Digne on one side, of the Montagne de Lure and Forcalquier Basin on the other.

▷ *A small road south of the village leads to N 96 and to Manosque.*

Across the Durance, a canal diverts the flow of the River Bléone and River Durance to the Oraison power station. Beyond the confluence of the Asse and the Durance, the road leaves the bank of the river to reach Manosque.

Manosque★ – See 👆 MANOSQUE.

② The Montagne de Lure and the Pays du Contadour

FROM MANOSQUE TO SISTERON 87km/54mi – about 2hr 30min – 👆 see local map

From Manosque, drive north along D 5 via the Col de la Mort d'Imbert which offers lovely **views** of Manosque and its surroundings. Turn right onto D 16.

Forcalquier★ – 🕭 *See FORCALQUIER.*

▷ *Leave Forcalquier along D 12, northwest of the town plan.*

Rochers des Mourres
These rock formations, eroded into strange shapes, stand on either side of the road.
On the way to Fontienne, the **view** extends to the Durance Valley on the right.

Fontienne
The small Romanesque chapel of this tiny village, perched on an escarpment, has a belfry-wall with twin openings; the castle goes back to the 13C.

St-Étienne-les-Orgues
This village marks the gateway of the Montagne de Lure. Its past prosperity was based on the production of numerous remedies based on aromatic and medicinal plants, which were sold by pedlars as far away as the Auvergne and Bourgogne regions. The 16C houses have mullioned windows and archivolts over the doorways. The **church** (🕭 *key available Mon to Fri from the Mairie (town hall) - ☎ 04 92 73 02 00)* has a polygonal chancel and the round towers of the 13C **castle** date from the 18C.

▷ *D 113 rises through the sloping lavender fields, then past pines and cedars and into dense forest.* Just beyond the Oratoire St-Joseph, a stony road on the right leads to Notre-Dame de Lure.

Montagne de Lure★
This impressive ridge, which prolongs Mont Ventoux eastwards over a distance of some 30km/19mi, is austere and practically uninhabited; as the altitude rises, holm oaks, scrubland, lavender fields and cedar trees gradually give way to pastures which release a strong scent of aromatic plants. The northern slopes are more densely forested with firs near the summits, replaced by beeches, larches, oaks and black Austrian pines lower down. The arid landscapes of the Montagne de Lure were extensively described by the Provençal writer Jean Giono, a native of Manosque.

Notre-Dame de Lure
(🕭 *key available in exchange for an identity document - ☎ 04 92 73 02 00, or tourist office - ☎ 04 92 73 02 57)*
The monks of Boscodon Abbey built a modest monastery here in 1165. The only part of this remaining is a large barrel-vaulted room located beneath the small hermitage, a more recent edifice. The abbey church, which became a pilgrims' chapel, has now recovered its original appearance through extensive restoration work.
The oak and three lime trees in front of the chapel are several centuries old.

▷ *Return to D 113 and continue upwards.*

Refuge de Lure
This small ski centre equipped with a few ski lifts and cross-country trails offers a wide **view**. A memorial to the 17C Belgian astronomer, Wendelin, who set up the **first observatory in France**, stands at the roadside 1.5km/0.9mi further on.

▷ *Continue for another 3.5km/2.2mi and leave the car on the platform of the telecommunications transmitter. Access is restricted in winter – the road between the Refuge de Lure and Vabelle is usually closed between 15 November and 31 May; enquire in St-Étienne-les-Orgues.*

Signal de Lure★★

The mountain's highest summit (1 826m/5 991ft) offers a vast **panorama** of Monte Viso, Mont Pelvoux, the Vercors Massif, the Cévennes range, Mont Ventoux and sometimes the Mediterranean coast. A little further on, to the left, is another good **view**: an opening in the mountains reveals the Jabron Valley.

Beyond the Pas de la Graille, the road goes down through a splendid beech forest to the Jabron Valley overlooked by the steep slopes of the Montagne de Lure.

▷ *Follow D 53 to Sisteron.*

Sisteron★★ – 👜 *See SISTERON.*

Hike

Walk to the Pénitents des Mées★

3hr on foot. Start from the camp site situated beyond Notre-Dame de la Salette on D 101. Leave the car at the side of the road.

🔼 Go down to the bottom of the valley and cross the low wall of the second reservoir to reach the north bank. From there, a path, marked in green, winds up *(keep to the right)* to the Forêt des Pénitents which is rich in Mediterranean vegetation. As you reach the pass (alt 600m/1 968ft), walk 91m/100yd to the left for striking views of the "Pénitents." Return to the pass and go down to the rocky ridge and the foot of the "Pénitents" *(a few steep sections)*. Continue left along the path *(facing the Durance Valley)* until you reach a surfaced road which skirts the old aqueduct and leads to the village of Les Mées. According to local legend, the rocks were formed when a group of monks fell in love with the beautiful Arab girls whom a local lord had brought back from his campaigns against the Saracens. St Donat punished the monks by turning them into stones as they walked in procession along the Durance.

The "Pénitents des Mées" – a miracle of geology or theology?

EMBRUN★

POPULATION 6 152
MICHELIN MAP 334 G5
LOCAL MAP SEE BARRAGE ET LAC DE SERRE-PONÇON

Embrun is picturesquely perched on a rocky ledge, 80m/262ft above the River Durance and the Lac de Serre-Ponçon. Its church, the finest in Dauphiné, testifies to its past influence as a religious centre. Today, the town is a pleasant summer resort offering a wide choice of water sports on the lake as well as canoeing on the Durance and hiking in the surrounding area. In winter, it is a centre of cross-country and Alpine skiing practised on the slopes of Les Orres and near the mountain village of Crévoux. *place Général-Dosse - 05200 Embrun July to Aug: daily 9am-7.30pm, Sun and public holidays 9.30am-noon, 4-7pm; Sept and 11 Dec to June: daily except Sun and public holidays 9am-noon, 2-6.30; Oct to 10 Dec: Sat 9am-noon, 4-6pm - ☎ 04 92 43 72 72 - www.ot-embrun.fr*

▶ **Orient Yourself:** Embrun lies on N 94, between Gap and Briançon, on the edge of the Parc national des Écrins and close to the lake of Serre-Ponçon, some 24 km/15 mi south of Guillestre at the threshold of the Queyras region.
- **Organizing Your Time:** You might lunch at Embrun, or take a picnic along on a hike or to one of the area's swimming beaches.
- **Especially for Kids:** The Tour Brune has a nature musem.
- **Also See:** Nearby Sights: L'ARGENTIÈRE-LA-BESSÉE, BARCELONNETE, CEILLAC, Vallée de FREISSINIÈRES, GAP, Route des GRANDES ALPES, GUILLESTRE, MONT-DAUPHIN, Route NAPOLÉON, Le QUEYRAS, Lac de SERRE-PONÇON, SEYNE, L'UBAYE, VAL D'ALLOS, VAR

A Religious Centre

During the Roman occupation, Embrun was an important town on the way from Briançon to Arles. It later became the main religious centre of the Alpes-Maritimes region and under the Holy Roman Empire, the archbishops of Embrun were granted temporal power over the whole region and the right to mint their own coinage.
From the 14C onwards, the pilgrimage to Notre-Dame-du-Réal attracted large crowds. The rank of canon conferred on King Louis XI during his visit was passed on to all his successors and is now bestowed on the president of France.
Owing to its geographical position, Embrun was attacked many times: by the Sarracens, by the Huguenots during the Wars of Religion and by the duke of Savoie, but only the Revolution deprived it of its special religious status.

Around the Old Town

Picturesque squares, brightly painted houses and pretty balconies; bubbling fountains and distant birdsong: it's hard to believe that the austere peaks of the Queyras are only a matter of miles away.

Place de l'Archevêché
The Belvédère du Roc offers a fine view of the Durance Valley and Morgon Mountain. The cathedral chapter held meetings in the 13C **Maison des Chanonges**. It is one of the rare examples of medieval domestic architecture in the area.

Tour Brune ★

🔲 🕐 *Mid-June to mid- Sept: daily except Mon 10.30am-12.30pm, 3-7pm, Sun 10.30am-12.30pm; rest of year enquire for time and charge. 2€, children 1€ - ☎ 04 92 43 23 31.*
This 12C tower is the former keep of the episcopal castle; it now houses a **Musée du Paysage,** devoted to the Parc national des Écrins. There is a fine view from the terrace *(viewing table).*

Rue de la Liberté and rue Clovis-Hugues ★

At no 6 rue de la Liberté, the governor's palace boasts a beautiful wooden **doorway**★ in Renaissance style, surmounted by a lion carved in the round. Continue along rue Clovis-Hugues and admire the 12C carved façade between no 29 and no 31. Further on, a beautiful 16C fountain in red marble decorates place St-Marcellin and there are interesting 14C corbelled houses along rue Caffe.

Cathédrale Notre-Dame-du-Réal ★ 45min

"Réal" is a distortion of *"royal:"* the church was once Notre-Dame-des-Rois, or kings, because of its fresco of the Adoration of the Magi, destroyed by Protestants in 1585. The edifice was built during the transitional period from the Romanesque style to the Gothic style (late 12C, early 13C). Its originality lies in the alternate use of black schist and white limestone. The steeple was rebuilt in the 19C, taking the 14C steeple as a model (💧 *see Introduction: Art and architecture).*

Portail "le Réal" ★

This is a remarkable example of Lombard art. The arch of the doorway is supported by pink marble columns; the front ones stand on two squatting lions. At the back are two slender columns resting on small figures one of which, held by two others, is said to be the dean of the cathedral chapter who refused to pay the workers. Pilgrims prayed in front of *The Adoration of the Magi* which used to decorate the tympanum; the painting is now reproduced as a mosaic inside the cathedral and the tympanum shows Christ surrounded by the symbols of the Evangelists.

Interior

🕐 *Daily 9am-6pm, guided tours of cathedral and treasury (1hr15min) July to Aug at 9pm Tue and 10am Thur, on request at the tourist office. 4.30€- ☎ 04 92 43 72 72.*
The Byzantine influence explains the absence of a transept. The chancel, in pure Romanesque style, was once covered with frescoes. The late-15C organ, bought with a bequest from Louis XI, is one of the oldest in France. Opposite, above the altar, there is a 16C picture depicting the Entombment of Christ.

Treasury ★

🕐 *July to Aug: Wed 10am-noon, Sun 3.30-5.30pm; rest of year, contact the tourist office for information. 3 € - ☎ 04 92 43 72 72.*
It was one of the richest in France before being plundered in the 16C by the Protestant troops of the duke of Lesdiguières. However, it still contains an important collection of religious objects, the Embrun Missal and 14C illuminated antiphonaries.

Chapelles des Cordeliers

Houses the tourist office. 🕐 *Hours same as tourist office (see above). No charge - ☎ 04 92 43 72 72.*
The side chapels of the former Franciscan church have survived; they are decorated with recently restored 15C and 16C **murals**★. The second chapel tells the story of St Anthony of Padua, the most famous Franciscan after St Francis himself.

Excursions

The tourist office sells maps covering the walks described below.

Les Orres ✳

🏠 *05200 Les Orres* 🕐 *Mon-Fri 9am-12.30pm, 2.30-6pm (Fri 5pm)* 🕐 *closed Sat-Sun and public holidays -* ☎ *04 92 44 01 61 - www.lesorres.com; reservation service -* ☎ *04 92 44 19 17*

▷ *17km/10.6mi southeast. Leave Embrun along N 94 towards Gap, drive for 2km/1.2mi and turn left onto D 40.*

The twisting road follows the Eyssalette Valley and affords lovely views of the northern part of the Lac de Serre-Ponçon. This winter resort (alt 1 600m/5 249ft), created in 1970 and named after the old village on the opposite slope, developed rapidly to form one of the main winter sports resorts of the southern Alps. Les Orres and its annexes of Le Pramouton (alpine skiing) and Champs-Lacas (cross-country skiing) offer a wide choice of activities including snowmobile, paragliding and

Address Book

For coin categories, see the Legend on the cover flap.

EATING OUT

⊖**Le Co'case** – *Bd Pasteur (pl. du Gén.-Dosse) -* ☎ *04 92 43 06 68 - closed Mar - Apr and Oct-Nov.* Fancy a cocktail before you eat? Settle in here and dip into the menu afterwards to read about salads, regional dishes, crêpes and a selection of home-made ice cream to tempt any food-lover. Food is served in a shaded courtyard.

⊖**Les Manins** – *Boissel-les-Manins - 05200 St-Sauveur - 8.5km/5mi S of Embrun on N 94, D 40 and left on D 39A -* ☎ *04 92 43 09 27, eric.boissel@free. fr – open Jul-Aug -* 🍴 *- reservations required from Sept to June.* Breathtaking view of the Lac de Serre-Ponçon from the terrace of this mountain chalet. The small charming dining room is entirely panelled in wood. Eclectic cuisine including charcuterie, pizzas, crêpes, and home-made desserts.

WHERE TO STAY

⊖ **Camping Les Esparons** – *05200 Baratier - 4km/2.5mi S of Embrun on N 94 then D 40 -* ☎ *04 92 43 02 73 - info@ lesesparons.com - open 15 Jun-1 Sept -* 🍴 *- reservations advised - 83 pitches.* This simple campsite offers spacious pitches bounded by apple trees. There is a swimming pool, and games for old

and young alike. In the village nearby (700m/770yd) there are facilities for tennis and riding.

⊖ **Camping Le Verger** – *05200 Baratier - 4km/2.5mi S of Embrun on N 94 then D 40 -* ☎ *04 92 43 15 87 - campingleverger@wanadoo.fr - 110 pitches – catering available on site.* Le Verger is a good choice for its selection of chalets in all sizes available for hire, with plenty of room in between them and with fireplace or without. Shaded pitches. Heated swimming pool and children's play area.

⊖⊖ **Hôtel Notre-Dame** – *Av. du Gén.-Nicolas -* ☎ *04 92 43 08 36 - closed 20 Dec-30 Jan, Sun evening and Mon out of season - 7rms -* ⊖⊖ *restaurant.* This family hotel slightly out of the town centre has a small garden in the front which can be used as a terrace in the summer. Rooms are small but comfortable. Traditional fare prepared by the proprietress.

⊖⊖ **Hôtel de la Mairie** – *Pl. de la Mairie -* ☎ *04 92 43 20 65 - courrier@ hoteldelamairie.com - closed 1-20 May, Oct and Nov - 24rms -* ⊖⊖ *restaurant.* Renovated rooms, light and well-kept, a pleasant restaurant with a terrace opposite a stone fountain, and a traditional cuisine as delicious as it is copious. This pretty house in the old town offers many advantages.

snowboarding. Summer activities include swimming, tennis, trap-shooting, riding and aerial sports.

Prelongis and Fontaine chair-lifts★

🎿 🕐 *Daily 9am-4.30pm, closed from end of Apr to mid-June and Sept-Nov. 7.50€ (for chairlifts) Alt 2 408m/7 900ft.* Fine views of the ski slopes running through a larch and pine forest below the Boussolenc Peak. From the top the view encompasses part of the Lac de Serre-Ponçon and the Embrun area.

Crévoux

▶ *13km/8mi. From Embrun, drive east (the road starts in front of a factory) via Coin, then join the route du Col de Parpaillon.* The small mountain village of Crévoux, a popular meeting place for skiers, is enclosed by the slopes of the Méale Mountain and the rocky wall of the St-André Peak, streaming with waterfalls.

🚶 The best views around Embrun

The beautiful Lac du Serre-Ponçon is surrounded by peaks which are relatively accessible and offer stunning prospects of the lake and countryside. Among the best are **Mont Guillaume** *(2 550m/8 366ft, 3hr on foot)* which gives views over the Durance and the lake from the mountain chapel at the summit, the **Pic de Morgon** *(2 324m/7 682ft, 2hr 30min, Route du Boscodon from the car park at L'Ours)* with a splendid view of the lake and the Aiguilles de Chabrières (🚶 *see Lac de SERRE PONÇON,* **2** *).*

VAL D'ENTRAUNES★★

MICHELIN MAP 341 A/B 1/3

Set in the middle of the **Parc national du Mercantour**, the Val d'Entraunes is one of the remotest areas of the Alpes-Maritimes *département*, even though the Côte d'Azur lies only 100km/62mi to the southeast. The D 2202, which follows the upper Var Valley through deep, narrow passages, is one of the main routes leading from the Alps to the Nice region. The itineraries below describe the section which will enable motorists to reach the Val d'Entraunes via the Col des Champs. 🏛 *Tourist office of Guillaumes: Mairie, 06470 Guillaumes* 🕐 *Daily 9am-noon, 2-6pm -* ☎ *04 93 05 57 76, www.pays-de-guillaumes.com*

▶ **Orient Yourself:** To get to Entraunes from Barcelonnette, take the route des Grandes Alpes and the col de la Cayolle, or go by the col d'Allos, Colmars and the col des Champs. From Puget-Theniers or Entrevaux, drive up through the gorges de Dalius.

😍 **Don't Miss:** The gorges de Daluis are spectacular; try to see the religious sites at Entraunes, St-Martin d'Entraunes, Châteaunef d'Entraunes and Guillaumes.

🕐 **Organizing Your Time:** You'll need a half-day to see the Val d'Entraunes, or an entire day if you pause in the Gorges de Daluis

Kids **Especially for Kids:** in the hameau de Villeplane, there are donkey rides at the Gîte itinérance - ☎ 04 93 05 56 01 - www.itinerance.net

👣 **Also See:** Nearby Sights: ANNOT, AURON, BARCELONNETTE, BEUIL, Gorges du CIANS, COLMARS, ENTREVAUX, Route des GRANDES ALPES, PRA-LOUP, PUGET-THÉNIERS, Vallée de la TINÉE, L'UBAYE, VAL-D'ALLOS

Excursions

Haute Vallée du Var

FROM COLMARS TO ST-MARTIN-D'ENTRAUNES *30km/18.6mi – allow 1hr*

The present road was built at the end of the 19C by the chasseurs alpins (Alpine troops) and runs alongside a rock face which appears to be about to crumble away at any moment. The surface is in very poor repair and free-roaming cattle have been known to wander across the road; please drive with extra care.

Colmars – *See COLMARS.*

From Colmars, D 2 rises in a series of hairpin bends, offering views of the Lance and Upper Verdon valleys, and passes through **La Ratery,** a little summer and winter resort and the starting point for a themed botanical walk.

Col des Champs★

Alt 2 045m/6 709ft. The road runs close to the pass at an altitude of 2 095m/6 873ft, through a completely barren landscape, on the border of the Alpes-Maritimes and Alpes-de-Haute-Provence *départements*. The view is limited to the north by the Tête des Muletiers and to the south by the Frema Summit (alt 2 747m/9 012ft).

From the pass, you can walk to **Mont Rénière** *(3hr there and back; starting point: 500m/547yd beyond the pass on the left)*, a comparatively easy climb rewarded by a fine overall view of the Val d'Entraunes..

Chastelonnette

This small cross-country ski resort, also known as **Val-Pelens** is overlooked by the Aiguilles de Pelens (2 523m/8 278ft).

As the road approaches the hamlet of **Le Monnard**, there is a lovely bird's-eye view of St-Martin-d'Entraunes and the Var Valley. The mountainous area forming the horizon separates the Var and Tinée basins.

St-Martin-d'Entraunes – *See below.*

From Col de la Cayolle to Puget-Théniers

51km/32mi – allow 3hr

Col de la Cayolle – *See Route des GRANDES-ALPES, Excursions.*

Estenc

The chalets of this hamlet stand on a glacial ridge. This is where the Var, the longest river of the Alpes-Maritimes *département,* has its source.

Entraunes

This village lies in a pleasant setting at the confluence of the River Var and River Bourdoux, below the Col de la Cayolle. The church has a strange asymmetrical bell-tower.

The **Chapelle St-Sébastien**, situated at the northern end of the village, has frescoes by **Andrea de Cella**, dating from 1516, cover the wall of the apse,

For coin categories, see the Legend on the cover flap.

WHERE TO STAY

Hôtel Vallière – *06470 St-Martin-d'Entraunes -* ☎ *04 93 05 59 59 - closed 16 Oct-30 Apr -* ▣ *- 13rms: restaurant.* This hotel with the pretty, bright façade offers a warm welcome and a view over the Mercantour mountains. The highway is nearby, but the comfortable rooms compensate for this. Traditional meals are served in the large dining room.

forming a kind of Renaissance altarpiece (St Sebastian's martyrdom surmounted by the Crucifixion).

The road runs through an austere mountain landscape; beyond a tunnel, the valley opens out into the St-Martin Basin.

St-Martin-d'Entraunes

The verdant setting of this village perched on a morainic mound offers a contrast with the mostly arid landscapes of the upper Var Valley. Note the Provençal Romanesque **church** with its blind façade and a Gothic side porch. The sundial bears the inscription: "The sun guides me, your pastor shows you the way". Inside, there is a fine altarpiece, the **Retable de la Vierge de Miséricorde**★, by François Bréa (c1555).

▶ *3.5km/2.2mi beyond Villeneuve-d'Entraunes, turn left onto D 74 which rises above the Barlatte Valley.*

Châteauneuf-d'Entraunes

The village lies in a desolate landscape, above the upper Var Valley. The Baroque church has an altarpiece in Primitive style (1524), in the style of of François Bréa.

▶ *Return to D 2202 and turn left.*

Guillaumes

This old fortified village, situated at the confluence of the River Var and River Tuébi, is today a summer resort overlooked by the ruined castle (fine view). A historical pageant takes place every year on 15 August, followed by a pilgrimage to the 18C **Chapelle Notre-Dame-du-Buyei**.

Gorges de Daluis ★★

The cliff road between Guillaumes and Daluis winds its way along the west bank of the upper Var, high above the clear green water of the river. Through the tunnels is where the road affords the finest **views**★★ of the red-schist gorge dotted with fresh greenery.

Daluis

Alt 800m/2 625ft. This hilltop village overlooked by the ruins of a castle, offers the opportunity of a pleasant break at the exit of the gorge. The **Grotte du Chat** nearby,

La Vierge de la Miséricorde by Francois Bréa, the most famous painter of the Nice Gothic school.

in which an underground river appears for a distance of more than 720m/787yd, is made up of a series of chambers. Between Daluis and Entrevaux, the road follows the river which veers left at Pont de Gueydan. The valley narrows near Entrevaux.

Entrevaux★ – *See ENTREVAUX.*

On the way to Puget-Théniers along N 202, there is a lovely **view**★★ of Entrevaux.

Puget-Théniers★ – *See PUGET-THÉNIERS.*

ENTREVAUX★

POPULATION 742
MICHELIN MAP 334 I9

Mother Nature and Monsieur de Vauban, the master engineer, both played their part in shaping the town's amazing **setting**★★. Entrevaux lies on the north bank of the River Var, at the foot of a strange rocky spur crowned by a citadel; the closely set houses of the lower town, defended by a wall, seem to have changed little over the centuries. Founded in the 11C, the town was granted its charter in 1542 by King François I in recognition of its defence against the imperial troops of Charles V. When war broke out between France and Savoie in 1690, Vauban, Louis XIV's foremost military architect, linked the castle and the town with a forti-fied wall, built the main gates and battlements. 🛈 *Porte Royale – 04320 Entrevaux – ☎ 04 93 05 46 73 - www.entrevaux.info. Telephone for opening times.*

▸ **Orient Yourself:** Entrevaux is between Puget-Theniers and Annot, on N 202.
🕐 **Organizing Your Time:** For a beautiful view★ of the town, take the route of the Col de Feline, signposted "Col de Buis."
🔎 **Also See:** Nearby Sights: ANNOT, BEUIL, CASTELLANE, Gorges du CIANS, CLUES DE HAUTE-PROVENCE, Val d'ENTRAUNES, Route NAPOLÉON, PUGET-THÉNIERS, ST-JULIEN-DU-VERDON, Vallée de la TINÉE, VILLARS-SUR-VAR

The Walled Town★ 30min

Ramparts

The drawbridge of the Porte Royale, flanked by two round towers, leads into the town. The guardroom beneath the archway houses the tourist office, from where it is possible to walk along the watch-path linking the three fortified gates: Porte de France, Porte Royale and Porte d'Italie. Near the watch-path are **medieval gardens** containing medici-nal plants, culinary herbs, vegetables and fruit.

Local Cuisine

The most famous culinary speciality of the town is "secca d'Entrevaux," thin slices of dried beef sprinkled with olive oil and a squeeze of lemon.

Old town

Three main streets: Haute-Rue, Basse-Rue and rue du Marché, go through the town, linked by a network of cool and dark alleyways. Most of the houses date from the 17C and the 18C.

Cathedral

Guided tours available, contact the tourist office - ☎ 04 93 05 46 73

Entrevaux was a bishopric from the 12C to the 1789 Revolution. The present church was built between 1610 and 1627 and later incorporated into the ramparts.

The walled town and citadel of Entrevaux

B. Kaufmann/MICHELN

The **interior**★ contains a wealth of classical and Baroque decoration. The gilt altarpiece of the high altar has a beautiful 17C painting in its centre, depicting the *Assumption of the Virgin Mary* by Mimault. On either side, note the 17C stalls carved by local craftsmen. On the left-hand wall hangs a Deposition believed to be by Jouvenet and, opposite, another Deposition by Philippe de Champaigne is said to be a gift from Louis XIV. To the left of the entrance, the retable of St John the Baptist, the patron saint of Entrevaux, and the silver bust of the saint are also noteworthy (💧 *see Introduction: Festivals*). The 1717 organ by Jean Eustache was recently restored.

Sights

Citadel★

🐾 *1hr Accessible throughout the year. 3€.* Perched 135m/443ft above the town, the castle is accessible via a rampart following a zigzag course and strengthened by about 20 fortified towers. The rampart rises from the magazine to the entrance of the castle defended by a redoubt with a drawbridge dating from 1693. *The walk to the top takes about 15min. Be very careful if you are with children: the buildings are being restored. As well, the steps up from the magazine are very steep.*
It is worth climbing up to the commander's house for the remarkable **views**★ of the Var Valley and the roofs of Entrevaux.

Musée de la Moto

Rue Serpente. 🕐 *Apr to Oct: 10am-noon, 2-6pm. No charge -* ☎ *04 93 79 12 70.*
This small museum houses an interesting collection of motorcycles, all of them in working order; the oldest in the collection dates back to 1901.

Oil and flour mills (Moulins à huile et à farine)

Near place Moreau, outside the walled town. Ask at the reception for a guided tour. 3€, children 2.50€ - ☎ *04 93 05 46 73.*
The flow of the River Chalvagne used to drive the oil and flour mills; one of them still produces oil.

ÉVIAN-LES-BAINS⧓⧓⧓

POPULATION 7 273
MICHELIN MAP 328 M2 – LOCAL MAP SEE THONON-LES-BAINS

Poetically known as the "pearl of Lake Geneva," Évian is remarkably well situated between the lake and the foothills of the Préalpes du Chablais. This famous spa town is also a lakeside and climatic resort, and during the season, a centre of fashionable entertainment whose influence extends all round the lake.

Opulent public buildings and palace hotels nestling amid greenery characterize this international holiday resort, where taking the waters is not the main preoccupation. In May, orchestras and soloists participating in the the famed Rencontres Musicales appear in public concerts. ▯ *place de la Porte d'Allinges - 74500 Evian-les-Bains* ⏱ *July to Aug: daily 9am-12.30pm, 4-7pm, Sat 9am-noon, 3-7pm, Sun and public holidays 10am-noon, 3-6pm; Oct to Apr: daily 9am-noon, 2-6pm (Sat 5pm); May, June and Sept: 9am-noon, 2-6.30pm, Sat 9am-noon, 2-6pm, Sun and public holidays 10am-noon, 3-6pm* ⏱ *closed 25 Dec, 1 Jan, 1 May, 11 Nov and All Souls Day -* ☎ *04 50 75 04 26 -www.eviantourism.com*

▶ **Orient Yourself:** Évian-les-Bains is about 45min from Exit 15 of A 40, or 10km/6.25mi from Thonon-les-Bains.
😊 **Don't Miss:** A boat ride on Lac Geneva is a delightful experience.
⏱ **Organizing Your Time:** Fridays in the summer, the little train tours the town.
🧒 **Especially for Kids:** The Pré-Curieux is both fun and educational.
👣 **Also See:** Nearby Sights: ABONDANCE, AVORIAZ, CHÂTEL, MORZINE, THONON-LES-BAINS, YVOIRE

The Spa Town

The nearby town of **Amphion-les-Bains** was the first spa resort of the Chablais region, which became fashionable as early as the 17C, when the dukes of Savoie regularly took the waters. The medicinal properties of Évian water were discovered in 1789, when a gentleman from Auvergne realised it was dissolving his kidney stones. However, Évian remained a small fortified town until 1865 when the lakeside promenade was built, partly over the water, thanks to Baron de Blonay who bequeathed his castle (situated where the casino now stands) to the town.

The treatment – The baths are open from 1 February to the end of November. Évian water, filtered by sand of glacial origin, is cold (11.6°C/52.8°F) and low in minerals. It is used for drinking and for bathing or showering, in the treatment of kidney or digestive complaints and other disorders which respond to hydrotherapy. Bottled Évian water is one of the main French mineral waters.

Along the Shore and on the Water

The Promenade★
The attractive lakeside walk is backed by the **Établissement thermal** (the baths), the **Villa Lumière**, now the town hall, and the Casino, three remarkable examples of spa-resort architecture of the late 19C and early 20C.
The new baths are situated in the **Parc thermal**. The pump room, designed by Maurice Novarina (also responsible for the Palais des Congrès), was erected in 1956

Office de tourisme, Évian

Évian and Lake Geneva

and the Espace Thermal in 1983. This is partly built below ground in order to preserve the appearance of the park.

Beyond the harbour where yachts find a mooring and where the lake's pleasure boats come alongside, the **Jardin anglais** offers a view of the Swiss shore. Large hotels are scattered inland on the lower slopes of the Pays Gavot.

Lac Léman★★★ (Lake Geneva)

Lac Léman, which covers 580km2/224sq mi and reaches depths of 310m/1 017ft, is 13 times larger than the Lac du Bourget; it is France's largest lake, even though almost two-thirds of its total area lies over the Swiss border. Shaped like a crescent, it is 72km/44.7mi long and 13km/8mi wide at its widest point; the narrower part between Geneva and Yvoire is known as the Petit Lac, the more open part as the Grand Lac. A natural phenomenon, known as the **"bataillère"** can be observed from the heights overlooking Montreux on the Swiss side and Meillerie on the French side: the muddy waters of the Rhône flowing into the lake seem to be completely absorbed by the lake. In fact, part of the river flow remains at a depth of 20m/66ft until the temperature drops in autumn and the undercurrent of river water blends into the cooling lake.

The areas bordering the lake enjoy a pleasantly mild microclimate: autumn in the Chablais can be glorious, in spite of frequent mist.

Boat trips★★★

🕐 *All year long, daily trips between Évian and Lausanne (35min). May to Sept: Haut-Lac Express (via Lausanne and the Château de Chillon) in a steamboat. Departures 11.45am and 4.15pm (4hrs). 33.10€ - ☎ 04 50 75 27 53 - www.cgn.ch*

The boats of the Compagnie Générale de Navigation link the French and Swiss shores of the lake and offer many cruises. From Évian, you can make a round tour of the lake, cross over to Lausanne-Ouchy or to go on night excursions.

Sights

La buvette Cachat (Information Centre about Évian water)

19 rue Nationale ♿ 🕐 Mid-June to mid-Sept: daily 10.30am-12.30pm, 3-7pm; 8 May to mid-June and third week of Sept: Mon-Sat 4.30-6.30pm 🕐 closed fourth week of Sept to 8 May. No charge - ☎ 04 50 26 80 29.

Address Book

For coin categories, see the Legend on the cover flap.

EATING OUT

La Bernolande – *1 pl. du Port - ☎ 04 50 70 72 60 - closed during school holidays in Feb and around 1 Nov, Thu in Sept-Apr and Wed.* If you have luck and fine weather you will be able to admire the view of the lake and the comings and goings of the ferries between Lausanne and Évian. Generous family-style cuisine.

Bourgogne – *Place Charles-Cotet - ☎ 04 50 75 01 05 - bourgogne@ wanadoo.fr .* A modern architect's interpretation of the Savoyard chalet, this restaurant has a great location at the beginning of the pedestrian shopping area. Appealing traditional menu in a modern setting. Rapid meals available at the brasserie.

Aux Ducs de Savoie – *R. du 23 Juillet 1944 - 74500 St-Gingolph - ☎ 04 50 76 73 09 - www.lelac.com/duc - closed 5-20 Jan, Mon and Tue.* This trim-looking chalet is a food-lover's paradise. It is popular with Swiss clients who cross the border to enjoy the refined menu. In summer, savour the fresh air on the terrace while enjoying a panoramic view of the lake. Children's menu.

WHERE TO STAY

Hôtel Continental – *65 r. Nationale - ☎ 04 50 75 37 54 - www.continental-evian.com - 32rms.* This building from 1868 has vast guestrooms that are well soundproofed. Those on the fourth floor, street side, have a nice view of the lake. Attractive old furniture collected by the proprietor.

Hôtel de France – *59 r. Nationale - ☎ 04 50 75 00 36 - www.hotel-france-evian.com - closed 12-20 Fev and 20 Nov-26 Dec - ℗ - 45rms.* This hotel on the town's main pedestrian street has a pretty garden growing on the site of the old palace of the Dukes of Savoie, a charming place to sit when the weather is fine. The rooms are light and pretty with modern furniture. Copious breakfast buffet.

Hôtel Alizé – *2 av Jean-Leger - ☎ 04 50 75 49 49 - www.hotel-alize-evian.com - closed 15 Nov-31 Jan - 22rms.* Just across from the boat landing and next to the thermal spa, this hotel has modern, renovated rooms brightly decorated; most face the lake.

Hôtel L'Oasis – *11 bd Bennevy - ☎ 04 50 75 13 38 www.oasis-hotel.com - open Apr-Sept - ℗ - 18rms.* On the heights of Évian, a charming hotel with gaily decorated modern rooms. Some face the lake, others are in two small houses nestled in the pretty shaded garden.

ON THE TOWN

Casino d'Évian – *Quai Baron-de-Blonay - ☎ 04 50 26 87 87 - www.casino-evian. com – Slot-machines: daily 10am-2am; traditional gambling: 8pm-2am; Liberté bar: noon-2am, and until 3am on Fri and Sat and during summer.* This internationally famous casino offers the classic range of activities to gambling enthusiasts. You can quench your thirst in the aptly named Jackpot bar or the Liberté, a bar-restaurant-tea room with a terrace overlooking the lake. Amateurs of waltzes, tangos or the paso doble will prefer the tea dances in the casino.

LEISURE

La Savoie – *See the information booth on the quai in July-August.* This boat is a faithful reproduction of the traditional ferries that once plied the lake. It is also one of the biggest heritage boats ever constructed in France.

Water sports – The **Cercle de la Voile** offers courses, regatas and lessons for sailors of all levels of experience. The **nautical centre** at Evian-Plage has a grassy lawn around 2 heated swimming pools. Finally, the **Cité de l'eau** at Amphion has a covered swimming pool, a wave pool, a diving tank, a sauna and a Jacuzzi.

CULTURAL EVENTS

Rencontres musicales d'Évian – *La Grange au Lac - ☎ 04 50 26 85 00 - www. evianroyalresort.com.* During the 2nd and 3rd weeks of May, Evian hosts a renowned festival of classical music, during which celebrated orchestras and musicians are in residence.

The centre is housed in the former pump room (1905) of the **Cachat spring**, an Art Nouveau building surmounted by a cupola. The spring is named after its owner, who improved the installations in 1824.

Église Notre-Dame de l'Assomption

Place des Anciens-Combattants This church is characteristic of early Gothic style in Savoie (end of 13C). Remodelled and restored for the last time in 1865, it has retained some of its original capitals; a Burgundian-style wooden Madonna carved in low relief, from 1493, can be seen in the side chapel on the right of the chancel.

Villa Lumière

🕐 *Daily except Sat-Sun 9-11.30am, 1.30-5pm - ☎ 04 50 83 10 00.*
Once owned by Antoine Lumière, father of the cinema pioneer, this grand 1896 villa now houses the town hall; the ground-floor rooms and the **grand staircase**★ are especially elegant, while the nest-door **theatre** is a splendid relic of 19C excess.

Musée Pré-lude

At the western end of the town, on N 5 coming from Amphion-les-Bains. 🕐 *July to Aug: daily except Mon 2.30-6.30pm; May to June and Sept: Sat-Sun 2.30-6.30pm. 3€ - ☎ 04 50 75 61 63.*
Tools and everyday objects, on display in a converted barn, give an impression of everyday rural life in the Chablais of the 19C.

Le Pré-Curieux Water Gardens★

♿🛥 *Guided tour (1hr45min, leaving from the pontoon opposite the casino) July to Aug: 10am, 1.45pm, 3.30pm; May to June and first 2 weeks of Sept: daily except Mon and Tue 10am, 1.45pm, 3.30pm. 10€, children 6€ - ☎04 50 75 04 26 - www.precurieux.com*
Kids This pretty garden of 3.5ha/9acres demonstrates the rich variety of marshland ecosystems. You reach the elegant, colonial-style villa on a solar-powered boat.

▶ *Leave Évian by ③ on the town plan, along N 5.*

Monument de la comtesse de Noailles

This small rotunda stands at the bottom of a garden which once belonged to the poet Anna de Noailles (1876-1933).

Bottling factory

♿🛥 *Guided tour (1 hr) by appointment at the company tour office, 22 av. des Sources, 74503 Évian-les-Bains: Jan to mid-Dec: daily except Sat-Sun and public holidays 9-10.30am, 2-3.30pm* 🕐 *closed 1 and 8 May, Ascension, 14 July, 15 Aug, 1 and 11 Nov. No charge - ☎ 04 50 26 93 23.*
This modern bottling factory, set up in Amphion-les-Bains, produces an average of 5 million litres of water per day, the highest output of any mineral water producer.

Excursion

④ **Falaises de Meillerie**★★ – *local map* 🧭*see THONON-LES-BAINS*

FROM ÉVIAN TO NOVEL *23km/14.3mi – about 1hr*
This itinerary takes you into the Franco-Swiss border zone (🧭*see Practical information).*

▶ *Leave Évian by ① on the town plan, along the lake shore.*

The road is lined with imposing properties and passes beneath a gallery linking the Château de Blonay (16C-19C) to the shore. Beyond Lugrin, the road skirts the foot of the Meillerie cliffs within sight of Montreux on the Swiss shore of the lake, overlooked by the Rochers de Naye.

Meillerie★

This fishing village, where Rousseau set part of his *Nouvelle Héloïse* (1764), nestles around its squat church (13C steeple) in a charming **setting**★ backed by the most impressive cliffs along Lake Geneva.

At the east end of the village, take the ramp off the main national road to drive down to the quayside where fishermen's nets are drying.

Beyond Meillerie, the view extends over the eastern part of the lake and the surrounding summits (Tour d'Aï).

St-Gingolph

This border village has two sets of public monuments apart from the church and the cemetery situated on the French side. The river Morge marks the frontier.

In the 18C, St-Gingolph was held to be one of the largest Swiss towns as young men wishing to enrol in the regiments of Louis XV's royal guard all claimed to be from the Swiss part of the town, as pay in Swiss francs was better than in French francs.

▷ *Follow D 30 to Novel.*

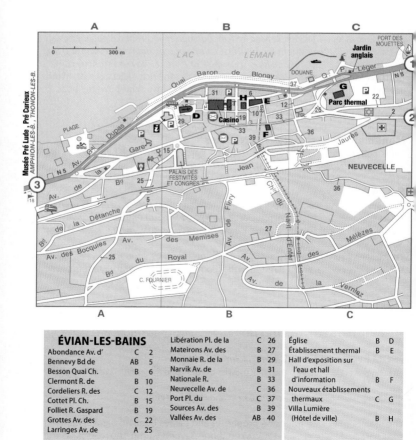

ÉVIAN-LES-BAINS			Libération Pl. de la	C	26	Église	B	D
Abondance Av. d'	C	2	Mateirons Av. des	B	27	Établissement thermal	B	E
Bennevy Bd de	AB	5	Monnaie R. de la	B	29	Hall d'exposition sur		
Besson Quai Ch.	B	6	Narvik Av. de	B	31	l'eau et hall		
Clermont R. de	B	10	Nationale R.	B	33	d'information	B	F
Cordeliers R. des	C	12	Neuvecelle Av. de	C	36	Nouveaux établissements		
Cottet Pl. Ch.	B	15	Port Pl. du	C	37	thermaux	C	G
Folliet R. Gaspard	B	19	Sources Av. des	B	39	Villa Lumière		
Grottes Av. des	C	22	Vallées Av. des	AB	40	(Hôtel de ville)	B	H
Larringes Av. de	A	25						

Novel
Splendid views of Lake Geneva. The village church has a typical Alpine bell-tower.

5 Pays Gavot★ *15km/9.3mi – 1hr 30min.*

The **Pays Gavot**, situated inland from Évian, is a plateau bounded to the south by the Dranse d'Abondance Valley and in the east by the cliffs of the Pic de Mémise. This open countryside, where woods and pastures predominate, is popular with hikers.

▶ *Leave Évian by ② on the town plan.*

The D 24 rises through a landscape of orchards. Two wide hairpin bends offer fine glimpses of the lake through the woods and give access to Thollon lying beneath the cliffs of the Pic de Mémise.

⌖ Thollon-les-Mémises
This resort, which consists of several hamlets overlooking Lake Geneva stretched out 600m/1 968ft below, has become an annexe of Évian, both in summer owing to its fine situation and in winter because of the proximity of the Mémise ski slopes.

Pic de Mémise★★
Alt 1 677m/5 502ft. *30min there and back on foot.*
🚡 The gondola brings visitors up to 1 596m/5 236ft on top of the Mémise cliffs. From there it is possible to reach the cross erected at the highest point and enjoy the **panorama** of the lake and of the Swiss shore from Nyon to Montreux, with the Jura mountains, Vaudois hills and Rochers de Naye in the background.

6 La Dranse d'Abondance

FROM EVIAN TO ABONDANCE *47km/29mi – allow 2hr*

▶ *Leave Evian by ② on the town plan and follow D 21 (Route de Thollon)*

Bernex
This holiday resort and small mountaineering centre is the starting point of the ascent of the **Dent d'Oche** (alt 2 222m/7 290ft).
From Vacheresse onwards, D 22 follows the deep wooded valley of the Dranse d'Abondance which opens up beyond Abondance. There are quite a few sawmills and chalets in typical local style with large roofs covered with light grey slates, gables marked with a cross and balconies with openwork wooden balustrades.

Abondance★ – *See ABONDANCE.*

FORCALQUIER ★

POPULATION 4 302
MICHELIN MAP 334 C9

This small Provençal town lies at the heart of a low area of rolling hills, a pretty site ★ bordered by the Montagne de Lure, the River Durance and the Luberon. The town, picturesquely built in the shape of an amphitheatre, surrounds a hill once crowned by a citadel. At the end of the 11C, the fortified town of Forcalquier became the capital of a comté (county) created by a branch of the Comtes de Provence dynasty and extending along the Durance from Manosque north to Sisteron, Gap and Embrun. The bishopric of Sisteron was split into two and the church of Forcalquier became a "co-cathedral," a unique precedent in the history of the Church. The Comté de Forcalquier and the Comté de Provence were united at the end of the 12C, under the leadership of **Raimond Bérenger V**, the son of Gersende de Sabran, Duchess of Forcalquier and of Alfonso II of Provence. The two territories were eventually bequeathed to the French crown in 1481.

Today, Forcalquier is a thriving agricultural and industrial centre and a lively little town where one of the most important markets in the area takes place on Mondays. It is also a busy tourist centre and the starting point for several excursions. In addition, jazz and classical music concerts and craft fairs are held every summer (see Planning Your Trip: Calendar of events). 13 place du Bourget - 04300 Forcalquier Daily 9am-noon, 2-6pm - ☎ 04 92 75 10 02 - www.forcalquier.com

▸ **Orient Yourself:** With Manosque 23km/138.3mi to the south and Sisteron 47km/29.4 mi to the north, Forcalquier makes a good base from which to explore the region: the plateau of Valensole is 30 km/18.75mi to the southwest, while the town of Sault is 54km/86.4mi to the northeast, over the plateau of Albion.

 Don't Miss: The view from the terrace of Notre-Dame-de-Provence is celebrated; See also the towns of Simiane-la-Rotonde for its fortifications; Banon for its cheeses; and Oppedette for its roofs

 Organizing Your Time: The Monday market is one of the biggest in Provence. If you plan to overnight in Forcalquier, opt for the "pays du Contadour" excursion in the afternoon, with "pays de Forqualquier" the following morning.

 Especially for Kids: The astronomy centre at Saint-Michel, part of the observatory of Haute-Provence, offers activities and evening star-gazing.

 Also See: Nearby Sights: CÉRESTE, Vallée de la Moyenne DURANCE, Monastère de GANAGOBIE, GRÉOUX-LES-BAINS, MANE, MANOSQUE, MONTBRUN-LES- BAINS, Route NAPOLÉON, RIEZ, SISTERON, Plateau de VALENSOLE

The Old Town

Église Notre-Dame

This former "co-cathedral" offers an interesting contrast between the Romanesque character of its massive rectangular tower and the slender appearance of its steeple crowned by a lantern. A lofty nave with a roof of broken-barrel vaulting, in typical Provençal Romanesque style, dates from the same period as the transept and the chancel which, built some time before 1217, are the oldest examples of Gothic style in southern France. The aisles were added in the 17C, as was the magnificent organ.

Cité comtale

The **Porte des Cordeliers** gate with its two pointed arches decorated with a torus is all that remains of the town's fortifications and marks the beginning of the medieval

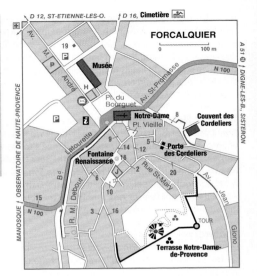

Address Book

For coin categories, see the Legend on the cover flap.

EATING OUT

L'Aïgo Blanco – *5 pl. Vieille -* ☎ *04 92 75 27 23 - closed 2-28 Oct, Mon evening in winter.* Behind the church of Notre-Dame, at the heart of the old town, this dining room in Provençal colours opens onto a terrace in fine weather. Generous regional fare is complemented in winter by a menu of Savoyard specialties.

La Tourette – *20 bd Latourette -* ☎ *04 92 75 14 00 - closed 1-15 Nov .* Warm welcome, decor in the colours of the Midi, traditional Provençal cuisine in this mid-town restaurant. The terrace under a spreading chestnut tree is pleasant on warm days.

WHERE TO STAY

Chambre d'hôte Campagne "Le Paradis" – *Quartier Paradis, at 700m/less than 1/2mi from town centre -* ☎ *04 92 75 37 33, campgneleparadis@ wanadoo.fr -* ⌧ *- 4rms, gîtes.* Everything evokes the past life of this farm, from the horse's manger to old photos to the barn, so the modern appearance of the guestrooms may come as something of a shock. There is always the option of one of the gîtes decorated in Provençal colours and with traditional furniture.

Auberge Charembeau – *4km/2.5mi E of Forcalquier on N 100 and a minor road -* ☎ *04 92 70 91 70 , contact@charembeau.com- closed 16 Nov-14 Feb. -* ⌧ *- 24rms.* This 18C farm in the middle of seven hectares (17 acres) of fields and hills has been restored in the Provençal tradition and offers comfort, greenery and quiet. Unfortunately there is no restaurant, but there are one or two rooms with kitchen facilities. Swimming pool and tennis court.

Chambre d'hôte Jas des Nevières – *Rte de St-Pierre - 04300 Pierrerue - 6km/4mi E of Forcalquier on D 12 then D 212 -* ☎ *04 92 75 24 99 - www.jas-des-nevieres.com- closed Nov-Mar -* ⌧ *- 4rms.* This old sheep farm set in a small village has been restored with great care and is now a haven of peace. Rooms are tastefully decorated in an understated style and exude genuine sophistication. On nice days, the breakfast is served on the covered terrace set up in a pretty interior courtyard.

GUIDED TOUR

Guided tour of town (2hrs) – *July to Aug: Tue 9.30am; Sept to June: Tue 10am. 3€ -* ☎ *04 92 75 10 02.* Guides from the tourist office take you around the old town, the cathedral, the citadel and historic old homes.

town. The narrow streets lined with tall houses were laid out to offer the best protection from the cold north-westerly wind or *mistral*. Many of the houses are in poor repair, but others have kept their paired windows and Gothic, Classical or Renaissance doorways. Walk along rue des Cordeliers leading to rue Passère and rue Bérenger then across place du Palais to Grande-Rue. A lovely 16C **Renaissance fountain**, in the shape of a pyramid crowned by St Michael slaying the dragon, decorates place St-Michel. Rue Mercière leads to place du Bourguet at the heart of the city.

Terrasse Notre-Dame-de-Provence

Rue St-Mary leads up to the site of the citadel where very little remains of the counts of Forcalquier's castle; below are the ruins of a tower which belonged to St Mary's Church, the town's first cathedral. Note the set of **bells** which the ringer plays with his fists in the traditional fashion *(concert on Sundays at 11.30am)*.

A 19C octagonal chapel dedicated to Notre-Dame-de-Provence stands at the top where the splendid **panorama**★ embraces the Forcalquier Basin and the surrounding mountains *(viewing table)*; there is a bird's-eye view of the town just below.

Cemetery★

Leave the town centre north along D 16 and turn left 200m/218yd further on. A superb central staircase leads to the lower part of the cemetery with its striking clipped yew alleys.

Sights

Couvent des Cordeliers

Closed for repairs; reopening scheduled for early 2007 - ☎ 04 92 75 02 38.
Franciscan friars, known as Cordeliers because they wore a knotted cord round the waist, settled in Forcalquier in 1236, probably at the invitation of Raimond Bérenger V. Their monastery, one of the first of its kind in Provence, was occupied until the 18C. The badly damaged 13C and 14C buildings were remarkably well restored in the 1960s.

The cloister was at the centre of the monastery. Several funeral recesses on the southwest and southeast sides were used as graves for the lords of Forcalquier. Note the graceful twin windows framing a Romanesque door on the side of the chapter-house. Part of the buildings can be visited: the library with its original ceiling, the scriptorium, the oratory (15C Virgin Mary with Child) and the refectory divided into three rooms.

Municipal Museum

Place du Bourget 🕐 *Closed for inventory; temporary exhibits only - ☎ 04 92 70 91 19.*
Housed in a former 17C convent, the museum contains utensils and decorative objects from the area (old tools, antique furniture, earthenware from Moustiers, Apt and Mane), a fine collection of coins and local archaeological finds.

Nearby Sights

St-Michel-l'Observatoire★

This pleasant old village built on a hillside is famous for its observatory, whose cupolas shine beneath the clearest skies in France. Narrow streets lead to the elegant, white **Église haute** crowning the hill. From the terrace of this 12C "upper church" there is a fine **view** of the area around Forcalquier, of the Montagne de Lure and of the Luberon. St Peter's Church, the **Église basse** at the heart of the village, was built in the 13C and 14C by the counts of Anjou who ruled Provence at the time. The pediment of the doorway is framed by a pointed archivolt. In the apse, there is a beautiful 15C wooden crucifix.

Chapelle St-Paul
1km/0.6mi south along D 105. Note the massive columns surmounted by Corinthian capitals, which belonged to a 12C priory.

Observatoire de Haute-Provence★
North of the village along D 305. Visit: 1hr. Visitors must climb 60 steps. ○ *Guided tour (1hr) April to Sept: Wed 2–4pm, Oct–Mar: Wed at 3pm* ○ *Closed public holidays. 4€, children 2.40€ - ☎ 04 92 70 64 00 - www.obs-hp.fr* The location of the observatory in St-Michel was justified by the quality of the air in the Forcalquier region. There are 14 cupolas containing astronomical instruments (among the largest in Europe), laboratories, workshops and living quarters. Many astronomers from France and other countries work here.

One of the telescopes, which has a diameter of 1.93m/6.5ft, was built with the latest electronic refinements and allowed researchers to identify the **first planet outside the solar system.** Spectrographs analyse light from the stars, thus establishing their chemical components, their temperature and their radial speed. A team of geophysicists is studying the upper strata of the atmosphere by means of laser sounding.

Kids The **Centre d'astronomie de Saint-Michel**, on the plateau du Moulin-à-Vent, offers themed activities and evening star-gazing guided by experts, by reservation only. ○ *July to Aug: observation of the Sun, star-gazing and lectures, ask for the schedule. Oct to June: 1 or 2 evening sessions per month. Evening star-gazing 9€, children 6-16 years old 7€. Observation of the Sun 5.60€, children 6-16 years old 4€ - ☎ 04 92 76 69 09 - www.centre-astro.fr*

From the entrance of the observatory, a path on the right leads to the modest but charming 11C **Chapelle St-Jean-des-Fuzils**, tiled with the traditional schist slabs known as *lauzes*.

Excursion

The Montagne de Lure and the Pays de Contadour

FROM FORCALQUIER TO SISTERON *64km/39.8mi – about 2hr –* 👣 *see Vallée de la Moyenne DURANCE,* ②

Pays de Forcalquier

FROM FORCALQUIER TO BANON *– 77km/47.8mi – allow 3hr*
This rich rural area, in striking contrast with the austere surrounding plateaux and Montagne de Lure, is dotted with charming hilltop villages, most facing east or south to shelter from the north-westerly wind.

▶ *From Forcalquier, follow N 100 towards Manosque.*

Mane★ – 👣 *See MANE.*

▶ *Turn onto D 13 then left 4.5km/2.8mi further on towards St-Maime.*

St-Maime
A few ruins and the castle chapel overlooking the village are the only remains of the Comtes de Provence's castle, in which the four daughters of Raimond Bérenger V were brought up in the traditional way (👣 *see FORCALQUIER*).

▶ *Return to D 13 and cross it to reach Dauphin.*

Dauphin

Built on another hilltop facing St-Maime, Dauphin has retained part of its 14C fortifications, its medieval streets and its keep, crowned by a balustrade and a statue of the Virgin Mary; from the top there is a wide open **view** of the surrounding area.

▶ *Follow D 5 and cross N 100.*

St-Michel-l'Observatoire★ – 👜 *See above.*

▶ *Follow D 105 south.*

Chapelle St-Paul – 👜 *See above.*

▶ *Turn right onto D 205.*

Lincel

This village, which nestles in a fold, has retained a small Romanesque church and a castle with a few 16C features.

▶ *Cross N 100, continue along D 105, then turn right onto D 907 and left towards Montfuron.*

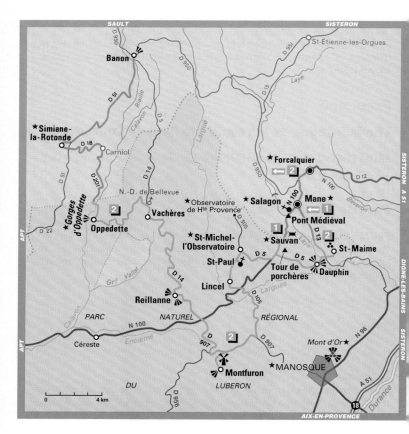

Montfuron

Fine restored **windmill**. ⏱ *Guided tour (15min) Sat 3-7pm - 1.50€, children .50€ - ☎ 06 16 56 47 90.* From the village, **view** of the heights of Haute-Provence to the northeast and of the Ste-Victoire Mountain to the southwest.

▶ *Return to D 907 and turn left; drive across N 100 and follow D 14.*

Reillanne

This village is built on the side of a hill crowned by the 18C Chapelle St-Denis, which replaced the castle; avenue Long-Barri leads past the Portail des Forges (all that remains of the castle) to the viewing table: panoramic **view** of the old village, of the Ste-Victoire Mountain to the south and Luberon to the west.

▶ *Continue along D 14 and make a detour to Vachères.*

Vachères

This old hilltop village acquired fame when the statue of a Gallo-Roman warrior, now in the Calvet Museum in Avignon, was discovered nearby. The local museum or **Musée communal** (&⏱ *May to Sept: 10am-noon, 3-6pm; Oct to Apr: 2-5pm, by appointment.* ⏱ *Closed mid-Dec to mid-Feb 2.30€ - ☎ 04 92 75 62 15.*) is housed in the village school; It contains archeological finds going back to prehistoric times, including flint, axes and a copy of the famous **Vachères warrior**, as well as fossils discovered locally.

▶ *From Notre-Dame-de-Bellevue on D 14, take a small road to Oppedette.*

Oppedette

This tastefully restored hamlet overlooks the Gorges d'Oppedette, 2.5km/1.5mi long and 120m/394ft deep in places, through which flows the Calavon. There is a fine **view**★ from the viewpoint near the cemetery; a marked path, starting beneath the viewpoint, leads to the bottom of the gorge.

▶ *Continue along D 201 and turn left onto D 18 at Carniol.*

Simiane-la-Rotonde★

This is one of the loveliest hilltop villages in Haute-Provence; perched on the edge of the Plateau d'Albion, it overlooks vast fields of mauve lavender. Above the tall houses stands the **Rotonde**★ (⏱ *Mid-June to Aug: daily 10am-1pm, 3-7.30pm; Apr to mid-June and Sept: daily except Tues 3-6pm. 3€ - ☎ 14 92 75 90 14)*, which is all that remains of the castle of the Sault family.

The **Rotonde**★ is the late-12C castle keep, of which the glacis is the only part visible from the outside. The interior is on two floors; on the upper level there are 12 recesses in Rayonnant Gothic style, separated by pilasters with carved capitals, and below, 12 ribs supporting a cupola with central oculus. A festival of ancient music takes place in summer.

The houses lining the steep streets have retained 17C and 18C carved doors. The **church** dates from the 16C, and there is a fine **view** of the Forcalquier region from the covered **market**.

▶ *Continue along D 51 to Banon.*

Banon

A 14C **fortified gate** and the restored medieval hospital can be seen at the top of the old village, which overlooks the new one; from the east end of the church there is a pleasant **view** of the tiled roofs backed by the Montagne de Lure. A tasty goat's cheese wrapped in chestnut leaves has been named after Banon.

Hike

Gorges d'Oppedette ★

About 3hr on foot from the viewpoint marked by a metal balustrade. Handrails guide visitors through difficult places. It is not advisable to go on this hike after a storm or when the weather is uncertain. There is no water available on the way. Hikers need a good sense of balance.

🚶 Follow the yellow markings; after three handrail-assisted sections, it is possible to return to the village along the blue-marked path on the left, or to carry on down along the yellow-marked path on the right to the bottom of the gorge dotted with pools (known as *gours*) and potholes. Beware of slippery surfaces as you go round the numerous *gours*. Beyond the bridge, follow the yellow-marked path on the left leading to the GR footpath, which leads through the *garrigue* (scrub) and offers fine views of the gorge. Return to the viewpoint along the surfaced road.

VALLÉE DE FREISSINIÈRES ★

MICHELIN MAP 334 H4

This small valley, "hanging" 200m/656ft above the River Durance and hidden behind reddish-ochre rocks typical of Mediterranean landscapes, is in fact an Alpine U-shaped valley scoured by a glacier, with a flat floor and contrasting sides: the south-facing *adret* dotted with houses and crops and the north-facing *ubac* covered with larch and pine woods. The municipality of Freissinières includes 13 hamlets which reflect the importance of sheep-farming in the area: sheep are kept in the vaulted basements of traditional houses, the upper floors being used as living quarters and for storing hay. 🏚 *Moulin des Ribes – 05310 Freissinières contact tourist office for hours -* ☎*04 92 20 95 49 - www.paysdesecrins.com*

▶ **Orient Yourself:** The town of St-Crépin is 11km/7mi south of Argentière-la-Bessée and 14km/8.75mi north of Guillestre, gateway to the Queyras region.

🕐 **Organizing Your Time:** Give yourself a half day to tour the region; if you climb to Dormillouse, accessible only on foot, you'll need the rest of the day.

👁 **Also See:** Nearby Sights: L'ARGENTIÈRE-LA-BESSÉE, BRIANÇON, Le BRIANÇON-NAIS, CEILLAC, EMBRUN, GUILLESTRE, MOLINES-EN-QUEYRAS, MONT-DAUPHIN, MONTGENÈVRE, Le QUEYRAS, SERRE-CHEVALIER, La VALLOUISE, VARS

Excursion

From St-Crépin to Dormillouse *25km/15.5mi – about 3hr*

St-Crépin

This village stands on top of a pink marble rock spur barring the Durance Valley. Note the beautiful doorway of the **church** and the bell-tower surmounted by a spire and four corner pinnacles.

▶ *Cross the River Durance and follow D 38.*

The road rises along a stony slope dotted with juniper bushes and tufts of lavender. Low stone walls are a reminder of the days when these slopes were covered with crops; the view covers the Guillestre Basin and Mont-Dauphin standing on top of its promontory.

The Rise and Fall of Dormillouse

In winter, Dormillouse has only one resident, yet this valley was once the centre of Protestant life in the area. The remoteness of the valley made it a natural refuge for renegades or dissidents during the long period of religious persecution. Followers of the Waldensian sect, who settled here and in the neighbouring Vallouise (see 🕲 La VALLOUISE) as early as the 13C, were joined by Huguenots in the 16C and the Col de Freissinières became a busy route. In the 19C, **Félix Neff**, a young clergyman from Geneva, came to the area and founded a teachers' training-college in Dormillouse in order to help the local population.

Gouffre de Gourfouran★

👣 *30min there and back on foot. Access is difficult and caution is recommended. Leave the car 500m/547yd beyond the hamlet of Le Chambon. Follow the path to a pile of stones. From there, walk across the fields to a rocky promontory overlooking the chasm and the Durance Valley.* The River Biaisse, which flows through the Freissinières Valley, joins the Durance Valley via a 100m/328ft-deep gorge with sheer sides of a striking reddish colour.

▶ *In Freissinières, take the road which climbs up the south-facing slope.*

From Les Roberts, there is an overall view of the valley blocked by the rocky knoll of Pallon.

▶ *Return to D 238*

The valley narrows beyond Freissinières. The road leads on through **Les Viollins** (old Protestant church) to the end of the valley, where a number of waterfalls flow together into the Biaisse.

Dormillouse★

1hr 30min there and back on foot.
🚶 The path leads to a group of houses, some of which are inhabited in summer. Note the small Protestant church and the restored water-mill *(the path continues to the Col de Freissinières).*

Hikes

Sentier des alpages★

5hr, no major difficulty; a car is needed to go back. Water is available on the way. Departure from "Champs-Queyras," just before the hamlet of Les Aujards (alt 1 568m/5 144ft). Destination is Dourmillouse (accommodation available).
🚶 This long hike on the south-facing slope makes use of the old footpaths linking the high-pasture hamlets and overlooking the Fressinières Valley and the River Biaisse. The path climbs to Les Garcines then crosses several streams just above the tree line. Beyond Les Allibrands, the path overlooks the chalets at La Got before reaching Dormillouse. You are likely to see samples of the rich local fauna: chamois, marmots, falcons, black redstarts and – if you are lucky – golden eagles. The itinerary also offers the opportunity of observing the results of the geological upheavals in the area: spectacular folds of sandstone alternating with black schist can clearly be seen from Les Allibrands on the opposite slope.

Grotte des Vaudois and Via ferrata de Freissinières

Leave the car in the car park at the entrance of Les Roberts. 1hr on foot along a stony steep path.

🏛 In the 15C, this cave was the refuge of followers of the Waldensian sect, pursued by members of the Inquisition.

The Via ferrata de Freissinières, the oldest in France, is well equipped and safe for beginners, in spite of some vertiginous sections; the course offers aerial views which should delight lovers of heights (👣 *see Planning Your Trip: Rock-climbing*).

ROUTE DU GALIBIER★★★

MICHELIN MAP 333 L/M 7/8

This road, one of the most famous in the French Alps, linking the Maurienne (the Arc Valley, (👣 *see La MAURIENNE) and the Briançonnais (👣 *see Le BRIANÇONNAIS*), takes you through an austere and totally unspoilt mountain area. The panorama unfolding from the Col du Galibier is one of the finest in France, particularly in the early morning or late afternoon. The itinerary starts with a steep climb from the Arc Valley to the wooded "hanging" valley of the Valloirette, a tributary of the Arc. As the road continues to rise in a series of dizzying curves, the landscape begins to look bleak, then utterly grim. The Écrins Massif comes into view beyond the Col du Galibier, a particularly impressive sight in the first or last hours of daylight. The route du Galibier is well known to cyclists as one of the most challenging stages of the Tour de France. This highlight of the sporting calendar, which borders on a national obsession, began in June 1903, with cyclists competing over a six-stage circuit of 2 500km/1 553mi. 🏛 *73450 Valloire* 🕐 *July-Aug: daily 9am-7pm, mid-Dec to mid-Apr: daily 9am-6.30pm; rest of year: daily except Sun 9am-noon, 2-6pm* 🕐 *closed public holidays except 14 July, 15 Aug -* ☎ *04 79 59 03 96 - www.valloire.net*

▸ **Orient Yourself:** D 902 takes you over the Col du Galibier to Valloire.
😊 **Don't Miss:** The baroque altarpiece in the church of Valloire is unique.
🕐 **Organizing Your Time:** Coming up from the south, you see clearly the passage from the Dauphiné to the Savoie regions, as bare, stony slopes give way to forests and pasture.
👣 **Also See:** Nearby Sights: L'ALPE-D'HUEZ, AUSSIOS, Le BOURG-D'OISANS, BRIANÇON, Le BRIANÇONNAIS, Route de la CROIX-DE-FER, Les DEUX-ALPES, Route DES GRANDES ALPES, La GRAVE, La Haute MAURIENNE, MODANE, L'OISANS, ST-JEAN-DE-MAURIENNE, SERRE-CHEVALIER

Excursions

From St-Michel-de-Maurienne to the Col Du Lautaret

41km/25.5mi – about 3hr. The Col du Galibier is blocked by snow from October to late May (sometimes until July).

The road rising to the Col du Télégraphe affords views of the escarpments of the Croix des Têtes towering over the narrow basin of St-Michel-de-Maurienne, with the Grand Perron des Encombres (alt 2 825m/9 268ft) behind it and, in the distance, the Péclet-Polset glaciers.

Col du Télégraphe★

Alt 1 566m/5 138ft. *There is a car park*. Climb to the top of the rocky knoll, on the north side, to get a bird's-eye **view** of the Arc Valley. Between the pass and Valloire, the road overlooks the Valloirette rushing through steep gorges towards the River Arc.

Valloire *

Conveniently situated between the Parc national de la Vanoise and the Parc national des Écrins, Valloire is the main tourist centre of the Maurienne region. It lies at the foot of the Rocher St-Pierre, which partly blocks the Valloirette Valley, and marks the transition between two typical Alpine landscapes: downriver, a wooded coomb and, upriver, a desolate corridor of pastureland with scree-covered slopes.

Dating mainly from the 17C, the Baroque **church**★ (🕙 *Mid-June to Aug: 10am-5pm - ☎ 04 79 59 03 96.*) is one of the most richly decorated in the Savoie region; note in particular the gilded-wood **retable**★★ over the high altar showing St Peter on the right and St Thècle, born in Valloire in the 6C, on the left. The calvary above the vestry door, dating from 1609, is believed to be a copy of Albrecht Dürer's *Christ*.

Beyond Valloire, there are clear views of the barren Grand Galibier Summit. As the road rises from Plan Lachat to the pass, it offers superb views of the Valloirette Valley in the distance.

🎿 Valloire is a well-equipped ski resort with a choice of red and black runs for experienced skiers in the Colérieux, Grandes Drozes and Plan Palais areas. Snow-cannon ensure adequate snow cover all winter. In addition, there are 40km/25mi of cross-country ski trails and the ski area is linked to that of Valmenier.

Col du Galibier ★★★

The road no longer goes through a tunnel but over the pass (alt 2 646m/8 681ft) which is the highest point of the **Route des Grandes Alpes** after the Col de l'Iseran (alt 2 770m/9 088ft). *Leave the car and walk up (15min there and back) to the viewing table* (alt 2 704m/8 871ft); nearby is an old boundary stone marking the border between France and Savoie. The splendid **panoramic view** includes the Aiguilles d'Arves and Mont Thabor to the north and the glaciers and snow-capped peaks of the Écrins Massif to the south.

At the north end of the old tunnel stands a monument to Henri Desgranges, editor of the sports newspaper *L'Auto* who organised the first Tour de France in 1903. Continue to the Col de Lautaret (*see Oisans,* **2***)*. There is a magnificent **view**★★★ of the Meije and the Glacier de l'Homme (Massif des Ecrins).

The Route du Galibier; a real test for the iron men of "Le Tour"

P. Lorne/EXPLORER

Hike

Pic Blanc du Galibier★★★

Alt 2 955m/9 695ft. *This 3hr hike is only suitable for experienced hikers. Difference in altitude: 400m/1 312ft; climbing boots recommended.*

🚶 Leave the car at the southern exit of the old tunnel and follow the marked path across the fields, aiming for a round summit on the left which it is advisable to climb on its left side *(steep climb)*: remarkable **panorama**★★ of the Meije and Mont Thabor. *People inclined to feel dizzy are advised to turn back here.*

The itinerary continues along a path following the narrow mountain ridge *(dangerous in wet conditions)*. The ascent to the summit of the Pic Blanc du Galibier is very steep but well worth it for the exceptional **panorama**★★★: Pic des Trois Évêchés and Aiguilles d'Arves in the foreground, Mont Thabor and the snow-capped peaks of the Vanoise to the northeast, Mont Blanc and the Grandes Jorasses further away.

On the way back, follow a narrow path on the left leading to the viewing table near the pass, then bear right to return to the car park.

MONASTÈRE DE GANAGOBIE★

MICHELIN MAP 334 D9
LOCAL MAP SEE VALLÉE DE LA MOYENNE DURANCE

The monastery stands on a remarkable site, on top of the Ganagobie Plateau, surrounded by broom, pines, holm oaks and lavender. The thousand year-old building, which was restored and re-inhabited in the 19C, houses one of the finest mosaics in the West.

▸ **Orient Yourself:** The monastery is 34km/21.25mi south of Sisteron and 27km/17mi north of Manosque. If you come from Forcalquier, 18km/11.25mi to the west, you can stop at Lurs and travel on to Ganagobie by a small country road.

🅿 **Parking:** A parking lot is some 15 minutes on foot from the monastery.

🕐 **Organizing Your Time:** You will need an hour to visit the monastery and stroll on the plateau.

⏱ **Also See:** Nearby Sights: CÉRESTE, DIGNE-LES-BAINS, Préalpes de DIGNE, Vallée de la Moyenne DURANCE, FORCALQUIER, GRÉOUX-LES-BAINS, MANE, MANOSQUE, Route NAPOLÉON, SISTERON, Plateau de VALENSOLE

A Bit of History

The presence of megaliths shows that the site was already inhabited in prehistoric times. From its medieval past it has retained the traces of a walled village (Villevieille), abandoned in the 15C, the remains of a Carolingian chapel and above all the Monastère de Ganagobie. The bishop of Sisteron was the first to found a community on the site back in the 10C but the present **monastery** was built in the 12C by monks of the Cluniac order. In the 14C, 15 monks worked on the land and in the forest, but 200 years later the buildings were practically abandoned; they were restored in the 17C. Following the 1789 Revolution, the church was saved just in time by the local people who decided to use it as their parish church. Today, the church and the monastery buildings, which are partly used by Benedictine monks, are being restored.

For coin categories, see the Legend on the cover flap

WHERE TO STAY AND EAT

⊝⊜ **Hôtel Le Séminaire** – *04700 Lurs - 7km/4mi S of the monastery on D 30 - ☎ 04 92 79 94 19 - info@hotel-leseminaire.com - closed Dec- Jan - 17rms- ⊝⊜⊜res- taurant.* This stone former seminary has a pretty garden adjoining it, sloping down to the swimming pool. The rooms are non-smoking only. Regional cuisine in the vaulted dining room or on the shaded terrace.

Tour 30min

🕐 *Daily except Mon 3-5pm, Sun 11am-noon, 3-5pm.*

Church

The decoration of the **doorway**★ is the most noticeable feature of the façade. The pointed arches are separated by stone festoons which also surround the door; on the tympanum, a formal, rather stern Christ in Glory contrasts with the freer representations of the adoring angels and the symbols of the Evangelists. The 12 apostles decorate the lintel.

The single nave, covered with broken barrel vaulting, is prolonged by a double transept and an oven-vaulted central apse. The carved ornamentation is extremely plain since the church was decorated with frescoes (only a few traces remain) as well as polychrome **mosaics**★★ in the chancel and transept, which date from the mid-12C and denote a strong Byzantine influence. It is easy to see how the rich tapestries brought back from the Crusades could have provided the inspiration for these designs. Elegant

Mosaic from Ganagobie showing St George slaying the dragon

Lonchamps Delahaye/CNMHS

tracery patterns frame a menagerie of mythical animals; note in particular St George slaying the dragon.

Walking Nearby

Viewpoints from the Plateau

The **Allée des Moines** leads from the left of the church to the edge of the plateau offering an aerial **view**★★ of the Durance Valley, the Valensole Plateau and the Préalpes de Digne, with the high Alpine mountains in the distance.

In the opposite direction, the **Allée de Forcalquier** leads to the western edge of the plateau; from this point, the **view**★ extends to the Forcalquier Basin and the Montagne de Lure. Megaliths still stand on the left of the path; on the right, hollows cut into the rock mark the site of prehistoric dwellings.

GAP

POPULATION 36 262
MICHELIN MAP 334 E5

There are few architectural traces of Gap's ancient past as the town was destroyed on several occasions, in particular during the Wars of Religion and in 1692 when the troops of Amedée of Savoie laid waste to the centre. However, Gap has retained the general plan of a medieval city with its narrow twisting lanes, now turned into pleasant pedestrian streets with a touch of Mediterranean flair.

The main administrative town of the Hautes-Alpes *département* is also a cathedral town and the headquarters of the Parc national des Écrins. As a tourist centre, it takes advantage of its situation near the Lac de Serre-Ponçon, the cross-country skiing area of Col Bayard and ski resorts such as Orcières-Merlette. *2a cours Frédéric-Mistral - 05002 Gap July to Aug: daily 9am-7pm, Sun and public holidays 10am-1pm; rest of year: daily except Mon and public holidays 9am-noon, 2-6pm - 04 92 52 56 56 - www.ville-gap.fr. Guided tours of the town (1hr30min) July to Aug: Tues 5pm, Thur-Fri 10am. 3.20€– Contact the tourist office.*

▶ **Orient Yourself:** Gap lies in a basin, at the heart of wooded farmland and at the intersection of two major roads, the Route Napoléon (Grasse to Grenoble) and D 994 (Valence to Briançon).

Don't Miss: The Musée départemental has remarkable archeological artifacts as well as artwork, and the Domaine de Charance has beautiful nature walks.

Organizing Your Time: You will need an hour to see the town, plus another hour for the museum and a third for the Domaine de Charance.

Especially for Kids: The Stade nautique de Fontreyne (see the Address Book) offers diversion for children and adults; children will also enjoy the Domaine de Charance, where there is lots of room to run.

Also See: Nearby Sights: Pays du BUËCH, Le CHAMPSAUR, Le DÉVOLUY, EMBRUN, MONTMAUR, Route NAPOLÉON, Lac de SERRE-PONÇON, SISTERON, Le VALGAU-DEMAR

Walking Tour

The old town

Few traces of the original medieval architecture remain, but the pattern of streets has changed little over the centuries. The pedestrian area, lined with brightly col-oured houses and shopfronts, comes alive with the bustle of shoppers during the Saturday market.

Cathedral

The 19C passion for Historicism was given full rein in this fusion of neo-Romanesque and neo-Gothic styles. Note the use of white, red and grey stone from the area, reminiscent of Embrun's cathedral, and step back to admire the 77m/253ft spire.

Hotel de Ville

The town hall has retained its fine 18C façade, emblazoned with the civic coat of arms.

Address Book

For coin categories, see the Legend on the cover flap.

EATING OUT

⊜ **Salon de thé Gondre-L'Ambroisine** – *R. du Col.-Roux -* ☎ *04 92 53 74 74 - ambroisie@online.fr - closed 18 Sept-7 Oct.* This is a mecca for food-lovers who will find it hard to resist the pastries and dainty cakes, generous salads, quiches and puff-pastry... All served in a freshly refurbished dining room.

⊜ **Le Tourton des Alpes** – *1 r. des Cordiers -* ☎ *04 92 53 90 91* . The tourton, a renowned local specialty, is a sort of fritter filled with various ingredients, and this establishment is dedicated to it. Don't hesitate to walk down the few steps to a table in this old vaulted cellar.

⊜ **Laiterie du Col Bayard** – *05500 Laye - 10km/6mi N of Gap by N 85 -* ☎ *04 92 50 50 06 - colbayard@wanadoo.fr- closed 12 Nov-18 Dec, evenings Tue, Wed and Thur, and Mon except during school and public holidays.* This cheese restaurant, just out of Gap, includes a shop selling local produce and a cheese-making operation you can visit: all activities are contained in one large, welcoming room.

⊜ **Café du Lycée** – *41 bd de la Libération -* ☎ *04 92 51 53 36 - closed Tue except Jul-Aug* . On the ground floor is a brasserie with ornamental woodwork and family portraits; in the basement is a lively watering hole for a younger clientele. Pleasant terrace for warm days.

WHERE TO STAY

⊜⊜ **Clos** – *20 ter av. Cdt-Dumont -* ☎ *04 92 51 37 04 - leclos@lemel.fr -* P *29rms -* ⊜⊜ *restaurant.* On the edge of town, this hotel offers functional rooms, many with balconies. Leafy garden with playground for children. Large, rustic dining room giving onto a terrace.

⊜⊜ **Hôtel Porte Colombe** – *4 pl. F.-Euzières -* ☎ *04 92 51 04 13 - hotel.portecolombe@wanadoo.fr - 27rms:* ⊜⊜ *restaurant.* This hotel right near the town centre pedestrian zone has fresh-looking soundproofed rooms. Panoramic terrace on the top floor, with a view of the village roofs and surrounding mountains.

⊜⊜ **Chambre d'hôte Le Parlement** – *At Charance - 4km/2.5mi NW of Gap on D 994 and a track to the right -* ☎ *04 92 53 94 20 - bruno.drouillard1@libertysurf.fr - 5rms.* This house in its leafy setting occupies the outbuildings of the neighbouring château. Large sophisticated rooms, sauna, pool table, swimming pool and children's playroom make it a delightful place to stay.

ON THE TOWN

Place Jean-Marcellin – *Pl. Jean-Marcellin* – Summer and winter alike, Place Marcellin and its numerous bars attract a large throng. Musical entertainment, themed evenings, karaoke and long terraces where you can sit and have a drink. The range of attractions on offer is considerable and makes for an enjoyable evening out.

SHOW TIME

In both summer and winter, the place Jean-Marcellin and its many bars welcome visitors night and day. Music, theme nights, karaoke or simply sitting with a drink on the long terraces, the possibilities are endless.

SHOPPING

Wednesday's market is mostly regular kitchen fare, while Saturday's is more varied with many craftspeople as well as producers of local specialties.

SPORT

Stade Nautique de Fontreyne – Kids *- Rte de Marseille -* ☎ *04 92 51 14 99 - opening hours vary according to the season; closed public holidays and one week in Sept.* This swimming complex has plenty to offer children, happily without neglecting their parents. The kids will love the two pools that are reserved for them, and especially the water chute; the grown-ups can enjoy the Olympic size open-air swimming pool and diving pool. Tennis, trampoline and miniature golf by the stadium.

Hiking – Around Gap, 8 easy walking trails are marked. The **balcons du Gapençais** offer 50km/31.25mi of foot and bicycle paths as well as horse trails. Information available at the tourist office.

Sights

Musée départemental★

6 av Maréchal-Foch ♿ ⏱ *July to mid-Sept: daily 10am-noon, 2-6pm; mid-Sept to June: 2-5.30pm, Sat-Sun 2-6pm.* ⏱ *Closed Tue and public holidays except 14 July and 15 Aug. 3€, children 1.50€ -* ☎ *04 92 51 01 58.*

Situated inside the public gardens of **La Pépinière**, this museum houses fine archaeological collections and antique earthenware.

Among the local finds in the archaeology section (basement) are a **double bust of Jupiter Ammon**★, the **stele**★ of Briançon, a Roman bas-relief from the 2C and some remarkable pieces of **jewellery**★ dating from the late Bronze Age.

A whole floor is devoted to fine collections of ceramics, mainly from Manisès (15C-18C), Nevers and Moustiers.

The **display of local ethnography**★ illustrates traditional daily life in the Queyras region from the 17C onwards, with carved **furniture**★★ and beautifully decorated objects. The third level houses an important collection of European painting from the 14C Italian school to French artists of the 19C. Other rooms are devoted to Alpine fauna, arms and armour and temporary exhibitions. The mausoleum★ of Francois de Bonne, duc de Lesdiguières, sculpted by Jacob Richier (1585-1640), is decorated with bas-reliefs illustrating the duke's most notable victories.

Excursions

Domaine de Charance★ *3km/2mi west of Gap*

▶ *From Gap, drive west along D 994 (towards Veynes) and turn right. In July-August, there is a shuttle bus; enquire at the tourist office.*

🄺🄸🄳🅂 Overlooking the valley, on the site of the old castle, destroyed by successive wars and replaced by a gracious 18C château, these English-style gardens occupy some 220ha/544 acres. After the French Revolution, rich owners embellished the gardens, which now include lawns, a forest, waterfalls, a lake and most spectacularly, a garden on four terraces with a view of surrounding mountains. The town of Gap purchased the estate in 1973 and has since developed it into an environment centre as well as a public park. Footpaths include a tour of the lake (*30min*), nature trails and a more ambitious climb up to the Pic de Charance (*3hrs*). The **information centre of the Parc national des Écrins** is housed in a pretty 18C building. The **Conservatoire botanique alpin** has a large collection of rare and exotic plants, as well as old roses, fruit-trees − including 550 varieties of apples − and local wild plants. Guided tours are offered.

▶ *From Gap, drive south towards Valserres then turn left onto D 11 and left again onto D 211.*

NOTRE-DAME DU LAUS *23km/14.4mi − about 1hr*

The hamlet of Laus has been a place of pilgrimage since 1664, when a young shepherdess called **Benoîte Rencurel** (1647-1718) had visions of the Virgin Mary. A church was built in 1666 with a chapel marking the spot where the vision appeared.

LES GETS ✻

MICHELIN MAP 328 N4 – SEE LOCAL MAP CLUSES

Unswayed by modish Morzine or futuristic Avoriaz, this little village has made it a point of honour to keep its authentic character and its restful, rural way of life. The well-equipped, family-friendly pistes are linked to Les Portes du Soleil; cross-country skiers can choose from 6 loops covering 20km/12.4mi in total. 🗊 *BP 27, Maison des Gets - 74260 Les Gets* 🕐 *July to Aug: daily 8.30am-12.30pm, 2-7pm, Sat-Sun and public holidays, 8.30am-7pm; mid-Dec to Mar: daily 8.30am-7pm; Apr-June and Sept-mid-Dec: daily except Sun and public holidays 9am-noon, 2-6pm* 🕐 *closed 1, 8 and 25 May, 1 and 11 Nov -* ☎ *04 50 75 80 80 - www.lesgets.com*

▶ **Orient Yourself:** Les Gets is 22km/13.75mi north of Cluses n D 902. The road through the Gorges du Foron is sometimes blocked by landslides or repairs.

🕭 **Don't Miss:** The Musée de Musique Mécanique has a certain eccentric charm.

🕐 **Organizing Your Time:** On Tuesdays, the church offers concerts featuring a huge organ with 1 000 pipes.

🅺🅸🅳🆂 **Especially for Kids:** Some farms welcome children as apprentices, with our without their parents. The tourist office has information.

⚭ **Also See:** Nearby Sights: AVORIAZ, CLUSES, Route des GRANDES ALPES, MORZINE, La ROCHE-SUR-FORON, Bassin de SALLANCHES, SAMOËNS, SIXT-FER-À-CHEVAL, THONON-LES-BAINS

The Museum

Musée de la Musique mécanique

294 route des Grandes-Alpes ♿ 🔊 *guided tour (1hr15min) July to Aug: daily 10.15am-12.15pm, 2.15-9.15pm; Sept-Oct: 2.15-7.15pm; mid-Dec to June: daily except Sat 2.15-7.15pm* 🕐 *closed Nov-mid Dec and 1 May. 6.50€ -* ☎ *04 50 79 85 75 - www.lemuseed-esgets.free.fr*

The 16C former "Maison des Soeurs" is now devoted to all forms of mechanical music; an interesting collection includes barrel organs, music boxes, player pianos, gramophones and orchestrions, as well as automata and animated scenes.

Hike

Mont Chéry ★★

Alt 1 827m/5 994ft. *10min gondola and chairlift ride or 2.5km/1.5mi by road to the Col de l'Encrenaz then 1hr 30min there and back on foot.* 🕐 *June to mid-Sept: 9.30am-5.30pm (continuous)* 🕐 *closed May and mid-Sept-mid-Dec. 7.90€ return -* ☎ *04 50 75 80 99 - www.lesgets.com.*

🖼 A vast **panorama**★★ of the limestone Faucigny mountains; the peaks in view are, from left to right, the Pointe de Nantaux, the Hautforts, at 2 464m/8 084ft the highest point in the Chablais, the Dents du Midi, Haut-Faucigny, Ruan, Buet, the Points de Sales with Mont-Blanc beyond, the Désert de Plate (⚭*see CLUSES,* ①*), Pointe Percée and the Pic de Marcelly.

WHERE TO STAY

🍽 🛏**Hôtel Bel'Alpe** – ☎ 04 50 79 74 11 - www.hotel-belalpe.com - closed 15 Apr- 2 June and 3 Sept-15 Dec - 🅿 - 35rms - 🛏restaurant. This family-friendly chalet offers simple rooms, most with a balcony. The restaurant has a view of the resort and a traditional local menu.

ROUTE DES GRANDES ALPES★★★

MICHELIN MAPS 332, 334, 340, 341

The Route des Grandes Alpes is the most renowned of the great routes crossing the French Alps. It links Lake Geneva with the Riviera via a road which follows the line of the peaks, often running alongside the border, and is only fully open at the height of summer. The challenge of crossing the French Alps along their entire length, from Lake Geneva to the Mediterranean, was taken up by the Touring Club de France in 1909. Tremendous difficulties along some sections of the route meant that the project continued for over a quarter of a century.

In 1934, mountain troops opened three passes until then inaccessible to tourists: the Col de la Cayolle, Col de l'Izoard (where an obelisk stands as a reminder of their achievement) and Col de Vars. In 1937, the President of the French Republic inaugurated the completed route from Évian to Nice, a journey which coaches took five whole days to cover. *Association Grande Traversée des Alpes - 14 r. de la République - 38000 Grenoble - ☎ 04 76 42 41 41 - www.routedesgrandesalpes.com*

▸ **Orient Yourself:** Stretching 600km/375mi from Thonon to Menton, the route goes over 16 mountain passes, including the Iseran pass at 2 770m/9 088ft, following peaks along the Italian border, where passes are generally blocked by snow from November until June.

🕐 **Organizing Your Time:** You can complete the itinerary in two days, but this is stressful and you miss a lot. See below.

👣 **Also See:** Nearby Sights: L'ARGENTIÈRE-LA-BESSÉE, Massif des ARAVIS, Les ARCS, AUSSOIS, BARCELONNETTE, BEAUFORT, BESSANS, BEUIL, BONNEVAL-SUR-ARC, BOURG-ST-MAURICE, BRIANÇON, Le BRIANÇONNAIS, Gorges du CIANS, La CLU-SAZ, CLUSES, EMBRUN, Val d'ENTRAUNES, Route du GALIBIER, Les GETS, La GRAVE, GUILLESTRE, Route de l'ISERAN, La Haute MAURIENNE, MODANE, MOLINES-EN-QUEYRAS, Route du MONT-CENIS, MONT-DAUPHIN, MORZINE, L'OISANS, Le QUEYRAS, Lac de SERRE-PONÇON, ST-VÉRAN, La TARENTAISE, THONON-LES-BAINS, TIGNES, Vallée de la TINÉE, L'UBAYE, VAL-D'ALLOS, VAL-D'ISÈRE, Massif de la VANOISE, VARS

Two-Day Itinerary

It is possible to go from Thonon to Menton in two days, by spending a night in Briançon; this, however, is a tiring journey which entails making sacrifices. For instance, it involves leaving out most of the excursions which really make the trip worthwhile, such as Chamonix with the Aiguille du Midi and the Vallée Blanche, or La Grave with the panoramic viewpoint at Le Chazelet... and only allows for carefully timed stops.

Five-Day Itinerary

◆ Thonon – Beaufort: *146km/91mi – allow 5hr 30min (tours included)*
◆ Beaufort – Val-d'Isère: *71km/44mi – allow 3hr (tours included)*
◆ Val-d'Isère – Briançon: *180km/111mi – allow 7hr 30min (tours included)*
◆ Briançon – Barcelonnette: *133km/83mi – allow 6hr 30min (tours included)*
◆ Barcelonnette – Menton: *206km/128mi – allow 6hr (tours included)*

Excursions

Across the Northern Alps

FROM LAKE GENEVA TO THE COL DU LAUTARET *347km/216mi*

The following route is only open in its entirety in summer. It crosses some of the most famous passes in the French Alps. Picturesque, unspoilt villages are separated by a bleak mountain landscape of exceptional beauty, at its most breathtaking at dawn or sunset.

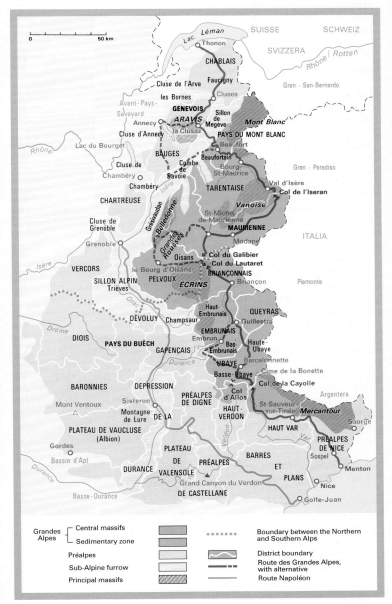

▶ *Follow D 902 from Thonon to Cluses.*

Thonon ♨♨ – ☙ *See THONON-LES-BAINS.*

Before leaving Thonon, stop in the Place du Château to take a last look at **Lake Geneva**★★★, Lausanne and the Swiss Jura. The damp, beech-lined gorge of the Dranse de Morzine leads into the **Chablais**★★, a pastoral region of the northern Préalpes and the grazing area of the famous Abondance breed of cattle.

Morzine ✲✲ – ☙ *See MORZINE.*

Les Gets ✲ – ☙ *See Les GETS.*

From Tanninges, the road enters the **Faucigny**★★ region, an area drained by the River Giffre, with landscapes shaped by glacial moraines through limestone folds.

Cluses – ☙ *See CLUSES.*

South of Cluses, the road enters the central massifs of the high Alps.

▶ *From Cluses, follow D 4 across the Col de la Colombière (☙ see Massif des ARAVIS).*

La Clusaz – ☙ *See La CLUSAZ.*

D 909 from La Clusaz to Flumet is one of the most famous routes in the French Alps. Try to reach the Col des Aravis in the afternoon to enjoy one of the finest views of the Mont Blanc Massif.

▶ *Take D 218B towards the Col des Saisies, via Notre-Dame-de-Bellecombe.*

There are glimpses to the right of the Aravis Massif and of the Gorges de l'Arly. The Col des Saisies (1 633m/5 358ft), overlooked by the Signal de Bisanne (1 939m/6 362ft), offers a fine viewpoint of the Beaufortain region.
Beyond Hauteluce, the road runs down to Beaufort, home of the famous Beaufort cheese.

Beaufort – ☙ *See BEAUFORT.*

Between Beaufort and Bourg-St-Maurice, the road goes through **Arèches** and the charming hamlet of **Boudin**★, then runs across the top of the Barrage de Roselend and along the **Cormet de Roselend**★ depression (☙ see BEAUFORT ⬛1⬛).

Bourg-St-Maurice – ☙ *See BOURG-ST-MAURICE.*

From Bourg-St-Maurice to Val-d'Isère, D 902 climbs in a series of hairpin bends and enters the Haute Tarentaise region.

▶ *For the next section of the route to Bonneval-sur-Arc, ☙ see Route de l'ISERAN, Excursions.*

The Gorges du Bachelard mark the northern boundary of the Parc du Mercantour

E. Baret/MICHELIN

Beyond Val-d'Isère, the road starts climbing to the Col de l'Iseran, the highest pass along the Route des Grandes Alpes (2 770m/9 088ft), and enters the Parc national de la Vanoise.

Bonneval-sur-Arc★★ – 🕭 See BONNEVAL-SUR-ARC.

From Bonneval-sur-Arc to Modane
56km/34.8mi along D 902 and N 6. 🕭 *See La Haute MAURIENNE, Excursions.*

▶ *Continue along the Arc Valley to St-Michel-de-Maurienne (17km/10.6mi). Turn left towards the Col du Galibier via Valloire and continue to the Col du Lautaret.*

Col du Galibier★★★
Alt 2 646m/8 681ft. 🕭 See Route du GALIBIER, Excursions.

Don't miss the alpine garden at the Col du Lautaret★★ (2 057m/6 749ft). Turn right from the pass towards La Grave then left just before the second tunnel to enjoy the lovely panorama of the Meije Massif.

Oratoire du Chazelet★★★ – See La GRAVE, Hikes

▶ *Return to the Col du Lautaret.*

Across the Southern Alps

FROM THE COL DU LAUTARET TO THE VALLÉE DE LA TINÉE

▶ *Follow N 91 to Briançon, then N 94 to Guillestre.*

South of the Col du Lautaret, the road enters the southern Alps. Oaks, ash trees and beeches can be seen along the Guisanne Valley, landscapes become brighter, valleys open out. This is the intra-Alpine zone.

Briançon★★ – 🕭 See BRIANÇON.

The road winds its way along the Durance Valley. Layers of marine sediment, shifted from east to west during the formation of the Alps, formed what is known as the **"nappes briançonnaises"** (consisting of schist and flysch).
The River Durance has dug its way through thick layers of limestone, flowing through a striking gorge (at L'Argentière-la-Bessée) before widening as it reaches the Guillestre Basin.

Mont-Dauphin★ – 🕭 See MONT-DAUPHIN.

Guillestre – 🕭 See GUILLESTRE.

This village lies at the exit of the **Combe du Queyras★★**, an impressive canyon through which flows the Guil.

▶ *An alternative route links Guillestre and Barcelonnette via Embrun (see Alternative route via the Lac de Serre-Ponçon).*

The Route des Grandes Alpes, which is 684km/425mi from start to finish, crosses 16 mountain passes, including the Col d'Iseran at a height of 2 770m/9 088ft. The altitude difference along the whole of the route is 10 675m/35 023ft.

Great Passes of the Southern Alps

– Col du Lautaret (2 057m/6 749ft)

– Col de Vars (2 111m/6 926ft)

– Col d'Allos (2 240m/7 349ft)

– Col de la Cayolle (2 326m/7 631ft)

– Col de la Lombarde (2 350m/7 710ft)

– Col d'Izoard (2 360m/7 743ft)

– Col Agnel (2 744m/9 003ft)

– Col de la Bonette (2 715m/8 907ft)

At the intersection with D 902, it is also possible to turn left towards Château-Queyras (⟨ see Le QUEYRAS, [1]), eventually reaching St-Véran *(15km/9mi east).*

St-Véran★★ – ⟨ See ST-VÉRAN.

▶ *Return to Guillestre by the same route and continue along D 902 towards Vars.*

Col de Vars
Alt 2 111m/6 926ft. The pass is the gateway to the Ubaye Valley in an arid landscape of meagre pastures dotted with blocks of sandstone and tiny pools. South of the pass, hamlets scattered across the south-facing slopes live on cattle-farming and handicraft. The upper Ubaye Valley, carved out of black schist, is obstructed by alluvial cones where mountain streams deposit debris. Note the strange rock formation of the Colonnes coiffées on the left, just before Les Prats.
The slender octagonal steeple in the village of **St-Paul** signals the beginning of the Haute Ubaye region.

Barcelonnette★ – ⟨ See BARCELONNETTE.

The narrow road runs along the bottom of the wild **Gorges du Bachelard**★, then winds round the Mont-Pelat Massif (3 053m/10 016ft), the main summit of the southern Alps.

Col de la Cayolle★★
Alt 2 327m/7 635ft.

▶ *There are numerous possibilities for hikes starting from the pass towards the Lac d'Allos and Lac des Garets (⟨ see Val d'ALLOS and below).*

Val d'Entraunes★★
The road follows the upper Var Valley lined with schist mountains until **St-Martin-d'Entraunes,** where it leaves the high Alps and enters the southern Préalpes. At **Guillaumes**, ignore the road on the right, which runs through the **Gorges de Daluis**★★ (⟨ see VAL D'ENTRAUNES, Excursions), carved out of red porphyry, and turn left towards Beuil. The road rises steadily to the Col de Valberg, affording varied views of the valley, the forested north-facing side offering a striking contrast with the south-facing slope covered with vineyards and orchards. Beuil lies at the beginning of the **Gorges du Cians**★★★ (⟨ see Gorges du CIANS), running south to join the River Var. On the way down to Roubion from the **Col de la Couillole** (alt 1 678m/5 505ft; ⟨ see BEUIL, Excursions), the road offers interesting views of the Vionène and Tinée valleys. The beauty of the wild landscape is enhanced by the contrasting colours of the rocks. Beyond **Roubion**★, perched on top of a rocky spur, at an altitude of 1 300m/4 265ft, the scenery is marked by red schist and waterfalls. **Roure**★ *(4km/2.5mi along a tiny road on the left, ⟨ see BEUIL, Excursions)* is another fine village with characteristic architectural features: houses have red-schist bases and are covered with *lauzes* (heavy slabs of schist).

The road winds its way alongside the Vionène, to its confluence with the River Tinée in St-Sauveur-sur-Tinée.

St-Sauveur-sur-Tinée – 🕭 *See Vallée de la TINÉE.*
The road follows the lower Tinée Valley for 4km/2.5mi before veering to the left towards St-Martin-Vésubie along the Valdeblore Valley. (🕭 *For the rest of the itinerary, see The Green Guide French Riviera.*)

Alternative route via the Lac de Serre-Ponçon

▶ *From Guillestre, it is possible to reach Barcelonnette via Savines-le-Lac and the Lac de Serre-Ponçon (27km/17mi detour).*

Embrun★
24km/15mi southwest of Guillestre. 🕭 *See EMBRUN.*

Beyond Embrun, the road crosses over to the south bank of the Durance then skirts the Lac de Serre-Ponçon. With its 3 000ha/7 413 acres, this is one of the largest reservoirs in Europe. As you come out of Savines-le-Lac, there is a splendid **view**★ of the Dévoluy Massif.
Further on, on the left-hand side of D 954, there is a group of *demoiselles coiffées*, rock columns characteristic of Alpine areas (🕭 *see Lac de SERRE-PONÇON, Nearby Sights*). The road then winds round the rocky promontory of Sauze-le-Lac marking the confluence of the River Durance and River Ubaye.

Barcelonnette★ – 🕭 *See BARCELONNETTE.*

Hike

Pas du Lausson and Col de la Petite Cayolle★★
4hr there and back on foot. Difference in altitude: 350m/1 148ft. Allow one day in order to derive full enjoyment from the beautiful landscapes.
🚶 From the car park at the Col de la Cayolle, walk towards the Pas du Lausson; lovely views of the Val d'Entraunes. Just before reaching the ridge, admire the exceptionally rich flora. From the summit, there is a remarkable **panorama**★★, in particular towards the east and the Lac du Lausson. From the edge of the plateau, it is possible to get a good view of the **Lac d'Allos** and its surroundings (🕭 *see VAL D'ALLOS*).
Go up, on the right, to the **Lac des Garets**; view of the Sommet des Garets and Mont Pelat. After skirting the lake towards the right, one eventually reaches the Col de la Petite Cayolle (2 642m/8 668ft). In clear weather, the view extends to Monte Viso.

▶ *Go down on the right to return to the Col de la Cayolle.*

LA GRAVE ✳✳

MICHELIN MAP 334 F1 – LOCAL MAP SEE L'OISANS

La Grave, which is the main ski resort in Dauphiné, is remarkably **well situated**✳✳ in the shadow of the Meije, one of the most impressive summits of the Écrins Massif and undoubtedly the most famous as far as mountaineers and tourists are concerned, for its peaks and glaciers offer spectacular views, particularly from the Oratoire du Chazelet. Beside the Meije, there are, in the immediate vicinity of La Grave, no fewer than 50 summits reaching heights ranging from 3 000m/9 843ft to 4 000m/13 123ft, although visitors with less of a head for heights can still enjoy some fine alpine panoramas. In spite of their tourist appeal, La Grave and its picturesque hamlets have avoided property developers and remained a small family resort with traditional houses. *N 91 - 05320 La Grave ◷ July to Aug, mid Dec to mid-April: daily 9am-noon, 2-7pm, Sun and public holidays 9am-noon, 3-6pm; mid-Apr to June: daily except Sun and public holidays 8am-noon, 2-6pm; Sept to mid-Dec: daily except Sun and public holidays 9am-noon, 2-5pm ◷ closed 1 and 8 May, Ascension, 1 and 11 Nov - ☎ 04 76 79 90 05 - www.lagrave-lameije.com*

▶ **Orient Yourself:** Located 28kn/17.5mi east of Bourg-d'Oisans on N 91, La Grave is the last village before the Col de Lautaret (11km/7mi), gateway to the Hautes-Alpes.

☞ **Don't Miss:** Ride the gondola up to the glaciers at la Meije.

◷ **Organizing Your Time:** You can take many excursions into the mountains. You will miss a lot if you don't spend at least four days in La Grave.

Kids **Especially for Kids:** Several climbing schools have programs for children.

☝ **Also See:** Nearby Sights: L'ALPE-D'HUEZ, Le BOURG-D'OISANS, BRIANÇON, Le BRIANÇONNAIS, Les DEUX-ALPES, Rout du GALIBIER, Route des GRANDES ALPES, L'OISANS, SERRE-CHEVALIER

The Village and the Slopes

☜☞ Ski area

In spite of having only a few ski lifts and ski runs, the ski area is nevertheless impressive owing to the difference in altitude (2 150m/7 054ft) between the Dôme de Lauze and La Grave.

Alpine skiing takes place on the slopes of the Meije and, in a more modest way, around Le Chazelet and the Col du Lautaret. There are also 20km/12.5mi of cross-country skiing tracks near Villar d'Arène, on the edge of the Parc national des Écrins. Finally there are numerous possibilities for ski touring *(enquire at the Compagnie des guides de l'Oisans)*. There are also 20km/12.5mi of cross country and snowshoe trails in the lower Arsine valley, across a wilderness area.

The cable car leads to two powder runs (Les Vallons de la Meije and Chancel) offering splendid views and the finest snow from late January to mid-May. This high-mountain area, which can be compared to the Chamonix Valley, is only suitable for competent skiers.

Runs on the Girose Glacier, above the cable car's upper station, are accessible in winter and summer to less advanced skiers.

For coin categories, see the Legend on the cover flap.

WHERE TO STAY

◷◷**La Meijette** – ☎ 04 76 79 90 34 - hotel.lameijette.juge@wanadoo.fr - open Mar-April, June-20 Sept, closed Tue except July-Aug- ▣ - 18rms- ◷◷restaurant. Splendid view of La Meije and its glacier from the terrace. Food is simple. The hotel, on the other side of the road, has comfortable, pine-paneled rooms.

Church

Surrounded by a small cemetery, this charming 12C Romanesque church, with its Lombard-style silhouette, low bell-tower and oven-vaulted apse, blends well into the splendid setting of the resort. Note the 15C font inside.

Next to it stands the 17C **Chapelle des Pénitents** *(Chapel undergoing restoration, ask at the presbytery to visit. ☎ 04 76 79 91 29.)* with frescoes all over the ceiling.

Excursions

There is a wide choice of **excursions** at moderate or high altitude. In summer, you need at least four days to explore the surrounding area; the main hiking itineraries lead to the **Plateau d'Emparis** *(starting from Le Chazelet)*, the **Col d'Arsine** *(starting from Pied du Col)* and the **Lac du Goléon** *(accessible from Valfroide)*.

In addition, La Grave is the ideal starting point for drives along the Romanche Valley, to the Col du Lautaret and Col du Galibier and to the resorts of Les Deux-Alpes and Serre-Chevalier.

Glaciers de la Meije★★★

⚞ Allow one day in order to explore all the possibilities of the site (1hr 10min there and back by cable car). 🕓 *Mid-June to mid-Sept. 18P return -* ☎ *04 76 79 91 09 - www. la-grave.com.*

The ride is in two sections: the first section leads to the Peyrou d'Amont Plateau (alt 2 400m/7 874ft), the second to the Col des Ruillans (alt 3 200m/10 499ft) on the northwest slopes of the Rateau Summit, offering on the way superb views of the Meije, Rateau and Girose glaciers. The view from the upper station includes the Aiguilles d'Arves due north, Mont Thabor to the northeast with the Vanoise summits in the distance and Mont Blanc further still, the Grandes Rousses and Belledonne mountains to the northwest.

Kids The **Grotte de glace** (🕓 *Second week July to second week Aug: 8am-3.45pm; third week June to first week July and third week Aug to mid-Sept: 10am-3.45pm (last admission 3pm)* 🕓 *closed mid-Sept to 2nd week June. 4€ -* ☎ *04 76 79 91 09 - www. grottedeglace.com)*, an ice cave decorated with many ice carvings, is easily accessible from the Col des Ruillans,

Several mountain restaurants offer superb panoramas as well as food.

⚞ From the Peyron d'Amont station lower down, it is possible to explore the area for half a day or a whole day along marked hiking trails *(ask for maps at the tourist office in La Grave).*

⚞ The **Trifides and Lauze ski lifts** offer an even more impressive **panorama**★★★ at an altitude of 3 550m/11 647ft, extending as far as the Grand Combin in the Swiss Alps.

Starting from Le Chazelet

Oratoire du Chazelet★★★

6km/3.7mi along D 33 branching off from N 91 to the Col du Lautaret at the exit of the first tunnel. The road goes through the village of **Les Terrasses** with its picturesque church. From the isolated Oratoire du Chazelet, there is a splendid **view** of the Meije Massif *(viewing table higher up, alt 1 834m/6 017ft).* Continue towards the village famous for its balconied houses. On the way down to the valley, it is possible to stop near the **Chapelle de Ventelon**, which offers another view of the Meije.

Hike to the Lac Lérié and Lac Noir★★★

3hr there and back. Difference in altitude: 700m/2 297ft. Leave the car at the entrance of Le Chazelet. Go towards the ski lifts at the other end of the village, cross the small bridge and follow footpath GR 54.

The Emparis Plateau is reached after climbing for 1hr; from here the walk becomes easier and offers clear views of the Meije. Another hour's walk leads to the spot with its height marked 2 300m/7 546ft; turn left at the signpost towards the Lac Lérié. Splendid **view** of the Lautaret road, the Rateau Summit and the vast Girose and Mont-de-Lans glaciers (summer ski area of La Grave and Les Deux-Alpes). Skirt the lake and admire the reflection of the mountains in the water as well as the striking view of the Romanche Valley.

▶ *Continue to the right towards the Lac Noir lying in a wild, desolate landscape dotted with edelweiss and gentians.*

View of the Meije Summit from the Oratoire du Chazelet

GRENOBLE★★

CONURBATION 419 334
MICHELIN MAP 333 H6

Standing at the confluence of the deep valley of the River Drac and River Isère, Grenoble's reputation as a forward-looking city, as well as the economic and cultural capital of the French Alps, has been growing since the Revolution; the dynamism of its research centres and the richness of its museums prove that it has lost none of its enthusiasm for progress. *14 rue de la République - 38000 daily 9am-6.30, Sun and public holidays 10am-1pm – Annexe at upper station of Bastille cable-car: June to Sept: 11am-1pm, 2-6pm, Sun 2-6pm closed 1 Jan, 1 May, 25 Dec - ☎ 04 76 42 41 41 - www.grenoble-isere.info – Guided tours (2hrs) July to Aug and Oct-June: contact tourist office for times. 7.50€*

▶ **Orient Yourself:** Enclosed by the rivers Drac and Isère and by the slopes of the Chartreuse range, the industrial and commercial centres of Grenoble are in the south (Échirolles, Point-de-Claix), to the east (Meylan) and where the rivers meet (Fontaine).

Don't Miss: The Musée de Grenoble and the Musée Dauphinois have remarkable collections; a walk along the heights of the Bastille is a highlight of any trip.

Organizing Your Time: The Notre-Dame district comes to life in the evening.

Especially for Kids: The Muséum d'histoire naturelle has a children's program; the beach at la Bifurk will provide fun and exercise.

Also See: Nearby Sights: CHAMBÉRY, Massif de CHAMROUSSE, Massif de la CHARTREUSE, Le GRÉSIVAUDAN, Lacs de LAFFREY, Route NAPOLÉON, PONT-EN-ROYANS, ST-PIERRE-DE-CHARTREUSE, Le TRIÈVES, Le VERCORS, VILLARD-DE-LANS, VIZILLE

A Bit of History

Origins – The town, founded by the Gauls at the confluence of the River Drac and River Isère, was fortified by the Romans and given the name of **Gratianopolis** (after Emperor Gratianus) which, in time, became Grenoble. During the Middle Ages, the

Address Book

For coin categories, see the Legend on the cover flap.

EATING OUT

La P'tite Ferme – *3 r. Jean-Jacques-Rousseau - ☎ 04 76 54 21 90 - laptiteferm@wanadoo.fr - closed Sun and Mon - reservations advised in evening.* This wine bar has a simple decor, and a wine list that is anything but. Traditional cuisine.

Le Valgaudemar – *2 r St-Hugues - ☎ 04 76 51 38 85 - closed Sun and Mon.* The farmhouse façade, wood panelling and photos of the Alps remind you that Valgaudemar is a valley in the Écrins park. Regional dishes such as tourtons filled with potato and cheese.

Ciao a Te – *2 r. de la Paix - ☎ 04 76 42 54 41 - closed Feb holidays, 3 weeks in Aug, Sun and Mon - reservations required.* This popular Italian restaurant in an old part of the city is near the Musée de Grenoble. Behind its timber front and hand-painted sign, it serves "fast" cuisine and of course pasta.

Café de la Table Ronde – *7 pl. St-André - ☎ 04 76 44 51 51 - www. cafetableronde.com - closed 1-15 Jan.* Huge mirrors on the walls reflect the regulars in lively discussion at the bar as well as photographs signed by Sarah Bernhardt, Raymond Devos and many other stars. Brasserie-style local cooking. The cabaret area claims to be one of the last homes of the classic French chanson. There are concerts on Thu, Fri and Sat.

Le Dialogue Café – *11 av Alsace-Lorraine - ☎ 04 76 46 18 03 - closed Mon evening and Sun - reservations advised.* Originally Le Strasbourg, this brasserie founded in 1904 has a new proprietor, but the interior is scarcely changed: wooden counter, banquettes in red velvet, and frescos. Brasserie style cooking, good choice of wine by the glass.

Bombay – *60 cours Jean-Jaurès - ☎ 04 76 87 71 80 - closed Aug and Mon - reservations required.* It is also possible to travel while seated at a table. Once across the threshold, you will be transported to distant climes by the tempting smell of Indian spices and the exotic flavours of the food.

Le Provençal – *16 cours St-André - 38800 Pont-de-Claix - 8km/5mi S of Grenoble on N 75 towards Sisteron - ☎ 04 76 98 01 16 - closed 2-10 Jan, 12-20 Apr, 2-24 Aug, Tue evening, Sun evening and Mon.* This restaurant behind a privet hedge in the suburbs of Grenoble offers cuisine from both Provence and Périgord, native regions of, respectively, Madame and Monsieur. As to decor, Madame's southern colours predominate.

WHERE TO STAY

Hôtel Acacia – *13 r de Belgrade - ☎ 04 76 87 29 90 - 20rms.* This hotel, located close to the cable-car of la Bastille was recently renovated. The guestrooms are modern, the reception area and breakfast room are decorated in Provençal colours.

Hôtel Patinoires – *12 r. Marie-Chamoux - ☎ 04 76 44 43 65 - www. hotel-patinoire.com - ⊡ - 35rms.* This austere modern construction in a residential area is a good address for those who want a calm night's sleep while remaining near the town centre. Small, practical rooms. Breakfast room decorated with hunting trophies.

Hôtel Trianon – *3 r. Pierre-Arthaud - ☎ 04 76 46 21 62 - info@hotel-trianon. com - closed 1-20 Aug and 26 Dec-2 Jan - 38rms.* This is a fairly peaceful hotel with some imaginatively themed rooms: Pastoral, Romantic, Butterfly and Louis XV. Others have a more classic look. Take your pick...

Hôtel Gambetta – *59 bd Gambetta - ☎ 04 76 87 22 25 - www. hotel-rest-gambetta.com - closed 17 July-6 Aug - 44rms - restaurant.* In spite of the liveliness of this district, you will rest undisturbed here. Rooms are well sound-proofed and air-conditioned. Large dining room with pale cherry-wood decor, traditional cuisine.

ON THE TOWN

The **Place Grenette** and the rue **Félix-Poulat** are pedestrian streets considered the "true" city centre. The **Place St-André** is popular in summer for its terraces, while in the antique-dealers area behind the Cathedral near the

Place Notre-Dame are found many pleasant cafes that stay open late. The weekly newspapers Le Petit Bulletin and Les Affiches de Grenoble (www.affiches.fr) list the entertainment in the Grenoble area.

La Soupe au Choux – *7 rte de Lyon - ☎ 04 76 87 05 67 - lasoupeauchoux@wanadoo.fr – Daily except Sun and Mon 6pm-1am*. This jazz club is a local institution. Well-known musicians appear here often; the rest of the time local groups display their jazz chops.

Le Tonneau de Diogène – *6 pl Notre-Dame - ☎ 04 76 42 38 40 - 8.30am-1am - closed 1 Jan and 25 Dec*. The only literary café in Grenoble is run by a former philosophy professor who organizes political and philosophical debates on Tue and Thur, frequented by local students. A bookstore is on the premises.

SHOPPING

La Noix de Grenoble-Desany – *6 bis pl. Grenette - ☎ 04 76 03 12 20 - Tue-Sat 9am-7pm, Mon 2-7pm - closed 2 weeks end of Jan and public holidays*. This confectioner-chocolate maker in the city centre offers a variety of local specialities, many of which incorporate the famous local walnuts: Noix de Grenoble, walnut cakes and Galets du Drac.

Christian Bochard – *19 r. Lesdiguières - ☎ 04 76 43 02 23* – M. Bochard is a chocolate inventor, and his most original creations are trademarked. For example, the Mandarin, a candied clementine filled with chocolate cream flavoured with Grand Marnier. There is also the Glaçon de Chartreuse, the glacier de Sarennes, fruit jellies, spice cake… An address to visit no matter what.

À l'Abeille d'Or – *3 r. de Strasbourg, quartier Étoile - ☎ 04 76 43 04 03 - daily except Sun and Mon 9.30am-12.30pm, 2.30-7.30pm - closed 1 week in Feb*. The interior of this shop is exactly as the grandparents of the present owners left it. You will find 14 sorts of honey, pollen, royal jelly, spice cake, barley sugar, licorice, many sorts of tea, preserves, and interesting condiments.

LEISURE

Maison de la montagne – *3 r Raoul-Blanchard - ☎ 825 825 588*. A centre providing information for people planning excursions on the mountain. The Bureau des Guides can be found here.

Kids **Plage de la Bifurk** – *2 r. Gustave-Flaubert (tramway stop MC2) - ☎ 04 76 23 57 16 - 6€* An urban beach open to all, with a lively, friendly ambiance.

town was repeatedly flooded by the River Drac, particularly in 1219 when the only bridge and most of the houses were destroyed.

"Dauphins" – In the 11C, the town came under the control of the counts of Albon, whose seat was the Château de Beauvoir on the edge of the Vercors. The English mother of Count Guigues III gave her son the affectionate nickname "Dolphin"; the name, translated into French, came to be the ruler's hereditary title and his territory was known as Dauphiné. **Humbert II**, the last Dauphin, sold the land to the king of France in 1349 and the title was thereafter conferred on the heir to the French throne.

The "Journée des Tuiles" (Day of the Tiles) – On the 7 June 1788, the news spread through Grenoble that the regional *parlements*, or high judicial courts, were to be closed down by order of Louis XVI. The people of Grenoble rebelled against the royal decree, climbed onto the roofs of the buildings and pelted the troops sent to subdue them with heavy tiles. The protest proved successful and the banished members returned to find jubilant crowds lining the streets, yet only three years later, in one of the ironic turns of local history, the *parlement* was dissolved by the leaders of the Revolution without any resistance from the town.

Industrialization – In the 19C, Grenoble developed into a prosperous industrial city. Glove-making, the town's speciality, became mechanised, while coal mines and cement factories changed the landscape of the surrounding area. Later on, paper mills, water power, electrometallurgy and electrochemistry increased the town's prosperity with the contribution of industries related to winter sports (⚡ *ski lifts*).

Grenoble today – The lively **place Grenette** and rue Félix-Poulat, the pedestrian streets of the old town, the many parks and flower gardens, the tree-lined avenues and wide boulevards give Grenoble the "feel of a real town and not that of a large village," as Stendhal once said. There is a new international trade centre, **Europole**, near the railway station. The **University**, founded in 1339 by Humbert II, includes highly specialised institutes of Alpine geography and geology and a centre of nuclear studies. The **Synchrotron**, a particle accelerator with a circumference of 850m/2 788ft standing near the Lyon-Grenoble motorway, symbolizes the dynamic approach of Alpine scientific research. The Winter Olympics of 1968 brought changes to the town's infrastructure and facilities, including a sports hall and a speed-skating rink, but also encouraged new trends in civic architecture.

Maison de la Culture – This imaginatively designed cultural centre, known locally as *"MC2,"* stands on elegant narrow columns. Black and white surfaces, cylinders and cubes contrast to make a striking modern structure.

Hôtel de ville – The town hall in Parc Paul-Mistral was designed by Maurice Novarina in collaboration with a number of other artists. A marble mosaic by Ettore Gianferrari and a bronze by Étienne Hadju decorate the central **patio**★. The Salle des Mariages displays a wall-hanging by Alfred Manessier; a tapestry by Raoul Ubac can be seen in the Salon de Réception.

An open-air museum – Grenoble's enthusiasm for modern civic art is on permanent view, as works by contemporary sculptors enliven urban spaces around the town, from the station square (Alexander Calder), Parc Paul-Mistral (George Apostu, Joseph Wyss) and the Quartier Alpin (Magda Frank) to the Olympic village and the main roads into the centre.

The Grenoble cable car: an unofficial emblem of the city

A Mountain at the End of Every Street

The setting

Stendhal's description of Grenoble sums up the unique charm of the town; the mighty escarpments of the Vercors dominate the skyline to the west, the sheer faces of the Néron and the St-Eynard rise up in the north and to the east stand the dark, often snow-capped peaks of the Belledonne range.

Panorama from the Fort de la Bastille *1hr*

The fort is accessible by cable car, by car or on foot. Car park next to the lower station. Cable-car: (6min, continuous) July to Aug: daily 9.15am (Mon 11 am)-midnight; June: daily 9.15am (Mon 11am)-11.45pm, Sun 9.15am-7.25pm; Apr-Mar and Oct: daily 9.30am (Tue 11am) -11.45pm, Mon 11am-7.25pm; Sun 9.30am-7.25pm; Nov to Feb: daily 11am-6.30pm; Mar: Mon and Tue 11am-7pm, Wed-Fri 9.30am-7pm, Sat-Sun 9.30am-7.25pm; Sept: 9.30am (Mon 11am)-11.45pm, Sun 9.30am-7.25pm closed 3 weeks in Jan. 5.80€ return, children 5-18 years 3.75€ - ☎ 04 76 44 33 65 - www.bastille-grenoble.com.

From the rocky promontory situated on the left as you come out of the upper station, the **view**★★ takes in the town, the confluence of the River Isère and River Drac and the transverse section of the Isère Valley framed by the Néron (right) and Moucherotte (left) summits.

▸ *Go up to the terrace above the restaurant.*

Information panels help visitors to detail the **panorama**★★ of mountains unfolding all round: Belledonne, Taillefer, Obiou, Vercors (Grand Veymont and Moucherotte) and even Mont Blanc, which can be seen through the Grésivaudan depression. There is a fine bird's-eye view of Grenoble, the old town and the 19C districts to the south and west, all overlooked by the high-rise tower blocks of the **Île Verte**.

Two marked paths lead back to town: one goes through the **Parc Guy-Pape** and Jardin des Dauphins *(about 1hr 30min)*, the other follows the **Circuit Léon-Moret** *(1 hr, people who dislike heights or who have trouble walking should avoid the 380-step monumental stairway)* which crosses the fortifications and ends at the Porte St-Laurent near the Église St-Laurent.

From the cable-car station, it is possible to walk towards the heights of Mont Jalla *(1hr)* for an even better panoramic view.

Other marked paths including GTA 2 go through the Bastille area *(specialised topographical guidebooks are available)*.

Old Town *1hr*

▸ *Start from place Grenette.*

From the Place Grenette to the rue Chenoise spreads a maze of streets dating from the Middle Ages to the 19C. Several courtyards in this area are open to discrete visits. Information is available at the tourist office.

Place Grenette

This lively square lined with shops is one of the favourite haunts of the locals who like to stroll and stop at the pavement cafés. This is also the spot where, on 19 June 1889, to the amazement of the inhabitants and the anger of the local gas companies, six lamps provided the first electric street lighting in the city.

▸ *Walk along Grande-Rue.*

Grande-Rue

This former Roman road is lined with fine old houses; no 20, facing a Renaissance mansion, is the **Maison Stendhal,** where the novelist, whose real name was Henri Beyle, spent part of his childhood in the apartment of his grandfather, Dr.Gagnon. The two fine courtyards date from the 15C and the 18C.

Rue J.-J.-Rousseau starts almost opposite; no 14 was Stendhal's birthplace (*not open to the public).*

▶ *Return to Grande-Rue.*

Several famous natives of Grenoble were born or lived along this street. The Hache workshop, home of the famous family firm of furniture makers, stands on place Claveyson.

Place St-André

In the centre stands a statue of Bayard, the "knight without fear and above reproach" (*see GRÉSIVAUDAN*). The appropriately chivalric-sounding Café de la Table Ronde (1739) is one of the oldest in France, and yet another address with a claim to literary fame; Stendhal liked to come here to sketch out his first drafts over a drink.

Palais de justice ★

Open first Sat in the month. This former palace of the Dauphiné Parliament is the finest building in Grenoble; the left wing is in Flamboyant-Gothic style and the right wing in early Renaissance style. Inside, note the interesting **wood panelling** ★ and ceilings.

Église St-André

The 13C chapel has a bell-tower surmounted by an octagonal spire; Bayard's funeral monument (17C) is in the north transept.

▶ *Walk round St-André to place d'Agier and go into the Jardin de Ville.*

Hôtel de Lesdiguières

This house was built in the 16C for the military hero, the Duc de Lesdiguières (1543-1626), but he prefered his sumptuous residence in Vizille. In the 17C, it was the seat of government for the Dauphiné, then served as the town hall until 1967.

▶ *Return to place St- André by rue Berlioz and turn right onto rue du Palais.*

The place aux Herbes is the oldest square in the city. The streets around nearby rue de la Brocherie were once the most sought-after in Grenoble. Some of the aristocratic town houses, or hôtels, have retained their Renaissance design; the courtyard of the Hôtel de Chasnel at **no6** is a fine example. Two more inner courts can be seen in the parallel rue Chenoise. No10 dates from the 17C; visitors can catch a glimpse of the staircase ★ at **no8, Hôtel d'Ornacieux**, through the glass panel of the front door.

Place Notre-Dame

Excavations carried out under the cathedral square have revealed the foundations of the Gallo-Roman walls surrounding Gratianopolis and important paleo-Christian remains; metal markers embedded in the paving of the square follow the outline of the walls. Standing with your back to the cathedral, you will notice a solitary tower, **Tour Clérieux**: it is all that remains of the episcopal buildings which stood here during the Middle Ages and included three churches: the Cathédrale Notre-Dame, the adjacent Église St-Hugues and the baptistery (destroyed in medieval times).

Cathédrale Notre-Dame

🕑*Open 2-6.30pm*. Remodelled many times and recently restored to its original aspect, the cathedral has retained some pre-Romanesque features such as the five adjacent naves and the base of the bell-tower; fortunately the cement façade added in the 19C was subsequently removed. In the chancel, note the 14m/45ft-high ciborium, an impressive example of flamboyant Gothic stonework. The Chapelle St-Hugues was once the nave of the 13C Église St-Hugues.

The elegant fountain, known as the fontaine des Trois-Ordres, in the centre of place Notre-Dame takes its name from its three figures who represent the traditional classes of society: the clergy, the nobility and the third estate. The former **bishop's palace** next to the Chapelle St-Hugues now houses the **Musée de l'ancien évêché** (👁*see below*).

Walk along **rue Barnave**, lined with charming old town houses. The Gothic **hôtel François Marc** at no22 dates from 1490; the archway bears a winged lion emblem, the symbol of St Mark the Evangelist. Beyond the door is a courtyard with an elegant spiral staircase.

▶ *Follow rue Duclos to rue Raoul-Blanchard.*

The former Jesuit college is now the Lycée International Stendhal. The walls and staircase were designed to work as a **sundial**, marking the solar and lunar calendars, religious festivals, feast days of the order and the time in the twelve towns in which the Society of Jesus had founded an institution. (🕑 *Guided tours; contact the tourist office*)

▶ *Return to place Grenette by rue de la République.*

Sights

The Left Bank of the Isèr

Musée de Grenoble ★★★

♿🕑 *Daily except Tues 10am-6.30pm. Guided tours available (1hr30min).* 🕑 *Closed 1 Jan, 1 May, 25 Dec. 5€, children uner 18 years no charge -* ☎ *04 76 63 44 44 - www.museedegrenoble.fr*

The Museum of Fine Arts, inaugurated in 1994, is located along the River Isère, at the heart of the old town. Its architecture is remarkably plain and lighting can be modified according to the works exhibited.

This is one of the most prestigious French regional museums: its collections of paintings from the 16C to the 20C include a particularly rich collection of modern and contemporary art, which is exceptional even by European standards.

16C and 17C painting

Italian painting is represented by Perugino. Tintoretto, Veronese, Carravaggio, Fra Bartolomeo and **Vasari** (*The Holy Family,* in typical Mannerist style). The collection from the 17C French school includes works by **Philippe de Champaigne**, **Georges de La Tour** and Claude Gellée, known as Le Lorrain. One of the highlights of the section is a series

Collection Musée de Grenoble

Psametik's Sarcophagus (c. 500 BC)

of pieces by **Francisco de Zurbarán**: - several paintings which form an altarpiece, originally from the monastery of Jerez de la Frontera.

19C painting
It extends from **neo-Classicism** to **Impressionism** and **Symbolism** and is represented by Ingres, Boudin, Monet, Sisley, Corot, Théodore Rousseau, Gauguin (Portrait of Madeleine Bernard) as well as by artists from Grenoble such as Ernest Hébert and **Henri Fantin-Latour**.

20C modern art
Donations and bequests have considerably enriched the museum so that most schools are represented by the most famous artists. **Fauvism** is illustrated by Signac, Vlaminck, Van Dongen and above all **Matisse** (Interior with Aubergines, 1911); the **Cubist School** is headed by Braque and **Dadaism** is reflected in the works of Picabia (Idyll), Grosz and Ernst. The Paris School is represented by **Chagall** and **Modigliani**. There are important works by **Picasso** and **Léger**. Klee, Miró and Kandinsky lead to **Abstract Art** with later representatives such as Taeuber and Domela.

Contemporary art
All the main trends from 1945 onwards, from **Lyrical Abstract Art** to **New Realism** and **Support-Surface** through **Pop Art** and **Minimalism**, are illustrated by major artists such as Dubuffet, Vasarely, Hartung, Atlan, Brauner (Woman with a bird), Wesselman, Boltanski (Monument), Raysse, Judd and many others.

Antiquities
In the basement. The extremely rich collection of **Egyptian antiquities** includes several royal steles, brightly decorated coffins and refined funeral masks.

Tour de l'Isle
Incorporated into the new museum, this medieval tower now houses more than 3 000 drawings including several masterpieces such as a 15C *St Jerome* from northern Italy.

Musée de l'Ancien Évêché – Patrimoines de l'Isère★★
&⬚ *Mon-Sat 9am-6pm (Tues 1.30-6pm), Sun 10am-7pm . ⬚ Closed 1 Jan, 1 May, 25 Dec. No charge. ⬚ Guided tours (1hr or 2hrs) first Sun of month at 3.30pm - ☎ 04 76 03 15 25 - www.ancien-eveche-isere.fr.*
Situated at the heart of the town's historic centre, this interactive museum is housed in the former bishops' palace; it offers an account of the regional heritage through a number of prestigious collections. In the basement, visitors can see in situ a paleo-Christian **baptistery**★, one of the oldest of its kind (4C).

St-Laurent District

Situated on the right bank of the River Isère this old district, flanked by the Porte de France to the west and the Porte St-Laurent to the east, is undergoing restoration work.
Access on foot: walk across the footbridge of the Citadelle and take the steps on the left leading to the museum. Access by car: along quai Perrière and rue Maurice-Gignoux.

Musée dauphinois★
30 rue Maurice-Gignoux &⬚ June to Sept: 10am-7pm; Oct to May: 10am-6pm ⬚. Closed Tues, 1 Jan, 1 May, 25 Dec. No charge. Guided tours (1hr) - ☎ 04 76 85 19 01 - www.musee-dauphinois.fr
This museum of regional art and traditions is housed in a former 17C convent, the **couvent de la Visitation de Ste-Marie-d'en-Haut**, built on the hillside in lovely sur-

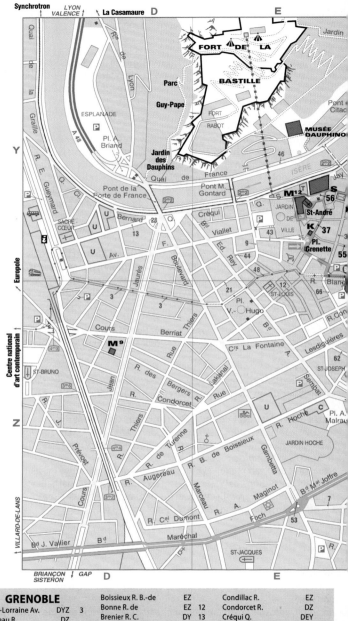

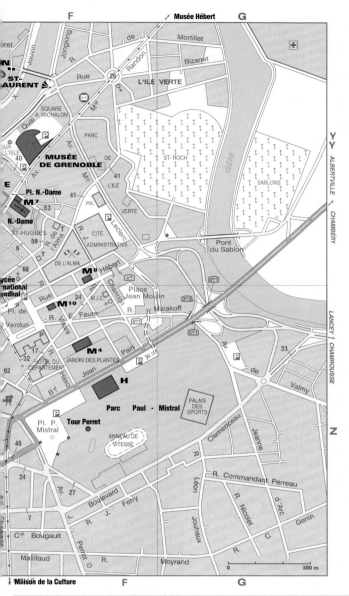

Perrot Av. J.	FZ		Sembat Bd A.	EZ		Valmy Av.de	GZ	
Poulat R. F.	EY	48	Servan R.	FY	59	Verdun Pl.	FZ	
Prévost R. J.	DZ		St-André Pl.	EY	56	Viallet Av. F.	DEY	
Randon AV. Mar.	FY		Ste-Claire Pl.	EY	57	Vicat R.	EZ	66
Rey Bd Ed.	EY		Strasbourg R. de	EFZ	62	Victor-Hugo Pl.	EZ	
Rivet Pl. G.	EZ	53	Thiers R.	DZ		Villars R. D.	FYZ	
Rousseau R. J.-J.	EY	55	Très-Cloître R.	FY	63	Voltaire R.	FY	68
Sablon Pont du	GY		Turenne R.	DZ				

Ancien palais du Parlement dauphinois	EY	S	La Casamaure	DY		Musée des Troupes de Montagne	FZ	M[10]
Cathédrale Notre-Dame	FY		Lycée international Stendhal	EFZ		Musée d'Histoire naturelle	FZ	M[4]
Centre national d'art contemporain	DZ		Maison de la Culture	FZ		Musée Hébert	GY	
Église St-André	EY		Maison Stendhal	EY	K	Musée Stendhal (Hôtel de Lesdiguières)	EY	M[12]
Église-musée St-Laurent	FY		Musée dauphinois	EY		Parc Guy-Pape	DY	
Europole	DY		Musée de Grenoble	FY		Parc Paul-Mistral	FGZ	
Fort de la Bastille	EY		Musée de l' Ancien Évêché -Patrimoine de l'Isère	FY	M[7]	Porte St-Laurent	FY	N
Hôtel de Ville	FZ	H	Musée de la Résistance et de la Déportation	FY	M[8]	Synchrotron	DY	
Hôtel d'Ornacieux	FY	E	Musée des Automates de Grenoble	DZ	M[9]	Tour Perret	FZ	
Hôtel François Marc	EY	D						
Jardin des Dauphins	DY							

roundings. The tour takes visitors round the cloister, the chapter-house and the Baroque chapel. The main rooms, devoted to regional heritage, display a rich collection of furniture and traditional tools. Long-term themed **exhibitions**★★ illustrate various aspects of life in the mountains. The splendid Baroque **chapel**★★ from the early 17C is the highlight of the tour and a popular venue for concerts. The murals illustrate the life of St François de Sales and were painted to celebrate his beatification. Note also the trompe-l'oeil painting above the chancel and the remarkable Baroque altarpiece.

Église-musée St-Laurent★★

☎ 04 76 44 78 68. Closed for repairs, reopening planned for 2008.
This building, one of the few of its kind in France, is particularly interesting owing to the extensive excavations which brought to light the numerous additions and alterations made to it. The **St-Oyand Crypt**★★, located beneath the east end of the present church, was built in the 6C-7C on the site of a pagan necropolis (excavation work in progress). This early medieval oratory is richly adorned with Roman and Merovingian decorative motifs skilfully blended with Carolingian elements. The church, surprisingly large by the standards of its time, is entered through the Romanesque porch surmounted by a bell-tower; from the gallery overlooking the nave, there is a fascinating overall view of the different architectural styles. The decoration of the chancel walls and ceiling dates from 1910, before the swastika motif in the design had taken on a political significance. In fact, this 3 000 year-old Hindu ideogram is thought to have represented "the origin of all things" or its literal Sanskrit meaning "well-being," ideas much more in keeping with the surroundings.

F. Pattou/Musée Dauphinois, Grenoble

Burial site in the Église St-Laurent

The "Grey Gold" of Grenoble

In the 19C, the Grenoble region was the birthplace of the French cement industry based on research carried out by Louis Vicat (1786-1861), who was looking for the lost secret of Roman cement. At the height of its production, natural cement from Dauphiné was exported to New York and South America.

Grenoble has retained several architectural and decorative reminders of this golden age including the neo-Moorish Chapelle Notre-Dame-Réconciliatrice (rue Joseph-Chaurion), the Tour Perret (1925), the former offices of Ciments de la Porte de France (Cours Jean-Jaurès) and the picturesque urinals – no longer in use – along the avenues of the Alpine metropolis.

Themed Museums

Musée de la Résistance et de la Déportation★

July to Aug: 10am (Tue 2pm)- 7pm; Sept to June: Mon-Fri 9am (Tue 2pm)-6pm, Sat-Sun 10am-8pm Closed 1 Jan, 1 May, 25 Dec. No charge. Guided tours first Sun of month at 2.30pm (no charge) - ☎ 04 76 42 38 53 - www.resistance-en-isere.fr.

This ultra-modern museum recreates original settings and sounds and explains the motives of members of the Resistance and the sacrifices entailed by their actions. The intense activity of the local Resistance movements is illustrated by several reconstructions; the German occupation is shown in relation to collaboration and deportation. Note the three authentic doors of the former Gestapo prison in Grenoble, covered with graffiti drawn by members of the Resistance. The importance of the military activity of the Resistance movements (highlighted by a huge relief map) and their preparatory work for the liberation of France are also shown. One room is devoted to the Monaco meeting which led to the fusion of the various movements. Children can follow a series of explanatory notes specifically directed at them.

Musée des Automates de Grenoble

Guided tours (1hr) 2-6.30pm (last admission 5.45pm) 5€, children 3€ - ☎ 04 76 43 33 33.

Hidden at the end of a narrow street, this museum houses a rich collection of automata and music boxes.

Musée d'Histoire naturelle

1 rue Dolomieu Mon-Fri 9.30am-noon, 1.30-5.30pm, Sat-Sun and public holidays 2-6pm. Closed 1 Jan, 1 May, 25 Dec. 2.20€, children no charge. No charge Wed afternoon from Oct to May - ☎ 04 76 44 05 35 - www.museum-grenoble.fr

Established early in the 19C, this museum reflects that period's passion for nature studies. The Salle des Eaux Vives on the ground floor contains several aquariums. Exceptionally fine collection of minerals and fossils. On the first floor, exhibits of stuffed animals in their natural habitats. The museum has been modernized, with electronic and multimedia aides to capture the interest of children.

Le Magasin - Centre national d'Art contemporain

West of the town centre along cours Berriat (no 155). Open according to the exhibition programme daily except Mon 2-7pm 3 € - ☎ 04 76 21 95 84 - www.magasin-cnac.org

Exhibitions of contemporary art are held under an immense glass roof inside a former industrial building, known as **Le Magasin**, designed in 1900 by the Eiffel Group.

Nearby Sights

St Martin-le-Vinoux – La Casamaures

8bis av du Général-Leclerc (off highway A 48). 38950 St-Martin-le-Vinoux ○ Guided tour 1hr 15min) Tue, Wed and every first Sat of month at 2pm; school holidays: Tue -Fri 2 pm ○ closed second to fourth week of Aug and mid-Dec to mid-Jan. 3€ - ☎ 04 76 47 13 50 - www.casamaures.org

This 1855 neo-Moorish villa from the heyday of cement construction offers a profusion of Moorish arches and moucharabies (window grills) based on designs from a palace in Istanbul.

La Tronche – Musée Hébert

Northeast of the Musée de Grenoble, along avenue Randon. Entrance in chemin Hébert. ♿○ June to Sept: daily except Tues 10am-6pm (Sun 7pm); Oct to May: daily except Tue 10am-6pm ○Closed Jan, 1 May, 25 Dec. No charge. ☎ 04 76 42 97 35 - wwwpatrimoine-en-isere.com.

A vast French-style park is the setting of the former home of the painter Ernest Hébert (1817-1908), a native of Dauphiné, and of the museum devoted to his works.

Lancey – Musée de la Houille blanche

16km/10mi. From Grenoble, follow D 523 towards Domène. In Lancey, turn right at the stoplights towards La Combe-de-Lancey and the paper mills. ☎ 04 76 45 66 81. Closed for renovations.

The term *houille blanche* (white coal) was coined by **Aristide Bergès** to describe water power. The engineer began building a chute above Lancey in 1869 (completed in 1875) to provide power for the paper mills. Later turbines were introduced. The museum illustrates Aristide Bergès' career and the history of water power in the 19C. His house (⚷ *not open to the public*) stands on the left of the entrance; the Art-Nouveau style of the hall is just visible through the window on the ground floor.

Sassenage

6km/3.7mi northwest by D 531 towards Villard-de-Lans. The town church is the final resting-place of **François de Bonne, Duc de Lesdiguières,** the last Constable of France.

Les Cuves

⬤⬤ 30min. Leave by the right bank of the Furon and return by the left bank. ○ Guided tour (1hr) July to Aug: 10am-6pm; Apr to May and Oct: Sat-Sun 1.30-6pm; June and Sept: daily except Mon 1.30-6pm. 5.10P, children 4.20€ - ☎ 04 76 27 55 37 - www.sassenage.fr This pair of caves, linked by a waterfall, is one of the "seven natural wonders of Dauphiné." The tour explores a vast underground maze of galleries full of stalactites, stalagmites and fossils and can be combined with a walk along the shady banks of the Furon.

Château

Park open to public. Built between 1662 and 1669, this was until recently the seat of the aristocratic Sassenage-Béranger family. According to legend, the local lords could trace their descent back to the beautiful, shape-changing fairy Mélusine, who is represented in relief above the entrance. The elegant château with tall dormer windows stands in a 19C landscaped park, below a rocky knoll and its ruined medieval castle. Fine views of the Vercors.

▷ *Leave Grenoble by boulevard Vallier and the N 532. Cross the Drac and take the D 106 towards St-Nizier-du-Moucherotte.*

St-Nizier-du-Moucherotte

15km/9.3mi west via Seyssinet.
This village, burnt down by the Germans in June 1944 and subsequently rebuilt, occupies a splendid open site on the plateau; it is one of the favourite winter and summer resorts of the residents of Grenoble.

Mémorial du Vercors

2km/1.2mi by D 106. This cemetery, containing the graves of 96 members of the Resistance, is situated on the first line of defence attacked by the Germans in July 1944.

Église

Despite extensive restoration work, the church has retained its traditional appearance; it also houses some interesting modern works of art. The stone cross outside dates from 1761.

Walks in the area

Viewpoint★★

A path, starting from the Bel-Ombrage Hotel leads to a viewing table giving extensive views of the Chartreuse, Mont-Blanc, Belledonne and Écrins massifs.

Sommet du Moucherotte★★

3hr there and back. Start from the car park at the top of the Olympic ski-jump and follow GR 91. The vast **panorama**★★★ unfolding from the summit includes Mont Blanc when the weather is clear, and at night the view of Grenoble is enchanting.

GRÉOUX-LES-BAINS ♒♒

POPULATION 1 921
MICHELIN MAP 334 D10

Gréoux has only one spring which releases 2.5 million litres/575 000gal of hot (37°C/98.6°F), sulphurous water used for the treatment of rheumatism, arthritis and respiratory complaints. Steles discovered last century, dating from AD 176 and dedicated to the nymphs of Gréoux, prove that the spa water was already famous in Roman times. Rediscovered centuries later, the resort became fashionable again during the 19C. Today the thriving town, which is favoured for its fine setting and sunny climate, has ever more hotels, luxury villas and shops as well as a wider choice of leisure activities. 🏠 *avenue des Marroniers – 04800 Gréoux-les-Bains– 🕐 June to Sept: daily 9am-12.30, 2.30-7pm, Sun and public holidays 9am-noon, 2-6pm (June and Sept 9am-noon); Apr to Mar and Oct: daily 9am-noon, 2-6pm, Sun and public holidays 9am-noon; Nov to Feb: daily 9am-noon, 2-6pm (Sat 5pm); Mar: 9am-noon, 4-6pm 🕐 closed Sun from Nov to Mar - ☎ 04 92 78 01 08. Guided tours of the town 🕐 June to Sept: every other Thur at 4pm; rest of year 2.30pm. 4€. Leaves from the tourist office.*

▸ **Orient Yourself:** Gréoux is 14km/8.75mi east of Manosque, on the edge of the Verdon gorges. Lac Sainte-Croix is 20km/12.5mi northeast by the D 952, passing through Riez.

🅿 **Parking:** Parking lots are found behind the tourist office and at the upper end of the village.

🕐 **Organizing Your Time:** Count one hour to see the town, and another to drive to Saint-Julien-le-Montagnier and admire the view

Kids **Especially for Kids:** Le Musée Santon-Crèche displays figurines illustrating daily life a century ago; L'Écomusée des Miniatures et Poupées has hundreds dolls to admire in thematic settings.

Also See: Nearby Sights: CÉRESTE, Vallée de la Moyenne DURANCE, FORCALQUIER, Monastère de GANAGOBIE, MANE, MANOSQUE, MOUSTIERS-STE-MARIE, RIEZ, Lac de STE-CROIX, Plateau de VALENSOLE, Grand Canyon du VERDON

Sights

Vieux village

The old village centre nestles at the foot of the castle. On rue Grande, an early 19C house, the **Maison de Pauline**, gives a glimpse into living arrangements a century ago, using items donated by local residents. ⏱ Mar to 20 Dec: daily except Sat-Sun and public holidays 10am-noon, 2-6pm. 2€. ☎ 04 92 78 10 92.

Castle

The former stronghold of the Knights Templar overlooking the village has retained its massive square keep in the northwest corner. When festivals are not being staged in the courtyard (👆 see Calendar of events), the castle is used as an exhibit space by local artists.

Troglodytic baths

A pool dating from the 1C AD, found near the present-day spa centre, shows the importance of the baths in the Gallo-Roman period. A stela found in the 19C celebrates the nymphs said to inhabit the spot.

Musée du Santon-Crèche de Haute-Provence

36 avenue des Alpes. 👆🚶 *Guided tour (30min) daily except Sun and Mon 10am-noon, 3-7pm; mid-Apr to June and Sept to Oct: daily except Sat, Sun and Mon 10am-noon, 2.30-5.30pm.* ⏱ *Closed Nov to mid-Apr, 1 May, 14 July and 15 Aug. 5€, children 7-12 years old 2.50€ -* ☎ *04 92 77 61 08.* Miniature village populated by some 300 santons illustrating daily life in the region at the turn of the last century.

Kids Écomusée des Miniatures, Poupées et Jouets du Monde

16 avenue des Alpes ⏱ *Mar to Nov: telephone for opening times* ☎ *04 92 78 16 52 or 06 84 62 71 23. 7€, children 5.50€.* Hundreds of dolls and toys, arranged in thematic scenes, fill 12 rooms.

E. Baret/MICHELIN

Santons – traditional Provençal figures in the Musée du Santon-Crèche

Excursions

St-Julien-le-Montagnier

579m/1 900ft, 14km/8.7mi south of Gréoux.
Wonderful **view**⋆ of the Plans de Provence, the Durance Valley, the Plateau de Valensole, Ste-Baume and Ste-Victoire from what used to be the village threshing floor. The square, lantern-shaped bell-tower of the 11C **village church** is a hallmark

Address Book

For coin categories, see the Legend on the cover flap.

WHERE TO STAY AND EAT

⊖ **Chambre d'hôte Bastide St-Donat** – *Rte de Vinon - 4km/2.5mi W of Gréoux on D 952 - ☎ 04 92 78 01 77 - www.bastidesaintdonat.com - ⊠ - 4rms.* The rooms in this former fortress are decorated in Provençal colours with antique furniture and red "tomette" tiles on the floors, providing a charming ambiance despite the road nearby. The garden perfumed by lavender bushes and a swimming pool complete the pleasant scene.

⊖⊖ **Hôtel Villa Castellane** – *Av. des Thermes - ☎ 04 92 78 00 31 - hotelcaste@ aol.com - closed Dec-Feb - ▣ - 17rms - ⊖⊖ restaurant.* At the heart of the spa resort, near the casino, this old hunting pavilion stands in the centre of a park. Guestrooms offer a high standard of comfort, as do the apartments available for a longer stay. Both restaurant and swimming pool are open only to guests.

⊖⊖ **Hôtel La Chêneraie** – *Les Hautes Plaines via Av. des Thermes - ☎ 04 92 78 03 23 - contact@la-cheneraie.com - closed 15 Nov-28 Feb - ▣ - 20rms - ⊖⊖ restaurant.* This modern hotel on the hillside above town has spacious, functional rooms. The balconies are very pleasant in fine weather and overlook a large swimming pool. Windows in the bright dining room overlook the old town and castle.

⊖⊖ **Alpes** – *Av. des Alpes - ☎ 04 92 74 24 24 - closed Dec- Mar - ▣ - 30rms - ⊖⊖ restaurant.* At the foot of the Templar castle, this hotel offers a renovated interior behind an old façade. Rooms are modern and sound-proofed. The restaurant offers Provençal cuisine in an appropriate decor. Pleasantly shaded terrace and family atmosphere.

ON THE TOWN

The **rue Grande** is lined with agreeable restaurants, crêperies and snackbars such as *La Marmite Provençale, La Main à la Pâte,* or *Myriam Miam.* You can sit out on terraces to watch passers-by.

---

of traditional Haute-Provence architecture. Inside, a carved, gilded altar from the 17C and a remarkably well-preserved rood beam still survive. The 13C **ramparts** are all that remains of the medieval stronghold. Follow the road to the point where it enters the village; there is a good view of the area from the fortified gate. ⏱ *Sat-Sun 9am-5pm, contact M or Mme Nicaud - ☎ 04 94 80 02 52*

Plateau de Valensole★ – *89km/55.3mi – about 5hr –* ♿ *see Plateau de VALENSOLE*

Plans de Provence

A sea of closely set trees stretches away as far as the eye can see. Here and there, villages set in fields, vineyards and olive groves form little islands.

LE GRÉSIVAUDAN★

MICHELIN MAP 333 J5/6

The phrase *chevalier sans peur et sans reproche* may sound familiar, but did you know that this "knight without fear and above reproach" first won his spurs in the Isère Valley? This sheltered depression, deeply eroded by Ice Age glaciers, is now the Alps' richest agricultural area; in the 19C, the region pioneered the development of water power for industrial use.

▶ **Orient Yourself:** To the east of the Isère River, D 523 stretches north from Grenoble along the line of the Belledonne mountain chain; on the west, A 41 and N 90 lead up to St Hilaire and Le Touvet

◉ **Don't Miss:** The road across the Croix de Revollat offers majestic scenery.

◉ **Organizing Your Time:** The sunset on the Belledone chain can be remarkable; as evening falls, try to be heading northeast to catch it.

▨ **Especially for Kids:** The steep funicular railway at St Hilaire is quite thrilling.

◔ **Also See:** Nearby Sights: ALLEVARD, Les BAUGES, CHAMBÉRY, Massif de la CHAMROUSSE, Massif de la CHARTREUSE, GRENOBLE, ST-PIERRE-DE-CHARTREUSE, VIZILLE

A Bit of History

Bayard's youth – Born in the Château de Bayard, near Pontcharra, in 1476, Pierre Terrail belonged to a long line of illustrious soldiers. As a child, he was only interested in riding and soldiering and soon became more skilled than his tutors, honing his skills and courtly graces as the Duke of Savoie's page. Charles VIII of France brought him to his court and, at the age of 16, Bayard took part in his first tournament, defeating one of the finest jousters in the kingdom. From then on, Bayard's daring feats won him a reputation as the last embodiment of heroic virtue in the final days of chivalry. King François I, no less an admirer than the rest of Europe's nobility, made him lieutenant-general of Dauphiné in 1515. He died on the battlefield in 1524.

Excursions

① At the foot of the Chartreuse★ – The Valley of a Hundred Châteaux

FROM GRENOBLE TO CHAPAREILLAN – *95km/59mi – about 2hr 30min*

This itinerary which runs along the Plateau des Petites Roches, beneath the Chartreuse Massif, offers constant views of the Belledonne range across the River Isère.

▶ *From Grenoble, drive along N 90 towards Chambéry.*

In Les Eymes, D 30 starts climbing to the Plateau des Petites Roches, a wide terrace covered with pastures, sheltering beneath the escarpments of the Chartreuse. Mont Blanc can be seen in the distance, to the northeast.

▶ *Turn left off D 30, 1km/0.6mi before St-Pancrasse, towards the Col du Coq.*

Col du Coq

The road winds along the slopes of the Dent de Crolles offering lovely views of the Isère Valley before reaching the pass (alt 1 434m/4 705ft).

▶ *Return to D 30.*

St-Pancrasse

The village lies on the very edge of the plateau, beneath the Dent de Crolles.

For coin categories, see the Legend on the cover flap.

WHERE TO STAY

⌂**Camping Les 7 Laux** – *38570 Theys - 3.8km/2mi S of Theys. 400m/440yd from the Col des Ayes -* ☎ *04 76 71 02 69 - camping.les7laux@ wanadoo.fr - open 15 Jun-15 Sept - reservations advised - 61 pitches.* The main attraction of this campsite near the Col des Ayes pass is its beautiful mountain setting. Well-kept standard facilities. Swimming pool.

Bec du Margain★★

🥾 *From D 30, 30min there and back on foot. Leave the car 150m/164yd past the football ground by the tennis courts and follow the path to the right through a pine wood.*
Walk along the edge of the escarpment to the viewing table situated 800m/2 625ft above the Isère Valley, with a superb **view** of the Vercors, Belledonne, Grandes Rousses, Sept-Laux, Bauges and Mont Blanc massifs.

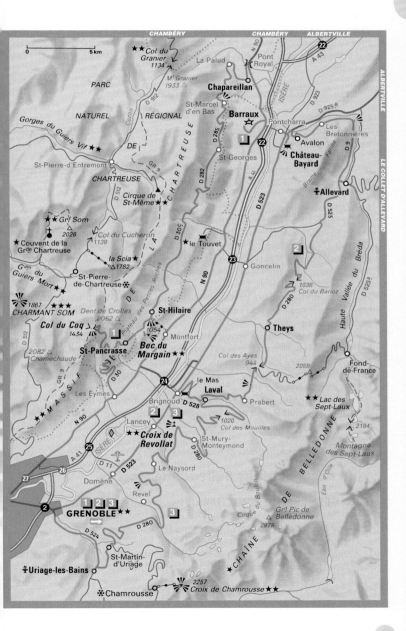

St-Hilaire-du-Touvet

This small health and ski resort is a great favourite with paragliding and hang-gliding enthusiasts. Since 1924 it has been linked to Montfort on N 90 by the steepest **funicular railway**★ (🕐 *June to Aug: 10am-7pm; Apr to June and Sept to Oct: 10am-6pm, Sun and public holidays 10am-7pm* 🕐 *closed rest of year. 10.90€ return, children 6.40€ - ☎ 04 76 08 00 02 - www.funiculaire.fr*) in Europe, which carries 40 people and negotiates a 65% gradient (83% at one point, inside a tunnel) over a distance of 1.5km/0.9mi. From the upper station, there is a striking **view**★ of the Grand Pic de Belledonne across the valley.

The road continues along the mountainside at the same average altitude of 900m/2 953ft, until the D 282 drops down towards St-Georges and Le-Petit-St-Marcel, where the Combe de Savoie and the peaks of the Bauges come into view. The D 285 carries on to La Palud; from there, it is possible to drive to Chambéry across the Col du Granier.

▷ *In La Palud, D 285 turns to the right towards Chapareillan.*

Chapareillan

The last Dauphiné village in the Grésivaudan lies just south of the former border between Dauphiné and Savoie at the "Pont-Royal".

▷ *The N 90 leads back along the river to Grenoble. Halfway along the road, a turn to the right leads to Touvet.*

Chateau de Touvet ★

&♿ 🌿 *Guided tour (45min) July to Aug: daily 2-6pm, closed Sat; Apr to June and Sept to Oct: Sun and public holidays 2-8pm. 6€, children under 10 years no charge - ☎ 04 76 08 42 27 - www.tourvet.com* The castle on the slopes of the Chartreuse Massif began as a simple 13C fort surveying the Grésivaudan; two round towers marking the entrance remain from the original defensive wall, but most of the present building dates from the 15C.

The castle was extensively remodelled in the 18C: the courtyard was enclosed, a main staircase was built inside and the **gardens**★ were adorned with a remarkable **water stairway**★ in the Italian style.

The gallery, adorned with Italian stucco work, houses archives including letters signed by Henri VIII of England and François I of France, which were preserved for posterity by Guigues Guiffrey, lord of the castle and ambassador to the English court.

The music room contains two harpsichords; one of them, made by Jan Couchet in 1652, is exquisitely decorated.

In the drawing room, there are a few pieces of furniture from the famous Hache workshop in Grenoble, and the walls of the dining room are decorated with Cordoba leather.

▷ *Return to St Bernard and continue along the D 30.*

② At the foot of the Belledonne Massif ★

FROM GRENOBLE TO PONTCHARRA *100km/62mi – about 3hr*

▷ *Leave Grenoble by the D 523 to Domène and Brignoud.*

This itinerary explores the slopes of the Belledonne range on the left bank of the River Isère. The D 528 climbs from Brignoud to Laval past the Château du Mas.

Laval

Lovely village with overhanging roofs and a charming manor, the Château de la Martellière. In the **church** *(Contact Mr. Chalaye - ☎ 04 76 71 48 60.)* there is a 15C mural depicting the Virgin Mary protecting the congregation.
Between Prabert and the Col des Ayes, there is a fine overall view of the Chartreuse Massif, including the Dent de Crolles and Chamechaude.

Theys

The village, which has retained many old houses, nestles in a green basin.

Allevard ‡ – 🚶 *See ALLEVARD.*

The spa and town centre of Allevard, not to mention the superb **panorama**★★ from the Collet d'Allevard (1 450m/4 757ft) are well worth a short detour.
Between Allevard and Pontcharra, D 9 goes round the heights of Brame Farine *(🚶 see ALLEVARD: Excursions)* and gives a fine **view**★ of the lower Gelon Valley.

▶ *From Pontcharra, follow a small road on the right to Château-Bayard.*

Château-Bayard

The road climbs from a square and passes Pontcharra's schools; as the climb ends, turn right then immediately left. Leave the car in the car park on the left of the buildings.
The doorway situated between the farm buildings and the former gatehouse *(now private property)* gives access to the terrace and the **Musée Bayard** *(🕐 July to Aug: daily except Tues 2-6pm; May to June and Sept: Sat-Sun and public holidays 2-6pm 🕐 closed Sept to May. No charge - ☎ 04 76 97 11 65 - www.ville-pontcharra.fr)*, housed in a 15C square building with mullioned windows, all that remains of the castle where the "knight without fear and above reproach" was born. The museum contains a few documents and an audio-visual presentation of his life and heroic military career. P**anorama**★ of the Grésivaudan and Chartreuse, Belledonne and Bauges massifs.

③ Croix de Revollat★

79km/49mi – about 2hr 30min. For the itinerary from Grenoble to Laval, see ②.

Laval – 🚶 *see ② above.*

After the Col des Mouilles the D 280 descends to the St-Mury valley. The Cirque du Boulon, with waterfalls streaming from the glacier, towers above the road and the three peaks of the Belledonne massif (2 913-2 978m/9 557ft-9 770ft) stand out sharply against the sky.

Croix de Revollat★★

50m/55yd to the right of D 280. The main interest of the itinerary lies in the **panorama** which unfolds from this viewpoint: the Grésivaudan below and, across the river, the Plateau des Petites Roches overlooked by the Chartreuse; the Vercors Massif to the left and the Bauges Massif to the right.

▶ *Drive straight on at the next cross, some 1.5km/0.9mi away.*

The road crosses the gorge at La-Combe-de-Lancey. After Le Naysord, the road climbs the terraced slope offering sweeping views of the Chartreuse. 2km/1.2mi further on there are bird's-eye views of Grenoble through the forest. Running above the beautiful Revel Valley, which ends in the forested slopes of the Belledonne, the D 280 heads out of the trees towards **Uriage-les-Bains** *(🚶 see Massif de CHAMROUSSE).*

▶ *In Uriage, turn right onto D 524 to Grenoble.*

GUILLESTRE

POPULATION 2 211
MICHELIN MAP 334 H5 – LOCAL MAP SEE LE QUEYRAS

Guillestre is situated at the centre of a ring of peaks and on the edge of the Queyras, Ecrins and Embrunais regions. The surrounding mountains protect the town from the worst of the weather – it is one of the driest places in the Alps – and make it a natural meeting place, where a thriving market (Monday) has been held since the Middle Ages. The town is also a good starting point for many hiking itineraries which explore the surrounding area. *(Details available at the tourist office.)* 🛈 *place Salva – 05600 Guillestre* 🕐 *July to Aug: daily 9am-8pm; rest of year: daily except Sun 9am-noon, 2-6pm -* ☎ *04 92 45 04 37- www.pays-du-guillestrois.com.*

▸ **Orient Yourself:** You will find Guillestre halfway between Gap and Briançon.
⌂ **Parking:** Parking lots are located at the top and the bottom the town.
🕐 **Organizing Your Time:** The driving can be difficult: talke your time.
👓 **Also See:** Nearby Sights: ABRIÈS, L'ARGENTIÈRE-LA-BESSÉE, BARCELONNETTE, BRIANÇON, Le BRIANÇONNAIS, CEILLAC, EMBRUN, Vallée de FREISSINIÈRES, Route des GRANDES ALPES, MOLINES-EN-QUEYRAS, MONT-DAUPHIN, MONTGENÈVRE, Le QUEYRAS, ST-VÉRAN, SERRE-CHEVALIER, Lac de SERRE-PONÇON, L'UBAYE, La VALLOUISE, VARS

🐾 Walking Tour

Very little remains of the medieval fortifications except for the **Porte du St-Esprit**, which guards the Route de Risoul. Place Albert and its monumental fountain mark the town centre. Built in the 16C, the **church** has a **porch**★ similar to that of Embrun, supported by four columns; two of them, in pink marble, rest on a base formed by squatting lions carved in Jura limestone. The doors are decorated with Renaissance panels; the lock in worked iron features a ferocious caricature of the archbishop!

Address Book

For coin categories, see the Legend on the cover flap.

EATING OUT

☕ **Catinat Fleuri** – ☎ 04 92 45 07 62 – *catinat-fleuri@wanadoo.fr - closed 28 Oct - 2 Nov.* This restaurant sits in the midst of a large family property with nature walks and sports facilities. Traditional dishes served in a comfortable round dining room decorated in rose colours.

WHERE TO STAY

☕☕ **La Grange de mon Père**– *Les Traverses - Hameau de Brudes - 05600 St-Clément-sur-Durance - 10km/6.25mi SW of Guillestre on D 902, then N 94, then the D 994 -* ☎ *04 92 45 37 80 -* ✈ *- 5rms -* ☕☕ *restaurant.* The proprietors have shown skill and originality in adapting this farm, parts of which date from the 17C, to the needs of a modern hotel. Decorated in lovely tones borrowed from the surrounding countryside. Home-cooked breakfast.

☕☕ **Hôtel Les Barnières** – ☎ *04 92 45 04 87 - hotel-lesbarnieres@wanadoo.fr - closed 15 Oct-26 Dec -* 🅿 *- 75rms -* ☕☕ *restaurant.* This hotel consisting of two chalets offers a superb panoramic view from the rooms or the terrace, stretching over the valley and the Alps. Relax in the swimming pool, spa bath or sauna. Or try one of the many sports on offer.

Hikes

Rue des Masques

An easy 2hr walk. Difference in altitude 250m/820ft. Walk from the tourist office to the gendarmerie along the rue des Champs-Élysées, then turn right onto the Chemin d'Eygliers. Continue to the top of the hill and follow the signs. The "road," a deep cleft in the rocks, appears almost man-made but is definitely a natural phenomenon; it penetrates 600m/1 969ft into the mountain and measures 5m/16ft from side to side. Return to Guillestre along the edge of the plateau and the path skirting the canal.

Mont-Dauphin★★

2hr on foot along a trail marked in orange. From Guillestre, follow D 902 towards Briançon until you reach the Chapelles district. Walk across the Plateau de la Chalp and take a footbridge across the Guil.

The trail to the Porte d'Embrun at the entrance of the fort lets you admire the natural defences of Mont-Dauphin from a different angle (*see MONT-DAUPHIN*).

Excursions

Le Cros

6km by D 37. Drive through Eygliers and continue to Le Cros along a demanding road. The **views**★ of Mont-Dauphin and its surroundings and the Guil gorges make the effort of the drive worthwhile.

Réotier★

Follow the D 902 to the N 94; turn right then left in front of the station. Follow signs for the **"Fontaine Pétrifiante du Réotier."** The water, high in mineral content, has formed strange concretions including a stalactite looking like a gargoyle.

Risoul 1850☀

14km/8.7mi along D 186.

05600 Risoul ⏱ *Daily in season 9am-7pm -* ☎ *04 92 46 02 60 - www.risoul.com*

The winding road offers panoramic views of Mont-Dauphin and its exceptional setting. The **Domaine de la Forêt Blanche** ski area (*see VARS*), is one of the largest in the southern Alps, with 160km/99.4mi of ski runs.

An unsurfaced road leads to the Col de Chérine and to the **Belvédère de l'Homme de Pierre** (alt 2 374m/7 789ft). From the viewing table, there is a superb **panorama**★★ extending north to the Vanoise Massif, south to Mont Ventoux and southwest to the Lac de Serre-Ponçon.

LES HOUCHES ✳

POPULATION 2 706
MICHELIN MAP 328 N5 – LOCAL MAP SEE MASSIF DU MONT-BLANC

The view of the massif from this resort at the foot of Mont Blanc is quite simply spectacular. Les Houches has extended across the widest and sunniest part of the Chamonix Valley, while still keeping its village character. Even if the setting is not on a par with that of Chamonix, Les Houches is a pleasant family resort; well equipped and, at only 1 000m/3 281ft, ideal for skiers who prefer not to take on the steeper, high-altitude slopes. 🛈 *BP 9, 74310 Les Houches* ⏰ *July to Aug and mid-Dec to mid-Apr: 8.30am-noon, 2.30-6.45pm; rest of year: Mon-Fri 9am-noon, 2-6pm, Sat 9am-noon -* ☎ *04 50 55 50 62 - www.leshouches.com. Guided tour of village July to Aug: Wed 10am.*

▶ **Orient Yourself:** Les Houches is 6km/3.75mi south of Chamonix on D 213.

🗺 **Don't Miss:** From Chavants, you have a great view over the Aiguilles de Chamonix.

Kids **Especially for Kids:** At the Parc de Merlet, children will see a variety of mountain animals such deer, chamois, llamas, ibex, marmots running around freely.

👣 **Also See:** Nearby Sights: ARGENTIÈRE, CHAMONIX-MONT-BLANC, CLUSES, Les CONTAMINES-MONTJOIE, MÉGÈVE, Massif du MONT-BLANC, ST-GERVAIS-LES-BAINS, Bassin de SALLANCHES

The Resort

🎿🏂 Ski area

The resort offers skiers a wide range of difficulties in the Lachat, Bellevue and Prarion areas, and 110 snow cannon are on standby to make good any lack of snow. The famous "green run" (black in fact!), brilliantly skied by Émile Allais in 1937, requires a high level of skiing skill. The ski area is linked to neighbouring resorts.

Address Book

For coin categories, see Legend on cover flap.

WHERE TO STAY

😐😐🛏**Auberge Le Montagny** – *Le Pont -74310 Les Houches -* ☎ *04 50 54 57 37 - www.chamonix-hotel.com - closed 20 Apr-6 June and 11 Oct-18 Dec -* 🅿 *- 8rms.* This farm dating from 1876 has been entirely refurbished by the proprietor, a carpenter. The peaceful rooms have exposed beams and pale timber roof trusses and pretty tiles in the bathrooms with matching friezes. Some have balconies with views of Mont Blanc.

😐😐🛏**Auberge Beau Site** – *Near the church 74310 les Houches-* ☎ *04 50 55 51 16 - www.hotel-beausite.com - closed 21 Apr-19 May and 11 Oct-19 Dec -* 🅿 *-*

18rms - 😐*restaurant.* This chalet is at the heart of the village. Guests sample the proprietor's cooking seated before the open fire in the restaurant or among flowers on the terrace in summer. Traditional-style rooms with colourful local fabrics. Swimming pool.

😐😐🛏**Hôtel du Prarion** – *Au Prarion – alt 1 860m/6 100ft – by cable car - 74170 St-Gervais-les-Bains -* ☎ *04 50 54 40 07 - www.prairon.com - open 26 June-5 Sept and 18 Dec-mid-Apr - 12rms - 😐restaurant.* At the summit of Le Prarion, an invitation to a night of utmost calm. There is a breathtaking panoramic view from the Aravis range to that of Mont Blanc. The rooms and food on offer are simple in the typical style of the mountains.

There are, in addition, some 30km/18.6mi of cross-country skiing trails.

Viewpoints

Le Prarion★★
Alt 1 967m/6 453ft. *30min there and back to the viewing table including a 20min cable-car ride.* ⏱ *At the end of 2006, a new 8-place gondola was opened between Les Houches and Le Prairon. For times, ask at the tourist office or ticket booth. 12.30€ return, children 8.60€ - ☎ 04 50 54 42 65.*
From the viewing table (alt 1 860m/6 102ft) next to the Hôtel du Prarion, there is an extended **view** of the Mont-Blanc Massif. In order to enjoy the **full panorama**★★★, follow the markings to the summit of Le Prarion *(about 1hr there and back on foot).*

Bellevue★★
Alt 1 812m/5 945ft. *1hr there and back including a 15min cable-car ride.* ⏱ *First week June to first week July: 7.30am-5pm; second week July to third week Aug: 7.30am-6pm; lst week Aug-third week Sept: 8am-5pm. 12.70€ return, children 8.90€ return - ☎ 04 50 54 40 32.*
🚠 It is possible to continue up to the Nid d'Aigle (Glacier de Bionnassay) and go back down via St-Gervais on board the Tramway du Mont-Blanc. *(See ST-GERVAIS).*

Kids Parc du Balcon de Merlet★★
6km/3.7mi – 10min there and back on foot. From the Houches station, drive 3km/1.8mi along the mountain road to Coupeau and turn right onto the partly surfaced forest road towards the Parc de Merlet. 🚶 *Leave the car in one of two lots and finish the climb on foot (300m/984ft)* ⏱ *July to Aug: 9.30am-7.30pm; May, June and Sept: 10am-6pm.* ⏱ *closed Mon in Sept. 5€, children 4-12years 3€ - ☎ 04 50 53 47 89.*
The Balcon de Merlet is a promontory covered with pastures, occupying a prime position opposite Mont Blanc. The park shelters typical mountain fauna (deer, mouflons, chamois, llamas, ibexes, marmots) roaming freely over a steep wooded area covering some 20ha/49 acres. From the terrace of the restaurant, or from the chapel (alt 1 534m/5 033ft), there is a superb close-up **view**★★ of the Mont-Blanc Massif.

ROUTE DE L'ISERAN★★★

MICHELIN MAP 333 L 5/6

This road, which goes over the Col de l'Iseran, was opened in 1937 to link the Tarentaise and Maurienne valleys and reaches the highest point (2 770m/9 088ft) of the Route des Grandes Alpes. A series of viewpoints along the route reveals the changing landscapes of the high mountains, at once austere and beautiful.

▶ **Orient Yourself:** The Col d'Iseran is on D 902, a winding route from Val d'isère south to Bonneville-sur-Arc.
🔎 **Don't Miss:** The belvedere of the Tarentaise is surprisingly easy to reach.
⏱ **Organizing Your Time:** Give yourself a half day to reach the Tête du Solaise
🐾 **Also See:** Nearby Sights: AUSSOIS, BESSANS, BONNEVAL-SUR-ARC, BOURG-ST-MAURICE, Route des GRANDES ALPES, La Haute MAURIENNE, La TARENTAISE, TIGNES, VAL D'ISÈRE, Massif de la VANOISE

Excursions

From the Barrage de Tignes to Bonneval-sur-Arc

32km/20mi – about 1hr 30min

The Col de l'Iseran is usually blocked by snow from early November to early July. It is recommended to take this road from Val-d'Isère to Bonneval.

The construction of D 902 running from the Barrage de Tignes to Val-d'Isère involved the building of eight tunnels (one of them is 459m/502yd long) and three avalanche barriers. The road therefore offers only intermittent views of the Vanoise Massif to the south and of Mont Pourri downriver.

The Gorges de la Daille open the way into the Val-d'Isère Basin.

Val-d'Isère✳✳✳ – *See VAL-D'ISÈRE.*

From Val-d'Isère to the Pont St-Charles, the road continues along the Isère Valley which becomes more and more desolate, and it is closed off upriver by the Pointe de la Galise. Beyond Le Fornet, there are stunning views of the Grande Motte at the heart of the Vanoise Massif and of the Tsanteleina Summit on the Italian border.

The road enters the Parc national de la Vanoise at the Pont St-Charles. *There is a car park for 150 cars just before the bridge.*

The road then rises along the southern slopes of the valley offering views of the Val-d'Isère Basin with the snow-capped Dôme de la Sache in the background and Mont Pourri just behind it.

Tête du Solaise★★

Alt 2 551m/8 369ft. *1hr 30min on foot there and back along a pleasant mountain path; you can reach the summit by cable car from Val-d'Isère (see VAL-D'ISÈRE).*

🚶 The **panorama** is similar to that which can be admired from the Belvédère de la Tarentaise *(see below)*, but there is a clearer view down the Isère Valley towards Tignes and its dam.

Belvédère de la Tarentaise★★
Alt 2 528m/8 294. *15min there and back on foot. Park the car as you come out of the bend.*

From the viewing table, the view extends all round from Val-d'Isère, the Lac de Tignes and the Pointe des Lessières in the foreground to the Vanoise Massif, Mont Pourri and the Grande Sassière range in the distance.

Col de l'Iseran★
Alt 2 770m/9 088ft. The harshness of the landscape is impressive. The snow cover remains throughout the summer on the Tarentaise side of the pass. The Chapelle Notre-Dame-de-l'Iseran was built in a sheltered spot in 1939. The Albaron Summit comes into view on the Maurienne side of the pass.

Pointe des Lessières★★★
Alt 3 041m/9 977ft. *From the Col de l'Iseran, 2hr 30min there and back on foot along a steep mountain path which can be dangerous for inexperienced hikers (vertiginous handrail-assisted sections towards the top). Climbing boots with non-slip soles are essential. The path starts behind the Chalet-hôtel de l'Iseran.*

This hike must only be attempted in clear weather; it offers an almost unique opportunity of climbing over 3 000m/9 843ft. The view from the summit is ample reward for one's efforts: the Vanoise Massif, Mont Pourri, the Italian side of Mont Blanc and the border range between the Grande Sassière and the Albaron.

The road continues across the Parc national de la Vanoise, offering views of the barren cirque of the upper Lenta Valley beneath the Grand Pissaillas Glacier.

Belvédère de la Maurienne★
Alt 2 503m/8 212ft. View of the Haute-Maurienne, the Ciamarella and Albaron summits and the Pointe de Charbonnel along the Italian border. Beyond the Pont de la Neige, the "hanging" Lenta Valley offers a landscape of high pastures againstthe snow-capped peak of the Albaron. Lower down, the road overlooks the austere upper Arc Valley which forms the setting of the village of Bonneval.

The view from the Pointe de Lessières

Fr. Isler/MICHELIN

ISOLA 2000 ✳ ✳

Isola 2000, built in 1972 in a beautiful mountain setting close to the Italian border, is the nearest Alpine ski resort to the Côte d'Azur region. It owes its popularity to its sunny climate and to its good-quality snow cover, which is partly due to the high altitude. *Espace Mercantour - Immeuble de Pévalos – 06420 Isola 2000 Dec to Apr: daily 9am-9pm; July to Aug: daily 9am-noon, 2-7pm; May to June and Sept to Nov: daily except Sat-Sun 9am-noon, 1.30-5.30pm closed 1 and 8 May, Ascension Day, 1 and 11 Nov - ☎ 04 93 23 15 15 - www.isola2000.com*

▶ **Orient Yourself:** Isola 2000 is less than 100km/62.5mi from Nice and 5min from Italy on the pleateau of Chastillon, overlooked by 15 mountain peaks. The resort is 17km/10.6mi from the village of Isola, on D 97.

🕐 **Organizing Your Time:** Spend some time in the village of Isola before exploring the resort and its sports facilities.

👍 **Also See:** Nearby Sights: AURON, BEUIL, Route de la BONETTE, Gorges du CIANS, ST-ÉTIENNE-DE-TINÉE, Vallée de la TINÉE

The Resort

⛷ Ski area

It is situated at an altitude ranging from 1 800m/5 906ft to 2 600m/8 539ft and extends towards the Vallon de Chastillon. Snow cover is frequently exceptional considering the southern latitude of Isola 2000, less than 100km/62mi from Nice. The ski runs (120km/75mi) are varied enough to satisfy the most demanding skiers (Génisserie and Méné black runs) and the less experienced (blue runs starting from Les Marmottes). Adequate snow-making equipment makes up for any lack of snow.

Hikes

In summer, Isola 2000 is the ideal **starting point for hikes** through the nearby Parc national du Mercantour and Parc naturel de l'Argentera on the Italian side or

---

Address Book

For coin categories, see the Legend on the cover flap.

WHERE TO STAY

⊜**Camping Lac des neiges** – *500m/1 640ft W of Isola on the D 2205, Rte d'Auron* – ☎*04 93 02 18 16 – 98 pitches – restaurant on site.* On the edge of a lake in bucolic mountain setting, this campground offers two distinct sites, for tents and for mobile homes. You can also rent well-equiped and comfortable housetrailers.

⊜⊜ **Hôtel du Soleil le Chastillon** –*Le Front de Neige* – ☎ *04 93 23 26 00- www.hotels-du-soleil.com - 54rms -*⊜⊜ *restaurant.* Just opposite the ski slopes here, this hotel combines comfort and flexability: you can rent apartments in the annexe, or well-equipped and comfortable guestrooms. Good choice of buffets at the restaurant.

⊜⊜**Pra Loup** – *Le Front de Neige* - ☎ *04 93 23 27 00 www.hotels-du-soleil. com- 97rms -*⊜⊜ *restaurant.* Alpine decor suits this hotel-club which offers guestrooms with views over the ski slopes, or apartments with more spartan comfort. Fitness centre with sauna. International cuisine, with a variety of buffets at the restaurant.

R. Palomba/FOC

Isola 2000

among the mountain lakes surrounding the resort. Many chamois roam around the area which used to be part of the Italian royal hunting grounds and has retained a network of well-marked paths *(map available from the tourist office)*.

Tête de Pélévos★

Alt 2 455m/8 054ft. *Take the Pélévos cable-car.* ⏰ *July to Aug (8min ride) 9.30-11.45am, 2.30-4.30pm, Sat-Sun and public holidays 9.30am-12.30pm, 2.30-4.30pm; Dec to Apr: 9am-4.30pm. 6€ return -* ☎ *04 93 23 25 25.*

🚶 From the upper station (alt 2 320m/7 612ft), follow a path on the right, which climbs towards the Marmottes lifts. Bear left at the second lift and go to the summit for a fine **panorama**★ of the ski area, the Lombarde and Malinvern summits.

Lacs de Terre Rouge★★

Difference in altitude: about 650m/2 133ft. Allow 4hr there and back.

🚶 Start from the restaurant called "La Bergerie" at the end of the resort and climb to the Hôtel Diva. From there, a marked path leads to the lakes lying at the foot of the Cime de Tavels and Mont Malinvern. Continue up to the **Baisse de Druos**★★ (alt 2 628m/8 622ft) which offers a fine view of the Argentera Nature Park on the Italian side and of Mont St-Sauveur and Mont Mounier on the French side.

Mont St-Sauveur★★

Alt 2 711m/8 894ft. *Allow 2hr on the way up and 1hr 30min on the way down. Difference in altitude: about 400m/1 312ft.*

🚶 Go up to the Marmottes 2 lift, as for the Tête de Pélévos described above, and continue to the Col Valette. From there, take a narrow path *(marked with a wooden signpost)* which runs along the mountainside towards Mont St-Sauveur *(⚠ caution is required at the beginning as the path is rather stony)*. Turn left at marker 89 and follow the short path running along the crest of the mountain. Extended **panorama**★★ from the summit including the Isola ski area in the foreground as well as a large area of the Parc national du Mercantour and, clockwise, the Gorges de Valabrès, the Valberg ski area, Mont Mounier, Auron, Monte Viso and the snow-capped Pelvoux.

Excursions

Col de la Lombarde

Alt 2 350m/7 710ft. 5km/3mi north of Isola 2000. Follow the narrow road which is the continuation of D 97 north of Isola 2000 and leads to the Italian border. It is possible to reach the pass on foot (3hr there and back) by following the easy marked path beyond the Belvédère chair lift.

The pass is framed on the right by the Lombarde Peak and on the left by the Lausetta Ridge, which provides fine walks or mountain-bike rides. Lovely overall **view** of the Isola 2000 cirque, overlooked by the Tête Mercière, and of the deeper valley on the Italian side.

Santuario di Santa Anna★★ (Italy)

12km/7.5mi to the north. 45min drive and 45min walk there and back. Have your identity papers with you.

From the Col de la Lombarde, the road runs through a splendid rocky landscape, skirts Lake Orgials and goes down through larch woods. In a bend, turn left towards Santa Anna. As you reach the sanctuary, turn left and continue to the end of the surfaced road. **View**★ of the sanctuary and of the mountains towering over it. Leave the car and walk for 20min to the beautiful **Lago di Santa Anna**★, lying below the Lausfer and Arène Grosse peaks. Walk along the shore to the end of the lake for the best view of it. The lake is the starting point for longer hikes.

Vallon de Chastillon★

17km/10.6mi. D 97 leads from Isola 2000 down to the village of Isola at the confluence of the River Guerche and River Tinée. The road runs down the steep Vallon de Chastillon, then widens as it leaves the high-pasture area. Many waterfalls cascade down the rock face. Isola's Romanesque bell-tower can be seen from afar.

Isola – *See Vallée de la TINÉE.*

LACS DE LAFFREY★

MICHELIN MAP 333 H7

The Laffrey lakes stretch from north to south along the Route Napoléon (*see ROUTE NAPOLÉON).* **The undoubted highlight of the lakes is the Chemin de Fer de la Mure, a little miracle of 19C railway engineering which offers sublime views from the comfort of a window seat.** *43 rue du Breuil - 38350 La Mure mid-June to Aug: Mon-Sat 9am-12.30pm, 2-7pm, Sun and public holidays 10am-1pm; mid-Sept to mid-June: weekdays 9am-noon, 2-5.30pm; Easter and 8 May: 9am-noon closed 1 Jan, 25 Dec, 1 May and 11 Nov - 04 76 81 05 71 - www.ville-lamure.com*

▶ **Orient Yourself:** The lakes comprise, from north to south: Lac Mort, Lac de Laffrey (the longest at 3km/2mi), Lac de Petichet and Lac de Pierre-Châtel.

Don't Miss: The coal-mine galleries at la Mine-Image are impressive.

Organizing Your Time: The lakes have popular beaches; a dip at the end of the day is particularly refreshing

Especially for Kids: A car for children has been added to the train de la Mure.

Also See: Nearby Sights: Le BOURG-D'OISANS, Le CHAMPSAUR, Massif de CHAM-ROUSSE, Massif de la CHARTREUSE, Le DÉVOLUY, GRENOBLE, Route NAPOLÉON, Le TRIÈVES, Le VALBONNAIS, Le VALGAUDEMAR, VILLARD-DE-LANS, Le VERCORS, VIZILLE

Excursions

1 **Route Napoléon** – *see ROUTE NAPOLÉON*

FROM LA MURE TO THE LACS DE LAFFREY – *15km – 45 min.*

2 **Route de la Morte**★

FROM LA MURE TO VIZILLE VIA THE COL DE LA MORTE – *45km – allow 2hr*

La Mure – *see ROUTE NAPOLÉON*

Between La Mure and the Col de Malissol (alt 1 105m/3 625ft) the D 114 offers views of the Obiou and the eastern escarpments of the Vercors Massif. From the Col de Malissol to the Col de la Morte, it runs along the narrow valley of the Roizonne.

La Morte
Lying at the foot of the Grand Serre and Taillefer summits, La Morte (alt 1 348m/4 423ft) offers beautiful ski runs. In summer, the ascent of the Taillefer starts here.

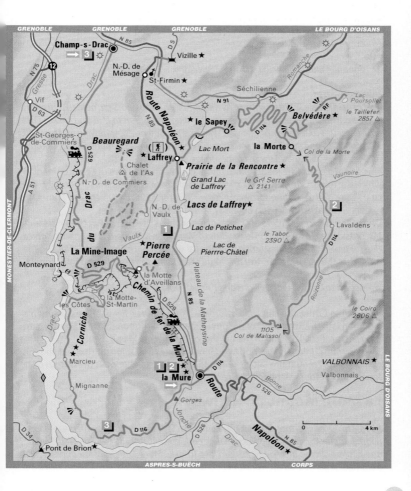

The forest road leading to the Lac Poursollet *(6km/3.7mi)* affords fine views of the Romanche Valley, but is only open in summer.

Viewpoint over the Vallée de la Romanche★★
By the first hairpin on the way down the Col de la Morte heading north. There are bird's-eye views of the Romanche Valley 1 000m/3 281ft below.
Road N 91 leads to Vizille.

Vizille★ – *See VIZILLE.*

▷ *To continue to Grenoble, make for Eybens and follow the D 5 through pleasant countryside; this is the final section of the Route Napoléon (see ROUTE NAPOLÉON).*

③ Corniche du Drac★★

FROM CHAMP-SUR-DRAC TO LA MURE *45km/28mi – about 2hr*

Between Champ-sur-Drac and Monteynard, the road rises gradually and offers views of the deep Drac Valley and of the extensive works carried out to harness the river at Notre-Dame-de-Commiers and Monteynard. On leaving Monteynard, the lake, with Mont Aiguille above, and the dam **(Barrage de Monteynard)** are visible on the right. Stop the car at the intersection of the road leading to La Motte-St-Martin to admire the splendid view.

▷ *Continue along D 529 to La Motte-d'Aveillans.*

Mine-Image
Kids *Les 4 Galeries - 38770 La Motte d'Aveillons ⟨⟩ June to mid-Sept: guided tours (1hr) every hour 10am-5pm; school holidays: at 2, 3 and 4pm; Jan to Mar and Nov to Dec: Sat-Sun at 2, 3 and 4pm; Apr and Oct: Wed and Sat-Sun at 2,3,4pm; May and last half Sept: daily 2, 3 and 4pm. Ticket can be combined with train de la Mure. 5.60€, children 3.20€ - ☎ 04 76 30 68 74 - www.mine-image.com.*
This site of a coal mine inaugerated under Napoleon recreates the environment in which the miners worked and shows the evolution of coal-mining technology. The coal seams were exploited from the early 19C until 1956, by which time some 318 miners were labouring along 60km/37.5mi of horizontal galleries.
One of the "seven wonders of Dauphiné," known as the **Pierre Percée**★★, stands just outside La Motte. *Take D 529 towards La Mure, then turn left at the signpost marked "Pierre Percée."* ⟨⟩A path starting from the car park leads to the ridge *(45min)*. Legend has it that the natural arch, 3m/10ft high, represents the devil turned into stone!

▷ *Return to La Motte-d'Aveillans and turn left onto D 116.*

Beyond Les Côtes, the cliff road affords striking **views**★★★ of the escarpments plunging into the River Drac, of the power station at Avignonet, of the Monteynard Dam and artificial lake and of the heights of the Vercors Massif.
The panorama unfolding beyond Mignanne includes the Obiou, the highest summit of the Dévoluy mountains (alt 2 790m/9 154ft). The road overlooks the Gorges de la Jonche just before reaching La Mure.

La Mure Mountain Railway★

⟨⟩ *July to Aug: departure from La Mure and from St-Georges-de-Commiers at 9.45am, noon, 2.30pm (4hrs round trip); May to June and Sept: dep from St-Georges Wed, Sat-Sun and public holidays at 9.45am, 2.30pm, dep from La Mure 2.30-5pm; Apr and Oct: dep from St-George Wed, Sat-Sun and public and school holidays 9.45am-2.30pm, dep from*

Chemin de fer de la Mure

La Mure Mountain Railway

La Mure Wed, Sat-Sun and public and school holidays. Reservations required. 10.50€ return, children 4-16 years 9€, family (2 adults, 2 children) 47€ return - ☎ 0 892 391 426 - www.trainlamure.com.

This railway line was opened in 1888 over a distance of 30km/18.6mi to transport coal from the mining site of La Mure to St-Georges-de-Commiers, and from there to the national network. At the time, it was a daring technical achievement; the line negotiates a difference in altitude of 560m/1 837ft by means of 12 curved viaducts and 18 tunnels, also curved. Early in the 20C, the La Mure Railway became the first railway in the world to be powered by high-voltage direct electric current. This modern power source still had its limits, however. Trains could only reach a speed of 40kph/25mph, and even this was only possible on the way down; until 1950 the uphill journey took 2hr 40min.

Once used to carry coal and to shuttle nuns and pilgrims visiting Notre-Dame-de-la-Salette (⟨ see Le DÉVOLUY, ②), the trains now operate as a tourist attraction. From St-Georges, the railway rises gradually to the highest point of the line at the Festinière Tunnel (924m/3 032ft). There are some spectacular sections such as those crossing the Gorges du Drac and the Vaulx Viaduct (170m/186yd over nine arches).

ROUTE DE LA MADELEINE ★

MICHELIN MAP 333 L5

Opened in 1969, this road links the Maurienne (N 6) and Tarentaise (N 90) valleys across moderately high mountains, an area of beautiful landscapes and charming hillside villages.

▶ **Orient Yourself:** The Route de la Madeleine follows D 213 from La Chambre over the Col de la Madeleine, then descends into the Isère valley.

⊘ **Don't Miss:** The view from the Col de la Madeleine takes in the massif of Mont-Blanc as well as those of Grande Rousses and Écrins.

⏱ **Also See:** Nearby Sights: ALBERTVILLE, La Vallée des BELLEVILLE, COURCHEVEL, Route de la CROIX-DE-FER, MÉRIBEL, ST-JEAN-DE-MAURIENNE, La TARENTAISE, Massif de la VANOISE

Excursions

Betweeen Arc and Isère

FROM LA CHAMBRE TO MOÛTIERS *53km/33mi – about 2hr. The Col de la Madeleine is blocked by snow from November to early June.*

D 213 climbs from La Chambre *(11km/6.8mi northwest of St-Jean-de-Maurienne)* in a series of hairpin bends and offers views of the Allevard and Grandes Rousses massifs through the Glandon Pass.

St-François-Longchamp

☞ This winter sports complex spreads out between St-François (1 450m/4 757ft) and Longchamp (1 610m/5 285ft) on the east side of the Bugeon Valley, beneath the Cheval Noir Summit.

Col de la Madeleine ★

Alt 2 000m/6 562ft (not to be confused with the pass of the same name between Bessans and Lanslevillard, see page 419). Covered with pastures, this wide gap between the Gros Villan and Cheval Noir (alt 2 832m/9 291ft) summits offers a remarkable view of the Mont-Blanc Massif to the northeast and of the Grandes Rousses and Écrins massifs to the south *(viewing tables)*.
Between Celliers and the Pas de Briançon, the cliff road clings to the western slopes of the Celliers Valley which are dotted with villages, the Beaufortain mountains barring the view downriver.

▶ *Drive to La Léchère via Notre-Dame-de-Briançon along D 97.*

La Léchère-les-Bains ♨

Lying deep down in the lower Tarentaise Valley, La Léchère is the newest Alpine spa resort, specialising in the treatment of vascular diseases, gynecological complaints and rheumatism. The springs were discovered after a landslide in 1869.

▶ *Follow the twisting road on the right, which rises to St-Oyen.*

Doucy

The 17C Baroque church is furnished in similar style: note the carved-wood polychrome retable over the **high altar** and the Rosary altar.

▶ *Continue along the road to Villaret (D 95B).*

This road, running along the ridge separating the Morel and Eau Rousse valleys, offers fine views of the Vanoise, Mont Jovet, part of Courchevel and the ski slopes of Méribel-les-Allues.

▶ *Drive to Valmorel via Le Meillet.*

Valmorel ☀

🏠 *73260 Valmorel* 🕒 *July to Aug and mid-Dec to April: 9am-12.30pm, 3.30-7pm; rest of year: weekdays except public holidays 9am-noon, 2-6pm -* ☎ *04 79 09 85 55 - www. valmorel.com*

1 400m/4 593ft. At times it seems as if Valmorel, built in 1976, has been part of the landscape for centuries. It is one of the most attractive modern resorts in the Alps, at the upper end of the verdant **Morel Valley** and surrounded by mountains. Trompe-l'œil façades in the Savoyard tradition brighten a traffic-free centre, which resembles an old alpine village. Fine old hamlets (Doucy, Les Avanchers) are dotted along the valley, which is renowned for its Beaufort cheese; tourism is expanding rapidly.

Snow to spare in Valmorel

🐾 Ski area

There is a wide choice of runs for skiers of all levels of proficiency. Experienced skiers prefer the area around St-François-Longchamp via the Madeleine chairlift and around the Massif de la Lauzière. The Morel teleski (T-bar) makes it possible to avoid the resort centre and go directly to the Gollet and Mottet ski areas. 162 snow-cannon more than make up for insufficient snow cover. You can practise night-skiing on the Planchamp runs and in the snowpark. The Valmorel ski area is linked to that of **St-François-Longchamp** and **Doucy-Combelouvière** to form the Grand Domaine *(area pass available).*

In summer, there is a wide choice of outdoor activities and excursions.

Crève-Tête ★★★

Alt 2 341m/7 680ft. *Take the Pierrafort gondola.* From the upper station (1 830m/6 004ft) it is easy to reach the Col du Golet which offers a fine view. The path to the summit is steeper, but the panorama is really superb. (♿ *See also la Vallée des BEL-LEVILLE.)*

▶ *Follow the Morel Valley (D 95) down to Aigueblanche.*

Barrage des Échelles d'Annibal

Built across a narrow passage of the Basse Tarentaise Valley, this dam diverts part of the flow of the River Isère to the power station at Randens on the Arc, through an 11.5km/7mi tunnel. The diversion was inaugurated in 1956.

Moûtiers – ♿ *See La TARENTAISE, Excursions*

MANE★

POPULATION 1 169

MICHELIN MAP 334 C9 – LOCAL MAP SEE FORCALQUIER

Built on an isolated rocky knoll standing in the centre of a plain, this village nestles round its medieval citadel, the last surviving example in Haute-Provence. The local stone, quarried near Porchères, was used in the construction of many buildings, including the Priory of Notre-Dame de Salagon and Sauvan Castle.

▶ **Orient Yourself:** Mane is 3km/2mi south of Forcalquier

🕭 **Don't Miss:** Be sure to see the Priory of Salagon and Sauvan Castle.

🕐 **Organizing Your Time:** Try to tour the Mane region in the afternoon because Sauvan Castle opens only at 3.30pm.

🕭 **Also See:** Nearby Sights: CÉRESTE, Vallée de la Moyenne DURANCE, FORCALQUIER, Monastère de la GANAGOBIE, GRÉOUX-LES-BAINS, MANOSQUE, Route NAPOLÉON, SISTERON, Plateau de VALENSOLE

Walking Tour

Église St-André

The 16C church has a Florentine doorway decorated with palm leaves. Inside, the Gothic chancel contains a fine marble altar.

Follow the paved street on the left of the church; the old Renaissance houses have carved lintels over the doors.

Citadel (🔒 not open to the public)

These well-preserved 12C fortifications were built from local stone; note the unusual mullioned windows and the two walls winding round the hillock. From the top there is a fine **view** of the Plateau du Vaucluse, the Luberon, the Observatoire St-Michel and the Durance Valley.

Excursions

N 100 south of Mane is lined with several monuments which bear witness to the rich historical background of the village.

Medieval bridge across the Laye

On the right of N 100; follow the signposting to the Auberge de la Laye.
The highest arch of this cutwater bridge is Romanesque.

Drystone huts

These circular constructions, half-hidden by the dense vegetation, can be seen to the north and east of Mane. They were built in the 18C and 19C with stones taken from the fields, both as shelters from the burning sun and as tool sheds. Inside, the roof is in the shape of a corbelled dome, like an igloo. There is a narrow window, a fireplace and a cupboard all made of stone. The height of these huts, or *cabanons* in French, varies from

Drystone hut

D. Faure/PHOTONONSTOP

3-7m/10-23ft and their circumference from 10-30m/33-98ft.

Hikers are asked not to pick up stones, even loose ones, not to climb onto walls and not to light fires near or inside them as the heat would split the stones.

Château de Sauvan★

🕐 *Guided tours (1hr30min) July to Aug: daily except Sat 3.30pm; Apr to June and Sept to Nov: Thur, Sun and public holidays 3.30pm; Dec to Mar: Sun and public holidays 3.30pm. 6€, children 3€ - ☎ 04 92 75 05 64.*

This classical building, dating from the early 18C, is shaded by ancient trees. A typical Mediterranean landscape reminiscent of Tuscany unfolds from the terrace. In 1793, the lady of the manor, who bore a striking resemblance to Queen Marie-Antoinette, offered to take her place in the Conciergerie; Marie-Antoinette refused her generous sacrifice and the countess fled the country. However, the lords of the Château de Sauvan were well liked in the area and the château was not destroyed during the Revolution. Neglected for many years, it was painstakingly restored in 1981.

Particularly noteworthy is the hall separated by pilasters with Ionic capitals from the imposing stone staircase overlooked by the first-floor gallery.

The fine reception rooms contain a rich collection of 17C, 18C and 19C furniture. French-style gardens adorned with fountains surround the château.

Tour de Porchères

At the end of a path on the right of the road, just beyond the Château de Sauvan. This massive rectangular keep, in Romanesque style, dates from the 12C; note the long voussoirs forming the arched doorway.

Prieuré de Salagon★

🕐 *May to Sept: daily 10am-noon, 2-7pm; Oct, Sat-Sun and school holidays: 2-6pm*
🕐 *closed Jan. 5€, children under 12 no charge - ☎ 04 92 75 70 50 - www.musée-de-salagon.com.*

The elegant Benedictine **priory**, founded in 1105, rebuilt in the 15C and later used as a farmhouse, was finally restored and turned into an ethnological museum in 1981. Note the unusual mullioned windows and stair turret. A medieval garden, and two gardens for medicinal and aromatic herbs were planted when the museum was opened. The west front of the **church**★ is decorated with a deeply inset rose-window and a doorway, similar to that of the Ganagobie Monastery (👆 *see Monastère de GANAGOBIE*). Inside, the capitals and engaged columns show a definite Provençal influence; the remains of simple 14C frescoes and engraved tableaux add to the charm. Gallo-Roman finds have been found in the chancel, with evidence of an earlier church dating from the 6C.

WHERE TO STAY

🪙🪙 **Mas du Pont Roman** – *Chemin Châteauneuf (Rte Apt)* - ☎ *04 92 75 49 46 - pont-roman@laposte.net -* 🅿 *9rms.* This traditional farmhouse, well off N 100, is near a Romanesque bridge. Pretty lounge and rooms furnished in Provençal style.

SHOPPING

Maison des produits de pays de Haute Provence - *Rte de Salagon* ☎ *04 92 75 37 60 – open daily 10am-7pm.* Some 40 local farmers and craftspeople sell their wares here.

MANOSQUE★

POPULATION 19 603
MICHELIN MAP 334 C10
LOCAL MAP SEE VALLÉE DE LA MOYENNE DURANCE

Nestling among foothills at the edge of the Luberon massif, a stone's throw from the River Durance, this peaceful little town has recently expanded owing to its position in the rich agricultural Durance Valley and the proximity of new, high-tech industries; in only twenty years its population has grown from 5 000 to 20 000.

This modernisation has altered the rural setting of Manosque, celebrated by the native born novelist, Jean Giono (1895-1970), and visitors taking a walk through the town will need sharp eyes to spot the charming little Provençal streets that the writer would have known. *place Dr Joubert - 04100 Manosque* *June to Sept: 9am-1pm, 2-7pm (until 6.30pm first half of June and last half of Sept); Oct to May: 9am-12.15pm, 1.30-6pm - ☎ 04 92 72 16 00 - www.manosque-tourisme.com. Guided tours of the town (1hr30min)* *June to Sept: Tue and Fri 3pm; rest of year Thur 2.30pm every second week. Contact tourism office. 3€.*

▸ **Orient Yourself:** At 80km/50mi from Marseille, Manosque is set among five hills. The ramparts are gone: a circular boulevard encloses the old town.

🐾 **Don't Miss:** The Saturday morning market at the Place Terreau is justly celebrated. Stop also at the Fondation Carzou and the Centre Jean-Giono; climb to the top of the Mont d'Or for the view of the town.

🕐 **Organizing Your Time:** Spend at least a half-day to see the town.

Kids **Especially for Kids:** The lake at Les Vannades has activities all year long.

👣 **Also See:** Nearby Sights: CÉRESTE, Vallée de la Moyenne DURANCE, FORCALQUIER, Monastère de la GANAGOBIE, GRÉOUX-LES-BAINS, MANE, Route NAPOLÉON, RIEZ, SISTERON, Plateau de VALENSOLE

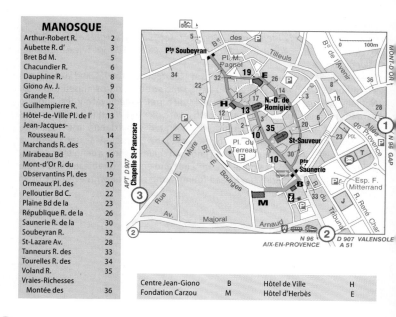

MANOSQUE	
Arthur-Robert R.	2
Aubette R. d'	3
Bret Bd M.	5
Chacundier R.	6
Dauphine R.	8
Giono Av. J.	9
Grande R.	10
Guilhempierre R.	12
Hôtel-de-Ville Pl. de l'	13
Jean-Jacques-Rousseau R.	14
Marchands R. des	15
Mirabeau Bd	16
Mont-d'Or R. du	17
Observantins Pl. des	19
Ormeaux Pl. des	20
Pelloutier Bd C.	22
Plaine Bd de la	23
République R. de la	26
Saunerie R. de la	30
Soubeyran R.	32
St-Lazare Av.	28
Tanneurs R. des	33
Tourelles R. des	34
Voland R.	35
Vraies-Richesses Montée des	36

Centre Jean-Giono	B	Hôtel de Ville	H
Fondation Carzou	M	Hôtel d'Herbès	E

Old Town ★ 1hr

Wide boulevards have replaced the ramparts which once enclosed the old town; the typically Provençal streets are narrow and lined with tall houses concealing secluded gardens, patios, beautiful cellars and galleries. The streets are linked by covered passages and extremely narrow alleyways known as *andrones*.

According to a local legend, King François I, on a visit to Manosque, was welcomed at the Porte Saunerie by the beautiful Péronne de Voland, who offered him the town keys on a velvet cushion. The king courted her and, not knowing how to turn him down, the consul's daughter exposed her face to sulphur fumes in order to spoil her looks. Since then, the town has been known as "the bashful Manosque."

Porte Saunerie ★
This 12C gate, which formed part of the original town walls, owes its name to the salt warehouses which once stood nearby. Note the twinned openings supported on slender columns and the machicolated side turrets.

Rue Grande
This lively, picturesque high street offers a wealth of old doorways, fine stairwells, courtyards and balconies. **No14** was the workshop where Giono's father used to mend shoes and where his mother ironed clothes. Note the wrought-iron balconies of the 16C-17C house at **no23**.

Église St-Sauveur
🕐 *Weekdays 8.30am-7pm.* 🚶 *Guided tours by request at the tourist office.*
The plain façade overlooks a square decorated with a fountain. Look for two blocks of stone set into the north wall of the church; one shows a pilgrim with his staff, the other a cockerel fighting with a snake. By the Gothic doorway are two impressive caryatids. The fine organ case, in carved gilded wood, dates from 1625. The square bell-tower is surmounted by a famous wrought-iron **campanile**, made in 1725 by a blacksmith from Rians.

Hôtel de Ville
The town hall, with its elegant 17C **façade** ★ and beautiful staircase, is one of the finest buildings in Manosque. A colourful **market** livens up the square three times a week.

Église Notre-Dame-de-Romigier ★
The church has a Renaissance doorway, but the nave was remodelled in the 17C and the aisles were added. The altar is a splendid 4C or 5C **sarcophagus** ★ in Carrara marble. According to legend, the **Black Madonna statue** ★ from which the church takes its name was discovered at the end of the 10C under a bramble bush, where it had been hidden when the Saracens invaded Provence in the 9C; it was later placed inside the church. The Virgin and Child both wear Merovingian crowns, which suggests that the sculpture is one of the oldest of its type in France.

Porte Soubeyran
The 12C gate, remodelled in the 14C like the Porte Saunerie, was later decorated with a lovely stone balustrade and a tower surmounted by a graceful onion-shaped top in wrought iron.

▶ *Turn back, then left onto rue Soubeyran.*

Gates and Doorways

In Manosque these are almost a local art form. Some of the finest examples can be seen at no5 rue Voland, which runs past St-Sauveur church, no12 rue J-J Rousseau, no2 rue des Ormeaux, no4 rue de la Saunerie and, in the Grande-Rue, nos 31 (the consul's house), 39 and 42.

Address Book

For coin categories, see the Legend on the cover flap.

EATING OUT

◠◠ **Le Luberon** – *21 bis pl. de Terreau - ☎ 04 92 72 03 09 - closed 6-20 Sept, Sun evening and Mon except mid-July to mid-Aug* . This restaurant in the old town offers food that evokes sunshine and an extensive wine list. Rustic furniture, coloured walls and paintings by local artists on exhibit. The regulars come here for the quality of the food.

◠◠ **Le Petit Laurageais** – *6 pl. du Terreau - ☎ 04 92 72 13 00 - closed school holidays in Feb, 1-20 July, 1-12 Nov, Sat and Sun lunchtime and Mon*. If you want a change from Provençal cooking, try this restaurant with the under-stated façade which offers excellently prepared specialities from southwest France, as well as Provençal dishes.

◠◠◠ **Dominique Bucaille** – *43 bd des Tilleuls – ☎04 92 72 32 28-dbucaille@wanadoo.fr – closed Feb holidays, from mid-July-mid-Aug, Wed evening and Sun, except public holidays*. A 17C thread-spinning factory has been converted to a charming restaurant with open kitchens. Menu changed daily.

WHERE TO STAY

◠**Hôtel du Terreau** – *Pl du Terreau - ☎ 04 92 72 15 50 - www.hotelmanosque.fr–closed 20 Dec-5 Jan – 20rms*. This hotel on a pretty square at the centre of old Manosque continues to improve the comfort it offers. Rooms are soundproofed. Many are decorated using traditional Provençal techniques: whitewash and wood.

◠**La Bastide des Collines**– *82 chemin de Valvéranne - ☎ 04 92 87 87 67 ⬦ - ◠restaurant*. Taste the pleasure of biologic cuisine with home-made ingre-dients. You can tour the gardens and taste the produce. Rooms are decorated in coloured themes. Lovely green lawn for a moment of repose.

◠**Chambre d'hôte La Maurissime** – *Chemin des Oliviers - 04180 Villeneuve - 12km/7.5mi NE of Manosque on N 96 then D 216 (Rte de Forcalquier) - ☎ 04 92 78 47 61 - closed 10 Jan- 1Mar - ⬦ - 4rms - ◠◠ restaurant*. This guesthouse dis-penses its friendly welcome and service with professionalism and good taste. The villa, of recent construction, is a good place for lounging on the terrace or dining. The rooms are decorated in Provençal style and face the garden.

◠◠◠ **Hôtel Le Pré St-Michel** – *1.5km/1mi N of Manosque on Bd M.-Bret and Rte Dauphin - ☎ 04 92 72 14 27 - pre.st.michel@wanadoo.fr ⬛ - 24rms*. This modern hotel with a Provençal appearance offers a pretty panorama overlooking Manosque. The rooms are large and decorated with care, with painted furniture, Provençal fabrics, worked iron details. Swimming pool.

SHOPPING

Rue Grande – *R. Grande* – The old town's main street, pleasantly shaded and closed to vehicular traffic, has numerous small shops dotted along it (off-the-peg clothes, articles for the home, crafts etc).

Market – *Place du Terreau at centre of the old town - Sat 5am-1pm*. This colourful market, rich with the scent of lavender and olive oil, embodies the essence of Provence. You will find almost everything here that features in Provençal cuisine and everyday life.

Le Moulin de l'Olivette – *Pl. de l'Olivette: leave Manosque towards Sisteron - ☎ 04 92 72 00 99 - open daily except Sun 8 am-noon, 2-6pm (Apr-Sept 2.30-6.30pm)*. This olive oil mill is among the biggest producers in Alpes-de-Haute-Provence. Since 2000, its extra-virgin AOC oil has regularly won the gold medal at the agricultural com-petition. The boutique sells, besides oil, Provençal pottery, crafts and objects made from olive wood.

Cave des Vigneron de Pierrevert – *04860 Pierrrevert - ☎04 92 72 19 06 – cave.pierrevert@wanadoo.fr – open daily except Sun 9am-noon, 2-6pm*. Located at the foot of the village, this shop offers a large choice of prize-win-ning regional wines.

Place des Observantins

A former monastery has been turned into the music and dance conservatory. The square is decorated with a lovely old fountain. The library and municipal archives are housed in the **Hôtel d'Herbès**, which has a fine 17C staircase inside.

Return to the Porte Saunerie via rue Jean-Jacques-Rousseau, rue des Ormeaux, past place des Ormeaux and along rue de la Saunerie, admiring some lovely doors on the way.

Sights

Fondation Carzou

7-9 bd Élémir-Bourges 🕐 *July to Aug: daily except Mon 10am-noon, 2.30-6.30pm; June and Sept: daily except Sun and Mon 2.30-6.30; Oct to May: daily except Sun, Mon and Tue, 2.30-6.30* 🕐 *closed 2 weeks at end of year. 4€ - ☎ 40 92 87 40 49.*

Jean Carzou, a French painter of Armenian descent, born in 1907, departed from Abstract painting and evolved his own intricate style, full of fantasy, against a monochrome background, to depict modern cities, Venice and Provence.

He decorated the former Couvent de la Présentation with murals on the theme of *The Apocalypse*. The interesting neo-Classical church, built in 1840, has a single nave surmounted by a dome on pendentives, a **coffered vault**, capitals decorated with acanthus leaves and a frieze running round the nave.

The Apocalypse

It took the artist seven years to complete this amazing fresco. Each decorated panel illustrates one of Carzou's favourite themes. The unity of the work is emphasized by the blue-green backgrounds, enhanced by the natural light from the dome.

Start with the left-hand side of the nave. In the left wing of the chancel the artist depicts destruction and massacres accomplished by Man; the four columns supporting the dome represent the Evangelists, in the apse he illustrates lust; the right side of the church is devoted to women's accomplishments. Most of the **stained-glass windows**✶ were also designed by Carzou; the four horsemen of the Apocalypse symbolize

Fondation Carzou, Manosque

The Tree-Woman, Fondation Carzou

the great genocides which have occurred in the history of mankind. The left wing announces the reconstruction of the world through love and work. Note the reference to Millet's *Angelus* in the corner of the left wall. The *Tree-woman* symbolizes the earth's revival. The lovers clasped in each other's arms represent the universality of Love. Eve appears triumphant whereas Adam, who faces her, is less sure of himself. More information about Carzou's work is available in the adjoining rooms.

Centre Jean-Giono

3 bd Élémir-Bourges ○ *July to Sept: daily except Mon 9.30am-12.30pm, 2-6pm; Oct-Mar: daily except Sun and Mon 2-6pm; Apr-June: daily except Sun and Mon 9.30am-12.30pm, 2-6pm.* ○ *Closed public holidays and Christmas holiday. 4€, children under 12 years 2€ - ☎ 04 92 70 54 54 - www.centrejeangiono.com –*

This fine Provençal house, dating from the 18C, houses a museum devoted to the life and works of Jean Giono.

On the ground floor (note the beautiful ceilings), Giono's life, written works and films are presented with the help of documents. The library contains manuscripts of his works and a collection of translations from all over the world. Most of the films to which he contributed, as well as interviews and television programmes, can be seen in the video library on request. The upper floor houses temporary exhibitions.

Those who wish to walk in the footprints of the great novelist can participate in **literary excursions** to sites in the area connected with his work.

Excursions

Chapelle St-Pancrace (also known as Chapelle de Toutes Aures)

2km/1.2mi southwest. Leave Manosque by ③ on the town plan and follow the sign-posted road.

Near this chapel, at the top of the hill, there is an extended **view**★ (almost 360°) of the Luberon, Manosque and the Préalpes de Digne beyond the Durance Valley and Valensole Plateau.

Mont d'Or★

1.5km/0.9mi northeast. Starting from rue Dauphine, climb up montée des Vraies-Richesses then follow a no-through road on the right to the last house on the right, known as Le Paraïs.

Le Paraïs

The house is still inhabited by the Giono family and discretion is therefore highly appreciated. ⟿ Guided tours (1hr30min) by appointment Fri. 2.30-5pm. ○ *Closed 1 May and Christmas holidays. No charge - ☎ 04 92 87 73 03.*

This is the house where Giono wrote most of his works from 1930 onwards. The tour goes through his library and the room where he wrote his last works, . His study is on the next floor; note the cast of his right hand and other mementoes. The roofs of the old town can be seen from the window, "fitting together" as the author said, "like the plates of a suit of armour."

The large tarred slabs which can be seen from the Sentier des Roches mark the area where crude oil and natural gas are being stored beneath the forest. Some 30 wells have been drilled to reach a vast layer of rock salt. Water is pumped in to dissolve the salt, which is then recovered and gradually replaced by oil and gas brought in by pipeline from the Étang de Berre. 10 million m3/353 million cu ft of oil and gas are held on the site.

Mont d'Or Summit★

The **view**★ gradually extends to embrace the old town and its roofs, the Durance Valley, the Luberon and, in the distance, the Ste-Victoire and Ste-Baume mountains.

Forêt de Pélicier

10km/6.2mi along D 5; 3hr. Drive out of Manosque along boulevard Martin-Bret; leave the car at the pass, called le Col de la Mort d'Imbert.

Part of a plan to reforest mountain areas, the forest consists mainly of Austrian pines, which are very hardy trees. From the Col de la Mort d'Imbert, follow the path on the right which skirts a former tile factory and its clay pits; turn left 400m/437yd further on and follow another path which goes through gypsum quarries, known as **gipières**, then round Escourteja Hill. Climb up to "Les Deux-Moulins" where an old building houses the **Centre de Découverte de l'Espace Pastoral** (Centre for the Discovery of Rural Environment). The tour continues along a forest road to the Sentier des Roches Aménagées. At the intersection of three tracks, you will find a map of the forest. Return to the Col de la Mort d'Imbert along the signposted track.

LA HAUTE MAURIENNE

MICHELIN MAP 333 L /M6 - SAVOIE (73)

The valley of the River Arc, known as La Maurienne, is one of the longest intra-Alpine valleys, deeply enclosed from end to end; in the height of the Middle Ages, traders and clerics, pilgrims and soldiers all passed this way on the road to Italy. There is a striking contrast between the beautiful natural environment and the major industrial complexes lining the valley, although the upper Maurienne between the Col de l'Iseran and the Col du Mont-Cenis has been spared intensive industrialization and still retains its traditional character. Churches and chapels draw art-lovers to the area, and skiers will not be disappointed by the valley's slopes.

🚊 73500 Termignon 🕐 *2nd week July to Aug: 9am-noon, 3-7pm; mid-Dec to mid-May: Mon-Sat 9am-noon, 2-6pm, Sun 10am-noon, 4-8pm; mid-Sept to Oct: Mon-Sat 9am-noon, 2-6pm; Nov to mid-Dec: Mon-Fri 9am-noon, 1.30-5.30pm; Apr-June: Mon-Fri 9am-noon, 2-6pm (open Sat from May to June)* - ☎ 04 79 20 51 67 - www.3petitsvillages.com

▸ **Orient Yourself:** This region stretches from Val d'Isère in the north, southwest towards Modane on the Italian border along the D 902 and N 6.

👁 **Don't Miss:** Stop to admire the naive murals recounting the life of St Sébastien at the church of Lanslevillard.

🕐 **Organizing Your Time:** If you can, drive south from Val d'Isère on D 902 over the Col d'Iseran, then turn south to the Col du Mont-Cenis on N 6, to avoid the heavily-used roads around Modane in the lower Maurienne.

🧒 **Especially for Kids:** There is a good nature train at the Termignon forest.

👣 **Also See:** Nearby Sights: AUSSOIS, BESSANS, BONNEVAL-SUR-ARC, Route du GALIBIER, Route des GRANDES ALPES, Route de l'ISERAN, MODANE, Route du MONT-CENIS, ST-JEAN-DE-MAURIENNE, TIGNES, VAL D'ISÈRE, Massif de la VANOISE

A Bit of History

Tourism and industry – The Maurienne lies on an important route between France and Italy across the Col du Mont-Cenis and, since 1980, via the Fréjus Tunnel, so that international traffic can now get through all year round by road and rail.
Between Avrieux, upriver from Modane, and Aiguebelle, near the confluence of the River Arc and River Isère, the course of the middle and lower Maurienne Valley is

415

Bonneval-sur-Arc and the Arc valley

dotted with some 10 factories (aluminium, steel and chemicals), using the energy produced by about 20 power stations.

Among the most important hydroelectric projects carried out in the area were the building of the generating station at Aussois (1951) and the underground power station at Randens (1954).

Busy river – The vast works undertaken to harness the Arc were completed by the building of a dam which created a huge reservoir of 320 million m3/259 200acft, at the foot of Mont Cenis, which supplies the power station at Villarodin-Bourget lower down the valley, near Avrieux.

Three more power stations, situated between Modane and St-Jean-de-Maurienne, regulate the course of the Arc. One of the most daring achievements of the harnessing programme was a 19km/11.8mi-long tunnel going through the Belledonne Massif and intended to divert part of the flow of the Arc to the Isère Valley on the other side of the mountains.

Excursions

Haute Maurienne ★

FROM BONNEVAL-SUR-ARC TO MODANE (The Trail of the Baroque)

56km/34.8mi – about 2hr not including the tour of the chapels decorated with murals in Bessans and Lanslevillard, the detour up the Route du Mont-Cenis and the recommended hikes.

Between December and March the D 902 may be blocked by snow from Bonneval-sur-Arc to Bessans.

Bonneval-sur-Arc ★ – *See BONNEVAL-SUR-ARC.*

There are many religious monuments left between Bonneval and Lanslebourg: Stations of the Cross, oratories and chapels erected by local people or by pilgrims who had safely travelled over the border passes.

▶ *Turn left past Notre-Dame-des-Grâces towards the Refuge d'Avérole.*

The **Col de la Madeleine** (not to be confused with the pass of the same name between Gros Villan and Cheval Noir, see page 408) between Bessans and Lanslevillard, with its piles of rocks scattered among larches, marks a transition in the landscape: downstream, the slopes appear more rounded, the vegetation is darker and the view extends further towards the **Dent Parrachée** (alt 12 087ft), the most southern peak of the Vanoise Massif, and, behind it, to the jagged Rateau d'Aussois.

Lanslevillard
Park at the church and continue on foot along the path behind the school.
The church and its high steeple, perched on a promontory, tower over the village. The **Chapelle St-Sébastien** (🕐 *To visit, contact the Mairie at Lanslevillard -* ☏ *04 79 05 93 78),* which looks very plain from the outside, was built in the 15C by a local man following a vow he made during an epidemic of plague. The **murals**✶, painted in tempera on all the walls, have retained their fresh colours and are still extremely vivid, with the martyrdom of St Sebastian on the right and the life of Christ on the other walls. Costumes and backgrounds are 15C, the expressions and gestures are as vivid as ever. The Renaissance coffered ceiling is remarkable.

Lanslebourg-Mont-Cenis
A garrison was stationed in this border town and a monument was erected to Flambeau, the army dog who, between 1928 and 1938, helped to carry the mail from the barracks up to the Sollières Fort (2 780m/9 121ft). The **Espace baroque Maurienne** (🕐 *Mid-June to mid-Sept: Mon-Wed 9.30am-noon, Thur, Fri, Sun 3.30-6.30pm; mid-Dec to Easter: Mon-Wed 9.30am-noon, Thur-Fri 3-9.15pm. 2.50€, children no charge -* ☏ *04 79 05 90 42 (when open) or* ☏ *04 79 05 91 75 (when closed))* is one of the starting points for the themed tour **"Les Chemins du baroque"** (🍃 *see Planning Your Trip).*

Val-Cenis✶
🍃 In 1967, the *communes* of Lanslevillard and Lanslebourg united under the name of Val-Cenis, a winter resort which occupies a central position in the Haute Maurienne region. It extends over 500ha/1 236 acres, at altitudes ranging from 1 400m/4 593ft to 2 800m/9 186ft, and a weekly pass giving access to most of the ski resorts in the Maurienne region is available. Europe's longest green run, the **Escargot** or "snail," comes down from the Col du Mont-Cenis *(10km/6.2mi)*; there are also several more difficult runs such as Jacquot, the Lac and the Arcelle. The north-facing aspect and the wind which frequently blows from Italy guarantee adequate snow cover, but the weather is often cold and changeable.

Termignon
The name of the town is said to come from the Latin *terminus,* "the end," and in the Middle Ages Termignon was indeed the last community in the Maurienne. The present **church** (🕐 *Mid-June to mid-Sept: daily except Sun and Mon 3-6pm -* ☏ *04 79 20 51 49.)* dates from the second half of the 17C; the **pine retable**✶ over the high altar is the work of Claude and Jean Rey; the other two are by Sébastien Rosaz.
🧒🚶 At Termignon, three marked **nature trails** (*Sentiers de la découverte -2hrs, half-day and full day*) take you into the Suffet forest and explain the history, climate and vegetation.
From Termignon, a winding road (D 83) leads to Bellecombe (alt 2 310m/7 579ft).

Refuge du Plan du Lac✶✶
(2hr there and back. Leave Termignon by the D 126 and stop at the car park in Bellecombe).
🚶 From the viewing table near the refuge, there is a splendid **panorama**✶✶ of the Dent Parrachée, Dôme de Chasseforêt, Vanoise glaciers and the Grande Casse and Grande Motte summits. The path then goes past the Entre-Deux-Eaux refuge through a pastoral landscape dotted with traditional chalets, where ibexes and chamois roam freely, to the Col de la Vanoise affording splendid **views** of the Grande Casse.

On N 6 south of Termignon in the village of Sollières-Sardières is a **Musée archéologique** where are displayed a wide variety of artifacts from a cave at Balmes where people lived 3 000 years ago. (*Mid-June to mid-Sept: daily except Tue 3-6.30pm; mid-Dec to mid-Apr: Wed-Thur 2.30-6pm. 4€, children under 16 years 2€ - ☎ 04 79 20 59 33*)

Beyond Sollières the route continues to Bramans *(8km/5mi)*. From here, take a detour on the D 100 to **St-Pierre-d'Extravache**. The modest 10C church, which is said to be the oldest in Savoie, has retained a well-preserved chancel and bell-tower.

▶ *Return to Sollières and follow D 83.*

The road rises among pastures and pine woods to the ledge where the pointed steeple of Sardières can be seen from afar, with the Ambin and Thabor summits in the distance.

▶ *Go into Sardières and follow the path leading to the monolith.*

Monolithe de Sardières★

This 83m/272ft-high pinnacle stands isolated on the southern edge of the Parc national de la Vanoise. It was first climbed in 1957.

Aussois★ – *See AUSSOIS.*

▶ *In Aussois, turn left in front of the church.*

The cliff road crosses the St-Benoît stream (fine waterfall facing a chapel) and dips into the Avrieux Basin.

▶ *Take a small road on the left leading to Avrieux.*

Avrieux

The **church** (*Guided tours by appointment at the Mairie - ☎ 04 79 20 33 16.*) is said to have been founded in the 12C by two English families connected with the Archbishop of Canterbury, Thomas Becket, to whom it is dedicated. The façade is decorated with 17C frescoes depicting the seven virtues and the seven capital sins, and the fine interior **decoration**★ is Baroque. On the west wall, there is a diptych dating from 1626 which retraces the life of St Thomas Becket; note also the 16C stone stoup and painted wooden statues of Saints Ours, Anne and Katherine.

The **Souffleries de Modane-Avrieux**, the most important wind-tunnels of their kind in Europe, were designed to try out and experiment on aeroplanes, helicopters, missiles, rockets and space shuttles before test flights are carried out. Elements of a huge wind tunnel, discovered in Austria by the Allies in 1945, were brought to this site where the nearby power station supplied the energy to produce wind power.

▶ *Just beyond Villarodin, turn left onto D 214 for La Norma.*

La Norma ✳

🏠 73500 la Norma - ☎ 04 79 20 31 46 - www.la-norma.com

This picturesque little resort, founded in 1971, occupies a favourable position on top of a plateau (alt 1 350m/4 429ft) overlooking the upper Maurienne Valley, 6km/3.7mi from Modane. In summer, the nearby Parc de la Vanoise offers hiking, rock climbing and mountain biking. 🔭 The **ski area,** which extends over 700ha/1 730 acres facing north-northwest, offers good snow cover (106 snow cannons) and 17 ski lifts for 65km/40.6mi of ski runs of varying levels of difficulty between 1 350 and 2 750m/4 429 and 9 022ft. In addition, there are exceptional **panoramas**★★ of the Thabor and Vanoise massifs.

Via ferrata du Diable

This rock-climbing course located near the Pont du Diable includes five one-way itineraries of varying difficulty and length *(3-6hr)*. Beginners should try the section linking Fort Marie-Thérèse to the Pont du Diable. Information is available from the Bureau des Guides (👆 *see Planning Your Trip*).

Modane – 👆 *See MODANE.*

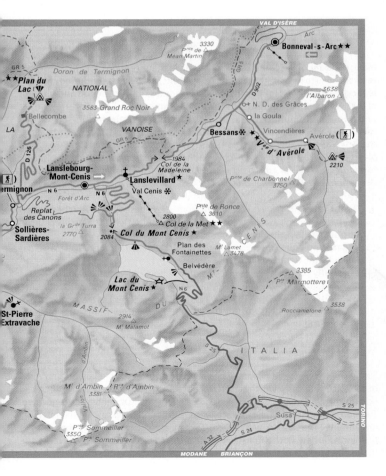

419

Highlight

The Esseillon Fortifications★

(☎ *July to Aug: guided tour of forts every Tue afternoon -* ☎ *04 79 20 30 80*) Between Aussois and Avrieux, the Esseillon is a rocky knoll crowned by impressive fortifications built by the Sardinian monarchy between 1817 and 1834 to repel a possible French invasion. There are five forts situated at different altitudes so that they could defend one another; when fully manned, 1 500 men with 170 artillery pieces would have been stationed here. The highest fortification, **Fort Marie-Christine** (☉*Mid-May to mid-Nov, and mid-Dec to mid-Apr: 8.30am-11pm; July to Aug, guided tours Tue afternoon* ☉ *closed 15 Apr to 15 May and Nov-15 Dec. No charge -* ☎ *04 79 20 36 44*), which overlooks Aussois, has been restored and now serves as a gateway into the Parc national de la Vanoise; it is also the starting point of many hikes. Opposite, on the south bank of the Arc, **Fort Marie-Thérèse** (☉ *June to Sept: daily except Mon 2-6pm. No charge -* ☎ *04 79 20 33 16 - www.avrieux.com*) is linked to the complex by the impressive Pont du Diable (☝*see La Norma above*).

MEGÈVE✳✳✳

POPULATION 4 509

MICHELIN MAP 328 M5 – LOCAL MAP SEE MASSIF DES ARAVIS

Inaugurated soon after the First World War, Megève remains a major French ski resort thanks to its many hotels and restaurants, as well as its enduring chic. The legacy of native son Émile Allais, the 1937 world skiing champion and initiator of the "French skiing method," lives on in the famed ski school. Forested slopes under rounded mountain peaks provide a charming setting, while spectacular views are easily accessible from ski lifts. The nearby pass (1 113m/3 652ft) links the Arly Valley to the Sallanches basin. 🏠 *rue Monseigneur-Conseil, PB 24 - 74120 Megève* ☉ *July to Aug: daily 9am-7pm, Sun and public holidays 9am-noon, 4-7pm; Sept to mid-Dec and May to June: daily except Sun and public holidays 9am-noon, 2-6pm; Dec to Apr: daily 9am-noon -* ☎ *04 50 21 27 28 - www.megève.com*

▶ **Orient Yourself:** Megève is 13km/8mi from Sallanches by N 212. Another route, D 113, narrow but pleasant, crosses the village of Cordon with its Baroque church.

☺ **Don't Miss:** Take the goldola to the summit of Mont Arbois.

☉ **Organizing Your Time:** From Megève, you can reach Savoie or the Massif des Aravis by the Gorges de l'Arly.

Kids **Especially for Kids:** The lake at Combloux offers a pleasant break.

☝ **Also See:** Nearby Sights: ALBERTVILLE, Massif des ARAVIS, ARGENTIÈRE, BEAUFORT, CHAMONIX-MONT-BLANC, La CLUSAZ, CLUSES, Les CONTAMINES-MONT-JOIE, Les HOUCHES, Massif du MONT-BLANC, ST-GERVAIS-LES-BAINS, Bassin de SALLANCHES

A Summer and Winter Resort

Sunny and safe, Megève's slopes appeal more to exponents of "relaxed skiing" than to daring athletes, although the resort has a deserved reputation for well-maintained ski runs and equipment. Its chalet-restaurants high on the mountain are renowned. There are many ski lifts, while snow cannon ensure good snow cover at this relatively low altitude . The ski area, with 300km/187.5mi of runs, extends over the slopes of the Mont d'Arbois, Rochebrune and the Aravis, and is linked by gondola or shuttle to the other resorts of the Mont Blanc Massif.

Address Book

For coin categories, see the Legend on the cover flap.

EATING OUT

Les Marronniers chez Maria – *18 impasse le Chamas -* ☎ *04 50 21 22 01 - May-mid-June, 3 wks in Oct and Tue out of season.* This rustic chalet at the heart of the resort is a crêperie with a bit more on the menu. Besides the usual crêpes made with wheat or rye flour, there are salads, omelettes and, on special order, a surprise house specialty.

Grange d'Arly – *10 r des Allobroges -* ☎ *04 50 58 77 88 - www.grange-darly.com - closed mid-Apr to mid-June, Sept to mid-Dec and noon.* This imposing chalet built of dark wood is a real treasure. Set in peaceful green surroundings, it has an elegant interior with pale woodwork. In the pretty dining room, or on the terrace in summer, you enjoy simple regional dishes. The guestrooms are also very attractive.

Au Vieux Megève – *58 pl de la Résistance -* ☎ *04 50 21 16 44 - vieux-megeve@py-internet.com - open 10 July-31 Aug, 15 Dec-10 Apr and noon.* Around a beautiful fireplace, in a traditional Megève decor with red tablecloths and wooden furniture, the same family has served guests for 30 years. Cheese dishes are a specialty.

Les Enfants Terribles – *Pl. de l'Église -* ☎ *04 50 58 76 69 - closed 15 Sept -20 Oct.* Jean Cocteau was the inspiration for this restaurant in the resort's pedestrian zone. There is a stained glass window in the ceiling and displays of books and lithographs by the artist. Colourful cocktails are served from behind a large bar, adding to the fun. In the vaulted 18C cellar, a wine bar.

La Sauvageonne-Chez Nano – *At Leutaz - 4km/2.5mi S of Megève on Rte du Bouchet -* ☎ *04 50 91 90 81 - www. saugageonne-refuge.com - open 28 June-16 Sept and 15 Dec-20 Apr.* This restored farm draws a smart clientele who come to admire its pastoral setting. Choose from a fine terrace or cosy dining room, where you will find a typical Alpine interior with wood paneling, open fireplace, paintings of chalets in the region and old ski equipment. You can choose from a menu featuring both local and more varied cuisine.

Idéal – *At the summit of Mont d'Arbois - 74120 St-Gervais - by the Mt d'Arbois or Princesse cable cars -* ☎ *04 50 21 31 26 - open July-Aug and 15 Dec-15 Apr, closed evenings.* This is a fine place to stop for a break on the ski slopes. The high altitude chalet combines a pleasant setting with prices that are reasonable by the standards of the resort. Skiers can enjoy the special dish or "kebab" of the day served in a welcoming dining room or on the vast terrace with its magnificent panoramic view.

WHERE TO STAY

Chambre d'hôte La Bérangère– *283 r. d'Anterne - 74480 Le Plateau-d'Assy 11.5km/7.2mi E of Sallanches by D 13 and D 43 -* ☎ *04 50 93 87 68 or 06 07 30 08 15 - www.berengeremb.com -* 5rms - meal. This large chalet and its outbuildings have large rooms that can shelter 2 to 15 people. The decor is Savoyard with lots of wood. Pretty view and sports facilities nearby.

Hôtel Chaumine – *36 chemin des Bouleaux, via Chemin du Maz -* ☎ *04 50 21 37 05 - closed 16 Apr-25 Jun and Sept-21 Dec -* 11rms. A pretty chalet with a friendly, home-like atmosphere at the end of a quiet track a few minutes away from the centre and well placed for the ski slopes. The decor is reminiscent of Scandinavia with pale golden wood panelling, large patchwork quilts and rustic furniture.

Hôtel Gai Soleil – *Rte du Crêt-du-Midi -* ☎ *04 50 21 00 70 - www.le-gai-soleil.fr - closed mid-Apr to mid-June and mid-Sept to mid-Dec -* 21rms - restaurant. This comfortable chalet with the attractive façade is about five minutes from the centre. The rooms vary in size and are plainly decorated with rustic wooden furniture. In summer, guests can enjoy the swimming pool and terrace.

Hôtel Gorges de la Diosaz – *74700 Sallanches -* ☎ *04 50 47 20 97- info@hoteldesgorges.com- closed 1st half May and 25 Oct-12 Nov, Sun evening and Wed -* 6rms - restaurant. A pretty family chalet in a quite, picturesque village. Rooms with an Alpine theme, wood-panelled dining room, flower-decked terrace in summer and cuisine carefully prepared by the proprietress.

☺☺**Chambre d'hôte Les Oyats** – *771 rte de Lady - 1.5km/1mi S of Megève towards Rochebrune then Rte des Perchets - ☎ 04 50 21 11 56 - lesoyats3@ wanadoo.fr - closed 1st wk Nov - ⌨ - 4rms€.* This farm chalet dates from 1800. The proprietor, a carpenter, has lovingly transformed the place. Rooms are large and well-equipped, as is the individual chalet also for rent. A kitchen is available to guests, with a view of the stable where two donkeys live.

☺☺☺**Hôtel Lodge Park** – *100 r. d'Arly - ☎ 04 50 93 05 03 - www. lodgepark.com - closed Apr-14 Dec - 🅿 - 39rms- ☺☺☺restaurant.* Hunting trophies, carvings of animals, log walls and comfortable furniture recreate the atmosphere of a Canadian hunting cabin. But don't be fooled, this is one of the best hotels in Megève, and the "natural" atmosphere in no way compromises the sophisticated luxury and high standard of service.

☺☺☺☺**Les Fermes de Marie** – *Chemin de Riante-Colline, via N 212 (rte d'Albertville) - ☎ 04 50 93 03 10 - www.fermesdemarie.com- open June-15 Oct and Dec-15 Apr - 🅿 - 61rms - ☺☺☺restaurant.* These chalets in the style of summer pasture farms, grouped in a little village on the hillside, offer the luxury and refinement of the best hotels and are very fashionable. Decorated in old Savoyard furniture, the chalets are authentic and utterly charming. Swimming pool and beauty centre.

SHOPPING

Au Crochon – *2748 Rte Nationale - ☎ 04 50 21 03 26 - megeve-decor@wanadoo. fr Open daily 9am-noon, 2-6.30pm - closed Sun except in summer, and public holidays except 14 July and 15 Aug.* Those who love articles hand-crafted from wood will be spoiled for choice here! Whether you are hesitating between a flower pot or a butter mould, a pair of clogs (for Grandma) or a small cask (for Grandpa), a toboggan or snowshoes, it boils down to whether you can fit it into your suitcase…

Flocon de neige – *133 r. Monseigneur-Conseil - ☎ 04 50 21 20 10 - daily 9.30am-12.30pm, 2.30pm-7.30pm, closed in May, Oct and Nov.* A vital stop for those with a sweet tooth: chocolates and confectionery, including the famous local speciality, the "Glaçon" (filled chocolate in a delicate "snowy" coating).

SPORTS AND LEISURE

The tourist office has detailed maps of trails for hiking and riding mountain bikes. Or you can tackle the Olympic swimming pool.

Lake – *74920 Combloux - open mid-June daily except Tue and Thur 11am-7pm; July to Aug: daily 11am-7pm.* This swimming area ("plan d'eau") is cleaned by aquatic plants, the first such "bio-lake" in France. It also has a splendid view of Mont-Blanc and a variety of sports facilities, including a gym.

Ice-skating rink – *25 r. Oberstdorf - ☎ 04 50 21 23 77 - palaismegeve@dial. olean.com - 4-6pm - closed May-Oct.* The Patinoire centrale de Megeve is an open-air skating rink at the heart of the village. There are also "Ice'Cars", a sort of bumper-car on ice.

In summer the area is popular for its bracing climate, nearby forest, opportunities for mountain hikes and drives and wide choice of sporting activities (tennis, swimming, skating). In recent years, it has become a centre for ballooning, paragliding and small aircraft. Megève is also a children's health and holiday resort.

Sights

Musée du Haut Val d'Arly

88 ruelle du Vieux-Marché. 🕐 *July to Sept and mid-Dec to Apr: daily except Sun 2.30-6.30pm* 🕐 *closed rest of year. 3.20€, children 2.50€ - ☎ 04 50 91 81 00.*
The museum houses collections of traditional objects displayed in reconstructed authentic settings along several themes: domestic life, agricultural tools, milk processing, textiles and winter sports.

Le Calvaire

This is a replica of the Stations of the Cross in Jerusalem, lined with 15 oratories and chapels decorated with paintings and sculptures (🖎 *unfortunately in poor condition*) made by local craftsmen between 1844 and 1863. From the lower chapel, there is a pleasant view of the upper Val d'Arly.

Hikes

Viewpoints Accessible by Gondola

Mont d'Arbois★★

Alt 1 833m/6 014ft. *Access by gondola from the Plateau du Mont d'Arbois.* 🕒 *July to Aug: 9am-1pm, 2-6pm (10 min departure every 30min). 10.20€ return -* ☎ *04 50 21 22 07.*
Splendid **panoramic view** of the Aravis and Fiz mountains as well as Mont Blanc. You can walk in 20min to the upper station of the cable car which goes back down to St-Gervais.

Croix des Salles★★

Alt 1 705m/5 594ft. *About 1hr 30min there and back, including 12min ride in the Jaillet gondola and 45min on foot.* 🕒 *Late June to early Sept: 9am-1pm, 2-6pm; mid-Dec to Mar 9am-6pm (10min, departure every 30min)* 🕒 *closed rest of year. 9.70€ return, children 8.40€ -* ☎ *04 50 21 01 50 or* ☎ *04 50 21 27 28.*
🚶 Having reached the upper station, continue on foot to the cross through pastures and woodland. View of the Fiz range and Mont Blanc Massif.

Rochebrune Super-Megève★

Alt 1 754m/5 755ft. *About 1hr there and back, including an 8min cable-car ride.* 🕒 *Mid-June to mid-Sept: 9am-1pm, 2-6pm; mid-Dec to mid-Feb: 9am-4.30pm; Feb to Apr: 9am-5.15 10.40€ return, children under 15 years 8.90€, under 5 years no charge -* ☎ *04 50 21 01 51.*
🚶 **View** of the Val d'Arly, the Aravis mountains and Mont Blanc.

For Experienced Walkers

A map on sale at the tourist office describes the many hiking trails in the area, including 30 from Megève without a gondola ride, and 8 from the Alloz parking lot.

Mont Joly★★★

Alt 2 525m/8 284ft. *4hr 30min there and back on foot from the Mont d'Arbois via a well-marked path. Climbing boots are recommended, particularly for the last, fairly steep part of the itinerary.*
🚶 The exceptional **panorama**★★★ unfolding from the summit (viewing table), includes the Mont-Blanc, Vanoise, Beaufortain, Écrins and Grandes Rousses massifs, the Belledonne range, the Chartreuse and the Aravis.

Mont de Vorès★★

Alt 2 067m/6 781ft. *5hr 30min on foot. Difference in altitude: 800m/2 625ft. This itinerary is not difficult but requires stamina. Board the cable car preferably before 10am. If it is not working, you can make a similar round tour from Leutaz.*
🚶 The path rises to L'Alpette and the Col de Véry on the way to the Mont de Vorès. Splendid **view** of the Mont-Blanc Massif to the east, with the Col du Joly and Lac de la Girotte in the foreground, and the Aravis mountains to the west. The path follows the mountain ridge to the Crêt du Midi which offers a remarkable **view** of Megève on the right and Le Planay on the left. Walk down to Les Fontanettes then up again to Rochebrune (🖎 *hard-going walk for about 1hr*) along a fairly steep path.

MÉRIBEL✳✳✳

MICHELIN MAP 333 M5– LOCAL MAP SEE MASSIF DE LA VANOISE

Méribel is an attractive ski resort situated in the Allues Valley, at the heart of the **Trois Vallées**✳✳✳ ski area (*see Massif de la VANOISE*), the largest in the world. British skiing enthusiasts were the first to realise the potential of the area for tourism. After the annexation of Austria by Germany in 1938, they stopped going to Austrian resorts and turned to the French Alps in their search for new slopes. Lord Lindsay discovered the Allues Valley with its 13 old hamlets and founded Méribel. After the war, regulations concerning architectural styles were laid down: all residential buildings must be chalets with ridged roofs and wood or stone façades. This architectural unity, along with extensive sports facilities, hiking trails and picturesque villages, have made Méribel a popular resort year-round. *BP1, 73550 Méribel Mid-Dec to Apr and July to Aug: 9am-7pm; Sept to mid-Dec: daily except Sat afternoon, Sun and public holidays: 9am-noon, 2-6pm; May to June: daily except Wed and Sat afternoons, Sun and public holidays: 9am-noon, 2-7pm - ☎ 04 79 08 60 01 - www.meribel.net*

▸ **Orient Yourself:** Méribel is 30min south of Moûtiers. Take D 915 in the direction of Brides-les-Bains, then take D 90, a pretty drive on a scenic ridge.

Don't Miss: An excursion on the Lac de Tueda is a pleasant interlude.

Organizing Your Time: If you are planning a hike starting from a mountain summit, double-check the opening times of the ski lifts.

Especially for Kids: If you are hiking with young children, there are several walks along easy forest trails.

Also See: Nearby Sights: La Vallée des BELLEVILLE, CHAMPAGNY-EN-VANOISE, COURCHEVEL, Route de la MADELEINE, La TARENTAISE, Massif de la VANOISE.

The Resorts

At the centre of Les Trois Vallées, **Méribel-Mottaret** is situated between 1 700-1 800m/5 577-5 906ft, on the edge of the Parc national de la Vanoise. A network of gondolas provides fast and comfortable links with Courchevel, la Tania, Les Ménuires and Val-Thorens. The areas of Mont Vallon, Mont de la Chambre, Roc des Trois Marches and Roc de Fer offer some of the finest ski slopes in Europe, ideal for competent skiers. They face north-south and west, so skiers remain in the sun all day. As a principal site for the Albertville Olympics in 1992, Méribel hosted the women's alpine skiing races on the difficult Roc de Fer run, as well as the ice-hockey matches in its skating rink.

The cross-country ski area is not very extensive but delightful; there are 33km/20mi of well-covered trails round the Altiport and Plan du Tueda, in a fine woodland setting (spruce and arolla pine), at an altitude of 1 700m/5 577ft.

The numerous chalet-apartments of Méribel are dotted around the forest between 1 450-1 600m/4 757-5 249ft; the only drawback is that, apart from La Chaudanne, there is no real resort centre. The road continues to the Altiport (mountain airport), where golf is played in summer. Themed flights are available in all seasons over the Trois Vallées, the Olympic sites and Mont Blanc.

Non-skiers can enjoy the superb landscapes of the Trois Vallées area. Various paths crisscross the forest or skirt the ski runs, and a special **pedestrian pass**, known as a *forfait piéton*, give hikers access to gondolas and chair-lifts in Méribel and Courchevel. In summer, Méribel is a popular **hiking base** (*see information in the Address Book*).

Address Book

For coin categories, see the Legend on the cover flap.

EATING OUT

⊝**Les Pierres Plates** – *La Saulire - winter: acces by 2 gondolas from Saulire sur Méribel -* ☎ *04 79 00 46 41 - www.chaudanne.com - closed May-June and Sept-Nov.* This bar and self-service restaurant on the summit of La Saulire at 2700m/8 858ft offers an incomparable view of the Vanoise glaciers and the Alps.

⊝**Le Martagon** – *Rte des Allues, Le Raffort -* ☎ *04 79 00 56 29 - closed 25 Apr-15 May, Sat-Sun out of season.* This brand-new chalet at the foot of the gondola is the ideal spot to relax after a day on the slopes. A large fireplace stands in the pine-panelled dining room, while in summer there is a pleasant terrace. Savoyard specialties and a traditional menu.

⊝⊜⊜**Le Blanchot** – *Rte de l'altiport - 3.5km/2mi N of Méribel -* ☎ *04 79 00 55 78 - le-blanchot@wanadoo.fr - open 18 Dec-25 Apr, July - Aug, closed Sun and Mon evenings.* The road leading to this restaurant, which is named for the species of hare that turns white as soon as the snow comes, winds through a pine forest, a summer golf course and a winter cross-country ski area. The food served is fairly plain at lunchtime and more elaborate in the evening.

WHERE TO STAY

Although Méribel is less jet-set than Courcheval, the price of lodging shoots skyward at the approach of winter. To find reasonable accommodation, contact the central reservation service at the tourist office.

⊝⊜**Hôtel Croix Jean-Claude** – *Aux Allues - 7km/4mi N of Méribel on D915a -* ☎ *04 79 08 61 05 - closed in June and 20 Sept - 28 Oct - 16rms-* ⊜*restaurant.* This is one of the oldest hotels in the valley, a fair distance from the slopes and popular with locals. Nights here are peaceful and the cuisine is in the local tradition, served on the terrace or in the rustic-style dining room.

⊝⊜⊜**Hôtel Adray Télébar** – *On the ski slopes (access on foot only) -* ☎ *04 79 08 60 26 - www.telebar-hotel.com - closed 21 Apr-19 Dec - 24rms -* ⊜*res-taurant.* You can get here on skis, and your luggage will catch up with you in a tracked vehicle. You will be greeted by a friendly family cosily settled in this chalet made entirely of timber, right in the middle of the ski slopes, opposite snow-clad peaks. Large terrace for sunbathing.

⊝⊜⊜⊜**Hôtel Yéti** – *Rd-pt des Pistes -* ☎ *04 79 00 51 15 - www.hotel-yeti.com - open July-Aug, 15 Dec-25 Apr - 27rms -* ⊝⊜⊜⊜*restaurant.* If you are not the sporty type, you can settle for a deck-chair on the panoramic terrace. Inside, the warm tones of pale waxed wood blend with the fabrics and carpets in the vaulted lounge. Spacious rooms with wood panelling. The cuisine is of high standard. Large swimming pool in summer.

ON THE TOWN

L'Éterlou – *La Chaudanne -* ☎ *04 79 08 89 00 - www.chaudanne.com - daily from 5pm in season - closed May-June and Oct-Nov.* This bar located in the hotel of the same name has an atmosphere that is both chic and convivial. Numerous themed evenings entertain patrons, and there is a small dance floor.

SPORTS AND LEISURE

Summer activities at Méribel are extensive. Besides hiking, there are the swimming pool, Olympic skating rink, golf course, gym and other facilities. Contact the tourist office for information.

Hiking – Nearly a quarter of the Méribel valley is included in the Parc national de la Vanoise, making it a centre for hiking and climbing. There are 20 hiking circuits in the area, through forests and pastures, while the summits of La Tougnète, la Saulire, and Mont-Vallon offer lovely views over the Mont-Blanc massif. High mountain trails are accessible to children as young as 6 years old. The *Guide des Sentiers*, on sale for 6.50€ at the tourist office, describes itineraries. The Bureau des Guides (*Maison du Tourisme,* ☎ *04 79 00 30 38*) organizes climbing courses for children and adults.There are also 117km/73mi of signposted mountain-biking tracks.

The Main Summits★★

La Saulire★★★
Access from Méribel by the Burgin Saulire gondola (closed in summer) or from Mottaret by the Pas du Lac gondola ⏱ in summer: Mon, Tue, Thur, Sun 9.30am-4.45pm. 9.20€ Splendid **panorama** (⎆*see COURCHEVEL).*

Mont du Vallon★★
Alt 2 952m/9 685ft. *From Mottaret, walk to the Plan des Mains alt 2 150m/7 054ft. Allow 1hr 15min in summer. In winter, access only by the Plattières gondola (second section, skiers only). Continue to the summit by the Mont Vallon gondola.*
On arrival, go to the panel "Réserve de Tueda": superb **view**★★★ of the Allues Valley, including the Aiguille du Borgne and the Gébroulaz Glacier to the south and the surrounding massif. Turn back and take a path towards the Lacs du Borgne, for a fine view of the Vallée des Belleville with the Aiguille d'Arves and Grandes Rousses Massif in the distance.

Roc des Trois Marches★★
Alt 2 704m/8 871ft. *In winter, access from Mottaret by the Plattières gondola (three sections).* Beautiful **circular view**, including the Vanoise glaciers and the Meije.

Tougnète★★
Alt 2 410m/7 907ft. *Access from Méribel by gondola; if possible, sit facing backwards rather than in the direction of travel.* ⏱ *July to Aug: Mon-Fri 9am-12.30pm, 1.30-5pm (two sections, 20min, continuous) 9.20€ return -* ☎ *04 79 08 65 32.*
On the way up, there is a view of Méribel and the villages dotted around the valley, with Mont Blanc and the Beaufortain in the background. From the upper station, the view extends over the whole Vallée des Belleville.

Y. Bontoux

Tueda Nature Reserve with the Aiguille du Fruit in the background

Skiers can also enjoy the various panoramas unfolding from the **Roc de Fer**★★, **Pas de Cherferie**★★, **Mont de la Challe**★, **Mont de la Chambre**★★ and **Col de la Loze**★★.

Hikes

Plan du Tueda★

At Mottaret, follow signs for Le Chatelet and park your car at the end of the road.
The **Réserve naturelle de Tueda** (*Maison de la Réserve at Lac de Tueda* 🕐 *July-Aug: 12.30pm-6pm -* ☎ *04 79 01 04 75 - www.vanoise.com*) was created in 1990 to preserve one of the last large forests of arolla pines in Savoie. These trees, which can reach the age of 600 years, are endangered because of their popularity for making furniture and musical instruments. The Tueda Forest surrounds a lovely lake overlooked by the jagged silhouette of the Aiguille du Fruit and by Mont Vallon. A **nature trail**, lined with many flower species, leads hikers through this fragile environment.

Col de Chanrouge★★

Alt 2 531m/8 304ft. *Start from the Plan du Tueda. On the way up, allow 2hr to the Refuge du Saut then 1hr 15min to the pass. On the way down, allow 2hr.* From the pass, there is a fine **view** of the Courchevel Valley, of the ski area of La Plagne (overlooked by the Sommet de Bellecôte) and of the Mont Blanc Massif.

MODANE

POPULATION 3 658
MICHELIN MAP 333 N6 – LOCAL MAP SEE LA MAURIENNE

This border town at the beginning of the middle Maurienne Valley, beneath the southern heights of the Vanoise Massif, is nearly overwhelmed by the dense traffic passing through the narrow valley of the Arc which links France and Italy. However, away from the main roads, the town centre still retains its Savoyard character. A short distance away, the resorts of la Norma and Valfréjus are set in pleasant landscapes. 🛈 *rue des Bettets – 73500 Valfréjus* 🕐 *July to Aug: daily 9am-noon, 2-6.30pm; school holidays in winter: 8.30am-6.30pm; Sept to mid-Dec and May-June: daily except Sat-Sun 9am-noon, 2-5pm -* ☎ *04 79 05 33 83*

▶ **Orient Yourself:** Modane is squarely on the Alpine highway A 43.
◔ **Don't Miss:** The Sentier nature de l'Orgère is an easy, pleasant walk
🕐 **Organizing Your Time:** You are only 30min from Italy by the Fréjus Tunnel.
◔ **Also See:** Nearby Sights: AUSSOIS, BESSANS, BONNEVAL-SUR-ARC, Route du GALIBIER, Route des GRANDES-ALPES, La Haute MAURIENNE, Route du MONT-CENIS, ST-JEAN-DE-MAURIENNE, Massif de la VANOISE

A Bit of History

Tunnel Routier du Fréjus –*Speed limit: 70km/44mph. Passing and parking forbidden. Closed to small vehicles and foot traffic. About 20min to cross.* Inaugurated in July 1980 after six years of construction work, the 2 870m/8mi-long road tunnel is shorter than the Arlberg tunnel (Austria) and the St-Gothard tunnel (Switzerland), but longer than the Mont Blanc tunnel. This Franco-Italian project was designed to ease road traffic when the Col du Mont-Cenis is blocked by snow.

The planned construction of a high-speed TGV rail link from Lyon to Turin via Chambéry will involve drilling a 50km/31mi tunnel through the mountains, starting at Modane. An exhibit describing the project has opened in a former rice factory in Modane at Place du 17 Sept 1943 (🕐 *Tue- Sat 9.30am-noon, 2.30pm-6.30pm,* 🕐*closed public holidays -* ☏ *04 79 05 84 31 - www.lyonturin-ferroviaire.com*)

The monumental **entrance to the railway tunnel** can be seen from the road. (Leave Modane and head towards Valfréjus; the road is on the left).

Excursions

Sentier nature de l'Orgère ⋆
From N 6 at Le Freney, turn right onto D 106, which rises steeply to the Orgère refuge (parking) over a distance of 13km/8mi.

🐾This nature trail *(2km/1.2mi)* winds through the Orgère Valley across meadows, woodland and pastures. The first part is lined with information panels. Ask the warden of the Maison du Parc for a leaflet giving details fo the trail.

Hike to the Col de Chavière ⋆⋆
Departure from the Orgère refuge: 3hr up (including 2hr to the Lac de Partie); 2hr down. Difference in altitude: about 900m/2 953ft. Climbing boots are recommended, not least because there is still snow on the ground until the end of July. Take a pair of binoculars to observe the fauna.

🚶 The path, with a view of the Râteau d'Aussois and the Aiguille Doran, climbs to the ruins of the Chalets de l'Estiva: **view** ⋆⋆ of Longe Côte and La Norma. When the path starts going down, after a further hour's walking, the Col de Chavière comes into view flanked by the snow-capped **Péclet-Polset** and high cliffs. Chamois and ibexes roam about the area. Beyond the Lac de Partie, the path climbs steeply to the pass (2 801m/9 190ft), giving a splendid view of the Pralognan Valley and Mont Blanc in the distance.

Valfréjus ⋆
🚠Alt 1 500m/4 921ft. *8km/5mi southwest of Modane by N 6.* The main attractions of this small ski resort, created in 1983, are its tasteful architecture, which fits in well with the landscape, and the nearby forest planted with spruces, larches and arolla pines. Between 2 000m-2 500m/6 562ft-8 202ft, the north-facing slopes enjoy good snow cover; there are 12 ski lifts and some 20 ski runs. In summer, Valfréjus is the starting point of hikes to the Pointe du Fréjus and Thabor Massif.

Punta Bagna ⋆⋆
Alt 2 750m/9 022ft. *The summit is accessible by gondola only in wintertime; in summer, only the first section operates.* 🕐 *July to Aug: Mon-Thur 9am-4pm (15min continuous); mid-Dec to Feb holiday: 9am-4pm (after Feb holiday until 4.30pm). In summer 5€ return, children under 12 years 3€; In winter 6€ return, children under 4€ -* ☏ *04 79 05 32 71.*

The **panorama** ⋆⋆ is superb. The Rochebrune and the Italian Alps are visible straight ahead, beyond the Col du Fréjus, to the left is the Pointe de Fréjus. From the terrace of the restaurant, you can see the northern summits of the Écrins Massif (Grande Ruine, Pic Gaspard, Meije and Rateau) to the southwest, and the Valfréjus ski area as well as the Péclet–Posset, Col d'Aussois, the Vanoise glacier, Grande Motte and Dent Parrachée to the north.

MOLINES-EN-QUEYRAS★

POPULATION 336
MICHELIN MAP 334 J4 – LOCAL MAP SEE LE QUEYRAS

Not far from St-Véran lie the seven hamlets of Molines. Their picturesque old houses are surmounted by large grain lofts, where crops continue to ripen after the harvest. There are few hotels but accommodation is available in private homes in the old village and surrounding hamlets. In winter, Molines offers skiing in a lovely woodland setting; the small ski area is linked to that of St-Véran.

🛈 *Clot-la-Chalpe - 05350 Molines-en-Queyras* 🕐 *Daily except Sun 9am-noon, 2-5pm - ☎ 04 92 45 83 22 - www.molinesenqueyras.com*

▸ **Orient Yourself:** Leave Château-Queyras, which is 36km/22.5km south of Briançon, on D 947 toward the east; at Ville-Vielle, turn south on D 5

💬 **Don't Miss:** St-Romain de Molines★ in the village is a fine example of a Baroque church interior.

🕐 **Also See:** Nearby Sights: ABRIÈS, BRIANÇON, Le BRIANÇONNAIS, CEILLAC, Vallée de FREISSINIÈRES, Route des GRANDES ALPES, GUILLESTRE, MONT-DAUPHIN, MONTGENÈVRE, Le QUEYRAS, ST-VERAN, VARS

Excursions

Route du Col Agnel★★ (Aigue Agnelle Valley)

15km to the Col Agnel – about 30min. Road closed in winter.

Drive to Pierre Grosse, which owes its name to the **erratic blocks** of igneous rock scattered over the surrounding pastures, then on to Fontgillarde, the valley's highest hamlet (1 997m/6 552ft). Beyond Fontgillarde, the road offers a fine **view** of the Pic de Château Renard, towering above the trees. A plaque, fixed to a rock on the right-hand side of the road, reminds passers-by that the armies of both Hannibal and Caesar marched through here on their way across the Alps.

The road continues to climb through a high-altitude mountain landscape, offering **views** of the snow-covered Pelvoux Massif to the northwest. It finally reaches the Agnel Refuge and, 2km/1.2mi further on, the Agnel Pass on the Italian border. Walk up to the **viewing table** (alt 2 744m/9 003ft) for a splendid **panorama**★★ of the Pain de Sucre and Monte Viso to the east, the Grand Queyras and Pointe des Sagnes to the northwest and the Pic de Rochebrune further away and the Meije and Mont Pelvoux in the distance.

Route de St-Véran★★

(Aigue Blanche Valley) – 💬*See Le QUEYRAS,* 2.

For coin categories, see the Legend on the cover flap.

WHERE TO STAY AND EAT

⊜⊜**Hôtel L'Astragale** – 05350 St-Véran- ☎ 04 92 45 87 00 - astragale@queyras. com - closed 16 Apr-16 June and 19 Sept-16 Dec. 🅿 - 21rms- ⊜⊜restaurant. This recently constructed chalet has considerable charm: comfortable furnishings, Alpine decor, large guestrooms equipped with VCRs, view of the mountains, tea-room and a friendly, no-smoking dining room with a fireplace. There are also lots of activities: hikes, snowshoeing, astronomy, etc.

The Caterpillar and the Larch or Why Evergreens Turn Brown in Summer

Hikers walking through the larch forests in July are sometimes horrified to see acres of blighted trees. What is this strange curse that strikes the "kings of the Queyras" every ten years?

The culprit is a creature called the larch budmoth. Its caterpillars hatch on the tree and gnaw into the buds, eating away at the needles and leaving only a dry husk. These give the tree its dull brown colour, but even a plague which destroys all the needles will not kill off a healthy larch. Pesticides are used to control the insects only in areas well off the beaten track.

Hikes

Pain de Sucre★★★

Alt 3 208m/10 525ft. *Leave the car on the roadside between the refuge and the Col Agnel. 1hr 45min to the top, 1hr 15min down. Difference in altitude: 600m/1 968ft. This itinerary is suitable for experienced hikers equipped with climbing boots; dry weather essential.*

The **Col Vieux**★ (2 806m/9 206ft) is easily reached in 30min; another 15min climb takes you to a ledge; carry straight on to a path which winds up to the Pain de Sucre *(very steep climb, caution is recommended)*. The magnificent **panorama**★★★, one of the finest in the Alps, includes Monte Viso and the Italian Alps to the east, the Brec and Aiguille de Chambeyron to the south and the Oisans Massif to the west. To the north, the view extends as far as Mont Blanc in clear weather. Go down along a marked path starting near the cross and leading back to the Col Vieux.

MASSIF DU MONT-BLANC★★★

MICHELIN MAP 328 O6

The Mont Blanc Massif surpasses in height all other European mountains, its highest peak reaching 4 807m/15 771ft, yet it owes its fame essentially to the wonderful variety of scenery offered by its domes, needles and glaciers. It was this landscape which inspired pioneering climbers to take on the challenge of Mont Blanc; countless mountaineers have followed in their footsteps. Motorists can enjoy an excellent overall view by driving up the Chamonix Valley, through which flows the Arve, or delight in the pastoral landscapes of the Val Montjoie (Bon Nant Valley).

The long "Round Tour of Mont Blanc" (320km/199mi), via the Grand and Petit St-Bernard passes, is highly recommended; but there is also the round tour of Mont Blanc on foot, which is a long and fascinating walk suitable for experienced hikers with plenty of stamina. You can also fly over the massif, starting from Megève or Sallanches airfield.

▶ **Orient Yourself:** At the end of A 41, the massif surges from the Le Fayet plain. To the north on N 205 is the valley of Chamonix, over the soaring Égrats viaduct; to the east on D 902 is St-Gervais and the Val de Montjoie.

- **Don't Miss:** Stop to admire the view at the arrival areas on the south flank of the Chamonix valley (Brévent, Flégère, Balme); the Mont-Blanc tramway, from Le Fayet or St-Gervais, takes you to the Bionassay glacier.
- **Organizing Your Time:** Always keep up with the weather report when starting a hike, and try to get an early start; most storms occur late in the day.
- **Especially for Kids:** Children will love the Mont Blanc tramway.
- **Also See:** Nearby Sights: ARGENTIÈRE, CHAMONIX-MONT-BLANC, Les CONTAMINES-MONTJOIE, Les HOUCHES, MEGÈVE, ST-GERVAIS-LES-BAINS, Bassin de SALLANCHES

A Bit of History

The First Ascent of Mont Blanc

In the mid-18C, it became fashionable for wealthy young men on a grand tour of Europe to stop in Chamonix, where they were shown the Mer de Glace by local guides. In 1760, a young scientist from Geneva, **Horace Bénédict de Saussure** offered a reward to the first person to reach the summit of Mont Blanc. A few local people attempted the climb but were all defeated by ignorance, fear, lack of equipment and the conviction that it was impossible to survive a night at such great heights.

In 1776, one **Jacques Balmat**, caught out by nightfall while looking for crystals in the mountains, showed that one could spend a night at very high altitude and survive. **Michel-Gabriel Paccard**, a doctor from Chamonix, found Balmat's experience interesting. He had spent many an hour surveying Mont Blanc with his telescope, trying to plot a path to the summit and the two of them took up Saussure's challenge; they left on 7 August 1786 and reached the summit the following evening, completely exhausted.

The following year, it was Saussure's turn to make the ascent accompanied by 18 guides laden with scientific equipment; using barometric instruments, he was able to confirm the height of the peak.

Many more attempts followed, some of them made by women such as **Marie Paradis** in 1809 and **Henriette d'Angeville** in 1838.

Saussure and his team climbing Mont Blanc

D. Rigault/Conservatoire d'Art et d'Histoire, Annecy

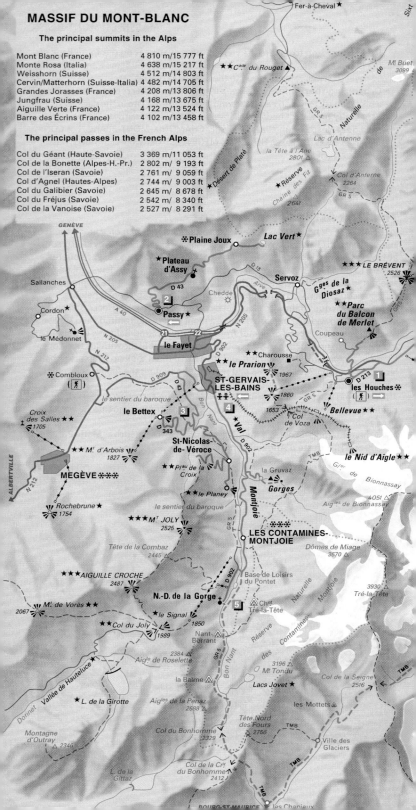

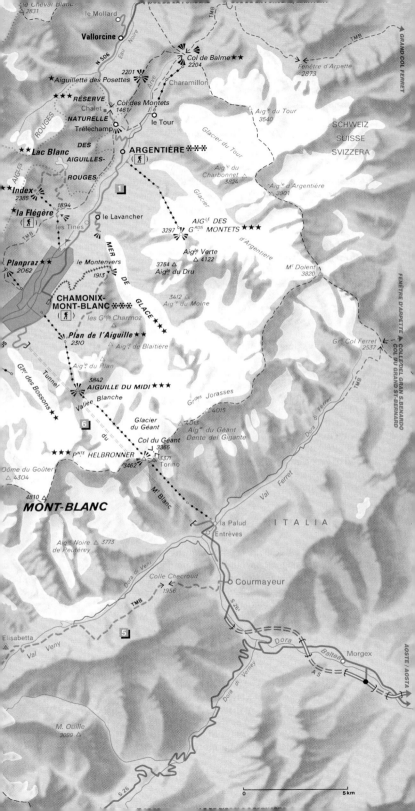

Geographical Notes

A young mountain range

The massif du Mont Blanc dates from 35 million years ago, quite recent in geological time. Young and partially eroded, as witness the jagged needles of Chamonix, the mountains experienced successive foldings and extreme pressures. The result is narrow valleys and parts of the range so compressed that in 1965, the Mont Blanc tunnel pierced it from one side to another. Finally, the mountains underwent a long period of glaciation, creating canyons, high passes and alpine meadows.

Mont Blanc... – Like the rest of the Alpine range, Mont Blanc has two different aspects. On the French side, it looks like a "gentle giant," impressively flanked by snow-covered domes underlined by a few rocky escarpments (Aiguille du Goûter and Aiguilles de Bionnassay) whereas the view from the Italian side is of a grim, dark wall bristling with rock pinnacles or needles (Aiguille Noire du Peutérey). The ascent from this side requires a lot of mountaineering skill, but endurance is more important if you want to climb Mont Blanc from Chamonix or St-Gervais.

...and its satellites – The Chamonix Valley owes its fame to the **"needles,"** (aiguilles) carved out of a kind of greenish coarse granite, known as *protogine*. Along the rock face of these splendid pinnacles, mountaineers can find the same hand and footholds year after year, for several decades. The most famous peaks are the Grépon, the Aiguille de Blaitière and the Aiguille du Dru. Three huge **glaciers** are sought after by summer visitors: the **Mer de Glace**, the longest (14km/8.7mi from the head of the Géant Glacier) and most popular, owing to the famous Montenvers scenery; the **Glacier des Bossons** (7km/4.3mi), the most picturesque, thrusting through the forest; the **Glacier d'Argentière** (11km/6.8mi), the most impressive, beneath the imposing north face of the Aiguille Verte. Since the last Ice Age, the size of these glaciers has changed considerably with the fluctuating climate; from the 16C to the mid-18C they stretched so far down that they destroyed houses built below them.

On the other side of the Arve Valley, the Aiguilles Rouges, which are the training ground of rock-climbers, offer some remarkable viewpoints such as the Brévent. South of Mont Blanc, the snow-covered Dômes de Miage form the typical background of the Val Montjoie.

Tunnel du Mont-Blanc

The Col du Géant (alt 3 365m/11 040ft), which is the lowest pass across the range, could not serve as a significant route for transporting goods owing to its high altitude. France and Italy therefore decided to finance the building of the 11.6km/7mi-long Mont Blanc Tunnel, which took place between 1959 and 1965. Chamonix is now only 20km/12.4mi from Courmayeur. The thickness of the layer of rock covering the tunnel is up to 2 480m/8 136ft below the Aiguille du Midi.

The Disaster

Nearly 2 million vehicles of all types went through the tunnel in 1998, but on 24 March, 1999, a traffic accident sparked off a fire which claimed the lives of 41 people. The tragedy forced the immediate closure of the tunnel, revealed the inadequacy of the ventilation and safety systems, which have now been entirely rebuilt, and reopened the debate about the problems of transport in the mountains.

Excursions

1 Route de Chamonix★★★

FROM ST-GERVAIS-LES-BAINS TO VALLORCINE 41km/
25.5mi – about 2hr – see local map

Le Fayet – &See ST-GERVAIS-LES-BAINS.

Beyond the modern power station at Passy, the road rises above the Chedde Plain, within sight of the long viaduct, carrying the Autoroute Blanche to Chamonix and of the splendid Chaîne des Fiz to the north, then makes its way through the Défilé du Châtelard and a tunnel to the Servoz Basin.

▶ *At Servoz Station, turn left towards D 13.*

The road now runs past Montées-Pélissier through the narrow valley carved out by the Arve on its way to Chamonix

▶ *Turn right onto D 213.*

Les Houches❋ – &*See Les HOUCHES.*

▶ *Continue along D 213 which joins N 205.*

The road runs close to the lower end of the Bossons Glacier and the view embraces the superb Aiguilles de Chamonix.

Chamonix and excursions❋❋❋ – &*See CHAMONIX-MONT-BLANC.*

Just beyond Chamonix, the slender spire of the Aiguille du Dru standing next to the **Aiguille Verte** forms a striking picture. The Aiguille Verte (alt 4 122m/13 523ft) was first climbed by two Swiss guides and an Englishman, Edward Whymper, who is best remembered for his successful ascent of the Cervin (Matterhorn) in 1865.

▶ *Beyond Les Tines, turn right onto the road leading to Le Lavancher.*

The road rises rapidly to **Le Lavancher** situated on a spur separating the Argentière and Chamonix basins. *Turn right before the Beausoleil Hotel.*
There are contrasting **views**★★ of the Chamonix Valley and its glaciers down-river and of the rocky peaks framing Argentière upriver, with the Glacier d'Argentière in the foreground beneath the Aiguille du Chardonnet.

▶ *Take the D 506 to Argentière*

Argentière❋❋❋ – &*See ARGENTIÈRE.*

As you leave Argentière, turn right towards Le Tour; the landscape becomes more austere and the Glacier du Tour comes into view.
From **Trélechamp**, there is a fine **vista**★★ of the high summits of the Mont Blanc Massif.
N 506 (⌂ *blocked by snow from December to April)* continues past Trélechamp through scrubland covered with rhododendrons and juniper bushes to the **Col des Montets** (alt 1 461m/4 793ft) overlooked by the Aiguilles Rouges.

Réserve naturelle des Aiguilles Rouges★★ – *See ARGENTIÈRE.*

The road follows the wooded valley of the River Eau Noire, offering views of the Swiss Alps.

Vallorcine
Drive past the station on the right and turn left towards Le Mollard. Turn round at the entrance of the hamlet.
The Vallorcine Church stands out against the impressive rock face of the Aiguille de Mesure at the northern extremity of the Aiguilles Rouges and Mont-Blanc massifs (*in order to prolong this excursion to Martigny across the Forclaz Pass, see The Green Guide Switzerland).*

2 Val Montjoie ★

FROM ST-GERVAIS TO NOTRE-DAME-DE-LA-GORGE *16km/10mi – about 45min – see local map*

St-Gervais-les-Bains♯♯ – *See ST-GERVAIS-LES-BAINS.*

▶ *Leave St-Gervais by ② on the town map, D 902 towards Les Contamines.*

Beyond Bionnay, a narrow wooded passage opens the way into the Contamines Basin in its picturesque mountain setting.

Gorges de la Gruvaz
🕐 *Open July to September* 🕐 *closed in winter and when there is danger of landslides - ☎ 04 50 47 01 58.*
🚶On the left, 1.5km/0.9mi from D 902. Caution: the first section includes several footbridges, the second a steep slippery path. Leave the car after La Gruvaz, in front of the entrance to the gorge.
The path starts by going through the woods, within sight of the stream; once above the tree line, it climbs up the schist slopes of the south side; look back to admire the gorge with St-Nicolas-de-Véroce in the distance. The path leads to a **viewpoint**★; upstream, the gorge forms a perfect V carved out of schist with the raging stream cascading down from the Miage Glacier.

Les Contamines-Montjoie✳✳✳ – *See Les CONTAMINES-MONTJOIE.*

▶ *Continue along D 902 to the end of the road.*

Notre-Dame-de-la-Gorge
Two pilgrimages to the Virgin Mary *(15 August and 8 September)* take place in this sanctuary, erected at the heart of a wooded valley. The interior decoration of the chapel is one of the finest examples of Baroque art in Haute-Savoie. The high altar (1707) and its **retable** adorned with twisted columns forms the main part of this harmonious ensemble.
Stay on the west bank of the Bon Nant and take a walk through the woods. This place is the starting point for many excursions, and the GR footpath which goes round Mont Blanc passes through here.

③ VAL MONTJOIE CLIFF-ROAD★★

FROM ST-GERVAIS-LES-BAINS TO THE PLATEAU DE LA CROIX (via St-Nicolas-de-Véroce) *15km/9.3mi – about 45min –* 🚶 *see local map*

This cliff road overlooking the Bon Nant Valley, known as Val Montjoie, offers clear views of the Mont Blanc Massif.

St-Gervais-les-Bains♨♨ – 🚶*See ST-GERVAIS-LES-BAINS.*

▷ *Leave St-Gervais by ③ on the town plan, towards Megève, then turn onto the first road on the left.*

The **Val Montjoie** has retained an interesting group of churches and chapels whose Baroque interior decoration is in striking contrast with the relatively plain façades.

St-Nicolas-de-Véroce

The village occupies a splendid high **position**★★ facing the Mont Blanc Massif. The 18C **church** has retained its original **Baroque altarpiece** situated inside the chancel decorated with paintings illustrating scenes from the life of St Nicholas. The **church treasury** (🕐 *July to Aug: Tues, Thur 3.30-6.30pm, Sat-Sun 4-6pm; guided tours for more than 5 people. No charge -* ☎ *04 50 93 20 63)* is displayed in a room of the presbytery, where monstrances adorned with gems, reliquaries, crucifixes (one of them decorated with the rare motif of the "brass serpent" from the Old Testament) and precious objects are exhibited next to less refined works which are the expression of popular faith (statue of Notre-Dame-des-Ermites).

▷ *Continue towards Le Planey.*

From the last bend before Le Planey, there is a panoramic **view**★★ of the whole Val Montjoie and its mountain frame (Mont Tondu, Arête des Fours, Aiguille de la Penaz and Aiguille de Roselette).

▷ *Return to St-Nicolas and take the road to the Plateau de la Croix.*

Plateau de la Croix

Leave the car near the chalet called "L'Étape" and walk to the base of the cross. The **view**★★ extends to Mont Blanc, the Aiguilles de Bionnassay, the Massif de Miage, the Chaîne des Fiz and the Aiguilles de Chamonix.

Hikes

④ A Short Round Tour of Mont Blanc on Foot★★★

Information about this hike is included in the topo-guide of the Tour du Mont Blanc GR path published by the Fédération Française de la Randonnée Pédestre (🚶see Practical information).

Starting from Les Contamines-Montjoie, follow D 902 for 2km/1.2mi, then GR 5 and TMB paths and S 26D (4.5km/2.8mi between Courmayeur and La Palud); a cable-car ride completes this itinerary. Remember that identification papers are needed to cross the Italian border.

This four-day tour is suitable for determined hikers with stamina and experience of mountain hiking.

Minimum equipment: climbing boots with non-slippery soles, spare warm clothing, rainwear, sunglasses and high factor sun cream.

The Aiguilles d'Argentière, Dru and Aiguille Verte from Planpraz

Suggested programme:
1st day – Les Contamines-Montjoie – Col du Bonhomme – Les Chapieux.
2nd day – Les Chapieux – Ville des Glaciers – Col de la Seigne – Refuge Elisabetta.
3rd day – Refuge Elisabetta – Checrouit cliff path – Courmayeur.
4th day – Courmayeur – La Palud – Cable-car ride across the range to Chamonix.
Start very early in the morning. The full round tour of the Mont-Blanc Massif takes 10 to 12 days including resting periods and excursions. It is only suitable for very experienced hikers with adequate equipment.

5 **Across the Mont Blanc Massif by Cable Car**

You can take an unforgettable one-day excursion from Chamonix by combining cable-car rides across the massif with a bus ride through the tunnel. *Inquire about the weather forecast before going. Rapid changes in altitude may affect blood circulation and can prove unexpectedly tiring; take as much time as possible and take care getting on and off the cable cars.*

The journey from Chamonix is broken up into several sections:

1. **Chamonix – Plan de l'Aiguille** – Difference in altitude: 1 300m/4 265ft – 9min cable-car ride.
2. **Plan de l'Aiguille** – Piton Nord de l'Aiguille du Midi – Difference in altitude: 1 500m/4 921ft – 8min cable-car ride. ⓘ *See CHAMONIX-MONT-BLANC.*
3. **Climb to the Piton Central of the Aiguille du Midi** – Difference in altitude: 65m/213ft – 35 seconds by lift. Terrace with panoramic view.
4. **Aiguille du Midi – Pointe Helbronner** – Difference in altitude: 1 300m/4 265ft – 35min gondola ride above the Glacier du Géant and the Vallée Blanche, offering one of the finest Alpine panoramas.
5. **Pointe Helbronner – Refuge Torino** – Difference in altitude: 100m/328ft – 3min cable-car ride. Terrace with panoramic view on the Pointe Helbronner.
6. **Refuge Torino – La Palud** – Difference in altitude: 2 000m/6 562ft – 15min cable-car ride in two sections.

MONTBRUN-LES-BAINS★

POPULATION 467
MICHELIN MAP 332 F8

Protected by the Montagne de Lure and Mont Ventoux, this Provençal village is spared the blasts of the mistral and the oppressive heat of summer. Standing at the confluence of the River Anary and River Toulourenc, Montbrun-les-Bains comprises the old village, clinging to the south-facing hillside beneath the castle ruins, and the new district spread in the green valley below, in contrast to the barren countryside around.

In summer, the holiday village and the recently reopened therapeutic baths bring life to the area. Already known to the Romans, the sulphur waters are excellent for the treatment of rheumatism, bronchitis, skin diseases and ear, nose and throat complaints, and in the late 19C, Montbrun was a popular spa town with baths resembling those of Baden-Baden. However, the First World War put an end to this thriving activity which was only resumed much later, in 1987. ⓘ *L'Autin – 26570 Montbrun-les-Bains* 🕐 *May to Oct: daily 9am-noon, 3-6pm, May to June and Sept to Oct: closed Sun; Nov to Apr: Mon and Fri, 3-8pm, Tue and Thur 10am-noon, in Mar and Apr, also open Sat 10am-noon -* ☎ *04 75 28 82 49-www. montbrunlesbainsofficedutourisme.fr*

▶ **Orient Yourself:** Situated on the flanks of Mont Ventoux, Montbrun is 12km/7.5mi north of Sault by D 942.
🕐 **Organizing Your Time:** The entire circuit will take you half a day.
👆 **Also See:** Nearby Sights: BUIS-LES-BARONNIES, FORCALQUIER, Route NAPOLÉON, SISTERON

🐾 Walking Tour

Place du Beffroi

The square gets its name from the 14C crenellated **Tour de l'Horloge**, which was one of the four fortified town gates. The old village high street begins here. From

The former spa town basks in the Provençal sun

B. Kaufmann/MICHELIN

the terrace there is an extended **view** of the Anary Valley and the hilltop village of Reilhannette standing out against the white silhouette of Mont Ventoux.

Church

The plain exterior, which is partly 12C, offers a striking contrast with the rich 17C interior decoration, recently restored. The walls of the nave are covered with wood panelling imitating pink and grey marble. Note in particular the superb **altarpiece**★ by a member of the famous Bernus family.

Castle

A few ruins and four round towers overlooking the village are all that remain of the mighty castle, which could accommodate more than 200 men with their horses. Built in the 14C, it was dismantled by Catholic troops during the Wars of Religion and partly rebuilt in 1564 by Charles Dupuy-Montbrun, the Protestant firebrand who forcibly converted the Baronnies region; the Renaissance ornamentation of the main doorway dates from this period.

Excursion

Haute vallée du Toulourenc *38km/23.6mi round tour – about 1hr 30min*

▶ *Leave from the top of the village and join D 159.*

The road goes through a fertile valley with many orchards.

Gorges du Toulourenc★

Squeezing its way between the Montagne de l'Ubac and the Montagne du Buc along a deep gorge overlooked by the cliff road, the impetuous River Toulourenc rushes over rocks.
As the road leaves the gorge, the imposing Château d'Aulan suddenly appears on top of a rocky spur.

Château d'Aulan

🕐 *July to Aug: guided tours 10am-noon, 2-7pm; rest of year: on request made 1 month in advance* 🕐 *Closed 15 Aug and 15 Nov to 30 Apr. 4€, children 2€ - ☎ 04 75 28 80 00.*
The original 12C castle was destroyed and the present castle was completely rebuilt in the 19C by the Suarez d'Aulan family who still own it. Inside, there is a fine collection of furniture and mementoes of the owners. Note a fine *Adoration of the Magi* by Leonard Bramer (17C Flemish School).
Next to the castle, the **church** (🕐 *guided tour July to Aug: 10am-noon, 2-9pm; rest of year by request - ☎ 04 75 28 80 00.*) has retained its 12C east end in spite of being remodelled in the 17C. It contains a beautiful 18C Baroque altar.
Beyond Aulan, the road runs through arid landscapes dotted with lavender fields.

▶ *Turn right onto D 546.*

Mévouillon

The village is named after a local family who owned the whole Baronnies region. A fortress, which stood on a ridge on the left-hand side of the road, was at the centre of bitter fighting during the Wars of Religion. Once considered impregnable, it has now completely disappeared.
The **National Hang-gliding Centre** of the Baronnies region is situated in Mévouillon, in a place known as Le Col.

▶ *Continue along D 546 then turn right onto D 542.*

The road follows the Méouge Valley. (Gorges de la Méouge, 👒 *see SISTERON,* 4).

Séderon
The Montagne de Bergiès (1 367m/4 485ft) towers above this peaceful mountain village.

▶ *Turn towards Montbrun-les-Bains at the intersection with D 546.*

When you reach the Col de Macuègne (alt 1 968m/3 504ft), turn left towards Ferrassières and stop 50m/55yd further on to admire the fine **views** of the gullied slopes of the Montagne d'Albion and Mont Ventoux.

▶ *Return to the pass.*

On its way to Montbrun, the road runs down the Anary Valley, dotted with picturesque peaks.

ROUTE DU MONT-CENIS ★

MICHELIN MAP 333 O6

A major international road linking France and Italy goes through the vast Mont-Cenis Basin now occupied by a huge artificial lake (see below). Climbing above the Haute Maurienne Valley, it offers clear views of the Vanoise Massif. Before the 19C, travellers had to climb up to the pass on the French side along a mule track and, from all accounts, it was worse on the way down: everyone (except, it seems, English travellers!) found the sledge ride organised by local monks positively hair-raising. Napoleon I ordered the construction of the present road (1803-11) with a carefully planned gradient averaging 8%.

▶ **Orient Yourself:** Between the summits of the Grande Turra and La Tomba, the Col du Mont-Cenis was once the frontier between Italy and France. Today it is crossed by N 6.
◉ **Don't Miss:** The view★★ of the Dent Parrachée and Bessans village just before the pass requires a short walk, but is worth it.
🕓 **Organizing Your Time:** Plan your excursion on a day with fine weather, both for reasons of safety and to enjoy the fine views.
👒 **Also See:** Nearby Sights: AUSSOIS, BESSANS, BONNEVAL-SUR-ARC, Route des GRANDES ALPES, La Haute MAURIENNE, MODANE, VAL D'ISÈRE, Massif de la VANOISE

Excursions

Route du Lac du Mont-Cenis ★

FROM LANSLEBOURG TO THE MONT-CENIS LAKE *16km/10mi – about 45min –* 👒 *local map see La MAURIENNE*
The Col du Mont-Cenis is usually blocked by snow from December to April.

Lanslebourg – 👆*See la Haute MAURIENNE, Excursions.*

▷ *Drive south out of Lanslebourg along N 6 towards Italy.*

The road rises through a conifer forest, including fine larches, then continues beyond the treeline.

▷ *Leave the car in a bend to the left (8km/5mi from Lanslebourg, ski lift arrival point).*

Beautiful **view**⋆ of the Vanoise glaciers reclining against the Dent Parrachée and of the Haute Maurienne extending towards Bessans through the narrow opening of the **Col de la Madeleine** (👆*see La Haute MAURIENNE)*, with ski slopes in the foreground below.
Stop just before the pass near a small monument; walk along the road leading to the Replat des Canons; 1km/0.6mi further on, there is a striking view⋆⋆ of the Dent Parrachée and Bessans village.

Col du Mont-Cenis⋆

Alt 2 084m/6 837ft. The pass used to mark the border between France and Italy, which is now a few kilometres further south. A badly maintained monument, originally erected in Mussolini's honour, is now dedicated to the achievements of the French alpine regiments. The view encompasses the green Mont-Cenis Basin, an ideal place for amateur botanists, framed by Mont Lamet and the Pointe de Clairy, the artificial lake, and to the south, through the opening of the Petit-Mont-Cenis Pass, the high summits of the Aiguille de Scolette (alt 3 508m/11 509ft) and Pointe Sommeiller.
The road skirts the lake past **Plan des Fontainettes,** where there is a busy transport café; the **"Salle historique du Mont-Cenis"** (🕐 *Mid-June to early Sept: 10am-12.30pm, 2-6pm 2.50€ - ☎ 04 79 05 92 95)* can be seen beneath the **chapel** of the priory built above the old hospice, which was flooded by the lake: it shows the Mont-Cenis area before and after the building of the dam. Small Alpine garden nearby.

Lac du Mont-Cenis⋆

From the EDF viewpoint (parking), there is a general **view**⋆ of the lake and the **dam.** The latter is slightly larger (1 485 000m 3/52 442 775cu ft) and much longer at the top (1 400m/1 531yd) but lower (maximum 120m/394ft) and narrower at the base (460m/1 509ft) than the Serre-Ponçon Dam in the southern Alps. It consists of a riprap dyke with clay in the centre to ensure watertightness. The lake has a maximum capacity of 315 million m3/255 371acft, mostly at the disposal of the French power station of Villarodin with about one sixth of the capacity being diverted to the Venaus power station in Italy.

Fr. Isler/MICHELIN

Lac du Mont Cenis

MONT-DAUPHIN ★

POPULATION 87
MICHELIN MAP 334 H4

Mont-Dauphin (alt 1 030m/3 379ft) is a mighty citadel situated on top of a promontory, commanding a superb **view**★★ of the Durance and the Guil. When the duke of Savoie's troops seized the towns of Gap, Embrun and Guillestre in 1692, King Louis XIV of France ordered Sébastien le Prestre de Vauban, his military engineer, to build fortifications along the border. Mont-Dauphin was one of nine strategic places where Vauban chose to build not just a fortress, but a fortified settlement from which the king's troops could guard the Queyras region, the Durance Valley and the road leading south across the Col de Vars. Vauban's vision of a true garrison town took shape, but failed to attract the local people, and when the army left Mont-Dauphin in 1980, efforts were made to bring in a civilian population, in particular craftsmen, for whom the **Caserne Campana** was turned into an exhibit centre. *quartier des Artisans d'Art – 05600 Mont-Dauphin– July to Aug and school holidays: daily 9.30am-noon, 2.30-6.30pm; rest of year: daily except Sat: 10am-noon, 2-5pm, Sun 2-5pm– ☎ 04 92 45 17 80.*

- ▶ **Orient Yourself:** Mont-Dauphin sits on the Plateau des Mille Vents, above the town of Guillestre.
- 🕐 **Organizing Your Time:** You'll need one to two hours to see the citadelle; try to take a guided tour.
- ⚭ **Also See:** Nearby Sights: ABRIÈS, L'ARGENTIÈRE-LA-BESSÉE, BARCELONNETTE, BRIANÇON, Le BRIANÇONNAIS, CEILLAC, EMBRUN, Vallée de FREISSINIÈRES, Route des GRANDES ALPES, GUILLESTRE, MOLINES-EN-QUEYRAS, MONT-GENÈVRE, Le QUEYRAS, ST-VÉRAN, SERRE-CHEVALIER, Lac de SERRE-PONÇON, L'UBAYE, La VALLOUISE, VARS

Tour of the Citadel 1hr

Guided tours of the citadel (1hr30min) – June to Sept: daily 10.30am, 2.30pm, 4.30pm; Oct to May: daily except Mon 2.30pm 🕐 closed 1 Jan, 1 May, 1 and 11 Nov, 25 Dec.

- ▶ *Go through the Porte de Briançon by turning off N 94 onto D 37.*

Moat

There is an interesting **view** of the moat from the bridge joining the gate and the guardhouse; note the scarp and counterscarp, the bastions and the lunette which communicates with the outside through an underground passage.

The town

The residential section of the citadel is split into four square blocks. Its buildings, each of which would have had a specific role in time of war, are built of pink marble from Guillestre, which looks lovely in the sunshine.

For coin categories, see the Legend on the cover flap

WHERE TO STAY AND EATING OUT

⊜**Hôtel Lacour and restaurant de la Gare** – At the station - 05600 Mont-Dauphin - ☎ 04 92 45 03 08 -renseignemens@hotel-lacour.com - closed Sat in May-June and Sept-20 Dec - 🅿 - 46rms- ⊜⊜restaurant. This hotel-restaurant between the road and the station is a good choice for its warm welcome, simple rooms and generous menus. The cheaper annexe has some rooms without bathrooms, popular with the young.

B. Kaufmann/MICHELIN

Mont-Dauphin

Powder magazine★

Only an earth mound and a few air pipes can be seen from the outside. The building looks fine from the inside; the upper room is covered with pointed vaulting and the lower room with a solid larch framework. A gallery running all the way round would have provided ventilation and, of course, light, as a naked flame from a lamp could have devastated the town; the locks were even made of bronze to prevent the tiniest spark from igniting the store. Exhibitions are held here in summer.

Arsenal

Built in the mid-18C, it comprised two wings set at right angles. One of them was destroyed by an Italian bomb dropped in 1940. The other building, with elegant œil-de-boeuf windows, houses an exhibition entitled **Vauban dans les Alpes** (*June to Sept: daily 9am-noon, 2-6pm. Guided tours in June and Sept: 10.30am, 2.30pm, 4.30pm; Oct to May: daily except Mon 10am-noon, 2-7pm. Guided tours: daily 2.30pm, Sun 3pm closed 1 Jan, 1 May, 1 and 11 Nov, 25 Dec. 4.60€, children no charge.*

A Military Genius

Architect and soldier, builder and destroyer of cities, **Sébastien Le Prestre de Vauban** (1633-1707) was an inspired and utterly untiring man. As Marshal of the army and chief military engineer to Louis XIV, he personally directed 53 sieges, designed countless bridges and public buildings, dug canals, reshaped harbours and built the famous Maintenon aqueduct. He reinforced the defences of over 300 towns and citadels and built 33 of his own, which maintained their daunting reputation as impregnable strongholds for 250 years after his death. An insightful military tactician, adapting his designs to changes in tactics or peculiarities of the terrain, he frequently worked from a star-shaped fortress design with bastions which could protect each other with their arc of fire. In Vauban's hands this basic Italian model was refined, strengthened with demi-lunes and redoubts, encircled by ditches and defended by outer walls. As the Sun King's wars of conquest extended France's borders, Vauban consolidated the new frontiers in Flanders, Alsace, the Ardennes, Franche-Comté, across the Alps and Pyrenees and along the coast. The topography of the Dauphiné and Haute Provence prevented him from planning defences with the aesthetic balance and precision which are his trademarks elsewhere. Nevertheless, twelve fortresses between Antibes and Briançon were built or rebuilt to his plans.

Church

The only part of the church designed by Vauban that was completed is the chancel, which explains the building's rather strange proportions; walls were raised for the transept and nave, but the stones were then used in the construction of munitions bunkers in 1873. In front of the first pew on the right is the fossil of an ammonite. There is a portrait of St Louis (Louis IX), to whom the church is dedicated, but, oddly enough, the figure in wig and regalia bears more than a passing resemblance to Louis XIV!

Plantation

Several tree species were planted as an experiment on this vast area of spare ground.

Caserne Rochambeau

On the outside, these large barracks form a defence wall overlooking the Porte d'Embrun and the ramparts above the gorge of the River Guil. Inside is a remarkable 260m/853ft-long wooden **framework**✱ which dates from 1820. It is based on a plan by King Henri II's famous architect, Philibert Delorme (1512-70), who designed a framework consisting of a succession of wooden arches held together by wooden dowels, which could easily be dismantled.

MONTGENÈVRE✱✱

POPULATION 497
MICHELIN MAP 334 I3 – LOCAL MAP SEE LE BRIANÇONNAIS

This small border town between France and Italy was the birthplace of French skiing. A young officer garrisoned in Briançon was so convinced of the usefulness of skis for travelling through snow-covered areas that he funded the equipment of seven of his men. In 1901, these *"chasseurs alpins"* **(Alpine troops) skied down the slopes of Montgenèvre in front of a panel of military experts. The demonstration was apparently conclusive since, in 1903, the War Ministry founded a school (which later became the École Française de Ski) and ordered all the Alpine troops to be suitably equipped; these measures were even extended to the local population. Technical improvements soon followed: first metal bindings, then the use of two poles instead of one. Today the town is one of the biggest skiing centres in the Briançonnais.**

▸ **Orient Yourself:** Situated between Briançon and Italy, Montgenèvre is set among summits approaching 3 000m/9 843ft.

🅿 **Parking:** Parking in the village centre is paying, but on the edge of town it is free.

🛇 **Don't Miss:** The heights of Chalvet and the Chalmettes, accessible by ski-lift, offer splendid views.

Kids **Especially for Kids:** The resort is designated "P'tits Montagnards,' meaning it offers ski and snow sports for children; in summer, families will enjoy the activities at the lakes.

⚜ **Also See:** Nearby Sights: L'ARGENTIÈRE-LA-BESSÉE, BRIANÇON, Le BRIANÇONNAIS, Vallée de FREISSINIÈRES, GUILLESTRE, MOLINES-EN-QUEYRAS, MONT-DAUPHIN, L'OISANS, LE QUEYRAS, SERRE-CHEVALIER, La VALLOUISE

🐟 The Resort

Montgenèvre is an important ski resort which forms part of the Franco-Italian **Voie Lactée** (Milky Way) together with the resorts of Clavière, Cesana, Sansicario, Sestrières and Sauze-d'Oulx (representing a total of 400km/249mi of ski runs and 92 ski lifts). The Montgenèvre ski area offers 100km/62mi of ski runs with good snow cover and 38 ski lifts, suitable for skiers of all levels. Experienced skiers like the 14 black runs, whereas beginners ski down the long green run of Le Lac (Les Anges area) and intermediate skiers prefer the beautiful Souréou run. There is also an ungroomed area (called, somewhat strangely, a "freeride" in French) for those who enjoy the challenge.

🎿 Finally, 17km/10.6mi of marked trail are open to **cross-country skiers**, with another 60km/37.5mi leaving from the village of Albert.

In summer, trails welcome hikers and mountain bikers, and the resort offers a variety of activities: swimming pool, tennis, obstacle running, climbing, deltaplaning...

The pass, which is open all year round, is on a busy commercial and tourist route. The obelisk situated near the French customs office is a reminder that the road was made suitable for wheeled vehicles in 1807.

Talking the Talk, Boarder Style...

The snow park's run is equipped with a quarterpipe, projump and gap, plus a little musical accompaniment. There's also a mogul contest on Thursdays.

⛰ Viewpoints Accessible by Gondola

Le Chalvet ★★

In winter, access daily by the Chalvet gondola and chair lift (alt 2 577m/8 455ft) ☎ 04 92 21 91 73; ⏱ July to 15 Aug: Mon, Wed, Fri 9.45am-12.30pm, 1.30-4.30pm. 5€. Then take the Chalvet chairlift , open 20 July-3 Aug, same hours as gondola.

🚶 *in summer access on foot: 4hr 15min there and back. Walk up to the viewing table (Check with the ski patrol that there are no avalanche hazards).*

Splendid **panorama**★★ of the Oisans region to the west, including the Bans, the Pointe de Sélé, the Pelvoux, the Barre des Écrins, the Agneaux, the Grande Ruine, the Rateau, the Pic Gaspard and the Meije. The Thabor and Aiguilles d'Arves can be seen to the north while, to the south, the view encompasses the Montgenèvre ski area overlooked by the Janus and Chenaillet summits, with the Pic de la Font Sancte, Pic de Rochebrune and Monte Viso in the background.

For coin categories, see the Legend on the cover flap.

WHERE TO STAY

◠◠ **Valérie** – *rue de l'Eglise- 05100 Montgenevre -* ☎ *04 92 21 90 02 - www. montgenevre.com –18rms and 1 suite.* Just outside the town centre and close to the ski-lifts, this hotel offers an alpine ambiance and modern comfort. South-facing rooms are sunnier, north-facing rooms are cheaper.

SPORT

Kids **Aire de loisirs des lacs** – *Zone des lacs -* ☎ *04 92 21 80 50 - daily 9am-7pm - closed 15 Sept-15 Jun.* This leisure complex gets the most out of the surrounding lakes and mountains, offering a large range of activities from pedalos to archery, via trout fishing, trampolining and mountain biking. Not forgetting also a 9-hole golf course covering 3 000m2/2mi.

Les Chalmettes gondola

Alt 2 200m/7 218ft. **View** of the Chalvet and Chaberton to the north, of Les Anges and Janus to the south. ⏱ *July to Aug: Tue, Thur and Sat-Sun 9.45am-12.30pm, 1.30-4.30pm. 5€-* ☎ *04 02 21 91 73*

Les Anges and Le Querelay★★

Alt 2 400m/7 874ft. *In winter, access to skiers via Les Anges drag lift (T-bar lift) or the Observatoire chairlift; in summer, access on foot.* Superb **panorama** of the Écrins, the Serre-Chevalier ski area, the Grand Peygu, the Col d'Izoard and the Pic de Rochebrune.

MONTMAUR

POPULATION 423

MICHELIN MAP 334 D5

This former medieval "barony" marks the transition between the Bochaine and Dévoluy regions. The ruins of the 11C stronghold overlook the village at the foot of the Montagne d'Auroze and the Pic de Bure. The nearby 18C manor was the birthplace of **Ponson du Terrail** (1829-71), a writer of romantic novels full of extraordinary adventures. ⓘ *Av Cdt Dumont - 05400 Veynes* ⏱ *Mon-Fri 9am-noon, 2.30-5.30pm, Sat 10am-noon -* ☎ *04 92 57 27 43*

- ▶ **Orient Yourself:** From Veynes, take D 994 east for 2 km. Turn left onto D 937.
- ⊕ **Don't Miss:** The château is interesting for its Renaissance decor and recent history.
- ⏱ **Organizing Your Time:** You can fit Montmaur into your tour of the Pays de Buëch.
- ⓖ **Also See:** Nearby Sights: Pays du BUËCH, Le CHAMPSAUR, Le DÉVOLUY, GAP, Route NAPOLÉON, Lac de SERRE-PONÇON, Le TRIÈVES

Castle

⏱ *July to end of Aug: guided tours (1hr) Aug: daily except Mon 3pm, 4pm and 5pm. 4.50€, children 3€ -* ☎ *11 92 58 11 42.*

The present castle dates from the 14C. Extended in the 16C and decorated in Renaissance style, it was more imposing than it is now, its two upper storeys having been destroyed in a fire. It looks quite austere from the outside, with its two round towers, mullioned windows and lovely 17C rusticated stone gateway, but the interior ornamentation is its main attraction. The four reception rooms are decorated with richly carved monumental fireplaces, French-style ceilings with ornamental beams, frescoes and friezes representing scenes on themes of war or morality. Doors carved with symbols, stucco work and *trompe-l'œil* add to the charm of the building. In the 1930s it became a health and beauty retreat which counted Jean Giono, screenwriter and director Henri-Georges Clouzot and the king of Belgium among its clientele. During the Second World War, the castle was occupied by a Resistance network.

Hike

Pic de Bure★★

4hr 30min from Montmaur, drive along D 320 towards the Col de Gaspardon (5km/3mi). Leave the car in the car park near the Maison Forestière des Sauvas (alt 1 320m/4 331ft). 🚶 A wide stony path rises to the north towards the cliffs of the Pic de Bure, on the west bank of the stream. After an hour's walk, you will reach the Roc des Hirondelles;

a path, marked in blue, leads across a small pass to the Plateau de Bure *(3hr 30min altogether)*. Continue eastwards for 45min to reach the summit of the Pic de Bure (alt 2 709m/8 888ft) which offers, in clear weather, one of the finest **panoramas**★★★ of the Alps, extending from the foothills of Mont Blanc in the northeast to the Cévennes *(to the right of Mont Ventoux)* and the Italian massifs.

▶ *Return by the same route.*

MORZINE ✳ ✳

POPULATION 2 948

MICHELIN MAP 328 N3– LOCAL MAP SEE LE CHABLAIS OR THONON-LES-BAINS

The town of Morzine and its neighbouring town of Montriond lie at an altitude of 980m/3 215ft, in a vast Alpine coomb flanked by the Pointe de Ressachaux and the Pointe de Nyon. Owing to its prime position at the intersection of six attractive roads, running through densely wooded valleys towards high-pasture areas, Morzine has, since the 1930s, been the main tourist centre and excursion base of the Haut Chablais region. ▤ *place de la Crusaz – 74110 Morzine* 🕐 *July to Aug and mid-Dec to Apr: 8.30am-7.30pm, Sat 8am-8pm; rest of year: Mon-Fri 9.30am-noon, 4-8pm, Sat 9.30am-noon, 2.30-5pm* 🕐 *closed Sun and public holidays -* ☎ *04 50 74 72 72 - www.morzine-avoriaz.com Guided tour of the old town Thur 10am, contact tourist office.*

▶ **Orient Yourself:** Morzine is 30km/18.75mi southeast of Thonon-les-Bains by D 902. However, if you take the lovely drive from Thonon via St-Jeoire, Taninges and Les Gets, the distance is 71km/44.4mi.

◉ **Don't Miss:** An afternoon on the shores of Lac Montriond is very pleasant.

🕐 **Organizing Your Time:** On Tuesdays at 5pm or Fridays at 10.30am, there is a tour of the slate quarry.

[Kids] **Especially for Kids:** Children will be thrilled by a ride in the summer toboggans or sleds.

◔ **Also See:** Nearby Sights: ABONDANCE, AVORIAZ, CHÂTEL, CLUSES, ÉVIAN-LES-BAINS, Les GETS, Routes des GRANDES ALPES, Bassin de SALLANCHES, SAMOËNS, SIXT-FER-À-CHEVAL, THONON-LES-BAINS, YVOIRE

The Resort

Capital of Haut-Chablais

Three tributaries of the Dranse de Savoie, the Dranse d'Abondance, the Dranse de Morzine and the Brevon, cross this landscape of woodland and meadows. These three long, deep valleys link the Haut Chablais region to the Valais and Faucigny. At the other end of the scale, the Hautforts (alt 2 464m/8 083ft) mark the highest point in the area.

⛷ Ski area

Morzine produced the 1960 Olympic downhill champion Jean Vuarnet, an early practitioner of the crouched "tuck" position. The resort's gentle slopes and beautiful landscapes make Morzine the ideal ski area for those who prefer a more relaxed style of skiing. Itineraries leading from Super-Morzine to Avoriaz are particularly enjoyable. Beginners can also have a go down the "Choucas" green run (from the summit of the Ran Folly). Experienced skiers are mainly drawn to the Creux and

Aigle runs or to Avoriaz at the heart of the **Portes du Soleil**✳✳ ski area, which has 650km/406.25mi of ski runs. Cross-country skiers can practise along 97km/60mi of fairly easy trails spread over five areas.

Ardoisière des Sept-Pieds
Take the Route des Prodains towards the Avoriaz cable-car. 🕐 *Guided tour July to Aug: Tue 5pm, Fri 10.30am; mid-Dec to Apr: Fri 10.30am. 5€ - ☎ 04 50 79 12 21 - www. ardoise-morzine.com* The route to the quarry rises over a wooded hill, and is lined by beautiful old buildings. Worked since the 14C, this slate quarry is one of the last in France. Morzine slate is light grey in colour.

Highlight

Three Viewpoints★★

Pointe de Nyon★
Access by cable car and chairlift. 🕐 *Nyon cable-car: closed in summer; mid-Dec to Easter: 9am-4.30pm (ticket for pedestrians 6€); La Pointe chairlift: closed in summer; mid-Dec to Easter 9am-4.30 - ☎ 04 50 79 00 38.*
Impressive view of the rocky barrier of the Dents Blanches and of Mont Blanc on one side, of Lake Geneva and of the Morzine Valley on the other.

Le Pléney★
1hr there and back. Access by cable car then on foot. 🕐 *June: 9am-4.30 pm; July to mid-Sept: 9am-5.30pm (10min, continuous). 7€ return, children 5€ - ☎ 04 50 79 00 38.*
From the upper cable-car station, walk alongside the Belvédère chairlift to a small mound crowned by a viewing table (alt 1 554m/5 098ft) offering a **panoramic view** of Avoriaz and the Dents Blanches to the east, of the Mont Blanc Massif to the southeast, of the Aravis range to the south and of the Pointe de Marcelly, Mont Chéry and Roc d'Enfer to the west. In clear weather, Lake Geneva is visible through the Dranse Valley. You can walk as far as the Chavannes gondola.

Address Book

For coin categories, see the Legend on the cover flap.

EATING OUT
⊜**Le Clin d'Œil** – *Opposite the post office - ☎ 04 50 79 03 10 - closed May, Oct-Nov and noon Dec-Apr.* This little restaurant in a converted barn on a quiet street is simple and friendly. The menu features a few local specialities and pizzas cooked over charcoal.

WHERE TO STAY
⊜**Camping les Marmottes** – *Essert-Romand, NW 3.7km/2.3mi on D 902, towards Thonon, then to left on D 329 - ☎ 04 50 75 74 44 - open 23 Dec-23 Apr, 24 June-3 Sept -⊞- 60 pitches.* This modest campsite is well-kept, with impeccable, modern sanitary facilities.

⊜⊜**L'Hermine Blanche** – *Chemin du Mas Metout - ☎ 04 50 75 76 55 - www. hermineblanche.com - closed 25 Apr-30 June and Sept-19 Dec - ⊞ - 25rms - ⊜⊜restaurant.* This chalet on the slopes offers nice, comfortable rooms, some with a balcony. The restaurant is simple and tidy, with a menu that changes every day. There is also a pleasant covered swimming pool and gym.

⊜⊜**Florimontane** – *Av. de Joux-Plane - ☎ 04 50 79 03 87 - www.renouveau-vacances.fr - closed mid-Apr to mid-May, Oct-mid-Dec.-⊞-41rms - ⊜⊜restaurant.* Three chalets linked by an underground passage offer wood-panelled rooms and 20 holiday apartments that are very practical for families. Gym, entertainment and guided hikes.

Chamossière★★

Alt 2 000m/6 562ft. *In winter, access is limited to skiers; in summer, the climb is on foot.* From the viewing table, splendid **panorama**★★ of the Dents du Midi, Dents Blanches, Buet, Aiguille du Midi, Mont Blanc and the Aravis range.

Excursions

Lac de Montriond and Col de la Joux Verte★★

20km/12.4mi – about 2hr. From Morzine, follow the road to Montriond (east bank of the Dranse). Turn right towards the lake immediately after Montriond Church.

Lac de Montriond★

Alt 1 049m/3 442ft. Framed by steep escarpments, the area surrounding the lake is well shaded and crisscrossed by footpaths. Continue to the **Cascade d'Ardent** *(stop by the viewpoint on the right-hand side of D 228)*. The waterfall, which is superb during the spring thaw, drops from a height of 30m/98ft.

The road then climbs up in a series of hairpin bends to a ledge gullied by a succession of waterfalls; there is a good view of the Roc d'Enfer downstream. Beyond the village of Les Lindarets, the road rises along the wooded slopes of the Joux Verte, within sight of the Mont de Grange to the north.

A road leaves the **Col de la Joux Verte** on the left towards Avoriaz.

Avoriaz✳✳ – ⓒ *See AVORIAZ.*

Route du Col de Joux-Plane★★

From Morzine to Samoëns via the Col de Joux-Plane

20km/12.4mi – about 1hr.

The narrow road *(D 354)*, which is passable in summer, rises very quickly above the Morzine Valley, winding across high pastures and some lovely wooded sections. It goes right round the Ran Folly in a 4km/2.5mi loop and over the pass of the same name (alt 1 650m/5 413ft) before reaching the Plateau de Joux Plane.

Col de Joux Plane★★

Alt 1 698m/5 571ft. The road runs between a small lake and a restaurant. From the restaurant, there is a remarkable **view** of Mont Blanc to the southeast, extending south to the Platé Massif and the resort of Flaine.

The road continues beyond the path on the left, which ends at the Col de Joux Plane, and runs down towards Samoëns offering bird's-eye **views**★ of the Eméru Coomb on the left and the Giffre Valley on the right.

Samoëns✳✳ – ⓒ *See SAMOËNS.*

② Route des Gets★

FROM MORZINE TO CLUSES *43km/26.7mi – about 1hr –* ⓒ *local map see CLUSES*

The Route des Grandes Alpes, D 902-N 202, links the Dranse de Morzine Valley to the Giffre and Arve valleys.

▶ *From Morzine, drive west along D 28 then take D 902 south towards Les Gets.*

The road affords views of the Roc d'Enfer (alt 2 244m/7 362ft), one of the most rugged Chablais summits.

Les Gets ❄ – ♿see Les GETS.

The road winds its way through the woods along the narrow Arpettaz and Foron valleys.

▶ *Turn right at the Pont des Gets onto D 328.*

The road climbs above the Foron then veers to the left to reach the vast Praz-de-Lys Basin covered with pastures. From the last bend, there is a wide **panorama**★ covering, from left to right, the Dents du Midi, Tour Sallière, Avoudrues, Mont Buet and Chaîne du Reposoir, with Mont Blanc in the distance.

🚶 The peaceful mountain village of **Praz-de-Lys** is overlooked by the Marcelly Peak (alt 2 000m/6 562ft), crowned by a monumental cross and accessible to experienced hikers (3hr there and back on foot).

▶ *Return to D 902 and drive towards Taninges.*

The heights of the Chaîne du Reposoir and Chaîne du Bargy line up on the horizon. Beyond Avonnex, there is an overall **view**★ of Taninges and of the Giffre Valley, backed by snow-capped high peaks.

Taninges
🛈 *Av des Thézières - 74440 Taninges* 🕐 *Mon-Fri 9am-noon, 2-6pm, Sat 9.30am-noon, 2-5pm; office at Praz de Lys* 🕐 *Mid-June to mid-Sept and mid-Dec to Apr: 10am-noon, 2.30-6pm, Sun 10am-noon, 2.30-7pm -* ☎ *04 50 34 25 05 - www.taninges.com*
This large village is a good starting point for summer walks. The old upper town has partly retained its traditional character,

Chartreuse de Mélan
🕐 *July to Aug: guided tour (1hr30min) Thur at 6pm. 3€. Access to gardens and temporary exhibits: daily 10am-noon, 2-7pm. 1.5€ -* ☎ *04 50 34 25 05 - www.taninges.com*
This Carthusian monastery was founded in the 13C by Béatrix de Fauciny to house her sepulchre and that of her son, who died accidentally at age 20. Following a fire, the present cloister was built in 1530. The vaulted 13C church is built of tufa blocks which give the place a quiet Romanesque dignity, reinforced by austere modern stained glass. A terrible fire in 1967 destroyed the living quarters.

Beyond Châtillon-sur-Cluses, the mountain setting of the small industrial town of Cluses can be fully appreciated. The road leads on to Cluses.

MOUSTIERS-STE-MARIE★★

POPULATION 625
MICHELIN MAP 334 F9
LOCAL MAP SEE GRAND CANYON DU VERDON

Moustiers nestles beneath a large gap in the limestone cliffs towering over the town; a 227m/745ft-long chain stretching across this amazing **setting**★★ holds a star suspended over Notre-Dame-de-Beauvoir. It was fixed into the rock in fulfillment of a wish made by a knight who returned to Moustiers from the crusades after many years as a prisoner. Moustiers owes its name to a monastery founded in the 5C by St Maxim, bishop of Riez, but it owes its fame to the manufacture of glazed **ceramics** which reached its peak in the 17C and 18C, disappeared at the end of the 19C and was revived in the 20C.

Built near the downstream exit of the Grand Canyon du Verdon (*see Grand Canyon du VERDON)*, **close to the Lac de Ste-Croix** (*see Lac de STE-CROIX)*, **the town is a very popular centre for excursions.** *Place de l'Église–04360 Moustiers* 🕐 *July to Aug: 9.30-12.30pm; Mar to June: 10am-noon, 2-5pm; Sept to Nov: 10am-noon, 2-6pm; Dec to Feb: 2-5pm - ☎ 04 92 74 67 84 - www.ville-moustiers-sainte-marie.fr*

- ▶ **Orient Yourself:** Moustiers-Sainte-Marie is 15km/9.4mi northeast of Riez.
- **Don't Miss:** The faïence museum is on everyone's list of places to see.
- 🕐 **Organizing Your Time:** Give yourself a half day to stroll around town.
- **Also See:** Nearby Sights: BARGÈME, CASTELLANE, GRÉOUX-LES-BAINS, Route NAPOLÉON, RIEZ, Lac de STE-CROIX, Plateau de VALENSOLE, Grand Canyon du VERDON

A Bit of History

Parc naturel régional du Verdon
Maison du Parc BP 14, 04360 Moustiers-Sainte-Marie - ☎ 04 92 74 68 00 – www. parcduverdon.fr
Founded in 1997, this regional nature park covers an area of 200 000ha/494 211 acres including the Grand Canyon du Verdon, the Plateau de Valensole, the Pays d'Artuby and the Préalpes de Castellane. The Verdon, which rises at an altitude of 2 500m/8 202ft and flows into the Durance, is the link between Provence and the Alps and the climate of this semi mountainous region (average altitude 700m/2 297ft, highest point: Mourre de Chanier 1 930m/6 332ft) still has a mild, Mediterranean feel. Cicadas chirr in the olive groves and the *garrigue* (arid, brush-covered land typical of region), wild boar rustle through the undergrowth, chamois climb across rocky ridges and grouse clatter through the larch woods. In the meadows, marmots stand on the qui vive amid the gentian and eagles can be seen circling around the peaks. Less noticeable is one of the smallest creatures in the park, a protected rare species of hairy snail.
Tourist information centres can be found by the five lakes in the park. Walkers, climbers and white-water fans will particularly love the Gorges du Verdon (*see Grand Canyon du VERDON)*.

Sight

Church★

Its warm-coloured massive bell-tower, characteristic of the Lombard Romanesque style, comprises three storeys with twinned openings and blind arcading resting on pillars or slender columns. The Romanesque chancel was replaced in the 14C by a Gothic chancel which forms an angle with the 12C nave. The base of the flat east end is decorated with twinned arcading opening onto rounded arches. Note the beautifully carved 16C and 18C stalls in the chancel and, in the nave, a 16C painting depicting Moustiers at that time, without the famous star. The room situated beneath the tower houses a collection of holy objects including a votive picture from 1702, 15C copper plates and local ceramics.

Musée de la Faïence★

J.-Ch. Gérard/PHOTONONSTOP

Moustiers faience decorated by J Olérys

🔧🕐 *Apr to Oct: daily except Tue 10am-12.30pm, 2-6pm; Nov to Mar: Sat-Sun and school holidays (daily except Tue) 2-5pm.* 🕐 *Closed Jan, 1 May, 25 Dec. 2€, children no charge -* ☎ *04 92 74 61 64.*

The museum of faïence, or glazed earthenware, is in the basement of the town hall. The displays are centred on the ceramic-makers who made Moustiers ceramics famous: the Clérissy family (1679-1783) who initiated the blue motifs on a white background; the Olérys family who introduced the polychrome motifs in 1738; the Fouque and Pelloquin families (1749-83) who used a yellow background; the Ferrat brothers (1761-94) who were strongly influenced by the technique and decoration of Strasbourg ceramics.

Chapelle Notre-Dame-de-Beauvoir★

30min there and back on foot from the large parking lot

🔼 This chapel on a ledge overlooking the town has been a place of pilgrimage since early medieval times, when it was known as Notre-Dame d'Entreroches, "Our Lady Between the Rocks." The wide stepped path leading to it offers glimpses of the village and of the Notre-Dame Gorge; it is lined with 14 Stations of the Cross decorated with ceramic scenes by Simone Garnier. At the end of the path, there is a terrace dating from the Middle Ages, planted with Mediterranean trees and ringed by the remains of the old ramparts; from there, the **view**★ takes in the rooftops of Moustiers, the Maïre Valley and the straight edge of the Valensole Plateau. Protected by an overhanging roof covered with glazed tiles, the Romanesque porch is surmounted by a bell-tower of the same period. The carved wooden door dates from the Renaissance.

The traditional festival known as "la Diane," which takes place every year on 9 September, is the culmination of a week of feasting, dancing and rejoicing to the sound of pipes and drums. A torch-lit procession to the chapel is followed by mass and celebrations.

Address Book

For coin categories, see the Legend on the cover flap.

EATING OUT

🍽 **La Grignotière** – *Quartier Ste-Anne, upper parking level* ☎ 04 92 74 69 12 - *closed 15 Nov-1 Mar, evenings in Mar-Apr and 15 Sept-15 Nov -* 🍴 *- A pleasant snack restaurant on the heights of the village; the terrace under the ancient olive trees is worth the climb. Grilled meats, sandwiches, crêpes.

🍽🍽 **Restaurant La Treille Muscate** – *Pl. de l'Église* - ☎ 04 92 74 64 31 - *la.treille.muscate@wanadoo.fr - closed Jan, evenings from 15-30 Nov and in Feb, Wed and Thurs evening out of season, Wed in season*. This friendly little Provençal bistrot serves regional cooking using only fresh ingredients. Pretty dining room linked to the terrace.

🍽🍽 **La Ferme Ste-Cécile** – *Rte de Castellane* - ☎ 04 92 74 64 18 - *contact@ferme-ste-cecile.com - closed Feb school holidays, 18 Nov-30 Dec, Sun evening out of season and Mon*. For those seeking a little peace and quiet outside Moustiers, beautiful natural suroundings can be admired from the terrace of this old farmhouse. Small Provençal dining rooms.

WHERE TO STAY

🛏 **Chambre d'hôte l'Escalo** – *R de la Bourgade* - ☎ 04 92 74 69 93 - *closed 15 Nov-17 Mar-* 🍴 *-4rms*. This typical Provençal village house has antique furniture in the rooms; the largest are on the second floor. Breakfast on the terrace overlooking the village is especially pleasant.

🛏 **Chambre d'hôte Monastère de Ségriès** – *6km/4mi SW of Moustiers on D 952* - ☎ 04 92 74 64 32 - *c.allegre@wanadoo.fr - closed Nov-Mar -* 🍴 *- 5rms - * 🍽 *restaurant*. Recapture the pleasures of unspoiled nature and silence in a forest of holm oaks, chosen as a place to settle by monks in the 19C. The real luxury here is space, both in the lounges and the rooms. There is a superb view of the cloister and of the valley.

🛏🛏 **Hôtel le Clos des Iris** – *Le Pavillon St-Michel* - ☎ 04 92 74 63 46- *closde-siris@wanadoo.fr - closed 1-26 Dec and Tue evening from 15 Nov to 15 Mar -* 🅿 *- 8rms*. This old farmhouse surrounded by trees and flowers has lovely rooms, each with a balcony. The bathroom fixtures in Salernes faïence are superb.

🛏🛏🛏 **La Ferme Rose** – *4km/2.5mi W of Moustiers on the Ste-Croix road* - ☎ 04 92 74 69 47 - *closed 5 Jan-30 Mar and 1 Nov-23 Dec -* 🅿 *- 12rms*. The decor here is determined by the owner's eclectic assortment of flea-market finds (miniature cars, old electric fans..). The bedrooms are comfortable and in traditional Provençal style.

SHOPPING

Faïence Bondil - *Pl de l'Église -* ☎ 04 92 74 67 02 - *bondilfaiencier@wanadoo.fr -daily 9.30am-1pm, 2-7pm*. Handmade faïence according to the old tradition. There is a collection of lamps by Jean-Pierre Bondil. You can visit the factory.

Faïencerie Lallier - *Quartier St-Jean* ☎ 04 92 74 66 41 - *lallier.faiencier. moustiers@wanadoo.fr - daily except Sat-Sun 8am-noon, 1.30-5.30pm, closed public holidays and Christmas vacation*. Factory visits. The boutique has some 700 models from the most traditional to very modern.

Excursions

Grand Canyon du Verdon★★★ – *154km/96mi round tour – 1 day –* ⌚ *see Grand Canyon du VERDON.*

Lac de Ste-Croix★★ – *70km/43.5mi round tour starting from Moustiers – about 3hr –* ⌚ *see Lac de STE-CROIX.*

ROUTE NAPOLÉON ★

MICHELIN MAPS 341 A/B 5 334 D/H 3/10

The Route Napoléon – Napoleon's road – follows the Emperor's route on his return from Elba, from the point where he landed in Golfe Juan to his arrival in Grenoble. The commemorative plaques and monuments bear the flying eagle symbol inspired by Napoleon's remark: 'The eagle will fly from steeple to steeple until he reaches the towers of Notre-Dame'. The road has always formed an important link between Grenoble and the Verdon and Durance valleys, but only became known as the Route Napoléon in 1913 and was not opened to motor traffic until 1932. The 325km/202mi can be covered in two days, at any time of the year. ⓘ *Association nationale des élus pour la route Napoléon (ANERN – comprised of 42 towns situated along the route)– Palais des Congrès, 22 cours H-Cresp, 06130 Grasse - ☎04 93 36 66 66 - www.route-napoleon.com*

▸ **Orient Yourself:** The full Route Napoleon starts at Golfe-Juan, on the Côte d'Azur and ends at Grenoble. The route is described from south to north. The first part, from Golfe Juan to the Col de Valferrière, is described in the Michelin Green Guide French Riviera.

⊘ **Don't Miss:** The towns of Castellane, Digne, Sisteron and Gap are almost required, but the villages of Volonne, Ventavon and Tallard are also worth seeing.

◷ **Organizing Your Time:** You will need two days to drive the route described here, although you may want to take more time.

♿ **Also See:** Nearby Sights: ANNOT, BARGÈME, Pays du BUËCH, BUIS-LES-BAR-ONNIES, CASTELLANE, Le CHAMPSAUR, Massif de CHAMROUSSE, Massif de la CHARTREUSE, CLUES DE HAUTE-PROVENCE, Le DÉVOLUY, DIGNE-LES-BAINS,

The Flight of the Eagle

After landing at Golfe Juan on 1 March 1815, Napoleon and his troops, preceded by an advance guard, set up a bivouac and made a brief stop at Cannes. Then, as the moon rose, between one and two o'clock in the morning, they broke camp. Wishing to avoid the Rhône area, which he knew to be hostile, Napoleon planned to get to the valley of the Durance by way of the Alps and made for Grasse. There he expected to find a road which he had ordered to be built when he was Emperor, but discovered that his orders had never been carried out. The little column struggled on, following mule tracks through deep snow. That evening, Napoleon waited impatiently for news from Sisteron, where the fort commanded the narrow passage of the Durance.

Sisteron, however, offered no resistance and, as he left the town, Napoleon realised that support for his cause was already growing; he felt that victory depended on his will power and that France would rally to him if he reached Grenoble. Travelling along a coach road once more, he received an enthusiastic welcome in Gap that night, slept in Corps the next day and on 7 March reached La Mure, only to find troops from the Grenoble garrison facing him at Laffrey. This was the setting for the famous episode which turned events in his favour. It happened on what came to be called the "Prairie de la Rencontre," near the Grand Lac de Laffrey, and is now commemorated by a monument. Seeing the road blocked by a battalion which greatly outnumbered his own escort; the Emperor took a calculated risk, walked forward and, pulling open his grey greatcoat, declared: 'Soldiers, I am your Emperor! If anyone among you wishes to kill his general, here I am!'. In spite of being ordered to fire by a young officer, the troops rallied to Napoleon shouting: 'Vive l'Empereur!' and marched with him to Grenoble. That same evening, he entered the town in triumph.

Préalpes de DIGNE, Vallée de la Moyenne DURANCE, EMBRUN, ENTREVAUX, FOR-CALQUIER, Monastère de GANAGOBIE, GAP, GRENOBLE, Lacs de LAFFREY, MANE, MANOSQUE, MONTBRUN-LES-BAINS, MONTMAUR, MOUSTIERS-STE-MARIE, ST-JULIEN-DU-VERDON, Lac de STE-CROIX, Lac de SERRE-PONÇON, SISTERON, Le TRIÈVES, Le VALBONNAIS, Plateau de VALENSOLE, Le VALGAUDEMAR, Grand Canyon du VERDON, VIZILLE

"Refuges Napoléon" – As a sign of gratitude for the enthusiastic welcome he received in Gap, Napoleon bequeathed to the Hautes-Alpes *département* a sum of money intended for the construction of refuges at the top of passes particularly exposed in winter. This sum, which was only accepted in 1854, was used to build refuges at the Col de Manse, Col du Lauraret, Col d'Izoard, Col de Vars, Col du Noyer, Col Agnel and Col de la Croix *(the last two are now in ruins and the refuge of the Col du Noyer has been replaced by a hotel).*

From the Col de Valferrière to Corps

210km/130mi – allow 1 day
Beyond the pass, the road goes through the **Clue de Séranon**. Napoleon spent the night (2 to 3 March) in the village of **Séranon** hidden in the midst of a pine forest. Further on, on the way down from the Col de Luens, the road affords views of Castellane nestling at the foot of its "rock," crowned by Notre-Dame du Roc.

Castellane★ – ⏱ *See CASTELLANE.*

On the way up to the **Col des Lèques** (alt 1 148m/3 766ft) there are lovely **views** of Castellane, the Lac de Castillon and the Préalpes de Provence.

Clue de Taulanne★

This opening cut through sheer rock leads from the Verdon Valley to the Asse Valley.

▶ *6km/3.7mi further on, cross the Asse to enter Senez.*

Rock formations in the Clue de Taulanne

B. Kaufmann/MICHELIN

Senez

This ancient Gallo-Roman town was one of the oldest and poorest bishoprics in France, finally dissolved in 1790. It came into the limelight in the 18C, when Bishop **Jean Soanen** refused to condemn Jansenism and was removed from office.
The **former cathedral** (👁️ *Guided tours by request at the Mairie -* ☎️*04 92 34 21 15*) dates from the early 13C. The east end is decorated with arcading in Lombard style, resting on slender engaged columns. A Gothic doorway gives access to the nave in typical Provençal Romanesque style. Inside, note the 17C stalls, altarpiece and lectern, as well as the 18C antiphonary, a book of (antiphonal) plainsong.

▶ *Return to N 85 and continue towards Digne.*

Barrême

The station houses an exhibition concerning one stage of the Cretaceous geological period, particularly well represented in the area.
Napoleon spent the night of 3 March 1815 here *(plaque on a house along N 85)*.
The Préalpes de Digne start beyond Chaudon-Norante. Napoleon went to Digne along the route followed by D 20. However, carry on along N 85.

Clue de Chabrières★

The gorge is framed by tall limestone cliffs.

Digne-les-Bains♨♨ – 🕐 *See DIGNE-LES-BAINS.*

▶ *Leave Digne by ③ on the town plan.*

The road *(N 85)* continues along the Bléone Valley, between the Plateau de Valensole and the Préalpes de Digne. The imposing Château de Fontenelle stands on the right-hand side of the road, just before Malijai.

Malijai

Napoleon spent the night of 4 to 5 March in the elegant 18C **château** (♿🕐 *Daily except Sat-Sun and public holidays 9am-noon, 3-6pm 9 (Fri closes at 5pm). No charge - ☎️ 04 92 34 01 12)*, famous for its stuccoed interior decoration.
Beyond Malijai, the view embraces the Durance Valley and extends towards the bluish mass of the Montagne de Lure. The road follows the Canal d'Oraison until it reaches L'Escale and the impressive dam across the river.

▶ *Leave the bridge to your left and drive north along D 24.*

Volonne

This village, clinging to a rocky spur picturesquely crowned by two old towers, is surrounded by lovely orchards. The ruined **Église St-Martin** is a fine specimen of early Romanesque style (11C); the nave flanked by side aisles is open to the sky.
Shortly after the Salignac Dam across the Durance, there is a splendid overall **view**★ of Sisteron and its remarkable setting.

Sisteron★★ – 🕐 *See SISTERON.*

The road *(N 85)* follows an EDF (French Electricity Board) feeder canal part of the way to Gap. 👁️ It is worth stopping at the viewing table situated at the exit of the village of Le Poët *(15min on foot)* to admire the **panorama** of the Gapençais and Embrunais heights and of the Écrins summits. After La Saulce, the road veers northwards.

Tallard

Tallard lies in the middle Durance Valley, surrounded by orchards and vineyards, which produce a popular white wine.

Église St-Grégoire

The church was erected in the 12C and partially rebuilt in the 17C. The main doorway (dated 1549 on the lintel) is the most interesting feature; it is decorated with Renaissance medallions depicting women, children and soldiers. Inside, the 17C pulpit and the 15C christening font supported by lions are particularly noteworthy. An Armenian pilgrimage takes place every year in September.

Castle

🕐 *July to Aug: daily except Tue 3-6pm – guided tours (1hr15min) at 6pm, reserve 1 month in advance. 2.50€, children 2€, guided tour 3.50€ - ☎ 04 92 54 10 14*

Its dismantled towers stand on a rock spur overlooking the Durance. Built in the 14C and 16C, it was taken time and again by both sides during the Wars of Religion and seriously damaged by the duke of Savoie's troops in 1692. The castle, which has been extensively repaired, is the venue of a summer festival of music. In the **chapel**, the Flamboyant style is represented by an elegant doorway surmounted by a pinnacle and finial standing between flame-like windows. Inside, note the beautiful keystones, carved capitals and fireplaces. The **main building** dates from the Renaissance. It has a rounded doorway surmounted by the arms of the Clermont-Tonnerre Family (who once owned the castle) and beautiful windows decorated with twisted mullions.

Round tour from Tallard via Urtis ★ *22km/13.7mi – about 1hr*

▷ *From Tallard, drive east across the Durance and turn left almost immediately.*

The D 346 rises above the river.

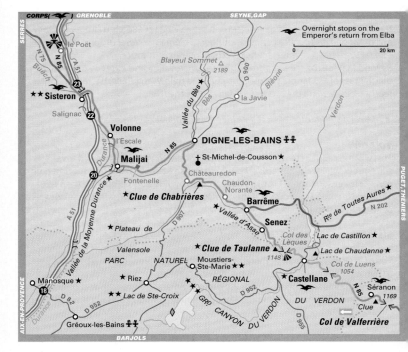

▷ *4km/2.5mi further on, turn right towards D 854 leading to Venterol.*

A bend to the left *(cross)* offers a fine **view**★ of the Durance. Just beyond Venterol, there is an extended **view**★ of a large section of the Durance Valley. Soon after Les Marmets, the road runs steeply down to the river and, 2.5km/1.5mi beyond Urtis, a small reservoir formed by a dam along the Durance comes into view.

▷ *Turn right at the intersection with the road to Curbans to rejoin the Tallard road within sight of the castle.*

Gap★ – 👆 *See GAP.*

WHERE TO STAY AND EAT
😊😊**Mas du Figuier** – *La Fontaine-04200 Bevons -* ☎ *04 92 62 81 28 - www.guidesprovence.com - closed Nov-Jan -* 🍴 *- 5rms -* 😊😊 *meal.* This pretty 17C mas, or traditional farmhouse, stands in a field of lavender. Pleasant Provençal-style rooms with warm colours, exposed rafters and tile floors. Moorish-style bathrooms. For a more unusual experience, rent the cabin suspended in an oak tree.

Beyond Gap, N 85 rises sharply to the **Col Bayard** (alt 1 248m/4 094ft, viewing table) and comes down again into the open valley of the upper Drac (👆 *see Le CHAMPSAUR).*

Les Baraques
Napoleon stopped here on 6 March 1815 and refused the offer made by local farmers to join his troops.
The escarpments of the Dévoluy (Montagne de Féraud) lie ahead, the Pic d'Olan in the Écrins Massif can be seen to the northeast, through the **Valgaudemar** Valley (👆 *see Le VALGAUDEMAR),* and the Obiou to the west of the **Lac du Sautet.**

Corps – 👆 *See Le DÉVOLUY.*

1 From La Mure to Grenoble

63km/39mi – allow a day – 👆 *see local map Lacs de LAFFREY or Le TRIÈVES.*
The road *(N 85)* winds its way above the Drac Valley, then crosses the Bonne Valley before running straight across the Matheysine Plateau.

La Mure
This lively market town, situated on the southern edge of the Plateau de la Matheysine, owed its prosperity to the nearby coal mines, which produced hundreds of thousands of tons of coal a year from 1901 until the last mine closed down in 1996. La Mure is the starting point of the mountain railway line running to St-Georges-de-Commiers (👆 *see see Lacs de LAFFREY, La Mure Mountain Railway).* Near the covered market, inside a historic building, the **Musée Matheysin** (🕐 *May to Oct: daily except Tue 1-6.30pm* 🕐 *closed 1 May. 2.30€ -* ☎ *04 76 30 98 15 - www.matheysine. com)* deals with local history, including mining, by means of many reconstructions, artefacts and recordings. The road to Laffrey runs along the plateau not far from the former mining complex of Le Villaret, the largest in the area, then along the lakes, sometimes hidden by vegetation, with the heights of the Chartreuse Massif filling the horizon ahead.
The austere Plateau de la Matheysine, with its north-south axis, is windswept and exposed to the full harshness of winter, and fully deserving of its nickname "the Siberia of the Dauphiné"; in spite of its relatively low altitude (below 1 000m/3 281ft) the lakes often freeze over during the winter months. The **45th parallel,** drawn at

an equal distance from the North Pole and the Equator, goes across the southern shore of the Lac de Pierre-Châtel.

Prairie de la Rencontre★

Two monuments bearing the imperial eagle symbol mark the access road. Napoleon's equestrian statue by Emmanuel Frémiet, visible from the road, is a reminder of the famous "meeting" which took place in this pleasant setting of lakes and mountains.

Laffrey★

This holiday resort is particularly popular with by anglers and bathers. A plaque on the wall of the cemetery recalls the speech addressed by Napoleon to the soldiers sent from Grenoble to stop him.

Point de vue de Beauregard

An easy walk *(about 2hr)* from Laffrey via the village of Notre-Dame-de-Vaux to the **Montagne de Beauregard**. Park the car near the Chalet de l'As and continue on foot to the top of the ridge which offers a splendid **view** of the plateau, the lakes and the Drac Valley.

Le Sapey★

The narrow road which branches off the N 85 to the right at Laffrey skirts the Lac Mort which supplies a power station in the Romanche Valley. From the end of the road, one can climb to the Chapelle du Sapey *(15min there and back on foot)* which provides a clear view of the Chamrousse-Belledonne and Taillefer massifs.

Vizille★ – See VIZILLE.

Napoleon went from Vizille to Grenoble along the route now followed by D 5, which offers, on the way down to Eybens, an overall view of Grenoble.

Grenoble★★ – See GRENOBLE

L'OISANS★★★

MICHELIN MAP 77 FOLDS 6, 7, 16 AND 17 OR 244 FOLDS 29, 40 AND 41

With a number of summits reaching or exceeding 4 000m/13 000ft, L'Oisans is the second highest massif in France after Mont Blanc. Since the creation of the **Parc national des Écrins** (*see Le VALGAUDEMAR)*, these imposing mountains with some 10km2/4sq mi of glaciers have become better known, but remain wilder, more unspoilt and less visited than their great rivals. The "glorious" **Meije** has a special place in the affections of mountaineers.

The summits of the massif form a huge horseshoe round the Vénéon Valley. The **Barre des Écrins** is the highest point of the massif (alt 4 102m/13 458ft); its icy solitude is so well concealed that from the road you catch only rare and fleeting glimpses of its peak, first reached in 1864 by the British mountaineer **Edward Whymper**. In fact, since Mont Blanc only became French after the annexation of Savoie in 1860, **Mont Pelvoux** was long regarded as the highest point in the French Alps. It was first climbed in 1828 by the French military engineer Captain Durand who soon acknowledged that the Barre des Écrins was higher. *Quai Girard - 38520 Le Bourg-d'Oisans July to Aug: Mon-Sat 9am-7pm, Sun and public* *holidays 10am-noon 3-6pm; mid-Dec to Apr: Mon-Sat 8.30am-noon, 2.30-6pm, Sun and public holidays 8.30-11.30am; rest of year Mon-Sat 9am-noon, 2-6pm -* ☎ *04 76 80 03 25 - www.bourgdoisans.com*

▶ **Orient Yourself:** The Oisans region is mostly within the high Écrins Massif, bounded by the valleys of the River Romanche, River Durance and River Drac.

🕙 **Organizing Your Time:** To enoy the thrill of the heights, you will have to walk, since the best views are not accessible by road.

ⓒ **Also See:** Nearby Sights: L'ALPE D'HUEZ, Le BOURG-D'OISANS, BRIANÇON, Le BRIANÇONNAIS, Les DEUX-ALPES, Le DÉVOLUY, Route du GALIBIER, Route des GRANDES ALPES, La GRAVE, MONTGENÈVRE, SERRE-CHEVALIER, Le VALBONNAIS, Le VALGAUDEMAR

Excursions

① Route de la Bérarde and Vallée du Vénéon ★★★

FROM LE BOURG-D'OISANS *31km/19.3mi – about 1hr 30min not including hikes. The last section beyond Champhorent is closed from November to May.*

The road follows the deep, austere Vénéon Valley, giving only occasional glimpses of the high summits; we therefore strongly advise you to go on the hikes suggested below, bearing in mind that some of them are meant for experienced hikers.

▶ *From Le Bourg-d'Oisans, drive eastwards along N 91 towards Briançon.*

The road to La Bérarde *(D 530)*, branching off from N 91 at Les Clapiers, enters the wide lower Vénéon Valley, which is in striking contrast with the narrow gorge of the Romanche; this is explained by the fact that, during the Ice Age, the Vénéon Glacier was longer than the Romanche Glacier. The small depression of the Lac Lauvitel appears straight ahead, overlooked by the Tête de la Muraillette.

Lac Lauvitel ★★
2.5km/1.5mi from D 530 then 3hr there and back on foot. At the bridge in Les Ougiers, turn right towards La Danchère and leave the car on the roadside. Beyond La Danchère, take the left fork via Les Selles.

🚶 This nature trail is lined with markers providing explanations on geology, local fauna and flora, which are detailed in a book on sale in information centres throughout the Parc national des Écrins.

The path follows the natural dam formed by successive landslides, which contains the Lac Lauvitel (60m/197ft deep in parts) set in a wild landscape.

▶ *Follow the La Rousse path back to La Danchère.*

Venosc
🏠 *38520 Venosc -* ☎ *04 76 80 06 82 - www.venosc.com*
Turn left off D 530 to a car park. 🚠 *You can also take the gondola,* **Télécabine de Venosc,** *from Les Deux-Alpes* 🕙 *Mid-June to Aug: 8am-8pm; Dec to Apr: 8am-6pm (10min, continuous). 6.90€ return -* ☎ *04 76 79 75 01.*

🚶 Walk up to the village which is a thriving centre of local handicrafts. A paved street leads to the church with its onion-shaped spire, which houses a fine altarpiece (17C Italian School). Slate quarrying in the Vénéon Valley was one of the main resources of the Oisans region from the 19C until the Second World War. Nowadays, the mining site has been entirely overgrown by trees.

Le Bourg-d'Arud

The village nestles inside a charming verdant basin.

The steepest climb of the route avoids the first glacial obstruction, a jumble of huge boulders. The road then runs through the Plan du Lac Basin, with the Vénéon meandering below, towards St-Christophe-en-Oisans, past the **Cascade de Lanchâtra** on the right and across the Torrent du Diable.

WHERE TO STAY AND EAT

⊝**La Cordée** – 38520 St-Christophe-en-Oisans - ☎ 04 76 79 52 37 - www.la-cordee.com -9rms . Frequented by Alpine guides since 1907, this multi-purpose commerce offers food and lodging, loans books and organizes meetings with the authors. Good local cuisine.

St-Christophe-en-Oisans★

🄸 *La Ville - 38520 St-Christophe-en-Oisans ◷ June to Sept: 10am-noon, 2-7pm; school holidays: 4-5pm; rest of year: telephone for info -* ☎ *04 76 80 50 01 www. berarde.com* Although it includes 15 hamlets, this vast *commune* (24 000ha/59 304 acres), one of the largest in France, barely has 30 inhabitants in winter, many of whom are professional guides from generation to generation. The **church** shows up against the Barre des Écrins; in the cemetery, young mountaineers who lost their lives in the Écrins Massif are buried next to local guide families such as the Turcs and the Gaspards.

A museum, **Mémoires d'aplinismes**, describes the valley, its mountaineering heros, and its history and culture. ♿◷ *July to Aug: 10am-noon, 2.30-7pm; June and Sept: 10am-noon, 2-6pm; other school holidays: 2-5pm; last admission one hr before closing ◷ closed 1 Jan, Easter Sun and Mon and 25 Dec. 3.60€, children under 10 years no charge -* ☎ *04 76 79 52 25*

Hike from Champhorent to the Refuge de la Lavey★★

Alt 1 797m/5 896ft. *3hr 30min there and back on foot (1hr 45min to reach the refuge); a fairly easy hike. Difference in altitude: 380m/1 247ft. Leave the car just outside Champhorent, in the car park laid out below D 530.*

🄺 The path leads rapidly down to the Vénéon. Markers signal the entrance of the Parc national des Écrins and the view extends towards the **Glacier du Fond** on the left and the **Glaciers des Sellettes** on the right. The path goes through a scree-covered area and the greenery becomes ever more sparse, with only tufts of Alpine sea holly and columbine to brighten up the landscape. A picturesque stone bridge leads over to the left bank of the Muande *(close the cattle gate behind you)*; a few lonely patches of grass are the only vegetation to be seen. The glacial hollow of the Lavey and its refuge come into view with the **Glacier d'Entre-Pierroux** and **Glacier du Lac** towering right above and the **Pic d'Olan** filling the horizon to the south. Colonies of marmots live on the northern slopes; you may be able to hear their shrill warning call.

▶ *Return to Champhorent along the same route.*

Beyond Champhorent, there is an overall view of the Lavey Valley and the glacial cirque at the end of it before the road goes through a small tunnel into a desolate gorge, followed by the greener Combe des Étages. The Dôme de Neige des Écrins (alt 4 012m/13 163ft) looms ahead in the distance.

La Bérarde

Once a sleepy hamlet, inhabited by the local shepherds, or "bérards" in the old dialect, La Bérarde is now a popular starting point for challenging mountaineering expeditions in the Écrins Massif *(see below)* and a lively place in summer.

② **Vallée de la Romanche**★★★

FROM LE BOURG-D'OISANS TO THE COL DU LAUTARET 57km/35.4mi
– about 2hr

This itinerary, combined with those of the Croix de Fer (*see Route de la CROIX DE FER*) and of the Galibier (*see Route du GALIBIER*), completes the unforgettable round tour of the Alps' great passes ("Circuit des Grands Cols").

The Col du Lautaret is now open throughout the winter, but can be closed for a few hours in the event of heavy snowfalls or poor visibility; watch out for information panels in Le Bourg-d'Oisans, Le Péage-de-Vizille and Champagnier or telephone for the recorded information at Lautartet - ☎ 04 92 24 44 44.

The Briançon road leaves the Bourg-d'Oisans Basin and runs through wild gorges; beyond La Grave, the valley widens, offering lovely views of the summits and glaciers of the Meije.

▶ *From Le Bourg-d'Oisans, drive along N 91.*

At first, the road runs southeast to the confluence of the River Vénéon and River Romanche, then turns eastwards, leaving the wide Vénéon Valley to the south.
Rampe des Commères – In the days of stagecoaches, tongue-wagging was the favourite pastime of travellers who had to step down and walk up this steep section, hence the name, which translates as "gossips' slope"!

Gorges de l'Infernet★
Fine **viewpoint**★ over this wild gorge in a tight bend, near a ruined oratory. The green Freney Basin offers a pleasant contrast.

▶ *At the Chambon Dam, take the road to Les Deux-Alpes.*

The Meije Massif from the Col du Lautaret

P. Tetrel/EXPLORER

Mont-de-Lans

This hilltop mountain village has retained a few old houses. The **Musée des Arts et Traditions populaires** (🕐 *July to Aug and Jan to Apr: 10am-noon, 3-7pm* 🕐 *closed rest of year. No charge -* ☎ *04 76 80 23 97*) illustrates daily life in the Oisans region during the 19C to the accompaniment of folksongs and stories; a permanent exhibition is devoted to local pedlars.

Climb up to the church and follow a narrow ridge to a high-voltage pylon for a fine **view**★ of Lake Chambon and the Gorges de l'Infernet.

▶ *Return to the N 91.*

Barrage du Chambon★★

The dam was built across a narrowing of the Romanche Valley in order to regulate the spates of summer and autumn and supply hydroelectric power stations. This gravity dam is 294m/965ft long at the top, 70m/230ft thick at the base, and 90m/295ft high (137m/450ft including the foundations). The reservoir, which covers an area of 125ha/309 acres, contains 54 million m3/43 778acft. Three hamlets, Le Chambon, Le Dauphin and Le Parizet were flooded when the dam was built.

▶ *Turn onto the D 25 at Le Freney.*

Beyond Mizoën, the cliff-road climbs up the deep ravine through which flows the Ferrand, affording close-up views of the Grandes Rousses.

Besse

This high **mountain village** (alt 1 550m/5 085ft) is characteristic of the area: the houses lining its narrow twisting lanes have wooden balconies and heavy roof structures, which used to be covered with lauzes (thick slabs of schist).

Maison des Alpages

On your left leaving the village, under the church. ♿🕐 *July to Aug: 10am-noon, 3-7pm; Sept to June: daily except Wed 2-6pm (9am-noon by appointment)* 🕐 *closed 1 Jan and 25 Dec. 3€ children 5-16 years 1€ -* ☎ *04 76 80 19 09*

Although stock farming is no longer a principal activity, it still has a strong cultural influence, which this museum describes with modern education exhibits. You can also arrange visits to sheep herders and cattle farmers through the regional Fédération des alpages de l'Isère.

▶ *Return to the Chambon Dam and continue along N 91.*

Combe de Malaval★

The rushing waters of the Romanche are almost level with the road all the way through this long gorge, past two impressive waterfalls on the north bank, the **Cascade de la Pisse**★ and **Cascade du Saut de la Pucelle**.

The Mont-de-Lans and the Girose glaciers are visible through gaps in the wall of rock to the right. The Meije and its glaciers come into view as one approaches La Grave.

La Grave and excursion★★ – ⟲ *See La GRAVE.*

Upstream from Villar-d'Arène, the road leaves the Romanche Valley which veers southeast along the Val d'Arsine; at the end of this glacial valley, the Pic des Agneaux (alt 3 663m/12 018ft) and the Pic de Neige Cordier (alt 3 613m/11 854ft) can be seen towering above the cirque of the Glacier d'Arsine.

Nearer the Col du Lautaret, the jagged peaks of the Combeynot Massif appear in the foreground.

Col du Lautaret★★

In spite of its relatively high altitude (2 057m/6 749ft), the Col du Lautaret is the busiest pass of the Dauphiné Alps and the road is now kept clear of snow throughout most of the winter. From July until the beginning of August, wild narcissi, anemones, lilies, gentians, rhododendrons and even edelweiss cover vast expanses and brighten up the rather austere landscape.

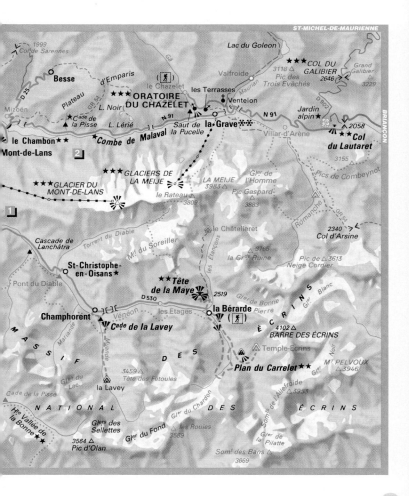

A path at the highest point of the pass leads off to the **Jardin alpin**★ *(05480 Villar d'Arene ⏱ June to Sept: 10am-6pm. 5€, children under 12 years no charge - ☎ 04 92 24 41 62)*. This famous garden, created early in the 20C and managed by the University of Grenoble, contains several rockeries and around 2 000 species of wild and medicinal plants from the Balkans, the Caucasus, the Himalayas and the Rocky Mountains, as well as varieties from closer to home. A research laboratory welcomes scientists and students. From the viewing table situated on top of a knoll, there is a striking **view**★★ of the Meije Massif surrounded by glaciers (Glacier de l'Homme).

The **Refuge Napoléon** is an information and exhibition centre devoted to the local fauna, flora and geology.

Hikes

These walks from Bérarde (👣 see 1) are suitable for moderately experienced hikers equipped with non-slip shoes.

Tête de la Maye ★★

Alt 2 517m/8 255ft. *North of La Bérarde. 4hr there and back (2hr 30min on the way up); suitable for hikers familiar with steep terrain and not liable to feel dizzy. Difference in altitude: 800m/2 625ft.*

🚶 The path starts before the bridge over the Étançons, winds its way across fields hemmed in by stone walls then runs along rows of arolla pines planted as avalanche barriers. *Bear left at the intersection with the path to Le Châtelleret;* 👁 *metal steps and safety cables make the following difficult sections a little easier, but caution is still required.*

From the viewing table at the summit, there is an overall **view**★★ of the Écrins Massif and of the peaks surrounding the Vénéon Valley: note in particular, from left to right, the **Grand Pic de la Meije** (3 983m/13 068ft), the **Glacier des Étançons**, the **Dôme des Écrins** (4 000m/13 123ft) and the **Glacier de la Bonne Pierre**.

It is possible to walk back along the east bank of the stream; at the intersection, bear left towards a bridge, then right to a footbridge and down to La Bérarde. Pleasant view of the Tête de la Maye on the right.

Plan du Carrelet and refuge ★★

Alt 2 000m/6 562ft – *South of La Bérarde. 2hr there and back. Difference in altitude: 300m/984ft. For the first half of the year, the névé (granular glacial snow) on the final stretch to the refuge means that this last leg of an otherwise easy walk should only be attempted by experienced and fully equipped hikers.*

🚶 Take the footpath starting beyond the Maison du Parc and following the east bank of the Vénéon. From the park's information panels, there is a fine view of the **Meije** and **Tête de la Maye** overlooking La Bérarde. The Meije has three peaks: the Meije Orientale to the east (3 890m), the Meije Centrale (3 974m), known to mountaineers as the Doigt de Dieu, "the finger of God," and the Meije Occidentale or Grand Pic de la Meije in the west. This last, with its steep, dramatic crags, is particularly impressive when seen in silhouette from La Grave. It was first climbed in 1877 – after 17 unsuccessful attempts – by one M. Boileau de Castelnau accompanied by two local guides, a father and son of the Gaspard family.

The U-shaped valley widens at the confluence of the Vénéon and Chardon. From the Plan du Carrelet refuge, the Chardon and Pilatte glaciers appear to fill the horizon to the south.

Retrace your steps, cross the stream and follow the path towards the Chardon Glacier. You then have to go over two footbridges in order to come back along the west bank of the Vénéon. Cross again as you reach the car park in La Bérarde. There is another view of the Meije and Tête de la Maye from here.

LA PLAGNE✳✳

MICHELIN MAP 333 N4 – LOCAL MAP SEE MASSIF DE LA VANOISE

The **Grande Plagne**✳✳, which covers an area of 10 000ha/24 711 acres, is one of the most extended ski areas in France. Gentle slopes and beautiful views embracing the Mont-Blanc, Beaufortain and Vanoise massifs lend a particular magic to its mountain landscapes, which can be explored on foot in summer and using snowshoes in winter. A superb variety of sports and activities detracts little from the pleasantly unspoilt character of the mountain village. *Le Chalet - 73210 La Plagne ⓒ July to Aug: Mon-Sat 9am-noon, 2-6pm, Sun 9am-noon; mid-Dec to Apr: daily 9am-noon, 2-6pm; rest of year: Mon-Fri 9am-noon, 2-6pm ⓒ closed 14 July and 15 Aug - ☎ 04 79 09 79 79 - www.la-plagne.com*

▶ **Orient Yourself:** La Plagne is 20 km/12.5mi south of Aime, in the Bellecôte Massif.
- **Don't Miss:** The summit of the Roche de Mio offers a great view.
- **Kids Especially for Kids:** Children will enjoy the ice cave on the Chiaupe glacier.
- **Also See:** Nearby Sights: Les ARCS, La Vallée de BELLEVILLE, BOURG-ST-MAURICE, CHAMPAGNY-EN-VANOISE, PRALOGNAN-LA-VANOISE, La TARENTAISE, Massif de la VANOISE

The Resorts

Ski area

The 1992 Olympic **bobsledding** competitions were staged in La Plagne. The 1 500m/0.9mi run, built for the occasion, is the only one of its kind in France. Visitors can try shooting through 19 hair-raising bends, or just watch from a safe distance; there is a good overall view near the intersection with the Plagne-Bellecôte road. Above 2 000m/6 562ft, the quality of the snow is exceptional and ideal for those who like moderately difficult runs (mainly blue runs). Experienced skiers can find a few suitable runs when snow cover is generous. Summer skiing takes place on the Glacier de la Chiaupe and Glacier de Bellecôte.

Created in 1961, La Plagne now includes six high villages and four lower ones. The high villages, situated at altitudes around 2 000m/6 562ft, enjoy good snow cover from December to May; being centrally located, they offer easy access to the whole ski area. Since 2003, La Plagne has been part of the **Paradski** area, which includes Peisey-Vallandry and Les Arcs.

Plagne Bellecôte, **Plagne Centre** and Aime 2000 have a more urban atmosphere, while Plagne 1800, Plagne Villages and above all **Belle Plagne** blend harmoniously with the landscape.

Snow conditions are not so good in the lower villages, situated at altitudes ranging from 1 250m/4 101ft to 1 450m/4 757ft, but they have other advantages. **Champagny-en-Vanoise**✳✳ (see CHAMPAGNY-EN-VANOISE) and, to a lesser extent, Montchavin have the charm of authentic Savoyard villages and offer superb views of the Vanoise Massif. Hikers can climb up to **Mont Jovet**✳✳, which offers a beautiful view of the Alps (a guidebook of the area's hiking itineraries is published by the tourist office).

For coin categories, see the Legend on the cover flap.

WHERE TO STAY

Chambre d'hôte Malezan – *Rte de la Plagne - 73210 Macot-la-Plagne - 16km/10mi N of La Plagne on D 221 - ☎ 04 79 55 69 90 - www.malezan.com - 2rms.* Expect a warm welcome in this simple, friendly establishment. Peace and quiet reign despite the nearby road, and you can rest after your althletic exersions. Leave your worries, and your cigarettes, at the door. Gîte available.

Viewpoints Accessible by Gondola

La Grande Rochette★★

Alt 2 508m/8 228ft. Access by Funiplagne gondola from Plagne Centre. ⏱ *July to Aug: (6mn,continuous) daily except Sun 9am-12.45pm, 2-5.15pm. 7€ return, children under 10 years no charge -* ☎ *04 79 09 67 00.*

From the upper station, climb to the viewing table on the summit. The splendid **panorama** includes the main summits of the Vanoise Massif (Mont Pourri, Bellecôte, Grande Motte, Grande Casse, Grand Bec) and extends to the Oisans (Meije), the Aiguilles d'Arves, the Étendard, Belledonne, Beaufortain and Mont Blanc massifs. The high villages of La Plagne can be seen below to the north and Courchevel to the southwest.

Télécabine de Bellecôte★★

Access from Plagne Bellecôte. ⏱ *July to Aug: daily except Sat. To Roche de Mio: 9am-4.45pm Roche de Mio to Glacier de Bellecôte: 9.20am- 4.20pm (45min). 10€ return, children under 10 years no charge -* ☎ *04 79 09 67 00.*

The exceptionally long gondola ride (6.5km/4mi) leads to Belle Plagne and then to the **Roche de Mio** (2 739m/8 986ft). Climb to the summit (viewing table) in 5min to enjoy the splendid **panorama**★★. The Sommet de Bellecôte (3 416m/11 207ft) and its glaciers can be seen in the foreground, with the Grande Motte, the Grande Casse, Péclet-Polset and the Trois Vallées further away to the south. Mont Pourri appears quite close to the northeast with Mont Blanc and the Grandes Jorasses in the distance.

Take the gondola leading to the **Col** and **Glacier de la Chiaupe** (alt 2 994m/9 823ft): beautiful **view** of the Vanoise.

PONT-EN-ROYANS★

POPULATION 917
MICHELIN MAP 333 F7 – LOCAL MAP SEE LE VERCORS

Picturesquely situated at the exit of the long gorge of the River Bourne, this village with its narrow streets and audacious architecture clinging to the mountain face has a definite southern atmosphere and great charm. 🏛 *Grand-Rue - 38680 Pont-en-Royans* ⏱ *Apr to Sept: Mon-Fri 10am-noon, 2-6pm, Sat-Sun 10am-12.30pm, 2-4pm; Oct to Mar: Mon-Fri 10am-noon, 2-5pm, Sat 10am-noon* ⏱ *closed Sun Oct to Mar, 15 Dec, 1 Jan -* ☎ *04 76 36 09 10*

▸ **Orient Yourself:** Situated between Romans-sur-Isère and Villard-de-Lans, Pont-en-Royans is a gateway to the Vercors region. Below the town is a lake formed by a dam on the Bourne River. Approach from the west for the best view.

🔍 **Don't Miss:** The Presles excursion offers lovely scenery.

Kids **Especially for Kids:** The Jardin des Fontaines pétrifiantes at the Château de la Sône will fascinate children with its strange rocks and many plants.

🦻 **Also See:** Nearby Sights: GRENOBLE, Le VERCORS, VILLARD-DE-LANS

Walking Tour

Viewpoints★★

The site★★

🐾At Pont Picard, take the steps leading to the embankment along the Bourne, from where it is possible to reach the medieval quarter. In spite of being partly destroyed

A. de Valroger/MICHELIN

Traditional houses line the narrow banks of the Bourne

during the Wars of Religion, the medieval quarter has retained a number of tall old houses clinging to the rock, overlooking the Bourne or dipping their narrow façades into the stream and forming a charming picture which once captured the imagination of the novelist Stendhal.

Trois Châteaux★
1hr there and back on foot. Steep paths going across screes; start with a series of steps from place de la Porte-de-France.

From the belvedere, there is a fine **view** of the Royans region and Isère Valley.

Excursions

St-Nazaire-en-Royans *9km/5.6mi west along D 531*
13 pl de l'Église - 26190 St-Jean-en-Royans ◷ *Mid-June to mid-Sept: 9am-12.30pm, 2-6.30pm, Sun and public holidays 10am-12.30pm; rest of year Mon-Sat 9am-noon, 2-6pm* ◷ *closed 1 May, 11 Nov, 25 Dec, 1 Jan - ☎ 04 75 48 61 39 - www.royans.com*. As one approaches St-Nazaire-en-Royans along D 531, old houses huddled on the bank of the River Isère appear framed by the arches of an imposing **aqueduct** carrying water from the Bourne into the Valence Plain.

The **Pont St-Hilaire-St-Nazaire** is an elegant single-arched bridge with a 110m/361ft span built across the confluence of the River Isère and River Bourne, now flooded by the more recent building of a dam.

Situated on the shore of the lake, beneath the aqueduct, the **Grotte préhistorique de Thaïs** (◷ *July to Aug:10.30-7pm; Easter weekend, Apr to June and Sept to Oct: daily except Mon 2-6pm, Sun and public holidays 10.30am-6pm (last admission 45min before closing)* ◷ *Closed Nov to Mar. 6.50€, children 3-13 years 4.50€ - ☎ 04 75 48 45 76 - www.grotte-de-thais.com.*) is a natural cave resulting from the chemical action of the water of an underground river; the deeply carved rock is, in some places, coloured in bright red and grey. Inhabited in prehistoric times, about 17 000 years ago, the cave has yielded a wealth of tools and engraved bones.

There are **paddle-boat trips** (◷ *mid-July to mid-Aug: boat leaves at 10.30am, 1pm, 3pm, 5pm; rest of summer: 10.30am, 2pm, 4pm; Apr to June and Sept to mid-Oct: Sun and public holidays, 2 or 3 trips a day. 9€, children 6 to 13 years 6€ - ☎ 04 76 64 43*

42.)on the artificial lake (220ha/494 acres), starting from the village of La Sône and going through an important bird sanctuary known as the **Roselière de Creux**.

The **Jardin des Fontaines pétrifiantes** (*June to Aug: 10.30am-7pm; May:10.30am-6.30pm; Sept: Mon-Fri 11.30am-6pm, Sat-Sun 10.30am-6.30pm; 1st 2 weeks Oct: 1-6pm. 6.50€, children 4.50€ - 43 76 64 43 42.*) is a green open space with 500 different species of plants and flowers, laid out round the petrifying springs at La Sône.

Round tour via Presles ★★ *32km/20mi – about 1hr 30min*

▶ *From Pont-en-Royans, drive along D 531 towards Villard-de-Lans and turn left onto D 292 immediately after the Pont Rouillard over the Bourne.*

The road climbs up the sunburnt slopes within sight of the escarpments overlooking the river. From the wide bend known as the "Croix de Toutes Aures," although there's no trace of a cross to be seen, the view extends from the rolling hills of the Royans region to the impressive gorge of the River Bourne overlooked by the Grand Veymont.

After a series of hairpin bends, the road finally reaches the Presles Plateau. It continues to rise beyond Presles through the Coulmes Forest to a small hamlet called Le Fas, where the view embraces a long stretch of the lower Isère Valley, including the imposing aqueduct of St-Nazaire-en-Royans.

The road then winds steeply down to St-Pierre-de-Chérennes across green fields, offering more picturesque views.

▶ *D 31 reaches N 532. Turn left almost immediately towards Beauvoir-en-Royans.*

Château de Beauvoir

The picturesque ruins of the 13C castle, razed by Louis XI, stand on top of an isolated hill overlooking the village. A square tower, a gate, a Gothic window, part of the former chapel and the old, ivy-covered walls are all that remain of the former residence of the "dauphins" (*see also GRENOBLE*). However the site is pleasant and affords a fine view of the meandering River Isère.

▶ *Return to N 532 and, in St-Romans, take D 518 leading back to Pont-en-Royans.*

Walnuts from Grenoble

Walnuts from Grenoble have, since 1938, been protected by a label guaranteeing their origin and quality *(appellation d'origine contrôlée)*. Three different kinds are grown in the region:

– the mayette, a large walnut with a thin shell and a refined taste;

– the parisienne, a round walnut with a brown shell, rich in oil;

– the franquette, an oblong walnut with a rough shell, which is the most sought-after by confectioners and the most widely cultivated.

The producing area straddles three *départements*; however, 60% of the annual production (around 10 000 – 15 000t) comes from just four communes: Pont-en-Royans, St-Marcellin, Vinay and Tullins.

The September harvest is followed by the washing, drying and conditioning process (there are two sizes: over 30mm/1.2in and between 20mm/0.8in and 30mm/1.2in).

This energy-giving fruit can be eaten fresh, within two weeks of the harvest, or dried and used in salads, cakes and confectionery (stuffed walnuts are a Grenoble speciality traditionally eaten during the Christmas period).

PRALOGNAN-LA-VANOISE

POPULATION 756
MICHELIN MAP 333 N5 – LOCAL MAP SEE MASSIF DE LA VANOISE

Set in an imposing glacial valley, this health and ski resort is the best starting point for fine hikes and mountaineering expeditions in the Parc national de la Vanoise, famous as an ibex reserve. The eastern edge of the Pralognan Basin is undoubtedly the most **picturesque area**★ with the cirques of the Grand Marchet and Petit Marchet in the foreground, backed by the Glaciers de la Vanoise. Pralognan, which attracts thousands of hikers and mountaineers, has been one of the liveliest summer resorts in Savoie for over a century. The first climbing attempts date from the late 19C; in 1860, the British mountaineer **William Matthews** and the Frenchman **Michel Croz** hewed their way up one of the peaks of the Grande Casse – now called Pointe Matthews – by carving no fewer than 1 100 steps, 800 of them with an axe. The small but sunny **ski area** offers remarkable possibilities for cross-country skiing. 🛈 *73710 Pralognan-la-Vanoise* 🕐 *All year round: 9am-noon, 2-6pm* 🕐 *closed Sat-Sun out of winter and summer seasons - ☎ 04 79 08 70 08 - www.prolognan.com*

▶ **Orient Yourself:** Located 27km/17mi east of Moûtiers on D 915, which follows the Doron Rivers and crosses vast forests.

😊 **Don't Miss:** Walk to the little village of Prioux.

Kids Especially for Kids: The Ouistiti trail crosses a forest and a via ferrata course designed for 6-8 year olds. The local Bureau des Guides also organizes outings for children.

👍 **Also See:** Nearby Sights: La Vallée de BELLEVILLE, CHAMPAGNY-EN-VANOISE, COURCHEVEL, La PLAGNE, La TARENTAISE, Massif de la VANOISE

Hikes

La Chollière ★

1.5km/0.9mi along a mountain road, then 30min on foot. Start from the Hôtel La Vanoise, cross the Doron and follow the road which winds up to La Chollière. Leave the car above the chalets.

🏔 A handsome group of mountains can be seen in the background behind the hamlet: the Pointes de la Glière and the Grande Casse (alt 3 855m/12 648ft, the highest peak of the Vanoise Massif). The surrounding pastures are famous for their wealth of wild flora, including narcissi and edelweiss in June and Alpine sea holly, known as the "Queen of the Alps," in August (👍*see Introduction: Vegetation*).

Mont Bochor ★

About 3hr there and back on foot or 6min by cable car. 🕐 *July to Aug: 8.10am-12.20pm, 1.50-5.50pm; June and Sept: 8.10-11.50am, 1.35-5.20pm (departure every 20min). 36F 6.10€ return, children under 13 years 4.60€ - ☎ 04 79 08 70 07.*

🏔 From the upper station, walk up to the summit (alt 2 023m/6 637ft, viewing table) for a bird's-eye view of the Pralognan Basin and the Doran de Chavière Valley, closed off upstream by the Péclet-Polset Massif and lined on the left by the huge Vanoise glaciers.

A 1.4km/0.9mi-long nature trail enables visitors to become familiar with this typical mountain environment. Information panels detail the geological and ecological wealth of the site.

Lac Blanc and Mont Parraché

Col de la Vanoise★★★

Alt 2 517m/8 258ft. *Start from Mont Bochor. If the cable car is not operating, start from the Fontanettes car park. 3hr up, 2hr 30min down to Pralognan.*

From the Barmettes refuge, the path rises steeply to the Lac des Vaches before reaching the pass; view of the Grande Casse Glacier and Pointe de la Réchasse. On the way down, there is a fine view of the Lauzière Massif with the Sommet de la Saulire, Dent de la Portetta and Aiguille du Fruit in the foreground. Martagon lily, columbine and houseleek are some of the wildflower species which can be seen along the route. Inexperienced hikers can come down via the Barmettes refuge and Fontanettes car park. Hikers with more experience of the mountains, on the other hand, can, in fine weather conditions only, enjoy a splendid hike via the Arcellin cirque and ravine.

Petit Mont Blanc★★

Alt 2 677m/8 783ft. *Start from Les Prioux.* 3hr up via the Col du Môme; 2hr down. *For a description of the* **panorama**★★ (☀ *see COURCHEVEL).*

Lac Blanc★★

Start from the Pont de la Pêche. A long and arduous climb; 3hr 15min up, 2hr 30min down.

Situated below the Péclet-Polset refuge, the Lac Blanc is one of the loveliest lakes in the Vanoise Massif. Walk along the right side of it and climb towards the Col du Soufre. View of the Aiguille de Polset, the Gébroulaz Glacier, the Col de Chavière, the Pointe de l'Échelle and the Génépy Glacier.

PRA-LOUP✳

MICHELIN MAP 334 H6 – LOCAL MAPS SEE L'UBAYE

In a dense larch forest, on the edge of a plateau (alt 1 630m/5 347ft) overlooking the Ubaye Valley, the 1960s resort of Pra-Loup is one of the most popular in the Alpes-de-Haute-Provence, owing its fame as much to its facilities the quality of its environment and to its long hours of sunshine as to an attractive setting. A natural ice rink marks the centre of an expanding town where fans of new winter sports will feel particularly at home. *Maison de Pra-Loup – 04400 Pra-Loup* 🕐 *Dec to Apr: daily 9am-7pm; July to Aug: daily 9am-noon, 2-6pm; rest of year: daily except Sat-Sun and public holidays 9am-noon, 2-6pm - ☎ 04 92 84 10 04 - www.praloup.com.*

▸ **Orient Yourself:** Pra-Loup is 8.5km/5.3mi from Barcelonnette by D 902 and D 109; note the lovely views over Barcelonnette and surrounding mountains.

Especially for Kids: The resort has the designation "P'tits Montagnards," meaning it offers facilities for children.

👆 **Also See:** Nearby Sights: BARCELONNETTE, Route de la BONETTE, COLMARS, Val d'ENTRAUNES, Lac de SERRE-PONÇON, SEYNE, L'UBAYE, VAL-D'ALLOS

View of the Grande Séolane from the Col des Thuiles

Y. Bontoux

The Resort

🐟 Ski area

Linked with that of La Foux d'Allos (🕯️ *see VAL-D'ALLOS*), it forms a vast area known as the **Espace Lumière**: 53 ski lifts and 170km/106mi of runs. However, the link with La Foux is generally only suitable for experienced skiers. Pra-Loup's own ski area, which rises to a maximum altitude of 2 500m/8 202ft, offers moderately steep snowfields ideal for intermediate skiers. Snow cannons ensure adequate snow cover down to the lowest part of the resort. The resort also boasts the most spectacular "big air" run in France and a snow park with its own sound system. Those who prefer ungroomed trails ("freeriding" in French) will want to head for four avalanche-free zones on the edge of the piste for miles of untouched snow.

In summer, Pra-Loup offers a wide choice of activities including mountain biking, white-water sports and paragliding as well as fine rambles along marked trails.

🚶 Hike

Col des Thuiles ★

This itinerary (6hr) is suitable for strong experienced hikers and requires a good sense of direction. The ascent to the pass, alongside the ski lifts, is arduous but the walk down through the Gimette Valley is quite pleasant. Take plenty of drinking water – the only opportunity to replenish supplies is at the Grande Cabane.

Address Book

For coin categories, see the Legend on the cover flap.

WHERE TO STAY

🍽️ **La Ferme du Couvent** – *Les Molanes* - ☎ *04 92 84 05 05* - *www.ferme-du-couvent.com* - *closed 1 week in June* - *5rms* - 🍽️🍽️*meal* - This 14C farm has kept the essential old architectural details: narrow windows, low doorways, slices of larch tree-trunk for the floor, cool rooms. The simple guestrooms open onto a terrace with view of the mountains. Meals in front of the fire.

🍽️🍽️**Hôtel Prieuré de Molanès** – *At Molanès* - ☎ *04 92 84 11 43* - *info@ prieure-praloup.com* - *closed 27 Apr-4 Jun and 19 Sept-10 Dec* - 🅿️ - *14rms* - 🍽️🍽️*restaurant*. Your stay will be comfortable and relaxed in this old 17C priory nestled in the heart of the Alps. Stone, wood, roughcast and panelling combine to create a warm decor typical of this mountain region. Lounge with open fire for winter evenings, and a swimming pool for the summer.

SPORT

Worth knowing – Pra-Loup is especially known for its huge ski area, which reaches as far as Foux-d'Allos. In summer, starting in July, there is also lots of activity, particularly for those who enjoy sports: white-water sports, hiking or mountain biking, hang-gliding, etc. There is also lots of shopping in the commercial malls, as well as bars and discothèques. For small children, strollers are available on loan, and there is a free childcare centre on Wednesday evenings in season.

Hiking – Leaving from Pra-Loup are 12 hiking trails. Information at the tourist office.

Angling – In summer, you can fish at no charge and without a fishing permit at the **Lac de Costebelle**. Take the gondola, followed by 40min of walking.

Nathy Loisirs – 🧒 - *Front-des-pistes* - ☎ *06 87 91 00 70 or 06 10 23 11 52* – *Mon-Fri 9am-12.30pm, 2pm-7pm (July to Aug open daily)* - *closed May-June and Sept-Nov*. This is a recreational paradise for 3-15 year olds. Whether toddler or teenager, the budding sportsperson can tackle activities such as mountain biking, pony rides, electric vehicles etc. All activities are run by qualified sports instructors.

An occasionally vertiginous path running along the mountain slope offers a fine **view**★ of the Agneliers area, the Gorges du Bachelard, the Cimet and Chapeau de Gendarme, eventually reaching the Col des Thuiles beneath the Grande Séolane. From here, make for the Rocher Jaumas, cross the Torrent de Langail and follow the yellow markings. A forest path leads steeply downhill for 100m/328ft, then turn right onto a path which crosses the Torrent des Bruns. Beyond the pine woods, a broad path leads to the Pas Lapeine. Carry on through the meadows, the larches and pines of the Gimette forest, across the stream and, after a rest at the Grande Cabane (2 138m/7 014ft), head towards Grande Séolane and the Col de Thuiles (2 376m/7 795ft). The path opposite the Grande Cabane leads back through the Vallon des Agneliers to the Lac de Pra-Loup.

PUGET-THÉNIERS ★

POPULATION 1 800
MICHELIN MAP 341 C4
LOCAL MAP SEE CLUES DE HAUTE-PROVENCE

This small town nestling beneath a rocky spur crowned with the ruins of a castle, at the confluence of the River Var and River Roudoule, is the starting point for excursions to the nearby mountains. Lively and distinctly southern, modern Puget–Théniers also has a historical treasure that is well worth seeking out; cross to the right bank of the Roudole and time seems to stand still in the streets of the old Jewish quarter. *Maison de Pays - N 202 (former train station)– 06260 Puget-Theniers Opening times vary with season; telephone for times –- ☎ 04 93 05 05 05 - www.provence-val-dazur.com.*

▶ **Orient Yourself:** The old town is on the right (west) bank of the Roudoule river, which here meets the Var river. By taking D 28, 8km/5mi to the east, you can drive through the gorges of the Cians.

🕐 **Organizing Your Time:** You will need one hour to see the town and another three hours to complete the excursion to the pays de la Roudoule.

Especially for Kids: Children will enjoy the steam tourist train.

⚘ **Also See:** Nearby Sights: ANNOT, BEUIL, Gorges du CIANS, CLUES DE HAUTE-PROVENCE, Val d'ENTRAUNES, ENTREVAUX, ST-JULIEN-DU-VERDON, Vallée de la TINÉE, VILLARS-SUR-VAR

Walking Tour

Old town★
The main concentratation lies on the west bank of the Roudoule and includes place A.-Conil and its lovely fountain as well as many old houses which have retained beautiful doorways and signs carved in stone.

Church
Built in the 13C by the Knights Templar, this Romanesque church was remodelled and richly decorated in the 17C (chancel vaulting and church furniture). It contains many works of art *(timed light switch at the entrance on the left)*.
Note the amazing **carved wooden calvary**★ consisting of three tiers representing the Crucifixion, the Entombment and the Resurrection. The faces of the different characters are very expressive and the representation of the thieves' bodies, tied to their crosses, and of Christ, carried by his disciples bending beneath the weight, is most realistic.

The high altar **retable of Notre-Dame-de-Secours**★, placed above a polychrome statue of the Virgin Mary carved out of an olive tree trunk, dates from 1525 and is believed to be the work of Antoine Rouzen. Note the beautiful representations of the Virgin Mary and of St James.

"L'Action enchaînée"★

This female nude by **Aristide Maillol**, a powerful figure with her hands bound behind her back, is dedicated to the memory of one of the town's most famous (or infamous) sons. **Louis-Auguste Blanqui** (1805-81), the anticlerical revolutionary who lived by the motto *"Ni Dieu ni maître"* "no God, no master" and helped to fan the flames of revolt in 1830, 1848 and 1870, spent more than 36 years in prison before being elected as member of parliament for Gironde. First unveiled – to the outrage of the pious – near the church, the statue now stands on a less contentious spot, in a charming square planted with very old plane trees on the edge of N 202.

Excursion

Pays de la Roudoule *45km/28mi round tour – about 3hr*

To the north of Puget-Théniers, a succession of unusual landscapes begins; the Roudole has scoured narrow gorges through folds of limestone, red sandstone and black marl, and several picturesque villages, surrounded by larches and olive groves, stand along its path.

▶ *From Puget-Théniers, drive along D 16.*

The road rises above Puget and offers a lovely view of the old town before entering the Gorges de la Roudoule.

▶ *Turn right onto D 116 towards Puget-Rostang.*

The road follows the Mairole Valley and goes through a strange landscape darkened by the presence of black marl formations, known as "robines."

Puget-Rostang

This hilltop village is overlooked by the square tower of a restored castle. The **Écomusée du Pays de la Roudoule** (♿ 🕐 *May to Sept: daily 10am-noon, 2-6pm; Oct to Apr: daily except Sat-Sun and public holidays 10am-noon, 2-6pm* 🕐 *Closed mid-Dec to mid-Jan. 4.50€, children 2.50€ - ☎ 04 93 05 07 38 - www.ecomusee-roudoule.fr.*), created to preserve and develop the area's traditional agriculture, rural architecture and cultural heritage, also organises exhibitions here.

From Puget-Rostang, a twisting road leads to **Auvare** (*13km/8mi there and back*), a village clinging to the

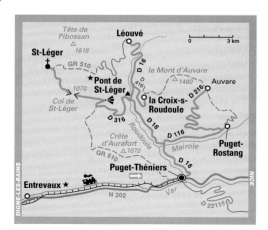

rock, where all kinds of fugitives used to find refuge.

▶ *Return to D 16 and continue along the Gorges de la Roudoule.*

Pont de St-Léger ★

This bridge occupies an amazing site. The Roman bridge can be seen below with the paved Roman road at either end.

▶ *Continue towards Léouvé and turn right onto D 416 to La Croix-sur-Roudoule.*

STEAM TRAIN

Kids **Steam Tourist Train** – *For times and prices, contact the train station in Puget-Théniers -* ☎ *04 93 05 00 46, or the office of the Chemins de fer de Provence at Nice -* ☎ *04 97 03 80 80* The Nice to Digne-les-Bains line, completed between 1890 and 1911, runs a train daily between Puget-Théniers and Annot.

Via Ferrata "Les Demoiselles du Castagnet" – contact the tourist office. Spectacular climb.

La Croix-sur-Roudoule

Perched high and backing onto the rock in a picturesque **setting**★, this village is still guarded by an old fortified gate. The small Romanesque **church**, which has a wall-belfry with twin openings, houses two panels from an altarpiece by François Bréa representing St John the Baptist on the right of the altar and St Michael on the left.
From the top of the village, there is an interesting **view** of the upper Roudoule Valley.

▶ *Return to D 16 and turn right.*

Léouvé

The Léouvé Cirque is carved out of red sandstone; copper was mined here from 1861 to 1929 and the tall chimneys of the foundry works can still be seen. An exhibition at the **Maison de la Mine** shows the grim reality of everyday life in the mines. 🕐 *July to Aug: daily 10am-noon, 2-5.30pm; Sept to Nov: daily except Mon 10am-noon, 2-5pm; Apr: Sun 10am-noon, 2-5pm; May to June: daily except Mon 10am-noon, 2.30-5.30pm. 2.50€, children under 7 years no charge.*

▶ *Return to the Pont de St-Léger and cross over.*

The road rises to the Col de St-Léger, from where a totally different landscape unfolds. The village of St-Léger lies in verdant surroundings framed by mountains.

▶ *Turn back towards Puget-Théniers.*

Just before the Pont de St-Léger, there is a fine view of the Roman bridge and of the Roman road, as well as of the village of La Croix-sur-Roudoule.

LE QUEYRAS★★★

MICHELIN MAP 334 I/J 4/5

This geographical, historical and human entity, centred round the Guil Valley, is one of the most authentic areas of the southern Alps, and one of the most culturally independent. Several tributary valleys, including the St-Véran Valley, converge towards the Guil Valley which, as one follows it downstream, is in turn imposing, charming, restful and austere. Even the weather has a distinctive character: the Queyras region has a reputation for blue skies and one of the sunniest climates in France, tempered by a certain coolness in the mountain air. Snow cover is excellent for six months of the year. *Place Jean-Léa - 05470 Aguilles Opening times vary, telephone for information - ☎ 04 92 46 70 34 - www. aiguilles.com*

▶ **Orient Yourself:** The Queyras region is an isolated bastion, accessible all year round through the Combe de Queras, and in summer also via the Col d'Izoard and the Col Agnel on the Italian border.

Don't Miss: Easy walks are found in the Parc naturel régional de Queyras.

Organizing Your Time: If you can, give yourself two days or a long weekend.

Especially for Kids: There are several nature walks in the Parc régional that children will enjoy. As well, older children can learn rock-climbing at the school "La Roche Écroulée" near l'Échalp. At La Chalp, childen can visit a wooden toy-making cooperative, "Les Jouets de Queyras."

Also See: Nearby Sights: ABRIÈS, L'ARGENTIÈRE-LA-BESSÉE, BRIANÇON, BRI-ANÇONNAIS, CEILLAC, EMBRUN, Vallée de FREISSINIÈRES, Route des GRANDES ALPES, GUILLESTRE, MOLINES-EN-QUEYRAS, MONT-DAUPHIN, MONT-GENÈVRE, ST-VÉRAN, SERRE-CHEVALIER, La VALLOUISE, VARS

A Bit of History

Unusual relief – The Queyras region is divided into two distinct areas. To the east, the Haut Queyras consists of folded sedimentary schist – made from deposits which once formed a **prehistoric seabed** – mixed with layers of volcanic porphyry; these were shaped into jagged summits and shiny mica-schist ridges overlooking rounded glacial valleys. The limestone that predominates in the Bas Queyras to the west pro-duced impressive but austere landscapes such as those of the Casse Déserte near the Col d'Izoard or the Combe du Queyras. The Espace géologique at Château-Queyras *(see below)* offers a detailed view of the region's natural history.

Moufflons

The **moufflon**, a wild sheep which can weigh up to 50kg/110lb, is another exam-ple of a successful newcomer; the twelve animals brought over from Corsica in 1973 increased to a colony of over 300 in a little over 20 years. Their splendid horns grow during their first year and, by the third year, curve right round to their neck. In winter, when their short, reddish fleece takes on a black-brown tinge, the search for food brings the moufflons down to the villages, where hay is often provided for them. When observing these surprisingly timid animals, remember to stay at least 50m/55yd away and be careful not to alarm them; you can use binoculars to get a closer look.

For coin categories, see the Legend on the cover flap.

WHERE TO STAY

🍽🍽 **Ferme de l'Izoard** – *La Chalp - 05350 Arvieux-en-Queyras -* ☎ *04 92 46 89 00 - www.laferme.fr - closed 25 Sept-15 Dec - 23rms-*🍽🍽 *restaurant.* Do not be misled by appearances: this chalet resembling a traditional farmhouse, with wood panelling and a stone slab roof, conceals modern rooms, all with balconies and some with a kitchenette. Heated swimming pool in view of the mountains. 🍽🍽🍽 **Chambre d'hôte La Girandole** – *At Brunissard - 05350 Arvieux-en-Queyras -* ☎ *04 92 46 84 12 - www.lagirandole.info - closed 15 Nov-15 Dec -* 🛏 *- 6rms.* This cosy guesthouse is full of character, with antique furniture and ornaments, fabrics in warm tones, soft sofas and a piano. In the rooms (all non-smoking) there are white walls and a prevailing lack of fuss or frills. Two gîtes available.

A land apart – The natural seclusion of the mountains has always encouraged a sense of independence from the world beyond; the medieval confederation of seven towns in the Aiguilles canton preserved a degree of autonomy until the 18C. Yet even the Queyras region was not spared the ravages of the Wars of Religion; an army of Huguenots, under the command of the Duc de Lesdiguières, seized Fort Queyras in 1587. After the revocation of the Edict of Nantes in 1685, many Protestant families emigrated to Switzerland or Germany.

During the 19C, the Queyras remained almost untouched by the Industrial Revolution; the region's first surfaced road, between Guillestre and Château-Queyras, was built only in 1856.

Arts and crafts – The Queyras region is particularly rich in folk art, comprising mainly objects made by peasants during the long winter evenings spent in their traditional houses (👉 *see Introduction: Handicraft*). Pieces of **furniture** made of larch wood or arolla pine are particularly famous (there are fine collections in the Musée Dauphinois in Grenoble, in the Musée Départemental in Gap and in the Musée des Arts et Traditions Populaires in Paris); they include box beds, wedding chests, spinning-wheels and cots, all decorated with geometric motifs carved with a knife.

This tradition has been perpetuated until today with the help of the Traditional Craftsmen's Union. There is a permanent display of their work in the **Maison de l'Artisanat** at Charpenel on D 947 towards St-Véran, near the intersection with D 5.
(*Summer: 10am-7pm; out of season: 10am-noon, 2-6pm. Closed 1 Jan and 25 Dec - ☏ 04 92 46 80 29 or 04 92 46 75 06 - Queyras.meubles@artisanat.com*).

There are many sundials in this exceptionally sunny region (300 days of sunshine a year). They were the work of travelling artists, often natives of Italy, and are decorated with mottos which express popular wisdom (*see Introduction: Traditional architecture, as well as the Practical information section*).

There are also numerous wooden **fountains**, with a rectangular basin and a circular bowl, which are fine examples of the skill of craftsmen from the Queyras region.

Croix de la Passion (or Croix des Outrages) – Queyras is famous for these crosses, usually found in front of churches, sometimes inside; fine examples of this devotional art can be seen at St-Véran and Ceillac. Each shows the symbols of Christ's Passion:

- the cock standing at the top is a reminder of Christ's words to Peter: "this night, before the cock crows, thou shalt deny me thrice" (Matthew XXVI, 34);
- the hand suggests Pontius Pilate's gesture at Jesus' trial;
- the coins symbolize the price of Judas' betrayal;
- the weapons, placed on either side of the central upright, represent those used for the Crucifixion;
- in some cases, a crown has been added as a reminder of Jesus' Crown of Thorns.

The Tour du Procureur – Several villages in the Haut Queyras region have a characteristic campanile built of larch logs and crowned with a bell, known as the Tour du Procureur.

Dating from the early Middle Ages, it is all that remains of the original village building. The sound of the bell called the villagers to a meeting where decisions concerning the community were taken: about baking day in the village oven, harvest time, sharing of communal duties and help for widows. The set of rules governing community work was called the "Ruido."

During the 19C, the tower was used for a different purpose in valleys where Protestants had returned; it was used as an ecumenical bell-tower. During the extensive flooding which occurred in 1957, the temporary absence of modern means of communication gave it back its original function.

Parc naturel régional du Queyras – By the mid-20C, isolation and depopulation had considerably slowed down the region's economy so that, in the 1960s, it was decided to modernize traditional agriculture, to develop handicrafts and above all tourism. The **Parc naturel régional du Queyras**, covering some 65 000ha/160 618 acres, was created in 1977 to provide information on the area, mark hiking routes, including the GR 5 and GR 58, and maintain refuges, as well as preserving the landscape and protecting endangered plant and animal species. The **flora** displays a great variety of Mediterranean and Alpine species, around 2 000 in all, and the **fauna** includes the usual mountain-dwellers such as the chamois and black grouse as well as rarer animals such as the black salamander. The ibex was successfully reintroduced in 1995; tourist information offices can provide information on where to watch these animals and how to avoid disturbing them.

1 Combe du Queyras★★

FROM GUILLESTRE TO CHÂTEAU-QUEYRAS *17km/10.6mi – about 1hr, not including the drive to Sommet-Bucher*

Guillestre★ – ◔ *See GUILLESTRE.*

▷ *From Guillestre, drive along D 902.*

Viewing table at Pied-la-Viste
It is located on top of a mound above the road. The imposing **Pelvoux-Écrins Massif**★ can be seen through the gap of the Durance Valley and Vallouise Depression. Between Pied-la-Viste and Maison du Roy, the valley becomes narrower and the road goes through several tunnels.

Maison du Roy
Tradition has it that King Louis XIII stopped at this inn on his way to Italy in 1629. A painting hanging inside is said to be a gift from the king.

▷ *D 60, which goes up the Ceillac Valley (◔ see CEILLAC-EN-QUEYRAS), branches off here. Continue along D 902.*

The road enters the **Combe du Queyras**★★, a long steep gorge. The narrowest part lies between La Chapelue and L'Ange Gardien, where there is barely room for the cliff road above the limpid and abundant flow of the river. Beyond the Rocher de l'Ange Gardien, the road offers a fine view of the splendid setting of Château-Queyras with its fort crowning the rocky height.

Château-Queyras★
🄸 *Chateau Queyras - 05350 Château-Ville-Vieille* ◔ *July to Aug: 9am-1pm, 2.30-6.30; rest of year: daily except Sat-Sun 9am-noon.*
The village nestles beneath **Fort Queyras**★ (◔ *July to Aug: daily 9am-7pm; May: Sat-Sun and public holidays 11am-6pm; June and Sept: 10am-6pm; Apr and Oct to early Nov: 1.30-5.30pm - ☎ 04 92 46 86 89 - www.chateauvillevielle.com. 4.20€, children 6-12 years 2.10€),* perched on a rugged knoll which almost completely blocks the entrance to the Guil Valley; this is the most characteristic **scenery**★ of the Queyras area. ☛*Leave the car on the right, just before climbing to the fort, or on the open space near the river.* This strategic hill at the gateway to the Durance valley has been fortified since medieval times and was occupied by a garrison until 1967. Its defences were improved and extended to the west by Louis XIV's military engineer Vauban in 1692, before being remodelled three times in the 18C and 19C. Beyond the drawbridge, a marked path leads past casemates and bastions to the crenellated 14C keep where exhibitions are held. Note the picturesque bartizan of the eastern bastion and go to the fortified outwork, or lunette, to get the best overall view of the fort.

Espace géologique★
Turn left at the church and park the car on the open space near the river, then walk back towards the village and go through the porch. ◔ *July to Aug: 10am-12.15, 2.30-6pm; rest of year: on request. 3.50€, children 2.50€ - ☎ 04 92 46 80 46*
The geological centre, housed in the crypt of the village church, illustrates the formation of the Alps through interactive displays presented in chronological order. One unusual exhibit gives you the chance to smell algae and plankton which were preserved in mud in the Arvieux area for 170 million years.

Sommet Bucher★

11km/6.8mi south – about 1hr there and back. The road is very difficult– please drive carefully.

The narrow road, shaded by larches and pines, climbs in a series of hairpin bends, offering fine glimpses of Château-Queyras and the Guil Valley. From the end of the road, climb to the viewing tables, situated on either side of a military building. The beautiful panorama includes Mont Viso and St-Véran village, framed by the Pic de Châteaurenard, Pointe de Toillies and Sommet de Razis, with the Pic de la Font Sancte to the south, Pelvoux-Écrins Massif to the west and Grand Pic de Rochebrune to the north.

2 The St-Véran Road★★

From Château-Queyras to St-Véran *15km/9.3mi – about 30min*

Château-Queyras★ – 🐾 *See* 1.

▶ *From Château-Queyras, drive east along D 947.*

Ville-Vieille

This village, administratively linked to Château-Queyras, forms part of **Château-Ville-Vieille.** A nature trail on the left just before the village, the **Sentier écologique des Astragales,** offers a pleasant 1hr 30min walk. 🔲 Views of the valley and of the Bric Bouchet Summit. Rare plant species can be seen along the way, in particular specimens of milk-vetch, pheasant's eye and Ethiopian sage. The path leads to **Pierre Fiche,** probably a prehistoric standing stone, which stood 7m/23ft high before it was broken. *A booklet containing explanations about the trail is on sale in the Maison de l'Artisanat in Ville-Vieille.*

▶ *Follow D 5.*

Note the **church** doorway, with its arches resting on carved heads, and the lovely sundial decorating the bell-tower.

The road rises along the north-facing slope covered with larches, offering a fine downstream view of the Guil Valley. Beyond a hairpin bend, it enters the Aigue Blanche Valley overlooked by the densely forested slopes of the Sommet Bucher.

At the exit of the Prats Ravine, note the **Demoiselle coiffée** (🐾 *see Lac de SERRE-PONÇON,* 3*),* a strange rock formation showing above the larches on the opposite slope. The end of the Aigue Blanche Valley is closed off by the Tête de Longet.

La Rua

Go through the village *(narrow street)* and admire the typical architecture of the St-Véran area including a few traditional mayes (barns entirely built with beams roughly joined together and covered with laths).

Église St-Romain-de-Molines★

Below the village to the right, this isolated church, rebuilt in the 15C, comprises a massive nave and an amazing campanile, next to a tiny enclosed cemetery. Inside, there is a wealth of Baroque decoration; note the imposing altarpiece, framed by twisted columns adorned with vine leaves and surmounted by a broken pediment. The chancel vaulting, restored in the 19C, is decorated with stucco work.

Molines-en-Queyras★ – 👤 *See MOLINES-EN-QUEYRAS.*

The road continues to climb through a lovely pastoral landscape, and the houses of St-Véran suddenly appear, scattered over the sunny side of the valley.

St-Véran★★ – 👤 *See ST-VÉRAN.*

③ Haut Queyras

From Château-Queyras to the Monte Viso Belvedere
30km/18.6mi – about 1hr

This itinerary takes you through the most open and most pleasant part of the Guil Valley, between Château-Queyras and Abriès, and offers splendid views of Monte Viso.

▶ *From Château-Queyras, follow D 947 towards Abriès.*

The road runs up the Guil Valley, densely forested with larches and pines on the north-facing side. There is a clear **view** ahead towards the heights lining the Italian border with the Bric Bouchet (alt 3 216m/10 551ft) soaring above.

Aiguilles★

Lying in pleasant surroundings and enjoying an exceptionally fine climate, Aiguilles is the liveliest resort of the Queyras region. The nearby larch woods are charming and, in winter, the sun shines generously on the ski runs. A large number of local inhabitants emigrated to South America at the beginning of the 19C; most of them came back at the end of the century, having made their fortune across the Atlantic (⊙ see BARCELONNETTE). They had sumptuous houses built in a style which was fashionable in large urban areas at the time. The best examples are: the town hall, the Château Margnat (on D 947) and above all the luxurious Villa Challe. Note also the amazing "Maison Eiffel," built entirely of metal for the 1898 Bordeaux Exhibition, but despite the name, not actually the work of Gustave Eiffel.

Beyond Aiguilles, note the contrast between the barren south-facing slope and the densely forested north-facing slope, the forêt de Marassan.

Abriès – ⊙ See ABRIÈS.

▶ *Continue along D 947.*

The Guil Valley turns southwest and the landscape becomes more austere.

L'Échalp

This is the last village in the valley and the starting point for excursions to the Monte Viso belvederes. 🚶 The hike to the **Chalets de la Médille**★ *(1hr 30min there and back on foot)*, affords a fine view of Monte Viso; take the first bridge over the Guil upstream of L'Échalp and follow the path which rises towards the Plateau de la Médille, a charming meadow surrounded by larches.

The road continues up the Guil Valley, which becomes narrower, passing near a huge rock, known as Kids **"La Roche écroulée,"** (⊙ *July to Aug: 1-5pm - ☎ 04 92 46 88 20.)* used for rock-climbing practice. The road is closed to traffic at the point where it crosses the Guil.

▶ 🚶 *Leave the car in the car park and continue on foot, in order to get a close-up view of the rocky ridge of Monte Viso. Mountain hiking enthusiasts can make a round tour via the Grand Belvédère, the Lac Lestio and the Refuge du Viso. A shorter and easier itinerary leads to the Petit Belvédère and the Pré Michel Nature trail. For other hiking possibilities, ⊙ see ABRIÈS.*

Petit Belvédère du mont Viso and Sentier écologique du Pré Michel★

🚶 *45min on foot and 1hr on the site. The Information Centre near the car park sells a booklet describing the nature trail.*

In addition to the view of Monte Viso, a great variety of plant and flower species are in bloom between late June and early August, including the martagon lily, delphinium and fritillary.

Hike to the Grand Belvédère, the Lac Lestio and the Refuge du Viso★★

5hr 30min there and back. Difference in altitude: about 700m/2 297ft. This round tour is varied and pleasant but does not offer outstanding panoramas.

🚶 You will reach the Grand Belvédère after 1hr 45min walk along a landscaped path (explanatory tables) running parallel to the road. From there the **view**★ extends to

Monte Viso (alt 3 841m/12 602ft) across the Italian border, which seems to close off the upper end of the Guil Valley.

After climbing for a while, take a path on the right which follows the stream. This easy itinerary is recognisable by the yellow markings along the way; after joining the path leading to the refuge and crossing the stream, one reaches the **Lac Lestio** (2 510m/8 235ft).

Retrace your steps and follow the path identified by red and blue markings, which leads to the refuge with a **view**★ of Monte Viso; go back along the road to the Grand Belvédère and the car park.

4 Arvieux Valley

From Château-Queyras to Brunissard *10km/6.2mi – about 1hr*

This valley is also on the Route de l'Izoard itinerary (*see Le BRIANÇONNAIS, 5*).

Château-Queyras★ – *See CHÂTEAU-QUEYRAS.*

▶ *2km beyond Château-Queyras, turn right onto D 902 towards the Col d'Izoard.*

Arvieux
This village and the surrounding hamlets are interesting for their traditional architecture represented by **arcaded houses** covered with larch shingles. Owing to its pleasant climate, Arvieux has become a lively summer resort and winter sports centre.

The 16C **church** has retained an 11C porch and doorway; note the naive-style carvings decorating the capitals.

La Chalp
Kids Situated above Arvieux, this village has been a toy making centre since the 1920s, set up to give inhabitants a trade to follow in winter; the wooden toys are decorated by hand (*see Introduction: Handicraft*). The cooperative centre offers a museum, demonstrations, and a boutique where you can purchase local products. *July to Aug: daily 9am-7pm; winter: daily 9am-12.30pm, 2-6.30pm, Sat opens at 10am, Sun and public holidays 2-6.30pm.* ☎ 04 92 46 73 86 - www.alpinchezlui.com

Brunissard
An interesting wooden campanile rises above village oven.

RIEZ

POPULATION 1 667
MICHELIN MAP 334 E10

Many historical paths have crossed at Riez: first a Celtic settlement, then a Roman colonial town. The foundation of a bishopric in the 5C, which survived until the Revolution, made Riez an economic as well as a religious force in the region. From here, every road leads out into the Parc naturel régional du Verdon; the Lac de Ste-Croix and the famous Verdon gorges are almost on the doorstep. *4, allée Louis Gardiol – 04500 Riez* *July to mid-Sept: daily 9am-1pm, 3-7pm, Sun 9am-noon; rest of year: daily except Sunday 8.30am-noon, 1.30-5pm -* *04 92 77 99 09 - www. ville-riez.fr –* *Guided tours on request from the tourist office.*

▸ **Orient Yourself:** This ancient town, overlooked by Mont St-Maxime, lies at the confluence of the River Auvestre and the River Colostre, between Gréoux-les-Bains, 20km/12.5mi to the southeast, and Moustier Ste-Marie, 15km/9.4mi to the northeast.

🙂 **Don't Miss:** The old town, today typically Provençal, has many traces of ancient Celtic, Roman and medieval construction.

🕐 **Organizing Your Time:** You will need at least two hours to see the town.

Kids Especially for Kids: At Quinson, the Musée de la Préhistoire des Gorges du Verdon, tells how the very earliest people in Europe lived; the Maison de l'Abeille et de la Truffe offers demonstrations of bee-keeping that thrill most children.

⚲ **Also See:** Nearby Sights: CASTELLANE, Vallée de la Moyenne DURANCE, FORCALQUIER, GRÉOUX-LES-BAINS, MANOSQUE, MOUSTIERS-STE-MARIE, Lac de STE-CROIX, Plateau de VALENSOLE, Grand Canyon du VERDON

Walking Tour

Old town★

Start from place Javelly or place du Quinconce, shaded by plane trees, and enter the old town through the 13C **Porte Aiguière**. Grand-Rue, the former main street, is lined with splendidly decorated houses: a corbelled house (no1), 16C **Hôtel de Mazan** (no12) with fine stucco work on the staircase, lovely façade decorated with twin windows (no25), windows surrounded by moulded friezes (no27). As you reach the 14C **Porte St-Sols**, turn right towards rue St-Thècle; a tiny square on the left

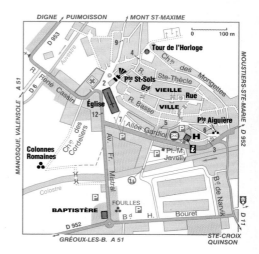

RIEZ	
Bouteuil Pl. E.	2
Colonne Pl. de la	3
Horloge R. de l'	4
Marché R. du	5
Pte-Aiguière R.	6
Quinconce Pl. du	7
St-Sébastien R. du Fg	9
Verdun Av. de	12

For coin categories, see the Legend on the cover flap.

WHERE TO STAY

🥄 Chambre d'hôte Le Vieux Castel

1 Rte des Châteaux–04500 Roumoules - 4km NE of Riez, Rte de Moustiers by D 952, edge of Roumoules - ☎ 04 92 77 75 42-http://vieuxcastel.free.fr - ⌁ - 5rms. This 17C estate once belonged to faïence-makers from Moustiers. Elegant rooms have plaster detailing and classic stenciling on the walls.

🥄🥄🥄 Chambre d'hôte Le Château d'Allemagne-en-Provence – *04500 Allemagne-en-Provence - ☎ 04 92 77 46 78 - www.chateaucountry.com – closed 1 Nov-15 Mar - ⌁ - 3rms.* You will be delighted by the large guestrooms furnished with character. In an annex, there are furnished apartments, as well as a swimming pool.

offers an interesting view of what remains of the town walls and of the **Tour de l'Horloge.** The **town hall** is housed in the former bishop's palace.

▸ *Go back to the church past the Porte St-Sols.*

Church

Rebuilt during the 19C, it has retained the bell-tower and apsidal chapels of the 15C cathedral.

Sights

Baptistère★

🔊 *Guided tours (30 min) mid-June to mid-Sept: Tue, Fri and Sat at 6pm; rest of year: tours on request at tourist office. 2€, children under 12 years no charge - ☎ 04 92 77 99 09.*
This is one of the few Merovingian buildings still standing in France. It probably dates from the 5C, but its cupola was rebuilt in the 12C. The square edifice comprises an octagonal room with four radiating chapels. Eight granite columns with marble Corinthian capitals form a circle round the christening font which has almost entirely disappeared.
A museum displays finds excavated on the site: altars, Roman inscriptions, sarcophagi, mosaics etc. Part of the Gallo-Roman town and the foundations of a cathedral dating from the 5C have been excavated opposite the baptistery.

Roman columns

Four beautiful granite columns, surmounted by white-marble Corinthian capitals and supporting an architrave, stand 6m/20ft high in a meadow. It is all that remains of a late 1C temple, believed to have been dedicated to Apollo.

Nearby Sights

Allemagne-en-Provence

12km/7.5mi northeast along D 952. A fine Renaissance **castle** ★(🕐 *Guided tours (1hr) July to mid-Sept: daily except Mon at 4 and 5pm; Apr to June and mid-Sept to mid-Nov: Sat-Sun and public holidays at 4 and 5pm. 6€, children 12-18 years old 3€- ☎ 04 92 77 46 78),* restored in the 19C, stands beside the River Colostre. The crenellated 12C keep was remodelled in the 16C and mullioned windows, surmounted by carved gables, were opened. The great hall, in Renaissance style, has a monumental **fireplace**★ decorated with gypsum carvings and framed by two mythological characters: Hercules and Minerva. Note the fine **spiral staircase** linking the medieval and Renaissance wings. Part of the park is laid out as a medieval herb garden.

The "Black Gold" of Haute-Provence

There are two kinds of truffle, known as **rabasse** in Provençal dialect.

The white truffle, picked in the spring, has little culinary value; it is used to train truffle hounds.

The rarer and tastier black truffle is gathered in December; it is used to enhance the taste of dishes and sauces.

Truffles, which are buried beneath oak and hazelnut trees, are the signs of a disease in these trees. Nowadays, the harvest takes place in fields containing trees which favour the growth of these sought-after mushrooms.

Montagnac, near Riez, is a famous centre of production in the Haute-Provence region.

Kids Maison de l'Abeille et de la truffe *2km/1.2mi northeast on the Puimoisson road.* ◷ *Guided tours (30 min) July to Aug: daily except Sun and Mon 10am-noon, 3-7pm; Mar to June and Sept to Oct: daily except Sun and Mon 3-7pm.* ◷ *closed public holidays. No charge -* ☎ *04 92 77 84 15.*
A bee-keeper and lavender-grower presents an exhibition about bee-keeping: the life of a bee (5 weeks in summer), what goes on inside a beehive (which houses as many as 50 000 working bees), the honey harvest (about 12kg/26lb per beehive) and the conditioning of honey to be sold. *Tasting and sale on the premises.*

Kids Musée de la Préhistoire des gorges du Verdon★ **at Quinson**
21km/13mi south on the D 11 ⅷ ◷ *July to Aug: daily 10am-8pm; Apr to June and Sept: daily except Tue 10am-7pm; Feb to Mar and Oct to mid-Dec: daily except Tue 10am-6pm* ◷ *closed 15 Dec through Jan. 7€, children 6-18 years 5€ -* ☎ *04 92 74 09 59 - www. museeprehistoire.com*
No dinosaurs here, but lots of cavemen. This impressive modern building, designed by Sir Norman Foster, expresses the aesthetics of Provençal architecture through an enormous curving stone wall which folds into the museum itself. The history of our distant ancestors is retraced, starting with their first appearance in Europe, up to the days of the Romans. Several dioramas, a dramatic film and a reconstructed prehistoric village★ (*on the banks of the Verdon, follow the signs "Parking du musée*) will fascinate children and adults alike.

Excursion

Mont St-Maxime
2km/1.2mi northeast along rue du Faubourg-St-Sébastien.
This 636m/2 087ft-high hill is a familiar landmark in the Riez area. The **Chapelle St-Maxime** has retained its Romanesque apse: the ambulatory is lined with six beautiful Corinthian columns, clearly taken from a much older building. From the shaded terrace in front of the chapel, the **panorama**★ extends over part of Riez, the Valensole Plateau, the Préalpes de Castellane, the Plans de Canjuers, the hills of the Haut Var area, the Luberon and the Montagne de Lure.

LA ROCHE-SUR-FORON ★

POPULATION 7 116
MICHELIN MAP 328 K4

This town of Reblochon, Beaufort and Tomme cheeses has a thousand year-old city at its centre. An important crossroads above the lower Arve Valley, La Roche-sur-Foron belonged to the Genevan nobility in the 11C and came to be as important as Geneva or Annecy in the 14C, becoming a Savoyard posession one hundred years later. In 1885, La Roche-sur-Foron was the first European town to enjoy electric lighting; a plaque in the castle park commemorates the event.

🛈 *place Andrevedan – 74800 La Roche-sur-Foron* 🕐 *June-Sept: Mon-Sat 9am-noon, 2-6pm(Sat 5.30), Sun office at Tour des Comtes de Genève is open 2-6.30pm; Oct-May: 8.30am-noon, 2-6pm, Sat 8.30-noon,* 🕐 *closed Sun in winter, 1 Jan, Easter Mon, 1 and 8 May, 11 Nov, 25 Dec -* ☎ *04 50 03 36 68 - www.larochesurforon.com. Guided tours of the town(1hr30min) July to Aug: Tue-Sun 2.30pm.4.50€ - Contact the tourist office.*

▸ **Orient Yourself:** This is a major road and railway hub located near Geneva (30min away), Bonneville and Annecy (15min away) on A 40 and A 41.

☺ **Don't Miss:** In the town, the Plain-Château district with its 16C and 17C houses is of interest. In the lovely countryside, you will find marked hiking trails.

Kids **Especially for Kids:** They will enjoy the Gorges du Bronze and the Mont-Saxonnex promentory.

👌 **Also See:** Nearby Sights: ANNECY, Lac d'ANNECY, Massif des ARAVIS, La CLUSAZ, CLUSES, Les GETS, MORZINE, ST-GERVAIS-LES-BAINS, Bassin de SALLANCHES, SAMOËNS, THONON-LES-BAINS, THORENS-GLIÈRES, YVOIRE

Old Town ★★ *1hr 30min*

A walk through the medieval town leads past many houses with ogee-arched mullioned windows. This charming district is being carefully restored; several houses and public buildings have been repainted with bright colours, in typical Piedmontese style.
The Plain-Château district is accessible from place St-Jean.

▸ *Follow rue des Fours on the left of the church to reach the tower.*

Go through the Porte Falquet into the school yard. The entrance to the tower is at the end, on the right.

Tour des comtes de Genève
🕐 *Mid-July to late Aug: Mon-Fri 2-6.30pm, Sat-Sun 10am-noon, 2-6.30pm; mid-June to mid-July, late Aug to mid-Oct: Sat-Sun 2-6.30pm. 2€ -* ☎ *04 50 25 82 29 - www.larochesurforon.com.*

The tower is all that remains of the castle of the counts of Geneva, built on the rocky spur which gave the town its name.
On the way down, take **rue du Plain-Château** (on the right) and admire the carved façades of the 17C houses; note in particular the **Maison des Chevaliers** (1565), once home to an order of knights founded by Amedée VI of Savoy.

For coin categories, see the Legend on the cover flap

WHERE TO STAY
🍽🍽 **Hôtel Le Foron** – *ZI du Dragiez -* ☎ *04 50 25 82 76 - www.hotel-le-foron.com - closed 15 Dec-15 Jan and Sun evening-* 🅿 *- 26rms.* On the outskirts of town, functional and soundproofed rooms.

▷ *Turn right at the end of the street towards the Château de l'Échelle.*
Retrace your steps and walk down rue du Cretet beyond the Porte St-Martin (remains of the 13C wall).

There are a couple of interesting houses in rue du Silence, in particular no30. Walk round the church and onto rue des Halles; a **stone bench** dating from 1558 has three **grain measures,** for 20, 40 and 80l/4.4, 8.8 and 17.6gal.

Église St-Jean-Baptiste

The arms of the counts of Geneva can be seen above the doorway of this early 12C church, surmounted by an onion-shaped steeple dating from the 19C which replaced the one destroyed in 1793. The chancel and the apse are Romanesque.
In rue Perrine, note the **Maison Boniface** (no79) in Renaissance style and the emblazoned lintels inside the courtyard. The picturesque halle aux grains (corn exchange), known as **"La Grenette,"** is near the town hall.
Walk onto the Pont-Neuf in order to admire the fine view of the Foron overlooked by terraced gardens.

Excursion

Le Salève★

The tiered cliffs of Mont Salève, towering above Geneva on the French side of the border, are one of the favourite haunts of Swiss tourists, especially rock-climbers. A road following the ridge leads past the main peaks: the Petit Salève, the Grand Salève and the Grand Piton, the highest of the three at 1 380m/4 528ft. All along the way, the route offers splendid views of the Arve Valley and the Faucigny heights to the east with the Mont Blanc Massif in the distance, and of Geneva and its lake to the west with the Jura mountains in the background.

Les Treize Arbres viewpoint★★

Follow the road from the hotel car park. 15min there and back on foot along the D 41.
Splendid **view** of the peaks between the Dents du Midi and Mont Blanc. The edge of the rock is a favourite spot for hangliders.

③ Route de Mont-Saxonnex★

From La Roche-sur-Foron to Cluses *36km/22.4mi – about 1hr 30min – local map see Cluses*

▷ *Drive east along N 203.*

Bonneville

The former capital of the Faucigny region is today an administrative centre, situated at a tourist-road junction and at the confluence of the River Borne and River Arve. A column, standing at the entrance of the bridge across the Arve, commemorates the harnessing of this mighty stream in the early 19C on the initiative of Charles-Félix, king of Sardinia, whose family ruled the Savoie until 1860.

▷ *From Bonneville, drive east along N 205; after crossing the motorway, turn right towards Mont-Saxonnex then right again to Brizon. Leave the car near a sharp bend to the right.*

Point de vue de Brizon ★

From the viewpoint at the side of the road, there is a bird's-eye view of the Gorges du Bronze with the Môle summits and Pointe de Marcelly in the distance across the Arve Valley.

▶ *Return to the Mont-Saxonnex road.*

Gorges du Bronze

Leave the car 100m/109yd beyond the first of four hairpin bends and climb onto a rock overlooking the deep wooded ravine.

Mont-Saxonnex ★

Kids This summer resort, popular for its high position overlooking the Arve Valley *(more than 500m/1 640ft above the river bed)*, includes two main villages: **Le Bourgeal** nestling below the church and **Pincru** at the beginning of the Gorges du Bronze. There are many easy hikes in this area, including a 2hr walk to **Lac Bénit**. Leave the car in front of the church and walk round the east end for a bird's-eye **view**★★ of the confluence of the Arve and Giffre.

After a dizzying view down to the Arve plain, the road runs through a wooded area and joins D 4 before passing a number of small metalworking workshops and finally reaching Cluses.

ST-ÉTIENNE-DE-TINÉE ★

POPULATION 1 528
MICHELIN MAP 341 C2

This charming Alpine town in the heart of the Mercantour region was rebuilt after a devastating fire which occurred in 1929. In summer, St-Étienne-de-Tinée is the ideal starting point of very interesting hikes, in particular from the Route de la Bonette. In winter, it offers a small **ski area** – highest point: **Cime de la Berchia**, alt 2 274m/7 461ft – linked to that of Auron by cable car and chairlift. *1 rue des Communes de France – 06660 St-Étienne -de-Tinée daily 9am-noon, 2-5.30pm - ☎ 04 93 02 41 96 - www.auron.com*

▶ **Orient Yourself:** Saint-Étienne-de-Tinée lies on the banks of a fast-flowing river, in a pleasant setting of pastures and terraced fields surrounded by mountains. Many people here still speak a Provençal dialect, called "gavot."

🕐 **Organizing Your Time:** If you visit the town and take one of the suggested walks, you'll need a whole day.

🕭 **Also See:** Nearby Sights: AURON, BARCELONNETTE, BEUIL, Route de la BONETTE, Gorges du CIANS, ISOLA 2000, Vallée de la TINÉE, L'UBAYE, VAL-D'ALLOS

Sights

Church

The most striking feature is the 4-tiered **steeple**★ in Lombard Romanesque style, surmounted by a tall octagonal stone spire surrounded by four gargoyled pinnacles; the date inscribed on the base of the steeple is 1492. Inside, the high altar in gilded wood bears the mark of Spanish influence; note, on the left, some carved wood panels depicting scenes of Christ's life surrounding a statue of the Virgin Mary with Child.

The Chapels

(*☞ guided tours by appointment at the tourist office - ☎ 04 93 02 41 96)* Well-preserved frescoes by Baleison and Canavesio in the **Chapelle St-Sébastien** include the creation of Adam and Eve on the vaulting, Jesus between the two thieves on the back wall and scenes from the life of St Sebastian on the right. The **Chapelle St-Michel** contains a small museum devoted to the penitent orders. The **Chapelle des Trinitaires**, which belonged to the former monastery (now a school), is decorated with fine carved wood panels 17C frescoes, including one showing the battle of Lepanto and two paintings depicting the life of the monks who used to buy back Christians enslaved on the Barbary Coast. The **Chapelle St-Maur** *(2km along the road to Auron – As for the other chapels.)* was decorated in the 15C with picturesque frescoes depicting the legends of St Maur and St Sebastian.

Three small museums illustrate aspects of traditional life (*🕐 guided tours (30 min): by appointment at the tourist office).* The **Musée des Traditions ,** housed in the former village bakery, explains the process of making rye bread and the **Musée du Lait** displays the equipment used in cheese-making. Finally, the **Musée de l'École** tells about school life in past days.

🚶 Hikes

There are numerous possibilities starting from St-Étienne-de-Tinée or Auron. A wide choice of itineraries is available from the tourist office in both resorts.

Starting from Le Pra

The Lacs de Vens★★
Leave the car in Le Pra, on the road to La Bonette (10km/6.2mi north of St-Étienne-de-Tinée). 6hr on foot via the Col de Fer. Difference in altitude: about 940m/3 084ft. Easy but long and taxing itinerary.

🚶 The path goes through a larch forest to reach the Plateau de Morgon *(after 1hr)* then past waymark no 33 to the Tortisse forest lodges. From there it is possible to go straight to the Refuge de Vens, but the detour via the **Col de Fer** (alt 2 584m/8 478ft) is recommended for the **view**★ it offers, even if the additional distance demands extra strength.

Lacs de Vens

Well-equipped hikers, who do not suffer from vertigo, can climb up to the Cime de Fer (alt 2 700m/8 858ft; *add 35min there and back on foot*), where a splendid **panorama**★★ includes Mont Vallonnet and the Lacs de Vens in the foreground, the road to the Col de Larche and the Tête de Moïse Summit further north.

From the Col de Fer, the path leads to the refuge and **Lacs de Vens**★★. The reflection of the mountains and of the sky in the clear waters of the lakes enhances the beauty of the landscape. Skirt the first lake and part of the second then turn right beyond a pile of huge rocks. The path divides several times; keep left every time in order to reach the top of the ridge. On the other side there is a splendid **view**★ of the Cime de la Bonette and Crête de la Blanche.

Go up the path, running just below, to waymark 23 and turn towards Le Pra. The path runs along the mountain slope in a splendid **setting**, then down to the Tortisse forest lodges. From there, retrace your steps to Le Pra.

Hike to the Refuge de Rabuons★★

This extension of the previous hike includes a night in the Refuge des Lacs de Vens. About 5hr on foot. Marked itinerary.

🚶 The main purpose in combining these hikes is to link the two highest mountain refuges in the Parc national du Mercantour along a route which overlooks the Tinée Valley and offers a succession of superb panoramic views. Walk along the right side of the middle and lower lakes, cross a footbridge then climb up to the Crête des Babarottes. On the way down, follow part of the *"Chemin de l'énergie"* to the Lac de Rabuons and the refuge of the same name.

The **"Chemin de l'énergie"** was built in the 1930s at high altitude, through very uneven terrain with retaining walls and tunnels, in order to supply a power station in St-Étienne-de-Tinée which was never completed.

Starting from the Camp des Fourches

The Pas de la Cavale★★

Alt 2 671m/8 763ft. *Leave the car at the Camp des Fourches, on the road to La Bonette (🕯 see Route de la BONETTE) and walk to the Col des Fourches (5min). Climbing boots recommended. 3hr 30min there and back on foot. Difference in altitude: about 750m/2 461ft.*

🚶 Walk down a narrow path, marked in white and red, to an old shack just below the Salso Moreno Cirque. The austere yet splendid landscape is very interesting from a geological point of view: sink-holes have resulted from the action of water and snow erosion. Colonies of marmots inhabit the area.

From waymark 37 onwards, the stony, slippery path climbs steadily to the Pas de la Cavale framed by the Rocher des Trois Évêques and the Tête Carrée. The **view**★★ embraces the Lacs d'Agnel, the heights lining the Italian border and the Auron ski area to the south, the Vallon du Lauzanier and the Brec de Chambeyron to the north. The Lac de Derrière la Croix lies just below.

ST-GERVAIS-LES-BAINS✢✢

POPULATION 5 276

MICHELIN MAP 328 N5 – LOCAL MAP SEE MASSIF DU MONT-BLANC

St-Gervais-les-Bains occupies one of the most open sites in the Alps, at the meeting point of the Autoroute Blanche and where the Val Montjoie widens out into the Sallanches Basin. Known for more than a century for its hot springs, the spa town is now regarded as the main health resort in the Mont-Blanc Massif and is sometimes called St-Gervais-Mont-Blanc. It welcomes children and is the starting point for many drives and cable-car rides offering outstanding views of the Mont-Blanc Massif. Mountaineers traditionally start the ascent of Mont Blanc from St-Gervais, via the Tramway du Mont Blanc, Tête Rousse and the Aiguille du Goûter. Finally, owing to its position at the centre of the network of cable cars and mountain railways linking Megève to the Chamonix Valley via the Mont d'Arbois, the Col de Voza and Bellevue, the town, together with its high-altitude satellites of Le Bettex, Voza-Prarion and St-Nicolas-de-Véroce, has become an important ski resort. *▌ 43 rue du Mont-Blanc – 74170 St-Gervais-les-Bains ◷ July to Aug: 9am-noon, 2-7pm; winter school holidays: 9am-8pm; outside school holidays: 9am-noon, 2-7pm; May to June and Sept to mid-Dec: Mon-Sat 9am-noon, 2-6pm ◷ closed 1 May - ☎ 04 50 47 76 08 - www.st-gervais.net*

▶ **Orient Yourself:** The hot springs are found at Le Fayet, exit 21 on A 40, but the town of St-Gervais is 4km/2.5mi off A 40 on D 902.

⊛ **Don't Miss:** You can tour the many Baroque sites in the area.

◷ **Organizing Your Time:** This is a good base from which to organize excursions to the many surrounding attractions.

Kids Especially for Kids: In bad weather, you can take children to the huge skating ring at St-Gervais. In nice weather, they can enjoy the Pontet recreation area at Contamines-Montjoie.

⚏ **Also See:** Nearby Sights: Massif des ARAVIS, ARGENTIÈRE, CHAMONIX-MONT-BLANC, CLUSES, Les CONTAMINES-MONTJOIE, Les HOUCHES, MEGÈVE, Massif du MONT-BLANC, LA-ROCHE-SUR-FORON, Bassin de SALLANCHES

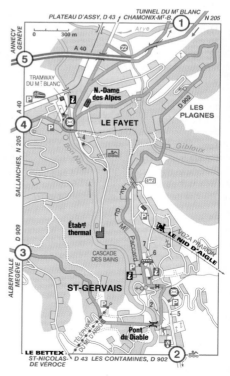

ST-GERVAIS-LES-BAINS	
Comtesse R.	2
Gontard Av.	4
Miage Av. de	5
Mont-Blanc R. et jardin du	6
Mont-Lachat R. du	7

St-Gervais

The town nestles round its church, on the last gentle slopes of the Val Montjoie above the wooded gorge through which flows the River Bon Nant, spanned here by the **Pont du Diable.** Looking up the valley from the bridge, there is a clear view of Mont Joly, Mont Tondu and the Dômes de Miage framing the Val Montjoie; downriver, the view extends to the escarpments of the Chaîne des Fiz (Pointe and Désert de Platé).

Le Fayet

This is the spa district. The **Établissement thermal** (hydrotherapy centre) is situated at the exit of the Bon Nant Gorge, inside a park with a lovely waterfall. The waters are used for the treatment of skin diseases and respiratory complaints. The local church, the **Église Notre-Dame-des-Alpes,** was designed in 1938 by Maurice Novarina; it is a good example of religious art at that time.

Excursions

Le Bettex★★★

8km/5mi along D 909 to Megève, then left along D 43 to Le Bettex. Instead of driving, you can also reach Le Bettex from St-Gervais by the **Mont d'Arbois cable car.** At

Address Book

For coin categories, see the Legend on the cover flap.

EATING OUT

Le Refuge du Boulanger – *85 av du Mont-Paccard - ☎ 04 50 93 61 29 - closed Tue out of season.* This tearoom-bakery is a stone's throw from the tourist office. In a setting of wood and brick, you will enjoy daily specials, salads, sandwiches, and a range of light meals, plus delicious pastries.

Auberge de Bionnassay – *3084 rte de Bionnassay - 3.5km/2mi S of St-Gervais towards Les Contamines then Bionnay - ☎ 04 50 93 45 23 - closed Oct-May, Mon in June and Sept.* This inn and farm dating from 1810 stands at a crossroads and is an ideal stopping place for hikers. The pleasant interior, with its small stable, reflects the charm of life in the mountains in years gone by.

Lou Grangni – *50 r. de la Vignette, 3e Fayet exit off highway, towards St-Gervais - ☎ 04 50 47 76 39 - closed 15 May-15 Jun, 15 Nov-15 Dec and Tue out of season .* Behind the timber façade of this restaurant in the centre of town you can watch the chef at work.Discover the joys of regional dishes or enjoy a more classic meal, but don't count the calories!

WHERE TO STAY

Hôtel Deux Gares –*74190 Le Fayet - ☎ 04 50 78 24 75 - www.hotel2gares. com - closed 23 Apr-1 May, 24 Sept-1 Oct and 29 oct-17 Dec -* 📛 *- 28rms -* restaurant. Just opposite the station for the famous Mont-Blanc tramway, this hotel has small, plain rooms; those in the annex have pretty wood carving. Nice covered swimming pool.

Hôtel Chez la Tante – *On Mont-d'Arbois via cable-car at the upper station (access on foot) - 74190 Le Fayet - ☎ 04 50 21 31 30 - chezlatante@wanadoo. fr - closed May-June and Oct-14 Dec - 26rooms half-pension.* Perched at 1 850m/6 070ft above sea level, this chalet offers a unique panorama of the Mont-Blanc range. You are guaranteed a breath of really fresh air in this magnificent site. Access via cable car and tracked vehicle, on skis or on foot. Accommodation is simple, as is the food.

LEISURE

Les Thermes de St-Gervais – *74190 Le Fayet - ☎ 04 50 47 54 54 - www.thermes-st-gervais.fr* You can try a range of spa and beauty treatments at the heart of Mont-Blanc, besides the traditional "cure."

Le Bettex you will have extremely varied views of the Mont Blanc, Fiz and Aravis massifs. You can then continue by cable car up to the **Mont d'Arbois**★★★ (alt 1 827m/5 994ft, viewing table) for an even finer **panoramic view.**

(🕐 *Mid-June to first week Sept and mid-Dec to mid-Apr:St Gervais-Le Bettex: 9am-12.30pm, 2-6pm; Le Bettex-Mt d'Arbois: 9am-12.45pm, 2-5.45pm (15min, every 30min). Both stages (St Gervais to Mt d'Arbois) 13.50€ return; 2nd stage only (Bettex to Mt d'Arbois) 8.50€ return -* ☎ *04 50 93 11 87).*

Col de Voza

Alt 1 653m/5 423ft. *Journey from Le Fayet or St-Gervais-Ville to the Nid d'Aigle (3hr there and back - see below) aboard the* **Tramway du Mont-Blanc** 🕐 *July to 3rd week Aug: 7.45am-6.40pm; mid-Dec to Mar: confirm times by telephone -* ☎ *04 50 47 51 83 - www.compagniedumontblanc.com.*

The electric tram on its way to the Nid d'Aigle (see below) stops at the Col de Voza; halfway up the mountainside, above the Bionnassay Valley, there are splendid **views**★★ of the Mont Blanc Massif.

The Nid d'Aigle★★ (Glacier de Bionnassay)

Alt 2 286m/7 828ft. *Allow 3hr there and back by the Tramway du Mont-Blanc (see above).*

This journey provides a good introduction to high-altitude mountain landscapes by opening up the wild setting of the Bionnassay Glacier *(from the upper station, 1hr there and back on foot to the moraine)* stretched out at the foot of the Aiguilles de Bionnassay *(spectacular avalanches)* and of the Aiguille du Goûter. **View** of the massifs surrounding the Bassin de Sallanches.

Gorges de la Diosaz★

On its way to join the River Arve, the Diosaz flows through a famous gorge with a **succession of waterfalls**★★, particularly abundant in July and August, when the dam upstream opens its floodgates

The entrance of the gorge can be reached by car (1km/0.6mi) from Servoz. 🕐 *3rd week May to Aug: 9am-6pm; Sept: 9.30am-5pm. 4.50€, children under 5 years no charge -* ☎ *04 50 47 21 13*

The itinerary, which has been equiped for safe walking, follows a path and overhanging galleries to several waterfalls including the Cascade des Danses, the Cascade de Barme-Rousse and the triple Cascade de l'Aigle, the most impressive of them all. The galleries continue as far as the natural bridge formed by a rock which fell in the 16C and stuck inside a fissure from which springs the **Cascade du Soufflet.**

St-Nicolas-de-Véroce and excursions

12km/7.5mi along D 909 to Megève, then left along D 43. 🕐 *See Massif du MONT-BLANC.*

ST-JEAN-DE-MAURIENNE

POPULATION 8 902
MICHELIN MAP 89 FOLD 17 OR 244 FOLD 30

Did you know that three of St. John the Baptist's fingers are still proudly pre-served in St-Jean-de Maurienne? The historic capital of the Maurienne region, situated at the confluence of the River Arc and River Arvan, owes its development to its role as diocesan town until 1966. *Ancien Évêché, place de la Cathédrale – 73300 St-jean-de-Maurienne ◷ July to Aug: 8.30am-6.30pm; June and Sept: 9am-noon, 2-6pm; Nov to May: 9am-noon, 2-6pm (Sat 4.30pm) ◷closed Sun and public holidays - ☎ 04 79 83 51 51 - www.saintjeandemaurienne.com.*

▶ **Orient Yourself:** The A 43 takes you directly to the town. In summer, it is more pleasant to arrive through the St-Jean valley, either from the south by the col de la Croix-de-Fer or from the north from Moûtiers by the Col de la Madeleine.
⊘ **Don't Miss:** The carvings on the choir stalls in the St-Jean-Baptiste cathedral are celebrated.
◷ **Organizing Your Time:** You will need a half day to cross from the valley of the Arc River to that of the Isère by the Col de la Madeleine.
⌾ **Also See:** Nearby Sights: AUSSOIS, Route de la CROIX-DE-FER, Route du GALIBIER, Route de la MADELEINE, La Haute MAURIENNE, MODANE

Sights

A long-term project to restore the town's historic centre has been a visible success; typical alpine houses boast colourful façades and pretty doorways.

Cathédrale St-Jean-Baptiste

For guided tours, enquire at the tourist office - ☎ 04 79 83 51 52 An isolated square tower (11C-12C), which was the bell-tower of the Église Notre-Dame and was partly dismantled during the Revolution, stands in front of the cathedral.
The cathedral, dedicated to the city's patron saint and dating from the 11C and 15C, was built over a **crypt** excavated in 1958; it is preceded by a peristyle built in 1771, beneath which stands a mausoleum dedicated to Humbert "White Hands," who

Opinel

Opinel – The Famous Knife from Savoie

At the end of the 19C, Joseph Opinel, a toolmaker from a nearby village, began to make folding pocket knives for his friends during the long winters. Opinel met with such success that he launched into the manufacture of knives in a big way and put the finishing touch to his prototype in 1890. Available in twelve different sizes, the knives sold well in local markets and fairs and soon became popular across the border in Italy and Switzerland. The Opinel trademark was added in 1905: the hand of St. John beneath a crown, symbolising loyalty to the house of Savoie, is also the insignia of the Canon of the cathedral. Chosen by the Museum of Modern Art in New York as a functional design classic, the knives are now pro-duced at Cognin, near Chambéry.

The misericords in the Cathédrale St-Jean-Baptiste are worth a closer look

founded the House of Savoie in the 11C. The interior, partly restored, contains some splendid 15C church furniture and two frescoes: one of them, on the north side, shows the Annunciation, the other, on the south side, depicts the Entombment. On the left-hand side of the apse is the **Ciborium**★, a delicate Flamboyant masterpiece carved in alabaster. Three of St John the Baptist's fingers used to be kept in the central recess (they are now in the vestry). The choir **stalls**★★ were carved between 1483 and 1498 by Pierre Mochet from Geneva; this superb piece of woodwork was restored in 1969. There are 43 high stalls and 39 low ones. The high backs are decorated with low-relief carvings depicting various saints whereas the backrests and misericords show a freer inspiration. There are two stalls under a baldaquin, near the high altar; the one on the right is the bishop's seat and the other is intended for the president of France, who is an honorary canon of the cathedral. On the north side of the church, the well-preserved 15C **cloister** has retained its original alabaster arches. A flight of steps in the south gallery leads to the crypt.

Musée Opinel
Avenue Henri-Falcoz   *Daily except Sun and public holidays 9am-noon, 2-7pm. No charge -* ☎ *04 79 64 04 78.*
The museum illustrates the history of the famous knives from Savoie produced by the Opinel dynasty of cutlers, who were natives of St-Jean-de-Maurienne.

Excursion

Route de la Toussuire★ *36km/22.4mi – allow 2hr*

▸ *From St-Jean, drive along D 926 then turn right towards La Toussuire.*

During the drive, the **Aiguilles d'Arves**★★ stand out from a broad horizon of mountains. The road rises above the St-Jean-de-Maurienne Basin offering bird's-eye views of the valley below.
The ancient hilltop village of **Fontcouverte**★ commands a panoramic view of the surrounding area. The ski area of **Le Corbier**, at the heart of the massif, is linked to that of the neighbouring resorts of **La Toussuire**, in a setting of barren slopes, and St-Sorlin-d'Arves. In all, 10 villages in the massif de l'Avan-Villards (1 100-2 600m/3 609-8 530ft) are included in the ski area of **Les Sybelles**, where there is

both downhill and cross-country skiing, as well as hiking in the summer (📍 ☎ 04 79 59 88 00 - www.les-sybelles.com)
On the way down to St-Jean-de-Maurienne, the road goes through **La Rochette;** note the isolated rock which gave its name to the hamlet.

ST-JULIEN-DU-VERDON ★

POPULATION 108
MICHELIN MAP 334 H9

A village which once clung to a hilltop now stands at the water's edge; a miracle worthy of St Julien himself, but one worked as part of the hydro-engineering project which saw the building of five dams in the space of 30 years and the creation of the Lac de Castillon. The hamlet at the foot of the white cliffs of Pinadoux is the perfect starting point for a tour of this remarkable man-made landscape. 📍 *Mairie – 04170 Saint-Julien-du-Verdon* 🕐 *Mon, Tue and Thur 8.30am-12.30pm, 1.30-7.30pm -* ☎ *04 92 89 05 82*

▶ **Orient Yourself:** At 900m/2 953ft, Saint-Julien sits on a little point of land spared from the flooding of the Lac de Castillon. It is 8km/5mi south of St-André-des-Alpes, from which you can return to Colmars following, in reverse, the excursion "Haute Vallée du Verdon."

🕐 **Organizing Your Time:** Give yourself a half-day to tour the lacs and the Route de Toutes Aures.

👌 **Also See:** Nearby Sights: ANNOT, BARGÈME, CASTELLANE, CLUES DE HAUT-PROVNCE, COLMARS, ENTREVAUX, Route NAPOLÉON, PUGET-THÉNIERS, Plateau de VALENSOLE, Grand Canyon du VERDON

Excursion

Lac de Castillon and Lac de Chaudanne ★

TOUR OF THE LAKES *47km/29.2mi – allow 3hr*
The road runs across the dam, then follows the right shore of the lake; a road to the left leads to the Col de Toutes Aures.

Barrage de Castillon
Stop by the belvedere to get a good view of the site; there are explanatory panels about the dam and the harnessing of the Verdon. This elegant arch dam is only 26m/85ft thick at the base. It is 200m/218yd long across the top and 100m/328ft high. The hydroelectric power station has a capacity of 77 million kWh.

Panorama from Blaron ★
Leave the car at the entrance to Blaron village and continue along the footpath (15min there and back). From the promontory there is a magnificent **view** of the Lac de Castillon, its tiny island and St-Julien-du-Verdon.

LEISURE

Base de loisirs Sirocco – *Lac de Castillon - le Cheiron -* ☎ *04 92 83 72 97 -* June to Aug: 9am-7pm. On the edge of the lake, this centre offers swimming, kayaking, canoeing and a picnic area. A snackbar is on site. The village **St-André-les-Alpes** has a famed hang-gliding centre, where you can watch spectacular flights.

> *Return to D 955 and continue along the edge of the lake.*

Castellane★ – 🕭 *see CASTELLANE*

St-Julien, now home to a water sports centre, is the only village on the slopes not to have been submerged by the flooding of the valley.

> *Go back along the same road and turn left onto D 102 towards Demandolx.*

The road rises in a series of hairpin bends. At the Croix de la Mission, there is a fine **view**★★ of the Lac de Castillon. On the way down towards the Lac de Chaudanne, there are bird's-eye **views**★★ of this dark green mountain lake.

Barrage de Chaudanne
The dam can no longer be visited due to security precautions. For information, contact ☎ *04 92 70 68 00.* This arch dam (total height 70m/230ft, length across the top 95m/104yd) is built across a gorge of the Verdon downstream from the Barrage de Castillon. The power station can produce 67 million kWh.

> *Return to St-Julien-du-Verdon by D 955.*

Route de Toutes Aures

FROM ST-JULIEN-DU-VERDON TO ENTREVAUX *30km/18.6mi – allow 1hr*
This road is a section of the "winter Alpine route" (N°202) linking the upper valleys of the River Verdon and the River Var.

> *From St-Julien, drive along N 202.*

Mountain streams, which are subject to fearsome spates, have cut across the barren plateaux at an angle to the mountain crests, carving deep valleys which often narrow to form wild gorges known as *"clues"* (🕭 *see CLUES DE HAUTE-PROVENCE).*

Clue de Vergons★
The road rises as it goes through the gorge, offering fine views of the lake and the lovely setting of St-Julien-du-Verdon.
The Romanesque **Chapelle Notre-Dame-de-Valvert** stands on the roadside just beyond Vergons.

Col de Toutes Aures
Alt 1 124m/3 688ft. Tilted rock strata – sometimes almost vertical – form a striking contrast with the forested slopes.

Clue de Rouaine★
The road runs between impressive cliffs.
Beyond Les Scaffarels, where one can see the famous Grès d'Annot (🕭 *see ANNOT),* the Coulomp Valley is deep and narrow, except where the river joins the Var (Pont de Gueydan). The road then follows the Var Valley, and the typically southern character of the arid landscape is enhanced by the Mediterranean sun.

Entrevaux★ – 🕭 *See ENTREVAUX.*

ST-PIERRE-DE-CHARTREUSE✳

POPULATION 770
MICHELIN MAP 333 H5 – LOCAL MAP SEE MASSIF DE LA CHARTREUSE

This charming resort sits in a peaceful valley surrounded by the soaring peaks of the Chartreuse Massif. In winter, there is fine skiing on the Scia, and in summer, 270km/168mi of marked paths lead out into beautiful forested landscapes.

▶ **Orient Yourself:** The village is easily accessible from Voiron or Grenoble. From Chambéry, you have to skirt the Chartreuse Massif on N 6, or you can cross the mountains on winding but very beautiful roads.

☺ **Don't Miss:** St-Hugues-de-Chartreuse is a major example of modern church architecture.

🕓 **Organizing Your Time:** Stop at the Belvédère des Sangles for a panoramic view of the Grande-Chartreuse monastery.

👒 **Also See:** Nearby Sights: ALLEVARD, CHAMBÉRY, Massif de CHAMROUSSE, Massif de la CHARTREUSE, GRENOBLE, Le GRÉSIVAUDAN, VIZILLE

The Town

The slopes of the Scia, at altitudes ranging between 900m/2 953ft and 1 800m/5 906ft, offer 35km/21.7mi of ski runs at all levels of difficulty, plus 80km/50mi of cross-country trails in St-Hugues. As well, many snowshoe hikes are organized around the area.

In summer, St-Pierre-de-Chartreuse is a popular touring and hiking base for excursions across the Chartreuse massif from Grenoble to Chambéry, across peaceful wooded countryside. The ascent of the **Dent de Crolles** or of **Mont Granier** is ideal for experienced hikers who do not suffer from vertigo.

There is a splendid **view**✳ of the elegant silhouette of Chamechaude (alt 2 082m/6 831ft) and of the rocky summit of the Pinea across the Col de Porte from the **Terrasse de la Mairie.**

Excursion

Église St-Hugues-de-Chartreuse

4km south. The 19C **church** (&🕓 Daily except Tue 10am-6pm. Guided tours (1hr) by appointment. 3.80€, children under 12 years no charge. 🕓 Closed 1 Jan and 1 May - ☎ 04 76 88 65 01 - www.arcabas.com.) looks quite ordinary from the outside, but, inside, the contemporary **sacred art**✳ with decoration in reds and golds is amazing; paintings, sculptures, stained glass and holy objects are all the work of a single artist, Jean-Marie Pirot Arcabas, who worked from 1953 to 1986.

For coin categories, see the Legend on the cover flap.

WHERE TO STAY AND EAT

⊖⊖**Hôtel Beau Site** - Pl. de l'Église - St-Pierre-de-Chartreuse - ☎ 04 76 88 61 34 - www.hotelbeausite.com closed 3-25 Apr and 18 Oct-19 Dec - 27rms - ⊖⊖ restaurant. The Sestier family has run this hotel opposite the church for four generations. The dining room has a view of the valley and forest. Ask for a room in the new section. Summer swimming pool.

Hikes

Grand Som★★

Alt 2 026m/6 647ft. *Difference in altitude: 1 175m/3 855ft. Taxing hike: 4hr ascent. The main interest of this itinerary lies in the panoramic view from the summit.*
From St-Pierre, drive west along D 520B for 3km/2mi; leave the car in the car park reserved for hikers of La Correrie .

Walk 300m/328yd back along the road and take the road on the right leading to the monastery, la Grande Chartreuse. Walk alongside it and turn right past a house on the left. The path leads to a calvary; climb to the top of the meadow on the edge of the forest. There is a fine **view** of the monastery.

Return to the road and continue in the direction of the Grand Som via the Col de la Ruchère. After walking for 30min and reaching two chapels, take the steep path *(marked in orange)* on the right; 15min later, turn right again onto a signposted path and shortly after that turn left onto a steep path leading to the Habert de Bovinan refuge *(45min)*. Continue until you reach the foot of the Grand Som. then take the path on the right marked with arrows painted on the rock. At the next intersection, take the stony path used by sheep. From the cross at the summit, there is a magnificent **panorama**★★★ of the whole Chartreuse Massif and a bird's-eye view of the monastery. Mont Blanc and the Belledonne range can just be seen on the eastern horizon.

Belvédère des Sangles★★

2km/1.2mi then 2hr 30min there and back on foot. Drive to La Diat and follow the road to St-Laurent-du-Pont. Leave the car beyond the bridge on the Guiers Mort, then cross back and take the Valombré Forest road.

It leads to the lovely **Prairie de Valombré** which offers the best **view**★ of the Grande Chartreuse Monastery, framed by the escarpments of the Grand Som on the right and the forested ridges of the Aliénard on the left.

The road ends at a roundabout. From there, a path climbs up to the **belvedere** overlooking the wooded gorge of the Guiers Mort.

Perquelin★

3km/2mi east. The path ends in the upper valley of the River Guiers Mort, beneath the escarpments of the Dent de Crolles.

The Scia★

*1hr 30min there and back, including a 45min ride on the **Essarts gondola and Scia chairlift** (Mid-Dec to Mar 9am-5pm Closed in summer.).*

It is easy to climb from the upper station of the second section of the gondola to the summit of the Scia (alt 1 782m/5 846ft), which offers a fine **panorama** of the Chartreuse, with the Taillefer, the Obiou and the Vercors to the south, the Dent du Chat and the Grand Colombier to the north.

ST-VÉRAN★★

POPULATION 267
MICHELIN MAP 334 J4
LOCAL MAP SEE LE QUEYRAS

St-Véran, lying at altitudes ranging from 1 990m/6 529ft to 2 040m/6 693ft, is the highest village in Europe. It owes its name to a 6C archbishop who is the hero of a local legend. **St Véran** is said to have fought and wounded a dragon which was terrorising the area. While the beast was flying off to Provence, 12 drops of blood dripped from its wounds. These later symbolised each of the places where shepherds used to stop when moving livestock from the Luberon to summer grazing in the Queyras. The houses are built in the midst of pastures on a gentle slope, which rises to 2 990m/9 810ft at its highest point, the **Pic de Châteaurenard**. In summer, the main attractions of St-Véran are the quality of its environment and the interesting hikes it offers. In winter, the resort's fairly easy and very sunny ski area is linked to that of Molines-en-Queyras. ▯ *05490 St-Véran* ⏰ *July to Aug: daily 9am-12.30pm, 2-6.30pm; rest of year: daily except Sun and school holidays 9am-12.30pm, 2-5.30pm -* ☎ *04 92 45 82 21.*

▶ **Orient Yourself:** At 2.5km/1.5mi outside of Château-Queyras, turn left on D 5 which will take you to St-Véran.

🅿 **Parking:** Traffic is banned in summer, except for temporary residents' vehicles, for which a disc must be obtained from the tourist office. There are several paying car parks at the entrance to the village.

🕐 **Organizing Your Time:** You'll need three hours to see the village and the Musée du Soum.

Kids **Especially for Kids:** Children will like the Musée du Soum.

⚓ **Also See:** Nearby Sights: ABRIÈS, BRIANÇON, Le BRIANÇONNAIS, CEILLAC, Route des GRANDES ALPES, GUILLESTRE, MOLINES-EN-QUEYRAS, MONT-DAUPHIN, Le QUEYRAS, VARS

St-Véran

G. Lucas/FOC.

🦢 Walking Tour

From June to the end of August, the road to the Chapelle Notre-Dame-de-Clausis is only open to the shuttle service vehicles *(paying)* and to ramblers.

The Italian border being quite close, hikers may wish to cross it and should therefore make sure they carry their identity papers at all times.

La Chalp and Le Raux

The two neighbouring hamlets are known locally for their handcrafted wooden furniture.

Old village★★

Built entirely of wood and stone, the village is considered one of the prettiest in France. Alpine farmhouses, facing south and built in a line stretching for 1km/0.6mi have long galleries in front of their storage lofts, where cereals go on ripening after the harvest. Each of St-Véran's six districts -- set well apart as a fire precaution -- has its own wooden fountain, *croix de la Passion* and communal oven. Many houses are decorated with elaborate sundials.

The road climbs up to the village square surrounded by the church, the town hall and the tourist office. The **church** at the centre of the cemetery dates from the 17C. The porch is supported by two columns resting on lions, which belonged to an earlier building. Inside, note the stone stoup, the 18C pulpit and the 17C **altarpiece**★ carved by Italian artists. The east-end wall is decorated with a sundial; its inscription, in the old dialect, celebrates "the highest village in which God's bread is eaten."

Sights

Musée du Soum★★

🕙 *July to mid-Sept: 10am-1pm, 2-8pm; mid-Sept to June: daily except Mon 2-5pm* 🕙 *closed Nov to mid-Dec. 3.80€, children 13-16 years 2.50€ - ☎ 04 92 45 86 42.*

On the right as you go in through the western car park. The name of the museum means "the end" (of one of the districts); built in 1641, this is the oldest house in the village.

The museum illustrates traditional life in St-Véran through a succession of rooms furnished in local style. It is representative of Haut Queyras houses, in spite of its typically local features: an outside pen for the household's pig; an inner courtyard floored with tree trunks and intended for cattle, and on the ground floor; a "shepherd's room" intended for seasonal workers, usually itinerant farmhands from Piedmont.

In the living room, note the box bed (1842) used by several members of the family, the fireplace – an unusual feature as the kitchen would normally be the only room to have a chimney – and the hay rack which is a reminder that humans and cattle cohabited in winter. Upstairs, the joiner's and the lapidary's workshops have been reconstructed.

Ancienne Maison traditionelle

🦢 *Guided tour (30 min) July to mid-Sept: 10am-1pm, 2-6pm; rest of year on request - ☎ 04 92 45 82 39. 2.50€, children 1.60€.*
Until 1976, the residents shared this house with their animals, in the traditional way. The members of the family who lived here guide visitors around their old home.

The Ibex in the Queyras

The ibex gradually disappeared from the Alps during the 17C. At the beginning of the 19C, there were fewer than 100 head in the Grand Paradisio Massif on the Italian side. The reintroduction of the ibex within the Parc naturel régional du Queyras took place in 1995 when 12 ibexes were transferred from the Parc national de la Vanoise. The animals are given electronic chips make it possible to locate them.

🥾 Hikes

Drive to the Col Agnel and hike to the Pain de Sucre★★★
Allow a minimum of 4hr.

🥾 Follow the 4km/2.5mi-long **Route des Amoureux**★ starting in St-Véran and offering views of the northern side of the Guil Valley overlooked by the Pic de Rochebrune. The road leads to Pierre Grosse. Turn right twice towards the Col Agnel *(for the rest of the itinerary, 👣 see MOLINES-EN-QUEYRAS).*

Chapelle Notre-Dame-de-Clausis
Alt 2 390m/7 841ft. *From June to Aug, road closed to motor vehicles. Access by shuttle (paying; The trip takes 20min then 15min on foot as the last section of the road is not suitable for wheeled vehicles) or on foot (3hr there and back).*

🥾 As the road runs past disused marble quarries and copper mines, spare a thought for the miners who worked here at high altitude, on meagre rations and who would get so covered in verdigris during their shift that they were known as "diables verts" (green devils). Colonies of marmots live in the area. The chapel, where a Franco-Italian pilgrimage takes place on 16 July, stands in the centre of a vast cirque within sight of the surrounding summits soaring to 3 000m/9 843ft.

Tête des Toillies round tour★★★
A splendid but taxing hike offering varied scenery: allow 5hr 30min for the walk and at least 1hr 30min for the breaks. Difference in altitude: 1 050m/3 445ft. Leave early in the morning, catching the shuttle to Notre-Dame-de-Clausis no later than 10am.

🥾 Leave the road on the last bend before the chapel and follow a path straight ahead, which leads to the Lac du Blanchet and to the refuge of the same name. Turn right before the refuge *(yellow markings)* towards the **Col de la Noire** (alt 2 955m/9 695ft) affording **views**★ of the impressive rocky summit of the Tête des Toillies and of nearby peaks.

The path drops steeply down to the **Lac de la Noire;** walk past the lake for another 10min and turn left then immediately head for the bottom of the valley. Shortly afterwards, there is a tricky passage through the rocks then the path runs along the mountainside to the Lac du Longet and disappears. Join another path leading to the **Col du Longet,** set in a wild landscape of screes dotted with lakes; **view** of Monte Viso.

Walk down for 10min and turn left towards the **Col Blanchet.** Allow 45min to climb up to the pass through pastures: striking **panorama**★★ of the Tête des Toillies soaring up to the sky, of the Pelvoux, Pic de Rochebrune, Monte Viso and the Italian Alps. *Allow 1hr 15min to return to the shuttle.*

Col St-Véran and Pic de Caramantran★★
Take the shuttle to the Chapelle Notre-Dame-de-Clausis. Continue on foot for 5min then, just before a bridge, take GR 58 (panel). Difference in altitude: about 700m/2 297ft.

It takes 1hr 30min to get to the pass: **view**★ of Monte Viso and Lake Castello on the Italian side. Follow the ridge line on the left, which leads in 30min to the Pic de Caramantran (alt 3 021m/9 911ft): superb **panorama**★★ of the surrounding peaks on both sides of the border.

Follow a path running between the two peaks of the Caramantran to the **Col de Chamoussière**★ offering a fine view of the Pain de Sucre, and return to the shuttle in 1hr 15min along the path marked in white and red.

LAC DE STE-CROIX★★

MICHELIN MAP 334 E10

The turquoise-coloured lake, into which flows the green River Verdon as it comes out of the famous canyon, is framed by the desolate heights of the Plateau de Valensole and Plan de Canjuers. Its shores are lined with pleasant beaches and popular summer resorts and its vast expanse is ideal for water sports. *Mairie – 04500 Ste-Croix-du-Verdon June to Sept: daily except Sun 10am-noon, 3-6pm, Sat 3-6pm; Jan to May: enquire at tourist office for hours closed rest of year - ☎ 04 92 77 85 29 - www.saintecroixduverdon.com*

▶ **Orient Yourself:** As large as the Lac d'Annecy, the Lac Ste-Croix stretches from the Grand Canyon du Verdon to the Gorges of the lower Verdon.

🕐 **Organizing Your Time:** Take an entire day. Spend the morning touring in your car, then picnic and spend the afternoon swimming or enjoying the peace.

Kids **Especially for Kids:** The villages of Ste-Croix and Bauduen both have beaches.

👍 **Also See:** Nearby Sights: BARGÈME, CASTELLANE, GRÉOUX-LES-BAINS, MOUTIERS-STE-MARIE, Route NAPOLÉON, RIEZ, Plateau de VALENSOLE, Grand Canyon du VERDON

Excursion

Tour of the Lake *70km/44mi – about 3hr*

Moustiers-Ste-Marie★★ – 👍 *See MOUSTIERS-STE-MARIE.*

▶ *From Moustiers, drive towards Riez then turn left towards Ste-Croix.*

The road rises in a series of hairpin bends, offering interesting views of Moustiers and its remarkable setting, then runs along the top of the plateau as the lake comes into view.

Ste-Croix-de-Verdon

This old hilltop village, which gave its name to the lake, is today almost level with the water. There is a beach along the shore.
The road goes down to the lake.

Lac de Ste-Croix

Barrage de Ste-Croix

The reservoir created by the dam contains 767 million m3/621 807acft of water supplying a power station which produces 150 million kWh per year.

▷ *Beyond the dam, turn right onto D 71.*

The road runs through the Gorges de Baudinard.
🚶 Beyond Baudinard, turn left onto the path leading to the chapel, which is best reached on foot *(allow 1hr there and back).*

View from Notre-Dame-de-Baudinard★

A small viewing platform has been set up on the roof of the chapel; the **view** extends over the Lac de Ste-Croix, the Plateau de Valensole, Plan de Canjuers and, beyond, towards the Alpine summits.

▷ *Return to the lake and continue eastwards.*

Bauduen

This Provençal village, formerly situated on high ground, is now on the edge of the lake. The **setting**★ is nevertheless remarkable. Old houses, their lovely rounded doorways flanked with hollyhocks, line the picturesque streets climbing towards the church, which stands out against the rocks overlooking the village. The lake shores are equipped for water sports.

▷ *The scenic road planned between Bauduen and Les Salles will avoid the detour via St-Andrieux, along D 49 and D 957.*

Les Salles-sur-Verdon

The old village of Les Salles is now lying 40m/131ft below the surface of the lake. A few architectural features (doors, tiles), as well as the church steeple and the village fountain were saved and used again when the new village was built on the shores of the lake. The entire valley was flooded after the dam was built in 1975; orchards and fields disappeared beneath the lake surface (2 200ha/5 436 acres)

▷ *Continue along D 957 to Moustiers past the leisure park.*

.BASSIN DE SALLANCHES★★

POPULATION 14 383
MICHELIN MAP 328 M5– LOCAL MAP SEE MONT BLANC

It is easy to see why Victor Hugo compared Sallanches to a colossal stage; the tiered escarpments form a vast amphitheatre to the north, with Mont Blanc, towering some 4 000m/13 000ft above the town, providing the most spectacular of backdrops. The scene is just as remakable on either side; to the west stands the Pointe Percée (alt 2 752m/9 029ft), the highest summit of the Aravis range. The **Chaîne des Fiz** extends its strange rocky heights to the east; the most striking of these is the **Désert de Platé**, a desolate and deeply fissured limestone plateau covering an area of 15km2/6sq mi.
The area has one more surprise in store on the nearby Lacs de la Cavettaz: enjoy swimming and summer sports at Mont-Blanc-Plage in sight of the "Giant of the Alps." 🛈 *31, quai de l'hôtel de ville – 74700 Sallanches* 🕐 *July to Aug: Mon-Sat 9am-noon,*

2-7pm, Sun 8.30am-12.30pm; Sept to June: Mon to Sat 9am-noon, 2-6pm ◷ *closed Mon in winter and public holidays - ☎ 04 50 58 04 25 - www.sallanches.com*

▶ **Orient Yourself:** Sallanches is 13km/8mi north of Comblous on N 212, and 18km/11.25 mi north of Megève.
⊚ **Don't Miss:** Inside the church Notre-Dame-de-Toute-Grace is remarkable religious work by some of the best-known modern artists..
🔲 **Especially for Kids:** The Centre de la nature montagnard at the Château Rubens has interesting exhibits about mountain animals.
⚭ **Also See:** Nearby Sights: ARGENTIÈRE, CHAMONIX-MONT-BLANC, Les CONTAMINES-MONTJOIE, Les GETS, Les HOUCHES, Massif du MONT-BLANC, MEGÈVE, MORZINE, La ROCHE-SUR-FORON, SAINT-GERVAIS-LES-BAINS, SAMOËNS, SIXT-FER-A-CHEVAL

Sights

Église St-Jacques

This imposing edifice, rebuilt in 1680, is decorated in Italian style. The christening chapel on the left as you go in houses a small Flamboyant ciborium and, inside a glass case, a collection of silver religious objects, including a 15C monstrance. A viewing table in place Charles-Albert gives a detailed overview of the Mont Blanc massif.

Château des Rubins

🔲 **Centre de la nature montagnard** (◷ *July to Aug: Mon-Fri 9am-6.30pm, Sat-Sun and public holidays 2-6pm; Sept to June: Mon-Fri 9am-noon, 2-6pm, Sat-Sun and public holidays 2-6pm.* ◷ *Closed 1 Jan and 25 Dec. 4.80€, children 2.80€ - ☎ 04 50 58 32 13 - www.centrenaturemontagnard.org.)* – This 17C castle displays, on two levels, an instructive presentation of ecosystems in mountainous areas.

Near Sallanches

Cascade d'Arpenaz★

From Sallanches take the D 205 towards Cluses as far as Luzier. Turn left towards Oëx; the waterfall is on the right of the road. This impressive 200m/656ft-high waterfall gushes from a curiously stratified channel in the rock. It has been a subject for artists since the 18C and was studied by 18C Swiss geologist Horace-Bénédict de Saussure, who found in its folds and stratifications evidence that the Earth's surface has undergone massive transformation over the eons; this was some of the earliest geological field-work.

Excursions

The Old Servoz Road★

13km from Sallanches – allow 30min

This itinerary follows the old Sallanches to Chamonix road, described by generations of travellers – particularly during the Romantic period – thrilled to be getting close to Mont Blanc.

From Sallanches, D 13 crosses the motorway and then the River Arve, 150m/164yd upstream of the old humpback bridge of **St-Martin,** painted and photographed many times over the past 100 years.

The road then climbs up the last slopes of the Plateau d'Assy and, between Passy and Servoz, it overlooks the narrow industrial Chedde Plain and the gorge through which the railway enters the Servoz Basin. Ahead is the narrow wooded valley of the Diosaz. Just beyond the hamlet of Joux, the imposing **Viaduc des Egratz** comes into view: this masterpiece of modern engineering, carrying the Chamonix motorway, is 2 277m/2 490yd long and some of its pillars are 68m/223ft high.

The road then goes through a wood, crosses a stream, offers glimpses of the Arve Valley towards the glaciers of the Dôme du Goûter and enters the verdant Servoz Basin.

Servoz
The village lies at the heart of a wooded basin beneath the cliffs of the Fiz mountains and the scree-covered slopes of the Pas du Dérochoir.

Maison de L'Alpage
🕐 *July to Aug and mid-Dec to mid-Apr: daily except Mon 9am-noon, 2.30-6.30 (closes Sun afternoon); rest of year: daily except Mon 9am-noon and 4.30-6.30* 🕐 *closed 1 Jan, Easter Mon, 1 and 8 May, Ascension, 1 Nov and 25 Dec. No charge -* ☎ *04 50 47 21 68*
In the picturesque village of Servoz, an old farmhouse has been transformed into a museum dedicated to the Alpine grazing traditions.

Route du Plateau d'Assy ★★

FROM PASSY TO PLAINE-JOUX *12km/7.5mi – allow 1hr 30min*
The D 43, branching off the Servoz road in Passy, rises onto wooded south-facing ledges, well sheltered from the wind and dotted with health establishments and family holiday homes. During the climb, the view gets gradually broader, embracing the Mont-Blanc Massif and the Chaîne des Fiz.

Pavillon de Charousse ★★
500m/547yd southwest of Bay. Leave the car in front of the Relais de Charousse and take the path on the left of the chapel leading to the wooded mound on which the house stands. Remarkable **panorama.** It is possible to walk along the edge of the escarpment, on the right of the house, to admire the view of Sallanches and the Aravis Massif.
As the road reaches Plateau d'Assy, the Aiguille Verte can be seen sticking up behind the Brévent.

Plateau d'Assy ★
This well-known health resort is spread over several terraces backing on to the Fiz range, at altitudes ranging from 1 000m/3 281ft to 1 500m/4 921ft; from this prime position, there is a magnificent **panorama** ★★ of the Mont Blanc Massif.

Address Book

EATING OUT
☕🍽 **La Chaumière** – *73 ancienne rte de Combloux- 74700 Sallanches -* ☎ *04 50 58 00 59 - closed 28 June-11 July, 23 Aug-1 Sept, Tue noon, Sun evening and Mon.* This inn close to the town hall was once a farm, then a post office. The rustic Savoyard-style dining room is a good setting for essentially traditional dishes.

WHERE TO STAY
☕🍽 **Hôtel Gorges de la Diosaz** – *74700 Sallanches -* ☎ *04 50 47 20 97 -infos@hoteldesgorges.com - closed 3-19 May and 25 Oct-12 Nov, Sun evening and Wed - 6rms -* ☕🍽*restaurant.* This family-style chalet in a small peaceful village is simple and charming. Enter through the bar to get to the typical dining room, the setting for traditional cooking. There is a terrace with flowers in summer. The rooms have mountain chalet-style decor.
☕🍽 **Hôtel Cordonant** – *Les Darbaillets - 74700 Sallanches - 4km/2.5mi from Sallanches on D 113 -* ☎ *04 50 58 34 56 - www. lecordant - open 16 May-20 Sept and 20 Dec-15 Apr -* 🅿 *- 16rms -* ☕🍽*restaurant.* This chalet with wood-panelled walls has a floral decor and windows with a view of the Mont Blanc range. In summer, you can eat dinner on the pleasant terrace with its abundance of plants. In winter, the hotel has a warm and cosy atmosphere. Good value for money.

The highlight of the town is the **Église Notre-Dame-de-Toute-Grâce**★,(⊙ Daily *9am-noon, 2-6.30pm, 5pm in winter - ☎ 04 50 58 80 61*) a good example of the contemporary revival of religious art. It was built between 1937 and 1945 by Maurice Novarina who took his inspiration from the region's traditional domestic architecture; the result is a solid, stocky church, adapted to Alpine climatic conditions and in harmony with traditional architecture, which is surmounted by a 29m/95ft-high campanile.

Famous contemporary artists contributed to the exterior and interior **decoration**★★: **Fernand Léger** made the mosaic which brightens up the façade, Lurçat decorated the chancel with a huge tapestry on the theme of the Woman triumphing over the Dragon of the Apocalypse. **Bazaine** designed the stained-glass windows lighting up the gallery, **Rouault** designed those situated at the back of the façade, notably in the side chapel on the north side. **Germaine Richier's** bronze crucifix, which caused a critical stir when first displayed, stands in front of the high altar, while **Bonnard, Matisse, Braque, Chagall** and **Lipchitz** are also represented. Walk round the building and go through the east-end doorway down to the crypt decorated with stained glass by Marguerite Huré and a representation of the Last Supper by Kijno.

The road then goes through a forested area, after which the Chamonix glacier comes into view.

Plaine-Joux⁕

A chalet at the centre of this small ski resort houses the Information Centre of the **Réserve naturelle de Passy** covering 2 000ha/4 942 acres.

Beyond Plaine-Joux, the road reaches an open area of high pastures giving glimpses of Mont-Blanc through the pines and close-up **views** of the cliffs of the Fiz range and the scree-covered Pas du Dérochoir.

Lac Vert★

The lake, surrounded by firs and overlooked by the escarpments of the Fiz mountains, is of a dark green colour *(you can walk round in about 15min)*.

Route du Combloux★★★

FROM SALLANCHES TO ST-GERVAIS *18km/11.2mi – allow 45min*

The roads running along the mountainside offer splendid and varied overall views of the massifs.

Désert de Platé

▷ *From Sallanches, drive south along N 212 towards Albertville.*

The approach to Combloux affords a **panorama**★★★ of the Aravis range, the Fiz mountains and the southern part of the Mont Blanc Massif.

Combloux ❊
This summer and winter resort, famous for its mild climate, has retained its traditional farms and old-world charm. The Baroque spire of the **church** is of typical 18C Alpine design; set against the backdrop of Mont Blanc, it has become one of the most popular images of Savoy. The elaborate retable decorating the high-altar also dates from the 18C. ❧❄The **Combloux- le Jaillet ski resort** (1 200-1 853m/3 937-6 079ft) specialises in family entertainment and skiing without risk. The ski area is linked to that of Jaillet (Megève) by numerous ski lifts. There are three separate cross-country loops totalling 15km/9.3mi. Experienced skiers looking for more of a challenge should head to **Évasion Mont Blanc** (1 100-2 353m/3 609-7 720ft) which offers 420km/261mi of runs, kept in good condition by 260 snow cannon.
3km/1.9mi away in La Cry *(turn right onto Route du Haut-Combloux)* is a **viewing table**★.

▷ *3km/1.9mi north of Megève, turn left towards Chamonix.*

Between Gemoëns and Le Freney there are views of the *cluse* (transverse valley) of the Arve, downstream of Sallanches, framed by the Aravis and Fiz mountains. The Dôme du Goûter, Mont Blanc and the Aiguille de Bionnassay and its glacier are visible on the other side.

▷ *D 909 reaches St-Gervais.*

St-Gervais-les-Bains ❧ – ❧ *See ST-GERVAIS-LES-BAINS.*

Round tour via Cordon ★★ *11km/6.8mi – allow 1hr*

▷ *From Sallanches, drive west along D 113 towards Cordon.*

The road winds its way along the ridge separating the gorges of the River Sallanche and River Frasse, as Mont Blanc comes into sight.

Cordon ★
This charming village, backed by the Aravis mountains, occupies an attractive **position**★ facing the majestic Mont Blanc Massif, amid orchards of cherry and walnut trees. ❧❄In winter, the resort offers possibilities of Alpine and cross-country skiing, as well as sleigh rides. The 18C **church** is a fine example of Savoyard Baroque style, including interesting paintings and a rich central **altarpiece** with twisted columns.

▷ *As you leave Cordon, follow the road to Combloux then turn left towards Nant Cruy. Drive through the village.*

The gilded onion spire of Cordon's church can be seen above the orchards.

▷ *The road runs down to an intersection (2km/1.2mi); turn right to the Chapelle du Médonnet (600m/656yd).*

Chapelle du Médonnet
The east end of this unassuming little chapel faces a magnificent **panorama**★★ which includes, from left to right, the Pointe d'Areu, the Chaîne des Fiz, the Aiguilles Rouges and the Mont-Blanc Massif from the Aiguille Verte to the Aiguille de la Bérangère.

▷ *Turn round to go back to Sallanches then right towards N 212.*

SAMOËNS ✳ ✳

POPULATION 2 323
MICHELIN MAP 328 N4– LOCAL MAP SEE LE FAUCIGNY

Samoëns lies at the bottom of a wide glacial valley through which flows the River Giffre. Each of its nine satellite hamlets, scattered over the forested slopes, has a chapel surmounted by a graceful onion-shaped spire. In spite of its considerable expansion, Samoëns has retained a wealth of traditional stone houses built by its famous stonemasons.

This tourist centre of the Haut Faucigny is the ideal starting point for relaxed hikes and splendid mountain excursions. The spectacular scenery of the nearby cirque du Fer-à-Cheval is justly celebrated. Summer activities include mountaineering, canoeing and rafting on the Giffre, swimming and tennis as well as paragliding and hang-gliding which have become a local speciality. In winter, 60km/37mi of ski runs and 90km/56mi of cross-country loops attract visitors, especially those with children. ▯ BP 42 – 74340 Samoëns 🕐 July to mid-Sept and mid-Dec to Apr: 9am-noon, 2.30-6.30pm; mid-Sept to mid-Dec and May to June: Mon-Sat 9am-noon, 2.30-6pm, Tue 9am-noon, 3.30-6.30pm, 🛇 closed Sun and public holidays - ☎ 04 50 34 40 28 - www.samoens.com. Guided tours of the town and surrounding villages 🕐 July to mid-Sept and mid-Dec to Apr: Mon, Tue, Wed. For hours, contact the tourist office.

▶ **Orient Yourself:** Samoëns is 21km/13mi from Cluses on D 902, then on D 907 until Taninges.

⊙ **Don't Miss:** The cirque Fer-a-Cheval, from which leave many hiking and walking trails, is a spectacular sight.

🕐 **Organizing Your Time:** Outdoor activities provide the principal attractions for the Giffre valley. Some activities require professional guides.

🧒 **Especially for Kids:** Samoëns was one of the first "P'tits Montagnards" resorts with special facilities for children. A children's centre provides playspace for youngsters.

☝ **Also See:** Nearby Sights: AVORIAZ, CLUSES, Les GETS, MORZINE, La ROCHE-SUR-FORON, Bassin de SALLANCHES, SIXT FER-À-CHEVAL

A Bit of History

The Stonemasons of Samoëns – Stone-cutting has been a local speciality since 1659, when the village's stonemasons and builders founded a brotherhood taking as their patron saints four Hungarian stonemasons who were martyred by the emperor Diocletian for refusing to sculpt a pagan idol. Members of this guild were called to work all over France, taking part in Vauban's military projects or building canals, and even went abroad, as far afield as Poland and Louisiana. The brotherhood also undertook benevolent work, looking after the sick and training the young; it had its own drawing school and a large library.

For coin categories, see the Legend on the cover flap.

WHERE TO STAY AND EAT

⊜⊜**Le Moulin de Bathieu** – 2km/1mi SW of Samoëns towards Vercland (follow Samoëns 1600) - ☎ 04 50 34 48 07 - www.bathieu. com - closed June-10 July and 4 Nov-mid- Dec - ℙ - reservations advised - 7rms- ⊜⊜restaurant. This former walnut oil mill offers a splendid view of the Dents Blanches mountains. Comfortable rooms, some with mezzanines. Traditional cuisine.

Chapelle de la Jaÿsinia, Samoëns

It was revived in 1979 when an association was created to preserve the architectural heritage of Samoëns and organise guided tours.

Walking Tour

Place du Gros-Tilleul★
Located at the centre of the village, the square owes its name to the lime tree planted here in 1438.

The **Grenette,** a 16C covered market restored in the 18C, stands on the south side; note the strange bulges on the central pillars: the arms of Samoëns were to be carved on these pillars, but the mason did not complete his work following a disagreement with the municipality over his contract. A lovely fountain stands in the centre of the square. The **church, Notre-Dame-de-l'Assomption,** next to the Château de la Tour on the north side of the square, was rebuilt in the 16C and 17C; at the foot of the 12C bell-tower, a graceful canopy covered with copper tiles shelters a 16C doorway with older features, including two lions supporting twisted columns.

The stained-glass windows on the left, dating from 1982, depict the four patron saints of the stonemasons' brotherhood. The baptistery chapel is in Flamboyant Gothic style. The 19C stoup was carved out of a single block of marble.

A sundial on the front of the **presbytery** indicates the time in 12 large cities of the world.

Jardin botanique alpin Jaÿsinia★
🕐 *May to Sept: 8am-noon, 1.30-7pm; Oct to Apr: 8am-noon, 1.30-5.30pm (last admission 1hr before closing; opening depends on snow accumulation). No charge. Guided tours* 👟 *July to Aug: Thur 10am-noon. 4€, children under 12 years no charge -* ☎ *04 50 34 49 86.*

These botanical gardens, complete with pools and waterfalls and covering an area of 3ha/7.5 acres, were created in 1906 on

A Local Speciality

What could be better at end of a tiring hike than a fortifying bowl of the local "soupe châtrée"? This nourishing soup is made with slices of bread soaked in onion sauce, covered with Tomme de Savoie, the local cheese, and browned under the grill. Wooden spoons are best to deal with the melted cheese.

sloping ground overlooking the village; they contain more than 5 000 species of mountain plants from the main temperate areas of the world. Walking past the **Chapelle de la Jaÿsinia,** one reaches the terrace and its ruined castle offering an extended view of Samoëns and the surrounding mountains. The garden was one of many gifts to the town from Louise Cognacq-Jaÿ, a local girl from a humble background who made her fortune as owner of the famous "La Samaritaine" department store in Paris. The **Maison de la Jaÿsinia** at the garden entrance contains documents relating to the village's benefactress.

Excursions

Les Vallons
2km/1.2mi along D 907 towards Sixt, then a road on the left. This hamlet is interesting for its lovely stone fountains and its chapel.

La Rosière★★ (view)
6km/3.7mi. Leave Samoëns along D 907 towards Sixt; turn left almost immediately towards Les Allamands, left again 750m/0.5mi further on and sharp right 1km/0.6mi after that. From la Rosière, there is a particularly fine view of Mont Blanc framed by the forested Rochers du Criou and the rock face of the Pointe de Sales.

Drive to the Cirque du Fer à Cheval★★ *13km/8mi from Samoëns – allow 45min*

▶ *Leave Samoëns by the D 907 heading southeast*

The Cascade de Nant d'Ant rushes down the rock on the opposite bank of the Giffre; the valley narrows as the road approaches the Gorges de Tines.

Gorges de Tines
This narrow gorge, through which the Giffre splashes, is best explored on foot. *Park the car in the car park just before the quarry and head right towards the footbridge over the river.*

Sixt-Fer-à-Cheval and Cirque du Fer à Cheval★★ – *13km/8mi east.* See SIXT-FER-À-CHEVAL.

Col de Joux Plane★★ – *10km/6.2mi via Chantemerle and D 354.* See MORZINE, Excursions

SERRE-CHEVALIER ✳✳✳

MICHELIN MAP 334 H3
LOCAL MAP SEE LE BRIANÇONNAIS

Situated in the Guisane Valley, between the Col du Lautaret and Briançon, Serre-Chevalier is the largest winter sports complex in the southern Alps. The resort, sheltered by the surrounding mountains, enjoys a microclimate characterised by 300 days of sunshine a year. Facilities and accommodation are spread over four main sites: Le Monêtier, Villeneuve, Chantemerle and Briançon. 🛈 *Centre Commercial "Serre d'Aigle" -BP 20 - 05240 Serre-Chevalier* 🕐 *in season: daily 9am-noon, 2-7pm; out of season: daily except Sun 9-noon, 2-6pm -* ☎ *04 92 24 71 88 - www. serre-chevalier.com.*

▶ **Orient Yourself:** The three municipalities composing the resort -- Saint-Chaffrey, La Salle-les-Alpes and Monêtier-les-Bains -- include 13 villages strung out along the River Guisane, on D 91 between Briançon and the Col du Lautaret.

🖼 **Don't Miss:** For a splendid view, take the gondola up to the summit of Serre-Chevalier.

🕐 **Organizing Your Time:** If you are just passing through Serre-Chevalier, spend a half day sight-seeing in the villages.

Kids **Especially for Kids:** The resort is designated "P'tits Montagnards" and has many facilities for children.

🐾 **Also See:** Nearby Sights: L'ARGENTIÈRE-LA-BESSÉE, BRIANÇON, Le BRIANÇON-NAIS, Vallée de FREISSINIÈRES, Route du GALIBIER, La GRAVE, GUILLESTRE, MONT-DAUPHIN, MONTGENÈVRE, L'OISANS, Le QUEYRAS, La VALLOUISE

The Resort

Serre-Chevalier is composed of four resorts: **Briançon**, which is known as **Serre-Chevalier 1200** since construction of the Prorel gondola; **Serre-Chevalier 1350** (Chantemerle-St-Chauffrey), **Serre-Chevalier 1400** (Villeneuve/LaSalle-les-Alpes) and **Serre-Chevalier 1500** (Le Monêtier-les-Bains). Each resort gives access to the entire skiable terrain. Traditional stone houses, nestling round 13C and 15C churches, stand next to modern shops, hotels and apartments.

🦅🎿 Ski area

The resort is equipped with 68 lifts giving access to 250km/155mi of north-facing runs suitable for skiers of all levels. Several are lit for night-skiing. No need to return to the base at lunchtime: there are 14 restaurants on the slopes. A bus shuttles tourists to and from their resort.

New snow sports are well-served, with a snowpark and half-pipe for boarders at Chevalier 1400, and a boarder cross at Serre-Chevalier 1350. On the upper reaches, there are trails for snowshoers, while 35km/22mi of cross-country skiing tracks connect St-Chauffrey and Lautaret. Other amusements include snow-scooter lessons for driving on ice, 25km/15.6mi of groomed trails for walking along the Guisane, and sledding for children at the bottom of the slopes at Serre-Chevalier 1400 and 1500.

After a hard day's skiing, warm pools and spas will relax your tired muscles. At Serre-Chevalier 1400, there is the Espace Thalassoforme, and at Serre-Chevalier 1500, the spa is called "Les Bains."

In summer, the valley offers a wide range of activities: mountain biking, canoeing and rafting on the Guisane, archery, riding tours, paragliding and hang-gliding. It is also a good place to start medium-altitude hikes in the Parc national des Écrins.

Address Book

For coin categories, see the Legend on the cover flap.

EATING OUT

☺☺ **Chazal** – *Les Guibertes - 05220 Monêtier-les-Bains -* ☎ *04 92 24 45 54 - closed 23 Jun-10 July, 24 Nov-15 Dec evenings and Mon.* This former sheep-fold houses a pleasant restaurant composed of two little rooms and a salon. The locally-inspired cuisine is varies daily.

WHERE TO STAY

☺☺ **Europe et des Bains**– *05220 Monêtier-les-Bains -* ☎ *04 92 24 40 03- hotel-de-leurope@wanadoo.fr - 29rms – ☺☺ restaurant.* This venerable hostelry, near the church, has been in the same family since 1850. Guestrooms are simple, with rustic furnishings. The cuisine is boarding-house style, and menus are traditional.

☺☺ **Alliey** – *05220 Monêtier-les-Bains -* ☎ *04 92 24 40 02 - hotel@alliey.com - 22rms - ☺☺ restaurant.* The interior of this village house is paneled in rustic wood; the pleasant guestrooms are decorated in Alpine style, and ther is a well-equiped spa. The restaurant serves imaginative food using local produce and aromatic herbs.

☺☺☺ **Christiana** – ☎ *04 92 24 76 33 - lechristiana@wanadoo.fr – open 24 June-10 Sept and 12 Dec-16 Apr –* ▣ *– 26rms – ☺☺ restaurant.* Rustic furnishings and large, comfortable rooms characterize this inn on the banks of the Guisane. The restaurant is decorated with old objects, and you can relax on a terrace in a garden along the river.

☺☺☺☺ **Auberge du Choucas** – *05220 Monêtier-les-Bains -* ☎ *04 92 24 42 73 - auberge.du.choucas@wanadoo. fr closed 2-28 May and 31 Oct-10 Dec - ☺☺☺ restaurant.* At the foot of the 15C church in the famous mountain village stands this inn redolent of local tradition. The rooms are warm and well lit, and the four suites on two floors are very practical. The dining room has a vaulted ceiling and stone walls and features an open fireplace decorated with a fine collection of copper pans and implements.

ON THE TOWN

Cocoon café – *C.C. "Le Prélong" - 05240 La Salle-les-Alpes -* ☎ *04 92 24 92 25 – open daily 8am-1am; in summer 10am-noon, 3pm-1am, closed mid Apr-mid Jun and Sept-Nov.* In tune with the seasons, this café offers a menu with the emphasis on coffee, tea and beer in the winter, and on cocktails in the summer, enjoyed on a terrace open to the sunshine. The interior combines relaxed comfort and good taste.

SHOPPING

La Maison des Artisans – *3 Pl du Marché - 05220 Monêtier-les-Bains -* ☎ *04 92 24 51 11 - daily except Sun and Mon 10am-noon, 3-7pm in winter, closed May to mid-June and mid-Sept to mid-Dec.* This is a cooperative where craftspeople and farm producers exhibit and sell their wares. Besides honey and preserves, there are turned wood pieces, pottery, original jewellery, unusual oil lamps etc. Displays change constantly, as the local producers regularly bring along their latest creations.

Longo Maï – *Filature de Chantemerle - 05330 St-Chaffrey -* ☎ *04 92 24 04 43 – daily except Sun 9.30am-12.30pm, 2.30-7pm - closed public holidays.* This mill produces items in pure wool coloured with natural dyes: shirts, sweaters, blankets, hats and so on. Guided tours every Friday at 5pm (2€) except in May-June and Oct-Nov.

SPORTS

The tourist offices of Serre-Chevalier sell a **Carte d'hôte** (guest card) which gives discounts on services and activities.

Summer ski-lift rides– ☎ *04 92 25 55 00 – July to Aug: 9.30am-5.30pm* At Serre-Chevalier 1400 and Serre-Chevalier 1500, the ski-lifts of the Casse-du-Bouef and Bachas will take you in 10min up to over 2 000m/6 562ft. At the top, hikers and mountain-bikers can descend on trails and enjoy the view without the fatique of climbing. Others may prefer to stop at the restaurant, then take the ski-lift down to the bottom.

Hiking and Mountain-biking – *Le Guide des itinéraires* which maps trails and gives information is available in tourist offices. 13€, or 8€ with the Carte d'hôte.

Bureau des Guides de Serre-Chevalier – ☎04 92 24 75 90. Qualified guides can accompany you on mountain activities: climbing frozen waterfalls, skiing treks and off-trail skiing, summer hikes.

Aventure Parc – Kids - 05240 La Salle-les-Alpes - ☎ 04 92 24 90 57 - www. aventure-parc.com – *opening times vary depending on the season - closed Nov-Apr.* About twenty varied activities (wooden bridge, rope bridge, bungy jumping etc) in this park, each a mini-ature adventure, mean that visitors will not be bored.

Pour barboter en famille (family swimming) – Kids - *052220 Le Monêtier-les-Bains -* ☎ *04 92 24 40 04, opening hours vary according to seasons.* Two lakes offer family water-sports: at the **Lac de Pontillas** in LaSalle-les-Alpes there are free swimming beaches, and the **Base de Loisirs** of Monêtier has a swimming pool with naturally warm water, open all year long.

Hikes

⚐ Sommet de Serre-Chevalier★★
Alt 2 483m/8 146ft. *Access from Chantemerle by a two-section* **cable car** (🕐 *July to mid-Aug: 9am-5.30pm; last 2 weeks of June and mid-Aug to mid-Sept: 9am-12.30pm, 1.30-5.30pm (10 minutes per section, departures every 20 min). 16€ per family, two sections -* ☎ *04 92 24 29 29.).*

⬛ From the upper station, climb to the viewing table: splendid **panorama**★★ of the Oisans Massif to the west, the Aiguilles d'Arves and Pic du Galibier to the northwest, the Vanoise to the north and the Queyras to the east.

Hike round the Eychauda Summit★★
5hr on foot on fairly level ground. A 1:25 000 map is strongly recommended. The hike starts in Chantemerle and ends in Le Monêtier; return to Chantemerle by coach (information from the tourist office).

⬛ Take the cable car to the top of Serre-Chevalier. From the viewing table, go down towards the Col de Serre-Chevalier and follow tracks leading to the path going round the Eychauda and walk up to the **Col de la Pisse** (alt 2 501m/8 205ft).

The path runs across the mountainside, offering lovely **views**★★ of Lake Eychauda and the Pelvoux Massif *(a few tricky sections)*, and finally reaches the **Col de l'Eychauda**, overlooking the Col du Lautaret road. A wide path leads down to a mountain restaurant. Go to the left, leave the path and take another one to the right *(GR 54, marked in white and red, sometimes in yellow)*. It follows the stream, crosses it and enters a pleasant larch forest.

Towards the end of the hike, continue straight on past a chapel and follow a small road going down to the left. When you reach a square with a playground, turn right, cross a small bridge and walk up rue de la Grande-Turière. As you join the Route Nationale, the coach stop is on your right, in front of the post office.

From Le Bez (Villeneuve) to Le Monêtier
Start from the rock-climbing school; 4hr there and back on foot; easy hike.

⬛ Walk towards Fréjus then take the path rising to the Clos de la Salette above the rock-climbing site; at the intersection, turn right to Le Monêtier. The viewpoint offers a panorama of the Guisane Valley. The path runs down to a stream, the Chanteloube, and continues into the Monêtier Valley.

Lac du Combeynot★★

5hr there and back along a path marked in blue. Please abide by the rules of the Parc national des Écrins: do not pick flowers, disturb the animals or bring dogs within the central zone of the park.

🚶 Start from Les Boussardes, 200m/219yd south of Le Lauzet. On the way up to the lake, hikers are likely to meet chamois (keep to the path). The Tête de Vallon rises above the splendid glacial lake (alt 2 555m/8 383ft and 16m/52ft deep).

Via ferrata de l'Aiguillette du Lauzet★

These high limestone cliffs are the favourite haunt of rock-climbers from the Briançon area. Via ferrata climbing has become very popular in the last few years and the car park near the starting point of the different courses is very congested (*see Planning Your Trip*).

Réserve naturelle du Combeynot★

This hike takes at least 7hr and should not be attempted by anyone without a good level of stamina, a good head for heights and experience of long walks. Start from the Refuge Napoléon at the Col du Lautaret. Not recommended in rainy weather or after a snowfall. Walkers must arrange to be picked up by car from Le Casset.

🚶 Walk across N 91, then due west along the marked Sentier des Crevasses. The path goes through the nature reserve and round the west side of the Pic du Combeynot before joining GR 54 at the Col d'Arsine. On the way up to the Refuge de l'Alpe du Villard *(food available)*, there are fine views of the Romanche Valley and numerous opportunities to observe high-altitude flora and birdlife. Continue to the Col d'Arsine and enjoy the splendid panorama of the glacial valleys, the Pic de Neige Cordier (3 613m/11 854ft) and the Arsine Glacier. The path then runs down to the lovely Lac de la Douche and back to the Guisane along the Petit Tabuc Valley.

BARRAGE ET LAC DE SERRE-PONÇON★★

MICHELIN MAP 334 F6

Forget any ideas you may have about artificial landscapes; no-one could fail to be charmed by the largest man-made lake in Europe, set against a line of mountain peaks reaching towards the sun. The picturesque road winds around the lake in a series of curves, turning away into the hills, only to reappear around the next bend for another view of the deep blue water, dotted with white sails.

▸ **Orient Yourself:** Located in the southern part of the Parc des Écrins, the lake lies on N 94; the towns of Gap, to the west, and of Barcelonnette, to the east, are each 20km/12.5mi away.

🚫 **Don't Miss:** The huge dam is an amazing sight, and well worth your time. The best look-out points from which to admire the beauty of the lake are Ivan-Wilhelm and Le Sauze-du-Lac. You will also want to see the strange rock formations called "les demoiselles coiffées" (the capped maidens) and the beautiful forest of Boscodon.

🕐 **Organizing Your Time:** A half day will take you around the lake.

Kids Especially for Kids: The whole family will enjoy a dip in the lake. You can also take children to the animal park called La Montagne aux Marmottes, and to the Muséoscope du lac.

Lac de Serre-Ponçon

Also See: Nearby Sights: BARCELONNETTE, CEILLAC, Le CHAMPSAUR, Le DÉVOLUY, Préalpes de DIGNE, EMBRUN, GAP, Route des GRANDES ALPES, GUILLESTRE, MONT-DAUPHIN, MONTMAUR, Route NAPOLÉON, PRA-LOUP, SEYNE, L'UBAYE, VAL-D'ALLOS, VARS

Highlights

Barrage de Serre-Ponçon★★

Work on a project to control the Durance, this most unpredictable of rivers, began in 1955, but nothing could check the torrential floods which devastated the region two years later. The project at Serre-Ponçon was the first time an earth dam with a waterproof core of clay was built on such a scale in France, applying a technique widely used in the USA. The dyke, made up of alluvial material from the river bed, is 600m/1 969ft long at the top, 650m/2 133ft wide at the base and 123m/404ft high. The clay core has a volume of 2 million m3/1 621acft against a total volume of 14 million m3/11 350acft. A mixture of clay and concrete is used to prevent seepage. The lake, created in 1960 and covering an area of 3 000ha/7 413 acres, is one of the largest reservoirs in Europe *(20km/12.5mi long, 3km/1.9mi at its widest point; capacity: 1 270 million m³/1 029 589cu ft).*

For coin categories, see the Legend on the cover flap.

WHERE TO STAY

⌂**Chambre d'hôte Les Carlines** – *Les Vignes - 05230 Prunières - 4km/2.5mi E of Chorges on D 9 then D 109 -* ☎ *04 92 50 63 27 -* ⌂ *- 5rms*. This chalet situated on the south slope of the Écrins range offers an idyllic panorama of the Lac de Serre-Ponçon and the Morgon peak. Rooms are clean and simple, and three open onto the garden. Breakfast on the terrace in summer.

⌂**Chambre d'hôte d'Arnica** – *Route du Col des Fillys - 04340 La Bréole - 3km/2 mi S of the Col du Fillys by D 7 -* ☎ *04 92 85 54 81 - www.chambres-hotes-arnica.com - closed 15 Nov-15 Dec - 4rms –* ⌂⌂ *restaurant*. This former sheep-fold sits on the most unspoiled shore of the lake. The rooms, under the rafters, are comfortably furnished and the bathrooms are well thought-out. Home-made preserves and bread, and a menu of "bio" dishes, either traditional or vegetarian.

La Maison des Énergies (Power station)

🕐 *July to Aug: guided tours (1hr) daily except Sun from 9.30am-5.30pm (last tour at 4.30pm); Sept to June: daily except Sat-Sun on request.* 🕐 *Closed public holidays. No charge -* ☎ *04 92 54 58 18 or* ☎ *06 13 48 35 19 - www.serre-poncon.com.*

Located at the foot of the dam, this museum explains its construction, history and functioning. As well as safeguarding the lower valley and improving irrigation, the dam is also an important energy provider. Imbedded in the rock of the south bank, its power station can produce 720 million kWh per year. In order to regulate the flow of the Durance downstream of the dam, a reservoir covering 100ha/247 acres was created on the site where the alluvial soil was removed.

The lake★★

The curved shape of the lake, its indented shores and the promontory marking the confluence of the Durance and the Ubaye have made it easier for this vast expanse of water to blend with the natural scenery and to offer at the same time a variety of water sports.

Excursions

1 **From the lower dam to Embrun** *39km/24mi – allow 1hr 30min*

D 3 to Chorges follows the downstream reservoir before rising sharply within sight of the riprap embankment of the dam.

Belvédère Ivan-Wilhem★★

This viewpoint (alt 847m/2 779ft), built along the axis of the ridge line of the dam and named after the engineer who designed it, offers a fine overall view. Films and models at the 🖼Kids **Muséoscope du Lac** (⟲ *guided tours (1hr) from 2nd week of July to Aug: 10 and 11 am and noon, 1.30-6pm (every 40min); June and Sept and 1st week July: daily except Tue 10 and 11 am 2, 3, 4 and 5pm; May daily except Tue 2, 3 and 4pm;*

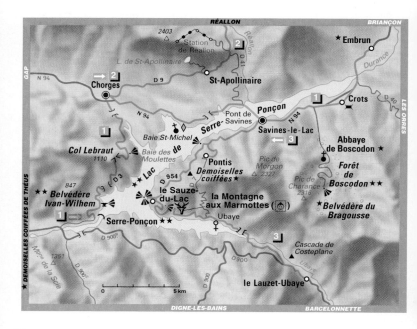

Feb to Mar: daily except Thur 2, 3 and 4 pm; Apr and Oct to Jan: daily except Tue and Thur 2, 3 and 4pm. 8.20€, children 6.20€ - ☎ 04 92 54 50 00 -www.museoscope-du-lac.com) immediately above offer reminders of the villages which were submerged under the lake.

Beyond the tunnel, the road veers away from the lake.

Col Lebraut

Alt 1 110m/3 642ft. From the pass, there is a view of the Gap Basin to the west and of the lake to the east. Further on *(1.2km/0.7mi)*, the **panorama**★ extends to the whole northeast arm of the lake.

Chorges

From its prosperous past, the village has retained a few old houses, a lovely 16C fountain and a hilltop church with a rounded 12C porch; to the right stands an imposing pink-marble stela, known as "Nero's stone," which may well be the pedestal of a Roman statue. Also noteworthy is the 14C bell-tower with its two tiers of windows and its narrow-stone bond.

From Chorges, the Savines road runs east towards the lake; note, on the right, a chapel standing on a tiny island in the **Baie St-Michel.** Further on, N 94 runs across the lake over the **Pont de Savines,** almost level with the water.

Savines-le-Lac

The village, which disappeared beneath the surface of the lake, was rebuilt here and has become a centre for water sports. 🄺🄸🄳 The beach has a lifeguard in summer.
Boat trips on the "Carline" are organised (🕐 *Mar to mid-Dec: non-stop trips with commentaries (1hr30min) at 10am, 2.30pm and 4.15pm; out of season, telephone for hours. 10.50€, children 7.80€. Société des Bateaux Carline - ☎ 04 92 44 26 88.)* .

Crots

Lying on the edge of the lake, this ancient village and its 14C church are overlooked by the 13C **Château de Picomtal,** extended in the 16C. 🄺🄸🄳 The beach has a lifeguard in summer.

Just before Embrun, the road crosses the Durance near the expanse of water reserved for sailing and water sports.

Embrun★ – 🕐 *See EMBRUN.*

2 **Vallée de Réallon** 18km/11mi – allow 1hr

▷ *Two alternative access roads: D 41 north from the Pont de Savines or D 9 from Chorges; choose the second one in preference.*

From Chorges, D 9 offers lovely views on its way to **St-Apollinaire,** a picturesque village overlooking the Lac de Serre-Ponçon; this section of the route sometimes forms part of the Monte-Carlo Rally. The pastoral Lac de St-Apollinaire can be reached along a road on the left.

Réallon

The church spire soars above the village which has retained its Alpine atmosphere and is now a pleasant family ski resort with 16 alpine trails and 25km/15.6mi of marked cross-country trails. All year long, the **panoramic chair-lift** takes passengers to 2,135m/7 005ft where there is a lookout point; there are also mountain bike and hiking trails.

Réallon has also been a famous archaeological site since the discovery last century of Bronze-Age precious objects, including a set of jewellery exhibited in the Gap Museum.

Aiguilles de Chabrières★★

5hr hike to be attempted in clear weather only. From Réallon, follow the path with yellow markings known as the "Tour des Aiguilles-Serre-du-Mouton"; detailed topo-guides are available at the tourist office. The itinerary goes across a deeply gullied limestone plateau to the ridge of the Aiguilles de Chabrières.

③ From Savines-le-Lac to Le Lauzet-Ubaye 25km/15.5mi
– allow 1hr

Savines-le-Lac – ⚫ *See drive* ①.

From Savines, D 954 winds along the indented shore of the lake; the **view**★ becomes gradually broader, embracing the wild southern part of the lake *(parking spaces on a bend to the left)*.

▶ *A small road branching off to the left leads to Pontis.*

Pontis

🧒 The old school houses the **Musée de la Vallée** (🕐 *July to Aug: 2-7pm. 2€, children 1€ - ☎ 04 92 44 26 94)*, a museum illustrating the life of schoolchildren and teachers in the 19C.

▶ *Turn back towards D 954.*

Demoiselles coiffées de Pontis★

For more details about these strange rock formations, *see Demoiselles coiffées de Théus below.* It is possible to get quite close to these 12 strange stone columns by following the stony path *(⏱ 30min there and back on foot; please do not touch the stones)*.

Le Sauze-du-Lac

A picturesque **site**★★, on top of a promontory overlooking the lake, at the confluence of the River Durance and River Ubaye. There is a fine **view**★ back towards Le Sauze from the road beyond.
The road winds steeply down the slope, offering a clear **view** of the Ubaye arm of the lake. On the opposite shore, the scenery is wild and the shoreline deeply indented.

Montagne aux Marmottes

🧒 ♿ 🕐 *July to Aug: 10am-7pm; Apr to June and Sept to mid-Nov: telephone for opening hours. 12€, children 3 to 15 years 8€ - ☎ 04 92 44 32 00.* The "Marmot Mountain" is an educational centre, studying and protecting animals from nature reserves and private collections. At certain hours, birds of prey and marmots are presented for close inspection. Also on show are a prehistoric cave dwelling, a beehive with a glass wall, a selection of minerals and fossils and a mountain fauna museum. Take a picnic if the weather is fine.

Ubaye

The church and the cemetery are all that remain of the flooded village.
The road runs through two tunnels *(single lane)* then across a bridge at the extremity of the lake. The **Cascade de Costeplane** flows through a deep gorge near the intersection of D 954 and D 900.

▶ *Continue along D 900 towards Barcelonnette.*

Le Lauzet-Ubaye

The village lies next to a small lake (*lauzet* in local dialect). A Roman bridge spans the river near the modern one ⏱️ *(15min there and back on foot).*

🕯️ *For a description of the lower-Ubaye itinerary from Le Lauzet-Ubaye to Barcelonnette, see L'UBAYE B.*

Sights Nearby

Demoiselles coiffées★

From the dam along the D 900 towards Tallard, then right towards Théus. Among the most remarkable geological wonders of the southern Alps, the **"demoiselles coiffées"** (capped maidens), sometimes called "cheminées de fées" (fairies' chimneys), are columns of soft material – in this case morainic debris – preserved from erosion by their harder rocky caps. These help to compress the soft material underneath making it last longer. However, the column quickly disappears once its cap has toppled over.

Leave the car at the **Salle de Bal★**, or ballroom, where there is a great concentration of these rock formations. It is possible to continue *(4.5km/2.8mi)* to the **Mont Colombis** transmitter (alt 1 733m/5 686ft) for a panoramic **view** of the Lac de Serre-Ponçon.

Abbaye de Boscodon★

Turn right onto the D 568 between Savines and Embrun. 🕐 *Abbey: daily except Sun morning, 8am-7pm; church, cloisters, exhibit, and boutique: daily 10.30am, 2.30-6pm.* ⏱️ *Guided tours July to Aug: daily except Sun 2.30-4pm; from mid-Nov to Easter, request a guided tour at the boutique. 5€, children no charge. Church visit no charge - ☎ 04 92 43 14 45.*

A local preservation society acquired the buildings in 1972 and teams of young people have worked hard to restore it ever since. The abbey is also home to a small community of Dominican nuns. The recently restored east end of the **abbey church** is remarkable; inside, one is overwhelmed by the architectural simplicity of this single-nave early Cistercian edifice and the amount of light pouring through its semicircular-arched windows. The chapter hall **(Aile des Moines)**, has been completely restored and is used as a reception and exhibition area. Excavations are still in progress in the lay community wing, **Aile des Convers.**

Forêt de Boscdon★★

▸ *From the abbey, take the forest road (surfaced) leading to Fontaine de l'Ours.* The forest, which formed part of the estate of the abbey and extends over 850ha/2 100 acres, is famous for its beautiful specimens of larch and fir trees. 600m/656yd further on, a ⏱️ **nature trail** guides walkers past 24 different types of tree and conifer. A **map** of the wood, showing the various walks, is on display in a hut.

Belvédère de Bragousse★

The gullied cirque forms a striking landscape enhanced by the beautiful colour of the soil; chamois can be seen (with the aid of binoculars) roaming around in the upper part of the cirque. The mountain stream, subject to sudden summer flooding when the snow melts, has been tamed by a series of dams; the first of these can be seen from the belvedere.

▸ *Drive another 500m/0.3mi to reach Fontaine de l'Ours; park the car at the end of the road.* 🥾 *A 2hr 30min walk along the Chantier de la Charance leads to the Cirque de Morgon (difference in altitude: 530m/1 739ft).*

SEYNE

POPULATION 1 440
MICHELIN MAP 334 G6

1 200m/3 937ft up in the verdant Blanche valley, Seyne is a sunny summer and winter resort (with an annexe at Grand-Puy), which keeps up its traditions, including its reputation for horse and mule breeding. *place d'Armes – 04140 Seyne-les-Alpes ◷ July to Aug: daily except Sun 9am-12.30pm, 2-6.30pm; rest of year: 9am-noon, 2-5pm - ☎ 04 92 35 11 00 - www.valleedelablanche.com.*

▸ **Orient Yourself:** Seyne lies on D 900, at 41km/25.6mi from Digne and 25km/15.6mi from the Lac du Serre-Ponçon.

▣ **Parking:** Free parking on the Place d'Armes, on the Digne side of the village.

◷ **Organizing Your Time:** Take two hours to see the village and its citadel.

✋ **Also See:** Nearby Sights: BARCELONNETTE, DIGNE-LES-BAINS, Préalpes de DIGNE, EMBRUN, PRA-LOUP, Lac de SERRE-PONÇON, L'UBAYE, VAL-D'ALLOS

A Bit of History

Mules from Seyne – The mule show (second Saturday in August) and the mule and horse fair (second Saturday in October) testify to a strong tradition which brought fame and prosperity to the town. The mule is a remarkable beast of burden, used in the past in mountain areas for farming and for carrying munitions and food to isolated mountain troops *(chasseurs alpins)*. Young mules, which are the sterile offspring of a male donkey and a female horse, were cared for and trained by specialists until the age of two. This activity remained vital until the 1950s, but the introduction of tractors and the progress made by artificial-insemination techniques caused it to decline rapidly. However, the development of tourism and pony-trekking in rural areas has recently given it a new lease of life.

Walking Tour

Vieille ville

Traces of Seyne's past as a defensive stronghold can still be seen in the centre of the old town. Closely set ranks of tall houses follow the line of the old town wall, of which only the crenellated southern gate, the **Porte Basse,** remains; the glacis under the fortifications is now a grassy park. Across the rue Basse stands the Chapelle des Dominicans, which contains an interesting **picture** of a penitential procession: the townspeople are depicted by class, with every citizen knowing his place in the social order. The **Maison de Pays** (☞◔✋ *guided tour on request. 3€ - ☎04 92 35 31 66)* houses an **Exposition mulassière** explaining everything there is to know about the history of mule-breeding.

Église Notre-Dame de Nazareth

◷ *In summer, ask for admission at the presbytery - ☎ 04 92 35 01 89.*
This 13C church in attractive pink and blue stone is a fine example of Alpine Romanesque architecture. The nave, surmounted by a broken barrel vault, contains a beautiful 17C set of stalls, pulpit and retable as well as a large single-block christening font. Note the strange monsters which stalk the sculpted capitals of the nave.

Citadel

🕐 *July to mid-Sept: daily except Mon and Tue 10am-noon, 3-6pm, guided tours (1hr); rest of year: on request at the tourist office. 3€, guided tour 4€, children under 10 years no charge -* ☎ *04 92 35 31 66.*

Commissioned by Vauban, military engineer of Louis XIV, in 1693, but rendered obsolete by the Treaty of Utrecht which handed nearby Ubaye to France, the citadel still has its 12C watchtower. It now plays host to summer exhibitions about the history of the fortress and mule-breeding in Seyne.

For coin categories, see the Legend on the cover flap.

WHERE TO STAY AND EAT

⊜ **Relais de la Forge** – *At Selonnet – 04460 Seyne - 4km/2.5mi NW of Seyne on D 900 -* ☎ *04 92 35 16 98 - lerelais@libertysurf.fr - closed 15 Nov-19 Dec, Sun evening and Mon except school holidays - 15rms-* ⊜ *restaurant.* This inn near a quiet village offers modest rooms; those upstairs have been renovated. Traditional fare in a dining room with a fireplace.

Excursion

Vallée de la Blanche

Near the Col des Maures, where the larches give way to open meadow, the little winter sports resort of Chabanon (1 600m/2 549ft) looks down into the Blanche valley. Rising at the Cabane des Mulets, not far from the Col des Maures, the Blanche cuts straight across the area around Seyne. To the north, downstream from Selonnet, it has cut deep gorges on its way to the Durance. The broad valley still bears traces of the glacier which once stretched as far as Col St-Jean.

🚠 St-Jean-Montclar

12km/7.5mi north along D 900.

This family ski resort, backed by the Dormillouse Massif, is situated on a plateau which is the starting point of the ski runs. The **ski area** is linked to that of **Le Lauzet,** situated on the north side of the Dormillouse Massif, via the Brèche runs. The village of **Montclar** has retained a 17C castle framed by two round towers (⚏ *not open to the public)* and the 13C Chapelle St-Léger.

A hike to the Dormillouse ★

🚠 (alt 2 505m/8 218ft) *The summit is accessible by chairlift to the Plateau de la Chau and then by a forest road (45min on foot).* From the 17C fort, there is a fine **view** ★ of the Ubaye Valley. The cliff below the fort is used for paragliding, and has even hosted a paragliding world championship.

SISTERON★★

POPULATION 6 964
MICHELIN MAP 334 D7
LOCAL MAPS SEE P 528 AND VALLÉE DE LA MOYENNE DURANCE

Sisteron is situated along a transverse section *(cluse)* of the Durance Valley which marks the transition between Dauphiné and Provence. Arriving from the south along D 4, one enjoys a remarkable view of the highly impressive **setting**★★: the town climbing up the steep side of a hillock crowned by a citadel facing the impressive Rocher de la Baume, whose almost vertical strata seem to rise from the river bed. Tall narrow houses, covered with tiles, nestle between the ruined 14C walls. *Place de la République – 04200 Sisteron ©July to Aug: daily 9am-7pm, Sun 10am-1pm, public holidays 10am-noon, 2-5pm; Sept to June: daily except Sun and public holidays 9am-noon, 2-6pm (5pm Nov to Feb) - ☎ 04 92 61 36 50 - www.sisteron.fr.*

▸ **Orient Yourself:** Sisteron is located on the Route Napoleon (N 85) between Gap, 50km/31.25mi to the north and Digne, 39km/24.4 mi to the southeast. Two tunnels facilitate passage through the village, one under the hill and its citadel, the other under the rock face opposite, on the A 51.

🅿 **Parking:** Free parking beneath the citadel, near the river.

◉ **Don't Miss:** Be sure to see the citadel, impressive in itself and which offers views over the town and countryside.

🕑 **Organizing Your Time:** Give yourself a half-day to see the town; each one of the suggested circuits requires another half-day.

▥ **Especially for Kids:** Children will enjoy the Musée Terre et Temps at Sisteron and the animal park at la Vallée Sauvage ⓒ see circuit ①.

ⓒ **Also See:** Nearby Sights: Pays du BUËCH, BUIS-LES-BARONNIES, DIGNE-LES-BAINS, Préalpes de DIGNE, Vallée de la Moyenne DURANCE, FORCALQUIER, Monastère de GANAGOBIE, GAP, MANE, MANOSQUE, MONTBRUN-LES-BAINS, Route NAPOLÉON, Plateau de VALENSOLE

Sisteron – the citadel and the banks of the Durance

A Bit of History

From Roman legions to GIs – During the Roman occupation, Sisteron, known as Segustero, was a major stopover along the **Domitian Way** linking Italy and the Rhône Delta. It became a bishopric in the 6C and was fortified by the lords of Forcalquier when it came into their possession some five hundred years later. After unification with Provence, the stronghold guarded the territory's northern border, until Provence itself was ceded to the king of France in 1483. The citadel was built during the Wars of Religion (late 16C). Napoleon, returning from the island of Elba in 1815, found

Address Book

For coin categories see the Legend on the cover flap.

EATING OUT

🍽 **Café-restaurant de la Paix** – *41 rue Saunerie -* ☎ *04 92 62 62 29 - closed 24-30 June, 25 Dec-1 Jan*. This unpretentious address is well known to locals who appreciate the generous traditional cuisine and seasonal dishes. The dining room is simply decorated, and prices stay the same in season and out.

🍽 **Les Becs Fins** – *16 r. Saunerie -* ☎ *04 92 61 12 04 - becsfins@aol.com - closed 14-24 Jun, 29 Nov-13 Dec, Sun evening, Thur evening and Wed except 14 Jul-15 Aug*. In a town where restaurants abound, this one certainly lives up to its name ("the gourmets"). The food served here is simple but tasty, attractively presented and reasonably priced. A large terrace fronts the partially pedestrianised street.

WHERE TO STAY

BUDGET

🛏 **Les Chênes** – *300 Rte de Gap - 2km/1.25mi NW of Sisteron -* ☎ *04 92 61 13 67 - closed 23 Dec-5 Feb, Sat from 1 Oct-19 Mar and Sun except July-Aug and public holidays - 23rms -* 🍽 *restaurant*. This is good place to stop not far from the Durance. The rooms are small, functional and soundproofed. The swimming pool and garden are shaded by old oaks. Enjoy traditional cuisine on the terrace in fine weather.

🛏 **Grand Hôtel du Cours** – *Pl. de l'Église -* ☎ *04 92 61 04 51 - hoteldu-cours@wanadoo.fr - closed 16 Nov-28 Feb - 51rms -* 🍽 *restaurant*. This hotel with 1960s decor stands at the heart of the historic old town. Ask for rooms at the back of the hotel, as these are more spacious and comfortable.

ON THE TOWN

La Citadelle – *126 r. Saunerie -* ☎ *04 92 61 13 52 - daily 7am-11pm; out of season, daily except Wed*. When approaching Sisteron from the north, you cannot miss this establishment with its terrace overlooking the Durance valley. While enjoying a cold drink, be sure to photograph the idyllic scene, subject of many a postcard.

SHOPPING

Pâtisserie Canteperdrix – *131 r. de Provence -* ☎ *04 92 61 02 49 - daily except Mon 8am-noon, 2.30pm-7.30pm; Sun 8am-noon - closed 1st week in Oct*. Specialties include the *brioche sisteronaise*, dotted with candied fruit, *Candeperdrillons* (almond-orange cookies), *croquettes Aujoras* (cookies with toasted almonds), calissons (small iced almond cakes), and for good measure a range of *génépi* liqueurs.

Rue Droite and Rue Saunerie – The streets of Sisteron's old town and especially the Rues Droite and Saunerie are good places for a stroll. Rue Droite is a shopper's paradise, while Rue Saunerie is lined with little bars tucked beneath stone vaults, shops selling local produce and craft workshops.

LEISURE

🧒 **Public beach** – *Lifeguards from mid-June to mid-Sept*. Sisteron's waterfront has walking trails and picnic facilities.

🧒 **Parcours Aventures** – *Montée de la Citadelle -* ☎ *06 09 30 81 45 - July to Aug: 9am-7pm* This adventure park just under the citadel offers four obstacle courses for all levels, from beginner to accomplished alpine commando.

luck was on his side when he entered Sisteron to discover that its royalist regiment had withdrawn the day before; the emperor was able to stop for lunch in the town before marching on to Grenoble. Towards the end of the Second World War, the town was partly destroyed by an Allied bombing raid on 15 August 1944 at a cost of 300 lives, but was then liberated by American troops a week later.

The programme for harnessing the Durance, completed in 1977, includes the underground power station at Sisteron, supplied by a pressure pipeline, and the Salignac Dam with its 118ha/292-acre reservoir. The town's economic activities are centred round the production of lamb meat and the food-processing industry.

A theatre and dance festival, **Les Nuits de la Citadelle,** takes place in the open-air theatre below the citadel. Chamber music concerts are given in the Église St-Dominique and the cathedral.

Walking Tour

Cathédrale Notre-Dame-des-Pommiers★
🕐 *From Easter to 1 Nov: 3-6pm -* ☎ *04 92 61 36 50*

This church, built between 1160 and 1220, is a fine example of Provençal Romanesque architecture. As so often in Provence, the influence of Lombard style is immediately apparent: an elegant doorway has alternate black and white voussoirs extended by half-rounded arches leaning against strong buttresses. The main pediment is also flanked by two half pediments; jambs and slender columns are decorated with carvings and capitals forming a continuous frieze representing a bestiary.

With its three naves, Notre-Dame is one of the largest churches in Provence. The square bell-tower is surmounted by a spire in the shape of a pyramid.

A slightly pointed barrel vault, supported by massive square pillars, rests over the dark nave flanked by narrow aisles. Paintings include works by Van Loo, Mignard

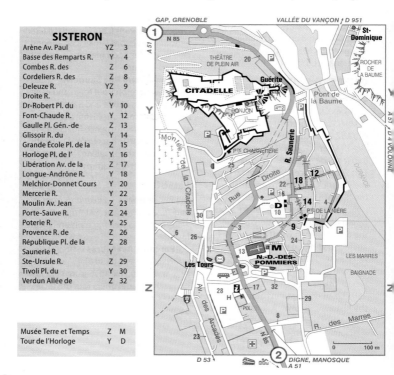

and Coypel. As for the unusual name of the church, it refers not to pommiers (apple trees) but rather to the *pomœrii,* the Latin word for the town walls.

Towers

Sisteron has retained five towers dating from 1370, which formed part of the town's fortifications; four of them stand just south of Notre-Dame, the fifth guards the foot of the citadel. Each bears an evocative name: during the Wars of Religion, the Protestants fled the town through the Porte Sauve, the "escaping gate"; women used to gather for a gossip at the Porte de la Médisance, or "scandalmongers' gate."

Old Sisteron★

For a self-guided tour (1hr), follow the arrows, starting on the left of Notre-Dame; guided tours of the old town are organised in summer by the Tourist Information Centre. The old town lies between rue Droite and the Durance; narrow streets running down to the river are lined with tall houses sometimes linked by vaulted passages known as **andrônes**. Note the elegant carved doorways (16C, 17C and 18C) along the way. Walk along **rue Deleuze** to the **Tour de l'Horloge**★ surmounted by a magnificent wrought-iron campanile bearing Sisteron's motto: *"Tuta montibus et fluviis"* (Safe between its mountains and its rivers). The **Longue Andrône**, a narrow arcaded passageway, branches off rue Mercerie. Continue along **rue du Glissoir** *(often icy in winter, as the name "slippery street" suggests)*, which has retained a 13C Romanesque façade (no 5). Beyond the square, rue Basse-des-Remparts leads to **rue Font-Chaude** then through a covered passageway up to **rue Saunerie;** Napoleon had lunch at no 64, the old **Hostellerie du Bras d'Or.** Note the attractive 16C door at no 2, rue Mercerie; the **porte d'Ornano** takes its name from the noble family who once lived here, and whose arms it bears.

Église St-Dominique

Situated on the opposite bank of the Durance, below the Rocher de la Baume, this former monastery church has retained a Lombard bell-tower. Concerts and literary evenings take place in summer.

The Citadel★ *1hr*

🕐 *May to Oct: (last admission 1hr before closing) July to Aug: daily 9am-7.30pm (June and Sept to 7pm; April-May to 6pm, October to 5.30pm) Nov: 10am-5pm. 4.90€, children 2.45€ - ☎ 04 92 61 27 57 - www.sisteron.com.*
The Porte Charretière leading into the citadel is accessible by car and on foot. In summer, a small tourist train provides a shuttle service between the town hall (Mairie) and the citadel. 🕐 *10am-noon, 2.15-6.30pm. 3€, children 2€ - ☎04 92 61 36 11*
There is nothing left of the 11C castle. The keep and the watch-path are late 12C and the mighty walls set around the rock are the work of **Jean Errard**, Henri IV's chief military engineer. New defences, designed by **Vauban**, Louis XIV's military engineer, in 1692, were added to the powerful 16C fortifications. Part of the citadel, including the chapel, was damaged by bombing in 1944 but later tastefully restored.
A marked tour leads up a succession of steps and terraces, offering views of the town and the Durance Valley, and on to the watch-path. Walk on below the keep, where Jan Kazimierz, prince of Poland, was imprisoned in 1639, to reach the terrace *(viewing table)* and enjoy the bird's-eye **view**★ of the lower part of town, the reservoir and

the mountains dominating the horizon to the north. The 15C **chapel**, partly rebuilt, with modern stained glass by Claude Courageux, is an exhibition centre.

Walk to the north side of the citadel, to the **"Guérite du Diable"** offering an impressive **view**★ of the Rocher de la Baume. The steps leading downwards were once part of an underground staircase, built to link the citadel to the Porte de Dauphiné, which was destroyed in 1944.

The citadel museum includes a room devoted to Napoleon's "Return from Elba" and an exhibition featuring horse-drawn vehicles.

Musée Terre et Temps ★

6 Place Gén-de-Gaulle - ◷ *July to Aug: daily except Wed 10am-1pm, 3-7pm; guided tours Tue 10.45am; Apr to June and Sept to Oct: daily except Tue and Wed 9.30am-12.30pm, 4-6pm. 3€, children 2€, guided tour 4.55€, children 3.55€ -☎ 04 92 61 61 30*

Kids In the Visitandine chapel, this museum set up by the Réserve Géologique de Haute-Provence explores the development of the idea of time, from geological time to modern timepieces. A Foucault's pendulum shows the rotation of the Earth. The museum is the starting point of the **Route du Temps**, ◷ see excursion ②

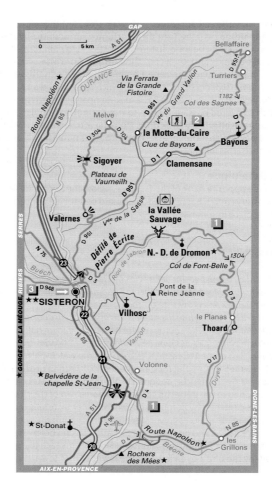

Excursions

1 **Prieuré de Vilhosc** *10km/6mi east along D 4 towards Volonne*
Guided tours by appointment with Mmme Giovale. ☎ *04 92 61 26 70.*

▶ *Drive 5km/3mi then turn left onto D 217; 4km/2.5mi further on, cross the Riou de Jabron and follow the signposted road on the right.*

The 3-naved **crypt** of an ancient monastery, located near the river beneath farm buildings, is a rare example of 11C early Romanesque art.
Continue along D 217 for 5km/3mi to reach the single-arched **Pont de la Reine-Jeanne** spanning the Vançon in a picturesque wooded setting.

2 **Haute vallée du Vançon**★ *92km/57mi round tour – allow 3hr*

▶ *Cross the bridge over the Durance and drive northeast along D 951 then D 3.*

This circuit follows a part of the Route du Temps, organized by the Réserve géologique de Haute-Provence, which is signposted from the departure point in Sisteron; the many footpaths and viewpoints are complemented by parking spaces along the road. If you wish to follow the complete route, continue along south towards Thoard. *A brochure describing the route is available at the Musée Terre et Temps and at the tourist office.*
The road rises, offering interesting **views**★★ of Sisteron and of the Buëch Valley in the foreground, with the Montagne de Lure to the southwest. Beyond the pass, there are bird's-eye views of the Riou de Jabron as it comes out of the Défilé de Pierre Écrite and flows towards the Durance.

Défilé de Pierre Écrite
The rock face of this deep gorge, on the left of the road near a small bridge, bears a Roman inscription celebrating Dardanus, a prefect of Gaul who converted to Christianity and who ordered the building of the first road through the gorge in the 5C AD. He founded Théopolis, a "city of God," the remains of which were discovered between Chardavon and St-Geniez.
Beyond St-Geniez on the right, Notre-Dame-de-Dromon can be seen at the foot of the Rocher de Dromon.

La Vallée Sauvage
Kids ⏱ *July to August: 10am-7pm; Apr to June and Sept to All Souls holiday: Wed and Sat-Sun 10am-7pm 5.60€, children 3-16 years 3.90€ - ☎04 92 61 52 85 - www.laval-leesauvage.com*
Just outside the gorge, this provides a nice stop for children, who can see and sometimes feed wild boars, mountain sheep, deer and farm animals along a 2km/1.25 mi circuit. There are picnic facilities and donkey and pony rides.

Notre-Dame-de-Dromon
Leave the car near a farm and continue on foot (15min there and back). Guided tours on request from mairie of Saint-Geniez - ☎ 04 92 61 27 97
This plain 11C chapel was a place of pilgrimage until the 19C. The vaulting dates from the 17C. The tiny crypt beneath the building, which has alabaster columns and capitals, is a fine example of early Romanesque art.

▶ *Continue along D 3.*

The road overlooks the wooded upper Vançon Valley, and the view extends through the Durance Valley to the Luberon and the Montagne Ste-Victoire.

The road, which narrows considerably beyond Authon, goes over the **Col de Font-belle** (alt 1 304m/4 278ft) and through the Mélan Forest.

▶ *At Le Planas, follow the small road to Thoard.*

Thoard

This picturesque old village has retained part of its medieval walls and a Romanesque keep which is now the bell-tower.

▶ *From Thoard, continue along D 17 to reach N 85 and follow the Route Napoléon (see ROUTE NAPOLÉON) back to Sisteron.*

③ **Pays de la Motte-Turriers** 85km/53mi round tour – allow 3hr

▶ *From Sisteron, drive north along D 951.*

The Sasse Valley, lying northeast of Sisteron, is an area modelled by erosion into a succession of ravines and gorges.

▶ *Turn right onto D 1.*

Clamensane

This village is perched on a rocky spur. The landscape becomes gradually wilder and more austere. Beyond the **Clue de Bayons,** the road enters an open basin.

Bayons

A large and beautiful abbey **church** overlooks the village square. Built in the 12C and 13C, it is a harmonious mixture of Romanesque and Gothic art: the nave is surmounted by a broken barrel vault and the chancel has a ribbed vault with an Agnus Dei on the fine keystone. The archivolt of the 14C porch is framed by lancet arcades.

▶ *Beyond Bayons, D 1 veers due north towards Turriers.*

The road rises in a series of steep hairpin bends, known locally as "tourniquets," to the Col des Sagnes, in its setting of gullied mountain slopes, before running down to Turriers and Bellaffaire (18C castle).

▶ *Beyond Bellaffaire, turn left onto D 951.*

The road follows the **Grand Vallon** Valley, famous for its orchards (apple, pear and peach trees).

▶ *Beyond La Motte, turn right onto D 104 to Melve then left onto D 304.*

Sigoyer

From the partly restored 15C castle, the **view**★★ extends to the Durance and, beyond, to the Baronnies and the Montagne de Lure.
The road runs down to Valernes through lavender fields.

Valernes

This hilltop village, which has retained part of its fortifications, offers a good view of the Sasse Valley.

▶ *Return to Sisteron along D 951.*

4 **Gorges de la Méouge** ★ *90km/56km round tour – allow 4hr*

▶ *From Sisteron, drive northeast on D 948 towards Ribiers; continue to Le Plan along the right bank of the Buëch then turn left onto D 942.*

The road winds through the gorge along the north bank of the rushing Méouge, a tributary of the Buëch. Several sections of the river are suitable for canoeing, particularly in the spring. There are excellent views of the water and the jagged rocks on the left bank, particularly at **Pomet.**

▶ *Carry on to Barret-le-Bas at the end of the gorge. It is possible to return to Sisteron via the north side of the Montagne de Chabre. Otherwise, continue to La Calandre, turn right onto D 170 towards the Col St-Jean and Laborel then follow the Céans Valley to Orpierre (☝ see BUIS-LES-BARONNIES, C) and Eyguiers, returning to Sisteron along N 75.*

SIXT-FER-À-CHEVAL★★

MICHELIN MAP 328 N4

Like many other communities in Savoie, this traditional village at the top of the Giffre valley has successfully reinvented itself as an attractive centre for walking and skiing holidays. Its main attraction, however, remains the **Cirque du Fer-à-Cheval** from which it takes its name. Hollowed out by an Ice Age glacier, this horseshoe-shaped ridge is celebrated for the waterfalls which splash down its steep, rocky face and wooded slopes. 🏛 *Place de la Gare - 74740 Sixt-Fer-à-Cheval* 🕐 *mid-Dec to Mar: 9am-12.30pm, 3-6.30pm; rest of year: daily except Sun and public D907.*

▶ The road ends in a cul-de-sac when it reaches the Cirque du Fer-a-Cheval, another 6.5km/4mi further on.
🔔 **Don't Miss:** The Cirque is a spectacular site not to be missed.
🕐 **Organizing Your Time:** Take the time to walk along the Fond de la Combe.
Kids **Especially for Kids:** The chalet at the Reserve has exhibits to explain the astonishing surroundings to children.

The Fond de la Combe, the source of the Giffre

Y. Tierry/MICHELIN

Also See: Nearby Sights: AVORIAZ, CLUSES, Les GETS, MORZINE, Bassin de SALLANCHES, SAMOËNS

Sights

Village of Sixt-Fer-à-Cheval ★

This charming village, located where the upper and lower Giffre rivers meet, clusters around the remains of its 12C abbey, a "daughter" to that of Abondance (see ABONDANCE). It is a centre for hiking and mountaineering in summer and for skiing in winter, but its greatest attraction is its extraordinary situation among cliffs and waterfalls, forests, high peaks and the great cirque carved by ancient glaciers.

For coin categories, see the Legend on the cover flap.

WHERE TO STAY

Mas du Figuier – *La Fontaine – 04200 Bevons - 7km/4.4mi W of Sisteron on N 85, D 946 and D 553 - ☎ 04 92 62 81 28 - closed Nov, Dec, Jan - - 5rms - restaurant*. A field of lavender spreads out before this 17C farmhouse. Rooms are pleasant with Provençal touches and Moorish bathrooms. You can request a cabin perched in an old oak tree.

Church

The village church still has its 13C nave. Beside it, handsome old houses face onto the square, where an ancient lime tree lends welcome shade in summer. A commemorative plaque on the wall of the church is dedicated to Jacques Balmat, the conqueror of Mont Blanc, who died in the mountains around Sixt while searching for gold.

Maison de la Réserve naturelle

Mid-June to Sept and mid-Dec to Apr: 9am-12.30pm, 3-6.30pm; May to mid-June and Oct to mid-Dec: daily except Sun and Mon 9.30-noon, 2.30-6pm. No charge - ☎ 04 50 34 91 90 or 04 50 34 49 36

Three-quarters of the Sixt area (9 200ha/22 734 acres) has been designated as a nature reserve. This visitors' centre in the middle of the village presents a short history of the area and an introduction to its flora, fauna and geology.

Hikes

The Limestone Alps of Faucigny

The limestone peaks in the French Alpine range reach their highest point in Faucigny (see also CLUSES, Excursions). Twisted and crumpled rocks have been shaped into a magnificent landscape of outcrops and steep cliff walls which climbers and hikers love to explore; ever-present on the skyline is the snow-capped peak of the **Buet** (3 099m/10 167ft), but the superb **Fer-à-Cheval** ★★ is the undisputed highlight. Dedicated walkers can follow part of the GR 5 route over the col d'Anterne (2 264m/7 428ft), linking the Sixt valley with the bassin de Sallanches or the Chamonix valley across the Chaîne des Fiz.

Réserve naturel de Sixt ★

Cirque du Fer-à-Cheval ★★

6.5km/4mi from Sixt on D 907. On leaving Sixt, there is a fine view of the pyramid-shaped peak of the Tenneverge (2 985m), and its Corne du Chamois, the "chamois horn," at the end of the basin. The limestone walls (500-700m/1 640-2 297ft) run with waterfalls; in June, as many as thirty stream down the cliffs and add to the magical attraction of the place. The cirque forms a near-perfect ring, broken only at its north end, where the Giffre has cut a path through the rock. The **Maison de la Réserve naturelle** presents exhibitions on mountain flora and fauna during the season.

Fond de la Combe★

1hr 30min on foot there and back

🚶 A marked path branches off at the end of the road, 50m/55yd beyond the kiosk, and leads to the Bout du Monde, "the End of the World," where the Giffre rises at the foot of the Ruan and Prazon glaciers.

Cascade du Rouget★★

5km/3mi from Sixt. Cross the Giffre in Sixt and follow the small road to Salvagny. Beyond Salvagny, the road runs down to the foot of this double waterfall, the largest in a whole chain of cascades which continues downstream.

LA TARENTAISE★★

MICHELIN MAP 333 L/M/N 4/5
LOCAL MAP SEE MASSIF DE LA VANOISE

The sinuous course of the upper Isère Valley is the main geographical feature of the Tarentaise region. The long and narrow defiles of the Haute and Basse Tarentaise provide a contrast with the more open Moyenne Tarentaise stretching from Moûtiers to Bourg-St-Maurice. This pastoral and wooded middle Tarentaise is the natural habitat of the fawn-coloured **Tarine cows,** one of the most carefully preserved mountain breeds in France which, owing to their high milk yield, have spread to areas outside the Alps, particularly in the southern part of the country. The Moûtiers area is the only industrialised part of the region, although hydroelectric power is produced in other areas such as Tignes (🕮 *see TIGNES*). The Tarentaise is also known as the home of the *"frontière,"* which has become one of the symbols of traditional life in Savoie. This black-velvet head-dress decorated with gold braid has probably been worn by women since the 16C. There's something of an art to wearing the bonnet, which may need up to an hour of careful adjustment before it sits perfectly. 🛈 *Av de Tarentaise - 73210 Aime* 🕐 *July to Aug: Mon-Sat 9am-12.30pm, 2-7pm, Sun 10am-12.30pm, 2.30-6pm; Sept to June: Mon-Sat 9am-noon, 2-6pm; mid-Dec to Mar: Mon-Fri 9am-noon, 2-6pm, Sat 10am-noon, 2-8pm.* 🕐 *Closed Sun except July to Aug and public holidays -* ☎ *04 79 55 67 00 - www.aimesavoie.com*

Fr. Isler/MICHELIN

Flocks on the high pastures

▶ **Orient Yourself:** The Tarentaise and the Maurienne regions, both cut by valleys, extend south on either side of the Vanoise Massif, towards the passes that have linked Italy and France since ancient times.

◉ **Don't Miss:** Stop to see the touching frescos at the basilica at Aime.

◷ **Organizing Your Time:** Roads are narrow, winding and crowded. Don't count on making fast time.

✋ **Also See:** Nearby Sights: ALBERTVILLE, Les ARCS, BEAUFORT, La Vallée des BEL-LEVILLE, BOURG-ST-MAURICE, CHAMPAGNY-EN-VANOISE, COURCHEVEL, Route des GRANDES ALPES, Route de l'ISERAN, Route de la MADELEINE, MÉRIBEL, La PLAGNE, PRALOGNAN-LA-VANOISE, TIGNES, VAL-D'ISÈRE, Massif de la VANOISE

Excursions

Moyenne Tarentaise ★

FROM MOÛTIERS TO BOURG-ST-MAURICE *41km/25.5mi – allow 2hr*

Beyond Aime, the itinerary leaves N 90 and follows secondary roads through orchards and fields on the south side of the valley, within sight of the wooded slope across the river, backed by the tall silhouette of Mont Pourri (alt 3 779m/12 398ft).

Moûtiers

Moûtierslies deep inside a basin, at the confluence of the River Dorons and River Isère. It used to be the capital of the Tarentaise region and a major religious centre whose feudal lords boasted the title of "princes of the Holy Roman Empire." Inside the **Cathédrale St-Pierre** note the wooden bishop's throne, dating from the 15C, and, on the left of the nave, a Romanesque Virgin Mary. On the first floor of the archbishop's palace is the **Musée d'histoire et d'archéologie**, (◷ *Ask for admission at the tourist ofice daily except Sun 10am-noon, 2-6pm* ◷ *closed public holidays. 2€, children under 15 years no charge -* ☎ *04 79 24 04 23 - www.ot-moutiers.com).* **The Musée des Traditions populaires de Tarentaise** *(*✋◷ *July-August: daily except Sun 9am-noon, 2-6pm; Sept to June: apply to the tourist office daily except Sun 9am-noon, 2-6pm* ◷ *closed public holidays. 2€, children under 15 years no charge -* ☎ *04 79 24 04 23 - www.ot-moutiers.com)* presents forgotten rural professions and ways of life.

Two spas in the lower Doron de Bozel Valley are within easy reach of Moutiers; **Brides-les-Bains**✚ (for obesity and circulatory complaints) and **Salins-les-Bains**✚, which offers stimulating salty waters, recommended in the treatment of gynaecological problems and complaints affecting the lymph glands. Salins-les-Bains was once a major salt producing centre, processing 1 000 tons per year until the 18C.

The **Chapelle St-Jacques** stands on a rocky spur at the entrance of the Étroit du Siaix Gorge, in front of the village of St-Marcel.

Étroit du Siaix

Stop 50m/55yd before the tunnel *(beware of falling rocks)* in order to appreciate the depth of this gorge, which is the narrowest passage of the whole Isère Valley.

On the way to Aime, the valley is blocked by two glacial obstructions. Beyond the first of these, within sight of the Mont Pourri Summit and glaciers lies the small **Centron Basin** which takes its name from the Celtic tribe who settled in the area.

Aime

Aime is the site of the **Ancienne basilique St-Martin**★★. This 11C church with its massive bell-tower is the best example of early Romanesque architecture in Savoie. The chancel and the apse are decorated with 12C and 14C frescoes – partly restored in the 19C – which illustrate scenes of the Old and New Testament (Adam and Eve, the massacre of the Innocents). Excavations have revealed traces of two previous edifices; the older of these, which may have been Roman, was used by the first

Christians, the "newer" building dates from the Merovingian period. The 11C **crypt,** with its plain square capitals, supports the chancel.

Housed in a former 14C chapel, the small **Musée Pierre-Borrione** (☞ *July to Aug: guided tours (1hr) on request at tourist office daily 10am-12.30pm, 2-6.30pm. 3€, children under 16 years no charge -* ☎ *04 79 55 67 00.)* displays Gallo-Roman and Merovingian finds.

▶ *Turn left onto D 218 towards Tessens and Granier, then take D 86.*

On leaving Valezan, the view extends over the other bank of the Isère, along the Ponturin Valley to the Bellecôte Massif (highest point: 3 416m/11 207ft). Beyond Montgirod, Bourg-St-Maurice gradually comes into view, backed by the Col du Petit-St-Bernard flanked on the left by the jagged silhouette of the Roc de Belleface.

Bourg-St-Maurice – ⓒ *See BOURG-ST-MAURICE.*

Haute Tarentaise ★

FROM BOURG-ST-MAURICE TO TIGNES *32km/20mi – allow 1hr, not including the hikes from Ste-Foy.*
From Bourg-St-Maurice there is a view of the Malgovert power station, which is fed by the Tignes dam. Beyond the town, D 902 leaves the broad valley and leads up in a series of tight bends to Ste-Foy.

Ste-Foy-Tarentaise
Built on high ground overlooking the east bank of the River Isère, between Bourg-St-Maurice and Val-d'Isère, and surrounded by traditional villages and hamlets, Ste-Foy-Tarentaise is the ideal starting point for pleasant excursions in the area.

La Sassière ★★
10km/6.2mi then 2hr there and back on foot. Leave Ste-Foy-Tarentaise towards the Col de l'Iseran and turn onto the first road on the left.
After driving for 2km/1.2mi, you will come within sight of **Le Miroir,** a large hamlet whose chalets, climbing up the south-facing slope, have wooden balconies.
The road continues to rise, eventually reaching the high-pasture area where houses are built of stone with small openings and flat roofs covered with *lauzes* (heavy slabs of schist) in order to withstand bitter winter conditions.

▶ *Leave the car at the end of the road and continue on foot.*

🚶 The path rises among clusters of rhododendrons. As you approach the Chapelle de la Sassière, the Rutor Glacier, situated across the Italian border and overlooking a pastoral landscape, suddenly comes into **view**★★.

Le Monal ★★
8km/5mi then 1hr there and back on foot. Drive south along D 902 then turn left to Chenal. Leave the car there and continue on foot.
🚶 From the hamlet, there is a remarkable **view**★★ of the Mont Pourri and its glaciers, in particular the waterfalls coming down from the Glaciers de la Gurra and the village of La Gurraz below.
Upstream of Ste-Foy, the wild wooded valley widens slightly between La Raie and the Pont de la Balme. Water can be seen cascading down the opposite slope from the Mont Pourri glaciers (the view is particularly interesting from Le Monal). Towards the end of the drive, the huge fresco of a giant decorating the Barrage de Tignes seems to bar the end of the valley.

✳✳✳**Tignes** – ⓒ *See TIGNES.*

THONON-LES-BAINS ♈♈

CONURBATION 53 834
MICHELIN MAP 328 L2

Thonon is the historic capital of the Chablais region as well as a health and spa resort specialising in the treatment of kidney and bladder diseases; the season lasts from 15 May to 15 September. In addition to the resort and the handsome lakeside villas, set back behind lush gardens, visitors should make time for the **Rives** district, near the harbour on Lake Geneva, which has retained a few picturesque fishermen's cottages. *1, place du Marché – 74023 Thonon-les-Bains July to August: Mon -Sat 9am-7pm, Sun 9am-6pm; rest of year: Mon-Sat 9am (Sat 10am)-12.30pm, 1.30-6.30pm closed Sun and public holidays - ☎ 04 50 71 55 55 - www.thononlesbains.com.*

▶ **Orient Yourself:** You can take the A 40 to Thonon-les-Bains, turning onto N 206 via exit 15, but expect dense traffic; the French side of Lake Geneva is heavily urbanized. You can also drive from Cluses, 60km/37.5mi to the south on D 902, passing through Morzine and the Aulps valley. Or, you can take one of the ferries from Ouchy on the Swiss side of the lake.

Don't Miss: Take the funicular between Thonon and the delightful port of Rives; on the edge of town, stop to see the Domaine de Ripaille with its arboretum.

Organizing Your Time: Monday evenings in July and August, the Abbey of Aulps is lit by flaming torches.

Especially for Kids: In July and August, the Thonon tourist offices organizes guided tours especially for children. There are also activities for children at the Abbey of Aulps.

Also See: Nearby Sights: ABONDANCE, AVORIAZ, CHÂTEL, CLUSES, ÉVIAN-LES-BAINS, Les GETS, Route des GRANDES ALPES, MORZINE, La ROCHE-SUR-FORON, YVOIRE

Around the Spa Town

The lake shore ★
On the way to Ripaille, there is a neatly appointed beach. The cruise ships which cross the lake moor in the well-preserved port of Rives, where professional fishermen also dock and sell their catch daily at 9.30am. From here, Thonon can be reached by car, by a picturesque **funicular** dating from 1888 (*July to Aug: 8am-11pm; mid-Apr-June and Sept: 8am-9pm; Oct to mid-Apr: 8am-12.30pm, 1.30-6.30pm, Sun 2-6pm (3min, every 4min). 1.80€ return - ☎ 04 50 71 21 54*) or even by walking up several inclines, preferably through the gardens laid out beneath the Château de Sonnaz.

Viewpoints ★★

Several viewpoints line the way from boulevard de la Corniche to the Jardin Anglais.

Place du Château
The castle of the dukes of Savoie which once stood on this site was destroyed by the French in 1589. In the centre of the square stands the statue of **Général Dessaix** (1764-1834), a native of Thonon, who joined French revolutionary forces when they occupied the Savoie and who was made a general by Napoleon.

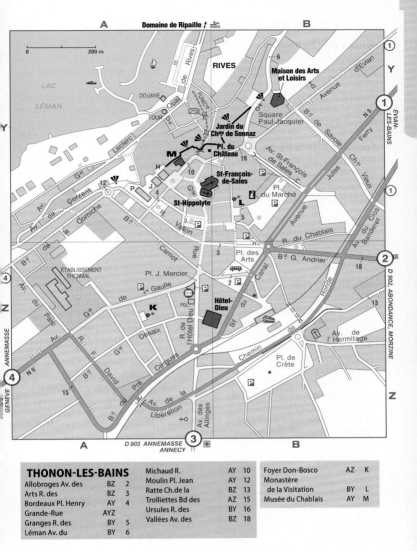

From the terraces, there is an open **view**★ of the Swiss side of Lake Geneva from Nyon to Lausanne. Below, the Rives district clusters round the brownish roofs of Rives-Montjoux Castle and Ripaille Castle can be seen to the right. The Vaudois Alps and Jura mountains form the panoramic background.

Jardin du château de Sonnaz and Jardin Paul-Jacquier

A pleasant place to relax; situated at the end of the vast open space of the Jardin Paul-Jacquier, the ancient Chapelle St-Bon, adjacent to a 13C tower (part of the town's fortifications), attracts water-colourists.

The Maison des Arts et Loisirs, designed by Maurice Novarina, a native of Thonon, was completed in 1966.

Other Sights

Musée du Chablais

🕐 *July to Aug: 10am-noon, 2.30-6pm; Dec to June and Sept: Wed-Sun 2.30-6pm (last admission 30min before closing)* 🕐 *closed public holidays and from Oct to mid-Dec. 2€ (children under 8 years no charge) - ☎ 69 50 70 69 49.*

Housed in the 17C Château de Sonnaz, this regional folk museum illustrates local history; a room is devoted to the prehistoric lakeside village period and to local Gallo-Roman finds.

Écomusée de la Pêche et du Lac (port of Rives)

🅺🅸🅳🆂 🕐 *July to Aug: Daily 10am-noon, 2.30-6pm; June and Sept: Wed-Sun 2.30-8pm - ☎ 04 50 70 26 96.* Occupying three former fishing huts, this little museum describes the resources, fishing, history, water quality and other facts about Europe's most celebrated lake. Lake fish swim about in aquariums.

Address Book

For coin categories, see the Legend on the cover flap.

WHERE TO EAT

☕**Le Moulin**– *Place du Marché - ☎ 04 50 26 29 43 - closed Sun and public holidays.* This pizzeria occupies an old mill made of stone on a little canal. There are two terraces, one on the street and one in a garden shaded by acacia trees. Simple decor inside. You can order from a varied menu.

☕ **Le Bétandi** – *2 r des Italiens - ☎ 04 50 71 37 71 - closed Sun noon in July-Aug.* Although close to the town centre, this little restaurant resembles an old Savoyard farmhouse. The menu offers typical local fare with the inevitable fondue, tartiflette and reblochonade as well as pizzas.

☕☕ **Château de Ripaille** – *☎ 04 50 26 64 44 - www.ripaille.fr - open July-Aug for lunch only.* The massive castle dominates this corner of Lac Geneva, and a "forfait découvert" gives you a taste of the château wine, a tour of the castle and lunch in a manicured garden.

☕☕**Auberge d'Anthy** – *2 r des Écoles 0 74200 Anthy-sur-Leman- ☎ 04 50 70 35 00 www.auberge-anthy.com - closed 4-20 Jan, Sun evening and Mon.* Here is a pleasant surprise: this bar serves well-prepared regional cuisine. The noon menu is quite reasonably priced, and the simple country decor is relaxing.

WHERE TO STAY

☕☕**À l'Ombre des Marronniers** – *17 pl. de Crête - ☎ 04 50 71 26 18 - info@hotel-marroniers.com- closed 28 Apr-8 May and 22 Dec-8 Jan -* 🅿 *- 17rms -* ☕☕*restaurant.* In this picturesque chalet set in the greenery of a flower garden, ask for one of the four very pretty rooms in typical local style. The rest of the hotel is clean but a bit out-of-date, like the restaurant. A good family place.

☕☕**Hôtel Arc en Ciel** – *18 pl Crête - ☎ 04 50 71 90 63 - www.hotelarcencielthonon.com - closed 28 Apr- 8 May and 22 Dec-6 Jan -* 🅿 *- 40rms.* Close to downtown, this is a modern hotel with a nice garden. Guestrooms are spacious and well-equiped, and most have a balcony. Sauna.

☕☕**Hotel À l'Écho des Montagnes** – *74200 Armoy - ☎ 04 50 73 94 55 - alechodesmontagnes@yahoo.fr - closed 17 Dec-10 Feb, Sun evening and Mon from 5 Oct-15 May -* 🅿 *- 47rms -* ☕☕*restaurant.* This imposing 19C house, set in a garden, is surrounded by village calm. It offers large rustic rooms and a friendly restaurant panelled in wood, with generous portions of regional cuisine incorporating vegetables from the garden.

ON THE TOWN

Maison des arts – *4 bis av d'Évian - ☎ 04 50 71 39 47 - www.mai-thonon.org - open daily except Sun and Mon 2-7pm, Thur 11am-7pm - closed Aug, 20 Dec-2 Jan and public holidays.* This centre offers a a varied programme of exhibits, plays, operas, variety shows etc.

Église St-Hippolyte

July to Aug: 10am-noon, 2-6.30pm. Romanesque crypt closed for repairs.
St François de Sales preached in this church and the local population renounced
Protestantism within its walls. The building illustrates different styles; the interior
decoration, dating from the 17C, includes stucco work as well as painted cartouches
and medallions over the nave **vaulting**★.
Note, on the right-hand side of the first nave, a 13C stoup bearing the arms of Savoie.
The pulpit dates from the 16C and the organ loft from 1672.
The three-naved Romanesque **crypt** (12C) was partly rebuilt in the 17C.

Basilique St-François-de-Sales

The neo-Gothic basilica is adjacent to Église St-Hippolyte. It contains the last work
painted by Maurice Denis, one of the founders of the Nabis movement: two large
frescoes entitled **Chemin de Croix** (1943), depicting Christ dying on the cross and
his apparition to the holy women after his resurrection. The christening font dates
from the 13C, the Virgin and Child from the 14C.

Monastère de la Visitation

It was erected in the 17C and recently restored. The chapel is surmounted by Gothic
ribbed vaulting.

Hôtel-Dieu

Occupying the site of the former Minimes Convent, founded in 1636, the edifice is
centred round a cloister whose upper part is decorated in Baroque style.

Foyer Don-Bosco

The small modern chapel of this institution is decorated with ceramics.

Excursions

Domaine de Ripaille★

*7km/4.3mi round tour. Go down to Rives and follow quai de Ripaille to the end then turn
left into the avenue leading to the Château de Ripaille.*
This monastery and castle comprises a group of imposing buildings in typical Savoyard style, set in the midst of fine vineyards.

Fondation Ripaille

*Guided tours (1hr) July to Aug: 11am and 2.30, 3.15, 4.45pm; Apr to June and Sept:
11am, 2.30 and 4pm; Feb to Mar and Oct to Nov: 3pm closed Dec to Jan. 6€, children
7-15 years 3 € - ☎ 04 50 26 64 44 - www.ripaille.fr*
The castle has, since 1976, been the headquarters of the Fondation Ripaille which
promotes a research centre concerned with ecology, geology and the development
of natural resources. A doorway in French classical style leads to the main courtyard.
The castle is on the right – four out of the seven towers are still standing – while
the monastery buildings are on the left; between 1619 and the Revolution, they
were occupied by Carthusian monks, hence the name of *chartreuse* by which they
are known today.

Castle

The interior was restored at the end of the 19C and decorated in neo-Gothic and
modern styles. There are exhibitions about the castle's history.

Chartreuse

The winepress and 17C kitchens are open to visitors.

Forest and arboretum

🕐 *May to Sept: 10am-7pm; Jan to Apr and Oct to Nov: 10am-4.30pm (last admission 1hr before closing. No charge -* ☎ *04 50 26 28 22*

Leave the grounds and take the first road on the left. The great storm of 1999 severely damaged the arboretum, which is just recovering. The Ripaille Forest, which was the hunting ground of the dukes of Savoie, covers an area of 53ha/131 acres. Marked paths lead to the arboretum whose trees, including firs, thujas, red oaks from America and black walnuts, were planted between 1930 and 1934. In a clearing nearby, the **monument national des Justes** commemorates the bravery of those who risked their lives to save French Jews from deportation during the Second World War.

VONGY

Église Notre-Dame-du-Léman is a graceful modern church decorated in tones of blue in honour of Our Lady. A large roof is supported by transverse gables and surmounted by a slender spire. The apse is adorned with a large mosaic depicting the Virgin Mary surrounded by local saints.

CHÂTEAU DES ALLINGES

7km/4.3mi south, leave Thonon by ③ on the town plan and following D 12. Take the first road on the right as you enter Macheron.

The hilltop was originally crowned by two castles belonging to rival feudal lords until 1355 when they both came into the possession of the count of Savoie. In 1594, St François de Sales made it his headquarters when he preached in the area.

Walk through the two fortified gates to the east platform offering an open **view** of the Bas Chablais region and the Dent d'Oche; the west platform affords an extended **view**★ of Lake Geneva, Thonon and the Jura mountains. The restored **chapel** has retained its oven-vaulted apse *(Light switch to the left of the door)* decorated with a late 10C Romanesque fresco, its rich colours and hieratic figures showing a clear Byzantine influence. Christ is represented in Glory, surrounded by the Evangelists, the Virgin Mary on the left, St John the Baptist on the right and personifications of the virtues below. Note the round stones embedded in the castle's east walls by a Carolingian catapult.

CHABLAIS

The Chablais★★, extending between Lake Geneva and the Giffre Valley, is the largest massif in the Préalpes with some imposing summits such as the Dent d'Oche and its twin peak the Château d'Oche. The complex geological structure comprises three distinct areas. The **Bas-Chablais** is a relatively low, hilly area bordering the southern shores of Lake Geneva (Lac Léman in French), where woods of chestnut trees alternate with vineyards along the Savoyard Riviera. The **Pays Gavot** is the name given to the area inland from Évian. The **Haut-Chablais** (highest point: the Hautforts, alt 2 464m/8 083ft), centred round Morzine, is an area of pastures and forests. Three rivers have cut their way through it: the Dranse d'Abondance, Dranse de Morzine and Brevon, all of which are tributaries of the Dranse de Savoie flowing into Lake Geneva.

1 Route des Trois Cols★ *55km/34.2mi round tour – about 3hr 30min.*

▶ *Leave Thonon-les-Bains by the road to Bellevaux*

The D 26 runs above the Gorges de la Dranse; here and there the route gives a glimpse of the picturesque valley of Bellevaux and the Dent d'Oche in the distance.

Bellevaux

The village lies on the west bank of the Brevon, in the charming green **valley**★ of the same name. The church, surmounted by a copper onion-shaped spire, contains some elegant woodwork and has retained a 14C chapel.

▷ *Turn right past the cemetery, cross the Brevon and take the forest road on the left.*

The road rises very steeply above the Bellevaux Valley.

Chalets de Buchille

Fine view of the Mont d'Hermone to the northwest.

Vallon de la Chèvrerie★

The upper Brevon Valley, guarded by the narrow pass of La Clusaz, was the secluded site chosen for the **Chartreuse de Vallon** dedicated to St Bruno in the 12C and abandoned in 1619 when the order moved to Ripaille. The road ends at La Chèvrerie, beneath a cirque over which the Roc d'Enfer towers at 2 244m/7 362ft.

▷ *Go back to the Col de Jambaz, turn left and almost immediately right onto D 32.*

Between the Col de Jambaz and the Col de Terramont, the road leaves the Risse Valley, briefly enters the Lullin Valley then the Vallon de Terramont. Further on, towards the Col du Cou, the road reveals the peaceful landscapes of the Vallée Verte framed by forested heights, including the Voirons, Mont d'Hirmentaz and Mont Forchat (the latter bearing a white statue of St François de Sales).

Col de Cou★

Alt 1 116m/3 661ft. Beyond the forested pass, there is a **view**★ of Lake Geneva with the Jura mountain range in the distance.
During the drive down from the pass (16km/10mi), the road offers glimpses through the trees of the lake, of the Yvoire promontory, of the Voirons and of the Jura mountains. Further down, there are lovely **views**★ of the pleasant Bas Chablais countryside overlooked by the ruins of the Château des Allinges.

▷ *In Mâcheron, turn left towards the Château des Allinges.*

S. Sauvignier/MICHELIN

Cow bells

Château des Allinges – ♿ *See above.*

▸ *Road D 12 leads to Thonon.*

[2] Gorges de la Dranse

From Thonon to Morzine

33km/20.5mi – allow 1hr 45min. Leave Thonon by ② on the town plan, D 902 towards Cluses.

The route follows the Dranse de Savoie Valley through a succession of narrow sections and small basins. From Thonon to Bioge, the road follows the wooded Gorges of the Dranse where impressive red and ochre cliffs tower over the rushing mountain stream.

Gorges du Pont du Diable★★

200 steps. (🕐 Guided tours (45min) May to Sept: 9am-6pm (July to Aug 7pm). 4.90€, children 6-15 years 3€, 16-20 years 4€ - ☎ 04 50 72 10 39 - www.lepontdudiable.com)
Enormous rocks, coloured in ochre, grey, green and blue by various deposits and eroded into all kinds of shapes, luxuriant vegetation and smooth vertical cliffs up to 60m/197ft high all contribute to make this visit fascinating; landslides have occurred in places, forming huge piles of boulders and a spectacular natural bridge known as the Pont du Diable.

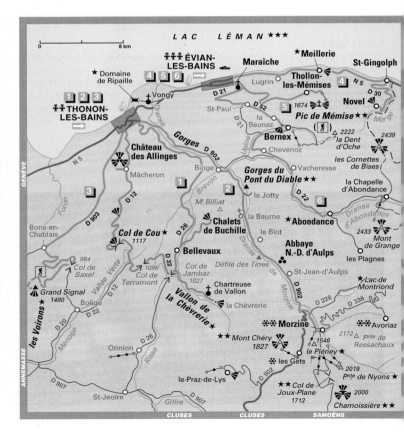

Stop further on by the Le Jotty Dam and the Église de la Baume, perched on a ledge. Beyond the Défilé de Tines (tunnel) are the ruins of Notre-Dame d'Aulps.

Abbaye Notre-Dame d'Aulps

🕐 *Admission only during guided tours July to Aug: Mon 10pm (tour with flaming torches); Fri 11am; Christmas and Feb holidays, June and Sept: Fri 11am; medieval festival 3rd week of Aug - ☎ 04 50 72 15 15 - www.valleedaulps.com.*

The ruins of the 12C-13C church are the only remaining part of this Cistercian abbey. The pilgrimage dedicated to St Guérin, a former abbot, now takes place in the neo-Gothic church of St-Jean-d'Aulps. Note the attractive rose window.

The road now leads into the broad, more densely populated Morzine valley with the Pointe de Ressachaux and Pointe de Nyon rising above it. Return by the same route or via Taninges and St-Jeoire.

Hike

③ Grand Signal des Voirons ★

▷ *Take the D 903 to Annemasse as far as Bons-en-Chablais. From Bons, drive southeast along D 20 towards Boëge.*

The road rises gently through the woods, offering lovely glimpses of the Bas Chablais and Lake Geneva. From the Col de Saxel, D 50 follows the line of the ridge to the right through a small wood; the view gradually extends to the east beyond the Chaîne du Reposoir to the Dents du Midi, Mont Buet and the snow-capped peaks of the Mont Blanc Massif.

🚶 *Leave the car at the end of the road, in the car park near the monastery. 1hr there and back. From the car park, take the path marked "voie sans issue" and head uphill through the wood. At the edge of the wood, follow a path 50m/55yd ahead on the left marked "Les Crêtes." After 200m/219yd this path joins the Chemin des Crêtes; turn right here. The path divides in front of the monastery building; take the left fork to the ridge and follow it to the right to the cross which marks the summit of the Grand Signal (1 480m/4 856ft).*

The **view** of Lake Geneva is partly blocked, but takes in the Mont Blanc Massif and the high chalk cliffs of Faucigny on the eastern and southern sides.

THORENS-GLIÈRES ★

POPULATION 2 560
MICHELIN MAP 328 K5

This small town lies on the banks of the River Fillière, a tributary of the Fier, at the point where the narrow valley opens out. It is the birthplace of St François de Sales who was christened and later ordained as a bishop in the parish church; its chancel, built in 1450, is the one that de Sales would have known. Nothing remains of the castle where François de Sales was born, but the Chapelle de Sales standing on the site, along the Usillon road, has become a place of annual pilgrimage; a procession in traditional costume takes place in Thorens on the same day *(Sunday following 15 August)*.

Thorens-Glières is also proud of its role as a focal point of resistance during the Second World War; the plateau around the town was the scene of bitter

fighting against the Wehrmacht and the Vichy militia. ▯ *22 pl de la Mairie - 74570 Thorens-Glières* ◷ *July to Aug: Mon-Sat 9am-12.30pm, 2.30-6pm, Sun 9am-12.30pm; May to June and Sept: Tue -Sat 9am-12.30pm, 2.30-6pm, closed Sun; Oct to Apr: Tue to Fri 9am-12.30pm, 1.30-5pm, closed Sun* ◷ *closed public holidays -* ☎ *04 50 22 40 31 - www.paysdefilliere.com*

▶ **Orient Yourself:** Thorens-Glières is 20km/12.5km northeast of Annecy on N 203, towards Roche-sur-Foron.

☺ **Don't Miss:** The Château of Thorens houses some remarkable art.

Especially for Kids: The commemorative trail at the Plateau des Glières should interest children and provide a useful history lesson.

◔ **Also See:** Nearby Sights: L'ALBANAIS, ANNECY, Lac d'ANNECY, Massif des ARAVIS, La CLUSAZ, CLUSES, La ROCHE-SUR-FORON

Château de Thorens★

&·⚑·⚐ *July to Aug: guided tours (1hr) daily 2-7pm (last admission at 6pm) 6€, children 7-15 years 3.50€ -* ☎ *04 50 22 42 02.*

The castle stands in an attractive setting, within sight of the Vallon de la Fillière and the Parmelan Mountain. The foundations date from the 11C, the round keep – unusual in Savoie – from the 13C, and the whole edifice was remodelled in the 19C.

The vaulted basement was originally given over to a guardroom and prison cells. The ground-floor rooms contain mementoes of St François de Sales, 16C tapestries from Brussels, a wealth of furniture and a collection of paintings; note in particular **St Stephen** by Marco d'Oggiono, 16C Lombard School, *Portrait of the Infanta Isabella* by Van Dyck and *Portrait of the Marquise de Grollier* by Madame Vigée-Lebrun. Two rooms are devoted to the architect of Italian unification, Count Cavour, who was related to the Sales family; portraits and letters are housed here, as well as the desk on which the treaty uniting France and Savoie was signed.

Plateau des Glières

14km/8.7mi east along a forest road.

During the Second World War, the high-pasture area of the Plateau des Glières was chosen by Resistance leaders as the site of one of their fortified camps. It was unsuccessfully attacked in February 1944 by Vichy security forces. A second attempt in March also failed. The Germans then sent 12 000 soldiers, and the 465 besieged men were forced to retreat in spite of putting up a fierce resistance. There were heavy losses on both sides and the surrounding towns and villages suffered fierce reprisals.

However, the local Resistance group became gradually stronger, regained possession of the plateau and eventually liberated the *département* with the help of other Resistance groups in the area; Haute-Savoie became the first French territory to be liberated without the help of the Allied forces.

The surfaced road ends at the **Col des Glières** (alt 1 440m/4 724ft), where a panel explains the sequence of the military operations which took place in 1944. The **memorial,** standing slightly below on the right, symbolises the V for Victory together with renewed hope and life. There is a chapel inside.

The Resistance fighters killed in 1944 are buried in the "Nécropole nationale des Glières."

A trail called "Nature et Paysages des Glières" (nature and landscapes of the Glières region) offers a marked itinerary which includes the main historic sites *(1hr 30min).*

TIGNES ✳ ✳ ✳

POPULATION 2 220

MICHELIN MAP 333 O5 – LOCAL MAP SEE MASSIF DE LA VANOISE

Almost every skier knows the name and its reputation as a modern winter resort; but few realise that Tignes was not always a sporting paradise. The old village, flooded in 1952 when the dam was built (🕯️ *see Excursions: Barrage de Tignes*), was replaced five years later by a ski resort which developed 6km/3.7mi higher up. The **setting**★★ could hardly be more delightful, near a lake surrounded by meadows, with the **Grande Motte** to the south and the **Grande Sassière** to the east. To the east of the lake, a cable car runs up to the peak of the Tovière. To the west, the Parc national de la Vanoise lies over the Col du Palet and the Col de Tourne. Golf and lake fishing are among the sports to be enjoyed in summer.

🛈 *BP 51 - 73321 Tignes Cedex* 🕐 *July to Aug: 9am-7pm; Dec to Apr: 8.30am-7pm; Sept to Nov: 8am-noon, 2-6pm (7pm in Nov); May to June: daily except Sat-Sun 8am-noon, 2-6pm -* ☎ *04 79 40 04 40 - www.tignes.net Information centres on the lake and at Val Claret, Lavachet and Les Brévières.*

▶ **Orient Yourself:** You can reach Tignes from the north via a long drive over the Tarantaise on N 90 to Bourg St-Maurice then D 902; if you come up from the Maurienne in the south, you will find D 902 between Bonneville-sur-Arc and Tignes is a difficult drive with tight hairpin turns.

🏠 **Parking:** You can take your car into town only to unload your luggage. You then park it in one of four covered lots.

🐾 **Don't Miss:** Go up to the glacier of the Grande Motte on the funicular.

🕐 **Organizing Your Time:** On a rainy day, escape to the new aquatic centre.

Kids **Especially for Kids:** Teen-agers especially will appreciate the latest rider sports available here: a skatepark, water jumps, etc.

Tignes

J.-M. Blache/PHOTONONSTOP

⚓ **Also See:** Nearby Sights: Les ARCS, BESSANS, BONNEVAL-SUR-ARC, BOURG-ST-MAURICE, Route des GRANDES ALPES, Route de l'ISERAN, La Haute MAURIENNE, La TARENTAISE, VAL-D'ISÈRE, Massif de la VANOISE

Lac de Tignes

This small natural lake lies at the centre of a treeless high-pasture basin backed by the snowfields of the **Grande Motte** sloping down to the Rochers de la Grande Balme. The setting of the **Grande Sassière** across the river is very similar. The Tovière Summit to the east, facing Val-d'Isère, is accessible by gondola. The Col du Palet and Col de la Tourne to the west give access to the Parc national de la Vanoise. In summer, the lake offers a variety of water sports and there is an 18-hole golf course nearby.

The Resort

Situated at an altitude of 2 100m/6 890ft, Tignes has gradually expanded into several districts spread around the lake: Tignes-le-Lac, Le Lavachet and Val Claret further south. The world championships of artistic and acrobatic skiing take place every

Address Book

For coin categories, see the Legend on the cover flap.

WHERE TO EAT

Tignes and its surrounding villages offer a vast array of restaurants: crêperies, saladeries, pizzerias, pubs, even Tex-Mex and Chinese food.

⊜⊜**La Chaumière** – *les Almes -* ☎ *04 79 40 01 44 - contact@vmontana.com - closed Dec-Apr.* This restaurant, composed of stone and wood, is located in the Village Montana, a complex of luxurious chalets. The cuisine is Savoyard, and on nice days you can sit on the terrace.

⊜⊜⊜**Gentiana** – *Montée du Rosset -* ☎ *04 79 06 52 46 - www.hotel-gentiana. com - closed 7 May-1 July, 27 Aug-20 Oct.* This family-run hotel-restaurant offers contemporary cuisine as well as Savoyard specialties, served in a panelled dining room with a lovely view of pastures. Rooms have been recently renovated. Covered swimming pool.

WHERE TO STAY

Through the Tignes Reservation service, you can reserve lodgings in a wide range of facilities: hotels, bed & breakfasts, hostels, private homes and campsites. Contact the tourist office.

⊜⊜ **Hôtel Le Paquis** – *Au Lac -* ☎ *04 79 06 37 33 - www.hotel-lepaquis. fr -closed 3 May-9 Jul and 31 Aug-9 Nov - 36rms-half-board.* This hotel on the slopes above the resort has been entirely refurbished and is run by friendly local people. The rooms are decorated in traditional local style and have painted wood panelling.

⊜⊜**Chambre d'hôte du Chalet Colinn** – *Rte de Val d'Isère, le Franchet -9.5km/6mi NE by Rte de Val-d'Isère, then take road to left -* ☎ *04 79 06 26 99 or 06 60 23 33 28 - www.chaletcolinn.com - reservations required - 5rms.* Lovingly renovated, this chalet has a spacious lounge with a bay window offering a magnificent montain view. The rooms are superb, all at ground level, opening onto a terrace with a hot tub.

ON THE TOWN

Grizzly's Bar – *Pl des Curlings, Val-Claret -* ☎ *04 79 06 34 17 – Nov-Apr 9am-2am - closed May-Oct.* Beneath the benevolent gaze of one or two bears carved from wood, skiers and hikers can take a break here and warm themselves by the fireside. There is also a fashion boutique and gift shop.

Le Panoramic – *Le Val Claret -* ☎ *04 79 06 47 21 - daily 9am-4.45pm - take the Grande Motte funicular.* The terrace of this bar-restarant is perched at 3 032m/9 945ft. In very cold weather, there is only one remedy: rikiki, hot chocolate with a shot of kirsch! Every Thursday there is a torch-lit procession downhill.

year in Tignes. The events include mogul skiing as well as ballet and jumping in the Lognan Olympic stadium.

Ski area

Tignes is linked to that of Val-d'Isère to form the famous **Espace Killy**✳✳✳ (*see Massif de la VANOISE*), one of the largest and most beautiful ski areas in the world, in a totally treeless high-mountain setting. Snow cover is excellent and available all year round (with summer skiing on the Grande Motte Glacier). Some 200 snow-cannons make it possible for skiers to ski down to the resort from October to May. Slopes are generally less steep than in Val-d'Isère, but some ski runs attract advanced skiers (Le Vallon de la Sache, Les Pâquerettes and La Ves). In addition, you can practise mogul skiing and ski ungroomed powder runs.

Highlights

Barrage de Tignes✳

The reservoir, known as the **Lac du Chevril**✳, holds 230 million m3/186 461acft, held back by a wall which is 180m/591ft high including its foundations. The massive downstream side of this arch dam, inaugurated in 1953, is decorated with a huge fresco covering 12 000m≤/129 120sq ft depicting **Le Géant** (the giant). Since painted in 1989, however, the poor giant has faded away considerably, and the details are hard to make out; the best view is from D 902 and the village of Les Brévières. The water falls a total height of 1 000m/3 281ft, first supplying the **Brévières** power station (yearly production: 154 million kWh), before travelling along a 15km/9mi-long tunnel to the **Malgovert** power station (yearly production: 750 million kWh).

In addition, the Chevril power station is partly supplied by the Réservoir de la Sassière (2 460m/8 071ft).

A **viewpoint** on the roof of the Chevril power station, just off D 902, offers an overall **view**✳ of the dam, its reservoir and the mountains.

The Grande Motte✳✳✳

🎿 This glacier is famous for its scenery and for its summer skiing. An underground **funicular railway** (*Late June to late Aug: 7.15am-4.45pm; last 2 weeks of June and late Aug to early Sept: 7.15am - 1.30pm (6min, every 20min) 15€ return, children under 13 years no charge.*), starting from Val Claret, runs over a distance of 3 400m/2.2mi to a viewing platform offering an overall view of the glacier. From there, a huge cable car (capacity: 125) takes skiers up to 3 450m/11 319ft, near the Grande Motte Summit (3 656m/11 995ft). The **panorama**✳✳ of the surrounding peaks is breathtaking.

The Tovière✳✳

Alt 2 696m/8 845ft. **Access from Tignes-le-Lac by the Aéro-Ski gondola in winter. Panorama** including the Espace Killy, the Grande Motte, Dôme de la Sache, Mont Blanc and the Grande Sassière.

Hikes

Col du Palet and Col de la Tourne✳✳✳

🥾 *Allow 1 day. Difference in altitude: 750m/2 461ft minimum. Experienced hikers can extend the itinerary if they wish: Col de la Grassaz or Lac de la Plagne are two splendid detours which can be included in the following tour.* Start from Tignes-le-Lac; 1hr 30min to the Col du Palet (alt 2 653m/8 704ft); from the pass, a further 30min to the **Pointe du Chardonnet**✳✳✳ (2 870m/9 416ft) *(for hikers not suffering from vertigo; mountain boots essential)*: exceptional panoramic view of the Tarentaise region. Less adventurous hikers can aim for the **Col de la Croix des**

Frêtes★★, 10min further on from the Col du Palet. Walk down to the Lac du Grataleu then up again to the **Col de la Tourne**★★ (2 656m/8 714ft), offering splendid views of the Espace Killy. On the way down, note the superb **Aiguille Percée** on the left.

Refuge de la Martin★★

Alt 2 154m/7 067ft. *5hr there and back from Tignes-le-Lac or Les Boisses.*

This undemanding hike offers lovely views of the Lac du Chevril, the surrounding summits and Mont Blanc in the distance. Walkers can continue as far as the edge of the glacier and admire the view (*Remember that it is highly dangerous for untrained walkers to venture onto a glacier*).

Excursions

Réserve naturelle de la Grande Sassière★★

From the Tignes Dam, follow the road to Val-d'Isère. Immediately beyond the Giettaz tunnel, turn left up a steep, narrow road towards the Barrage du Saut (6km/3.7mi), at an altitude of 2 300m/7 546ft (car park).

The nature reserve covering 2 230ha/5 511 acres was created in 1973, and the beauty of the environment has been totally preserved in spite of important investments in hydroelectric projects. Overlooked by the **Grande Sassière** (3 747m/12 293ft) and **Tsanteleina** (3 605m/11 827ft) summits, it extends to the Glacier de Rhêmes-Golette on the Italian border.

Lac de la Sassière★★

Alt 2 460m/8 071ft. *1hr 45min there and back on foot from Le Saut; go up along a path following the stream and return by the EDF road on the opposite bank.*

This undemanding hike leads to a pleasant lake with the Aiguille de Dôme towering above it.

Glacier de Rhême-Golette★★

Alt about 3 000m/9 843ft. *1hr 30min steep climb from the Lac de la Sassière; it is dangerous to go onto the glacier.*

Beautiful scenery with the Grande Casse and Grande Motte in the distance.

VALLÉE DE LA TINÉE★★

MICHELIN MAP 341 C/E 2/4

The River Tinée flows southwards from the Col de la Bonette to its confluence with the Var. Gorges and open basins alternate along this green valley covered with forests of chestnuts, firs and larches. Hilltop villages line the way on both sides of the river, their simple little churches often brightened with frescoes★ on the inside.

▶ **Orient Yourself:** The villages of the Tinée valley are often perched at the end of winding roads that branch off D 2205, which follows the river.

Don't Miss: Try to stop at a few of the "villages perchés;" each one is different.

Organizing Your Time: To visit each village, you need two days. Be aware that driving along the winding road is tiring.

Also See: Nearby Sights: AURON, BARCELONNETTE, BEUIL, Gorges du CIANS, CLUES DE HAUTE-PROVENCE, Route de la BONETTE, Val d'ENTRAUNES, ENTREVAUX, Route des GRANDES ALPES, ISOLA 2000, PUGET-THÉNIERS, ST-ÉTIENNE-DE-TINÉE, L'UBAYE, VILLARS-SUR-VAR

Excursion

A Drive through the Gorges *143km/89mi – allow 1 day*

This itinerary, which begins at the confluence of the Tinée and the Var, requires a full day as the detours to hilltop villages involve taking narrow, winding roads.

▶ *From the Pont de la Mescla, drive along D 2205.*

Gorges de la Mescla★

The road runs along the bottom of the gorge, beneath overhanging rocks; the name Mescla, a Provençal word meaning "mix," refers to the joining of the two rivers.

▶ *At the Pont de la Lune, turn right onto D 32.*

La Tour

This isolated village, perched on a rocky spur above the Tinée Valley, has retained its medieval character and boasts a charming square, lined with arcades, a shaded fountain and *trompe-l'œil* façades.

The Romanesque-Gothic **church** (🕐*To visit, contact the presbytery -* ☎ *04 93 02 04 84*) is decorated with three beautiful Renaissance retables and two 15C stoups. Several 16C water-powered oil-mills are still in working order.

The **Chapelle des Pénitents-Blancs** (*As for the church.*) stands along D 32 at the northeast end of the village. The side walls are covered with **frescoes**★ by Brevesi and Nadale, dating from 1491, depicting 20 scenes from the Passion. Older frescoes, painted on the east-end wall, illustrate the Last Judgement.

▶ *Return to D 2205 and drive north to Pons-de-Clans then turn left onto D 56.*

The road winds its way to Bairols in a series of spectacular hairpin bends, amid olive, oak and chestnut trees.

Bairols

This hilltop village (alt 830m/2 723ft) has been tastefully restored. It offers bird's-eye **views**★ of the valley below. The old flour-mill has been turned into a restaurant and the oil-mill into a bar.

▶ *Rejoin D 2205 and turn immediately right onto D 55 to Clans.*

Clans

🕐*To visit the church of Cians, as well as the chapels of Sainte-Antoine and Saint-Michel, contact the Mairie -* ☎ *04 93 02 90 08, or the Collégiale -* ☎ *04 93 98 05 91.*

This pleasant village, overlooking the steep Clans Valley on one side and the Tinée on the other, is surrounded by a large forest of spruces, larches and firs and framed by mountains. Note its many fountains, which date back to medieval times.

The Romanesque **church** was rebuilt in Baroque style, so the beautiful doorway, dating from 1702, is preceded by a portico. The interior decoration is rather elaborate: the chancel contains two panels of a retable from the Nice School; in the side chapel on the left of the chancel

Life of St Anthony – a fresco from the Chapelle St. Antoine

E. Baret/MICHELIN

and there is a Baroque altarpiece in 17 parts. 11C **frescoes** representing hunting scenes have been discovered behind the high altar, together with a 15C Christ in Glory. The organ case was made in 1792 by **Honoré Grinda** from Nice. *Walk along the left-hand side of the church to the end of the surfaced road.* **Chapelle St-Michel** stands at the top of the village. The flat east end is adorned with 16C **frescoes**; the Archangel Michael can be seen in the centre, weighing souls. From the terrace, the **view** embraces Clans, the Tinée Valley with Bairols and the Pointe des Quatre Cantons across the river.

On the left of the Pont-de-Clans road stands **Chapelle St-Antoine** (500m/547yd from the village). The small rustic chapel has a wall-belfry and a large porch. The interior is extensively decorated with 15C **frescoes**★ depicting virtues and vices and scenes from the life of St Anthony, with texts in the old local dialect.

▷ *Return to D 2205 once more and, a little further on, turn left to Ilonse.*

Ilonse

Ilonse lies in a beautiful mountain setting, at an altitude of 1 210m/3 970ft. From the viewing table at the top of the village several hilltop villages can be seen standing out against dark forest patches.

▷ *Back to D 2205; continue towards St-Sauveur-sur-Tinée.*

The Valdeblore road on the right links the Tinée and Vésubie valleys. Red schists add colour to the landscape.

St-Sauveur-sur-Tinée

Situated at the confluence of the River Tinée and River Vionène, this village is a maze of twisting lanes lined with tall buildings with projecting roofs. It houses an information centre of the **Parc national du Mercantour**.

The 15C **church** has a Romanesque bell-tower decorated with gargoyles. Inside, the rich ornaments include the **Retable Notre-Dame** (1483) by Guillaume Planeta. A painting of the betrothal of St Catherine, showing Tinée as it was in the 17C, can be seen behind the wrought-iron grille of the chapelle St-Joseph

Beyond St-Sauveur, D 30 winds westwards along the Vionène and across the Col de la Couillole (*see BEUIL, Excursions*), linking the Tinée and Cians valleys. D 2205 follows the Tinée through the dark and barren corridor of the **Gorges de Valabres**★, between Mont Gravières and the Cime des Lauses and Mont St-Sauveur.

Isola

The lovely Romanesque bell-tower of the church, destroyed by a flood of the Guerche, stands at the entrance of the village. The rounded twinned windows with carved capitals are typical of the Lombard influence.

The road on the left leads to the **Cascade de Louch**★; the water falls from a hanging valley, 100m/328ft above the Tinée.

▷ *To reach Isola 2000★★ (see ISOLA 2000), turn right onto D 97 and follow the Vallon de Chastillon.*

The road runs close to the Italian border, which is lined with snow-capped peaks. Mountain streams come rushing down the slopes on both sides of the River Tinée and the valley widens within sight of St-Étienne-de-Tinée.

Auron★ – *See AURON.*

Via Ferrata d'Auron
The climb is made up of seven separate sections, which can be completed in three to four hours, combining the thrill of close contact with the rock and the security of a safety line. France's longest via ferrata bridge (46m/151ft) is guaranteed to impress.

St-Étienne-de-Tinée★ – *See ST-ÉTIENNE-DE-TINÉE.*

Beyond St-Étienne-de-Tinée, the road rises above the Tinée Valley, towards the Col de la Bonette (*see Route de la BONETTE, Excursions*).

LE TRIÈVES★★

MICHELIN MAP 333 H9

The River Drac and River Ébron have carved deep trenches through the green Trièves Depression. To the west, the landscape ressembles the Savoyard High Alps; guarding the approaches of the Vercors Massif like a bastion is **Mont Aiguille** (alt 2 086m/6 844ft), one of the "Seven Wonders of the Dauphiné." This isolated table mountain inspired one of the earliest mountaineering expeditions in France. In 1492, King Charles VIII came to Notre-Dame d'Embrun on a pilgrimage and, hearing tales of supernatural manifestations on the top of the mountain, ordered Antoine de Ville to lead an expedition of ten men. These early alpinistes reached the top, only to find not the dancing angels of local legend but a charming meadow dotted with flowers and a flock of chamois. *R du Breuil - 38710 Mens* *July to Aug: Tue-Sat 10am-noon, 3-7pm; Sept to June: Tue, Sat 10am-noon, 3-6pm* *closed public holidays - ☎ 04 76 34 84 25 www.alpes-trieves.com*

▶ **Orient Yourself:** The region is crossed by N 75, heading south from Grenoble.
▶ **Don't Miss:** Stop at Mens, the historical capital of Trièves.
▶ **Organizing Your Time:** You can cross the Arc River at only two points on D 526 and D 537.
▶ **Especially for Kids:** The water park at the Lac du Sautet offers exercise.
▶ **Also See:** Nearby Sights: Pays du BUËCH, Massif de CHAMROUSSE, Le DÉVOLUY, GRENOBLE, Lacs de LAFFREY, MONTMAUR, Route NAPOLÉON, Le VALGAUDEMAR, Le VERCORS, VIZILLE

Excursions

1 Route du Col de la Croix Haute★

MONESTIER TO THE COL DE LA CROIX HAUTE *36km/22.4mi – about 1hr 30min*

Monestier-de-Clermont
The surrounding woods offer numerous possibilities for shaded walks and the nearby village of Avignonet to the northeast has an excellent belvedere overlooking the Drac, the Monteynard Dam and its reservoir *(water sports)*.
The road leading to the Col de la Croix Haute affords a vast panorama of mountains, with the splendid escarpments of **Mont Aiguille** in the foreground on the right.

Col de la Croix Haute (1 179m/3 858ft) – Its landscape of pastures and dark fir forests is characteristic of northern Alpine scenery.

② Upper Gresse Valley

ROUND TOUR STARTING FROM MONESTIER *61km/38mi – about 2hr*

▷ *From Monestier-de-Clermont, drive northwest along D 8.*

The road goes through St-Guillaume, a typical village of the Trièves region, with its stocky houses covered with steep, tiled roofs. It then rises above the Gresse Valley to Miribel-Lanchâtre *(lovely views)* and runs down again to St-Barthélemy.

▷ *Turn left onto D 8B.*

Address Book

For coin categories, see the Legend on the cover flap.

WHERE TO STAY AND EAT

⌖**Hôtel Au Gai Soleil du Mont Aiguille** – *At La Richardière - 38930 Chichilianne - 4km/2.5mi NW of Chichilianne on B-road -* ☎ *04 76 34 41 71 - www.hotelgaisoleil.com - closed Nov-20 Dec -* 🅿 *- 20rms -* ⌖*restaurant*. This family hotel occupies an outstanding site at the foot of Mont Aiguille, from where you can leave on hikes. In winter, you can take off your cross-country skis on the threshold.

⌖**Hôtel de l'Auberge de Mens** – *38710 Mens -* ☎ *04 76 34 81 00 - aubergedemens@wanadoo.fr - closed Jan - 10rms -* ⌖⌖*restaurant*. On the village square, this large house offers modern, well-equipped rooms. In winter, you can huddle near the woodstove. The renovated dining room has a daily menu and a shaded terrace.

⌖**Chambre d'hôte la Ferme de Ruthières** – *Lieu-dit Ruthières - 38930 Chichilianne - 4km/2.5mi NW of Chichilianne by B-road -* ☎ *04 76 34 45 98 - www.fermederuthieres.com - closed 25 Dec -*✒*- 4rms -* ⌖⌖*main meal*. This former stable will charm you with its pretty vaulted rooms, pillars in tufa and decorative tiles. The guestrooms, spacious and plain, look over the Vercors plateau. At the table, farm produce.

⌖⌖**Chambre d'hôte Le Château de Pâquier** – *38650 St-Michel-les-Portes - 12km/7.5mi N of Monestier-de-Clermont on N 75 and B-road -* ☎ *04 76 72 77 33 - http://chateau.de.paquier.free.fr - reservations required in winter - 5rms:* ⌖⌖ *main meal*. This small Renaissance castle at the end of a track is surrounded by a pretty garden. Downstairs, there is a fine French-style ceiling, mullioned windows and a spiral staircase, which leads you up to the tastefully furnished rooms. One of the bedrooms is in the old chapel.

⌖⌖**Hôtel Au Sans Souci** – *38650 St-Paul-lès-Monestier - 2km/1mi NW of Monestier-de-Clermont on N 75 and D 8 -* ☎ *04 76 34 03 60 - au.sans.souci@wanadoo.fr - closed 10 Dec-Jan, Sun evening and Mon except Jul-Aug -* 🅿 *- 14rms-* ⌖*restaurant*. For a short break in the countryside, you might try this peaceful vine-clad hotel. The decor is typically Alpine, with beams, solid wooden tables and floral wallpaper in the bedrooms. Tennis court and a swimming pool. Good value for money.

⌖⌖**Chambre d'hôte Ferme de Préfaucon** – *Préfaucon - 38710 Mens - 2km/1mi S of Mens on D 66 towards St-Baudille-et-Pipet -* ☎ *04 76 34 62 50 - www.prefaucon.com -*✒*- 5rms. half-board*. This renovated farm boasts a large vaulted hall supported on a single column, typical of the Trièves. It offers nature lovers and hikers a welcome at the foot of Mont Obiou. Food served uses organic products grown in the kitchen garden and home-raised lamb.

SHOPPING

La Ferme du Serre Monet – *From the Dolomites parking lot, take the road to the left - 38650 Gresse-en-Vercors -* ☎ *04 76 34 39 20* At this chalet at 1 260m/4 134ft , you can observe daily farm life, feed animals and purchase local produce. Some rental chalets.

Prélenfrey

This small summer resort lies at the heart of a **vale**★ beneath the escarpments of the Vercors Massif (Arêtes du Gerbier). The Échaillon flows through a narrow gorge, through which there is a pleasant view of the Drac valley.

▶ *Continue along D 8B to the Col de l'Arzelier.*

🚗 The road rises to the Col de l'Arzelier (ski area), then runs down to Château-Bernard, offering more fine views of the Vercors.

▶ *Follow D 242 towards St-Andéol.*

The pastoral landscapes of the Trièves are backed by the impressive cliffs of the Vercors, including the Grand Veymont (alt 2 341m/7 680ft), the massif's highest peak. D 242 goes over the Col des Deux to join the road leading to Gresse-en-Vercors.

Gresse-en-Vercors

Note the strange local means of transport known as *trinqueballes*, which look vaguely like sledges and are designed to cope with uneven ground. The Maison du Parc naturel régional du Vercors is in the village centre.

Col de l'Allimas★

From the pass there is a striking view of Mont Aiguille, followed by fine views of the Trièves on the way down to St-Michel-les-Portes.

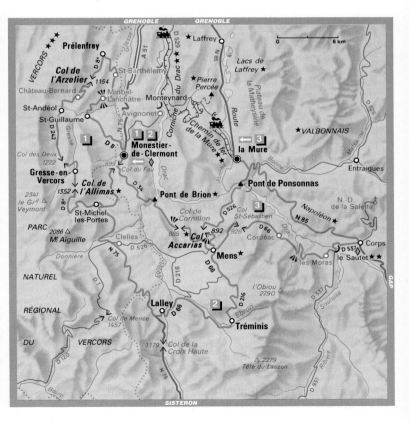

Pony trekking near Tréminis

▷ *Return to Monestier along N 75 towards Grenoble.*

③ Across The Trièves ⋆

FROM MONESTIER-DE-CLERMONT TO CORPS *46km/28.6mi – about 1hr 30min*

▷ *From Monestier, drive south along N 75 then turn left onto D 34.*

Pont de Brion⋆

This suspension bridge, looking surprisingly light, spans the sombre gorge of the Ébron. It used to be 126m/413ft above the river bed, but since the building of the Monteynard Dam on the Drac downstream, the level of the Ébron has been raised by 60m/197ft.

Near the Col de Cornillon, there is a clear **view** on the left of the Corniche du Drac and the reservoir of the Monteynard Dam.

Mens⋆

The capital of the Trièves region was a stopping point on the Roman road; the old covered **market**⋆ and the 17C townhouses in the rue du Bourg hint at the prosperity and importance which Mens once enjoyed. The **Café des Arts**, mentioned in Jean Giono's *Triomphe de la Vie,* features a mural (1896) by Gustave Riquet depicting local landscapes and farming scenes.

Musée du Trièves⋆

♿🕐 *May to Sept: daily except Mon 3-6pm; Oct to Apr: Sat-Sun 2-5pm; school holidays: daily except Mon 2-5pm* 🕐*closed 1 Jan, Easter Mon, 1 May, 1 and 11 Nov, 25 Dec. 2.30€, children under 12 years no charge -* ☎ *04 76 34 88 28.*

This museum presents the history of Trièves, from prehistoric times to the 21C, including the wars of religion that have divided the country's people.

▷ *Beyond Mens, drive northeastwards along D 66.*

Between the Col de St-Sébastien and Cordéac, the road skirts the Obiou Massif before passing the terraced fields above the left bank of the Drac.

Barrage et lac du Sautet and Corps★★ – 👃*See Le DÉVOLUY* 2.

4 **From La Mure to the Col de la Croix Haute** *65km/40mi – allow 2hr*

La Mure – 👃*See Route NAPOLÉON* 1

Between La Mure and the Pont de Ponsonnas, the snow-capped southern peaks of the Écrins Massif can be seen through the Valbonnais Corridor.

Pont de Ponsonnas
This bridge spans the gorge of the Drac 100m/328ft above the river bed.

Col Accarias★
Alt 892m/2 927ft. Extended **view**★ of the Trièves enclosed by the Obiou, the Grand Ferrand and the Tête du Lauzon.

▶ *From Mens, drive south along D 66, then turn left onto D 216.*

Tréminis
Tréminis lies in the upper Ébron Valley, which is covered with fir forests and overlooked by the limestone escarpments of the Dévoluy. This **setting**★ is one of most attractive of the whole area and the resort is a pleasant place to spend a summer holiday.

▶ *Return to D 66 and continue towards Lalley.*

Col de la Croix Haute – 👃*See* 1.

L'UBAYE★★

MICHELIN MAP 334 H/I 6/7

The valley of the River Ubaye, a tributary of the Durance, forms the most northern region of the Provençal Alps. It is an area of deeply gullied marly slopes, of huge alluvial fans covered with scrub, but also of fine conifer forests and rocky peaks, conveying an impression of spaciousness to travellers used to the deep valleys of the northern Alps.

The Ubaye region remained cut off during the long winter months until 1883, when the road linking Barcelonnette to the Durance Valley *(D 900)* was completed. This isolation also had a political side; the region was within the Duchy of Savoy's sphere of influence from the 14C to the 18C and maintained strong links with Piedmont in Italy. ▉ *R. Principale - 04850 Jaussiers* 🕒 *July to Aug: 8.30am-12.30pm, 2.30-7pm (Sun 9.30am-12.30pm; rest of year: daily except Sun 8.30am-noon, 2.30-6pm* 🕒 *closed public holidays (except 14 July and 15 Aug) -* ☎ *04 92 81 21 45 - www.jausiers.com*

▶ **Orient Yourself:** The Barcelonnette Basin lies at the intersection of the international Gap-Cuneo Route (D 900-S 21) and the Route des Grandes Alpes (D 902), between the Col de Vars to the Col de la Cayolle.

👁 **Don't Miss:** Be sure to visit the Musée de la Vallée, the Fort du Tournoux and the remarkable Pont du Châtelet.

🕐 **Organizing Your Time:** It will take you a day to complete all the excursions.

👣 **Also See:** Nearby Sights: BARCELONNETTE, Route de la BONETTE, EMBRUN, Val d'ENTRAUNES, Route des GRANDES ALPES, GUILLESTRE, MONT-DAUPHIN, PRA-LOUP, ST-ÉTIENNE-DE-TINÉE, Lac de SERRE-PONÇON, SEYNE, Vallée de la TINÉE, VAL D'ALLOS, VARS

Excursions

1 The Lower Ubaye Valley

FROM LE LAUZET-UBAYE TO BARCELONNETTE *21km/13mi along D 900 – about 30min*

Le Lauzet-Ubaye – 👣 *See Barrage et Lac de SERRE-PONÇON,* 2

Beyond Serre-Ponçon the gorges become narrower and the landscape takes on a very different aspect. Before the construction of the road in 1883, travellers had no choice but to brave a dangerous, 23km/14mi path through the gorges of the Durance and negotiate some infamous, life-threatening stretches. The road skirts the south bank of the Ubaye flowing between wooded slopes, within sight of the snow-capped summits of the Petite and Grande Séolane. Between Le Lauzet and Le Martinet, you can watch from several viewpoints the numerous rafters and canoeists on the river. Just before Le Martinet is the rock known as Tête de Louis XVI; but don't worry, this "head" is unlikely to roll.

Le Martinet
As you drive through the village, look right up the Grand Riou Valley sloping down from the Montagne de la Blanche. Before the bridge, a road runs down to an important water sports park.

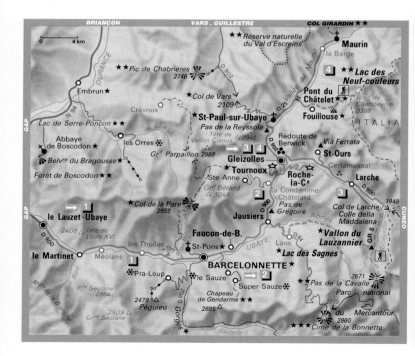

The landscape becomes more open beyond Les Thuiles and the view embraces the Barcelonnette Basin at the heart of the valley. To the right, the ski resort of **Pra-Loup** ☀ (☙ *see PRA-LOUP*) can be seen clinging to the steep slopes of the Péguieu. On its way to Barcelonnette, the road runs between the tributary valleys of the Riou Bourdoux (☙ *see BARCELONNETTE*) and of the Bachelard.

Barcelonnette★ – ☙ *See BARCELONNETTE.*

② Barcelonnette Basin

FROM BARCELONNETTE TO LES GLEIZOLLES *15km/9.3mi – about 1hr*

Barcelonnette★ – ☙ *See BARCELONNETTE.*

The road *(D 900)* runs across the Barcelonnette Basin where crops alternate with scree.

Faucon-de-Barcelonnette
This ancient village going back to Roman times is said to owe its name to the numerous birds of prey (falcons) inhabiting the area.
An elegant 12C **campanile** overlooks the village. Note the carved cover of a Gallo-Roman sarcophagus on the right of the church doorway.
The characteristic silhouettes of the Pain de Sucre and Chapeau de Gendarme summits can be seen on the horizon to the south.

Jausiers
The Arnaud brothers, who pioneered the mass emigration of the local population to Mexico in 1805 (☙ *see BARCELONNETTE*), were natives of this village, which has been twinned with Arnaudville in Louisiana since 1995.
Several buildings testify to the success of the emigrants in the New World (Villa Morélia, Villa Manon).
Beyond Jausiers, wooded basins alternate with deep gorges. The strategic importance of the narrow **Pas de Grégoire** and **Pas de la Reyssole** (☙ *see* ④, *Upper Ubaye Valley*) was at the origin of the construction of the Fort de Tournoux.
    A road branching off D 900 at La Condamine leads to the small ski resort of **Sainte-Anne.**

Musée de la Vallée★ – ⏰ *July to Aug and school holidays: 10.30am-noon, 5-6.30pm; Jan to May: Wed and Sat 3-8pm; June and Sept: daily except Mon, Tue and Sun 3-6pm.* ⏰ *closed Oct to Dec, 1 Jan, 1 May. 1.50€, children free.* In a house on the main square, this branch of the Barcelonnette museum offers wide-ranging information on the area, including geologic and fossile displays, life of yesteryear, winter sports, and the story of the development of hydraulic works that tamed the floods that forced a large part of the population to immigrate to Mexico.

Fort de Tournoux★
🔲*Turn left before the bridge over the Ubaye, 1km/0.6mi beyond La Condamine-Châtelard, leave the car on the open space. Follow the twisting track which goes up to the middle fort. This is only possible on days when there are guided tours (from 1h30 to 3h30 duration). Hiking boots recommended.* ⏰ *Last week of June to first week of Sept and Christmas and All Souls holidays: for times, ask M. Noyez -* ☎*06 87 35 93 99 or at the tourist office* ☎ *04 92 81 03 68 - 6€ and 11€, children under 12 years 3.50€ and 6.50€.*
These extensive fortifications, straddling a ridge line at the confluence of the Ubaye and Ubayette valleys, are a real feat of engineering: there is a difference in height of 700m/2 297ft between the barracks on the river and the upper fort. The main part was built from 1843 to 1865 and the different batteries are linked by underground

passages and steps (including a flight of 808 steps). Other batteries were added later on the heights surrounding the fort. The tour includes the middle fort with its monumental gate, several other buildings and the ramps giving access to the upper fort; from the upper batteries, there is a splendid **view**★ of the two valleys.

Fort de Roche-la-Croix

7km/4.3mi along a forest road branching off D 900 to the right, just before the intersection with D 902. ◷ *same visiting conditions as for the Fort de Tournoux, above. 6€, children 3.50€.*
This fort, built between 1931 and 1940, formed part of the Maginot line of defence in the Alps; it was designed to survive as independently as a submarine at sea. The tour illustrates the fighting which took place here in 1940 and 1945.

Fort de Tournoux

Other fortifications along the Ubayette Valley may be open to the public during the season *(inquire at the tourist office in Barcelonnette).*

③ Ubayette ★

FROM LES GLEIZOLLES TO THE COL DE LARCHE *(on the Italian border)*
11km6.8mi – about 30min
The road *(D 900)* follows the Ubayette Valley lined with villages destroyed in 1944 and rebuilt after the war.

St-Ours

A narrow twisting road, branching off D 900, leads to this isolated hamlet, famous for its fortifications which withstood attacks by the Italians in 1940. On the north side of the Rochers de St-Ours, a path gives access to the base of the **Via ferrata de St-Ours** offering rock-climbers two different courses, *l'Ourson* and *l'Aiguille de Luce.*

Tour of the fortifications

3km/1.9mi round tour starting from the village. The fort of **St-Ours-Haut** *(◷ Same conditions as for the Fort de Tournoux and the Fort de Roche-la-Croix, above. 6€, children under 12 years 3.50€),* an infantry and artillery station, forms the central part of the fortifications. It was used together with the Roche-la-Croix Fort to block the Col de Larche. At Saint-Ours-Bas is a branch of the **Musée de la Vallée**★, which describes military life.
A path up the north side of the Rocher de St-Ours leads to the **Via Ferrata de St-Ours** (car park at the end of the village) offering two different routes, "L'Ourson" and "L'Aiguille de Luce."

⚞Larche

This is the last French village on the way to the Italian border, beyond the Col de Larche (1 948m/6 391ft), on the Italian side, lies the lovely Lago della Magdalena. In winter, this centre for nordic skiing (alt 1 700m/5 578ft) offers 30km/19mi of cross-country trails and two snowshoe circuits. In summer, there are many lovely walks.

4 Upper Ubaye Valley ★★

FROM LES GLEIZOLLES TO MAURIN *28km/17.4mi – about 3hr.*

The Briançon road *(D 902)*, follows the upper Ubaye Valley. The **Redoute de Berwick** on the right formed part of fortifications built at the beginning of the 18C in anticipation of the union of the Ubaye region with France. The road and the river then go through the corridor formed by the **Pas de la Reyssole**.

St-Paul-sur-Ubaye

This pleasant village is the starting point of numerous excursions. The **church**★ dates from the early Middle Ages but the chancel was rebuilt in the 15C and the vault in the 16C, at the end of the Wars of Religion. The doorway is surmounted by a three-lobed rose-window. Note the partly Romanesque octagonal bell-tower with twinned openings, surmounted by a pyramid. Inside, there is a 17C rood beam, interesting 16C paintings and some fine woodwork including a larch ceiling.

The former barn of the Maison Arnaud houses the **Musée de la Vallée Albert-Manuel** (⏱ *July to Aug: 3-7pm. 3€, children no charge -* ☎ *04 92 84 36 23)*, a branch of the Musée de la Vallée de Barcelonnette devoted to agriculture and forestry. It displays tools and machinery from the Ubaye region and illustrates traditional techniques, some of which are also demonstrated at a picturesque fair of local produce takes place every year on the third Sunday in August.

⚜ In winter, the nordic ski centre (alt 1 400m/5 593ft) offers 17km/10.6mi of trails and a 3km/2mi snowshoe track.

▶ *From St-Paul, continue along D 25 and the River Ubaye.*

The road goes through a succession of small hamlets overlooked by the slender steeples of their remarkably well-restored churches, in particular the façades, often decorated with frescoes.

Pont du Châtelet ★★

This site is famous throughout the region; the single-arched bridge, built in 1880, spans the gorge 100m/328ft above the stream. Onthe way up, there are splendid views★★ over the Ubaye of the Tête de Panyron (alt 2 787m/9 144ft) and the Pic de la Font Sancte (alt 3 387m/11 112ft).

Pines of Haute-Provence

Five varieties of pine may be found in the region. You might spot:

An Austrian or **black pine**, regularly used for reforestation and easily identified by its sticky buds and its hard, sharp, dark green needles, which can grow up to 15cm/6in long.

A **Swiss mountain pine**, with its short, shiny needles and rounded hooks on its cones.

An **Aleppo pine**, which has reddish-brown bark, a twisted trunk and grows well in dry soil, but only below 500m/1 640ft. Its soft, comparatively pale green needles grow in pairs.

A **Scots pine**, which prefers higher altitudes. It also bears needles in pairs, although they are darker and more curved than on an Aleppo pine. Its bark peels off in thin strips.

A **larch**, with its distinctive bunches of light green needles and its furrowed, reddish brown trunk. The larch is the only pine which loses its needles in winter.

▷ *Turn right towards Fouillouse for an excellent view of the valley around St-Paul.*

Fouillouse★

This high-mountain hamlet (alt 1 907m/6 257ft) lies on the edge of a desolate glacial cirque overlooked by the Brec de Chambeyron (alt 3 389m/11 119ft). The houses occupy the south-facing slope; note the charming 16C Église St-Jean-Baptiste. *Food is available at the inn-café in a former shepherd's hut.*

▷ *Return to the valley and turn right towards Maurin.*

The road rises towards Maurin through a lonely mountain landscape, enhanced by the Mediterranean light, until suddenly the view opens onto the valley, framed by rocky slopes. Farmsteads with tall chimneys and grey schist roofs on larch timbers stand by the roadside. A 3hr hike from the hamlets of La Barge and Maljasset leads to the **Col Girardin★★**.

Église de Maurin

The church stands on an isolated site, surrounded by the old cemetery. An inscription in Provençal tells how an avalanche destroyed the previous 12C church in 1531. This explains why the present edifice, although built in the 16C, has a Romanesque appearance.

🏃 Hikes

Vallon du Chambreyon and the Lac des Neuf Couleurs★

6hr there and back starting from Fouillouse. Leave the car at the entrance of the village. It is possible to make it a two-day trip by booking a night in the Refuge du Chambeyron. It may be necessary cross névés (glacial snowpacks) and it is therefore essential to wear climbing boots.

🔲 Go through the village and take the path on the left winding its way through a pine wood to a ledge. After climbing for 2hr, hikers will reach the **Refuge du Chambeyron** and **Refuge Jean-Coste** overlooking Lac Premier. The superb mountain landscape is framed by the Aiguille de Chambeyron (3 412m/11 194ft) to the north and the Brec de Chambeyron (3 389m/11 119ft) to the east. The Brec de Chambeyron was always regarded as impossible to climb until two climbers from Fouillouse reached the top in 1878, to be followed the next year by the American mountaineer **William A.B. Coolidge**.

The path runs northeast to Lac Long. From the top of a mound on the left there is a fine view of Lac Noir. Continue along the path which goes past the Lac de l'Étoile before reaching the magnificent **Lac des Neuf Couleurs★★** (2 834m/9 298ft). It is possible to continue climbing for another hour to the **Col de la Gypière** (2 927m/9 603ft), in clear weather only; hikers must be used to walking across steep screes.

▷ *Return to Fouillouse by the same route.*

Keeping the Lakes Crystal-Clear

The high Alpine lakes, without plant life or sediment to cloud the waters, reflect the sky with all the clarity of a mirror, sometimes even taking on a hint of turquoise. But this remarkable purity has its disadvantages. The low oxygen content means that any waste which is thrown into the water, even biodegradeable material, may take years to be broken down, during which time it may damage the delicate biological balance of the lake.

Hike to the Lac du Lauzanier★

In Larche, turn right after the border post and leave the car in the Pont Rouge car park (alt 1 907m/6 257ft), 6km/3.7mi further on. 2hr walk to the Lac de Lauzanier along GR 5-56.

🚶 A great number of sheep spend the summer in this area of the Parc national du Mercantour; the grass is dense and the path is lined with typical high-pasture huts. Continue along the green valley, past a series of waterfalls. The **lake** (alt 2 284m/7 493ft) fills one of the finest glacial depressions in this part of the Alps. The small chapel used to be a place of pilgrimage.

Experienced hikers can continue to the **Pas de la Cavalle**★★ (*see ST-ÉTIENNE-DE-TINÉE, Hikes). Allow at least 2hr there and back.*

🚲 Mountain Bike Tour

Parpaillon round tour★

There is a difference in altitude of almost 1 000m/3 281ft over a distance of 30km/18.6mi. Start from Ste-Anne towards the Chapelle Ste-Anne and the Pont Bérard. This cycle tour is interesting on two counts: it satisfies sports enthusiasts and offers them the opportunity of discovering the Parpaillon military road, build by the *chasseurs alpins* (mountain troops) at the end of the 19C to link the upper Ubaye Valley and the Embrun region from La Condamine to Crévoux.

LE VALBONNAIS★

MICHELIN MAP 333 I8

The lower valley of the River Bonne, a tributary of the Drac, is known as the **Valbonnais,** whereas its upper valley, upstream of Entraigues, is called **Valjouffrey.** This is a region of deep valleys and wild landscapes characteristic of the Dauphiné mountains. At the turn of the 19C, farming supported a population around ten times its present size in near self-sufficiency; the development of forestry brought a need for roads to the outside world. The natural environment has survived the changes well, still offering space to roam for hikers as well as the ibexes reintroduced to the valley in 1989 and 1990. A beautiful road passes through the valley of the Malsanne, a tributary of the Bonne to the Bourg-d'Oisans (*see BOURG D'OISANS*) region via the Col d'Ornon. 🏠 *38740 Valvonnais* 🕐 *mid-July to mid-Aug: 9am-non, 2-7pm; rest of year: Tue-Fri 9am-noon, 2-5pm* 🕐 *closed Christmas vacation - ☎ 04 76 30 25 26 - www.ot-valbonnais.fr*

▶ **Orient Yourself:** The region is south of Grenoble, along N 85, from which branch out a maze of secondary roads reaching into the mountains.

🔎 **Don't Miss:** The museum village of Valsenestre opens a window on the past.

🕐 **Organizing Your Time:** The road from Le Bourg-d'Oisans to Valbonnais, D 526, by the Col d'Ornon is magnificent.

⛷ **Also See:** Nearby Sights: L'ALPE d'HUEZ, Le BOURG-D'OISANS, Le CHAMPSAUR, Massif de CHAMROUSSE, Les DEUX-ALPES, Le DÉVOLUY, Route NAPOLÉON, Lacs de LAFFREY, L'OISANS, Le VALGAUDEMAR, VIZILLE

Excursion

FROM LA MURE TO LE DÉSERT *55km/34mi – about 1hr 30min*

La Mure – *See Route NAPOLÉON,* **1**.

Between La Mure and Le Pont-Haut, N 85 offers panoramic views, south towards the imposing Obiou and east towards the snow-capped peaks of the Écrins Massif (Roche de la Muzelle, Pic d'Olan).

Pont-Haut
Capped columns (the demoiselles coiffées , literally "capped maidens"), more common to the south, are forming in the nearby ravines (*see Lac de SERRE-PONÇON,* **3**).

▶ *At Pont-Haut, turn onto D 526.*

Valbonnais
Together with Entraigues, Valbonnais is the region's trading centre. As you leave, note the small lake below on the right where the Bonne has been dammed.

Entraigues
This unassuming village is pleasantly situated on a sunny ledge overlooking the confluence of the River Bonne and River Malsanne.

▶ *From Entraigues, follow D 117 towards Valjouffrey. At the Pont de la Chapelle, turn left onto D 117A and follow the Valsenestre road.*

Route de Valsenestre★
The road rises above the **Gorges du Béranger**★, then runs along the wooded slopes (larches and firs). Many waterfalls can be seen on the way. Valsenestre, situated at the entrance of a vast glacial cirque, is the starting point of numerous mountain excursions.

▶ *Return to D 117.*

Hike

Haute vallée de la Bonne★★
3hr there and back on foot. Parking compulsory at the entrance of Le Désert-en-Valjouffrey.
🚶 This pleasant, relaxed itinerary follows the bottom of the glacial valley carved through the crystalline massif.

Le Désert-en-Valjouffrey (1 267m/4 157ft) is the last village along the upper Bonne Valley; barns still line the main street, testifying to the strong rural traditions. Some still bear the year in which they were built and the farmer's initials.
Beyond the hamlet, the U-shaped valley can be seen clearly; it is blocked by an impressive rock wall reaching over 3 000m/9 843ft. On the left, the alluvial cone of a side valley is cultivated thanks to the patient stone-extracting done by the farmers. The dark-grey Aiguille des Marmes (3 046m/9 993ft) soars above the area. On the right, the Bonne flows at the centre of a vast stony river bed. Beyond the park's gate, the landscape becomes wilder *(please read the park regulations carefully)*; at such high altitudes, the stunted, twisted trees become more and more scarce. Heather and juniper grow on the south-facing slope whereas the shadier north-facing slope

is dotted with rhododendrons. The path goes across a scree before reaching the **Cascade de la Pisse**★ on the left.

Walk over the footbridge then through a small pine wood: the trees owe their twisted trunks to the fact that they had to adapt to severe conditions. The meagre pastures give way to bare rock within sight of the imposing Pic d'Olan (3 564m/11 693ft) overlooking the **Cirque de Font-Turbat** glacial cirque.

▶ *Return to Le Désert along the same path.*

PLATEAU DE VALENSOLE★

MICHELIN MAP 334 D9

This region is a vast plateau sloping from east to west and towering 200-300m/656-984ft above the River Durance. The Asse Valley splits it into two: the north includes arid wooded areas and a few inhabited valleys; the south is flatter and more open with vast fields of cereals and lavandin (cultivated lavender), dotted with almond trees. The best time to drive across the plateau is at almond blossom time in March, or in July when the scent of the lavandin flowers fills the air.

▶ **Orient Yourself:** The plateau is defined by three river valleys: the Bléone in the north, the Durance in the west and the Verdon in the south. The valley of the River Asse runs down the middle.

🕐 **Organizing Your Time:** Take a day and picnic at the Lac d'Esparron; in the afternoon, plan to visit the château of Allemagne-en-Provence, which has limited visiting hours.

Kids **Especially for Kids:** Children will enjoy the Maison de l'Abeille et de la Truffe at Puimoisson.

🖐 **Also See:** Nearby Sights: CASTELLANE, CÉRESTE, DIGNE-LES-BAINS, Préalpes de DIGNE, Vallée de la Moyenne DURANCE, FORCALQUIER, Monastère de GAN-AGOBIE, GRÉOUX-LES-BAINS, MANE, MANOSQUE, MOUSTIERS-STE-MARIE, Route NAPOLÉON, RIEZ, ST-JULIEN-DU-VERDON, Lac de STE-CROIX, SISTERON, Grand Canyon du VERDON

For coin categories, see the Legend on the cover flap.

WHERE TO STAY

⌓**Camping Le Soleil** – *Rte de Quinson - 04800 Esparron-de-Verdon - ☎ 04 92 77 13 78 - campinglesoleil@wanadoo.fr - open May-Sept - reservations advised - 100 pitches - catering available on site.* This campsite has an exceptional position on the shores of the lake. The pitches are either marked out or on terraces and are shaded by pines and oak trees. Facilities for water sports and games, a snack bar and a pleasant terrace.

⌓⌓⌓⌓**Chambre d'hôte Château d'Esparron** – *04800 Esparron-de-Verdon - ☎ 04 92 77 12 05 - www.esparron.com - closed 1 Nov-Easter - 5rms.* This castle has belonged to the Castellane family since the 15C and still boasts its keep and main courtyard. A monumental spiral staircase leads to the bedrooms which are vast, with four-poster beds, fireplaces and antechambers. They are decorated with furniture some of which is original to the château.

Excursions

Through the lavender fields *89km/55mi – allow 5hr*

Valensole

This large village, spread over a gently sloping hill, is the birthplace of Nelson's great rival during the Napoleonic Wars, Admiral de Villeneuve (1763-1806), who was defeated and captured at the battle of Trafalgar. St. Mayeul, the founder of the abbey of Cluny (965), was also a native of the town. The townhouses, some with 17C or 18C doors, stand in the shadow of the church and its massive tower; the flat Gothic apse is lit by six lancet windows. The stalls in the chancel date from the 16C.

▶ *From Valensole, drive northeast along D 8.*

The road skirts the edge of the Valensole Plateau and runs through fields of cereals and lavandin, offering interesting **views** of the Asse Valley.

▶ *Turn right onto D 953 towards Puimoisson then left to St-Jurs.*

St-Jurs

From the church overlooking this ancient hilltop village, the **view**★ extends over the Valensole Plateau and the southern Alps.

▶ *Return to D 953.*

Puimoisson

In the 12C, Puimoisson belonged to the Knights of the Hospital of St John at Jerusalem. The 15C church stands on a vast square planted with nettle trees, but it was not always as peaceful as it seems today. In the 16C, building work uncovered the buried relics of two saints. Pilgrims flocked to the tiny village until the local people lost patience and secretly reinterred the relics, which remain hidden to this day.

▶ *Continue along D 953.*

Riez – ᛒ *See RIEZ.*

▶ *Drive southeast along D 952.*

The road follows the Colostre Valley which abounds in lavender distilleries.

The Bees Move to Summer Pastures Too

Between early June and mid-July, a feverish activity invades the Plateau de Valensole as beehives are set up everywhere, in time for the flowering of aromatic plants. The honey "season" starts in spring with the flowering of rosemary and reaches its height at the end of June when the lavender fields are in bloom.

At that time, some 250 000 beehives are set up on the plateau; they belong to 500 beekeepers from the nearby *départements* and even from abroad, who rent the land from the farmers. The transport of beehives is strictly regulated; lorries can only operate at night for obvious security reasons but also because the bees do not return to the beehive until after dusk.

Allemagne-en-Provence – *See RIEZ.*

▶ *Continue along D 952 through fields of lavandin and tulips alternating with vineyards.*

St-Martin-de-Brômes★

Note the date and various inscriptions over the doors of the village's old Romanesque or classical houses. The Romanesque **church** (*May to mid-Sept: guided tour daily except Mon 3-7pm; rest of year: enquire at the Mairie - ☎ 04 92 78 02 02.*), dating from the 11C, has a lovely rustic east end and a steeple surmounted by a stone pyramid. Inside, note the carved corbels and, behind the altar, an interesting polychrome tabernacle. The 14C **Tour templière** (*Guided tours (1hr30min) daily except Mon and public holidays 3-7pm.1.50€ - ☎ 04 92 78 02 02.*), once part of the castle, houses a Roman grave found in 1972, dating from the early 4C AD.

▶ *Drive southeast along D 82 to Esparron.*

Esparron-de-Verdon

The old village built on either side of a ravine is overlooked by the **Château des Castellane.** Today, Esparron is a small resort for sailing and fishing enthusiasts on the shore of the Gréoux artificial lake.

▶ *Go back along the same road and turn left towards Gréoux after 6km/3.7mi.*

Barrage de Gréoux

It is 260m/853ft thick at the base, 67m/220ft high and 220m/722ft long. The reservoir holds water from the River Verdon, which supplies the power station at Vinon (producing 130 million kWh) and the Canal de Provence. There is a fine **view**★ of Esparron-de-Verdon and the Chateau

The road reaches the lower Verdon Valley and leads to Gréoux.

Gréoux-les-Bains‡‡ – *See GRÉOUX-LES-BAINS.*

▶ *Return to Valensole along D 8 which follows the Ravin de Laval.*

LE VALGAUDEMAR★★

MICHELIN MAP 334 E/F4

The Séveraisse, a clear mountain stream, penetrates deeper than any other tributary of the upper Drac into the Écrins Massif; this is the reason why the Valgaudemar Valley is such a popular mountaineering area. The scenery changes dramatically at Villar-Loubière. Downstream, the deep pleasant valley is covered with pastures separated by rows of poplars and dotted with picturesque villages lost amid clusters of trees; upstream, the valley becomes almost oppressively narrow as the river runs between screes collected at the foot of south-facing slopes and densely forested north-facing slopes. *Pont-des-Richards - 05800 Saint-Firmin ◷July to Aug: 9.30am-12.30pm, 2-6pm;in winter, during school holidays: Mon, Wed, Fri 8am-noon, 2-5pm, Sat 9am-noon, Sun 10am-noon; rest of year: Mon, Wed, Fri 8.30am-noon, 2-5pm, Sat 9am-noon - ☎ 04 92 55 23 21 - www.valgaudemar.com*

▸ **Orient Yourself:** At 30km/18.75mi north of Gap on N 85, turn east on D 985A to climb into the Vallée of the Séveraisse.
- **Organizing Your Time:** You will need a day to enjoy the beauty of the region.
- **Also See:** Nearby Sights: Le CHAMPSAUR, Le DÉVOLUY, GAP, Lacs de LAFFREY, Route NAPOLÉON, L'OISANS, Le TRIÈVES, Le VALBONNAIS

A Bit of History

Parc national des Écrins

05800 La-Chapelle-en-Valgaudemar ◷daily except Sat-Sun and Wed 8.30am-noon, 2-6pm - ☎ 04 92 55 23 21 - www.valgaudemar.com
Created in 1973, this is France's largest national park, covering an area of 92 000ha/227 332 acres, a third of which are in the Isère *département* and two thirds in the Hautes-Alpes *département*. This high mountain region includes numerous peaks above 3 000m/9 843ft including the Meije, Pelvoux, Bans, Olan and Agneaux peaks and the highest of them all, the Barre des Écrins which reaches 4 102m/13 458ft. Within the park, which was formerly known as the Parc domanial du Pelvoux, there are glaciers covering an area of 12 000ha/29 653 acres, such as the Glacier Blanc on the north side of the Barre des Écrins, and lakes such as Lac Lauvitel, Lac de Vallon and Lac de l'Eychauda.
The Massif du Pelvoux, situated at the heart of the park, offers marvellous possibilities for mountain climbing, whereas the diverging Vénéon, Valgaudemar and Vallouise valleys are ideal starting points for hiking. More than 1 000km/621mi of

WHERE TO STAY

Hôtel du Mont-Olan – *05800 La Chapelle-en-Valgaudemar - ☎ 04 92 55 23 03 - open 10 Apr-15 Sept - P - restaurant*. Join the many hikers who make a stopover in this mountain village and share with them the friendly, lively atmosphere of these two chalets nestling in the bottom of the valley. Modest but comfortable rooms, laundry, traditional dishes and snack menu.

Ferme-auberge Les Clarines – *At Entrepierres - 05800 St-Jacques-en-Valgaudemar - 1km/0.6mi S of St-Jacques-en-Valgaudemar - ☎ 04 92 55 20 31 - www.auberge-clarines. com - reservations required- 4rms - main meal*. This farm-inn offers accommodation and meals. You can choose among a studio, a gîte for 6 people and simple, clean rooms with a mountain view. Regional cuisine served family style with home-prepared products.

footpaths are available inside the park, including the GR 54 "Tour de l'Oisans," the GR 50 "Tour du Dauphiné" offering a wider round trip and the "Tour du Vieux Chaillol" which leads through Champsaur.

A combination of Alpine and Mediterranean climates encourages an extremely varied flora; hardy, resistant species and plants vulnerable to the cold can often be found on the shady and the sunny slopes of the same valley. 1 800 different species of flowering plants grow here, including the lady's slipper, the orange lily, the wormwood, the Alpine columbine and the Alpine sea holly.

This rich habitat also supports 7 000 chamois as well as golden eagles. More than 50 000 sheep spend the summer in the area; in October, their trek down from the high summer pastures is marked by picturesque fairs in the villages of La Chapelle-en-Valgaudemar and St-Bonnet.

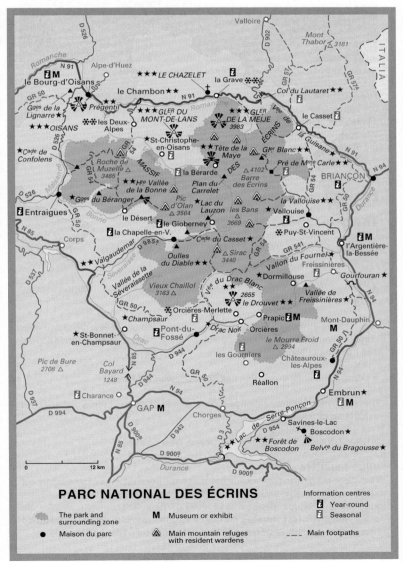

PARC NATIONAL DES ÉCRINS

The park and surrounding zone

● Maison du parc

Ⓜ Museum or exhibit

⚠ Main mountain refuges with resident wardens

Information centres

🛈 Year-round

🛈 Seasonal

--- Main footpaths

B. Kaufmann/MICHELIN

The Valgaudemar in autumn – Pic d'Olan in the background on the right

The peripheral zone, which covers an area of 178 000ha/439 838 acres, comprises the upper valleys of the Drac, Romanche, Malsanne, Guisane and Durance rivers where several winter resorts have developed in recent years.

Information and exhibition centres are located at entrances to the park, including the **Maison du parc national des Écrins** near the village of Vallouise. In summer, guided tours are organised by the Guides de l'Oisans.

Excursion

The Upper Séveraisse★★

FROM THE ROUTE NAPOLÉON TO LE GIOBERNEY *27km/16.8mi – allow 1hr 30min*

▷ *Leave N 85 3km/1.9mi north of Chauffayer (between Gap and Corps), turning right onto D 16.*

This narrow twisting road, which follows the left bank of the Séveraisse and goes through several villages, is nicely shaded. The elegant pyramid of the Pic d'Olan (alt 3 564m/11 693ft) looms ahead.

▷ *Cross the Séveraisse at L'Ubac and turn left towards St-Firmin.*

The church of St-Maurice-en-Valgaudemar, standing next to a huge lime tree, forms a charming picture.

▷ *Turn back onto D 16 and continue towards Villar-Loubière.*

Villar-Loubière

The village clinging to the rockside forms a picturesque setting with the heights of the Écrins Massif in the background: Pic de Bonvoisin, Glacier des Aupillous, Pic des Aupillous and Sommet des Bans (3 669m/12 037ft). Villar-Loubière is also the site of Valgaudemar's **last working mill,** used to grind corn but also as a walnut and hazelnut press for oil. Restored in 1979, the thatched mill dates back to 1838.

Les Andrieux

The Aiguille du Midi des Andrieux towering above this hamlet deprives it of any sun for **100 days every year,** as the locals say, from November to February.

La Chapelle-en-Valgaudemar

This mountaineering centre is ideally located beneath the Pic d'Olan. An office of the Parc national des Écrins is located here(🌙 *for information, see above*). Note how many of the house and stable doorways are sheltered by "tounes," the large, arched porches which are typical of the village.

Les Oulles du Diable★★

🌿 From La Chapelle it is easy to walk to **Les Portes,** which has retained a few lovely old houses *(1hr there and back)*; fine view of the Pic d'Olan on the left and of the Cime du Vallon. Beyond the hamlet, a path leads down to the bridge spanning the **"Oulles du Diable"**★, a series of potholes carved by erosion, where the River Navette whirls round with a thundering noise.

Upstream of La Chapelle-en-Valgaudemar, D 480 offers views of several waterfalls gushing down from the slopes or from the glaciers; beyond the Cascade de Combefroide, the road enters the wildest part of the valley and climbs along the northern slope.

Cascade du Casset★

This fine waterfall can be seen on the left, at the intersection with the road leading to Le Bourg.

Chalet-hôtel du Gioberney

It lies inside a wild and austere glacial **cirque**★★, nearby waterfalls include the famous **"Voile de la Mariée"**★, ("Bride's Veil") which owes its name to its long, frothy train.

The *chalet-hôtel* (alt 1 700m/5 577ft) is the starting point for many excursions into the Écrins Massif.

Hikes

Lac du Lauzon★

2hr 30min there and back on foot; start upstream of the Chalet-hôtel du Gioberney, on the left.

The High-Pasture Lookout

Marmots, who live in colonies above 1 000m/3 281ft, have evolved an unusually exact warning system: one single strident cry announces the presence of a golden eagle or other bird of prey, whereas a series of cries warns of the arrival of a four-legged predator such as a fox or a dog.

Marmots lead a strictly regulated family life. The colony, which forms the social unit, includes several families living in communicating burrows up to 10m/11yd long. During their six-month hibernation period, their body temperature falls to 4°C/39.2°F and they lose around half their weight. At the end of the mating season, which lasts from mid-April to the mid-May, three to four baby marmots are born to every couple.

The species is protected throughout the Alpine nature parks and reserves. The southern part of the Parc national des Écrins, in particular the Valgaudemar region, is known to shelter large colonies.

🚶 From the lake (alt 2 200m/7 218ft) there is a splendid **view**★★ of the glacial cirque which closes off the Valgaudemar Valley: the Bans, Pigeonnier and Rouies massifs.

Refuge de Vallonpierre★

2 280m/7 480ft. *3hr on foot to the refuge by the direct path. Hikers wishing to continue beyond the refuge will need experience of crossing névés (mounds of glacial snow) and scree slopes.*

🚶 The relatively easy walk up to the refuge offers a good view of the **Glacier de Sirac,** one of the most impressive glaciers in the Écrins massif. The "Sentier du Ministre" joins the winding GR 54, which in turn leads to the Lac de Vallonpierre; the pleasant refuge on the shore is a relaxing place to stop in summer.

LA VALLOUISE★★

MICHELIN MAP 334 G3

The valley of an important tributary of the Durance, which penetrates deep into the Écrins Massif, was named Vallouise in the 15C after Louis XI, who was king of France at the time. The verdant landscapes are reminiscent of Savoie but the luminous sky is characteristic of the southern Alps. Large villages and spacious stone-built houses, typical of the Briançonnais region (🔖 *see Introduction*), add to the charm of the area. The ski resort of Puy-St-Vincent (🔖 *see PUY-ST-VINCENT*) has contributed to the development of tourism. 🔖 *place de l'Église – 05290 Vallouise* 🕐*Daily except Sun and Mon 9am–noon, 2-6pm -* ☎ *04 92 23 36 12 - www.paysdesecrins.com.*

▸ **Orient Yourself:** At l'Argentière, leave N 94 which links Gap and Briançon, cross the Durance and take D 994 which rises up towards the four municipalities in the valley.

😊 **Don't Miss:** Be sure to see the murals of the church at Les Vigneaux; the lovely houses of Vallouise; the wild countryside of the Pré de Madame Carle.

🕐 **Organizing Your Time:** The circuit will take you 3 hours, and you will want time to see the mountains as well.

🌿 **Also See:** Nearby Sights: L'ARGENTIÈRE-LA-BESSÉE, BRIANÇON, Le BRIANÇON-NAIS, Vallée de FREISSINIÈRES, GUILLESTRE, MONT-DAUPHIN, MONTGENÈVRE, Le QUEYRAS, SERRE-CHEVALIER, VARS

A Bit of History

The Vaudois – Not to be confused with the Swiss from the Vaud canton, these Vaudois or Waldenses were members of a sect founded in the 12C by a rich merchant from Lyon, **Pierre Valdo** (or de Vaux) who believed that salvation depended on the renunciation of all worldly possessions and put his beliefs into practice. Vaudois worship centred on praying, reading the Scriptures and lay preaching, and it was this last that brought Valdo's followers into conflict with the Church authorities. As this new sect, which was a forerunner of the Reformation, spread throughout the Lyon region, the Church became worried and the Pope denounced the schismatics, excommunicating Pierre Valdo in 1184.

The Vaudois scattered and took refuge in nearby regions, settling in remote valleys where they were forgotten for two centuries. Ultimately, however, the persecution began again in earnest; the campaign led by the Catholics of Grenoble in 1488 inspired merciless crusades against the "heretics," who were rooted out and slaugh-

tered. The valley of the Gyronde, where many of the new sect had settled, was devastated and came to be known as *Val pute*, or "the bad valley." Louis XI brought the grim persecution to an end, and the area was renamed in his honour.
The final blow came in the 17C, after the Revocation of the Edict of Nantes: 8 000 soldiers were sent to "cleanse" the Vallouise, Valgaudemar and Champsaur valleys and the Vaudois took refuge over the border in the valleys of Piedmont in Italy.

Farmhouses – The three-storey houses still common in Vallouise are a reminder of the region's strong farming traditions. The vaulted ground floor would have served as accommodation for the animals, the first floor, often with a larch balcony painted with flowers, provided living quarters for the family and the top floor, or "baouti" in local dialect, was designed to be used as a grain store.

Excursion

From l'Argentière-la-Bessée to the Pré de Madame Carle *38km – allow 3hr*

▶ *From L'Argentière, drive along D 994E which follows the Vallouise Valley.*

The road crosses the Durance and the Gyronde near their confluence. Note on the right the ruins of some 14C fortifications improperly called **Mur des Vaudois,** which might equally have been built to keep out marauding mercenaries, or in a vain attempt to halt the spread of the plague.
As you drive through La Bâtie, the twin peaks of Mont Pelvoux come into view with, further south, the Sommet des Bans and the Pic des Aupillous.

▶ *Turn right towards Les Vigneaux.*

Les Vigneaux
The outside wall of the 15C **church**, to the right of the traditional réal (porch), is decorated with **murals** on the theme of vices and their punishments.

▶ *At Pont des Vigneaux, follow the road leading to Puy-St-Vincent.*

The cliff road rises through a larch forest, opposite the beautifully coloured escarpments of the Tête d'Aval and Tête d'Amont.
The view becomes more open and the Glacier Blanc can be seen overlooked by the Pic de Neige Cordier.

Puy-St-Vincent※
The fast-expanding ski resort and the summer hiking routes in the nearby Parc national des Écrins have greatly contributed to the development of this village. The Combe de Narreyoux, a lovely pastoral conservation area, also offers fine walks through the beautiful countryside of a high valley. The traditional and peaceful village, **Puy-St-Vincent 1400,** comprises the main resort's hotel sector. It is linked by chairlift to Puy-St-Vincent 1600. Go round the Église des Prés for a lovely **panorama**★ of the Vallouise, framed by mountains: the Pelvoux, Glacier Blanc and Pic de Clouzis to the northwest, the Sommet des Bans to the west, the Pic de Peyre-Eyraute to the east. Then park the car near L'Aiglière and walk up through the meadow to the 16C **Chapelle St-Romain,** which is used for exhibitions. There is a splendid **panorama**★ of Vallouise, overlooked by the Pelvoux, Condamine and Montbrison summits. (▶*Follow the road to Puy-St-Vincent 1600 and park the car on the right, at the intersection of the Narreyoux Valley road*). Finally, admire the remarkable 15C **frescoes**★ in the **Chapelle St-Vincent** (🕐 *Tue 3-5pm*).

Mountain landscape near the Pré de Madame Carle

The modern resort of **Puy-St-Vincent 1600,** situated above the old village and sheltered from the wind by Mont Pelvoux, faces the ski runs on two levels; in winter and summer, a gondola gives access to the upper part of the **ski area,** just below the Pendine (2 749m/9 019ft). The forested ski area is well known for the quality of its snow cover, due to its northern aspect and its location near the Écrins Massif. It comprises 31 runs suitable for all levels of skiing; international competitions, such as the women's world downhill championship, have been held on the steepest runs. There are 30km/18.6mi of cross-country trails, in particular on the Tournoux Plateau at an altitude of 1 800m/5 906ft.

▶ *From Puy-St-Vincent, drive down to Vallouise.*

The **Maison du Parc national des Écrins** (*July and Aug: 10am-noon, 3-7pm; Sept to June: daily except Sat-Sun and Mon 1.30-5.30pm. No charge - ☎ 04 92 23 32 31*) stands on the left, near the intersection with D 994E. It houses exhibitions relating the flora, fauna and geology of the area and also to the traditional architecture inside the park. Various shows and activities are designed to make children aware of the environment. A nature trail (30min walk) offers an introduction to the natural environment.

Vallouise★

This picturesque village has retained a wealth of architectural interest, including large houses with arcades and sundials.
The 15C-16C **church of St-Étienne**★ with an elegant porch is a fine example of Lombard style in the Alps. Note the splendid wrought-iron chimera's head **lock**★ on the carved door.
The chapel on the right of the entrance, dedicated to souls in Purgatory, is covered with frescoes and houses a 15C polychrome Pietà carved in wood. Note the old grain measures and the lengths marked out at the foot of the bell-tower.

▶ *Continue along D 994T running close to the Gyr. Beyond Le Poët-en-Pelvoux, turn right towards Les Choulières.*

The road climbs in a series of hairpin bends and offers **close-up views**★★ of the Grande Sagne, the twin peaks of the Pelvoux, the Pic Sans Nom and the Ailefroide.

▶ *Turn back at Les Choulières and rejoin D 994T.*

Pelvoux

Pelvoux is a family resort with twelve ski runs, covering a difference in altitude of 1 050m/3 445ft; some slopes are floodlit at night. A 5km/3.1mi off-piste route is reserved for accomplished skiers and snowboarders. There are also 60km/37.5mi of marked cross-country trails.

Ailefroide★

This hamlet, which seems crushed by the Pelvoux foothills, makes an ideal mountaineering base.

D 204T follows the bottom of the valley which becomes wilder as it gains altitude; larches become rarer. The jagged Pic de Clouzis soars quite near on the right.

Pré de Madame Carle★★

This hollow, once filled by a lake and since planted with larches is today a stony, avalanche-prone **landscape**★★, characteristic of the Dauphiné mountains. Legend has it that the field is named after a local woman whose husband, a rich nobleman, was consumed with anger on returning from his campaigns and learning of her infidelity. He revenged himself by depriving his wife's horse of water before she went on one of her favourite rides through the fields of Ailefroide. Dying of thirst, the horse plunged into the fast-flowing river and drowned its rider.

Hikes

While the following hikes do not require an understanding of mountaineering techniques, as long as the glaciers are avoided, the correct equipment is absolutely essential. Walkers should not attempt the following itineraries without good hiking boots, rainproof clothing and sunglasses.

The Vallouise offers numerous possibilities for hikes along 250km/155mi of paths and it is also a superb mountaineering area. It is one of the rare valleys of the southern Alps to afford views of snow-capped high mountains and many glaciers all year round. It is also fascinating from a geological point of view, and its varied flora and fauna (chamois) are an added attraction.

Glacier Blanc★★

Fine hike, very popular in summer; 4hr there and back on foot. Difference in altitude: 676m/2 218ft to the refuge. Start from the Pré de Madame Carle, waymarked path. Average difficulty.

The path crosses the mountain stream and climbs up the lateral moraine of the glacier, then, leaving the path leading to the Glacier Noir on the left, it winds its way to the Glacier Blanc, once linked to the Glacier Noir but now receding. Continue to the refuge; difficult sections are fitted with metal ladders. Standing on a ledge on the right, the former **Refuge Tuckett** (alt 2 438m/7 999ft) has been turned into a mountaineering museum. In July 1862, the British mountaineer Francis Tuckett and his French guides set up camp here before attempting the ascent of the Barre des Écrins. From the refuge, there is a fine **view**★★ of the glacier and the north side of Mont Pelvoux.

Glacier Noir★★

Start from the Pré de Madame Carle (parking area); 1hr 45min up a steep path; 1hr 15min on the way down. Narrow path not suitable for people prone to vertigo.

Follow the same itinerary as for the Glacier Blanc but turn left towards the Glacier Noir and walk alongside it. It takes its name, "the black glacier," from the thick layer of stones which covers it. The **Pic Coolidge** (named for the American climber WAB Coolidge,1850-1926, who made some 1750 ascents in the Alps) stands straight ahead with the **Ailefroide** and **Mont Pelvoux** on the left.

There is a fine view of the southern Écrins peaks on the way up.

Refuge des Bans★

Alt 2 076m/6 811. *From Vallouise, drive west along D 504 and park the car at the end of the road (Entre-les-Aigues, alt 1 615m/5 299ft). This hike requires a certain amount of stamina: 2hr on the way up and 1hr 30min on the way down. Difference in altitude: 540m/1 772ft.*

The Sommet des Bans is already visible from the car park. There is a great variety of wild flowers along the path which runs close to the mountain stream then climbs a rocky escarpment to reach the refuge; **view**★ of the Glacier des Bruyères, the Pic and Glacier de Bonvoisin.

Lac de l'Eychauda★

Alt 2 514m/8 248ft. *From Vallouise, drive along D 994T along the Gyr Valley towards Ailefroide, then turn right to Les Choulières. Park the car at the Chalets de Chambran car park (1 720m/5 643ft). Continue on foot: 2hr 30min to the lake; 1hr 45min on the way down. Try to start this walk as early as possible, as the path is exposed to the full glare of the sun and can be gruelling in the midday heat.*

The ascent is very tiring and monotonous, but the beauty of the lake makes up for it. Walk along the right side of the lake towards the Col des Grangettes to get a good view of the **Glacier de Séguret Foran**, which feeds the lake.

Col des Grangettes★★

Alt 2 884m/9 462ft. *45min climb from the Lac de l'Eychauda. Steep, stony path suitable for experienced hikers equipped with non-slip boots.*

Splendid **panorama**★★: the Guisanne Valley in the foreground, backed by Mont Thabor, the Col du Lautaret and Col du Galibier. On a clear day, you can just see Mont Blanc in the far distance.

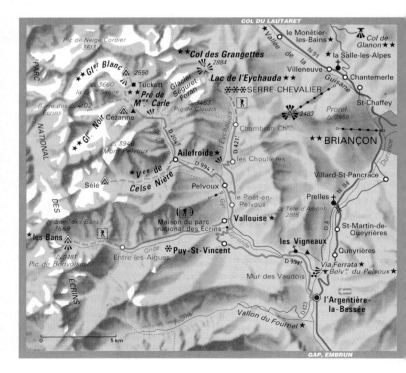

VAL–D'ALLOS ✳ ✳

POPULATION 709
MICHELIN MAP 334 H7

Situated in the upper Verdon Valley, on the edge of the Parc national du Mer-cantour, the Val d'Allos includes Allos village and two nearby ski resorts, Le Seignus and La Foux-d'Allos. Owing to its sunny climate, its beautiful landscape, overlooked by the Trois Évêchés, the Grande Séolane and Mont Pelat, and its extensive facilities, the Val d'Allos has become one of the most popular resorts in the southern Alps. 🛈 *Place du Presbytère, Maison de la Foux - 04260 Allos* 🕐 *July to Aug and mid-Dec to Mar: 8.30am-noon, 2-6.30pm, Sun and public holidays 9am-noon, 3-6pm; Sept to mid-Dec and Apr to June: daily except Sun and public holidays 9am-noon, 2-5pm -* ☎ *04 92 83 02 81 - www.valdallos.com*

▶ **Orient Yourself:** From Barcelonnette in the north, the road D 908 is steep and winding. It is easier to take D 955 and N 202 from Castellane in the south, then D 908, via Saint-André and Colmars. By this route, you cross first Allos (Allos 1400), then Le Seignus (Val-d'Allos 1500) and finally La Foux d'Allos (Val d'Allos 1800).

🐾 **Don't Miss:** Walk around the old village of Allos, and hike to the splendid Lac d'Allos.

🕐 **Organizing Your Time:** To enjoy the wonderful scenery, spend at least a day in the Val d'Allos.

🧒 **Especially for Kids:** The ski resorts of Allos are "P'tits Montagnards," meaning they have facilities for children.

👣 **Also See:** Nearby Sights: BARCELONNETTE, Route de la BONETTE, COLMARS, EMBRUN, Val d'ENTRAUNES, Route des GRANDES ALPES, PRA-LOUP, ST-ÉTIENNE-DE-TINÉE, Lac de SERRE-PONÇON, SEYNE, UBAYE

Parc National du Mercantour

The newest of the national parks, founded in 1979, covers 68 500ha of the Alpes-Maritimes and Alpes-de-Haute-Provence départements. The park, which was part of the Italian royal hunting estates until 1861, renewed the transalpine connec-tion in 1987 by agreeing to work in partnership with the Parco naturale delle Alpe Marittime, with which it shares 33km/20.5mi of common boundary.

The altitude of this high mountain region ranges from 500m/1 640ft to 3 143m/10 308ft and the park offers beautiful views of cirques, glacial valleys and deep gorg-es. It is home to around 6 300 chamois, 300 ibexes and 1 250 moufflons, all well adapted to the Mediterranean climate. Lower wooded areas are inhabited by red deer and roe deer, as well as smaller mammals such as the blue hare, the stoat and the marmot. Among the more common birds are the black grouse and the snow-partridge, and visitors may also spot the short-toed eagle and the golden eagle; the bearded eagle was successfully reintroduced during the summer of 1993. Wolves are also returning, crossing the border from Italy where this protected species is growing in number. Of the 2 000 species of plants in the area, ranging from olive trees to rhododendrons, the rare saxifraga florulenta was chosen as the park's emblem. Walkers can choose from 600km/373mi of paths, not to mention several nature trails, like those at Lac d'Allos and the Col de la Bonette. Two long-distance hiking routes, GR 5 and GR 52 ("Sentier panoramique du Mercantour") also cross park territory.

Information: Information centre in Entraunes: open every day from 3pm to 7pm ☎04 93 05 53 07; Col de la Cayolle refuge: 15 June-15 Sept., ☎ 04 92 81 24 25.

Lac d'Allos

The Resorts

Allos★

Alt 1 400m/4 593ft. This old village is the starting point for many excursions including the popular hike to the Lac d'Allos.

In summer, the outdoor leisure park, set in green surroundings round a large expanse of water, offers swimming plus water chutes, canoeing and also tennis.

The 13C **Église Notre-Dame-de-Valvert** (🕐 *July to Aug: Sun 11am-noon, during religious services*) is an interesting example of Provençal Romanesque art.

🎿 Ski area

Cross-country skiers have 19km/12mi of marked trails at their disposal near the village, which is linked by gondola to Le Seignus and the ski runs.

🎿 Le Seignus

Alt 1 500m/4 921ft. This long-established family resort inaugurated the first ski lift of the upper Verdon region in 1936. The gondolas remain open in summer for hikers and mountain-bikers.

Ski area

Situated just above Allos village, Le Seignus offers a limited but varied ski area; 12 ski lifts and some 25 runs (including the Valcibière red run) between 1 500m/4 921 and 2 400m/7 874ft. The first section is equipped with snow cannon.

🎿 La Foux-d'Allos★★

Alt 1 708m/5 604ft. La Foux is a modern resort, situated between Allos and the Col d'Allos, whose wooden houses decorated with small balconies blend well with the surroundings.

Ski area

Situated inside a glacial cirque, overlooked by the Trois Évêchés Massif, the ski area is spread over five slopes, which catch the sun in turn. It is linked to that of Pra-Loup (🇫🇷 *see PRA-LOUP*) to form the **Espace Lumière,** one of the largest ski areas in France with a total of 180km/112.5mi of runs. The snowfields around La Foux are ideal for advanced skiers, particularly the runs starting from the upper station of the Observatoire gondola and the Pouret chairlift. Snowmaking guarantees resort-level snow until late in the season.

Observatoire gondola⋆
Alt 2 600m/8 530ft. **View** of the Tête de l'Estrop, the Préalpes de Digne, the Grande Séolane and Mont Pelat from the top station.

Nature trail
Park the car near the tennis courts and the Pont de Labrau chair-lift as you go into the resort (on the Allos side).
This hike enables visitors to get to know the area surrounding La Foux-d'Allos and its history.

🥾Hikes

Through the Parc du Mercantour

Lac d'Allos⋆⋆
This excursion attracts many tourists from mid-July to mid-August. Leave very early. Drive east along D 226 for 13km/8mi; twisting road, narrow and steep from Allos onwards. From the end of the road (parking) allow 1hr there and back on foot and 30min to read the panels and admire the landscape.

🥾 Situated at the heart of the Parc national du Mercantour, the 60ha/148 acre **lake**, which has a maximum depth of 50m/164ft, is the largest natural lake in Europe at that altitude (2 230m/7 316ft). The lake and the surrounding jagged peaks form a splendid barren landscape. The azure-coloured expanse of water is supplied by

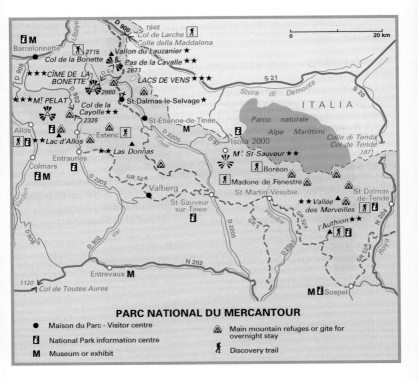

PARC NATIONAL DU MERCANTOUR

● Maison du Parc - Visitor centre

🛈 National Park information centre

M Museum or exhibit

⚠ Main mountain refuges or gite for overnight stay

🥾 Discovery trail

melting snow and numerous springs. Another glacial lake situated below has been replaced by a bog. This and other phenomena concerning Alpine geology and flora are explained on panels dotted along the **nature trail** linking the car park and the lake. Experienced hikers can combine this excursion to the Lac d'Allos with the one described below.

Mont Pelat★★★

Alt 3 050m/10 007ft. *5hr there and back Difference in altitude: 925m/3 035ft. Leave the car in the same car park as for the previous excursion. The yellow and green-marked path is not too taxing but it is steep and stony towards the end and climbing boots are strongly recommended.*

From the summit, the magnificent **panoramic view**★★★ of the roads leading to the Col d'Allos, Col de la Cayolle and Col de la Bonette and of the surrounding summits extends in clear weather to Mont Blanc, Monte Viso and Mont Ventoux. A recently discovered underground glacier runs beneath the surface of Mont Pelat. Twenty-two ibexes, fitted with transmitters, were reintroduced into the Mont Pelat Massif in 1994. This is just one of several projects designed to encourage the survival of this species in the Mercantour (upper Var, upper Verdon and upper Ubaye valleys).

Excursion

Route du Col d'Allos★★

FROM BARCELONNETTE TO COLMARS *44km/27mi – about 2hr*

Please exercise **extreme caution** *at crossroads. The Col d'Allos is blocked by snow from November to May.*
Through the rugged landscape between Barcelonnette and the upper Verdon Valley the twisting, narrow track clings to a near-vertical rock face. Extra care is needed, but exhilarating views are guaranteed.

Barcelonnette★ – *See BARCELONNETTE.*

Leaving Barcelonnette and the Ubaye Valley, D 908 climbs above the wild, forested **Gorges du Bachelard**★ (*see Route des GRANDES ALPES*).
After the bridge across the Fau, road D 908 makes a detour via the Vallon des Agneliers, overlooked by the ridge of the Grande Séolane (alt 2 909m/9 544ft), before affording more breathtaking bird's-eye views of the deep Gorges du Bachelard.

Col d'Allos★★

Alt 2 247m/7 372ft. From the platform of the refuge situated just below the pass *(viewing table)*, there is a fine **panorama**★ of Barcelonnette to the north, of the Pain de Sucre and Chapeau de Gendarme to the northeast and of the Grand Cheval de Bois to the east. The Grande Séolane and the ski area of La Foux d'Allos can be seen from the pass itself.
The road continues down to the pastures where the Verdon takes its source.
As one approaches Colmars, the road affords a lovely view of the fortified town.

Colmars★ – *See COLMARS.*

VAL-D'ISÈRE✳✳✳

POPULATION 1 800
MICHELIN MAP 333 O5
LOCAL MAPS SEE ROUTE DE L'ISERAN AND MASSIF DE LA VANOISE

Val-d'Isère is one of the most prestigious Alpine ski resorts, located in the deep valley of the upper River Isère at an altitude of 1 850m/6 070ft beneath the imposing Rocher de Bellevarde, Tête du Solaise and Grande Sassière summits. Beyond its narrow entrance, the valley is surprisingly vast, spread out and open. The heart of the resort, transformed for the 1992 Albertville Olympics, is characterized by two- and three-storey stone houses with charming carved wooden balconies protected by overhanging roofs. Besides the resort centre, Val-d'Isère includes the old hamlet of Le Fornet to the east and the modern La Daille to the north. *BP 228 - 73150 Val d'Isère July to Aug and Dec to Apr: 8.30am-7.30 (Sat in winter 8pm); rest of year: Mon-Fri 9am-noon, 2-6pm, Sat 9am-noon, 2-6pm, Sun 10am-noon, 3-6pm (closed Sat-Sun from Mar to May and Oct to Nov) - ☎ 04 79 06 06 60 - www.valdisere.com*

▶ **Orient Yourself:** Val d'Isère is 32km/20mi south of Bourg St-Maurice by D 902, a good road with heavy traffic during school holidays. In summer, you can also take the spectacular D 902 up from the south over the Col d'iseran.

Don't Miss: Take the cable car up to the Rocher de Bellevarde.

Organizing Your Time: In summer, if you choose the route over the Col d'Iseran, start early in the morning. Later in the day, traffic can be dense.

Especially for Kids: Children can learn to ski in the summer on the Pissaillas glacier. They will also enjoy the adventure park in the Forêt de Rogoney.

Also See: Nearby sights: Les ARCS, AUSSOIS, BESSANS, BONNEVAL-SUR-ARC, BOURG-ST-MAURICE, Route des GRANDES ALPES, Route de l'ISERAN, La Haute MAURIENNE, Route du MONT-CENIS, La TARENTAISE, TIGNES, Massif de la VANOISE

Val-d'Isère

J. Kérébel/PHOTONONSTOP

The Resort

Ski area

Val d'Isère owes its reputation as a resort both for families and for high-level skiers to its abundant snow cover and extensive snowfields, linked with the Tignes area to form the **Espace Killy**★★★; the Face de Bellevarde, "S" de Solaise, the Épaule du Charvet and Tunnel runs are all impressive tests of skill. Some 30 passes and summits soaring to 3 000m/9 843ft, within a 10km/6mi radius of the resort in the Vanoise Massif, ensure plenty of choice for cross-country enthusiasts.

The **Critérium de la Première Neige,** a major international ski race, has been held on the Oreiller-Killy run in early December every year since 1955, and the men's Alpine events of the 1992 Olympic Games were held along the spectacular **Face de Bellevarde** slopes.

In summer, Val-d'Isère is also a lively holiday resort with summer skiing on the Pissaillas Glacier, using man-made snow on parts of the run. In addition, Val d'Isère is also part of the beautiful **Route de l'Iseran**★★★ (see Route de l'ISERAN).

Highlight

Viewpoints accessible by cable car

Rocher de Bellevarde★★★

Alt 2 826m/9 272ft. ⏱ July to Aug: daily except Sat 9.30am-12.30pm, 2-4.30pm (continous) 6€, children 5-12 years 4.50€ return. 1hr there and back, including a 5min cable-car ride. In winter (4th weekend Nov to mid-May) access also by **Funival** mountain railway starting from La Daille (4.5min) - ☎ 04 79 06 00 35

From the upper station, steep flights of steps lead to the viewing table in 5min. The splendid **panoramic view**★★★ includes Val-d'Isère 1 000m/3 281ft below, and the summits all around.

Tête du Solaise★★

Alt 2 551m/8 369ft. 45min there and back, including a 6min cable-car ride. ⏱ From 4th weekend Nov to mid-May: 9am-5pm - ☎ 04 79 06 00 35.

During the journey and from the platform of the café situated on the summit, the magnificent view embraces the Isère Valley, Val-d'Isère and the Lac du Chevril, the Bellevarde Olympic run immediately opposite and a panorama of the Grande Sassière, Mont Pourri, the Grande Motte and the Pointe de la Sana.

Col de l'Iseran★

Access by the Fornet cable car and the Vallon de l'Iseran gondola in winter. In summer it is preferable to drive up to the pass along the impressive Route de l'Iseran (see Route de l'ISERAN).

From the pass, skiers can go up to the Grand Pissaillas Glacier (3 300m/10 827ft) where they can enjoy superb **views**★★ of the Haute Maurienne and Haute Tarentaise.

Hikes

There is little to inspire walkers in the ski area itself, but some excellent itineraries begin in the Parc national de la Vanoise, a few kilometres from Val-d'Isère.

Refuge de Prariond and Col de la Galise★★

Park the car by the Pont St-Charles on the way to the Col de l'Iseran. 1hr on foot up to the refuge then 2hr to the pass. Difference in altitude: 900m/2 953ft. 2hr on the way down.

🚶 The steep path goes through the Gorges du Malpasset, where ibexes roam freely, to the foot of the Glacier des Sources de l'Isère. Beyond the refuge it becomes steeper until it reaches the Col de la Galise (alt 2 990m/9 810ft).

Col des Fours★★
Taxing hike requiring a lot of stamina. From the centre of Val-d'Isère, drive south to Le Manchet (3km/1.9mi, parking area). 1hr 30min on foot up to the Fonds des Fours refuge then 1hr to the pass. Difference in altitude: 1 100m/3 609ft. 2hr on the way down. Take along a waterproof windcheater and warm clothing, as the wind at the top of the pass can be bitterly cold.

🚶 At the refuge, pause to take in the **view**★ of the Grande Sassière, the Mont-Blanc Massif, the Dôme de la Sache and Bellevarde. The path then veers to the left and climbs to the pass (3 000m/9 843ft): splendid **view**★★ of a lake surrounded by the Glacier de la Jave and of the Maurienne and Tarentaise mountains. Chamois are frequently seen in the area.

MASSIF DE LA VANOISE★★★

MICHELIN MAP 333 M/N/O 4/5/6

Numerous Neolithic stone monuments, cairns and stone roads high on the mountain show that the Vanoise has been a centre of human activity for thousands of years. The magnificent landscapes have drawn mountaineers at least since the 19C. When France's first national park was created here in 1963, a principal goal was preservation of the last ibexes in the Alps; yet this animal, the first emblem of the park, is only one of a thousand species of flora and fauna in the park's 53 000ha/130 966 acres. The public has also benefited from conservation efforts. The splendid surroundings bring tourists for hiking and breathtaking rock-climbing, not to mention exhilarating skiing on the 1 000km/621mi of runs in the area. 🏠 *Maison de la Vanoise - 73500 Termignon* 🕐 *Mid-June to mid-Sept: Mon-Sat 9am-noon, 2-6pm, Sun 10am-noon, 4-6pm; mid-Sept to mid-Dec: Mon-Fri 9am-noon, 2-6pm; mid-Dec to Easter: Mon-Sat except Thur morning 9am-noon, 2-6pm, Sun 10am-noon, 2-6pm - ☎ 04 79 20 51 67 - www.vanoise.com*

▸ **Orient Yourself:** The Vanoise Massif occupies nearly a third of the Savoie. It extends from the Isère Valley in the north to the Arc Valley in the south. To the east, it runs up against the Italian national park of Grand Paradis.

☺ **Don't Miss:** Any of the belvederes in the park is spectacular.

🕐 **Organizing Your Time:** When on a hike, plan carefully; time passes fast and the weather is capricious.

Kids **Especially for Kids:** The five nature centres have exhibits aimed at children.

⚲ **Also See:** Nearby Sights: Les ARCS, AUSSOIS, Vallée des BELLEVILLE, BESSANS, BONNEVAL-SUR-ARC, BOURG-ST-MAURICE, CHAMPAGNY-EN-VANOISE, COURCHEVEL, Route des GRANDES ALPES, Route de l'ISERAN, Route de la MADELEINE, La Haute MAURIENNE, MÉRIBEL, MODANE, Route du MONT-CENIS, PRALOGNAN, La TARENTAISE, TIGNES, VAL-D'ISÈRE

Ski Area

The peripheral zone of the Vanoise Massif includes an exceptionally fine skiing area with three major assets: its size, the quality of its facilities and its dependable snow cover. The Maurienne Valley to the south of the park, specialises in charming family resorts, while the Tarentaise, arching over the north and Bourg St-Maurice towards the east, has, since the 1930s, developed an impressive number of winter sports resorts. The 1992 Winter Olympics centred at Albertville confirmed the exceptional quality of the region's attractions. The Espace Olympique Pass gives access to the following areas: the Trois Vallées, the Espace Killy, the Espace La Plagne-les-Arcs, Pralognan, Ste-Foy-Tarentaise, La Rosière, Valmorel and Les Saisies.

Tourist offices supply the "Guide du skieur Trois-Vallées" to help you plan your route through the ski area. The well-marked runs are generally open from December to May; if possible, ask one of the "pisteurs" on patrol about snow conditions and any avalanche warnings. Once on the slopes, keep track of the time and the weather so that you return to your base in good time.

Espace Killy ✳✳✳

This skiing area, linking that of **Tignes** ✳✳✳ and **Val-d'Isère** ✳✳✳, has gained international fame because of its size (100 sq km/39sq mi), its high-quality snow cover (all year skiing on the Grande Motte Glacier) and its superb high-mountain scenery. There are some 100 ski lifts and 300km/186mi of runs.

Val-d'Isère is particularly suitable for advanced skiers while Tignes has easier runs and skiers are able to ski right down to the resort.

Trois Vallées ✳✳✳

This ski area, covering 400 sq km/154sq mi and extending over the **St-Bon Valley (Courchevel** ✳✳✳**, La Tania),** the **Allues Valley (Méribel** ✳✳✳**)** and the **Belleville Valley** ✳✳✳ **(St-Martin-de-Belleville** ✳**, Les Ménuires** ✳✳ and **Val-Thorens** ✳✳✳**),** is the largest in the Alps: 210 ski lifts including 37 gondolas and cable cars, 300 runs and itineraries totalling 700km/435mi. These are extremely varied: there are large runs for all levels of proficiency, technical runs – among the most difficult in the Alps – and numerous possibilities of off-trail skiing in conservation areas, as well as 110km/68mi of cross-country skiing trails. The Trois-Vallées owe their success to the efficient links among resorts, to their excellent snow conditions and to a superb diversity of mountain landscapes and life.

In addition to the two main ski areas of the Trois Vallées and the Espace Killy, the Tarentaise offers a choice of first-class resorts such as **La Plagne** ✳✳ and **Les Arcs** ✳✳✳**/Peisey-Nancroix** ✳.

There are also smaller resorts which are interesting from a sightseeing point of view and enjoy very good snow cover conditions, such as La Rosière ✳ and Valmorel ✳.

The National Park

The **peripheral zone (1 450km²/560sq mi)** offers an impressive range of first-class accommodation and sports facilities. The Tarentaise region alone includes some of France's largest and most prestigious winter sports resorts, whereas picturesque hamlets and villages like Bonneval-sur-Arc and Le Monal take life at a more restful pace. Churches and chapels including St-Martin-de-Belleville, Champagny, Peisey-Nancroix, Bessans and Lanslevillard are proof of a remarkable architectural and artistic heritage. Five information centres known as **"portes du Parc,"** are located at Orgère (near Modane), at Fort Marie-Christine (Aussois), at Plan du Lac (above Termignon), at Rosuel (Peisey-Nancroix) and at Le Bois (Champagny-le-Haut).

The **central zone (530km²/205sq mi)** is essentially a high-mountain area, with 107 summits above 3 000m/9 843ft and glaciers covering an area of 88km³/34sq mi.

The name Vanoise refers to the huge ice cap extending from the Col de la Vanoise to the Col d'Aussois. The most famous summits are: Mont Pourri (3 779m/12 398ft - Les Arcs area) and the Sommet de Bellecôte (3 416m/11 207ft - La Plagne area) in the north; the Aiguille de la Grande Sassière (3 747m/12 293ft - Tignes area) in the northeast; the Grande Casse (3 855m/12 648ft - Pralognan area) and the Grande

Lac Blanc and the Col de Soufre (& see PRALOGNAN-LA-VANOISE)

Motte (3 656m/11 995ft - Tignes area) in the centre; the Pointe de la Sana (3 456m/11 339ft) and the Pointe de Méan Martin (3 330m/10 925ft) in the east, and finally the Massif de Péclet-Polset (3 562m/11 686ft - Val-Thorens area) and the Dent Parrachée (3 684m/12 087ft - Aussois area) in the south.

Below 2 000m/6 562ft, there are some beautiful forests with a variety of species including spruce, larch and arolla pine, notably at Méribel and Peisey-Nancroix. An exceptionally rich flora includes some very rare arctic species such as the buttercup and the catchfly, as well as the familiar gentians, rhododendron and anemones, sprouting freely by the side of the road and, here and there, the famous edelweiss.

The fauna has increased considerably since creation of the park: the 1963 population of 40 ibexes has grown to 2 000. Hikers are likely to meet marmots along their way, but spotting rarer species, such as the ptarmigan, rock partridge, black grouse and golden eagle, requires a great deal of patience and a fair knowledge of animal life in mountain areas.

Excursions

Roads running through the picturesque Isère and Arc valleys are ideal for a drive around the park, but the heart of the massif cannot be explored by car; the best scenery is only available to skiers in winter and hikers in summer. The following sections may be useful:

La Tarentaise★★ (& see La TARENTAISE)

La Haute Maurienne★ (& see La MAURIENNE)

Route du Petit-Saint-Bernard★★ (& see BOURG-ST-MAURICE: Excursions)

Route du Mont-Cenis★ (& see Route du MONT-CENIS)

Route de l'Iseran★★★ (& see Route de l'ISERAN)

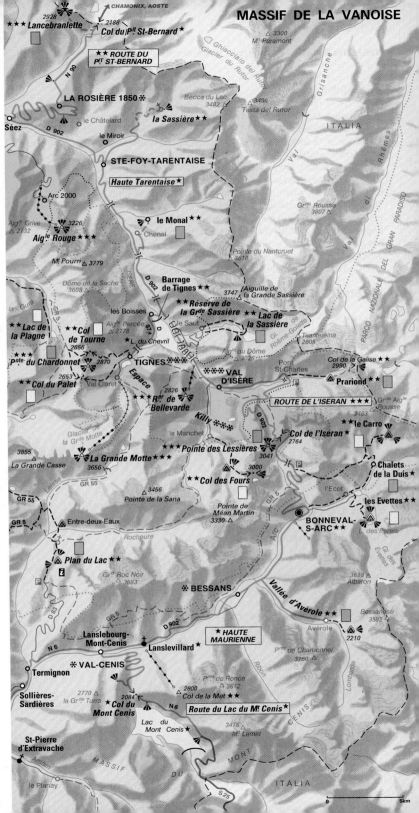

Vallée des Belleville✳✳✳ (&see La Vallée des BELLEVILLE)

Hikes★★★

The Vanoise massif offers an almost limitless variety of paths to explore. It can be hard to know where to start, but first-time visitors should consider basing themselves in Pralognan, Champagny, Peisey-Nancroix or Bonneville-sur-Arc, although Tignes, Les Ménuires at St-Martin-de-Belleville, Méribel and Courchevel, better known as ski resorts, also make good starting points for walking expeditions. Paths in the central zone are the most frequented, so consider setting out on one of the quieter routes on the periphery, where the landscape is every bit as beautiful.

The best time for a walking holiday is between 4 July and 15 August, when the flowers are in bloom. Bear in mind that there may still be snow on the ground until the beginning of July, which can add to the difficulty of walks above 2 000m/6 562ft, but a holiday in early summer or early autumn does at least have the advantage of avoiding the crowds at the height of the season. The best hikes described in this guide are listed below and graded according to their length and level of difficulty.

🚶 Family rambles

These short and easy itineraries are suitable for families with children, but you should be properly equipped all the same.

Lac de la Sassière★★ (Tsee TIGNES)

Le Monal★★ (&see LA TARENTAISE)

Refuge de Prariond★★ (&see VAL-D'ISÈRE)

Plan du Lac★★ (&see la Haute MAURIENNE)

Refuge d'Avérole★★ (&see BESSANS)

Fond d'Aussois★★ (&see AUSSOIS)

Chalets de la Duis★ (&see BONNEVAL-SUR-ARC)

Plan de Tueda★ (&see MÉRIBEL)

🚶 Hikes

These itineraries require stamina and physical fitness but are not technically difficult.

Col de la Vanoise★★★ (&see PRALOGNAN-LA-VANOISE)

Col du Palet and Col de la Tourne★★★ (&see TIGNES)

Col de Chavière★★★ (&see MODANE)

Crève-Tête★★★ (&see Route de la MADELEINE or La vallée des BELLEVILLE)

Lac de la Plagne★★ (&see Les ARCS)

Refuge du Carro★★ (&see BONNEVAL-SUR-ARC)

🛗 Main Viewpoints Accessible by Lift

★★★ Cime de Caron – 🛗 *See La vallée des BELLEVILLE: Val-Thorens*

★★★ Bellevarde – 🛗 *See VAL-D'ISÈRE*

★★★ Aiguille Rouge – 🛗 *See Les ARCS*

★★★ La Grande Motte – 🛗 *See TIGNES*

★★★ La Saulire – 🛗 *See COURCHEVEL*

★★ Mont du Vallon – 🛗 *See MÉRIBEL*

★★ Sommet de Bellecôte Gondola – 🛗 *See La PLAGNE*

Refuge des Évettes★★ (🛗 *see BONNEVAL-SUR-ARC*)

Lacs Merlet★★ (🛗 *see COURCHEVEL*)

Col des Fours★★ (🛗 *see VAL-D'ISÈRE*)

🚶 Itineraries for experienced hikers

These itineraries require stamina and include difficult sections (extremely steep or vertiginous paths). They do not, however, require any knowledge of rock-climbing or mountaineering techniques *(non-slip climbing boots essential)*.

Pointe du Chardonnet★★★ (🛗 *see TIGNES*)

Pointe de l'Observatoire★★★ (🛗 *see AUSSOIS*)

Pointe des Lessières★★★ (🛗 *see Route de l'ISERAN*)

Three-day round tour of the Vanoise glaciers

This itinerary is suitable for experienced hikers in good physical condition. Before leaving, it is essential to book overnight stays in refuges (ask at the Pralognan tourist office - ☎ 04 79 08 79 08 - www.pralognan.com) and to inquire about the weather forecast over several days. Leave very early in the morning in order to reach the refuge before 7pm (reservations are cancelled after that time). See the advice on hiking given in the Practical information section.

First day: Pralognan – **Mont Bochor**★ (by cable car) – **Col de la Vanoise**★★★ – **Refuge de l'Arpont.**

Second day: Refuge de l'Arpont – La Loza – La Turra – **Refuge du Fond d'Aussois**★★★.

Third day: Refuge du Fond d'Aussois – Col d'Aussois – **Pointe de l'Observatoire**★★★ – **Les Prioux** – **Pralognan.**

VARS ✹ ✹

POPULATION 941
MICHELIN MAP 334 I5

Situated between Guillestre and Barcelonnette, near the pass (2 109m/6 919ft) that links l'Ubaye and the Haut-Embrunnais, Vars is one of the main winter and summer resorts of the southern Alps, highly regarded for its sunny climate, the quality of its facilities and the beauty of its natural environment. *Cours Fontanarosa – 05560 Vars* ⏱ *July to Aug and Dec to Apr: 9am-7pm; daily except Sat-Sun 9am-noon, 2-6pm -* ☎ *04 92 46 51 31 - www.vars-ete.com or wwww.vars-ski.com*

▸ **Orient Yourself:** The resort is spread over three traditional hamlets (Ste-Marie, St-Marcellin and Ste-Catherine) and a modern resort (Les Claux) at altitudes ranging from 1 600m/5 249ft to 1 800m/5 906ft.

⊙ **Don't Miss:** Take time to admire the wild scenery of the Col de Vars, and the Réserve naturelle du Val d'Éscreins.

⊙ **Organizing Your Time:** It would be unfortunate to hurry through the area; give yourself a half-day on the footpaths of the Réserve naturelle du Val d'Escreins.

Kids **Especially for Kids:** The ski area is designated "Station Kid," and welcomes children.

⚭ **Also See:** Nearby sights: ABRIÈS, L'ARGENTIÈRE-LA-BESSÉE, BARCELONNETTE, BRIANÇON, Le BRIANÇONNAIS, CEILLAC, EMBRUN, Vallée de FREISSINIÈRES, Route des GRANDES ALPES, GUILLESTRE, MOLINES-EN-QUEYRAS, MONT-DAUPHIN, Le QUEYRAS, ST-VÉRAN, Lac de SERRE-PONÇON, L'UBAYE, La VALLOUISE

The Resort

⌖Ski area

Ste-Marie-de-Vars and **Les Claux** alone offer direct access to the ski runs.

Linked to the slopes of **Risoul** under the name of **Domaine de la Forêt Blanche,** the resort includes 56 ski lifts and 180km/112.5mi of runs with adequate snow cover. Its mostly quite gentle slopes are ideal for intermediate skiers who love beautiful scenery. Vars also boasts a number of high-speed runs on which the **Speed-skiing** World Cup is held.

In summer, Vars is an excellent hiking base. In addition to skiing and rambling, the resort offers a wide choice of summer and winter activities including skating, snowmobiling, swimming, riding, paragliding and squash. Mountain bikers can test their stamina on the longest course in Europe (32km/20mi).

Excursions

The Col de Vars may be blocked by snow from December to April.

▸ *From Guillestre, drive south along D 902.*

Between Guillestre and Peyre-Haute, there are views of the fortified city of Mont-Dauphin (⚭ *See MONT-DAUPHIN)* perched on its promontory, of the Durance Valley upstream of Embrun and of the Guil Valley. The road rises up to a rocky ridge separating the Rif-Bel (Val d'Escreins) and Chagne valleys.

Peyre-Haute viewing table

15min there and back on foot; 100m/109yd upstream of Peyre-Haute (panel), climb onto the mound on the left. The **view**★ includes, from left to right, the Ailefroide, the Pic sans Nom, Mont Pelvoux, and the Pic de Neige Cordier with the Glacier Blanc coming down from it.

The next few bends offer views of the snow-capped summits of the Écrins Massif. The **Route du Val d'Escreins**★★ *(see below)* branches off on the left.

The road goes through the hamlets which make up the resort of Vars.

Vars★★

From Vars to the pass, the road runs along the foot of the slopes, equipped with ski lifts between Ste-Marie and the Refuge Napoléon.

Musée du KL (Refuge Napoléon)

This museum just off N 902, before the pass, is devoted to speed skiing, from its origins in the 1930s to the latest refinements of the **Kilomètre Lancé** or "flying kilometre." Open to amateurs as well as speed specialists, the Pic de Chabrières is

---

Address Book

For coin categories see the Legend on the cover flap.

EATING OUT

Chez Plumot – 05560 Les Claux - ☎ 04 92 46 52 12 - open 1 July-1 Sept, 7 Dec-27 Apr and summer evenings. This popular spot has a cozy dining room and a mezzanine level, and offers traditional and Savoyard dishes as well as some from the Southwest. If it is available, try the *tarte tatin*. Fast service and menu option at lunchtime.

Caribou – 05560 Les Claux - ☎04 92 46 50 43 - hotelcaribou@villagesclub-sdusoleil.com – closed 25 Apr-25 June and 31 Aug-18 Dec. In the elegant dining room or on the terrace, you will enjoy traditional cuisine. There are also some guestrooms available if you would like to prolong your stay.

WHERE TO STAY

Les Escondus– 05560 Les Claux - ☎ 04 92 46 67 00 - hotel.les.escondus@wanadoo.fr - closed 26 Apr-27 Jun and 16 Dec-24 Apr - 🅿 - 22rms - restaurant. Simple, practical rooms, some with balconies, piano bar. The restaurant offers traditional dishes and Alpine specialties in a wood-paneled dining room or on the terrace opposite the forest.

Le Vallon – 05560 Ste-Marie-de-Vars - ☎04 92 46 54 72 - info@hotelvallon.com - closed 27 Apr-30 June and 29 Aug-16 Dec - 🅿 - 34rms - restaurant. At the foot of the ski-hill, this large hotel offers an Alpine ambiance and decor. Renovated rooms with large windows, lounge with billard table and game room. Traditional cuisine in a dining room decorated with mountain photos.

Hôtel l'Écureuil – 05560 Les Claux - ☎04 92 46 50 72 - hotel.ecureuil@wanadoo.fr – closed 27 Apr-27 June and 9 Sept-7 Dec - 🅿 -21rms. This chalet off the beaten track has a traditional decor with wood panelling and warm ambiance. A pleasant lounge-bar with fireplace, rooms decorated with colourful fabrics.

SHOPPING AND ON THE TOWN

Le Point Show – Cours Rohner – depending on the shops, closed mid Apr-Jun and Sept-mid Dec. This shopping arcade is without a doubt the resort's liveliest. In fact, it not only offers shops of every kind, but also bars and small restaurants, as well as a cinema, games arcade and swimming pool.

SPORTS

Indiana Forest – 🅺🅸🅳 - La Charpenterie - ☎ 06 09 52 35 62 - www.indian.forest.com– Jun-Sept: daily 9am-7pm. Inspired by archaeological adventurer Indiana Jones, this adventure circuit is riddled with pitfalls and obstacles such as rope ladders and footbridges made from lianas. Children over age 5 will have great time while the grown-ups can also put their skills to the test.

the site of the world's fastest ski run, but be warned: the 1.4km/0.87mi slope has an average gradient of 52%, reaching a dizzying 98% at its steepest point. No wonder, then, that racers need a full 850m braking zone to slow down. *(For more on the refuges Napoléon, ⓒsee Le BRIANÇONNAIS, 5).*

Col de Vars★

Alt 2 111m/6 926ft. In the middle of meagre pastures dotted with blocks of sandstone stands a monument commemorating the renovation of the road by Alpine troops. On the way down to l'Ubaye, the pastoral landscape remains austere. The truncated summit of the Brec de Chambeyron (alt 3 390m/11 122ft), preceded by a long ridge, can be seen to the east.

Between Melezen and St-Paul, there is an interesting group of "demoiselles coiffées" (capped maidens) on the roadside. It is possible to park the car before the small bridge and walk close to them *(ⓒsee SERRE-PONÇON, 3 and Sights Nearby).*

St-Paul – *ⓒSee L'UBAYE, 4*

Réserve naturelle du Val d'Escreins★★

▶ *From Vars, drive down towards Guillestre along D 902; turn right onto a small road following the Val d'Escreins.*

The Rif-Bel Valley, which is inaccessible for eight months of the year, became the **Réserve naturelle du Val d'Escreins** (2 500ha/3 707 acres – ⓒ *Mid-May to mid-Oct: from dawn to dusk. No charge - ☎ 04 92 46 51 31 - www.vars-ete.com.*) in 1964 and was later combined with the Parc naturel régional du Queyras.

At the end of the valley, the forested slopes give way to barren summits, including the **Pic de la Font Sancte** (alt 3 387m/11 112ft). The name, meaning "holy fountain," comes, according to tradition, from a spring discovered by a young shepherdess, which became a place of pilgrimage in times of drought. ⚑ The climb to the summit is only suitable for experienced hikers, who are rewarded with one of the finest panoramas in the Alps.

⚑The reserve, open to visitors in summer, offers 37km/23mi of marked footpaths linking this valley to that of Ceillac in the north and Maurin in the east. Accommodation is available during the season at the Basse Rua refuge, allowing seasoned walkers to climb to the Col des Houerts *(map available from tourist information centres).*

St-Marcellin-de-Vars

This ancient hamlet has retained its mountain-village atmosphere.

⚑ A pleasant **walk to the castle ruins**★ starts in St. Marcellin. *Leave the car in one of St-Marcellin's car parks. Allow 1hr 30min there and back on foot (steep path).*
Walk along the right side of the church. The path is marked in yellow. After the first bend to the left, carry straight on *(do not go towards the house up on the right).* The path crosses a small road. Continue to the summit where you will find explanations about the ruined castle and enjoy an extended **view**★ of the various hamlets around Vars, of Guillestre and of Mont-Dauphin.

⚑Hikes

Pic de Chabrières★★

In winter: access via the 🚡 **Chabrières gondola** *(ⓒJuly to Aug: (departure every min, length 30 seconds) daily except Mon and Sat 10am-5pm. 5€ - ☎ 04 92 46 51 04 - www.sedev.fr.), the Crévoux and Chabrières chairlifts. In summer: access via the Chabrières gondola, then on foot (3hr 30min there and back). Climbing boots recommended.*

▣ The upper station of the **Télecabine de Chabrières** stands at the foot of the **Kilometre lancé** speed-record trial run; view of Ste-Marie, Ste-Catherine, the Col de Vars and the Crêtes de l'Eyssina.

The **Pic de Chabrières** (alt 2 727m/8 947ft) offers a magnificent **panorama**★★ of the "Forêt Blanche" ski area backed by the Pic de la Font Sancte, the Queyras Massif, the snow-capped Pelvoux and the peaks surrounding the Lac de Serre-Ponçon, which is visible from the **Col de Crévoux**★.

Hike to the Tête de Paneyron★★

Alt 2 787m/9 144ft. *Leave the car at the Col de Vars. 3hr 30min there and back on foot. Difference in height: 677m/2 221ft. It is advisable to wear mountain boots.*

▣ Walk down towards Barcelonnette for a few minutes and turn left onto a wide path which, after around 20min, leads to a shepherd's house; above and to the right are some cairns which mark the way. After a 10min walk across pastures, you will find a clearer path which climbs very steeply as it nears the summit. Beautiful **panorama**★★ of the ski area from the Pointe de l'Eyssina to the Val d'Escreins and of the road to the Col de Vars, from Guillestre to the River Ubaye.

▷ *Return by the same route.*

LE VERCORS★★★

MICHELIN MAP 332 F/G 2/3

Rising above Grenoble like a fortress, the massive limestone plateau of the Vercors forms the largest regional park in the northern Alps. Daring cliff roads follow the deep gorges carved by tributaries of the lower Isère and run deep into thick beech and conifer forests. Its southern uplands, arid and deserted, feel like the plains of the Midi; the forested northern heights have the open, untouched look of the Canadian wilderness. The Vercors attracts Alpine and cross-country skiers who brave the bitter winters in search of peace and quiet and natural beauty. ▤ *rue du Cinéma, 38880 Autrans* ◷ *July to Aug: daily 9am-12.30pm, 2-7pm; mid-Dec to Mar: daily 9am-noon, 2-6pm; Sept and Nov: daily except Sun 9am-noon, 2-6pm; Apr to Mar: daily except Sun 9am to noon, 2-6pm; June daily except tue 9am-noon, 2-6pm - ☎ 04 75 48 22 54 - www.vercors-net.com*

▷ **Orient Yourself:** The area is to the west and southwest of Grenoble. Take D 531 from Grenoble through the Gorges d'Engins; from the Rhone valley, take D 518 southeast through Pont-en-Royons; from the south, D 518 leads up from Die by the Col de Rousset.

⊘ **Don't Miss:** If the route of the Grands Goulets is closed, take the Combe-Laval route, which is equally vertiginous.

◷ **Organizing Your Time:** The roads are beautiful, but whether clinging to rock faces or passing over high plateaux, they all demand that you take your time.

▨ **Especially for Kids:** There are donkey rides for children, or a visit to the museum of mechanical toys in Lans-en-Vercors would interest them.

⊙ **Also See:** Nearby Sights: Massif de CHAMROUSSE, Massif de la CHARTREUSE, DIE, GRENOBLE, Lacs de LAFFREY, PONT-EN-ROYANS, Le TRIÈVES, VILLARD-DE-LANS, VIZILLE

A Maze of Caves

The "crust" of the Vercors Plateau consists of a gently undulating layer of limestone from the Cretaceous period, up to 300m/984ft thick in places, which forms impressive cliffs in the gorges and along the edge of the massif. Water flows freely through these calcareous rocks, streams disappear into sink-holes known as *scialets* similar to the *chourums* of the Dévoluy region, and reappear as resurgent springs. The most striking example of this phenomenon is the underground **Vernaison**; identified in the depths of the Luire Cave, it reappears in the Bournillon Cave, 20km/12mi further on, which makes it one of the major underground rivers in France.

The exploration of the **Gouffre Berger**, which opens on the Sornin Plateau (west of Sassenage), led the Spéléo-club de la Seine to a depth of 1 141m/3 743ft.

Stronghold of the Resistance

The strategic advantage of the Vercors Massif, thinly populated and easy to defend, became apparent to the local resistance movements, or *maquis*, as early as 1942 and several defensive camps were established from 1943 onwards.

Two keen amateur mountaineers, the writer Jean Prévost and the architect Pierre Dalloz, and the head of the Secret Army, General Delestraint, hatched a scheme, known as the **"plan Montagnards,"** to establish an allied bridgehead in the Vercors.

By March 1944 there were two Resistance groups in the Vercors, totalling 400 men. After D-day (June 6), there were 4 000 volunteers receiving military training from professional soldiers. A first German assault on St-Nizier was beaten back on the 15 June; and on 3 July the "République du Vercors" was proclaimed and supplied with Allied airdrops of light armament and material. The area was soon surrounded by two German Alpine divisions numbering 15 000 men and, on 21 July, German gliders used the airfield intended for allied planes to drop special commandos and SS troops. After three days of fierce fighting, the outnumbered Resistance fighters retreated towards the Forêt de Lente while the St-Martin Hospital was evacuated south to the Grotte de la Luire. The hospital was stormed by a commando unit on 27 July: one Resistance fighter managed to survive by hiding in a fissure in the rock, but

Address Book

For coin categories, see the Legend on the cover flap.

EATING OUT

☺☺**Le Pertuzon** – *Av. du Vercors - 38112 Méaudre -* ☎ *04 76 95 21 17 - closed 2-8 June, 15 Nov-15 Dec, Sun evening, Tue evening and Wed out of season.* This hotel-restaurant in a little village near the lush greenery of a river gorge offers simple, well-cooked meals in a non-smoking dining room decorated with bright pictures, or in fine weather on the terrace. Rooms are very plain, but will do in a pinch.

WHERE TO STAY

☺**Chambre d'hôte entre Chiens et Loups** – *Panenat -38880 Autrans-1km/.5mi SW of Autrans -* ☎ *04 76 95 36 64 - www.entrechiensetloups.fr.st - closed Apr-May and 12-24 Sept -* ☺ *- reservations required - 4rms -* ☺☺ *meal.* This modern wooden house, at the edge of a forest, is perfect for those seeking calm and wide-open spaces. The rooms are pleasant, and services include fishing lessons and rides on a dogsled.

☺☺**Hôtel Les Tilleuls** – *La Côte - 38880 Autrans -* ☎ *04 76 95 32 34 - closed 11 Apr-3 May, 24 Oct-16 Nov, Tue evening and Wed out of season and school holidays -* ℗ *- 18rms-* ☺☺*restaurant.* Near the heart of this resort, this attractive building has functional, well-kept rooms. Wood-panelled dining room, classic cuisine with game in season and a house specialty: the caillette, a sort of Gallic haggis.

the remaining patients, two doctors and a priest were killed and the nurses deported to Ravensbrück concentration camp. Reprisals continued until 19 August. A number of memorials in the Vercors Massif commemorate these events.

Highlight

Parc naturel régional du Vercors

Maison du Parc - 225 Chemin des Fusillés - 38250 Lans-en-Vercors - ☎ 04 76 94 38 26 - www.parc-du-vercors.fr
Created in 1970, the park covers an area of 175 000ha/432 425 acres and includes 72 municipalities situated in the limestone Massif du Vercors and also in the Royans, Trièves and Diois regions.
A number of local museums document the area, five nature trails have been set up and the high plateaux, overlooked by Mont Aiguille, are now designated as a nature reserve. The Vercors has also gained a reputation for cross-country skiing, thanks mainly to the resorts of Autrans and Villard-de-Lans; the area is crisscrossed with marked trails and cross-country ski clubs. Several hiking footpaths go through the area, including the GR 91 which crosses the high plateaux.

A remarkable ecosystem – Forests cover more than half the total area of the Vercors Massif and offer great variety: beeches and firs are gradually replaced by pines in the south of the region. There are more than 1 800 different plant varieties including some very rare protected species: the lady's slipper, martagon lily and forest tulip. The Vercors is one of the rare areas where the six species of wild hoofed animals living in France can be found: chamois, deer, roe-deer, wild boars, moufflons and ibexes. Birds of prey are also well represented: golden eagles, peregrines, eagle owls, Bonelli's eagles (in the south) and a few bearded vultures. Since 1994, griffon vultures have also been gradually reintroduced to the park's skies.
Wolves have also made a come-back recently due to declining agriculture and the increase in wild prey. However, wolves venturing off the high plateaux into valleys have developed a taste for sheep; the park is working with shepherds to find an accomodation. In the Italian Alps, wolves are even more numerous, but cohabit with flocks of sheep, which points to a possible solution.

1 Grands Goulets★★★

From Villard-de-Lans to Pont-en-Royans *36km/22.4mi – allow 2hr – see local map*

▸ From Villard de Lans (*see VILLARD-DE-LANS*), drive along D 531 towards Pont-en-Royans. (This road is closed until 2008. Instead take the route of Combe Laval, then drive towards La Chapelle over the Col de Carri, or take the route of the Gorges de la Bourne towards St-Julien-en-Vercors up to the bridge over the Goule Noire.)

Beyond Les Jarrands, the road runs beside the Méaudre through a deep gorge, which narrows until there is only just room for the road and the stream.

The Grands Goulets

S. Sauvignier/MICHELIN

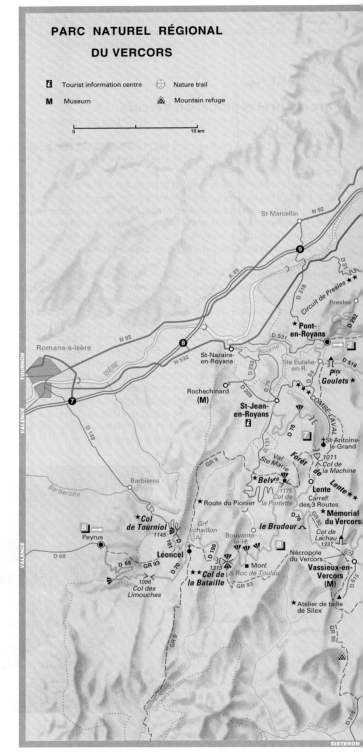

PARC NATUREL RÉGIONAL
DU VERCORS

ⓘ Tourist information centre   **❀** Nature trail

M Museum   **⛰** Mountain refuge

0   10 km

St-Marcellin   N 92

❾

Circuit de Presles ★★

Presles

D 292

★ **Pont-en-Royans** D 531

❽

St-Nazaire-en-Royans

Ste Eulalie-en-R.

D 518

★★★ **Pits Goulets** ★

Romans-s-Isère

ISÈRE

N 92

N 532

Rochechinard **(M)**

D 253

D 209

Bourne

Cholet

St-Jean-en-Royans ⓘ

D 76

COMBE-LAVAL

★ St-Antoine-le-Grand

D 131

Val Ste Marie

Forêt

☖ 1011 Col de la Machine

7

★ **Belve**

de

Lente ★★

Lente

Carref: des 3 Routes

★ **Mémorial du Vercors**

1175 Col de la Portette

★ **Route du Pionier**

GR 9

Barbières

Barberolle

★ **Col de Tourniol**

1145

101

Grd Echaillon

le Brudour ⌒

D 76

GR 95

Col de Lachau 1337 ⛰

Bouvante-le-Ht

8

Nécropole du Vercors

Vassieux-en-Vercors (M)

D 615

8 →

Peyrus

Léoncel

D 68

D 190

1313

★★ **Col de la Bataille**

GR 93

Roc de Toulau

Mon!

Atelier de taille de Silex

D 68

GR 93

1086 Col des Limouches

D 70

Sune

Gervanne

GR 9

⛰

D 518

Drôme

7

VALENCE
TOURNON
VALENCE

D 149

SISTERON

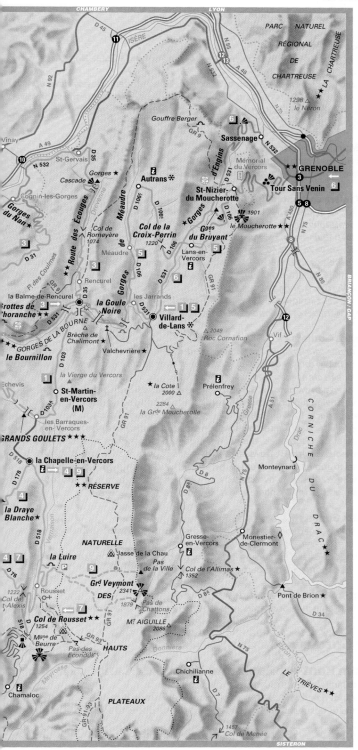

▶ *At the Pont de la Goule Noire, bear left along D 103.*

La Goule Noire

This large spring is visible downstream of the Pont de la Goule Noire, level with the river bed.

The cliff road rises above the south bank of the Bourne, offering lovely views of cliffs known as the Rochers du Rang. Before St-Martin-en-Vercors, note the impressive rock, standing like a statue; it is known as the Vierge de Vercors, "the Virgin Mary of the Vercors."

St-Martin-en-Vercors

This was the French headquarters during the 1944 fighting. The last European brown bear in the French Alps was seen here in 1938.

La Tanière enchantée

Kids ♿ ⌖ *guided tours (1 hr) June to Aug: 9.30am-noon, 1.30 to 6.30pm; Jan to May and Sept: 10am-noon, 2-6pm; Oct to Dec: Wed, Sat-Sun, public holidays and school holidays: 10am-noon, 2-6pm.* ◷ *Closed 1 Jan, 25 Dec. 5.80€, children under 15 years 4.20€ - ☎ 04 76 94 18 40.*

This exhibition uses mechanical reconstructions and the display of stuffed animals to illustrate the often difficult relationship between men, bears and other animals in the Vercors sharing the same habitat.

Beyond Les Barraques, D 518 enters the Grands Goulets.

Parking facilities at the entrance of Les Barraques.

Grands Goulets★★★

⚠*Extreme care is required as you drive through the Grands Goulets. Stopping points for one or two cars are on the right-hand side of the road driving towards Les Barraques. The tunnels are not designed for large vehicles.*

This deep narrow gorge is the most impressive natural sight of the Vercors region. Before driving through, walk as far as the second bridge over the Vernaison *(15min there and back)*. Daylight barely reaches the road through the thick vegetation and when you suddenly enter the gorge on a blazing summer's day, the effect is striking. Near the last tunnels, the cliff road clings to the rock face above the river bed (numerous waterfalls). Downstream, the ravine opens out; look back after the last tunnel to appreciate the depth of the gorge. The road continues high above the valley, whose arid slopes, overlooked by rocky escarpments high in colour, contribute to the southern atmosphere which pervades the scenery.

Petits Goulets★

The sharp-edged rocky slabs plunging almost vertically into the river are remarkable.

Beyond Ste-Eulalie, the smiling Royans countryside offers a strong contrast with the last *cluse* (gorge) of the Bourne, looking like a natural gateway.

Pont-en-Royans★ – ♿*See PONT-EN-ROYANS.*

The following itinerary describes the return journey to Villard-de-Lans.

☑ Gorges de la Bourne★★★

From Pont-en-Royans to Villard-de-Lans

24km/15mi – allow 1hr 30min – ♿ see local map.

This gorge, lined with thick layers of coloured limestone, gets deeper and deeper as one heads upstream along the Bourne, which is reduced to a trickle in summer.

After Pont-en-Royans, the D 531 enters the gorge immediately and follows the river. The valley widens slightly before Choranche, then becomes narrow again and the road leaves the river bed to climb along the steep north bank, where many waterfalls cascade down the cliffside in rainy weather.

Grotte du Bournillon

1km/0.6mi south of D 531, then 1hr there and back on foot. Turn onto the private road leading to the power station, cross its yard and turn right; the path giving access to the cave starts on the left, on the other side of a bridge over the Bournillon (parking allowed, but beware of falling rocks). Continue left along a steep, difficult path at the base of the escarpments to reach the huge **entrance**★ (100m/328ft high) of the cave. Walk as far as the footbridge to appreciate the size of this enormous arch. The Bournillon spring, now piped, was the continuation of the underground river Vernaison which has its source in the Grotte de la Luire. Opposite the semicircular walls around the spring are the red rocks of the cirque de Choranche.

Grottes de Choranche★★

2.5km/1.5mi from D 531 across the Bourne (car park); continue on foot.
There are seven caves in all at the foot of tall cliffs overlooking the village of Choranche. Two of them are open to the public. *Temperature in the caves is not much above freezing. Wear warm clothing and non-slip shoes.*
The **Grotte de Coufin**★★ *(&* ⏲ *Apr to Oct: guided tours (1hr, departure every 30min) For information about hours, telephone or consult the Website. 7.70€, children 5-14 years 4.80€ - ☎ 04 76 36 09 88 - www.choranche.com)* is the most spectacular cave in the Vercors Massif. Its name, somewhat disconcerting for English-speakers, means "narrow neck" and refers to the cave entrance. Discovered in 1875, it includes a vast chamber where thousands of snow-white **stalactites**★★, 1-3m/3-10ft long, are reflected in the water of a lake. The tour continues along a winding gallery where light effects create a supernatural atmosphere. The visit ends with an **audio-visual show**★. An aquarium contains an olm, a blind cave-dwelling salamander with external gills. Outside, there is an exhibition about prehistoric people who lived in the area; a very pleasant and interesting walk along the scientific **nature trail** *(allow 1hr)* provides an introduction to the flora, fauna and geology of the area.

Grottes de Choranche

P. Labriel/Grottes de Chorance

The **Grotte du Gournier** contains a beautiful lake, 50m/164ft long and 8m/26ft deep, fed by an underwater spring. This underground network, known to stretch over 18km/11mi, consists of a succession of waterfalls with a considerable difference in altitude, but you will need the right equipment and an experienced guide to explore the caves properly.

The road then runs through the basin of La Balme at the confluence of the Rencurel and Bourne valleys (🐾 *see Route des Écouges below*), then enters the Goule Noire Gorge. Note the large Calvaire de Valchevrière, which commemorates the battles of July 1944, standing on the opposite bank. After the Pont de la Goule Noire and the Grotte de la Goule Blanche, its water now used to generate electricity, the road continues to Villard-de-Lans (🐾 *see VILLARD-DE-LANS*).

3 Route Des Écouges et Du Nan★★

Round Trip From La Balme-de-rencurel To N 532

21km/13mi – allow 1hr – 🐾 *see local map*

This itinerary opened in 1883 includes one of the most vertiginous sections in the Vercors region, but promises superb views of the Bas-Dauphiné.

▷ *From La Balme, drive north along D 35.*

The road runs up the Rencurel Valley along to the **Col de Romeyère** (alt 1 074m/3 524ft), where a forest road leads to the vast Coulmes Forest. The valley itself is densely forested and now uninhabited. At Pont Chabert-d'Hières, the Drevenne leaves this wide coomb and veers left through a spectacular **gorge**★ towards the Isère Valley, running along the side of the cliff. There are bird's-eye **views**★★ of the Isère Valley and the hills of the Bas Dauphiné.

Bridge over the Drevenne

It is worth stopping for a moment to admire the **waterfall** dropping from a height of 50m/164ft.

▷ *Just beyond St-Gervais, the road joins N 532 along the east bank of the Isère to Cognin-les-Gorges. Continue on the D 55 to Malleval.*

Gorges de Nan★

The Nan, a mountain stream flowing down from the western foothills of the Vercors, is followed from a great height by a small picturesque cliff road. The stretch along the left bank of the River Isère is still more spectacular.

D 22 rises in a series of hairpin bends along the escarpment overlooking the Nan Valley. Stop between the second and third tunnels on the most impressive section of the route, on the edge of a precipice with a drop of 200m/656ft. A second, less vertiginous narrow defile leads to the cool and verdant upper valley. The road continues upwards through meadows to Malleval, from where a relatively new road, built in 1983, gives access to the Coulmes Forest and the D 31 leads up to the Vercors Plateau (in summer only).

▷ *The route along the D 292 via Presles is described in reverse order under* 🐾*PONT-DE-ROYANS.*

At the crossroads with the D 531, turn left towards La Balme-de-Rencurel and **Gorges de la Bourne**★★★ (🐾 *see* 2 *above*).

4 Route du Col de Rousset★★

From Chapelle-en-Vercors to the Col de Rousset
24km/15mi – allow 1hr 30min – 👣 *see local map*

▶ *From Les Barraques-en-Vercors, drive south along D 518.*

La Chapelle-en-Vercors
This tourist centre located near the Forêt de Lente was bombed and burnt down in July 1944. Two plaques in a farmyard (Ferme Albert), one of the rare places which was not destroyed, honour the memory of 16 inhabitants of the village who were shot.

▶ *Follow D 518 towards Grotte de la Luire and Col du Rousset.*

Grotte de la Luire
0.5km/0.3mi off D 518 on the left and 15min there and back on foot; allow 30min more to see the Decombaz Chamber. 🕐 *July and Aug: guided tours (30min) 9.30am-6.30pm; May to June: 9.30am-noon, 1.30-6pm; Apr and Sept: 10am-noon, 1.30-5.30pm.* 🕐 *Closed Oct to Mar: 5.20€, children 3.40€ -* ☎ *04 75 48 25 83.*
The cave is interesting from a geological and a historical point of view. In July 1944, the Nazis killed or deported the wounded and the staff of the Resistance movement hospital set up inside the cave (👣 *see above: Stronghold of the Resistance).*
The **Decombaz Chamber** is 60m/197ft high under a natural vault; deep inside it, there is a chasm which led cave explorers 470m/1 542ft down to what is thought to be the underground Vernaison. During periods of exceptional spates, the water of the river rises up the chasm and overflows into the cave.

▶ *Continue south along D 518 to the Col de Rousset station and go through the tunnel.*

Col de Rousset★★
Alt 1 254m/4 114ft. *Leave the car at the tunnel exit and walk to a viewpoint (1 367m/4 485ft).* The Col de Rousset marks the climatic limit between the northern and southern Alps: the green landscapes of the Vercors on the northside, the arid **Bassin de Die**★★ on the southside.
🎿 The ski runs of the recent **Col de Rousset** ski resort are on the slopes of the **Montagne de Beurre,** near the pass. In summer, a new vehicle takes advantage of the available slopes: the **"trottinherbe,"** a cross between a mountain bike and a scooter.
From the viewing table, situated on the edge of the plateau, an impressive **panorama**★★ unfolds: the Grande Moucherolle to the north, the Grand Veymont to the east (in the foreground) and the heights of the Diois to the south with Mont Ventoux on the horizon.

▶ *Head north and turn left onto D 76 to Vassieux-en-Vercors.*

The road leads gradually uphill through the woods above the Vernaison, crosses the Col de St-Alexis and heads down through stony fields into the valley of Vassieux. 500m/550yd from the town, on the left side of the road, lie the remains of German gliders from the Second World War.

Vassieux-en-Vercors
🏛 *Av du Mémorial - 26420 Vaissieux-en-Vercors* 🕐 *July to Aug: Tue-Sat 9am-noon, 2-6pm, Sun 9am-noon; Christmas and Feb holidays: daily except Sun 9am-noon, 2-6pm; rest of year: contact the tourist office at la Chapelle-en-Vercors -* ☎ *04 75 48 22 54* 🕐 *closed public holidays except 14 July, 15 Aug -* ☎ *04 75 48 27 40*

In 1944, while fierce fighting was going on in the region, the Resistance built an airfield for the Allies near Vassieux, but early on the morning of 21 July it was used by German gliders filled with commandos. The resistance fighters, at first believing them to be their liberators, realised their mistake too late: the German troops killed the population and burnt the village to the ground. Vassieux was entirely rebuilt and a monument, surmounted by a recumbent figure by Émile Gilioli, was erected to the "Martyrs of the Vercors, 1944"; a commemorative plaque on the town hall square bears the names of the 74 civilian victims.

The **church**, built after the war, is decorated with a fresco by Jean Aujame *(The Assumption)* and bears a touching commemorative plaque.

The **Musée de la Résistance du Vercors** *(&🕐 Mid-July to mid-Aug: 10am-7pm; Apr to mid-July, mid-Aug to Oct: 2-6pm; Feb-Mar, Nov to Dec: Wed-Sun 2-5pm. 2€, children under 8 years no charge - ☎ 04 75 48 28 46.)* was founded by a former member of the Secret Army. It deals with the events which took place in the region in 1944, as well as the horror of the Nazi camps and the joy of the Liberation.

Musée de la Préhistoire du Vercors ★ *3km/1.9mi south of Vassieux by D 615*
🕐 *July to Aug: 10am-6pm; Apr: daily except Tue 10am-12.30pm, 2-5pm; May to June and Sept: daily except Tue 10am-12.30pm, 2-6pm; Oct to Mar: Sat-Sun 10am-12.30pm, 2-5pm; school holidays: 10am-12.30pm, 2-5pm 🕐 closed Nov to mid-Dec. 1 Jan, 25 Dec. 5€, children 6-15years 2.50€ -☎ 04 75 48 27 81 - www.prehistoire-vercors.fr*
Excavations in 1969 revealed numerous flints shards and blades spread over an area of 100m2. The specialised knife and dagger blades cut in this 4 000-year-old workshop show a remarkable degree of skill; some were clearly only for display, and probably had a symbolic meaning. They were traded all over Europe. Other such workshops have been found, but this one is remarkable because because it happened to be the spot where local peasants tossed rocks removed from their fields, so remained undisturbed. Displays, films, practical demonstrations and reconstructions of pre-historic dwellings reveal the working methods of these early craftsmen.

1km/0.6mi north along D 76, the **Cimetière national du Vercors** contains the graves of 193 Resistance fighters and civilian victims who died during the operations of July 1944.

▷ *Follow D 76 to the Col de Lachau.*

Mémorial de la Résistance du Vercors ★ (Col de la Chau)

3km/1.9mi from Vassieux; from the cemetery, take D 76 on the left. Car park at the pass.
&🕐 *May to Sept: 10am-6pm; Jan to Mar: daily except Mon and Tue (except during school holidays)10am-5pm; April and Oct to 11 Nov: 10am-5pm 🕐 Closed 12 Nov to mid-Dec, 1 Jan, 25 Dec. 5€, children 8-15 years 2.50€ - ☎ 04 75 48 26 00.*
The memorial stands out like the prow of a ship against the dense Forêt de Lente. Built by a group of architects from Grenoble at an altitude of 1 305m/4 282ft, it is covered with junipers and pines which grow naturally in the Vercors Massif. The intentionally plain building is devoted to the Vercors Resistance Movement and to national events which took place at the time. Themed reconstructions and dioramas cover collaboration with the Germans, interrogations by the Milice (French paramili-tary organisation created by the Vichy Government) and the role of women in the Resistance movements; recorded individual accounts and contemporary films recall the "République du Vercors" which lasted until 23 July 1944.
On the way out, the names of 840 civilian victims are inscribed in recesses along a large wall. From the terrace, the view embraces the Vassieux Valley.

▷ *Turn right after the cemetery and take the D 178 towards La Chapelle-en-Vercors and follow the signs to la Draye Blanche.*

Grotte de la Draye Blanche ★
🕐 *July to Aug: guided tours (50min) 9am-7pm; Sept to Mar: 10am-noon, 2-5pm; Apr to June: 9am-6pm. 6.50€, children 4€ -* ☎ *04 75 48 24 96.*

One of the most ancient caves in the Vercors region, la Grotte de la Draye Blache was discovered in 1918 by one Fabien Rey, who had the foresight to block off the entrance. The cave remained perfectly preserved until it was finally opened to the public in 1970 and is now directly accessible from the car park via a tunnel. This most recent work led to the discovery of another cave containing animal remains from many thousands of years ago, a find which sheds new light on the prehistory of the Vercors. The tour includes the **Grande Salle**★, a vast chamber, 100m/110yd long, in which calcite comes in different colours, white, ochre or blue-grey. A stalagmite, 12m/40ft high and 2m/6.5ft thick, looks like a petrified waterfall.

5 Gorges de Méaudre

From Villard-de-Lans to Grenoble
46km/29mi – allow 5hr – 👣 *see local map.*

▷ *From Villard, drive west along D 531.*

The road follows the River Bourne. At Les Jarrands, where the valley suddenly narrows, turn right onto D 106 which goes up the **Gorges de Méaudre** through pastoral scenery. Beyond Méaudre, bear left onto D 106C and continue through 🎿**Autrans**★, a popular cross-country skiing resort, before rejoining the main D 106.

Col de la Croix Perrin
Alt 1 220m/4 003ft. The pass is a vast clearing between slopes clad with splendid forests of firs. In Jaume, D 106 veers to the right, goes through **Lans-en-Vercors** then rises above the Furon Valley, offering bird's-eye views of the picturesque Gorges d'Engins and Gorges du Bruyant.

Lans-en-Vercors

La Magie des automates
🧒 🕐*Daily except Mon 2-6pm, Sun and public holidays: 10am-6pm; school holidays: 10am-6pm* 🕐 *closed Oct. 7€, children 2-14 years 5€ -* ☎ *04 76 95 40 14 - www.mag-iedesautomates.com*

Lively mechanical toys represent scenes from the circus, traditional occupations and a Santa's village with 1500 figurines.

Route de la Molière
Turn north towards the Mortier tunnel for a pleasant 8km/5mi detour across a lovely plateau dotted with old houses, up to a viewpoint overlooking the Massif du Mont Blanc, the Chartreuse, Belledone and the Val d'Autrans.

St-Nizier-du-Moucherotte – 👣*see GRENOBLE, Nearby Sights.*

On the way down to Grenoble, there are views of the Grenoble Basin where the River Isère and River Drac meet. In the foreground on the right are three peaks known as the Trois Pucelles or "Three Maidens," the site of a climbing school.

Tour Sans Venin
🚶*15min there and back on foot.*

One of the Seven Wonders of Dauphiné. According to legend, a crusader brought back soil from the Holy Land and, by spreading it round his castle, rid the area of venomous snakes, hence the name "tower without venom." From the foot of the ruined tower, the **view**★ extends south to the Dévoluy.

6 Gorges d'Engins

FROM GRENOBLE TO VILLARD-DE-LANS 32km/20mi – allow 2hr

▷ *From Grenoble, drive northwest to Sassenage along D 532, which runs parallel to the Casque de Néron along the Isère valley.*

Sassenage – 🚶see GRENOBLE, Nearby Sights

Gorges d'Engins★
The smooth rock walls of this deep trench frame the verdant valley of the Furon.

Gorges du Bruyant
🚶 A convenient footpath, linking D 531 and D 106, leads to the bottom of the gorge *(1hr there and back).*
From Jaume to Villard-de-Lans, the road follows the Lans Valley, whose gentle slopes are clad with dense forests of fir, within sight of the peaks marking the eastern edge of the Vercors. Note the stepped gables of traditional houses.

7 Route du Combe Laval★★★

From the Col de Rousset to St-Jean en Royans

41km/25.5mi – allow 3hr – 🚶 see local map

▷ *Drive north and bear left onto D 76 to Vassieux-en Vercors, passing the memorial.*

Grotte du Brudour
🐾From the bridge across the Brudour, 30min there and back on foot along a very pleasant path. Take along a flashlight. It leads to a cave where water from nearby Urle bubbles up as a resurgent spring. Follow the left-hand gallery to a chamber containing a small lake *(30min there and back)*. The Brudour itself soon disappears into various sink-holes to reappear as the Cholet below the cirque of the Combe Laval.

From the Carrefour des Trois Routes to St-Jean-en-Royans

After heavy rain, look out for the waterfall just before **Lente**, a small forestry village; the cascade disappears straight into a funnel-shaped sinkhole known as a *doline*.

Combe Laval

B. Bodin/FOC

Forêt de Lente★★
The forest consists essentially of firs and beeches; the timber was used in the 19C by the navy and the coal industry. The great storm of 1982 devastated the forest, and 220,000 trees have since been replanted.

Combe Laval★★★
The spine-chilling journey starts from the **Col de la Machine**. The road, hewn out of the rock face, literally hangs above the gorge of the upper Cholet from a height of 600m/1 968ft. Note the Cascade du Cholet, a resurgent spring of the Brudour. After going through several tunnels, the road suddenly overlooks the whole Royans region, offering bird's-eye **views**★★ of this deeply burrowed area and of the Bas Dauphiné plateaux (Chambaran Forest). To the north are the deep furrows dug through the mountain by the River Bourne and River Vernaison.

St-Jean-en-Royans
Lying below the cliffs of the Vercors Plateau, this small town is the starting point of magnificent excursions on foot or by car. The town is also celebrated for its unique cuisine, including Royans *raviole*, adapted from the ravioli introduced by Italians working in the Vercors forests. The chancel of the church is decorated with fine 18C woodwork from a former Carthusian monastery. There is an interesting **viewpoint** on top of the **Toura** Hill accessible via the cemetery lane.
Situated 5km/3mi west along D 209, **Rochechinard** is overlooked by the ruins of an 11C-12C **castle**; its small country church and its presbytery form a lovely picture with the cliffs of the Combe Laval in the background; the **Musée de Royans** (☞ *July to Aug: guided tours (1hr) daily except Mon 3-7pm. 3.5 € - ☎ 04 75 48 62 53.)* contains a collection of tools and regional costumes as well as reconstructions of traditional interiors.
There is a fine excursion to be made south of St-Jean *(17km/10.6mi on D 131 and D 331)* along a cliff road known as the Route du Pionniera, which overlooks the Lyonne Valley. *It is possible to make it a round tour by returning via the Combe Laval (see above) or via the Col de la Bataille (see drive* 8 *).*

Monastère St-Antoine-le-Grand
Take the D 54 to Combe de Laval and follow signs for the Gorges de Laval along the D 2 and D 239. ♿🕐 *All year long: 11.30am-12.30pm, 4-5.30pm (mid-Sept to mid-June 4.50pm). 3.50€, children under 12 years no charge -* ☎ *04 75 47 72 02.* This short diversion leads to a Greek Orthodox monastery, constructed between 1988 and 1990, with unusual murals painted by two Russians who took six years to complete the work.

8 Col de la Bataille★

From Peyrus to the Carrefour des Trois Routes
45km/28mi – allow 2hr – ♿ see local map

▷ *From Peyrus, drive along D 68.*

The road rises in a series of wide hairpin bends above a wooded vale. About half a mile before it reaches the plateau, there is an extended view of the Valence Plain with the Cevennes in the background. The Col des Limouches gives access to the Léoncel Valley, whose meagre pastures, dotted with box and juniper bushes, look distinctly Mediterranean.

Léoncel
From its Cistercian abbey founded in 1137, the village has retained a vast Romanesque **abbey church**★ (🕐 *All year long: 9am-12.30pm, 2.30-7pm -* ☎ *04 75 44 51 10)* dating from the late 12C, surmounted by a stocky square bell-tower topped by a pyramid. Built in stages from 1150 to 1210, the interior demonstrates the changing taste in

Before Going

- Water is rare on the Vercors plateaux: an extra supply is never superfluous.
- Do not go off marked paths, even when going across open spaces.
- Sheepfolds which look deserted always belong to shepherds; if you want to stop for a break or to take cover, make sure you do not leave anything behind.
- When a flock or herd approaches, make a wide detour round it without sudden movements or noises.
- Paragliding, camping and fires are forbidden and dogs are not allowed inside the reserve's perimeter. Mountain bikes are only permitted on the "Grande Traversée du Vercors" (GTV).

architecture: the oven-vaulted apse and apsidal chapels are typical of Provençal Romanesque style, whereas the quadripartite vaulting of the nave already bears the mark of Gothic art. Note the arms of the abbey chiselled into the wall near the door, on the right, plus a 16C lectern and a fine modern icon in the northern transept.

▷ *From Léoncel, follow D 101 to the Col de Tourniol.*

Col de Tourniol★
The **view** extends beyond the Vercors foothills across the Valence Basin.

▷ *Return to Léoncel.*

The road climbs up the eastern slope of the valley and reaches the densely forested plateau.

Col de la Bataille★★
The road is closed from 15 November to 15 May.
A tunnel gives access to the pass (alt 1 313m/4 308ft) overlooked by the Roc de Toulau. The **panorama** is impressive.
From the pass to Malatra *(2km/1.2mi)*, the **cliff road**★★ winds it way above the Bouvante Cirque and its small lake; there are three viewpoints along this section, before the road veers north towards the Col de la Portette.

Belvédère de la Portette★
15min on foot there and back from the Col de la Portette. Leave the car in the last bend and follow the stony path which starts behind a forest marker; bear right 200m/219yd further on. From the belvedere, the **view** looks down over the Val Ste-Marie, with the Royans region and Isère Valley beyond; note the huge modern bridge of St-Hilaire-St-Nazaire.

▷ *From the pass, it is only a short distance to the Carrefour des Trois Routes.*

Hikes

9 Réserve naturelle des Hauts-Plateaux★★

This desolate area, covering 16 600ha/41 020 acres and situated at altitudes ranging from 1 200m/3 846ft to 2 300m/7 546ft, was declared a nature reserve in 1985 in order to safeguard the balance which existed between traditional activities (foresters and shepherds) and natural ecosystems. No road goes through it and there are no permanent dwellings.

The area consists of karst-like limestone plateaux, dotted with fissures and sinkholes into which surface water disappears, and includes the two highest summits of the Vercors Massif, the Grand Veymont (2 341m/7 680ft) and Mont Aiguille (2 086m/6 844ft); it is bounded by impressive cliffs on the east and west sides.

Wildlife is less diverse here than in the rest of the Vercors. The main species of fauna are the black grouse, the blue hare and the chamois, as well as around 100 ibexes and the recently reintroduced wild vultures. Cave-dwellers, on the other hand, are plentiful, in particular the many species of bat.

Many marked footpaths such as GR 91 and 93 crisscross the high plateaux, but in the absence of access roads, hikes are inevitably lengthened and often involve camping overnight. Specialised topo-guides are available at tourist offices.

From Rousset to the Col des Escondus

The excursion described below is relatively easy and should only take half a day; start from Rousset, where you can leave the car. Difference in altitude: 400m/1 312ft.

Aim for the Chapelle St-Alexis, cross a stream then walk south along its east bank to the end of the Combe Male and then to the Col des Escondus at the intersection of GR 93. Impressive views of the hamlet of La Grange and the Montagne de Beurre. Follow the path going north through the woods to the Chalet des Ours *(You can also go west to the Col de Rousset across high pastures)*. Take the path running behind the chalet towards the Combe Male and follow it back to your starting point.

Grand Veymont★★

Allow 1 day – Difference in altitude: 1 000m/3 281ft – Altitude at the starting point: 1 350m/4 429ft.

From La Chapelle-en-Vercors, drive along D 518 towards the Col de Rousset; 1km/0.6mi before Rousset, turn left onto a narrow forest road signposted "Route forestière de la Coche." Follow it to the vast car park of the Maison Forestière de la Coche (9km/5.6mi). Leave the car there. Make sure you have warm clothing with you; the summit is exposed to high winds.

Continue on foot to the Maison Forestière de Pré Grandu. Walk east along the marked path running across the plateau, past rocks and pine woods; the stern wall of the Grand Veymont bars the horizon straight ahead. On the way down through the central depression, make for the **Nouvelle Jasse de la Chau,** where you can get a fresh supply of water.

Behind the information panel, a path climbs towards the **Pas de la Ville,** the last stage before the summit, exposed to high winds. A path on the right of the iron cross leads up to the summit but it is worth walking a few extra metres east beyond the pass for some wonderful bird's-eye views of the Trièves Valley.

The climb to the summit along the scree-covered slope requires particular care. Several cairns mark the summit (2 341m/7 680ft); the impressive **panorama**★★★ includes the major part of the Alps from Mont Blanc in the northeast to Mont Pelvoux and the Meije facing the Grand Veymont, with the solitary Mont Ventoux in Provence. But the most striking silhouette is undoubtedly that of Mont Aiguille (2 086m/6 844ft) in the foreground.

The way down to the south is very steep. At the foot of the ridge, take the path on the right which runs west to the Pas de Chattons and joins GR 91 just before La Grande Cabane. Continue westwards and turn right at the intersection. The path runs north for 5km/3mi to meet the large path leading to the Maison Forestière du Pré Grandu.

GRAND CANYON DU VERDON★★★

MICHELIN MAP 334 E/F10

The River Verdon, a tributary of the Durance, has carved magnificent gorges through the limestone plateaux of the Haute-Provence region, the most spectacular being the Grand Canyon which extends for 21km/13mi from Rougon to Aiguines. The sight of this vast furrow lined with sheer walls in wild unspoilt surroundings is unique in Europe; in the words of Jean Giono: "Here, it is more than remote, it is elsewhere..." *Maison des Gorges du Verdon – 04120 LaPalud-sur-Verdon ⏱15 June to 15 Sept: daily except Tue 10am-1pm, 2-7pm; 15 Mar-14 June and 16 Sept-15 Nov: daily except Tue 10am-noon, 2-6pm. 4€, children under 15years 2€ - ☎ 04 92 77 32 02 -www.lapaludsurverdon.com*

▶ **Orient Yourself:** On its north side, the Grand Canyon can be followed on D 952 and D23, while the D 71 runs along the south side.

Don't Miss: From the Balcons de la Mescla, admire the churning waters below; the view of the canyon between the two Fayet tunnels is spectacular; the highest point on the route is the Cirque de Vaumale; there are also extraordinary views from the Col d'Illoire and from viewing points between Moustier-Sainte-Marie and La Palud.

Organizing Your Time: You will need a day to follow the gorges from both sides of the river. If you enjoy hiking and adventures, stay at least another day.

Especially for Kids: Take children to the Maison des gorges du Verdon and on the nature walks of Châteauneuf-les-Moustiers at La Palud and of Les Lézards at Rougon.

Also See: Nearby Sights: BARGÈME, CASTELLANE, CLUES DE HAUTE-PROVENCE, GRÉOUX-LES-BAINS, MOUSTIERS-STE-MARIE, Route NAPOLÉON, RIEZ, ST-JULIEN-DU-VERDON, Lac de STE-CROIX, Plateau de VALENSOLE

A Bit of History

How can so deep a gorge have been carved out by so small a river? The reason is that when the Alpine area folded during the Tertiary tectonic upheaval, the huge layers of limestone deposits rose slowly and the existing river bed sank deeper and deeper. The Verdon subsequently widened and modelled the sinuous corridor through which it now flows. Intense erosion carved huge caves in the cliffside, and water penetrating through the karst of the plateau created a vast network of underground caves and galleries.

The width of the gorge varies from 6/20ft to 100m/328ft at water level and from 200m/656ft to 1 500m/4 921ft at the top of the cliffs. Its depth varies from 250m/820ft to 700m/2 297ft.

Edouard Martel (1859-1938), a founder of speleology, was the first to explore the 21km/13mi-long gorge. In 1928, part of the canyon was equipped to receive visitors, but still only on foot; the main viewpoints were signposted. In 1947, the cliff road (D 71), known as the Corniche Sublime, was hewn out of the rock, thus opening the way to motorists. The north bank road, on the other hand, was only completed in 1973. In 1997 the Parc naturel régional du Verdon was inaugurated to safeguard the outstanding natural site of the Grand-Canyon du Verdon.

Excursions

Route de la Corniche Sublime ★★★ *81km/50.3mi – half a day*

This itinerary is almost perfect from a tourist's point of view, the road twisting and turning to reach the most impressive viewpoints. The bird's-eye views of the canyon are amazing, but you are unlikely to have this idyllic route all to yourself: the Gorges du Verdon attract over one million visitors every year.

FROM CASTELLANE TO THE BALCONS DE LA MESCLA

Castellane★ – *See CASTELLANE.*

▶ *Leave Castellane by ② on the town plan and drive along D 952.*

The road follows the north bank of the Verdon meandering beneath impressive escarpments. The rocky ridge of the Cadières de Brandis can be seen on the right.

Porte de St-Jean★
Beyond this narrow passage cut through limestone heights, the river takes a wide turn to the left and flows southwards.

Clue de Chasteuil★
This long transverse gorge is lined with vertical rock strata.

Address Book

For coin categories, see the Legend on the cover flap.

EATING OUT

◎◎**Auberge du Point Sublime** – 04120 Point-Sublime - ☎ 04 92 83 60 35 - point.sublime@wanadoo.fr - closed 16 Oct-14 Apr, Thur noon and Wed. This small traditional restaurant on the road that follows the Gorges du Verdon has a delightful lounge with a panoramic view and a shaded terrace. The guestrooms are simple, functional, and comfortable.

WHERE TO STAY

◎◎**Auberge des Crêtes** – 04120 La Palud-sur-Verdon - 1km/0.6mi E on D 952 - ☎ 04 92 77 38 47 - aubergedescretes@ wanadoo.fr - closed 4 Oct-3 Apr - ▣ - 12rms - ◎◎ restaurant. This is an unpretentious and practical inn on the Gorges du Verdon road. The rooms are simple and have simply fitted bathrooms. There is a large terrace at the front and a shaded patio at the back of the house. Good cooking and friendly atmosphere.

◎◎◎**Chambre d'hôte Mme Colombéro** – Campagne l'Enchastre - 04120 La Palud-sur-Verdon - 12km/7.5mi N of La Palud on D 123 (towards Châteauneuf) then D 17 - ☎ 04 92 83 76 12 - closed 1 Oct-15 Apr - ⌀ -5rms - ◎◎ meals for hotel guests. Those who love unspoiled nature and peace and quiet will be delighted with this guesthouse in the middle of nowhere at the end of a very narrow road. The modern house stands on a farm estate 1 100m/3 608ft above sea level. The rooms are plain but comfortable and decorated in colourful tones.

◎◎◎◎**Hôtel Les Gorges du Verdon** – 04120 La Palud-sur-Verdon - 1km/0.6mi S of La Palud - ☎ 04 92 77 38 26 - bog@worldonline.fr - closed 25 Oct -8 Apr - ▣ - 27rms - ◎◎ restaurant. Before embarking on one of the numerous adventurous activities open to you in the Gorges de Verdon, enjoy the peace and quiet of this hotel on the hillside above the river gorge. Traditional cuisine. Swimming pool, garden, tennis courts.

▶ *In Pont-de-Soleils, turn left into D 955.*

The road leaves the Verdon to follow the green Jabron Valley. On the right, the hilltop village of **Trigance** is overlooked by an imposing medieval castle remodelled in the 16C, now turned into a hotel.

Comps-sur-Artuby
This ancient village, which once belonged to the Knights Templar and later to the Knights Hospitaller, nestles at the foot of a rock crowned by the 13C **Église St-André**; the nave, surmounted by a pointed vault, ends with an oven-vaulted apse. Note the christening font.

From the church, there are fine views of the Artuby Gorge and the entrances of several caves.

D. Faure/SCOPE

Falaise des Cavaliers, Gorges du Verdon

▶ *From Comps, drive west along D 71.*

A bend in the road affords a wide **view**⋆ of the arid Préalpes de Castellane and Préalpes de Digne.

Balcons de la Mescla⋆⋆⋆
On the right side of the road and on either side of the Café-Relais des Balcons.
From these rock terraces, there are bird's-eye views of the Mescla 250m/820ft below, the name taken from the Provençal word for "mix" and given to the confluence of the Verdon and its tributary the Artuby. The Verdon takes a sharp bend round a narrow promontory and the view embraces the upstream part of the gorge, 400-500m/1 312-1 640ft deep. The upper viewing terrace offers the most impressive view.
The road then runs towards the Artuby.

FROM THE BALCONS DE LA MESCLA TO MOUSTIERS-STE-MARIE
🔁 *The road may be blocked by snow from December to March.*

Pont de l'Artuby⋆
🅿*Car park at the end of the bridge.* This remarkable piece of engineering in reinforced concrete comprises a single arch with a 110m/361ft span thrown across the Artuby Canyon lined with vertical cliffs. Anyone keen to get a closer look at the gorge may like to know that this is a popular bungee jumping spot. The road goes round the Pilon du Fayet to reach the Verdon Canyon.

Tunnels de Fayet
Between the two tunnels and immediately beyond there is a breathtaking **view**⋆⋆⋆ of the curve of the canyon near the Étroit des Cavaliers.

Falaise des Cavaliers⋆
The road follows the edge of the cliff where there are two viewpoints. Turn right towards the Restaurant des Cavaliers. From the terrace, there is a striking **view** of the 300m/984ft-high cliff.
Over the next 3km/1.9mi, the road runs 250-400m/820-1 312ft above the gorge; it is one of the most impressive sections of the whole itinerary.

Falaise de Baucher⋆
Lovely view of the Pré Baucher Basin upstream.

Pas de l'Imbut
Bird's-eye view of the Verdon overlooked by huge sheer cliffs; the river disappears 400m/1 312ft below under a pile of fallen rocks.
Further on, the road leaves the edge of the cliffs and one loses sight of the gorge for a while.

The Acrobats of the River Verdon

For a long time, the bottom of the gorge and the river bed provided the local population with their main means of support: boxwood and wild honey.

It required a great deal of skill and courage to reach the virtually inaccessible sites where box and honey could be found. Honey gatherers moved about on a plank held by a hemp rope, whereas box cutters climbed up and down a succession of long poles fitted with bars. The most daring among them worked their way along the cliffs by driving spikes into the rock; they were the forerunners of today's rock-climbers whose demonstrations up and down the Falaise de l'Escalès win the admiration of onlookers.

Cirque de Vaumale★★

The road enters the cirque after a sharp bend to the left and the view then embraces the downstream section of the gorge. The road reaches its highest point at an altitude of 1 204m/3 950ft. The gorge backed by the heights of the opposite bank forms a superb landscape.

As it comes out of the cirque, the road leaves the gorge once more and winds its way westwards, offering **views**★ of the Lac de Ste-Croix and, further away, of the Luberon, the Montagne de Lure and Mont Ventoux beyond the Durance Valley.

Col d'Illoire★★

The road comes out of the gorge for good. Stop and admire the Grand Canyon once more.

The **view**★ now embraces the flat expanse of the Plateau de Valensole, with a line of bluish heights on the horizon.

Aiguines

This village, in a superb **site**★ overlooking the vast expanse of the Lac de Ste-Croix, has retained its old-world charm, twisting lanes, old houses and a 17C castle with four corner towers covered in colourful tiles. Aiguines was famous for the work of its wood-turners who used boxwood from the nearby forests. The Musée des Tourneurs (*temporarily closed*) presents the various species of wood used by turners and illustrates their work. It contains lathes and a collection of objects, from bottle cases and powder boxes to tool handles and potato-mashers. Animated models show the process of collecting and turning the wood.

A video show is devoted to the speciality of Aiguines: **nail-studded boules** for playing *pétanque*!

Beyond Aiguines, the road winds down to the Lac de Ste-Croix.

▶ *Turn right onto D 957.*

Lac de Ste-Croix★★ – 🍷 *See Lac de STE-CROIX.*

There is a fine **view**★ of the entrance of the canyon from the bridge across the Verdon; the road then follows the Maïre Valley and skirts the outdoor leisure park of Moustiers-Ste-Marie.

Moustiers-Ste-Marie★★ – 🍷 *See MOUSTIERS-STE-MARIE.*

North Bank★★★ 73km/45mi
– allow half a day

The direct road *(D 952)* from Moustiers to Castellane only runs close to the Grand Canyon at each end. However, the "Route des Crêtes" *(D 23)* offers an unforgettable round tour from La Palud-sur-Verdon via a number of viewpoints.

PARC NATUREL RÉGIONAL DU VERDON

🛈 Tourist information centre
🚶 Discovery trail
🚢 Boat trip
M Museum or exhibit
⛵ Canoe and kayak hire

FROM MOUSTIERS-STE-MARIE TO LA PALUD-SUR-VERDON

Moustiers-Ste-Marie★★ – ⓒ *See MOUSTIERS-STE-MARIE.*

On the way down the Maïre Valley, the scenery is unmistakably Provençal with its lavender fields and twisted olive trees. The view embraces the edge of the Plateau de Valensole, overlooking the vast turquoise expanse of the Lac de Ste-Croix, and takes in Aiguines and its castle as well.

Belvédère de Galetas★

This viewpoint marks the entrance of the gorge. View of the gateway of the Grand Canyon and of the Lac de Ste-Croix in a picturesque landscape of ochre-coloured cliffs.

The road enters the Cirque de Mayreste and climbs steeply.

Belvédère de Mayreste★★

15min on foot there and back along a marked stony path. First overall upstream view of the deep furrow.

Belvédère du col d'Ayen★

5min on foot there and back. Interesting upstream view of the twisted course of the canyon; however, the bottom remains out of sight.

The road veers away from the Verdon towards the cultivated area surrounding La Palud-sur-Verdon.

La Palud-sur-Verdon

This family resort is the ideal starting point of hikes through the canyon and a good base for rock-climbers.

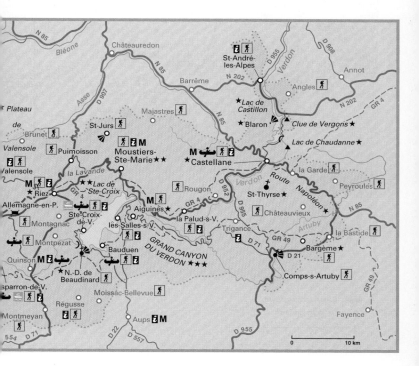

A 12C Romanesque bell-tower is all that remains of the original church. The 18C castle and its four corner towers overlook the village.

Kids Maison des gorges du Verdon★

(◔ *see above for opening times*) This is an essential stop for getting the information you need to appreciate the great spectacle of the Verdon gorges: brochures, a bookshop, exhibits and a nature trail as well as photos, videos and models to explain all aspects of the gorges: geology, botany, history, local traditions and more.

🚶 *1hr30min* All the family will enjoy the nature trail at Châteauneuf-les-Moustiers, an abandoned village where life in olden times is imaginatively described. A brochure is available at the Maison des Gorges.

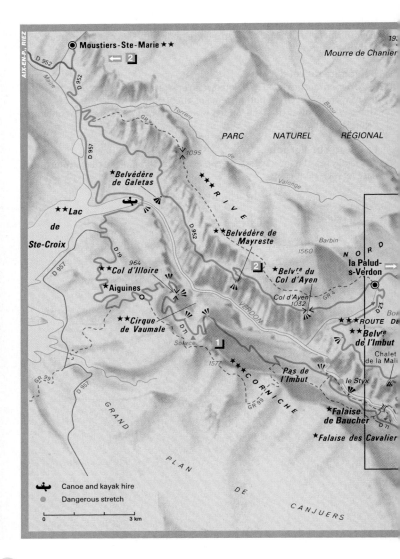

Canoe and kayak hire
Dangerous stretch

0   3 km

ROUTE DES CRÊTES★★★ (Round tour starting from La Palud-sur-Verdon)

A succession of belvederes or viewing points line this itinerary; they are sometimes situated so high above the gorge that it feels as if you were looking at an aerial view. The main belvederes are listed below.

▶ *From La Palud, continue along D 952 towards Castellane then turn right into D 23.*

The road rises through lavender fields and woodland areas.

Belvédère de Trescaïre★★★
Looking upstream, the Verdon is seen to flow through a jumble of fallen rocks and disappear under the vault of the Baulme aux Pigeons Cave, in the Samson Corridor.

In summer, take a moment to watch the rock climbers inching their way up the rock face.

Belvédère de Carelle★★

Bird's-eye view of the river meandering deep down in the gorge. To the left is the Auberge du Point Sublime and, above it, the hilltop village of Rougon. It is one of the main free-climbing sites in the Grand Canyon.

Belvédère de l'Escalès★★★

It is situated on top of the sheer cliffs below which runs the Sentier Martel. In summer, numerous rock-climbers add to the interest of the site.

Belvédère de la Dent d'Aire★★

Alt 1 300m/4 265ft. The golden cliffs of the Dent d'Aire and of the Barre de l'Escalès can be seen towering on the left; straight ahead is the narrow corridor of the Baumes-Frères.

Belvédère du Tilleul★★

The confluence of the Verdon and Artuby, known as the "Mescla," lies ahead and the single-arched Pont de l'Artuby behind. The Verdon changes course to the northwest.

Belvédère des Glacières★★

Impressive view of the Mescla and its enormous promontory, of the Verdon and Plan de Canjuers. When the weather is clear, you can see the Mediterranean Sea.
🚶The road runs past the Chalet de la Maline, which is the starting point of the hike through the Grand Canyon (♿see Sentier Martel).

Belvédère de l'Imbut★★

The Verdon disappears under a pile of fallen rocks and the Sentier Vidal and Sentier de l'Imbut can be seen running along the opposite bank. The **view** embraces the mighty cliffs of the Baou Béni. Upstream, the narrowing of the **"Passage du Styx"** affords glimpses of the Pré Baucher.
The road veers away from the Verdon to return to La Palud-sur-Verdon.

FROM LA PALUD-SUR-VERDON TO CASTELLANE

Don't miss the fine **view** on the next bend: the picturesque hilltop village of Rougon suddenly appears ahead, slightly to the left, and the road runs within sight of the gorge once more.

Point Sublime★★★

15min there and back on foot. Leave the car in the car park near the Auberge du Point Sublime. Follow the signposted path on the right across the deeply fissured Plateau des Lauves to the belvedere towering 180m/590ft above the confluence of the Verdon and its tributary the Baou. Splendid **view**★★★ of the entrance of the Grand Canyon and of the Samson Corridor.

▷ *Return to the car and follow D 17 to Rougon.*

Rougon

Alt 960m/3 150ft. This "eyrie," overlooked by medieval ruins, affords a fine **view**★ of the entrance of the Grand Canyon from the slope above the car park. *Access to the ruins can be tricky as there is no path, so extra care is required.*

▷ *Return to D 952 and follow it towards Castellane.*

Couloir Samson★★

Just before the Tunnel du Tusset, a dead-end road branching off to the right leads to the confluence of the Verdon and the Baou (car park); it meets the path running along the river from the Chalet de la Maline.

From this spot, the narrowing of the Grand Canyon downstream looks wild and impressive as huge rocks lie across the river bed.

Useful Tips for a Successful Hike into the Canyon

Duration – Allow 2hr extra as a safety precaution, to make sure you will return before nightfall. Stick to the times indicated for each section of the itinerary so as not to be caught by surprise. Follow the itinerary in the direction that is recommended (usually the easiest) to avoid encountering awkward crossings and having to make too great an effort climbing out of the gorge.

Equipment – Take some food and 2litres (4 pints) pints of water per person (the river water is not suitable for drinking), one or two torches, additional clothing (the tunnels are quite cool; other places sunny and hot) and climbing boots.

Strictly prohibited – Camping on unauthorized sites, lighting a fire, digging up fossils. Hikers are also asked to refrain from taking shortcuts (it tends to increase the gullying of slopes), crossing the river except via bridges and picking flowers (they fade rapidly anyway) as many species are protected.

Domestic animals – Dogs must not be taken along the footpaths in the gorges (Martel, Imbut). In any case, they would find the terrain too difficult.

Children – Going into the gorge with children under 10 is not recommended; the Sentier Imbut is too difficult for them.

Variation of the water level – Water released by the Chaudanne or Castillon plants can cause a sudden rise in the level of the Verdon; the flow of the river is liable to increase from 10-100m3/353-3 531cu ft per second. The EDF recorded information only lists forecast rates of flow, so it is essential, when stopping for any length of time, to choose a few rocks at water level as markers and watch them carefully. Releases from the dams are not preceded by warning signals.

The **Sentier de l'Imbut**, which is only suitable for experienced hikers, is accessible under special conditions *(see hike 4)*.

Recorded information – Weather forecast in St-Auban: ☎ 08 92 68 02 04. Rate of flow of the Verdon (EDF service): ☎ 04 92 83 62 68.

Taxis – A shuttle service operates between the Auberge du Point Sublime, La Palud-sur-Verdon and the Chalet de la Maline in summer; taxis run all year round: ☎ 06 07 65 19 49, or ☎ 04 92 77 14 20. This enables hikers to return to where they left their cars.

Maps and topo-guides – In addition to the local maps included in this chapter, it would be useful to buy the Moustiers-Ste-Marie local map (1:50 000) and the Grand Canyon du Verdon map by A Monier. "Le Guide du Verdon" by JF Bettus, is on sale in La Palud-sur-Verdon; another useful guide is "Randonnées pédestres dans le pays du Verdon," published by Édisud.

Exploration of the bottom of the gorge – It can be done mostly on foot, but swimming is necessary in places, so it is closer to canyoning (see *Planning Your Trip*). Whatever the conditions and the length of the exploration planned, it is a sporting feat which entails danger and requires a thorough knowledge of the techniques of white-water sports. Training from a qualified guide is essential.

Rock-climbing sites – The main one is the Belvédère de Carelle, where it is easy to film rock-climbers at work; there is also the Belvédère de Trescaïre and the Falaise de l'Escalès.

Beyond the tunnel, the cliff road runs down towards the river.

Clue de Carejuan★

The limestone strata are strangely coloured. The water cascades over fallen rocks and its clear, green surface is temporarily disturbed.

After the heavy spates of Autumn 1994, the banks of the stream had to be reinforced.

For the section of the itinerary from Pont-de-Soleils to Castellane, see the drive entitled Corniche Sublime.

Hikes Through the Grand Canyon★★★

1 Sentier Martel★★★

Between the Chalet de la Maline and the Point Sublime, GR 4, known as the Sentier Martel, offers tourists who do not mind a tiring day's hike an unforgettable close contact with the Grand Canyon.

FROM THE CHALET DE LA MALINE TO THE POINT SUBLIME

5hr hike, not counting resting time, along a difficult itinerary; see local map – torch essential, a headlamp even better. GR 4 is marked in white and red.

From the steps going down to the river, there are fine views of the Pas de l'Estellié.

The Canyon du Verdon from the Sentier Martel

G. Kosigki/FOC

Ignore the path branching off to the right towards the Estellié Footbridge; it leads to the Restaurant des Cavaliers and the Corniche Sublime.

At the Pré d'Issane (*after 1hr30min walking*), the path runs close to the river and follows it through the Étroit des Cavaliers with sheer cliffs towering 300m/984ft above. The gorge widens and the path reaches the Talus de Guègues, a scree framed by steep slopes.

Continue upstream past the vast Baumes-aux-Bœufs Cave and take the second path to the right leading to the **Mescla**★★★ (*30 min there and back*), where the flow of

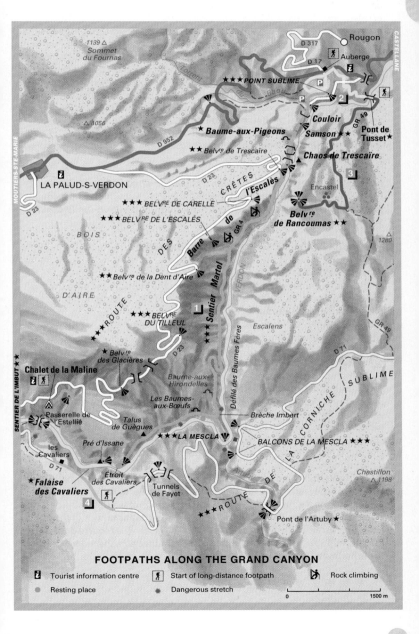

FOOTPATHS ALONG THE GRAND CANYON

🛈 Tourist information centre	🚶 Start of long-distance footpath	🧗 Rock climbing
● Resting place	✳ Dangerous stretch	

0 — 1500 m

the Verdon mixes with that of the Artuby. There is a splendid view upstream of the Défilé des Baumes-Frères.

▶ *Retrace your steps to the intersection and turn right.*

The path winds its way up to the Brèche Imbert *(steps)*: superb view of the Baumes-Frères and the Barre de l'Escalès. The canyon, overlooked by very high cliffs (400-500m/1 312-1 640ft), becomes wider and the walk *(1hr30min)* is a bit monotonous, until the cliffs narrow. The Chaos de Trescaïre, on the right, is an extraordinary jumble of fallen rocks. The hilltop village of Rougon can be seen in the distance. Next come two tunnels; inside the second, metal steps lead to the **Baume-aux-Pigeons**★, a vast cave, 30m/98ft high, situated at the foot of a 350m/1 148ft-high cliff. From the bottom of the stairs, you can see, on the opposite bank, the huge blocks which fell when the roof caved in. This cave and the collapsed roof indicate that in the past the Verdon partly flowed underground. From the last opening, there is a view of the **Couloir Samson**★★, a very narrow corridor with smooth vertical sides. Beyond the tunnel, the path goes over the footbridge across the Baou and climbs to the parking area. The hike ends at the **Belvédère du Point Sublime**★★★.

▶ *Walk to the inn where you can call a taxi. You can join D 952 from the Auberge du Point Sublime by taking shortcuts.*

If you wish to go to La Palud-sur-Verdon without going past the Point Sublime, take the path on the left just before the footbridge over the Baou; it goes up along the south bank of the stream and joins D 952 4km/2.5mi from La Palud-sur-Verdon. This shortens the hike by 3km/1.9mi.

2 Sentier de Découverte des Lézards

From the Point Sublime★
🚶 Kids This well-marked nature trail starts from the Plateau des Lauves. A small explanatory booklet is available at the Auberge du Point Sublime or at the tourist office in La Palud-sur-Verdon.
Another itinerary leads to the Pont de Tusset along GR 49.
These round tours usually take between 1hr and 3hr 30min.

3 Belvédère de Rancoumas★★

East bank starting from the Point Sublime★★
3hr 30min there and back. It is possible to start from the Point Sublime car park and to walk south, following GR 49 markings, or to drive towards the Couloir Samson (D 23B) and park the car on the last bend before the straight stretch ending in the car park.
🚶 2km/1.2mi before reaching the car park, take GR 49 on the left, marked in white and red; it leads through an oak forest down to the **Pont de Tusset**★, a bridge dating from the early 17C.
The path starts rising through a forest of pines, maples and beeches, then joins a wide track. Leave the marked path and follow the track on the right; it crosses a stream before reaching the ruins of Encastel. Go up to the edge of the cliff.
The natural Belvédère de Rancoumas offers a striking **panorama**★★ of the whole Falaise de l'Escalès with the Sentier Martel running below. The **Mourre de Chanier** (alt 1 930m/6 332ft), the highest summit of the Verdon region, soars in the distance to the northwest.

▶ *Return along the same route.*

④ **Sentier de l'Imbut** ★★ *3km/1.9mi.*

This itinerary is very difficult and should be attempted only if you are fit, well-equipped and experienced on this sort of terrain. Several points overhanging the river are somewhat technical (ladders, handrails).

The path must be followed in one direction only, *i.e.*, exit via the Vidal steps.

Do not take domestic animals or children under 10 on this hike.

Do not undertake this hike if the forecast flow rate reaches *40m³/1 413cu ft per second.*

Qualified guides are available (*contact the Maison des gorges de Verdon*).

▸ *You can cross the Verdon over the Estellié footbridge and follow the Sentier Martel to the Chalet de la Maline.*

Start from the Auberge des Cavaliers, 2.5km/1.5mi to the Estellié footbridge including 340m/372yd downwards. The itinerary runs entirely on the south bank, along a cliff path equipped with handrails in several places.

This is the most secluded and impressive part of the canyon where one can see huge beech trees, caves, groves of hazelnut trees and potholes. The itinerary follows the long Styx Corridor and reaches the Imbut Beach, where the path ends. This is the point where the water disappears down a sump. Exercise great caution if you wish to go over the jumble of rocks forming the "Chaos de l'Imbut."

The return journey up the steep Vidal steps requires a considerable effort to negotiate the difference in altitude of 400m/1 312ft; the steps are often 50cm/20in high and the only help comes from a steel handrail.

▸ *Walkers can also cross the Estellié footbridge and continue along the Sentier Martel to the Chalet de la Maline.*

VILLARD-DE-LANS

POPULATION 3 798
MICHELIN MAP 333 G7

The tourist capital of the Vercors region has the best facilities of all the resorts in the Dauphiné Préalpes. Its dry, sunny climate, clean air and sheltered position at the foot of the Cornafion, Gerbier and Moucherotte make it an ideal resort for children and adults; outdoor activities include skiing, paragliding, cave exploration, canyoning and ballooning. In the 1980s, Villars-de-Lans and Corrençon-en-Vercors joined forces to form a single holiday resort with a greater variety of ski slopes, hikes and climbing routes. 🛈 *101 place Mure-Ravaud - 38250 Villard-de-Lans* 🕐 *July to Aug: 9am-12.30pm, 2-7pm; Christmas and Feb holidays: 9am-7pm; rest of year: Mon-Sat 9am-noon, 2-6pm, Sun 9am-noon - ☎ 0811 460 015 - www.villarddelans.com*

▸ **Orient Yourself:** Villard-de-lans is 36km/22.5mi soutwest of Grenoble. Start from Sassenage to reach the Gorges d'Engins by D 531, or from Seyssinet to reach the Tour sans Venin and St-Nizier de Moucherotte on D 106.

Don't Miss: The exhibit on the Villarde cow at the Musée du Patrimoine.

🕐 **Organizing Your Time:** from the town centre, you can make short trips (1 or 2hr) to see the principal sites of interest.

Also See: Nearby Sights: Massif de CHAMROUSSE, Massif de la CHARTREUSE, GRENOBLE, Lacs de LAFFREY, PONT-EN-ROYANS, Le VERCORS, VIZILLE

Museum

Maison du patrimoine

1 Place de la Libération ◷ July to Aug: daily except Mon 3-7pm; Dec to Mar: Tue-Sat 3-6.30pm; out of season: Fri and Sat 3-6pm. 3.05€, children under 10 years no charge - ☎ 04 76 95 17 31

This small museum has a rather unique exhibit devoted to the Villarde cow (*see Introduction, Local Economy*), which Alpine farmers valued for its strength and resistance as a work animal, as well as for its ability to provide milk and meat, a truly all-round beast. There is also the inevitable collection of old objects, photographs, pictures and tools that testify to the daily life in Vercors only one or two generations ago. The development of the resort is also traced.

Excursions

Cote 2000★ *4.5km/2.8mi southeast*

From Villard-de-Lans, take the avenue des Bains to the end of the valley. Turn left onto D 215 to Corrençon and left again to the gondola station. Take the **Cote 2000 gondola** (◷ *July to Aug: 9am-12.45pm, 2-5.30 (10 min, continuous). 5.50€ - ☎ 04 76 94 50 50*) to the mountain station and continue on foot *(1hr there and back for the ride and the walk)*.

The **view** embraces the undulating plateaux of the Montagnes de Lans and Vercors to the north and west and stretches as far as the distant brown line of the Cevennes

---

Address Book

For coin categories, see the Legend on the cover flap.

EATING OUT

Le Bacha – *42 pl. de la Libération - ☎ 04 76 95 15 24 - bacha-rest@wanadoo. fr - closed 2 wks in May and 3 wks in Dec.* This family restaurant on a small and lively square in the village centre has rustic decor and a vaulted basement dining room. Take a seat on the terrace in season.

Auberge des Montauds – *Au Bois-Barbu - 38250 Villard-de-Lans - ☎ 04 76 95 17 25 - aubergedesmontauds@ wanadoo.fr - closed 15 Apr-1 May, and Nov-15 Dec.* On the heights over Villard, this inn is literally at the end of the road. Beyond is only nature and calm. Generous traditional and Alpine cuisine to enjoy next to the fire, or on the terrace in summer. Renovated guestrooms, one equipped for the handicapped.

WHERE TO STAY

Hôtel de la Villa Primerose – *147 av. des Bains - ☎ 04 76 95 13 17 - www.hotel-villa-primrose.com - closed 15-30 Apr and Oct-20 Dec - 18rms.* Take a seat in the verdant garden or on the terrace to admire the view of the mountains. Tennis courts are opposite the hotel and both cross-country and downhill skiing are close by in winter. Guests can use the kitchen, which is practical.

Chambre d'hôte Le Val Ste-Marie – *Au Bois-Barbu - 38250 Villard-de-Lans – near the start of the cross-country ski trails - 4km/2.5mi W of Villard-de-Lans on D 215E towards Bois-Barbu then La Glisse mountain refuge, track to the left after the signpost to Caisse - ☎ 04 76 95 92 80 - http://levalsaintemarie.villard-de-lans. fr - 3rms - main meal.* This two hundred year-old farm has been well restored and is a comfortable place to stay. Nature lovers can make the most of the surrounding countryside in summer and of the cross-country ski trails in winter. In the evening, guests dine with their hosts. Library, garden, terrace.

The Return of the Bear

Since it was last seen near St-Martin-en-Vercors in 1938, the European brown bear has completely disappeared from the French Alps. This animal, which lives in forests, is particularly shy and can sense human presence several hundred yards away. Occasionally carnivorous, it lives mainly on plants and looks for them in remote and steep wooded areas. The Haut-Vercors region, which is totally desolate in winter and has no permanent settlements, offers the ideal conditions for the return of the bear, which is represented by statues in many villages. However, the Parc naturel régional du Vercors authorities, who have drawn up plans for its possible return, are first looking for the support and active involvement of the local population, particularly farmers.

Route de Valchevrière ★

▶ *Leave Villard-de-Lans by the avenue des Bains. At the junction at the end of the valley, follow the D 215C towards Le Bois-Barbu.*

A small scenic road is lined with the Stations of the Cross dedicated to the victims of the fighting which took place in 1944. Views of the Gorges de la Bourne and the Méaudre valley.

Calvaire de Valchevrière ★
(8km/5mi west along D 215C) The twelfth cross was erected on the last position held on 23 and 24 July 1944 by members of the Resistance. View of the Gorges de la Bourne and of Valchevrière. The chapel, now the fourteenth station of the cross, was the only building to survive the fire that destroyed the old village.

Brèche de Chalimont ★
Continue to the Chalets de Chalimont. Turn right along a forest road *(1hr there and back on foot – the road is also suitable for cars in dry weather)*. A narrow ridge offers extended views of the whole area.

Gorges de la Bourne ★★★

From Villard-de-Lans to Pont-en-Royans – 🚶 *Itinerary described in reverse under VERCORS, ②*

VILLARS-SUR-VAR

POPULATION 507
MICHELIN MAP 341 D4

Set in the midst of rocks, vines and olive groves, Villars-sur-Var was once a stronghold of the mighty Grimaldi family. The remains of the old walls and the Porte St-Antoine guard a peaceful village, perched on a sunny mountain terrace above the Var, only 40 minutes' drive from Nice. 🏛*Mairie – 06710 Villars-sur-Var* 🕐 *daily except Sat-Sun 8.30am-12.30pm, Thurs also open 1-4pm.*

▶ **Orient Yourself:** From Villars, you can drive to the Vallée de la Tinée by way of Tournefort; alternatively, you can head for the Gorges du Cian through Touët-sur-Var, 9km/5.6mi to the east.

- ▣ **Parking:** The old town is closed to cars; park just above the village.
- ◷ **Organizing Your Time:** You will need an hour to see the village; then relax at a café and sample a glass of Clos-Saint-Joseph, the only wine in the Alpes-Maritimes with an AOC designation.
- ◔ **Also See:** Nearby Sights: ANNOT, BEUIL, Gorges du CIANS, CLUES DE HAUTE-PROVENCE, ENTREVAUX, PUGET-THÉNIERS, Vallée de la TINÉE

The Old Town

Within the walls, a walk along the cobbled streets, closed to traffic, leads past a number of doorways with carved 18C and 19C porches.

Church

◷ *If the church is closed, enquire at the presbytery -* ☎*04 93 84 44 32*
The highlight of the rich interior decoration is a large **high-altar retable**★ made up of 10 panels in Franciscan style, painted by an unknown artist; the central panel represents a splendid **Entombment**★★, below are St. Claire and St. Francis to the left and St. Lucy and St. Honoratus to the right. The polychrome woodwork bears the arms of the Grimaldi, a powerful family bitterly opposed to the dukes of Savoie from the 14C to the 17C. The **Annunciation altarpiece**★ (Nice School c 1520), located on the left of the chancel, is also remarkable, as are the three paintings above it; a Nativity, a Pietà and a depiction of the Flight into Egypt. The Madonna with rosary (late 16C) on the right of the chancel, was a favourite subject of the Nice Gothic school.

Excursions

Thiéry★

14km/8.7mi northwest along D 226. A place of narrow streets and covered alleyways, this isolated village overlooking the Gorges du Cians **(viewpoint)** has stood on the hilltop since the 11C.

Route de Tournefort★

This picturesque road *(D 25)* linking the River Var and River Tinée across the foothills of the Pointe des Quatre-Cantons, some 10km/6mi upstream from their confluence, presents some of the best of the local landscape. 11km/6.8mi west of the Pont de la Mescla, the road branches off from N 202 and climbs the slopes towards Villars.

Villars-sur-Var – ◔*see above*

D 26 winds its way along the forested slopes of Mont Falourde, offering glimpses of the Chapelle de la Madone d'Utelle across the River Tinée.

Massoins

From this mountain village, there is a fine **view** of the Var Valley. The ruins of a 14C castle stand above the centre.

▷ *2km/1.2mi further on, turn right onto a small road.*

Tournefort

The village clings to a steep rock spur. Near the chapel, the **view**★ embraces the Var and Tinée valleys framed by mountains, the Madone d'Utelle and the hilltop village of La Tour (◔*see Vallée de la TINÉE*).

▷ *Return to D 26 and follow it down to the Tinée Valley.*

VIZILLE

POPULATION 7 495
MICHELIN MAP 333 H7 – LOCAL MAP SEE LACS DE LAFFREY

This small industrial town has retained one of the major historic buildings of the Dauphiné region, the château of François de Bonne de **Lesdiguières** (1543-1627). Until 1972, it was one of the national estates at the disposal of the French President. ▤ *Place du Château - 38220 Vizille* ◷ *July to Aug: 10.30am-12.30pm, 2-6pm (Sat 7pm), Sun 9am-1pm; rest of year: Mon-Sat 10.30am-12.30pm, 2-6pm* ◷ *closed public holidays -* ☏ *04 76 68 15 16 - www.ot-vizille.com*

▶ **Orient Yourself:** Vizille is 15km/9.4mi south of Grenoble on the Route Napoléon (N 85)
◉ **Don't Miss:** The Musée de la Révolution française★ in the Château offers an interesting modern perspective on that tumultuous event.
◷ **Organizing Your Time:** The town of Vizille is interesting in itself, and worth an hour or two of your time.
ঌ **Also See:** Nearby Sights: Le BOURG D'OISANS, Massif de CHAMROUSSE, Massif de la CHARTREUSE, GRENOBLE, Le GRÉSIVAUDAN, Lacs de LAFFREY, Route NAPOLÉON, ST-PIERRE-DE-CHARTREUSE, Le TRIÈVES, Le VALBONNAIS, Le VERCORS, VILLARD-DE-LANS

A Bit of History

The Duc de Lesdiguières rose from the minor aristocracy to become one of the most colourful characters of his time. A staunch supporter of the Reformation who had made his name at 22 as a Huguenot leader, he was made governor of Dauphiné by King Henri IV and for the next thirty years exercised his authority with vigour and such cunning that he was nicknamed the "Fox." Lesdiguières was created duke, peer of the realm and marshal of France, but his ambition was not yet satisfied. In 1622

Château de Vizille

P. Demarchez/FOC

he finally became constable of France, the last person to hold this office, but only after renouncing the Protestant faith.

In 1602 he supervised the building of the Château de Vizille, exacting forced labour from the local villagers to get the job done by warning them, "You will come, or you will burn." His son-in-law Marshal Créqui added the monumental staircase leading down to the park. In 1780, the château was bought by Claude Périer, a wealthy financier from Grenoble who lent it to the États du Dauphiné for their historic meeting in 1788.

The major event in the history of this little town took place on 21 July 1788, one year before the French Revolution began. The meeting of the regional assembly, which was banned in Grenoble, took place instead in the Château de Vizille. Discussions between 165 members of the nobility, 50 clergymen and 325 representatives of the middle and lower classes went on from 8am to 3am the next morning. The resolution finally voted by the **Assemblée de Vizille** protested against the suppression of Parliament by Louis XVI, called for a meeting of all the regional assemblies and demanded individual freedom for all French citizens. For having expressed wishes that the whole nation adopted a year later, Vizille can rightly be called the "cradle" of the French Revolution.

Château★ *1hr*

Guided tour (1hr30min) Apr to Oct: daily except Tue 10am-12.30pm, 1.30-6pm; Nov to Mar: daily except Tue 10am-12.30pm, 1.30-5pm. Closed 25 Dec-1 Jan and public holidays from Nov to Mar. No charge - ☎ *04 76 68 07 35.*

The original buiding, constructed in several stages over two centuries, burned down in 1825. It was rebuilt, but another fire in 1865 destroyed its two wings and resulted in its present asymmetric silhouette, flanked by a round and a square tower. One of the entrances is decorated with a bronze low relief by Jacob Richier, depicting Lesdiguières on horseback. The austere main façade faces the Romanche whereas a more elegant Renaissance façade overlooks the park. Recently, the entrance courtyard was completely renovated.

Interior
It is divided into two parts: the **Musée de la Révolution française**★ and the old château.

The museum is arranged in a modern style on four levels. It offers an interesting vision of the tumultuous period that inspired artists over a half-century to produce work both supporting and opposing the revolutionary spirit. On the ground floor, French and English earthenware is on display in the Orangery; on the same floor, in the "salle des Colonnes" carved out of the rock, are displayed some large canvases, stored for the Musée du Louvre and the Château de Versailles. The next floor is devoted to artworks inspired by the French Revolution. Upstairs are temporary exhibitions as well as the Liberté gallery where there is an educational exhibit describing major events of the Revolution.

The historic part of the old château on the top floor comprises several reception rooms including the Grand Salon des Tapisseries (17C tapestries, portraits of Lesdiguières) and the Salon Lesdiguières (Louis XIII furniture), the terrace (lovely view of the park with the Mont Thabor in the distance) and the library (Louis XIV panelling).

Park★
June to Aug: 9am-8pm; Apr to May and Sept to Oct: daily except Tue 9am-7pm; Nov to Mar: daily except Tue 10am-5pm closed 1 May. Off-limits to bicycles and animals. Guided tour in a little train (35 min). 2.50€, children 1.60€. In the vast park (100ha/247

acres), extending south of the château, deer, moufflons and herons roam freely and huge trout can be seen swimming in the lake.

Jardin du Roi
Access during the summer. Medieval ruins of the old feudal fortress crown the "King's Garden," a rocky promontory overlooking the old town of Vizille, north of the present building.

Excursion

Jarrie
This charming little village is the site of the Clos et la Maison Jouvin, dating from the 19C. In its vast park is the **Musée de la Chimie** (*Wed and Sat 2.30-5.30, guided tours by appointment during the week for families - ☎ 04 76 68 62 18*) which displays exhibits about the chemical industries in the Grenoble area, particularly the history of chlorine, a principal component of products from the Atofina plant in Jarrie. . The late 14C **Château de Bon-Repos** (*Access 3rd Sun of each month, except public holidays. No charge. closed Aug.*) with its four round towers is visible from the town. A public campaign saved the château from certain destruction in 1976.

Notre-Dame-de-Mésage
2.6km/1.6mi south along N 85. Ask for the key at the Mairie : daily except Wed and Sun 1.30-5.30pm, Sat 8.30-11.30am - ☎ 04 76 68 07 33. The church stands on the right of the main road; note its fine Romanesque stone bell-tower.
Slightly further on, the **Chapelle St-Firmin**★, a 13C chapel of the Knights Templar, has an elegant east end.

YVOIRE★★

POPULATION 650
MICHELIN MAP 328 K2

Yvoire occupies a splendid position on the shores of Lake Geneva, at the tip of the promontory which separates the "Petit Lac" and the "Grand Lac." Flowers abound in this picturesque village which has retained its medieval character. Its restaurants are renowned for their fish specialities, and in summer the marina is kept busy by yachtsmen from Switzerland and Savoie. Due to crowds, you should try to visit during the off-season. *place de la Mairie – 74140 Yvoire July to Aug: daily 9.30am-6.30pm; Sept to Oct and Apr to June: Mon-Sat 9.30am-12.30pm, 1.30-5pm, Sun noon-4pm; Nov to Mar: Mon -Fri 9.30am-12.30pm, 1.30-5pm closed Sat-Sun and public holidays - ☎ 04 50 72 80 21 - www.presqueileleman.com.*

▸ **Orient Yourself:** Approach the town from Douvaine, passing through the village of Nernier, or come from Exevenex.

Parking: Leave your car in the paying lot just outside the town wall, to your right coming from Thonon.

Don't Miss: Stop to admire the waves lapping at the port.

Organizing Your Time: The beach at Excevenex is pleasant in late afternoon.

Especially for Kids: The children will enjoy the Jardin des cinq sens.

Also See: Nearby Sights: ABONDANCE, AVORIAZ, CHÂTEL, ÉVIAN-LES-BAINS, MORZINE, La ROCHE-SUR-FORON, THONON-LES-BAINS

The Medieval Village★★

Yvoire has retained part of its 14C fortifications, including two gateways, the **castle** (☞ *not open to the public*) with its massive square keep flanked by turrets, and a few old houses.

Take a stroll through the lively streets lined with workshops; now and then a lovely square decorated with flowers offers views of the lake.

The **Église St-Pancrace** adds the finishing touch to this attractive picture; the chancel dates from the 14C but the building was only completed at the end of the 17C.

From the end of the pier, where boats offering trips round the lake have their moorings (☞ *see ÉVIAN: Practical information*), there are views of the Swiss

Fr. Isler/MICHELIN

The château at Yvoire

Address Book

For coin categories, see the Legend on the cover flap.

EATING OUT

☞**Les Jardins du Léman** – Grande-Rue - ☎ 04 50 72 80 32 - lesjardinsduleman.com - closed mid-Dec to mid-Jan - reservations advised in season. This restaurant has recently redecorated its dining rooms and has added two summer terraces, one on the pedestrian street and the other overlookng the château and Lake Geneva. Generous traditional fare.

☞**Le Denieu** – 74140 Bonnatrait - 7440 Sciez-sur-Léman - 6km/4mi SE of Yvoire on D 25 and N 5 - ☎ 04 50 72 35 06 - le.deniue@wanadoo.fr. Enter this imposing, harmoniously proportioned house on the main road and you will be charmed by lovely rooms with aged wood decor where old farming implements recall an agricultural past. Specialities from the Savoie region.

☞☞ **Les Flots Bleus** – 74140 Excenevex - ☎ 04 50 72 80 08 - www.flotsbleus-yvoire.com - closed Nov - 14 Apr. The best feature of this restaurant is its huge shaded terrace, shaded by vines, overlooking the lake and marina.

Fish dishes are a specialty. Also some guestrooms with lake-inspired decor.

☞☞☞**Restaurant du Port** – R. du Port - ☎ 04 50 72 80 17 - hotelduport. yvoire@wanadoo.fr - closed Nov-mid-Feb and Wed out of season. This is an ideal site on the marina next to the lake, and the terrace and flower-decked façade make the most of it. Fish dishes are a specialty. Pretty guestrooms.

WHERE TO STAY

☞☞☞**Hôtel Le Pré de la Cure** – ☎ 04 50 72 83 58 -www.pre-delacure. com - closed 15 Nov-3 Mar - 🅿 - 25rms - ☞☞restaurant. This modern house opposite one of the fortified gateways of the old town is set in a pleasant garden. The rooms are quite spacious and functional; 8 have balconies with a view of the lake. Friendly welcome and well-prepared regional food served in an enclosed veranda or on the terrace facing Yvoire and Lake Geneva.

SPORTS

You can enjoy public beaches in the sectors "Sous les Prés" and "La Pointe," where you can try all sorts of water sports.

shore backed by the Jura mountains. Day excursions are organised along the opposite shore.

Jardin des Cinq Sens★

Rue du Lac. 🚶 🕐 *May to mid-Sept: 10am-7pm; last half of Apr: 11am-6pm; mid-Sept to mid-Oct: 1-5pm (last admission 30min before closing). 9€, children 4-16 years 5.50€, 8€ in spring and fall, children 4.50€, also family tickets -* ☎ *04 50 72 88 80 - www. jardin5sens.net*

The former kitchen garden of the castle has been turned into a reconstruction of a medieval enclosed garden where monks used to grow vegetables and herbs. Gentian and rhododendrons grow in the Alpine garden, from where there is a fine view of the castle. Next comes the **Labyrinthe végétal**, a maze on the theme of the five senses: the Jardin du goût (taste) with its strawberries, raspberries and apple trees, the Jardin des textures (touch) with its subtle variety of foliage, the Jardin des couleurs (sight) with its harmonious range of colours changing with the seasons (geraniums, roses, bluebells) and the Jardin des senteurs (smell) with its lilies, honeysuckle and daphnes; at the centre of the garden, an aviary, full of pheasants and turtledoves, symbolises the sense of hearing. Other themed gardens: an Alpine garden, a planting of white roses against luxuriant foliage and a medicinal herb garden.

Excursions

The Presqu'ile du Léman

At Douvain, leave N5 in direction of Chens sur Léman. Follow D25 to Yvoire.

Although overshadowed by Yvoire, the villages of Chens-sur-Léman, Messery and Nernier offer ports, marinas and medieval streets for pleasant strolls.

Le château de Chens-sur-Léman This imposing ediface saw serious damange in the 16C and during the French Revolution. In the 15C it belonged to the dukes of Savoie, then passed to their Swiss banker. Since 1700, it has belonged to the same family. Renovated in the 20C, it is surrounded by a large garden (🕐 *Gardens open May to June, 1st week of July and Sat-Sun in Sept 10am-6pm. 2€ -* ☎ *04 50 94 0407*)

Excenevex★

3km/1.9mi southeast along D 25.

This charming lakeside resort, sheltering in the Golfe de Coudrée, is famous for having the most extensive beach on the French side of Lake Geneva. The coast is lined with luxury holiday villas.

France's last manufacturers of gold leaf, which is used for bookbinding, picture-framing and decorative wrought-iron, have been working here since 1939 (🔑 *not open to the public*). Some of the gold leaf produced in Excenevex was used for the restoration of Versailles.

INDEX

INDEX

ACCOMMODATIONS

INDEX

RESTAURANTS 38

MAPS AND PLANS

LIST OF MAPS

COMPANION PUBLICATIONS

Motorists who plan ahead will always have the appropriate maps to hand. Michelin products are complementary: for each of the sites listed in The Green Guide, map references are indicated which help you find your location on our range of maps. The image below shows the maps to use for each geographical area covered in this guide.

To travel the roads in this region, you may use any of the following:

• the regional maps at a scale of 1:275 000 nos 523 and 527, which cover the main roads and secondary roads, and include useful indications for finding tourist attractions. These are good maps to choose for travelling in a wide area. At a quick glance, you can locate and identify the main sights. In addition to identifying the types of road ways, the maps show castles, churches and other religious edifices, scenic viewpoints, megalithic monuments, swimming beaches on lakes and rivers, swimming pools, golf courses, racetracks, airfields, and more.

And remember to travel with the latest edition of the map of France no 721, which gives an overall view of the Alpine region and the main access roads which connect it to the rest of France (1:1 000 000 scale). Atlas formats are also available, spiral bound, paperback, hardback and the new, convenient Mini France (all including the Paris region, 50 town plans and an index of place names).

Michelin is pleased to offer a route-planning service on the Internet: www.ViaMichelin.com Choose the shortest route, a scenic route, a route without tolls, or the Michelin recommended route to your destination; you can also access information about hotels and restaurants from the *Michelin Guide*, and tourists sites from *The Green Guide*.

Bon voyage!

Legend

Selected monuments and sights

◉ ⟳ Tour - Departure point

🏛 ⛪ Catholic church

🏛 ⛪ Protestant church, other temple

✡ ✉ ☪ Synagogue - Mosque

▬▬ Building

■ Statue, small building

✝ Calvary, wayside cross

◎ Fountain

—●—▪— Rampart - Tower - Gate

⋈ Château, castle, historic house

∴ Ruins

⌣ Dam

✿ Factory, power plant

✩ Fort

∩ Cave

▣ Troglodyte dwelling

ππ Prehistoric site

▼ Viewing table

Ⓦ Viewpoint

▲ Other place of interest

Sports and recreation

🏇 Racecourse

⛸ Skating rink

≋ ≋ Outdoor, indoor swimming pool

🎥 Multiplex Cinema

⛵ Marina, sailing centre

⛺ Trail refuge hut

□–■–■–□ Cable cars, gondolas

□–+++++–□ Funicular, rack railway

🚂 Tourist train

◇ Recreation area, park

🐘 Theme, amusement park

🐂 Wildlife park, zoo

❀ Gardens, park, arboretum

🕊 Bird sanctuary, aviary

🚶 Walking tour, footpath

☺ Of special interest to children

Abbreviations

A   Agricultural office (Chambre d'agriculture)

C   Chamber of Commerce (Chambre de commerce)

H   Town hall (Hôtel de ville)

J   Law courts (Palais de justice)

M   Museum (Musée)

P   Local authority offices (Préfecture, sous-préfecture)

POL.   Police station (Police)

🛡   Police station (Gendarmerie)

T   Theatre (Théâtre)

U   University (Université)

	Sight	Seaside resort	Winter sports resort	Spa
Highly recommended ★★★	★★★	⚏⚏⚏	❋❋❋	ⵚⵚⵚ
Recommended ★★	★★	⚏⚏	❋❋	ⵚⵚ
Interesting	★	⚏	❋	ⵚ

Additional symbols

🛈	Tourist information
══ ══	Motorway or other primary route
❶ ❶	Junction: complete, limited
⊨══⊨ ══	Pedestrian street
⊥═══⊥	Unsuitable for traffic, street subject to restrictions
▥▥▥ ┄┄┄	Steps – Footpath
🚆 🚉	Train station – Auto-train station
🚌 🚌 S.N.C.F.	Coach (bus) station
─┼─┼─	Tram
Ⓜ	Metro, underground
🅿R	Park-and-Ride
♿	Access for the disabled
✉	Post office
☎	Telephone
✉	Covered market
⋅✕⋅	Barracks
△	Drawbridge
∪	Quarry
✕	Mine
🄑 🄕	Car ferry (river or lake)
⛴	Ferry service: cars and passengers
⛵	Foot passengers only
③	Access route number common to Michelin maps and town plans
Bert (R.)...	Main shopping street
AZ B	Map co-ordinates

Hotels and restaurants

Hotels- price categories:

	Provinces	Large cities
⊖	<40 €	<60 €
⊖⊖	40 to 65 €	60 to 90 €
⊖⊖⊖	65 to 100 €	90 to 130 €
⊖⊖⊖⊖	>100 €	>130 €

Restaurants- price categories:

	Provinces	Large cities
⊖	<14 €	<16 €
⊖⊖	14 to 25 €	16 to 30 €
⊖⊖⊖	25 to 40 €	30 to 50 €
⊖⊖⊖⊖	>40 €	>50 €

20 rooms :	Number of rooms
⊏ *6.85 €*	Price of breakfast; when not given, it is included in the price of the room (i.e., for bed-and-breakfast)
120 sites :	Number of camp sites
rest.	Lodging where meals are served
reserv	Reservation recommended
⊄	No credit cards accepted
🅿	Reserved parking for hotel patrons
⌇	Swimming Pool
▤	Air conditioning
⇸✕	Hotel: non-smoking rooms Restaurant: non-smoking section
♿	Rooms accessible to persons of reduced mobility

The prices correspond to the higher rates of the tourist season

MICHELIN

Michelin North America
One Parkway South – Greenville, SC 29615 USA
☎ 800-423-0485
www.MichelinTravel.com
michelin.guides@us.michelin.com

Manufacture française des pneumatiques Michelin

Société en commandite par actions au capital de 304 000 000 EUR
Place des Carmes-Déchaux – 63000 Clermont-Ferrand (France)
R.C.S. Clermont-Fd B 855 200 507

© Michelin, Propriétaires-éditeurs
Dépot légal janvier 2007 – ISSN 0763-1383
Printed in France: janvier 2007
Printing and Binding: IME
Printed in: France